SAS® Language and Procedures: Usage 2

Version 6, First Edition

SAS Institute Inc.
SAS Campus Drive
Cary, NC 27513

The correct bibliographic citation for this manual is as follows: SAS Institute Inc., *SAS® Language and Procedures: Usage 2, Version 6, First Edition,* Cary, NC: SAS Institute Inc., 1991. 649 pp.

SAS® Language and Procedures: Usage 2, Version 6, First Edition

ISBN 1-55544-445-8

1st printing, July 1991

The SAS® System is an integrated system of software providing complete control over data access, management, analysis, and presentation. Base SAS software is the foundation of the SAS System. Products within the SAS System include SAS/ACCESS®, SAS/AF®, SAS/ASSIST®, SAS/CPE®, SAS/DMI®, SAS/ETS®, SAS/FSP®, SAS/GRAPH®, SAS/IML®, SAS/IMS-DL/I®, SAS/OR®, SAS/QC®, SAS/REPLAY-CICS®, SAS/SHARE®, SAS/STAT®, SAS/CALC,™ SAS/CONNECT,™ SAS/DB2,™ SAS/EIS,™ SAS/INSIGHT,™ SAS/PH-Clinical,™ SAS/SQL-DS,™ and SAS/TOOLKIT™ software. Other SAS Institute products are SYSTEM 2000® Data Management Software, with basic SYSTEM 2000, CREATE,™ Multi-User,™ QueX,™ Screen Writer,™ and CICS interface software; NeoVisuals® software; JMP®, JMP IN®, JMP SERVE®, and JMP Ahead™ software; SAS/RTERM® software; the SAS/C® Compiler, and the SAS/CX® Compiler. MultiVendor Architecture™ and MVA™ are trademarks of SAS Institute Inc. *SAS Communications®, SAS Training®, SAS Views®,* and the SASware Ballot® are published by SAS Institute Inc. All trademarks above are registered trademarks or trademarks, as indicated by their mark, of SAS Institute Inc.

A footnote must accompany the first use of each Institute registered trademark or trademark and must state that the referenced trademark is used to identify products or services of SAS Institute Inc.

The Institute is a private company devoted to the support and further development of its software and related services.

IBM® and OS/2® are registered trademarks of International Business Machines Corporation. PRIMOS® is a registered trademark of Prime Computer Inc. Realtor™ is a trademark of the National Association of Realtors. UNIX® is a registered trademark of AT&T. VMS™ is a trademark of Digital Equipment Corporation.

Doc S19, Ver 1.01, 01JUL91

Contents

Part 4 · Producing Reports 249

Part 6 · Creating a Customized SAS Environment   487

Part 7 · Appendix   541

Reference Aids

Displays

Figures

Tables

Credits

Documentation

Composition	Gail C. Freeman, Susan H. Hoggard, Cynthia M. Hopkins, Nancy Mitchell, Pamela A. Troutman, David S. Tyree
Graphic Design	Creative Services Department
Proofreading	Patsy P. Blessis, Carey H. Cox, Heather B. Dees, Josephine P. Pope, Toni P. Sherrill, David A. Teal, John M. West, Susan E. Willard
Technical Review	James J. Ashton, Stephen Beatrous, David C. Berger, Lynne E. Bresler, Dave Brumitt, Gloria N. Cappy, Brent L. Cohen, Tom Cole, Ginny Dineley, Douglas R. Dotson, Darwin E. Driggers, David A. Driggs, Alan R. Eaton, Ceci Edmiston, Scott W. Ellis, Gloria Faley, Ann Ferraro, Donna O. Fulenwider, James C. Gear, Bary Allan Gold, John E. Green III, Thomas J. Hahl, Christina N. Harvey, Maureen Hayes, Darylene C. Hecht, Amerie Helton, Linda C. Helwig, Brian Hess, F. W. Hester, Kevin Hobbs, Lindi Ingold, Charles A. Jacobs, Susan E. Johnston, Brenda C. Kalt, Paul J. Karlok, Christina A. Keene, Jennifer L. Aquino Kendall, Paul M. Kent, Bradley W. Klenz, Ken Larsen, Marty Light, Julie A. Maddox, Jeffrey R. McDermott, James A. McKenzie, Jean Moorefield, Mark Moorman, Cynthia H. Morris, Susan M. O'Connor, Len Olszewski, Sally Painter, Randall D. Poindexter, Denise M. Poll, Jeffrey A. Polzin, Terry D. Poole, Meg Pounds, Bill Powers, Lisa M. Ripperton, Heman Robinson, Eddie Routten, Tim Rowles, Alissa W. Schleich, David C. Schlotzhauer, Mark L. Schneider, James D. Seabolt, Douglas J. Sedlak, David Shamlin, W. David Shinn, Veronica L. Shores, John Sims, Joseph G. Slater, Mike Stockstill, Dee Stribling, Tina Tart, Annette Tharpe, Bruce Tindall, Toby Trott, Maggie Underberg, Stephen A. Vincent, Keith Wagner, Linda Walters, Mark Watson, Bud Whitmeyer, Helen F. Wolfson, Donna E. Woodward, Ken D. Worsham, Dea B. Zullo
Writing and Editing	Deborah S. Blank, Caroline Brickley, Matthew R. Clark, Fonda J. Daniels, Paramita Ghosh, Christina N. Harvey, Carol Austin Linden, N. Elizabeth Malcom, Susan H. McCoy, Eric Schwoebel, Judith K. Whatley, John S. Williams

Software Development and Support

Complete software development, support, and quality assurance credits for base SAS software are listed in the reference guides for this product. Refer to *SAS Language: Reference, Version 6, First Edition* and the *SAS Procedures Guide, Version 6, Third Edition.*

Using This Book

Purpose

SAS Language and Procedures: Usage 2, Version 6, First Edition provides
instructions and examples for accomplishing tasks of moderate difficulty for
special purposes as you use the SAS System. This task-oriented book builds on
more basic information provided in *SAS Language and Procedures: Usage, Version
6, First Edition* and documents base SAS software beginning with Release 6.06.
This guide does not attempt to cover all features of the SAS System, all statements
for a procedure, or all options for a statement. Instead it focuses on selected tasks
and demonstrates a straightforward way of accomplishing them.

"Using This Book" contains important information to assist you as you read
this guide. This information includes the experience required with base SAS
software before using this book, the organization of the book, and the conventions
used in text and example code. "Additional Documentation," found at the end of
"Using This Book," provides references to other books that contain information on
related topics.

Audience

SAS Language and Procedures: Usage 2, Version 6, First Edition is written for

☐ users who have at least an introductory-level knowledge of the SAS System

☐ experienced SAS users who want to learn new tasks.

Prerequisites

Before you use this book, you need to learn how to invoke the SAS System at your
site. Contact the SAS Software Consultant at your site for instructions. In
addition, you should be familiar with the concepts and use of tools presented in
SAS Language and Procedures: Usage, Version 6, First Edition. Prerequisites listed
within chapters in this book, unless otherwise stated, refer to *SAS Language and
Procedures: Usage*.

How to Use This Book

The following sections provide an overview of the information in this book and explain the organization.

Organization

This book is divided into seven parts. Each of the first six parts has one or more chapters to develop the topic for the part. The seventh part is an appendix that includes raw data and DATA steps not shown in the chapters. The parts and chapters of the book are as follows:

Part 1: Introduction to the SAS System

Part 1 introduces you to the components of base SAS software, what it produces, and the primary methods of running the SAS System.

Chapter 1, "What Is the SAS System?"

Part 2: Reading Raw Data

Part 2 describes techniques for reading various configurations of raw data to create a SAS data set. It tells how to create and store data using the SAS System.

Chapter 2, "Reading Data in Different Record Formats and in Hierarchical Files"

Chapter 3, "Reading Varying-Length Fields and Repeated Fields"

Chapter 4, "Handling Missing and Invalid Values and Missing Records"

Chapter 5, "Reading Multiple Raw Data Files"

Part 3: Using Advanced Programming Techniques

Part 3 offers programming techniques to solve different data-handling problems.

Chapter 6, "Converting Variable Values"

Chapter 7, "Grouping Variables to Perform Repetitive Tasks Easily"

Chapter 8, "Classifying Variables into Categories"

Chapter 9, "Reshaping Data"

Chapter 10, "Performing a Table Lookup"

Chapter 11, "Smoothing Data"

Chapter 12, "Taking Random Samples"

Part 4: Producing Reports

Part 4 teaches you how to produce various types of reports, including summary reports, detail reports on subsets of data, exceptions reports, calendars, and time plots.

Chapter 13, "Translating Data Values for Meaning and Readability"

Chapter 14, "Reporting on Subsets of SAS Data Sets"

Chapter 15, "Producing Exceptions Reports"

Chapter 16, "Producing Multi-Panel Reports"

Chapter 17, "Producing Summary Reports Using Descriptive Procedures"

Chapter 18, "Producing Calendars"

Chapter 19, "Plotting the Values of Variables Over Time"

Part 5: Working with Files

Part 5 teaches you ways to use base SAS software to manipulate external files, how to use the spell checking facility, and how to work with certain SAS files.

Chapter 20, "Working with External Files"

Chapter 21, "Using a Spell Checking Facility"

Chapter 22, "Managing SAS Catalogs"

Chapter 23, "Comparing SAS Data Sets"

Part 6: Creating a Customized SAS Environment

Part 6 teaches you how to create customized windows and customize a SAS environment for individual users.

Chapter 24, "Creating Customized Windows"

Chapter 25, "Customizing a SAS Environment for Individual Users"

Part 7: Appendix

Part 7 lists the DATA steps or raw data used to create data sets that are not listed within the chapters.

Appendix, "Raw Data and DATA Steps"

Reference Aids

SAS Language and Procedures: Usage 2 provides a number of reference aids to help you find the information you need.

Table of Contents — lists parts titles and chapter titles as well as page numbers for the major parts of the book.

Table of Reference Aids — lists page numbers for all displays, figures, and tables.

Glossary — provides concise definitions of the terms used in discussions of base SAS software.

Index — provides page numbers where specific procedures, statements, options, and tasks are discussed.

The inside cover graphics provide functional overviews of the SAS System. The inside front cover depicts the entire SAS System. The inside back cover illustrates how base SAS software is organized.

Each chapter provides special reference aids to help you find specific information.

Table of Contents — lists the page numbers of sections within a single chapter.

SAS Tools — appears at the end of all chapters. This section summarizes the elements of the SAS System discussed in the chapter by illustrating the syntax of each element. Note that the syntax summaries in this section are specific to usage presented in the chapter and usually do not include all possible arguments for a statement or procedure. For complete syntax, including all available options, refer to *SAS Language: Reference, Version 6, First Edition*; the *SAS Procedures Guide, Version 6, Third Edition*; and *SAS Language and Procedures: Syntax, Version 6, First Edition*.

For a detailed discussion of the syntax conventions used in the SAS Tools section, refer to "Syntax Conventions" later in "Using This Book."

Learning More — appears at the end of all chapters. This section lists other sources of information for topics discussed in the chapter. In addition, this section can contain brief summaries of related topics that may interest you. When a related topic is introduced, it also includes a reference to other documentation where you can learn more about the topic.

Conventions

This section explains the various conventions used in presenting text, SAS language syntax, examples, and printed output in this book.

Typographical Conventions

You will see several type styles used in this book. The following list explains the meaning of each style:

roman	is the standard type style used for most text in this book.
UPPERCASE ROMAN	is used for SAS statements, variable names, and other SAS language elements when they appear in the text. However, you can enter these elements in your own SAS code in lowercase, uppercase, or a mixture of the two.
italic	is used for special terms defined in the text or in the glossary and to emphasize important information.
`monospace`	is used to show examples of SAS code. In most cases, this book uses lowercase type for SAS code, with the exception of some title characters. You can enter your own SAS code in lowercase, uppercase, or a mixture of the two. The SAS System ignores case except in character values. Therefore, enter any titles, footnotes, and character variable values exactly as you want them to appear in your output. Monospace is also used to show the values of character variables in text.
`red monospace`	is used in examples to highlight SAS code that is introduced in text.

Syntax Conventions

Type styles have special meanings when used in the presentation of base SAS software syntax. The following list explains the style conventions for presenting syntax in this book:

UPPERCASE BOLD	identifies SAS keywords such as the names of statements and procedures (for example, **PROC PRINT**).
UPPERCASE ROMAN	identifies arguments and values that are literals (for example, DATA=).

italic identifies arguments or values that you supply. Items in italic can represent user-supplied values assigned to an argument (for example, *SAS-data-set* in DATA=*SAS-data-set*) or nonliteral arguments (for example, VAR *variable*;).

The following symbols are used to indicate other syntax conventions:

< > (angle brackets) identify optional arguments. Any argument not enclosed in angle brackets is required.

| (vertical bar) indicates that you can choose one value from a group. Values separated by bars are mutually exclusive.

. . . (ellipsis) indicates that the argument or group of arguments following the ellipsis can be repeated any number of times. If the ellipsis and the following argument are enclosed in angle brackets, they are optional.

The following examples illustrate these syntax conventions:

□ **FILE** *'output-file'* <*PRINT* <*HEADER=label*>>;

□ **FORMAT** *variable-list-1 format-1* <*. . . variable-list-n format-n*>;

□ **PUT** <*variable-list* | *_ALL_*>;

FILE, FORMAT, and **PUT**
are all primary parts of the language so they appear in boldface type.

'output-file'
is required because it is not enclosed in angle brackets. The italic type indicates that you supply the value for this argument.

<HEADER=*label*>
is optional because it is enclosed in angle brackets. The uppercase roman type for HEADER= indicates that the argument must be spelled as shown. If you use HEADER=, you must supply the name of a statement label to replace *label*.

<PRINT <HEADER=*label*>>
are optional because they are enclosed in angle brackets, but if you use HEADER=, you must also use PRINT.

variable-list-1 format-1
is required and must have both a list of one or more variable names and a format.

<*. . . variable-list-n format-n*>
indicates that you can optionally specify multiple sets of variables and formats, but they must occur in pairs with each list of variables followed by a format.

<*variable-list* | *_ALL_*>
is separated by a vertical bar to indicate that you can use only one of these two arguments. The angle brackets indicate that both arguments are optional. Therefore, you can specify a list of variables with the PUT statement, you can specify PUT _ALL_, or you can simply specify PUT with no arguments.

Conventions for Examples and Output

The examples in each chapter build on previous examples in the chapter to teach you how to combine statements and options to achieve the results you want. You can run any of the examples in this book as you read the chapters. The following conventions are used to simplify your use of examples:

☐ This book shows all of the code that creates all data sets.

☐ This book uses two methods to show the raw data used to create data sets: the CARDS statement and the INFILE statement. If the raw data for a data set are lengthy, this book lists the data in the appendix, not in the main text of the chapter.

☐ This book uses the following forms of the INFILE and FILE statements to simplify showing how to access an external file:

INFILE *'input-file'*;
FILE *'output-file'*;

These forms of the statements enable you to directly specify the name of the file as it is known on your operating system. Refer to the SAS documentation for your operating system for information on specifying filenames. Note that these forms of the INFILE and FILE statements are available in all environments except VSE. Under VSE, you must use operating-system control language to access external files. Refer to the SAS documentation for the VSE environment for more information.

☐ Examples use permanent data sets when subsequent examples in a chapter use the same data set. When a data set is reused, it is created only once and used throughout the rest of the chapter. To help you find the data set more easily, a reference to the page where the data set is created is included in the index under the listing "sample SAS data sets."

☐ Most examples use a LIBNAME statement to assign a libref to a SAS data library:

LIBNAME *libref 'SAS-data-library'*;

Some examples use a FILENAME statement to assign a fileref to an external file:

FILENAME *fileref 'external-file'*;

For more information about specifying the name of a SAS data library or an external file in these statements, see the SAS documentation for the operating system you use. Note that this use of the LIBNAME and FILENAME statements is available in all environments except VSE. Under VSE, you must use operating-system control language to make these assignments. Refer to the SAS documentation for the VSE environment for more information.

Each page of output produced by a procedure is enclosed in a box. In each chapter, the procedure output is numbered consecutively starting with 1, and most output is given a title. Also, most of the output in this book is produced using the following SAS system options:

☐ LINESIZE=76

☐ PAGESIZE=60

☐ NODATE.

In examples where other options are used, the options appear in the SAS code that produces the output.

In examples that illustrate log output, the line numbers shown in the log will probably not match the line numbers of your log when you run the same example, regardless of the method you use to run the system. The difference in line numbers in the log is not important.

Additional Documentation

SAS Institute provides many publications about products of the SAS System and how to use SAS software on specific hosts. For a complete list of SAS publications, you should refer to the current *Publications Catalog*. The catalog is produced twice a year. You can order a free copy of the catalog by writing to the following address:

SAS Institute Inc.
Book Sales Department
SAS Campus Drive
Cary, NC 27513
(919)677-8000

Base SAS Software Documentation

In addition to *SAS Language and Procedures: Usage 2*, you will find these other documents helpful when using base SAS software:

☐ *SAS Language and Procedures: Introduction, Version 6, First Edition* (order #A56074) helps you get started if you are unfamiliar with the SAS System or any other programming language.

☐ *SAS Language and Procedures: Usage, Version 6, First Edition* (order #A56075) provides task-oriented information that shows you in a step-by-step format how to use base SAS software to perform common tasks.

☐ *SAS Language: Reference, Version 6, First Edition* (order #A56076) provides detailed reference information on SAS language statements, functions, formats, informats, display manager, or any other part of base SAS software except procedures.

☐ *SAS Procedures Guide, Version 6, Third Edition* (order #A56080) provides detailed reference information on SAS procedures.

☐ *SAS Guide to TABULATE Processing, Second Edition* (order #A56095) provides more information about the TABULATE procedure.

☐ *SAS Guide to the SQL Procedure: Usage and Reference, Version 6, First Edition* (order #A56070) provides information on the SQL procedure.

☐ *SAS Guide to Macro Processing, Version 6, Second Edition* (order #A56041) provides more information about macro variables and statements.

☐ *SAS Programming Tips: A Guide to Efficient SAS Processing* (order #A56150) suggests more than 100 tips for improving the efficiency of your SAS programs.

☐ *SAS Language and Procedures: Syntax, Version 6, First Edition* (order #A56077) provides a quick, but complete, reference to the syntax for portable base SAS software.

☐ SAS documentation for your host system provides details for your specific host operating system.

Documentation for Other SAS Software

The SAS System includes many software products in addition to the base SAS System. Several books that may be of particular interest to you are listed here:

☐ *SAS/ASSIST Software: Your Interface to the SAS System* (order #A56086) provides information on using the SAS System in a menu-driven windowing environment that requires no programming.

☐ *Getting Started with the SAS System Using SAS/ASSIST Software, Version 6, First Edition* (order #A56085) provides step-by-step instruction for performing the most commonly used tasks of the SAS System using SAS/ASSIST software.

☐ *SAS/FSP Software: Usage and Reference, Version 6, First Edition* (order #A56001) provides information on using interactive procedures for creating SAS data sets and entering and editing data or for creating, editing, and printing form letters and reports.

☐ *SAS/AF Software: Usage and Reference, Version 6, First Edition* (order #A56011) provides information on building windows for your own applications.

☐ *SAS/GRAPH Software: Reference, Version 6, First Edition, Volume 1* and *Volume 2* (order #A56020) provides information on creating presentation graphics to illustrate relationships of data.

☐ *SAS/STAT User's Guide, Version 6, Fourth Edition, Volume 1* and *Volume 2* (order #A56045) provides information on methods of statistical analysis.

Part 1

Introduction to the SAS® System

Chapter 1   **What Is the SAS® System?**

Chapter 1 What Is the SAS® System?

Introduction

The SAS System is an integrated system of software products that enables you to access, manage, analyze, and present all of your data. With the SAS System you can perform data entry, retrieval, and management; report writing and graphics design; statistical and mathematical analysis; business forecasting and decision support; operations research and project management; and applications development. At the core of the SAS System is base SAS software, the software product you learn to use in this book.

In this chapter
This chapter introduces the capabilities of base SAS software, outlines various types of output, and addresses methods of running the SAS System. This basic discussion will refresh you on some of the key facts about the SAS System.

Understanding Base SAS Software

Base SAS software contains a data access and management facility, a programming language, and data analysis and reporting utilities. Learning to use base SAS software enables you to work with these features of the SAS System. It also prepares you to learn other software products in the SAS System, since all SAS software products follow essentially the same rules.

Understanding How the SAS System Organizes Data

The SAS System organizes data into a rectangular form called a *SAS data set*. In a SAS data set, each row represents information about an individual entity and is called an *observation*. Each column represents the same type of information and is called a *variable*. Each separate piece of information is a *data value*. In a SAS data set, an observation contains all the data values for an entity; a variable contains the same kind of data value for all entities. Figure 1.1 illustrates a SAS data set. The data describe participants in a 16-week program at a weight-loss center. The data for each participant are an identification number, name, team name, and weight at the beginning and end of the program.

One more important concept to remember about a SAS data set is, as Figure 1.1 also shows, every SAS data set contains a descriptor portion.

Figure 1.1
Structure of a SAS Data Set

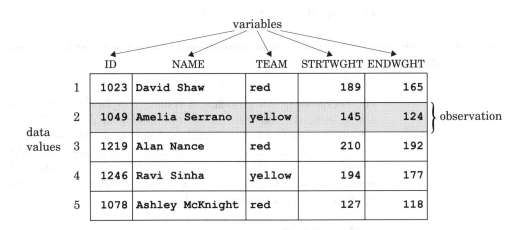

The descriptor portion consists of details the SAS System records about a data set, such as the names of all its variables, the attributes of all the variables, the number of observations in the data set, and the time the data set was created or updated. Depending on the operating system you use, additional information about SAS data sets may be stored.

Understanding How to Build a SAS Data Set

To build a SAS data set with base SAS software, you use statements in the SAS programming language. The following example creates a SAS data set named WGHTCLUB with the information on the participants in the weight-loss program. The DATA statement tells the SAS System to begin building a SAS data set named WGHTCLUB.

```
data wghtclub;
```

The INPUT statement identifies the fields that are read from the input data and names the SAS variables that are created from them. In this example, the variables are IDNO, the identification number of the participant; NAME, the name of the participant; TEAM, the color that identifies the participant's team; STRTWGHT, the weight of the participant at the beginning of the program; and ENDWGHT, the participant's weight after completing the program. The dollar signs after NAME and TEAM indicate that those are character variables, meaning that their values are not necessarily numeric. The numbers specify the columns in which the values for the variables are entered.

```
input idno 1-4 name $ 6-24 team $ strtwght endwght;
```

The following assignment statement calculates the weight each person lost and assigns the result to a new variable called LOSS.

```
loss=strtwght-endwght;
```

The CARDS statement indicates that data lines follow. This approach is useful when you have only a small amount of data.

```
cards;
```

The data lines follow the CARDS statement and match the specifications given in the INPUT statement.

```
1023 David Shaw          red 189 165
1049 Amelia Serrano      yellow 145 124
1219 Alan Nance          red 210 192
1246 Ravi Sinha          yellow 194 177
1078 Ashley McKnight     red 127 118
;
```

Here is the complete program that produces the SAS data set WGHTCLUB with the information on the participants in the weight-loss program:

```
data wghtclub;
    input idno 1-4 name $ 6-24 team $ strtwght endwght;
    loss=strtwght-endwght;
    cards;
1023 David Shaw          red 189 165
1049 Amelia Serrano      yellow 145 124
1219 Alan Nance          red 210 192
1246 Ravi Sinha          yellow 194 177
1078 Ashley McKnight     red 127 118
;
```

A SAS program or a portion of a program that begins with a DATA statement and usually ends with a RUN statement is called a *DATA step*. A DATA step can be bounded by another DATA step or a PROC step (discussed later in this chapter).

Note: By default, the data set WGHTCLUB is temporary; that is, it exists only for the current job or session.

Understanding the Programming Language

The statements that created the data set WGHTCLUB are part of the SAS programming language. The SAS language includes statements, expressions, functions, options, and formats—elements that many programming languages share. However, the way you use the elements of the SAS language depends on certain programming rules. The most important rules are listed in the next two sections.

Rules for SAS Statements

□ SAS statements end with a semicolon.

□ SAS statements can be entered in lowercase, uppercase, or a mixture of the two.

□ Any number of SAS statements can appear on a single line.

□ A SAS statement can be continued from one line to the next, as long as no word is split.

□ SAS statements can begin in any column.

□ Words in SAS statements are separated by blanks or by special characters (such as the equal sign and the minus sign in the calculation of the LOSS variable in the WGHTCLUB example).

Rules for SAS Names

□ SAS names are used for SAS data set names, variable names, and other items.

□ A SAS name can contain from one to eight characters.

□ The first character must be a letter or an underscore (_).

□ Subsequent characters must be letters, numbers, or underscores.

□ Blanks cannot appear in SAS names.

Understanding the Data Analysis and Reporting Utilities

The SAS programming language is both powerful and flexible. You can program any number of analyses and reports with it. The SAS System can also simplify programming for you with its library of built-in programs known as *SAS procedures*. SAS procedures use data values from SAS data sets to produce preprogrammed reports, requiring minimal effort from you.

For example, the following PRINT procedure step displays the values of the variables in the SAS data set WGHTCLUB:

```
proc print data=wghtclub;
   title 'Weight-Loss Data';
run;
```

Output 1.1 shows the results.

Output 1.1
*Displaying the
Values in a
SAS Data Set*

```
                          Weight-Loss Data                              1

   OBS    IDNO    NAME              TEAM      STRTWGHT    ENDWGHT    LOSS

    1     1023    David Shaw        red         189        165       24
    2     1049    Amelia Serrano    yellow      145        124       21
    3     1219    Alan Nance        red         210        192       18
    4     1246    Ravi Sinha        yellow      194        177       17
    5     1078    Ashley McKnight   red         127        118        9
```

The following program is another example of a SAS procedure step. In this example, the TABULATE procedure calculates the mean starting weight, ending weight, and weight loss for each team and produces a table showing these statistics.

```
proc tabulate data=wghtclub;
   class team;
   var strtwght endwght loss;
   table team, mean*(strtwght endwght loss);
   title 'Mean Starting Weight, Ending Weight, and Weight Loss';
run;
```

Output 1.2 shows the results.

Output 1.2
*Displaying the
Mean Values for
Each Team*

```
     Mean Starting Weight, Ending Weight, and Weight Loss          1

     ----------------------------------------------------------
     |              |                   MEAN                   |
     |              |------------------------------------------|
     |              |  STRTWGHT  |  ENDWGHT   |    LOSS    |
     |--------------+------------+------------+------------|
     |TEAM          |            |            |            |
     |--------------|            |            |            |
     |red           |    175.33  |    158.33  |     17.00  |
     |--------------+------------+------------+------------|
     |yellow        |    169.50  |    150.50  |     19.00  |
     ----------------------------------------------------------
```

A portion of a SAS program that begins with a PROC statement and ends with a RUN statement, a DATA statement, or another PROC statement is called a *PROC step.** Both PROC steps that create Output 1.1 and 1.2 comprise the following elements:

□   a PROC statement, which includes the word PROC, the name of the procedure used, and the name of the SAS data set containing the values. If the DATA= option and the data set name are omitted, the procedure uses the SAS data set most recently created or updated in the program.

□   additional statements that give the SAS System more information about what to do, such as, CLASS, VAR, TABLE, and TITLE statements.

---

*   For some procedures in the SAS System, a RUN statement executes the preceding group of statements but does not end the PROC step.

□ a RUN statement, which indicates that the preceding group of statements is ready to be executed.

Producing Output with the SAS System

A SAS program can produce some or all of the following kinds of output:

□ a SAS data set. A SAS data set contains data values stored as a table of observations and variables. It also stores descriptive information about the data set, such as the names and arrangement of variables, the number of observations, and the date the data set was created. The SAS data set can be temporary or permanent and can be stored on disk or tape. The first example in this chapter creates the data set WGHTCLUB.

□ a SAS log. By default, the SAS System creates the SAS log as a record of the SAS statements entered and messages from the SAS System about the execution of the program. It can appear as a file on disk, a display on the monitor, or a hardcopy listing. The exact appearance of the SAS log varies according to the site, but a typical SAS log for the program in this chapter looks like Output 1.3.

Output 1.3
An Example
SAS Log

```
5        options nomemrpt nostimer nodate number pageno=1;
6        data wghtclub;
7            input idno 1-4 name $ 6-24 team $ strtwght endwght;
8            loss=strtwght-endwght;
9            cards;

NOTE: The data set WORK.WGHTCLUB has 5 observations and 6 variables.

15       ;
16       proc print data=wghtclub;
17           title 'Weight-Loss Data';
18       run;

NOTE: The PROCEDURE PRINT printed page 1.

19       proc tabulate data=wghtclub;
20           class team;
21           var strtwght endwght loss;
22           table team, mean*(strtwght endwght loss);
23           title 'Mean Starting Weight, Ending Weight, and Weight Loss';
24       run;

NOTE: The PROCEDURE TABULATE printed page 2.
```

□ procedure output. SAS procedure output contains the result of the analysis or the report produced. It can take the form of a file on disk, a display on the monitor, or hardcopy. The appearance of procedure output varies according to the site and the options specified in the program, but Output 1.1 and 1.2, shown earlier in this chapter, illustrate typical procedure output.

□ other SAS files, such as catalogs. SAS catalogs contain information that cannot be represented as tables of data values. Examples of items that can be stored in SAS catalogs include function key settings, letters produced by SAS/FSP software, and graphics output produced by SAS/GRAPH software.

□ external files or entries in other databases. The SAS System can create and update external files and some databases created by other software products. The information is stored on disk or tape.

Using the SAS System

There are two different ways to use the SAS System. One way is to write SAS programs; the other is to use SAS/ASSIST software, an easy, menu-driven interface to SAS features. This book shows you how to write SAS programs.

Figure 1.2
Two User
Interfaces for the
SAS System

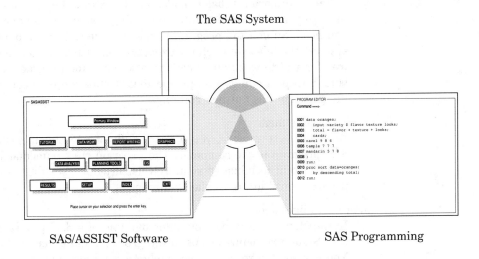

SAS/ASSIST Software   SAS Programming

Running SAS Programs

When using SAS software, you have a choice of several methods of running SAS programs and displaying output.

Figure 1.3
Methods of
Running the
SAS System

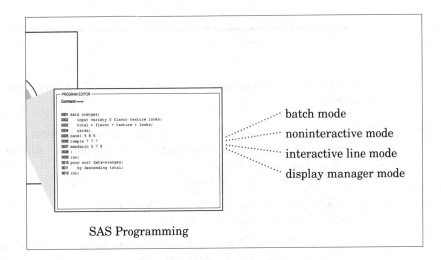

SAS Programming

The methods differ in the speed with which they run, the amount of computer resources they require, and the interaction you have with the program (that is, the kinds of changes you can make while the program is running). The examples in this book produce the same results, regardless of the way the programs are run. The following list briefly describes four methods of running the SAS System:

batch mode
> To run a program in *batch mode*, you prepare a file containing a SAS program including any statements in the operating system's command language that you need. Submit the program to the computer. The computer's operating system schedules your job for execution and runs it. Your terminal session is free for you to work on something else while the program runs. The results of your SAS program go to a prespecified destination; you can look at them when the program has finished running.

noninteractive mode
> In *noninteractive mode*, you prepare a file of SAS statements and submit the SAS program to the computer. The program runs immediately and occupies your current terminal session. You usually don't see the results of your SAS program until it has finished running.

interactive line mode
> In *interactive line mode*, you enter one line of a SAS program at a time. The SAS System recognizes steps in the program and executes them automatically. You can see the results immediately on your monitor.

display manager mode
> In *display manager mode*, you interact directly with the SAS System via a series of windows. Display manager mode is a quick and convenient way to write, submit, and view the results of your SAS programs.

The programs in this book can be run using any of the methods previously described. This book uses display manager for all examples.

Summary

The following points summarize features of the SAS System discussed in this chapter:

□ The components of base SAS software are a data access and management facility, a programming language, and data analysis and reporting utilities. Using base SAS software prepares you to learn how to use other software products in the SAS System.

□ A SAS program can produce a SAS data set, a SAS log, procedure output, other SAS files, and external files.

□ The SAS System offers many ways to run programs including SAS/ASSIST software, batch mode, noninteractive mode, interactive line mode, and display manager mode.

SAS Tools

This section summarizes syntax for the statements and procedures discussed in this chapter. This section in subsequent chapters omits some of the most basic elements that are described in this chapter.

Statements

variable=expression;
> is an assignment statement that evaluates an expression and stores the result in a variable. *Variable* names a new or existing variable. *Expression* is any valid SAS expression.

CARDS;
> indicates that data lines follow.

DATA *SAS-data-set*;
> tells the SAS System to begin a DATA step and create a SAS data set.

INPUT *variable-1* <$> <*column-specifications*> < . . . *variable-n*> <$> <*column-specifications*>;
> describes the arrangement of values in an input record and assigns input values to corresponding SAS variables. *Variable* names the variable whose value is read.

RUN;
> tells the SAS System to begin executing the preceding group of SAS statements.

TITLE <'*text*'>;
> specifies a title line printed on SAS procedure output and other output.

Procedures

PROC *procedure* <DATA=*SAS-data-set*>;
> tells the SAS System to invoke a particular SAS *procedure* to process the *SAS-data-set* specified in the DATA= option. If you omit the DATA= option, the procedure processes the most recently created SAS data set. A portion of a SAS program that begins with a PROC statement and ends with a RUN statement, a DATA statement, or another PROC statement is called a PROC step.

PROC PRINT <DATA=*SAS-data-set*>;
> prints a listing of the values of the variables in a SAS data set.

Learning More

This section provides references for learning more about topics presented in this chapter.

□ This book continues a mid-level introduction to the most commonly used parts of base SAS software, as presented in *SAS Language and Procedures: Usage, Version 6, First Edition.* For an easier but more limited introduction, see *SAS Language and Procedures: Introduction, Version 6, First Edition.* For complete reference information on the features shown here and related features, see *SAS Language: Reference, Version 6, First Edition*, and the *SAS Procedures Guide, Version 6, Third Edition*.

□ For a detailed discussion of the structure of SAS data sets and SAS data libraries, see *SAS Language: Reference*, Chapter 6, "SAS Files." Chapter 6 also describes SAS indexes, which form an important component of the SAS data set model.

□ For additional information about entering data using the INPUT statement, refer to *SAS Language: Reference*, Chapter 9, "SAS Language Statements."

□ *The SAS Guide to TABULATE Processing, Second Edition* and the *SAS Procedures Guide* provide more information about the TABULATE procedure.

Part 2
Reading Raw Data

14

Chapter 2 Reading Data in Different Record Formats and in Hierarchical Files

Introduction

To create a SAS data set from records that vary in layout, you need to use conditional processing to read the records accurately. In the simplest case, a file may consist of records in which the information is similar but the data fields are laid out differently. These records are typically independent of each other. A more complex case consists of hierarchical files. In hierarchical files, the data occur in varying layouts in the records, and some records are specifically related to others. These related records occur in groups.

In this chapter
This chapter demonstrates how to read data records in different formats and discusses different ways to store hierarchical data in one or more SAS data sets.

Prerequisites
To understand the examples in this chapter, you need to be familiar with the following DATA step features:

□ the flow of action in the DATA step

□ the effect of the single trailing @ in an INPUT statement

□ the use of pointer controls in an INPUT statement

□ the effect of the RETAIN statement on values of variables in the program data vector.*

Reading Data from Independent Records in Different Formats

To create a SAS data set from records of raw data, you must correctly describe the location of the data fields in an INPUT statement. When a file contains records in different formats, you must determine the layout of the current record in order to execute the appropriate INPUT statement.

The records read in this example contain sales totals from the hardware and software divisions of four regional sales offices. The file was composed from other files and shows that one record format was used by the hardware divisions and another by the software divisions. For example, the hardware division records (denoted by the H following the region number) contain only the region number and division letter, followed by three numbers representing the sales totals for January, February, and March.

```
----+----1----+----2----+----3----+----4
REGION1H 34567.55 38210.75 46758.89
```

However, the software division records (denoted by an S following the division number) were constructed differently and contain the regional number, the division letter, and a number representing a month, followed immediately by the sales total for that month.

```
----+----1----+----2----+----3----+----4
REGION1S 1 1789.45 2 1058.85 3 5023.35
```

---

* In Version 6 of the SAS System, the program data vector is a logical concept and does not imply a contiguous physical storage area.

Here is the entire file containing January, February, and March sales totals for the hardware and software divisions of four regional sales offices:

```
----+----1----+----2----+----3----+----4
REGION1H 34567.55 38210.75 46758.89
REGION1S 1 1789.45 2 1058.85 3 5023.35
REGION2B 34567.55 38210.75 46758.89
REGION2S 1 1789.45 2 1058.85 3 5023.35
REGION3H 34567.55 38210.75 46758.89
REGION3S 1 1789.45 2 1058.85 3 5023.35
REGION4H 34567.55 38210.75 46758.89
REGION4S 1 1789.45 2 1058.85 3 5023.35
```

Note that in the third record the region number is followed by a B instead of an H or S. This intentional error is used to demonstrate how you can provide for error handling.

To read this file and create a SAS data set, follow these steps:

□ identify the record layout

□ conditionally read one of two types of records

□ provide error-handling.

Identify the Record Layout

Begin the DATA step and name the data set to be created with a DATA statement. Identify the input file with an INFILE statement:

```
data regional;
   infile 'input-file';
```

Before you can read all the fields in a record, you need to determine which kind of record you are trying to read. To do so, read a field whose value identifies the type of record being read, and assign that value to a variable. Hold this record in the input buffer while you decide how to read the rest of it by using a single trailing at sign (@).

In this example the value in the eighth column reveals the layout of the rest of the record. The following INPUT statement brings a record into the input buffer, reads a value from the eighth column, and assigns that value to the variable DIVISION:

```
input @8 division $1. @;
```

The next step is to test the variable value and use the results of that test to determine how to read the rest of the record. In this example, the value of DIVISION determines how to read the rest of the record.

Conditionally Read One of Two Types of Records

After assigning to a variable the value that reveals the format of the record, test that value and conditionally execute the INPUT statement that correctly reads the rest of the record. One way to execute statements conditionally is to use a SELECT group.

Begin a SELECT group with a SELECT statement. Specify the variable to test in the SELECT statement. Specify each condition and each action to take in a WHEN statement. When a condition is true, the statement or statements following the condition in that WHEN statement are executed.

```
select (variable);
   when (value-1) action-to-take-1;
   when (value-n) action-to-take-n;
   otherwise;
end;
```

If one of the specified conditions is not met, the DATA step stops processing and writes a note to the log notifying you of the problem. To prevent this, always use an OTHERWISE statement in a SELECT group. Note that a SELECT group, like a DO group, ends with an END statement.

In this example, a SELECT group conditionally executes the correct INPUT statement to read a record from a hardware or software division, based on the value of DIVISION (H or S).

```
select (division);
   when ('H') input @10 jan feb mar;
   when ('S') input @12 jan +2 feb +2 mar;
   otherwise;
end;
```

The next section shows how to use an OTHERWISE statement to provide an alternative course of action when one of the specified conditions is not met.

Provide Error-Handling

If an observation does not meet one of the conditions specified in the WHEN statements, you can use an OTHERWISE statement to specify an alternative course of action. For example, you can use an OTHERWISE statement to handle errors by taking the following steps:

□ write a message to the log

□ write the erroneous record to a file

□ eliminate the unwanted observation.

Write a Message to the Log

You can flag a problem by writing a message to the SAS log. The following OTHERWISE statement writes a note to the SAS log when the value of DIVISION does not equal **H** or **S**.

```
select (division);
    when ('H') input @10 jan feb mar;
    when ('S') input @12 jan +2 feb +2 mar;
    otherwise put 'Erroneous Value for DIVISION at Record ' _n_ +(-1) '.';
end;
```

Note the use of the automatic variable _N_ to indicate which record contains the error in the original data file. You can use _N_ this way if each iteration of a DATA step reads a single record. The value of _N_ is automatically set to the number of the current iteration of the DATA step.

Note also the use of the pointer control $+(-1)$ in this PUT statement. It moves the pointer back one space so the period at the end of the message follows the variable _N_ without an intervening space.

Write the Problematic Record to a File

To help you resolve the problems in the raw data after running your job, you create a file that consists of all the problematic records. Specify an external file in a FILE statement and write each problematic record to that file with a PUT _INFILE_ statement. The _INFILE_ specification causes the contents of the current input record to be written to the file. To specify multiple statements in an OTHERWISE statement, use a DO group.

```
otherwise
    do;
        put 'Erroneous Value for DIVISION at Record ' _n_ +(-1) '.';
        file 'output-file';
        put _infile_;
    end;
```

Prevent an Incorrect Observation from Being Written

The last step is to protect the integrity of your output data set by preventing an incomplete observation from being written to it. In this example, when neither of the WHEN statements executes, no second INPUT statement reads the rest of a record to assign values to the variables JAN, FEB, and MAR. The presence of an OTHERWISE statement prevents the DATA step from stopping when no WHEN condition is met; however the incomplete observation is still output automatically at the bottom of the DATA step. To prevent this, use a DELETE statement. This statement returns control to the top of the DATA step without writing the current observation to the data set. Here is the entire program with the error-handling feature in place:

```
data regional;
    infile 'input-file';
    input @7 region $1. division $1. @;
    select (division);
        when ('H') input @10 jan feb mar;
        when ('S') input @12 jan +2 feb +2 mar;
        otherwise
            do;
                put 'Erroneous Value for DIVISION at Record ' _n_ +(-1) '.';
                file 'output-file';
                put _infile_;
                delete;
            end;
    end;
run;
```

This DATA step writes the following lines to the SAS log:

```
Erroneous Value for DIVISION at Record 3.
NOTE: 8 records were read from the infile input-file.
NOTE: 1 record was written to the file output-file.
NOTE: The data set WORK.REGIONAL has 7 observations and 5 variables.
```

It also writes the only problematic record to an external file

```
REGION2B 34567.55 38210.75 46758.89
```

Output 2.1, produced by the following statements, demonstrates that the data set REGIONAL was built correctly:

```
proc print data=regional;
    title 'First Quarter: Regional Sales';
run;
```

Output 2.1
Creating a Data Set from Records in Different Formats

```
                        First Quarter: Regional Sales                    1
        OBS    REGION    DIVISION      JAN         FEB         MAR
         1       1          H        34567.55    38210.75    46758.89
         2       1          S         1789.45     1058.85     5023.35
         3       2          S         1344.45      958.85     4893.35
         4       3          H        55643.55    49761.75    53221.89
         5       3          S         2433.45     1539.85     6444.35
         6       4          H        21003.55    22453.75    34522.89
         7       4          S         1154.45      854.85     4176.35
```

Reading Hierarchical Files

A *hierarchical file* is a special case of a file in which records have different formats. In a hierarchical file, related records of different formats occur in record groups. To create a SAS data set from a hierarchical file, you must be able to do the following:

□ read differently formatted records successfully

□ construct observations in a way that maintains the relationship between the data.

The examples in this section demonstrate techniques for reading hierarchical records and maintaining the connection between related data under the following circumstances:

□ when writing the header information to one SAS data set and detail records as separate observations to another data set

□ when reading an entire group of records that contain an end-of-record marker before writing an observation

□ when reading an entire group of records that do not contain an end-of-record marker before writing an observation.

Key concepts are explained in the following section "Understanding Hierarchical Files."

Understanding Hierarchical Files

Before you can understand the examples of creating SAS data sets from hierarchical files, you need to understand the structure of hierarchical files and the different ways you can create SAS data sets from them.

The Structure of Hierarchical Files

The two basic types of records in a hierarchical file are the *header record* and the *detail record*. A group of related records begins with a header record and typically contains one or more detail records. Usually each record contains a field that indicates the record type. The header record (or records) contains information that is relatively stable and unchanging; detail records typically contain more transitory information. For example, header records may contain a customer's name, account number, and other reference information. Each detail record may contain information about a single event or item, such as the type and amount of an item purchased. Figure 2.1 illustrates the structure of hierarchical data records.

Figure 2.1
Structure of
Hierarchical Data
Records

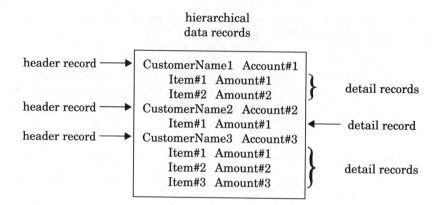

Ways to Create SAS Data Sets from Hierarchical Data Records

Using a DATA step, you can choose how to construct a SAS data set from hierarchical records. This discussion points out the advantages and disadvantages of each method based on ease of access of information and efficient use of storage space. When determining how to construct a data set from your own data, you should also consider how you want to analyze the data or which SAS reporting procedures you plan to use.

One method involves reading a hierarchical file to create two SAS data sets, one for the information read from the header records and a second for information from the detail records. This method requires creating a means of linking the related data that you are writing to separate data sets. Therefore, you must have a *key variable*, a variable written to both data sets, that links the header information in one data set to the related detail information in the other. This method saves storage space because you store header information only once and you don't have to create numerous variables with missing values by putting all the detail records in a single observation. Figure 2.2 demonstrates this method.

Figure 2.2
Creating Separate
Data Sets from
Header Records
and Detail Records

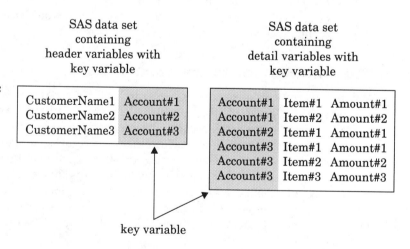

If you store information this way, however, you must read from two SAS data sets instead of only one to access this information.

Another way to create a SAS data set from data in hierarchical records is to read all the records in a given group and construct a single observation that contains the header information and the information from all detail records. This method can be convenient because you need to read from only one data set to access all the information. Figure 2.3 demonstrates this method.

Figure 2.3   *Creating an Observation from a Header Record and All Related Detail Records*

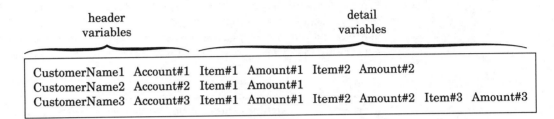

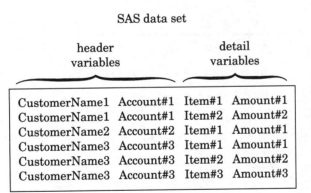

This method, however, is impractical if your data vary greatly in the number of detail records. For example, if one group contains ten detail records, but most of the others contain only two or three records, this method would waste a great deal of space in the rectangular structure of an uncompressed SAS data set.

Another way to create a single data set from hierarchical data is to create observations that contain both the header information and a single detail record. Figure 2.4 illustrates this arrangement.

Figure 2.4
Creating an Observation from a Header Record and a Single Detail Record

SAS data set

header variables		detail variables	
CustomerName1	Account#1	Item#1	Amount#1
CustomerName1	Account#1	Item#2	Amount#2
CustomerName2	Account#2	Item#1	Amount#1
CustomerName3	Account#3	Item#1	Amount#1
CustomerName3	Account#3	Item#2	Amount#2
CustomerName3	Account#3	Item#3	Amount#3

The advantage of this method, like the previous one, is that you have to read only one data set to process or report on these data. The repetition caused by storing the header information with each record, however, is not a very effective use of storage space. Consider using this method only if your header information is very brief. This method is not illustrated in this chapter.

Creating Separate SAS Data Sets from Header and Detail Records

As shown in Figure 2.2, one way to create a SAS data set from a hierarchical file is to create two data sets from a single hierarchical file. Create one to contain header information, the other to contain information from the detail records. For example, one file can store information about customers and another can store information about each order.

To illustrate, look at the order information in a hierarchical file of a computer supply company that sells hardware, software, and publications. When an order is placed, essential information about the company placing the order, such as the address and the person placing the order, is taken down, as well as information concerning the orders placed. The header records contain the following fields:

Field	Description
code	signifies the first header record in a new record group
account	number of the customer's account
company	name of the company placing the order
contact	name of purchasing agent
phone	purchasing agent's phone number

Each detail record represents a sale for either the hardware (H), publications (P), or software (S) division. A detail record contains the following fields:

Field	Description
dept	code for dept of item ordered
item	inventory number of the item ordered
quantity	quantity of the item ordered

Here are the raw data records used in this example:

```
----+----1----+----2----+----3
C 1845
  Watson's Mechanical Inc.
  Connie Lee
  9194678911
```

```
H VEN59M590768 1
P 1555441249 5
H VEN42M577621 1
H VEN21M000793 1
S MFF00512EDTR 25
C 1231
  Berstein, Epson and Epson
  Richard Long
  9199428083
H VEN34M590769 1
P 1555441253 3
P 1555441256 3
H VEN34M000792 1
S MFF00075WDPR 25
----+----1----+----2----+----3
```

The following steps describe how to store this information in two SAS data sets, one containing the header information and one containing an observation for each item ordered:

□ Describe the variables to be stored in each of the two SAS data sets and identify the input file.

□ Determine the record type.

□ Build an observation from the header information and write it to one data set.

□ Build an observation from each detail record and write it to the other data set.

□ Provide a means of handling errors.

Describe the Data Sets and Identify the Input File

First, name the two output data sets that you want to create. Specify which variables you want to write to each data set by using the KEEP= data set option. Remember that the data sets must contain one variable in common, the key variable. This variable enables you to use both data sets in the future to associate the appropriate customer information in one data set with the order information in the other. Also, specify the hierarchical file you want to read in an INFILE statement.

```
data customer(keep==account company contact phone)
     orders(keep=account dept itemno quantity);
   infile 'input-file';
```

In this example, ACCOUNT is the key variable.

Determine the Record Type

Before you can correctly read a record in a hierarchical file, you must determine the type of the current record. As shown previously in this chapter, to do this you must read a value from the record that reveals the record type and hold this record for further processing. In this example, this is the first record:

```
----+----1
C 1845
```

The following INPUT statement reads a value that reveals the type of the current record:

```
input a1 type $ a;
```

As shown earlier in this chapter, you can use conditional processing in the form of a SELECT group to read the rest of each record correctly. In this example, the value of TYPE is used to determine which kind of record is being read and then to execute the statements that correctly build an observation. The following template shows the structure of the SELECT group used here:

```
select;
   when (type='C')
      do;
         statements that build header observations
      end;
   when (type in ('S','H','P'))
      do;
         statements that build detail observations
      end;
   otherwise;
end;
```

Note that the syntax shown for this SELECT group is different from the previous one in this chapter. Both the variable name and value appear in the WHEN statement, not in the SELECT statement. As shown in the second WHEN statement, this syntax enables a single WHEN statement to express more than one value for the variable being tested.

The statements that build each observation are described in the following sections.

Build an Observation from Header Records

In this example, each observation storing customer reference information should contain the following variables:

Variable	Type	Description
ACCOUNT	character	number of the customer's account
COMPANY	character	name of the company placing the order
CONTACT	character	name of purchasing agent
PHONE	character	purchasing agent's phone number

The first records are the header records from the first record group and look like this:

```
----+----1----+----2----+----3
C 1845
   Watson's Mechanical Inc.
   Connie Lee
   9194678911
```

The first WHEN statement in the SELECT group executes when the first header record is read and begins building an observation that is written to the data set that contains header information. In this example, the first WHEN statement executes when TYPE is equal to C. This WHEN statement contains an INPUT statement to read the header records and assign values to variables and then uses an OUTPUT statement to write an observation to the customer reference data set.

```
select;
   when(type='C')
      do;
         input @3 account $4. / @3 company $30. / @3 contact $25. /
               @3 phone $10.;
         output customer;
      end;
```

When you use a DATA step to write to more than one data set, you must specify the output data set with an OUTPUT statement to direct an observation to a particular data set.

Build Each Detail Observation

In this example, each observation created from a detail record should contain the following variables:

Variable	Type	Description
ACCOUNT	character	number of the customer's account
DEPT	character	code for department of item ordered
ITEMNO	character	inventory number of the item ordered
QUANTITY	numeric	quantity of the item ordered

The detail records look like this:

```
----+----1----+----2
H VEN59M590768 1
P 1555441249 5
H VEN42M577621 1
H VEN21M000793 1
S MFF00512EDTR 25
```

Note that each detail record contains all the values needed to create an observation except for the key variable ACCOUNT. To build an observation from each detail record, you must read the necessary values from a detail record, make the values of the key variable available, and write the resulting observation to the correct data set.

Read Values from Each Detail Record

The first field has already been read and assigned to TYPE. An INPUT statement can read the second and third fields and assign values to ITEMNO and QUANTITY. Because the value for TYPE reveals the department from which an item was purchased, the value for DEPT can be set equal to that of TYPE.

```
when (type in ('S','H','P'))
   do;
      input @3 itemno : $12. quantity;
      dept=type;
```

Note that the INPUT statement uses the colon (:) format modifier and the informat $12. to read the variable ITEMNO. Using this format modifier enables you, among other things, to assign a length longer than the default to a character variable and still take advantage of the scanning feature of list input.

The next two sections continue building this DO group.

Make the Value of the Key Variable Available

Once you have read all the information you need from a detail record, you need to consider how to obtain a value for the key variable, the variable that associates information in one data set to the related information in the other data set. Usually the value of the key variable is obtained from a header record. Because variable values are set to missing at the top of each iteration of the DATA step, the key variable is set to missing before you can use its value to create an observation from any of the detail records. To prevent this value from being set to missing at the beginning of the next iteration of the DATA step, use a RETAIN statement.

In this example, ACCOUNT is the key variable. This value is contained in the first header record in each record group and cannot be obtained from a detail record. Because it is read from the first header record, however, it is reset to missing before a detail record is read. To include the value of ACCOUNT in an observation created from a detail record, use a RETAIN statement to specify that ACCOUNT's value should be retained in the program data vector from one iteration to the next.

```
retain account;
```

Once ACCOUNT is assigned a value, that value is retained until an INPUT statement reads another header record and assigns ACCOUNT a new value.

Write the Observation to the Correct Data Set

As shown previously, when creating more than one data set with a DATA step, you must use an OUTPUT statement to specify where an observation should be written. In this example, an OUTPUT statement writes each observation created from a detail record to the ORDERS data set.

```
when (type in ('S','H','P'))
   do;
       input @3 itemno : $12. quantity;
       dept=type;
       output orders;
   end;
```

Provide Error-Handling

As shown earlier in this chapter, you can use an OTHERWISE statement in a SELECT group to handle errors. You can flag problems in the SAS log by using a PUT statement. To prevent an erroneous observation from being written to the data, use a DELETE statement.* Here is the entire program that creates and prints the SAS data sets CUSTOMER and ORDERS:

```
data customer(keep=account company contact phone)
     orders(keep=account dept itemno quantity);
   retain account;
   infile 'input-file';
   input @1 type $ @;
```

---

* The DELETE statement is not actually required in this example because no statements follow the SELECT group. It is shown here, however, because in longer programs it may be necessary to use DELETE in code that handles errors.

```
        select;
           when (type='C')
              do;
                 input @3 account $4. / @3 company $30. / @3 contact $25. /
                       @3 phone $10.;
                 output customer;
              end;
           when (type in ('S','H','P'))
              do;
                 input @3 itemno : $12. quantity;
                 dept=type;
                 output orders;
              end;
           otherwise
              do;
                 put 'Error in record ' _n_ 'as follows:' _infile_;
                 delete;
              end;
        end;
run;

proc print data=orders;
   title1 'Data Set Containing Detail Information';
   title2 'and the Key Variable';
run;

proc print data=customer;
   title1 'Data Set Containing Header Information';
   title2 'and the Key Variable';
run;
```

Output 2.2 shows the results.

Output 2.2
Creating Two SAS Data Sets

```
                Data Set Containing Detail Information              1
                        and the Key Variable

        OBS    ACCOUNT      ITEMNO      QUANTITY    DEPT

         1      1845     VEN59M590768       1        H
         2      1845     1555441249         5        P
         3      1845     VEN42M577621       1        H
         4      1845     VEN21M000793       1        H
         5      1845     MFF00512EDTR      25        S
         6      1231     VEN34M590769       1        H
         7      1231     1555441253         3        P
         8      1231     1555441256         3        P
         9      1231     VEN34M000792       1        H
        10      1231     MFF00075WDPR      25        S
```

```
                Data Set Containing Header Information             2
                        and the Key Variable

    OBS    ACCOUNT        COMPANY            CONTACT       PHONE

     1      1845    Watson's Mechanical Inc.  Connie Lee   9194678911
     2      1231    Berstein, Epson and Epson Richard Long 9199428083
```

Creating One SAS Data Set When the File Contains Markers

Because it is more convenient to access a single file to retrieve information, you may choose to create a single SAS data set from hierarchical records. As shown previously in Figure 2.3, you can store all the information from each record group in a single observation. Especially if the amount of detail information in each record group is fairly uniform, this method is a particularly efficient way to store your data.

To create a single observation from an entire record group, you must be able to

□ determine when the end of a record group is reached

□ override the automatic output at the end of each iteration of the DATA step so that you can write an observation only when a complete group of records has been read.

How you determine when the end of a record group is reached relies on whether or not the file contains markers between record groups. The following example demonstrates reading hierarchical data that contain markers between record groups to create a single SAS data set. The next example in this chapter demonstrates reading the same data without the convenience of such markers.

Raw Data Example

This example reads a hierarchical file containing expense account information for each trip a company representative made during a given month. The header record contains a code that identifies it as a header record, the representative's name, and the destination. Each detail record reports an amount spent on airfare (A), ground transportation (T), hotel (H), food (F), or entertainment (E). There is only one detail record for each type of expense in each record group. The last detail record in each group is followed by a record containing a pound sign (#). Here are the contents of the raw data file read in this example:

```
----+----1----+----2----+----3----+----4----+
Z Harry Smith        Las Vegas
A 459.70
T 25.00
H 239.50
F 110.15
E 120.00
#
Z Sandra Jones       San Francisco
A 776.80
T 75.50
H 659.75
F 195.00
#
Z Benson Vale        Chicago
A 329.70
T 35.00
H 355.50
F 136.15
E 75.00
#
----+----1----+----2----+----3----+----4----+
```

The data set to be created from these data contains the following variables:

Variable	Type	Description
NAME	character	name of employee
CITY	character	trip destination
AIRFARE	numeric	air travel costs
GROUND	numeric	ground travel costs
HOTEL	numeric	hotel costs
FOOD	numeric	food costs
ENTERTMT	numeric	entertainment costs

The following tasks describe how to construct such a data set from these data:

□ Determine the record type.

□ Conditionally read information from the header records and check for errors.

□ Conditionally read information from each of an undetermined number of detail records and write an observation.

Determine the Record Type

As shown previously, begin the DATA step and specify the input file. Read a record, assign a value to a variable, and test that value to determine the kind of record being read. Then hold the record for further processing with a single trailing @. In this example, the variable TYPE is used to determine the type of record being read. This variable is not needed in the output data set, so the DROP= data set option specifies that it not be written to the output data set.

```
data expense(drop=type);
   infile 'input-file';
   input type $1. a;
```

Conditionally Read the Header Record and Check for Errors

To begin building an observation correctly, you must start with a header record. In this example, if TYPE is equal to Z, the record is a header record, and the appropriate INPUT statement executes and assigns values to the variables NAME and CITY.

```
select (type);
   when ('Z') input name & $23. city & $15.;
```

Note that an ampersand (&) precedes each informat in the INPUT statement. This format modifier enables you to use list input to read character values that contain an embedded blank.

If the first record isn't a header record, you don't want to begin building an observation. Provide for this possibility with an OTHERWISE statement. In this example, the following statements begin building an observation with a header record and provide the same type of error-handling feature as shown earlier in this chapter:

```
select (type);
   when ('Z') input name & $23. city & $15.;
   otherwise
      do;
         put 'Missing header record. Erroneous record follows:';
         put _infile_;
         delete;
      end;
end;
```

Conditionally Read Detail Records and Write an Observation

The next step is to continue building an observation by reading all of the detail records in a record group. To accomplish this you must do the following:

□ read a detail record and assign values to the appropriate variable

□ read all detail records in a group before writing an observation.

Read Each Detail Record

To read each detail record and assign values to the appropriate variable, use a SELECT group. In this example, the record is a detail record if TYPE is equal to A, T, H, F, or E. The following SELECT group conditionally executes the appropriate INPUT statement for each possible type of expense in a detail record to assign a data value to the appropriate variable. As shown earlier, you can use an OTHERWISE statement to handle errors.

```
select (type);
   when ('A') input airfare;
   when ('T') input ground;
   when ('H') input hotel;
   when ('F') input food;
   when ('E') input entertmt;
   when ('#');
   otherwise put 'Error in detail record as follows: ' _infile_;
end;
```

Note that the last WHEN statement prevents the OTHERWISE statement from writing a note to the log each time a marker between record groups (#) is read.

Read the Entire Record Group before Writing an Observation

To build an observation from an entire record group, you need to continue reading a record, testing its type, and executing the correct INPUT statement until you reach the end of a record group. To do this, embed the statements that read each detail record in a DO UNTIL group. This example specifies that the DO UNTIL loop executes until the value read for a record type is a pound sign (#).

```
do until(type='#');
   input type $1. @;
   select (type);
      when ('A') input airfare;
      when ('T') input ground;
      when ('H') input hotel;
      when ('F') input food;
      when ('E') input entertmt;
      when ('#');
      otherwise put 'Error in detail record as follows: ' _infile_;
   end;
end;
```

At the end of each iteration of the DATA step in this example, all records will have been read for a record group. A single observation that contains all the expenses reported for a single trip is automatically written to the data set EXPENSE. Processing returns to the top of the DATA step and continues until each record group has been read and the end of the file is reached.

Here is the entire DATA step that reads these data and constructs observations that contain all the information for each business trip. The PRINT procedure displays the resulting data set.

```
data expense(drop=type);
   length name $ 23 city $ 15 type $ 1;
   infile 'input-file';
   input type $1. @;
   select (type);
      when ('Z') input name & $23. city & $15.;
      otherwise
         do;
            put 'Missing header record. Erroneous record follows:';
            put _infile_;
            delete;
         end;
   end;
   do until(type='#');
      input type $1. @;
      select (type);
         when ('A') input airfare;
         when ('T') input ground;
         when ('H') input hotel;
         when ('F') input food;
         when ('E') input entertmt;
         when ('#');
         otherwise put 'Error in detail record as follows: ' _infile_;
      end;
   end;
run;
proc print data=expense;
   format airfare ground hotel food entertmt dollar8.2;
   title 'Travel Expenses';
run;
```

Output 2.3 shows the resulting data set. Note that the expense figures are formatted to show that they are monetary amounts.

Output 2.3
Creating a Single Observation from a Group of Records

```
                              Travel Expenses                             1

OBS    NAME       CITY          AIRFARE  GROUND   HOTEL     FOOD ENTERTMT

 1   Harry Smith  Las Vegas     $459.70  $25.00 $239.50 $110.15 $120.00
 2   Sandra Jones San Francisco $776.80  $75.50 $659.75 $195.00       .
 3   Benson Vale  Chicago       $329.70  $35.00 $355.50 $136.15  $75.00
```

Creating One SAS Data Set When the File Contains No Markers

In the previous example, the data contained markers that separated one record group from the next. However, sometimes your data do not contain such markers. In such cases you must use other means for determining when you have reached the end of a record group and, therefore, when to write an observation. Here are the same data you saw in the previous example, with one exception: there are no markers between record groups.

```
----+----1----+----2----+----3----+----4----+
Z Harry Smith           Las Vegas
A 459.70
T 25.00
H 239.50
F 110.15
E 120.00
Z Sandra Jones          San Francisco
A 776.80
T 75.50
H 659.75
F 195.00
Z Benson Vale           Chicago
A 329.70
T 35.00
H 355.50
F 136.15
E 75.00
----+----1----+----2----+----3----+----4----+
```

To create a single observation from each record group when the groups are not separated by markers, you must read the header record belonging to the next record group before you can know when to write an observation. One way to accomplish this is to read one record per iteration and then write an observation when you reach the next header record. When you use multiple iterations of the DATA step to build a single observation, you must ensure that variable values needed for the current observation are not reset to missing each time the DATA step begins a new iteration. To solve these problems, use the following steps:

□ Determine the record type.

□ Conditionally read information from a header record.

□ Conditionally read information from a single detail record.

□ Provide error-handling.

□ Control resetting values between iterations.

□ Write an observation when all related records have been read.

Determine the Record Type

As shown previously, begin the DATA step, determine the record type, and hold a record so you can read the rest of it with another INPUT statement:

```
data expense(drop=type);
   infile 'input-file';
   input type $1. @;
```

Conditionally Read Information from a Header Record

As shown previously, you can use a SELECT group to read information from each type of record. The following WHEN statement reads a header record in this example:

```
select (type);
   when ('Z') input @3 name & $23. city & $15.;
```

Conditionally Read Information from a Single Detail Record

The following WHEN statements execute the appropriate INPUT statement to read detail records in this example:

```
select (type);
   when ('Z') input @3 name & $23. city & $15.;
   when ('A') input airfare;
   when ('T') input ground;
   when ('H') input hotel;
   when ('F') input food;
   when ('E') input entertmt;
   otherwise;
end;
```

Provide Error-Handling

As shown previously, use an OTHERWISE statement to provide error-handling:

```
select (type);
   when ('Z') input @3 name & $23. city & $15.;
   when ('A') input airfare;
   when ('T') input ground;
   when ('H') input hotel;
   when ('F') input food;
   when ('E') input entertmt;
   otherwise put 'Erroneous record follows:' / _infile_;
end;
```

Control Resetting Values between Iterations

By default, values read from previous iterations are set to missing after each iteration. An observation, therefore, will contain only values for the last detail record read. For this reason, you must override the default action of the DATA step and control explicitly when values are retained in the program data vector.

To prevent values in the program data vector from being reset to missing after each iteration, use a RETAIN statement. Once you retain the values, you must clear them each time you begin building a new observation. Therefore, use assignment statements to reset retained values to missing. This example sets the retained values to missing each time a header record is read.

```
data expense(drop=type);
   length name $ 23 city $ 15;
   retain name city airfare ground hotel food entertmt;
   infile 'input-file' end=lastone;
   input type $1. @;
   select (type);
      when ('Z')
         do;
            name=' '; city=' ';
            airfare=.; ground=.; hotel=.; food=.; entertmt=.;
            input @3 name & $23. city & $15.;
         end;
      when ('A') input airfare;
      when ('T') input ground;
      when ('H') input hotel;
      when ('F') input food;
      when ('E') input entertmt;
      otherwise put 'Erroneous record follows:' / _infile_;
   end;
run;
```

Write an Observation

When you use multiple iterations of the DATA step to gather the information necessary to produce a single observation, you cannot use the automatic output at the end of each iteration of the DATA step to produce the observations you want. You must explicitly write an observation when you have read all the detail records in a record group.

When there are no markers between record groups in your data, you must read the next header record in the file before you can know that you are ready to write an observation. Therefore, you can use an OUTPUT statement to create an observation each time a header record is read after the first iteration of the DATA step. Use the automatic variable _N_ in an IF-THEN statement to ensure that no observation is written on the first iteration of the DATA step since only a header record has been read at that time.

```
select (type);
   when ('Z')
      do;
          if _n_ gt 1 then output;
          name=' '; city=' ';
          airfare=.; ground=.; hotel=.; food=.; entertmt=.;
          input a3 name & $23. city & $15.;
      end;
```

A single OUTPUT statement would be the only one required if not for the problem caused by the last observation created. The last record group in a hierarchical file is not followed by a header record; therefore, the only way you can know that you have finished reading the last record group is by reaching the end of the input file. To create an observation after the last detail record is read for the last record group, use the END= variable to determine when the last record is being processed and execute an OUTPUT statement when that variable is equal to 1 (or true). Use the END= option in an INFILE statement to create a variable whose value is automatically set to 1 when the last record is processed:

```
infile 'input-file' end=lastone;
```

Then, execute an OUTPUT statement at the bottom of the DATA step when LASTONE, the END= variable in this case, is true:

```
if lastone then output;
```

Here is the complete DATA step that creates the data set EXPENSE and the PROC PRINT step that displays it.

```
data expense(drop=type);
   infile 'input-file' end=lastone;
   length name $ 23 city $ 15;
   retain name city airfare ground hotel food entertmt;
   input type $1. a;
   select (type);
      when ('Z')
         do;
             if _n_ gt 1 then output;
             name=' '; city=' ';
             airfare=.; ground=.; hotel=.; food=.; entertmt=.;
             input a3 name & $23. city & $15.;
         end;
```

```
            when ('A') input airfare;
            when ('T') input ground;
            when ('H') input hotel;
            when ('F') input food;
            when ('E') input entertmt;
            otherwise put 'Erroneous record follows: ' / _infile_;
         end;
         if lastone then output;
   run;

   proc print data=expense;
      format airfare ground hotel food entertmt dollar8.2;
      title 'Travel Expenses';
   run;
```

Output 2.4 shows the resulting data set.

Output 2.4
Reading All
Related Records to
Produce
Observations

```
                              Travel Expenses                            1

   OBS    NAME       CITY          AIRFARE  GROUND   HOTEL    FOOD ENTERTMT

    1   Harry Smith  Las Vegas     $459.70  $25.00 $239.50 $110.15 $120.00
    2   Sandra Jones San Francisco $776.80  $75.50 $659.75 $195.00    .
    3   Benson Vale  Chicago       $329.70  $35.00 $355.50 $136.15  $75.00
```

Summary

The following points summarize how to handle the special problems presented by reading files containing records in different formats, including the special case of hierarchical files:

□ To read files that contain different types of records, determine the record type and conditionally execute the appropriate INPUT statement. Use the single trailing @ to hold a record in the input buffer while reading a field that reveals the record type. To conditionally process the INPUT statement appropriate to the current record type, use IF-THEN statements or SELECT and WHEN statements.

□ You can detect certain types of errors and prevent those records from affecting your output data set. In a SELECT group, use OTHERWISE and DO statements to specify a group of statements that will execute when the value for the record type is invalid. Use PUT and FILE statements to write messages to the log when an error occurs and to write the record containing the mistake to an external file.

□ One way to create SAS data sets from hierarchical records is to create a separate observation from each record, writing header records to one data set and detail records to another. The two data sets must have a variable in common, the key variable, that allows you to determine the relationship between the header and detail information. Use an OUTPUT statement and specify the appropriate data set rather than use the automatic output feature of the DATA step.

□ Another method of creating a SAS data set from a hierarchical file is to read all the records in a given group of records in a hierarchical file and then create a single observation. How you determine when you have reached the end of a group of records affects whether you can use the automatic output feature in the DATA step or you must explicitly output observations.

□ To determine when you have reached the end of an INPUT file, use the END= option in an INFILE statement. You can then base an action, such as executing an OUTPUT statement to write an observation to the data set, on the value of the END= variable.

SAS Tools

This section summarizes syntax for the statements and procedures discussed in this chapter.

Statements

DO UNTIL (*condition*);
   SAS statements
END;
   executes the enclosed SAS statements until the specified condition is true. The condition can be any valid SAS expression, enclosed in parentheses. The condition is evaluated at the bottom of the loop, after the enclosed statements have been executed. If the condition is true, the DO loop is not executed again. Because the condition is evaluated at the bottom of the loop, the enclosed statements are always executed at least once.

FILE '*output-file*';
   identifies the output file for PUT statements in the current DATA step. Specify in quotes the name by which the operating system identifies the physical file. Note that if you do not specify a FILE statement, PUT statement output is written to the SAS log.

INFILE '*input-file*' END=*variable*;
   specifies the external file in which the input data are located. The END= option creates a variable, whose name you specify, that is automatically set to 1 when the last record from an input file is being processed. You can use the value of END= to allow a statement to execute only during the last iteration of the DATA step. When the DATA step reads only one input file, the END= variable is set to 1 during the last iteration. Note that the END= variable is available only for the duration of the DATA step, that is, it is not written to the data set.

INPUT *specifications* @;
   reads a record of raw data either from an external file or instream data lines. Use the single trailing @ sign to hold the current record, preventing the next INPUT statement from reading a new record. This is important in conditional processing where you need to read a value from a record to determine which INPUT statement should be executed for reading the rest of the record.

The *specifications* introduced in this chapter include the ampersand (&) and colon (:) format modifiers.

&

enables you to read a character value that contains a blank when using list input. The value must be terminated with at least two blanks. This format modifier can be used with or without an informat.

:

enables you to use an informat when using list input to read a data value.

PUT __INFILE__;

writes the contents of the current record in the input buffer to the SAS log by default, or to an external file, or to the procedure output file.
PUT __INFILE__ is especially useful with other statements for error-handling.

RETAIN *variable-list*;

causes a variable whose value is assigned by an assignment statement to retain its value from the current iteration of the DATA step to the next iteration.

SELECT <*variable*>;
  WHEN-*1 (value-1) action-to-take*;
  <**WHEN**-*n (value-2) action-to-take*;>
  <**OTHERWISE** <*action-to-take*>;>
END;

is known as a SELECT group. Like a series of IF-THEN and ELSE statements, a SELECT group tests for conditions and then takes appropriate action. Especially if you have many conditions to specify, your code may be easier to read if you use a SELECT group. The *action-to-take* may be expressed in a single executable statement or in a DO group.

The OTHERWISE statement provides an alternative action when none of the valid conditions are met and is especially useful for error-handling. If you do not want to supply an alternative action, it is recommended that you use a null OTHERWISE statement to prevent the DATA step from stopping when none of the valid conditions are met.

SELECT;
  WHEN *(variable=value-1) action-to-take*;
  <**WHEN** *(variable* IN *(value-2, . . . , value-n)) action-to-take*;>
  OTHERWISE <*action-to-take*>;
END;

To express multiple conditions in a single WHEN statement, you can use this alternate syntax for a SELECT group. Note that the name of the variable being tested is not specified in the SELECT statement. If the variable is a character variable, remember to enclose each value in quotes.

Data Set Options

DROP=*variable-list*
    specifies the variables that should not be processed or written to an output data set.

KEEP=*variable-list*
    specifies the variables to be processed or to be written to an output data set. When used following a data set name in a DATA statement, the KEEP= option specifies which variables should be part of the observation written to the data set. Using KEEP= in a DATA statement is especially useful when you are creating more than one data set in a single DATA step or when you create some variables only for computational purposes that you want to use during the course of the DATA step but not store in the output data set.

Learning More

This section provides references for learning more about the topics presented in this chapter.

□ For complete information on writing specifications for an INPUT statement, see Chapter 9, "SAS Language Statements," in *SAS Language: Reference, Version 6, First Edition.*

□ For more information on how to specify an external file in an INFILE or FILE statement (*input-file* or *output-file* in the examples in this chapter), see the SAS companion for your host operating system.

□ For more information on options available under all host operating systems for the FILE and INFILE statements, see Chapter 9 in *SAS Language: Reference.* For information about options for these statements that are specific to an operating system, see the SAS companion for your operating system.

□ For more information on select group processing, see the SELECT statement in Chapter 9 of *SAS Language: Reference.*

Chapter 3 Reading Varying-Length Fields and Repeated Fields

Introduction

Sometimes you need to create a SAS data set from raw data that are configured in a way that made recording the data easy but presents certain problems when trying to read them. For example, you may need to read character fields that vary in length from one record to the next. You may also need to generate data for statistically designed experiments. These experiments are designed to require the least amount of effort in recording the data. To create a SAS data set from such data, however, you need to know how to generate additional data while reading the data that were recorded. This chapter demonstrates techniques for reading data in both of these circumstances.

Records in which the data are arranged in repeated patterns may be easy to read, but your programs can get lengthy and repetitive. This chapter demonstrates how to read such data in a way that reduces repetition in your programming statements. The final data-reading task demonstrates how to read records that contain a varying number of repeated fields. The solution to this task combines techniques used in reading varying-length fields and data arranged in repeated patterns.

In this chapter

This chapter demonstrates techniques for reading data in the following configurations:

□ reading records that contain a varying-length character field

□ reading data that occur in repeated patterns

□ reading data for which additional values must be generated

□ reading records that contain a varying number of fields.

Prerequisites

To understand how to perform the data-reading tasks in this chapter, you need to be familiar with the following features and concepts:

□ DO loops in DATA step processing

□ list and formatted input

□ pointer controls in INPUT statements

□ data set options.

Reading Varying-Length Fields

Data records that contain a character field that varies in length from one record to the next create a problem when you try to read the data to create a SAS data set. The problem is that it is more difficult to describe the fields in an INPUT statement than when the fields are a uniform length in all records. If the data contain delimiters, you can usually read the records accurately with modified list input. If the data do not contain delimiters, however, as in the examples in this section, you must find another solution to be able to read the varying-length field accurately in all records.

The following examples show you how to read data records having a varying-length character field under these circumstances:

□ when the length of the field is given

□ when the length of the field is not given.

Reading a Varying-Length Field
When the Length Is Given

Some data records contain a field whose value indicates the length of the varying-length field. When this is the case, you can simply read that field and use the value in conjunction with a SAS informat to read the varying-length character field.

In this example, the data records contain the following four fields:

Field	Description
name length	length of the character field containing the employee's name
department	employee's department
name	employee's first and last names
phone	employee's telephone extension

Here are the raw data records:

```
----+----1----+----2----+----3
100156Gene Short7450
180156Suzette Milanovich7451
110156Jason Blank7447
070156Lee Lai7463
```

Note that there are no delimiters between the four fields and that the third field, containing the employee's name, varies in length.

To read such records, first read the field that reveals the length of the varying-length field in the current record and assign it to a variable. In this example, the first field, assigned to the variable NAMELEN, reveals the length of the varying-length character field that occurs later in the record.

```
data employee(drop=namelen);
   input namelen 2. other variables and informats;
```

Once the length of the varying-length field is known, you can use the $VARYING. informat to read a value from that field and assign it to a variable. This example uses the $VARYING. informat and the value supplied by the variable NAMELEN to read a value and assign it to the variable NAME.

```
   input namelen 2. dept $4. name $varying18. namelen phone $4.;
```

Note that the informat is expressed as $VARYING18. Specify a width with this informat that is large enough to accommodate the longest field you expect to read with it.

The $VARYING. informat in conjunction with a variable whose value supplies the correct length (NAMELEN) enables the INPUT statement to read the character value as though the INPUT statement were coded specifically for each record. In the first record, the value for the variable NAME is read as if it were described as follows in the INPUT statement:

```
name $10.
```

In the second record, the value for NAME is read as if it were described as follows in the INPUT statement:

```
name $18.
```

Here is the entire DATA step that reads these data, as well as the PRINT procedure that prints the report.

```
data employee(drop=namelen);
   input namelen 2. dept $4. name $varying18. namelen phone $4.;
   cards;
100156Gene Short7450
180156Suzette Milanovich7451
110156Jason Blank7447
070156Lee Lai7463
;

proc print data=employee noobs;
   title 'Phone List';
run;
```

Output 3.1 shows the results.

Output 3.1
Reading a
Varying-Length
Field

```
                           Phone List                              1

            DEPT    NAME                    PHONE

            0156    Gene Short              7450
            0156    Suzette Milanovich      7451
            0156    Jason Blank             7447
            0156    Lee Lai                 7463
```

Reading a Varying-Length Field When the Length Is Not Given

Usually records containing a field that varies in length from one record to the next do not also contain a field that reveals the varying field's length. You must, therefore, determine the field length yourself before you can read the record. This is an easy matter when the following conditions exist:

□ the data reside in a file that has a variable instead of a fixed-record format

□ the other fields in each record have a fixed length

□ the records contain no trailing blanks.

By using the length of each record and the combined length of the other fields, you can calculate the length of the varying-length field in each record and use it with the $VARYING. informat.

The raw data records in this example are similar to those in the previous example, with two exceptions:

□ They do not contain a field that indicates the length of the varying-length character field.

□ They reside in an external file that contains varying-length records.

The raw data records are as follows:

```
----+----1----+----2----+----3
0156Gene Short7450
0156Suzette Milanovich7451
0156Jason Blank7447
0156Lee Lai7463
```

First, determine the length of the entire record. To do this, use the LENGTH= option in the INFILE statement and specify a variable name. When an INPUT statement reads a record, the LENGTH= variable is given a value.

```
data employe2(drop=namelen totlen);
infile 'input-file' length=totlen;
input @;
```

The LENGTH= variable is named TOTLEN in this example. Note that this variable is created by the INFILE statement but that it does not acquire a value until an INPUT statement reads a record. For this reason, you cannot use the value of the LENGTH= variable until after an INPUT statement has executed.

Next, calculate the length of the varying-length field. First, manually calculate the sum of the fixed-length fields. Then, subtract the combined lengths of the known fields from the LENGTH= variable and assign that value to a variable in an assignment statement. The following assignment statement subtracts 8, the combined length of the known fields, from the value of TOTLEN, and assigns the value to the new variable NAMELEN.

```
namelen=totlen-8;
```

Third, read the varying-length field by using the $VARYING. informat and a variable whose value represents the length of the varying-length field in the current record. This example reads a value for NAME by using the $VARYING. informat and the value calculated for NAMELEN. Here is the complete program that creates and displays the data set EMPLOYE2.

```
data employe2(drop=namelen, totlen);
   infile 'input-file ' length=totlen;
   input @;
   namelen=totlen-8;
   input dept $4. name $varying18. namelen phone $4.;
run;

proc print data=employe2 noobs;
   title 'Phone List';
run;
```

Output 3.2 shows the results.

Output 3.2
Reading a
Varying-Length
Field in a
Varying-Length
Record

```
                                     Phone List                              1

               DEPT    NAME                    PHONE

               0156    Gene Short              7450
               0156    Suzette Milanovich      7451
               0156    Jason Blank             7447
               0156    Lee Lai                 7463
```

Reducing Repetition When Reading Data in Repeated Patterns

Sometimes data occur in repeated patterns in data records. Reading these data to create a SAS data set is usually easy, but your programs may be lengthy and repetitive. You can reduce such repetition in your DATA step programs by using DO loops.

As an example, consider the following manufacturing data. These data record the weight of oil cans filled by machine. The machine fills 8-ounce cans of two-cycle engine oil additive. Each hour for twelve hours four sample cans are selected and weighed.

Each record in the raw data contains the following fields:

Field	Description
hour	the hour in which the samples are taken
weight1-4	weights of four sample cans

The quality control department wants to analyze these data. The first step is to create a SAS data set that contains a single observation for each measurement taken. As shown in Figure 3.1, a DATA step must create four observations from each record.

Figure 3.1
Creating Four
Observations from
a Single Record

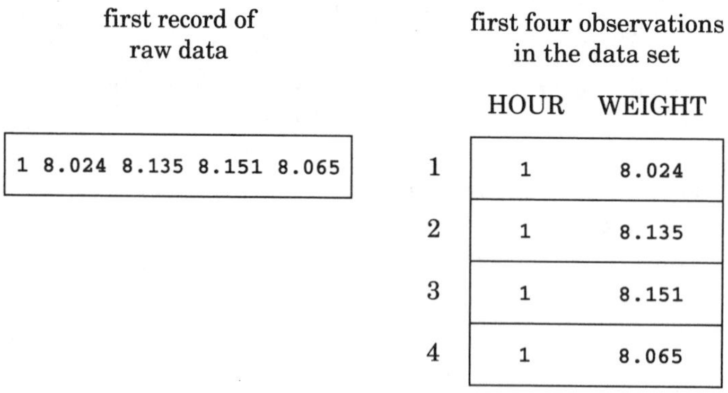

first record of
raw data

```
1 8.024 8.135 8.151 8.065
```

first four observations
in the data set

	HOUR	WEIGHT
1	1	8.024
2	1	8.135
3	1	8.151
4	1	8.065

The first INPUT statement reads a value from the first field and assigns it to HOUR. The value for HOUR is the same for all four observations to be created from the first record.

```
data oil1(drop=i);
   input hour @;
```

The next step is to read each value for WEIGHT (four in each record) and write an observation after each is read. An iterative DO loop enables you to write a single pair of INPUT and OUTPUT statements to read a value and write an observation multiple times. Here is the complete program that creates the data set OIL1 and prints a report.

```
data oil1(drop=i);
   input hour @;
   do i=1 to 4;
      input weight @;
      output;
   end;
   cards;
1 8.024 8.135 8.151 8.065
2 7.971 8.165 8.066 8.157
3 8.024 8.135 8.151 8.065
4 7.971 8.165 8.066 8.157
5 8.024 8.135 8.151 8.065
6 7.971 8.165 8.066 8.157
7 8.024 8.135 8.151 8.065
8 7.971 8.165 8.066 8.157
9 8.024 8.135 8.151 8.065
10 7.971 8.165 8.066 8.157
11 8.024 8.135 8.151 8.065
12 7.971 8.165 8.066 8.157
;

proc print data=oil1;
   title 'Four Sample Weights Taken for 12 Hours';
run;
```

Output 3.3 shows the results.

Output 3.3
Reducing Repetition When Reading Data

```
            Four Sample Weights Taken for 12 Hours              1

            OBS     HOUR     WEIGHT

             1       1       8.024
             2       1       8.135
             3       1       8.151
             4       1       8.065
             5       2       7.971
             6       2       8.165
             7       2       8.066
             8       2       8.157
             9       3       8.024
```

(continued on next page)

(continued from previous page)

```
10      3       8.135
11      3       8.151
12      3       8.065
13      4       7.971
14      4       8.165
15      4       8.066
16      4       8.157
17      5       8.024
18      5       8.135
19      5       8.151
20      5       8.065
21      6       7.971
22      6       8.165
23      6       8.066
24      6       8.157
25      7       8.024
26      7       8.135
27      7       8.151
28      7       8.065
29      8       7.971
30      8       8.165
31      8       8.066
32      8       8.157
33      9       8.024
34      9       8.135
35      9       8.151
36      9       8.065
37     10       7.971
38     10       8.165
39     10       8.066
40     10       8.157
41     11       8.024
42     11       8.135
43     11       8.151
44     11       8.065
45     12       7.971
46     12       8.165
47     12       8.066
48     12       8.157
```

Generating Data for Statistically Designed Experiments

Experiments can be statistically designed so that repetitive recording is kept to a minimum. To create a SAS data set from these data so that you can analyze the results, you must be able to generate unrecorded data values at the same time that you read the data that were recorded.

The first example below is over-simplified to demonstrate the basic principle of using programming statements to generate data. The second example consists of actual experiment data that show the real power of the DATA step to generate data.

Generating Values for a Single Variable

This example demonstrates how to generate values for a variable while reading recorded values from raw data. It uses data similar to the data in the preceding example. The data records have one difference, however. Note that each data line shows only the four weights taken each hour not the number of the hour itself.

```
----+----1----+----2----+
8.024 8.135 8.151 8.065
```

Read the Recorded Values

The previous example showed how to use a DO loop to read repeated fields and create four observations from each record:

```
do i=1 to 4;
   input weight @;
   output;
end;
```

Generate an Additional Value

Since the hour in which the measurements were taken is not available in each record, the next step is to generate that value and assign it to HOUR. Because each record contains weight measurements taken each hour, the program needs to change the value of the variable HOUR each time it reads a complete record. A second DO loop accomplishes this:

```
do hour=1 to 12;
   do i=1 to 4;
      input weight @;
      output;
   end;
end;
```

The variable HOUR is set to 1 at the beginning of the first DO loop. The inner DO loop generates four observations from the first record and stops iterating. Then the index variable of the outer DO loop is checked. Because its value has not reached the stopping value, the variable HOUR is incremented by 1. Then the inner DO loop iterates again, reading the second record and generating four more observations. This continues until the DO loop reads the twelfth record, after which the value of the index variable exceeds the stopping value.

Release a Held Input Record

Here is the example, as created thus far. Note that, unlike the previous example, the DATA step itself iterates only once. All input records are read within the iterations of the outside DO loop.

```
data oil2(drop=i);
   do hour=1 to 12;
      do i=1 to 4;
         input weight a;
         output;
      end;
   end;
   cards;
data lines
   ;
```

This program works, but it writes a note to the log reporting that the INPUT statement was forced to go to a new line to continue reading. When all the records are read by iterations of a DO loop instead of iterations of a DATA step, the record held by the single trailing @ is not released automatically when the next iteration begins. A null INPUT statement is useful for releasing a held record at the appropriate time. Here is the complete program that creates and prints the data set OIL2.

```
data oil2(drop=i);
   do hour=1 to 12;
      do i=1 to 4;
         input weight a;
         output;
      end;
      input;
   end;
   cards;
8.024 8.135 8.151 8.065
7.971 8.165 8.066 8.157
8.024 8.135 8.151 8.065
7.971 8.165 8.066 8.157
8.024 8.135 8.151 8.065
7.971 8.165 8.066 8.157
8.024 8.135 8.151 8.065
7.971 8.165 8.066 8.157
8.024 8.135 8.151 8.065
7.971 8.165 8.066 8.157
8.024 8.135 8.151 8.065
7.971 8.165 8.066 8.157
;

proc print data=oil2;
   title 'Four Sample Weights Taken for 12 Hours';
run;
```

Note that this DATA step results in the same output data set as the preceding example (Output 3.3).

Generating Values for Multiple Variables

This example demonstrates using programming statements to generate data values for statistically designed experiment data.

Raw Data Example

The data used in this example, from Cochran and Cox (1957, p.176),* record the effect of electric current on denervated muscle.** Each record lists only twelve values, each value being the weight of a muscle after a current was passed through it. For example, here is the first data record:

```
----+----1----+----2----+----3----+----4
72 74 69 61 61 65 62 65 70 85 76 61
```

For each value of the variable WEIGHT, the appropriate value must be generated for the variables TIME, CURRENT, and NUMBER by programming statements. Each observation in the resulting SAS data set contains the following numeric variables:

Variable	Description
TIME	length of time the current is applied to the muscle, ranging from 1 to 4
CURRENT	level of electric current applied, ranging from 1 to 4
NUMBER	number of treatments per day, ranging from 1 to 3 times
WEIGHT	weight of the muscle

Because of the way the experiment is designed, it is easy to generate the correct values for the TIME, CURRENT, and NUMBER for each value of WEIGHT. You

---

* Cochran, W.G. and Cox, G.M. (1957), *Experimental Designs*, 2d Edition, New York: John Wiley & Sons, Inc., 176.

** Due to their length, only part of the data are shown in this example.

can see the pattern by looking at the observations that should be generated by the 12 values for WEIGHT in the first record:

```
OBSERVATION    TIME    CURRENT    NUMBER    WEIGHT
          1       1          1         1        72
          2       1          1         2        74
          3       1          1         3        69
          4       1          2         1        61
          5       1          2         2        61
          6       1          2         3        65
          7       1          3         1        62
          8       1          3         2        65
          9       1          3         3        70
         10       1          4         1        85
         11       1          4         2        76
         12       1          4         3        61
```

Read Each Recorded Value and Write an Observation

Each input record contains 12 values for WEIGHT. The following program creates an observation for each value read and assigned to WEIGHT:

```
data one;
   do i=1 to 12;
      input weight @;
      output;
   end;
   cards;
72 74 69 61 61 65 62 65 70 85 76 61
more data lines
;
```

Each iteration of this DATA step reads a single record and generates 12 observations. The next section shows you how to use additional DO loops to generate unrecorded data values.

Generate Unrecorded Values for Each Observation

Because of the design of the experiment, an iterative DO loop can generate the unrecorded values for the variables NUMBER, CURRENT, and TIME. The value for NUMBER, the number of treatments, ranges from 1 to 3, and treatments are done consecutively. The value for the variable CURRENT ranges from 1 to 4 and is incremented by 1 after each set of three treatments.

```
data one;
   do current=1 to 4;
      do number=1 to 3;
         input weight @;
         output;
      end;
   end;
```

```
    cards;
72 74 69 61 61 65 62 65 70 85 76 61
more data lines
    ;
```

At the end of the first iteration of the DATA step, twelve values for WEIGHT have been read and a new record must be read. Each new record requires a new value for the variable TIME, which represents the length of time the current is applied. The value for TIME ranges from 1 to 4 and is incremented by 1 after each set of 12 treatments. Note that, as in the previous example, a null INPUT statement releases the input record held by the single trailing @. Here is the complete program that creates a data set from the statistically designed experiment data and then displays it.

```
data one;
   do time=1 to 4;
      do current=1 to 4;
         do number=1 to 3;
            input weight @;
            output;
         end;
      end;
      input;
   end;
   cards;
72 74 69 61 61 65 62 65 70 85 76 61
67 52 62 60 55 59 64 65 64 67 72 60
57 66 72 72 43 43 63 66 72 56 75 92
57 56 78 60 63 58 61 79 68 73 86 71
   ;

proc print data=one;
   title1 'Weight of Denervated Muscle';
   title2 'After Application of Electric Current';
run;
```

Output 3.4 shows the results. It is easy to discern the design of the experiment from the resulting output.

Output 3.4
Generating Values
for Multiple
Variables

```
                      Weight of Denervated Muscle                    1
                  After Application of Electric Current

          OBS     TIME     CURRENT     NUMBER     WEIGHT

           1        1         1           1          72
           2        1         1           2          74
           3        1         1           3          69
           4        1         2           1          61
           5        1         2           2          61
           6        1         2           3          65
           7        1         3           1          62
           8        1         3           2          65
           9        1         3           3          70
          10        1         4           1          85
          11        1         4           2          76
```

(continued on next page)

(continued from previous page)

12	1	4	3	61
13	2	1	1	67
14	2	1	2	52
15	2	1	3	62
16	2	2	1	60
17	2	2	2	55
18	2	2	3	59
19	2	3	1	64
20	2	3	2	65
21	2	3	3	64
22	2	4	1	67
23	2	4	2	72
24	2	4	3	60
25	3	1	1	57
26	3	1	2	66
27	3	1	3	72
28	3	2	1	72
29	3	2	2	43
30	3	2	3	43
31	3	3	1	63
32	3	3	2	66
33	3	3	3	72
34	3	4	1	56
35	3	4	2	75
36	3	4	3	92
37	4	1	1	57
38	4	1	2	56
39	4	1	3	78
40	4	2	1	60
41	4	2	2	63
42	4	2	3	58
43	4	3	1	61
44	4	3	2	79
45	4	3	3	68
46	4	4	1	73
47	4	4	2	86
48	4	4	3	71

Reading a Varying Number of Fields

To read a record of raw data in a DATA step, you must be able to describe the location of the fields in each record. If records contain a varying number of fields, you do not know what any individual record looks like when it is being read. Describing fluctuating records is more complex than describing uniform records.

Raw Data Example

Consider the following records of expense report data. Each record contains the following fields:

Field	Description
name	employee's name
code	expense category
amount	amount of the expenditure

Valid expense categories are Entertainment, Hotel, Travel, and Food. Each type of expenditure is reported only once in each record. The number of expenditures reported, however, differs from one record to the next. Here are the records:

```
----+----1----+----2----+----3----+----4----+
Smith E 45.75 H 375.00 T 985.00 F 157.95
Wyerbach T 16.65 F 23.63
Lee H 975.00 T 235.50 F 295.00
```

The goal is to create a SAS data set that contains one observation for each expenditure reported in the records. Output 3.5 shows the data set to be created.

Output 3.5
Reading a Varying Number of Fields

```
                      Reported Travel Expenditures                    1

            OBS    NAME        CODE    AMOUNT

             1     Smith        E       45.75
             2     Smith        H      375.00
             3     Smith        T      985.00
             4     Smith        F      157.95
             5     Wyerbach     T       16.65
             6     Wyerbach     F       23.63
             7     Lee          H      975.00
             8     Lee          T      235.50
             9     Lee          F      295.00
```

The following steps describe how to read the expenditure data to create the data set shown in Output 3.5:

□   create an observation for each expenditure

□   make the process more efficient

□   provide an error-handling feature.

Create an Observation for Each Expenditure

The DATA step begins building an observation by reading a record, assigning a value to the variable NAME, and holding the record for further processing when the repeated fields are read.

```
data expense;
   infile 'input-file';
   length name $ 15 code $ 1;
   input name @;
```

Note that the LENGTH statement creates two character variables, NAME and CODE, with lengths different than the default (8 bytes). Once you declare the type and length of a character variable in a LENGTH statement, you can specify simply the variable name in a subsequent INPUT statement.

The next step is to read the repeated fields in the same record, assign values to the variables CODE and AMOUNT, and write additional observations until there are no more data values to be read in the current record. A DO UNTIL statement can accomplish this. When the variable CODE has a missing value, all fields in the record have been read. This condition, therefore, can control the iterations of the DO UNTIL loop.

```
data expense;
   infile 'input-file';
   length name $ 15 code $ 1;
   input name @;
   do until(code = ' ');
      input code amount @;
   end;
```

Because the DO loop iterates until CODE equals missing, the last observation created from each record always contains missing values for CODE and AMOUNT. To prevent these observations from being written to the data set, use an IF-THEN statement. An observation is written to the data set only when the value for CODE is not missing.

```
data expense;
   infile 'input-file';
   length name $ 15 code $ 1;
   input name @;
   do until(code = ' ');
      input code amount @;
      if code ne ' ' then output;
   end;
```

There is still one problem to solve. Because this example uses list input to read these records, the pointer moves past the end of each record scanning for a value for CODE. Automatically, a new record is read into the input buffer to continue scanning. To prevent this from happening, use the MISSOVER option in the INFILE statement.* Here is the DATA step as discussed so far:

```
data expense;
   infile 'input-file' missover;
   length name $ 15 code $ 1;
   input name @;
   do until (code = ' ');
      input code amount @;
      if code ne ' ' then output;
   end;
run;
```

---

* The MISSOVER option is discussed in detail in Chapter 2, "Reading Data in Different Record Formats and in Hierarchical Files."

Make the Process More Efficient

This DATA step works, but it can be improved. Note that there are two checks made here. One is made by the DO UNTIL statement; the second is made by the IF-THEN statement.

```
data expense;
   infile 'input-file' missover;
   length name $ 15 code $ 1;
   input name a;
   do until(code = ' ');
      input code amount a;
      if code ne ' ' then output;
   end;
run;
```

With two changes to this code, the DO UNTIL statement can prevent an observation with missing values for CODE from being written to the data set, eliminating the second check altogether.

First, the order of the INPUT and OUTPUT statements in the DO UNTIL loop should be reversed. The DO UNTIL statement checks the value of CODE at the bottom of the loop. If the INPUT statement is the last statement, the check is performed by the DO UNTIL statement after CODE gets a new value but before an observation is written by the OUTPUT statement.

Second, the INPUT statement that precedes the DO UNTIL loop needs to read the first pair of repeated fields and assign values to CODE and AMOUNT so that the OUTPUT statement can write a complete observation the first time it executes for a new record.

```
data expense;
   infile 'input-file' missover;
   length name $ 15 code $ 1;
   input name code amount a;
   do until(code = ' ');
      output;
      input code amount a;
   end;
run;
```

Provide an Error-Handling Feature

As long as each record this DATA step reads contains at least one pair of values for CODE and AMOUNT, there is no problem. However, when it tries to read an erroneous record containing a name but no values for CODE and AMOUNT, the problem is not detected, and an observation with missing values for CODE and AMOUNT is written to the data set. Using a DO WHILE statement instead of a DO UNTIL statement, however, solves this problem. Because a DO WHILE statement checks the condition before the statements in the loop execute, not after, it prevents any observations built by the first INPUT statement from being written to the data set with a missing value for CODE. Here is the program that creates and displays the resulting data set.

```
data expense;
   infile 'input-file' missover;
   length name $ 15 code $ 1;
   input name code amount a;
   do while(code ne ' ');
      output;
      input code amount a;
   end;
run;

proc print data=expense;
   title 'Reported Travel Expenditures';
run;
```

Output 3.6 shows the results.

Output 3.6
Reading a Varying
Number of Fields

```
                        Reported Travel Expenditures                           1

            OBS     NAME        CODE     AMOUNT

             1      Smith        E        45.75
             2      Smith        H       375.00
             3      Smith        T       985.00
             4      Smith        F       157.95
             5      Wyerbach     T        16.65
             6      Wyerbach     F        23.63
             7      Lee          H       975.00
             8      Lee          T       235.50
             9      Lee          F       295.00
```

Summary

The following points summarize how to use the data-reading techniques discussed in this chapter:

□ To create a variable whose value is equal to the length of the current input record, use the LENGTH= option in an INFILE statement.

□ To read character fields that vary in length from one record to the next, use the $VARYING. character informat. Often you can use the LENGTH= option in the INFILE statement in conjunction with the $VARYING. informat because it enables you to easily determine the length of the current input record.

□ To write more compact programs for reading repeated fields in raw data, use the iterative DO statement. You can use an iterative DO statement not only to make your program more compact, but also to generate values for variables in the data set, as shown in the example of statistically designed experiment data.

□ When using list input to read a varying number of repeated fields, you can use the MISSOVER option to prevent a new record from automatically being read when the pointer moves past the end of a record. The DO WHILE and DO UNTIL statements enable you to express a condition under which the statements should stop iterating without requiring you to specify a fixed number, as in an iterative DO statement.

□ The iterations of a DO loop can be controlled by expressing a condition in a DO WHILE or DO UNTIL statement. When choosing between the statements, remember the significance of when the condition is checked. With the DO WHILE statement, the condition is checked at the top of the loop. With the DO UNTIL statement, the condition is checked at the bottom of the loop. Statements in a DO UNTIL loop always execute at least once.

SAS Tools

This section summarizes syntax for the statements and informats discussed in this chapter.

Statements

DO UNTIL (*condition*);
  SAS statements
END;
  executes the enclosed SAS statements until the specified condition is true. The condition can be any valid SAS expression, enclosed in parentheses. The condition is evaluated at the bottom of the loop, after the enclosed statements have been executed. If the condition is true, the DO loop is not executed again. Because the condition is evaluated at the bottom of the loop, the enclosed statements are always executed at least once.

DO WHILE (*condition*);
  SAS statements
END;
  executes the enclosed SAS statements as long as the specified condition is true. The condition can be any valid SAS expression, enclosed in parentheses. The condition is evaluated at the top of the loop, before the enclosed statements are executed. If the expression is true, the DO loop is executed. If the condition is false the first time it is evaluated, the DO loop is not executed at all.

INFILE '*input-file*' <*options*>;
  identifies the file containing the input data and allows you to specify options that control how the data records are read.
  The following INFILE statement options are discussed in this chapter:

LENGTH=*variable*
  creates a variable whose value is automatically set to the length of the current input record. The LENGTH= variable is created by the INFILE statement but is not assigned a value until an INPUT statement executes. The LENGTH= option is useful in conjunction with the $VARYING. informat when reading varying-length records.

MISSOVER
  prevents the input pointer from going to the next record if it doesn't find values in the current line for all INPUT statement variables. Instead, missing values are assigned to variables for which no values appear on the current input line.

INPUT *specifications @;*

reads a record of raw data either from an external file or from instream data lines. Use the single trailing @ sign to hold the current record, preventing the next INPUT statement from reading a new record. This is important in conditional processing where you need to read a value from a record before reading the rest of the record or writing an observation.

INPUT;

a null INPUT statement can be used to release an input record held by a single trailing @ in a previous INPUT statement. A new iteration of the DATA step automatically releases a record held with a single trailing @. If you use the iterations of a DO loop instead of the DATA step itself to read all the input records, using a null INPUT statement is a convenient way to release the held records.

LENGTH *variable* <$> *length;*

specifies the number of bytes to be used for storing a variable. Follow the name of a character variable with a $.

Informats

$VARYINGw.

is an informat that allows you to read a character variable that varies in length from record to record. If you specify a width *w*, specify the longest length that might be required as *w*. If you do not specify a width, the DATA step uses the length of the character variable to which the value is being assigned. You must follow the $VARYING. informat with the name of a numeric variable whose value is equal to the length appropriate for the field being read in the current record.

Learning More

This section provides references for learning more about the topics presented in this chapter.

□ For complete information on writing specifications for an INPUT statement, see Chapter 9, "SAS Language Statements," in *SAS Language: Reference, Version 6, First Edition.*

□ For more information on options available for the INFILE statement under all operating systems, see Chapter 9 in *SAS Language: Reference.* For information about options for these statements that are specific to an operating system, see the SAS companion for your host operating system.

□ For more information on how to specify an external file in an INFILE statement (*input-file* in the examples in this chapter), see the SAS companion for your host operating system.

Chapter 4 Handling Missing and Invalid Values and Missing Records

Introduction

Sometimes data contain missing data values or contain unmatched records when records need to be read in pairs. Reading these data can cause inaccuracies in the SAS data sets you build. So that you can protect the integrity of your SAS data sets, this chapter demonstrates techniques for dealing with some common problems related to missing values and records.

Techniques for dealing with related issues are also covered in this chapter. For example, if you want to detect erroneous values in your data, you may find it useful to distinguish between data values that were in error and others that were simply missing. In certain applications, such as survey or testing data, you may find it useful to distinguish between values that were missing for different reasons and to preserve these differences in a SAS data set.

In this chapter
If you are using brief, compact data, you may be able to detect and correct manually the kinds of problems described here before they cause mistakes to multiply in your output SAS data set. However, if you are handling large amounts of data that cannot easily be checked field by field, you may find techniques in this chapter especially useful. For practical reasons, the examples in this chapter use a

small collection of data to demonstrate the techniques for handling invalid numeric values, uncoded missing values, and missing records in the following circumstances:

□ distinguishing between types of missing values

□ distinguishing between invalid numeric values and missing values

□ minimizing the effect of missing data values on the integrity of your SAS data set when reading data with list input

□ reading matched data records that may contain missing records.

Prerequisites

To understand the examples in this chapter, you need to be familiar with the following features and concepts:

□ list and formatted input

□ pointer controls in the INPUT statement

□ the assignment statement

□ specifying character strings and variable values in a PUT statement

□ the OPTIONS statement.

Raw Data Example

The examples in this chapter use data from a marketing research company. Five testers were hired to test five different products for ease of use and effectiveness. They were asked to give the product a rating, based on certain guidelines.

Each record contains the following fields:

Field	Description
id	identification number of tester
period	identification of test period
test1-test5	5 fields that contain a rating for a tested product

The records are read to create the following variables:

Variable	Type	Description
ID	character	identification number of tester
FOODPR1	numeric	rating for first food processor
FOODPR2	numeric	rating for second food processor
FOODPR3	numeric	rating for third food processor
COFFEEM1	numeric	rating for first coffee maker
COFFEEM2	numeric	rating for second coffee maker

In the examples in this chapter, the data values change slightly from example to example so that each can demonstrate techniques for handling a specific type of problem in the input data.

Distinguishing between Types of Missing Values

Raw data often contain missing values. Depending on the application, there can be different reasons for a value to be missing, and you may need to be able to record these differences. For example, questionnaire data can contain missing values because the respondent failed to answer some questions, answered others in invalid ways, or answered some illegibly. If it is important to your application to be able to distinguish between types of missing values, you can use the MISSING statement.

Ordinarily, a missing numeric value must be represented in input data by a period. The MISSING statement enables alphabetic characters to be read and stored as special missing values rather than invalid numeric values.

For example, consider the marketing research data described previously. If a tester is absent, there is no rating to report, and the value is recorded with an X for "absent." If the tester was unable to test the product adequately, there is no rating, and the value is recorded with an I for "incomplete test." The following program reads these data and displays the resulting SAS data set. Note the special missing values in the first and third data lines.

```
options pagesize=20;

data period_a;
   missing X I;
   input id $4. +3 foodpr1 foodpr2 foodpr3 coffeem1 coffeem2;
   cards;
1001 A 115 45 65 I 78
1002 A 86 27 55 72 86
1004 A 93 52 X 76 88
1015 A 73 35 43 112 108
1027 A 101 127 39 76 79
;

proc print data=period_a;
   title 'Results of Test Period A';
   footnote1 'X indicates TESTER ABSENT';
   footnote2 'I indicates TEST WAS INCOMPLETE';
run;
```

Output 4.1 shows the results.

```
                                 Results of Test Period A                              1

            OBS     ID     FOODPR1     FOODPR2     FOODPR3     COFFEEM1     COFFEEM2

             1     1001      115         45          65           I           78
             2     1002       86         27          55          72           86
             3     1004       93         52           X           76           88
             4     1015       73         35          43          112          108
             5     1027      101        127          39           76           79




                             X indicates TESTER ABSENT
                           I indicates TEST WAS INCOMPLETE
```

Output 4.1 demonstrates that in the first and third observations alphabetic characters (I and X) are stored as special missing values for numeric variables. Note that not all SAS procedures differentiate between special missing values.

Distinguishing between Missing and Invalid Numeric Data

When a missing value is read in raw data and assigned to a variable, the variable is set to missing. When an invalid numeric value is read in raw data and assigned to a variable, the variable is also set to missing. For this reason, you cannot distinguish in the output data set between values that were missing in the raw data and values that were invalid. Knowing which values were invalid can help you track down errors in your data and correct them.

As an example, here is a DATA step that reads the marketing research data, this time containing an invalid numeric value and a properly coded missing value in the first data line:

```
data period_a;
   input id $4. +3 foodpr1 foodpr2 foodpr3 coffeem1 coffeem2;
   cards;
1001 A 115 4r 65 . 78
1002 A 86 27 55 72 86
1004 A 93 52 63 76 88
1015 A 73 35 43 112 108
1027 A 101 127 39 76 79
;
```

When this DATA step executes, the lines written to the SAS log demonstrate that both of these values result in missing values assigned to the variables FOODPR2 and COFFEEM1, respectively. Note that the first line under the column ruler shows the current input record, and the second line shows the variable values in the current observation.

```
NOTE: Invalid data for FOODPR2 in line 5 12-13.
RULE:----+----1----+----2----+----3----+----4----+----5----+----6----+--
5    1001 A 115 4r 65 . 78
ID=1001 PERIOD=A FOODPR1=115 FOODPR2=. FOODPR3=65 COFFEEM1=. COFFEEM2=78
_ERROR_=1 _N_=1
```

To distinguish between variable values that were created from invalid numeric values and ones that were created from originally missing values, you should indicate that you want invalid numeric values to be translated into special missing values. Missing values are stored as periods by default. Use the INVALIDDATA= SAS system option to specify that invalid numeric values be treated as special missing values and that they be stored as either an alphabetic character or an underscore instead of a period.

The following DATA step uses the INVALIDDATA= SAS system option in an OPTIONS statement to specify that invalid numeric values be stored as an X instead of a period. The PRINT procedure displays the resulting SAS data set.

```
options invaliddata='X';

data period_a;
    input id $4. +3 foodpr1 foodpr2 foodpr3 coffeem1 coffeem2;
    cards;
1001 A 115 4r 65 . 78
1002 A 86 27 55 72 86
1004 A 93 52 63 76 88
1015 A 73 35 43 112 108
1027 A 101 127 39 76 79
;

proc print data=period_a;
    title 'Results of Test Period A';
run;
```

As Output 4.2 demonstrates, you can now distinguish between a value that was originally an invalid numeric value and one that was missing.

Output 4.2
Distinguishing between Invalid Numeric and Missing Values

```
                            Results of Test Period A                         1

        OBS     ID     FOODPR1     FOODPR2     FOODPR3     COFFEEM1     COFFEEM2

         1     1001      115          X          65           .           78
         2     1002       86         27          55          72           86
         3     1004       93         52          63          76           88
         4     1015       73         35          43         112          108
         5     1027      101        127          39          76           79
```

Protecting Data Integrity When Reading Uncoded Missing Values with List Input

List input is a popular method for reading data into a SAS data set because it is easy to use. However, the characteristic that makes list input easy to use, scanning until it locates a value, causes incorrect observations to be built when it is used to read input data lines in which missing values have not been properly coded.

The next section explains why the problem occurs and is followed by two examples that suggest ways to minimize errors.

Understanding How Errors Are Propagated

List input reads a value until it reaches a blank and then reads and discards blanks until the pointer encounters the next nonblank column. For this reason, fields that are left blank are not properly recorded as missing. They are simply regarded as blanks between data values, causing the next value that occurs to be assigned to the wrong variable. When the scanning feature moves the pointer to the end of the input line without finding enough values, the system automatically reads a new record into the input buffer to search for the next value. This default action compounds the original error.

To understand how incorrect observations are constructed, look at the following program. It reads the marketing research data and prints the resulting data set. Note that the second record contains only four ratings, not five, and that the missing values have not been properly coded with periods. When the records are read, incorrect observations are constructed.

```
data period_a;
   input id $4. +3 foodpr1 foodpr2 foodpr3 coffeem1 coffeem2;
   cards;
1001 A 115 45 65 83 78
1002 A 86 27 55    86
1004 A 93 52 63 76 88
1015 A 73 35 43 112 108
1027 A 101 127 39 76 79
;

proc print data=period_a;
   title 'Results of Test Period A';
run;
```

As a result of this DATA step, the following line is written to the SAS log:

```
NOTE: SAS went to a new line when INPUT statement reached past the
      end of a line.
```

As in this example, this note may indicate a problem in the input data. Output 4.3 displays the resulting inaccurate data set.

Output 4.3
Reading Data with the FLOWOVER Option

```
                        Results of Test Period A                        1

    OBS     ID    FOODPR1    FOODPR2    FOODPR3    COFFEEM1    COFFEEM2

     1     1001     115        45         65          83          78
     2     1002      86        27         55          86        1004
     3     1015      73        35         43         112         108
     4     1027     101       127         39          76          79
```

Output 4.3 demonstrates that an incorrect observation is constructed from the second data line and part of the third data line and that no observation is created for the third data line. This action is the result of the FLOWOVER option, which is in effect by default when using list input to read data.

There are two fool-proof solutions to correct this problem in input data. You can correct the raw data file so that all missing values are properly coded with a period. Or you can read the data with column or formatted input if the data are aligned so that this is possible. The problem is easy to correct in this example because the amount of data is so small. These solutions, however, are impractical when you are working with large data files. When you must use list input on data that may contain miscoded missing values, use one of the following methods to minimize the detrimental effects on your data set:

□ Prevent the pointer from going to a new line, set all remaining variables to missing, and continue to build the data set.

□ Discard the erroneous observation and stop building the data set altogether.

The following two sections describe methods for minimizing errors by using alternatives to the FLOWOVER option.

Minimizing Errors While Continuing to Build the Data Set

One way to try to minimize the errors created in an output data set is to override the default action taken when the input pointer moves past the end of the current record. Use the MISSOVER option in the INFILE statement to

□ prevent the system from automatically reading the next record into the input buffer

□ set the rest of the variables in the INPUT statement to missing for the current observation.

This DATA step uses the MISSOVER option in the INFILE statement to read the same data lines as shown in the last section. Note that the INFILE statement specifies CARDS instead of the name of an input file. By using the CARDS option, you can take advantage of options that affect how the INPUT statement reads data even when reading data that follow a CARDS statement. Here is the complete program that creates and prints the data set PERIOD_A.

```
data period_a;
   infile cards missover;
   input id $4. +3 foodpr1 foodpr2 foodpr3 coffeem1 coffeem2;
   cards;
1001 A 115 45 65 83 78
1002 A 86 27 55    86
1004 A 93 52 63 76 88
1015 A 73 35 43 112 108
1027 A 101 127 39 76 79
;

proc print data=period_a;
   title 'Results of Test Period A';
run;
```

Note that when you use the MISSOVER option, no message is written to the log when a data record does not contain a value for each variable in the INPUT statement. Output 4.4 shows the resulting data set.

Output 4.4
Reading Data with the MISSOVER Option

```
                         Results of Test Period A                              1

    OBS     ID     FOODPR1     FOODPR2     FOODPR3     COFFEEM1     COFFEEM2

     1     1001      115         45          65          83           78
     2     1002       86         27          55          86            .
     3     1004       93         52          63          76           88
     4     1015       73         35          43         112          108
     5     1027      101        127          39          76           79
```

Compare Output 4.3 to Output 4.4. Using the MISSOVER option prevents the uncoded missing value in the second data line from causing the third record to be read incorrectly as well. The second observation is still incorrect, but the errors have been restricted to a single observation.

Minimizing Errors by Stopping the Building of the Data Set

A second way to minimize the number of incorrect observations created is to stop the DATA step entirely by using the STOPOVER option in the INFILE statement. When the input line does not contain a value for each variable in the INPUT statement, the STOPOVER option prevents the observation from being written to the data set and stops the DATA step from further processing.

The following program reads the marketing research data, uses the STOPOVER option to stop processing when an input line does not contain enough values, and prints the resulting data set.

```
data period_a;
   infile cards stopover;
   input id $4. +3 foodpr1 foodpr2 foodpr3 coffeem1 coffeem2;
   cards;
1001 A 115 45 65 83 78
1002 A 86 27 55    86
1004 A 93 52 63 76 88
1015 A 73 35 43 112 108
1027 A 101 127 39 76 79
;

proc print data=period_a;
   title 'Results of Test Period A';
run;
```

As a result of this DATA step, the following lines are written to the SAS log, reporting that the input pointer reached the end of a record without reading the required number of values:

```
ERROR: INPUT statement exceeded record length.
       INFILE CARDS OPTION STOPOVER specified.
RULE:----+----1----+----2----+----3----+----4----+----5----+----6----+----7
9    1002 A 86 27 55    86
ID=1002 FOODPR1=86 FOODPR2=27 FOODPR3=55 COFFEEM1=86 COFFEEM2=. _ERROR_=1
_N_=2
NOTE: The SAS System stopped processing this step because of errors.
WARNING: The data set WORK.PERIOD_A may be incomplete.  When this step was
         stopped there were 1 observations and 6 variables.
```

Output 4.5 shows the resulting data set. Note that using the STOPOVER option prevents an observation built from incomplete input records from being written to the data set.

Output 4.5
Reading Data with the STOPOVER Option

```
                         Results of Test Period A                          1

   OBS     ID     FOODPR1     FOODPR2     FOODPR3     COFFEEM1     COFFEEM2

    1     1001      115          45          65          83           78
```

As you can see, using the MISSOVER and STOPOVER options cannot correct the problem of incomplete records of raw data. However, the MISSOVER option can prevent one incomplete record from corrupting multiple observations, and the STOPOVER option can prevent any incomplete observations from being written to the data set. The log messages from both can help you locate the problem records in your input data.

Protecting Data Integrity When Reading Matched Records

Sometimes a program must read more than one input record to construct a single observation in a SAS data set. For example, information about the same entity, such as a patient or inventory item, may be contained in two records instead of one. To create an accurate data set in which each observation contains all the information about a single item, you must create observations only from matched records. As long as the data records are properly sorted and there are no missing records, the resulting data set should be accurate. If, however, a record is missing in the input data, the observations from that point on may be inaccurately built. To ensure the accuracy of an output data set, use a DATA step to construct observations only from the appropriately related records, discarding any unmatched ones. To do this, follow these steps:

□ read a record

□ begin building an observation if the record is correct

□ take alternate action when the record is incorrect

□ read the next record

□ build an observation when a match is found

□ take action when no match is found.

Input Data Example

This example uses an expanded version of the marketing research data used throughout this chapter. These data include test scores for a second test period (B) in which the same testers rated five more products, two microwave ovens and three dishwashers. Instead of a single record for each tester, there are now two records for each tester. Here are the data:

```
----+----1----+----2----+----3
1001 A 115 45 65 83 78
1001 B 55 113 82 45 77
1002 A 86 27 55 72 86
1004 A 93 52 63 76 88
1004 B 69 127 101 32 68
1015 A 73 35 43 112 108
1015 B 47 98 78 51 73
1027 A 101 127 39 76 79
1027 B 58 101 109 47 69
```

The goal is to create a single observation for each tester that contains the tester's identification number and all ten test scores. Note that the third record, the one for tester 1002 during test period A, is not followed by a matching record for this tester during test period B. If a DATA step reads these records to construct a data set without checking the records for a match, observations from this point on will be incorrect.

Read a Record

The first step is to begin the DATA step and read enough of a record to determine whether to begin building the observation. A single trailing @ holds the record for further processing.

```
data alltests;
    input id1 $4. +1 period1 $1. @;
```

Begin Building an Observation If a Record Is Correct

In this example, the DATA step should begin building an observation only if a record contains the ratings from test period A. An IF-THEN statement tests the value of PERIOD1. If PERIOD1 is equal to **A**, an INPUT statement reads the rest of the fields and assigns values to the other variables:

```
if period1='A' then
    input foodpr1 foodpr2 foodpr3 coffeem1 coffeem2;
```

Take Action When the Record Is Incorrect

You also must provide an alternative action when a record read by the first INPUT statement is not correct. Instead of assigning values to the rest of the variables, you want to stop trying to build the current observation and try again with the next record. To do this, use a DELETE statement in an ELSE statement:

```
else delete;
```

The DELETE statement protects the output data set because it does two things:

□ stops processing the current observation

□ causes processing to resume at the beginning of the DATA step without writing the current observation to the data set.

The DELETE statement does not, however, help solve the problem of the record that is out of order. To help you find and correct the error in your input data, you can use a PUT statement to write a note and the contents of the problematic record to the log. Here are the statements discussed thus far, with the error-handling statements in place:

```
data a_and_b;
    input id1 period1 $1. @;
    if period1='A' then
        input foodpr1 foodpr2 foodpr3 coffeem1 coffeem2;
    else
```

```
do;
    put 'Following record deleted; not for test period A:'   / _infile_;
    delete;
end;
```

Note that the PUT statements must precede the DELETE statement. Since the DELETE statement signals that processing should stop for the current observation and resume at the beginning of the DATA step, any statements that follow it in the ELSE DO group never execute.

Read the Next Record

When an appropriate record has been read for beginning to build an observation, the DATA step continues building the observation. The next step is to read another record, searching for an appropriate record to complete the observation being built. This example reads the next record with an INPUT statement, assigns values to the variables ID2 and PERIOD2, and holds the record with a single trailing @.

```
input id2 $4. +1 period2 $1. a;
```

Build an Observation When a Match Is Found

Use an IF-THEN statement to determine if a matched pair of records has been read. In this example, if the value for ID2 in the second record matches ID1 in the first record and if PERIOD2 is equal to B, the records match; therefore, an INPUT statement reads the rest of the data values from that record and assigns them to the appropriate variables.

```
if id1=id2 and period2='B' then
    input mw_oven1 mw_oven2 dishwhr1 dishwhr2 dishwhr3;
```

Take Action When No Match Is Found

You also must provide an alternative action when no match is found. In this example, the following two records are read on the second iteration of the DATA step:

```
----+----1----+----2----+----3
1002 A 86 27 55 72 86
1004 A 93 52 63 76 88
```

Since there is no record containing ratings from period B for tester 1002, there is no match on this iteration. When no match is found, the DATA step should

□ discard the first record on the assumption that there is no match in the file

□ return to the top of the DATA step

□ begin the comparison process over again, this time with the current record in the input buffer as the first in the series of records to be compared.

A LOSTCARD statement accomplishes all of these actions. This example uses the LOSTCARD statement in an ELSE statement:

```
if id1=id2 and period2='B' then
    input mw_oven1 mw_oven2 dishwhr1 dishwhr2 dishwhr3;
else lostcard;
```

The LOSTCARD statement also writes the contents of the current record to the SAS log. You may find it useful to use a PUT statement to reveal something about the discarded record. This example identifies the tester and test period in the discarded record by using a PUT statement to write the values of ID1 and PERIOD1 to the SAS log. Here is the entire program that creates and prints the data set A_AND_B. Note the statements that handle errors when the records don't match.

```
data a_and_b(drop=id2 period1 period2 rename=(id1=id));
    input id1 $4. +1 period1 $1. @;

    /* Test for beginning of new observation. */

    if period1='A' then
        input foodpr1 foodpr2 foodpr3 coffeem1 coffeem2;
    else
        do;
            put 'Following record deleted; not for test period A:';
            put _infile_;
            delete;
        end;
    input id2 $4. +1 period2 $1. @;

    /* Test for matching records.            */

    if id1=id2 and period2='B' then
        input mw_oven1 mw_oven2 dishwhr1 dishwhr2 dishwhr3;
    else
        do;
            put 'ERROR IN DATA RECORDS ' id1= period1=;
            lostcard;
        end;
    cards;
1001 A 115 45 65 83 78
1001 B 55 113 82 45 77
1002 A 86 27 55 72 86
1004 A 93 52 63 76 88
```

```
1004 B 69 127 101 32 68
1015 A 73 35 43 112 108
1015 B 47 98 78 51 73
1027 A 101 127 39 76 79
1027 B 58 101 109 47 69
;

proc print data=a_and_b;
   title 'Results of Test Periods A and B';
run;
```

The following lines are written to the SAS log when the DATA step executes:

```
ERROR IN DATA RECORDS ID1=1002 PERIOD1=A
NOTE: LOST CARD.
RULE:      ----+----1----+----2----+----3----+----4----+----5----+----6----+
33         1004 A 93 52 63 76 88
NOTE: The data set WORK.A_AND_B has 4 observations and 11 variables.
```

Output 4.6 shows the results of the PROC PRINT step.

Output 4.6
Creating a Data
Set without
Mismatched
Records

```
                     Results of Test Periods A and B                              1

                                      C    C    M    M    D    D    D
                   F    F    F    O    O    W    W    I    I    I
                   O    O    O    F    F    _    _    S    S    S
                   O    O    O    F    F    O    O    H    H    H
                   D    D    D    E    E    V    V    W    W    W
     O             P    P    P    E    E    E    E    H    H    H
     B    I        R    R    R    M    M    N    N    R    R    R
     S    D        1    2    3    1    2    1    2    1    2    3

     1    1001    115   45   65   83   78   55  113   82   45   77
     2    1004     93   52   63   76   88   69  127  101   32   68
     3    1015     73   35   43  112  108   47   98   78   51   73
     4    1027    101  127   39   76   79   58  101  109   47   69
```

Note that there is no observation for tester 1002 because the input data contain a single unmatched record for that tester.

Summary

The following points summarize how to read missing values, invalid numeric values, and missing records:

□   If it is important to your application to be able to distinguish between values that are missing for different reasons, use the MISSING statement to specify that an alphabetic character or an underscore be recorded as a valid missing numeric value.

□   Invalid numeric values are recorded as missing values in a SAS data set. To be able to distinguish between values that are missing in the original input data and ones that are invalid, use the INVALIDDATA= system option in the OPTIONS statement. It assigns a special missing value (either an alphabetic character or an underscore) to a numeric variable when the raw data contain an invalid numeric value.

□ Uncoded missing values present special problems for using list input. To provide some protection for the integrity of your output data set when input data contain uncoded missing input values, use the MISSOVER or STOPOVER options in the INFILE statement. Use the MISSOVER option to set all remaining variables in the INPUT statement to missing. Use the STOPOVER option to prevent an observation from being written to the data set when the input line does not contain a value for each variable in the INPUT statement and to stop the DATA step from further processing.

□ When reading a fixed number of multiple input records to construct a single observation, you can prevent observations from being erroneously constructed from mismatched input records by using the LOSTCARD statement.

SAS Tools

This section summarizes syntax for the statements and system options discussed in this chapter.

Statements

DELETE;
stops processing the current observation, causes the SAS System to return to the top of the DATA step to begin a new iteration, and does not write the current observation to the data set.

INFILE *input-source<options>*;
identifies the source of the input data and allows you to specify options that control how the data records are read. The *input-source* can be either an external file, expressed as a fileref or the name of the physical file, or instream data lines, expressed as CARDS. The CARDS argument allows you to take advantage of data-reading options even when you are reading instream data lines instead of an external file.

The following INFILE statement options are discussed in this chapter:

FLOWOVER
specifies that when the input pointer moves past the end of an input record a new record is automatically read into the input buffer. FLOWOVER is the default action taken.

MISSOVER
prevents the input pointer from going to the next record if it doesn't find values in the current line for all INPUT statement variables. Instead, no new input record is read into the input buffer, and all remaining variables in the INPUT statement are set to missing.

STOPOVER
specifies that when the input pointer moves past the end of an input record a new record is not read into the input buffer. The current observation is not written to the data set, and the DATA step is stopped.

LOSTCARD;
>　resynchronizes the input data when the SAS System encounters a missing record while reading multiple records to create a single observation.

MISSING *character-1* <*. . . character-n*>;
>　allows the specified character to be read and stored as a special missing value for numeric variables. Using the MISSING statement allows you to distinguish between different types of missing values in your input data and to code them with an alphabetic character (lowercase or uppercase) or an underscore. These values are read and stored as special missing values instead of invalid numeric values.

PUT _INFILE_;
>　writes the contents of the record currently in the input buffer to the SAS log, by default. PUT _INFILE_ is especially useful with other statements for error-handling.

System options

INVALIDDATA=*'character'*
>　specifies an alphabetic character or an underscore to be used as a special missing value assigned to a numeric variable when otherwise an invalid numeric value would be assigned to it. This option is useful because it allows you to distinguish in a SAS data set between values that were originally invalid numeric values in your raw data and ones that were missing in the raw data.

Learning More

This section provides references for learning more about topics presented in this chapter.

□　For more information on missing values, see Chapter 2, "The DATA Step," and Chapter 4, "Rules of the SAS Language," in *SAS Language: Reference, Version 6, Third Edition.*

□　For information on how individual procedures in base SAS software handle missing values, see the appropriate chapters in the *SAS Procedures Guide, Version 6, Third Edition.*

□　To help you locate and correct problems in input data, you can produce an exceptions report. See Chapter 15, "Producing Exceptions Reports," for more details.

Chapter 5 Reading Multiple Raw Data Files

Introduction

If you are responsible for analyzing data that come from different sources, such as different departments within a division, you probably need to be able to read more than one raw data file to construct a SAS data set. One approach is to read each file in a separate DATA step and then merge or concatenate those SAS data sets to create the complete data set you need. Using multiple DATA steps instead of one may be easier to program, but it is less efficient. This chapter, therefore, shows you how to read multiple raw data files in a single DATA step to create the desired SAS data set from the start.

In this chapter
This chapter demonstrates how to create a SAS data set when reading multiple raw data files concurrently or consecutively.

Prerequisites
To understand the examples in this chapter, you need to be familiar with the following features and concepts:

- □   list and formatted input

- □   the colon modifier used in modified list input

- □   the concatenation operator (||) used for character values

□ the FILENAME statement

□ the assignment statement

□ the KEEP= data set option.

Understanding How to Build Observations from Multiple Raw Data Files

When your raw data reside in separate files, you can create a SAS data set by reading all the files in a single DATA step. You can do this in several ways, depending on the results you want to achieve. First, you can read files concurrently so information from both files can contribute to each observation, as shown in Figure 5.1.

Figure 5.1

Reading Raw Data Files Concurrently to Create Each Observation

file 1

| BA01 | 2000 | 190 |
| BA02 | 17000 | 1700 |

file 2

| BA01 | Barnet and Sons | 555-1111 |
| BA02 | Baxter Brothers Asphalt | 555-5555 |

SAS data set

| BA01 | 2000 | 190 | Barnet and Sons | 555-1111 |
| BA02 | 17000 | 1700 | Baxter Brothers Asphalt | 555-5555 |

A second method (shown in Figure 5.2) involves reading files consecutively. In this case, observations created from the second file are appended to the set of observations created from the first file.

Figure 5.2

Reading Raw Data Files Consecutively to Create Separate Observations

file 1

16	101	Alvarez, J.T.	4.65	45.0
16	103	Marcos, D.	7.50	11.0
16	41	Ritter, E.S.	3.50	13.5

file 2

17	79	Carrithers, E.A.	3.50	13.5
17	56	Ianelli, L.O.	3.35	26.5
17	23	Smith, L.O.	4.65	45.0

SAS data set

16	101	Alvarez, J.T.	4.65	45.0
16	103	Marcos, D.	7.50	11.0
16	41	Ritter, E.S.	3.50	13.5
17	79	Carrithers, E.A.	3.50	13.5
17	56	Ianelli, L.O.	3.35	26.5
17	23	Smith, L.O.	4.65	45.0

Reading Raw Data Files Concurrently

Related data values that you need in a report are often stored in separate files. For example, one file may contain orders received on a given day, while a larger master file contains the necessary customer information for billing or shipping purposes. To analyze such data or construct a complete report, you need to use information from both files to construct a SAS data set. To do this, use the following steps:

□ read from the first file

□ search the second file for a match

□ test for a match and take the appropriate action based on the value of the key variables

□ prevent reading past the end of the second file.

Raw Data Example

A company that quarries limestone needs to construct a billing report from data stored in two separate external files. One file contains a record for each order filled that day; the other contains customer reference information. The following table describes the fields in each record in the daily order file and the corresponding variable created in the DATA step:

Field	Description	Variable
id	customer's identification number	IDDAILY
amount owed	amount to bill the customer	AMTOWED
tons	number of tons delivered	TONS

Here are the raw data records from the daily order file. Note that the records are sorted by the customer's identification number.

```
----+----1----+----2
BA01  2000   190
BA02 17000  1700
CA01 33000  3500
CN01  7000   600
ZA01  7500   635
```

The customer reference file contains more complete information about all the company's customers. The following table describes the fields in each record in this file and the corresponding variables created in the DATA step:

Field	Description	Variable
id	customer's identification number	IDREF
customer	customer's name	NAMEREF
address	first part of the customer's address	(not read)
location	city, state, and ZIP code of the customer	(not read)

Here is a sample of the raw data records from the customer reference file.* Note that the records are sorted by the customer's identification number.

```
----+----1----+----2----+----3----+----4----+----5----+----6----+----7----+
AP01 Appleton Construction    P.O. Box 1923     Apex, NC 27516
BA01 Barnet and Sons          P.O. Box 1172     Raleigh, NC 27742
BA02 Baxter Brothers Asphalt  P.O. Box 95       Fuquay-Varina, NC 27732
CN01 Concord Concrete         P.O. Box 13       Concord, NC   27832
DE01 Drummens Hauling         P.O. Box 42118    Durham,  NC   27704
          more data records
WE01 Wellington Builders, Inc P.O. Box 9221     Raleigh, NC 27742
YA01 Yang Brothers Grading    P.O. Box 229      Chapel Hill, NC 27514
```

Output 5.1 shows the report to be generated.

Output 5.1
Data Set Created from Two Raw Data Files

```
                      Amount Owed by Customer                        1

      NAME                    IDDAILY   AMTOWED   TONS

      Barnet and Sons         BA01      $2,000     190
      Baxter Brothers Asphalt BA02      $17,000   1700
      CA01 (name unknown)     CA01      $33,000   3500
      Concord Concrete        CN01      $7,000     600
      ZA01 (name unknown)     ZA01      $7,500     635
```

Read from the First File

Identify the first file with an INFILE statement and then use an INPUT statement to read a record and assign to variables the data values you need. This example reads values for the customer's identification number, the amount charged, and the tons shipped from the daily order file:

```
data rptdata(keep=iddaily amtowed tons name);
infile 'daily-order-file';
input iddaily $4. amtowed tons;
```

---

* Refer to the Appendix for a complete listing of the input data.

This INPUT statement assigns the customer's identification number to the variable IDDAILY. It becomes the key variable the program uses to identify the corresponding record to read in the customer reference file.

Search the Second File for a Match

The next step is to search the second file for a record that contains a matching value for the key variable. To do this you must

□ identify the file to be searched

□ control the reading of the search file

□ retain needed values between iterations.

Identify the File to be Searched

First, identify the file to be searched with an INFILE statement:

```
infile 'customer-reference-file';
```

Control the Reading of the Search File

You must control how the file being searched for a match is read. One way is to use a DO UNTIL or a DO WHILE loop, using a condition that ensures you don't read past the appropriate location in the second file.

Here the goal is to match a customer's record in the customer reference file with that customer's current record from the daily order file. The following DO UNTIL statement reads a record from the customer reference file until the value of IDREF matches the value of IDDAILY:

```
do until(idref eq iddaily);
   input idref $4. name $25.;
end;
```

As long as a match occurs, this method works without any problems. If there is no match, however, the program reads the entire file, stopping only when it reaches the end of the file. To prevent the DATA step from reading past the appropriate point in the second file, use a DO WHILE statement and specify the LT (less than) condition rather than the EQ (equal) condition.

```
do while(idref lt iddaily);
   input idref $4. nameref $25.;
end;
```

This program continues reading records from the customer reference file only while IDREF is less than IDDAILY. The pointer stops here and begins reading at this point when the INPUT statement reads from this file during the next iteration of the DATA step.

Retain Needed Values between Iterations

This method works fine for a single iteration. However, because values are set to missing each time the DATA step begins a new iteration, you probably need to retain the value of one or more variables.

In this example, IDREF is set to missing at the beginning of each iteration. To retain the current value of IDREF so it can be used by the DO WHILE statement to make a comparison, a RETAIN statement is required. In this example, the RETAIN statement should also retain the value of the NAMEREF variable so its value is available for the current observation. (Remember that if IDREF is already equal to the new value for IDDAILY, the DO WHILE loop won't execute the second INPUT statement at all.)

```
data rptdata(keep=iddaily amtowed tons name);
   retain idref nameref;
   infile 'daily-order-file';
   input iddaily $4. amtowed tons;
   infile 'customer-reference-file';
   do while(idref lt iddaily);
      input idref $4. nameref $25.;
   end;
```

Test for a Match and Take the Appropriate Action

The next step is to test for a match between the key variables and take the appropriate action. You can use IF-THEN and ELSE statements to do this. If there is no match, there is probably an incorrect value in one file or a missing record in the other. In either case, you probably want to flag the error so you can correct it later. You can use an ELSE statement to do this.

This example tests for a match between the value of IDREF and IDDAILY. If the values of IDDAILY and IDREF match, the variable NAME is assigned the value of the variable NAMEREF. If there is no match, the ELSE statement flags the problem in the resulting data set by constructing the value of the NAME variable differently. An assignment statement begins with the value of IDDAILY and appends the character string `(name unknown)` to it.

```
if iddaily=idref then name=nameref;
else name=iddaily || '(name unknown)';
```

Here is the entire program that creates and prints the RPTDATA data set:

```
data rptdata(keep=iddaily amtowed tons name);
   retain idref nameref;
   infile 'daily-order-file';
   input iddaily $4. amtowed tons;
   infile 'customer-reference-file';
   do while(idref lt iddaily);
      input idref $4. nameref $25.;
   end;
   if iddaily=idref then name=nameref;
   else name=iddaily || ' (name unknown)';
run;
```

```
proc print data=rptdata;
   title 'Amount Owed by Customer';
   id name;
   format amtowed dollar7.;
run;
```

Output 5.2 shows the results.

Output 5.2
Creating an
Incomplete Data
Set

```
                               Amount Owed by Customer                              1

              NAME                      IDDAILY    AMTOWED    TONS

              Barnet and Sons           BA01        $2,000     190
              Baxter Brothers Asphalt   BA02       $17,000    1700
              CA01 (name unknown)       CA01       $33,000    3500
              Concord Concrete          CN01        $7,000     600
```

However, one problem exists with this data set. No observation is shown for the final record in the daily order file. The next section illustrates how to prevent this error when no matching record is found in the reference file.

Prevent Reading Past the End of the Second File

The final record in the daily order file contains the following information:

```
----+----1----+----2
ZA01  7500    635
```

No observation is written to the data set for this record because the last record in the reference file contains the value YA01 for IDREF:

```
----+----1----+----2----+----3----+----4----+----5----+----6----+----7----+
YA01 Yang Brothers Grading     P.O. Box 229        Chapel Hill, NC 27514
```

Therefore, the INPUT statement reading the customer reference file comes to the end of the file before it satisfies the DO WHILE condition, and the DATA step automatically stops.

```
do while(idref lt iddaily);
   input idref $4. nameref $25.;
end;
```

To remedy this situation, add a condition to the DO WHILE statement that prevents the INPUT statement from attempting to read past the end of the file being searched for a match. Use the END= option in the INFILE statement to create a variable whose value is automatically set to 1 when the end of the external file is reached. Then use that condition to prevent the DO WHILE loop from continuing to execute past the end of the file:

```
infile 'customer-reference-file' end=endref;
do while(idref lt iddaily and endref ne 1);
   input idref $4. nameref $25.;
end;
```

Because the DATA step does not end prematurely, the IF-THEN statement and the ELSE statement can execute and build the final observation:

```
if iddaily=idref then name=nameref;
else name=iddaily || ' (name unknown)';
```

Here is the entire program that creates and prints the RPTDATA data set:

```
data rptdata(keep=iddaily amtowed tons name);
   retain idref nameref;
   infile 'daily-order-file';
   input iddaily $4. amtowed tons;
   infile 'customer-reference-file' end=endref;
   do while(idref lt iddaily and endref ne 1);
      input idref $4. nameref $25.;
   end;
   if iddaily=idref then name=nameref;
   else name=iddaily || ' (name unknown)';
run;

proc print data=rptdata;
   title 'Amount Owed by Customer';
   id name;
   format amtowed dollar7.;
run;
```

Output 5.3 shows the results.

Output 5.3
Creating a
Complete Data Set

```
                       Amount Owed by Customer                          1

       NAME                     IDDAILY    AMTOWED     TONS

       Barnet and Sons            BA01      $2,000      190
       Baxter Brothers Asphalt    BA02     $17,000     1700
       CA01 (name unknown)        CA01     $33,000     3500
       Concord Concrete           CN01      $7,000      600
       ZA01 (name unknown)        ZA01      $7,500      635
```

Note that this data set now contains an observation for the final record in the daily order file.

Reading Raw Data Files Consecutively

Another common data reading task requires reading raw data from multiple files that are formatted the same way to create a data set for a report or processing. For example, budget or payroll data can be sent from each department to a central office for processing. If you do not need an intermediate SAS data set created from each file, you can read the files consecutively and create a SAS data set that contains all the data in a single DATA step. To read multiple raw data files consecutively, you need to

□ build each observation

□ read each file without going past the end-of-file marker

□ supply the names of the external files to be read consecutively.

Raw Data Example

For example, four branches of an ice cream franchise send information to a central office that produces checks for all part-time employees. The raw data files include the following fields:

Field	Description	Variable
store	store number	STORE
id	employee's number	EMPLOYID
name	employee's name	NAME
rate	hourly wage	RATE
hours	number of hours an employee worked in a week	HOURS

All the raw data records are in the format shown here. These records are from the first file used in this example:*

```
----+----1----+----2----+----3----+----4
16 79 Carrithers, E. A.  3.50 13.5
16 101 Alvarez, J. T.  4.65 45.0
16 56 Ianelli, L. O.  3.35 26.5
16 83 Patel, H.  7.50 11.0
16 105 Huang, L.  3.35 3.0
```

---

* Refer to the Appendix for a complete listing of the input data.

Build Each Observation

First, write the statements that build each observation as if you were creating a data set from a single raw data file. Identify the file and assign values to variables.

This example reads some values with an INPUT statement and calculates others with assignment statements. It calculates the gross pay and assigns the value to the variable GROSS. It also calculates the pay-after-deductions and assigns the value to ACTUAL. The following statements create the data set PARTTIME by reading records of raw data from a single external file:

```
filename payroll 'store-1-input-file';

data parttime;
   infile payroll;
   input store $ employid $ name & $25. rate hours;
   gross=rate*hours;
   actual=gross-(gross*.06);
run;
```

Control Reading the Records in Each File

To read multiple raw data files consecutively in a single DATA step, you can use a DO WHILE loop to read an entire file and use the looping action of the DATA step itself to change the current input file. Place the statements that create each observation in a DO WHILE loop. Specify an OUTPUT statement to write each observation since you are no longer using the automatic output feature of the DATA step to do so.

```
do while(all-records-have-not-been-read);
   input store $ employid $ name & $25. rate hours;
   gross=rate*hours;
   actual=gross-(gross*.06);
   output;
end;
```

You must specify a condition that controls the iterations of the DO WHILE loop, enabling it to execute the statements enclosed in the loop only until the end of the current input file is reached. If you allow the INPUT statement within the DO WHILE loop to attempt to read from a file after the end-of-file is reached, the DATA step halts. You must prevent this by specifying the END= option in the INFILE statement to create a variable whose value is automatically set to 1 when the end of the current input file is reached. When the value of the END= variable is used to control a DO WHILE loop, the value of the variable is checked at the top of each iteration. When that value equals 1, the DO WHILE loop stops iterating, preventing the INPUT statement from attempting to read past the end of a file.

The following statements read an entire file and build each observation:

```
infile payroll end=theend;
do while(theend ne 1);
   input payroll $ employid $ name & $25. rate hours;
   gross=rate*hours;
   actual=gross-(gross*.06);
   output;
end;
```

Supply the Names of the Files Consecutively

The only remaining task is to change the current input file for each iteration of the DATA step. Do this by reading the name of a new raw data file with each iteration and assigning it to a variable. Then specify this variable with the FILEVAR= option in the INFILE statement.

The FILEVAR= option defines a variable whose value is checked each time the INFILE statement executes. If the variable value has changed, the current input file is closed and a new one, whose name is supplied by the variable value, is opened. Although the file to be read is actually determined by the value of the FILEVAR= variable, you must include a fileref in the INFILE statement. As a rule, you can simply assign this fileref in a FILENAME statement to the first file in the group you want to read:

```
filename payroll 'store-1-input-file';
```

```
data parttime;
   more SAS statements
   infile payroll end=theend filevar=variable;
   more SAS statements
```

You can assign a value to the FILEVAR= variable just as you would to any variable. This example takes advantage of the automatic looping action of the DATA step to assign values to the FILEVAR= variable. Each loop of the DATA step uses an INPUT statement to read the name of a file from instream data lines and then to assign it to the variable EACHFILE. When the INFILE statement executes, as it will once for each iteration of the DATA step, the value of EACHFILE is checked. With each iteration, EACHFILE receives a new value. The current file is then closed and a new file is opened.

The following statements read four raw data files consecutively to create the data set PARTTIME and then print it.

```
filename payroll 'store-1-input-file';

data parttime;
   input eachfile : $44.;
   infile payroll end=theend filevar=eachfile;
   length store $ 2 employid $ 3;
   do while(theend ne 1);
      input store employid name & $25. rate hours;
      gross=rate*hours;
```

```
            actual=gross-(gross*.06);
            output;
        end;
        cards;
store-1-input-file
store-2-input-file
store-3-input-file
store-4-input-file
;

proc print data=parttime;
    format gross actual dollar10.2;
    title 'Payroll: Weekly Part-Time';
run;
```

Output 5.4 prints the resulting data set.

Output 5.4
Reading Multiple
Files Consecutively

```
                            Payroll: Weekly Part-Time                        1

OBS  STORE  EMPLOYID   NAME               RATE   HOURS      GROSS     ACTUAL

  1    16      79      Carson, E. A.      3.85   13.5     $51.98     $48.86
  2    16     101      Alvarez, J. T.     4.65   45.0    $209.25    $196.70
  3    16      56      Ianelli, L. O.     3.90   26.5    $103.35     $97.15
  4    16      50      Daniels, J. T.     4.10   20.5     $84.05     $79.01
  5    16      83      Patel, H.          7.50   11.0     $82.50     $77.55
  6    16     105      Huang, L.          4.00    3.0     $12.00     $11.28
  7    16      22      Woods, H.          5.50   15.0     $82.50     $77.55
  8    17      79      Covington, T. A.   3.85   13.5     $51.98     $48.86
  9    17     101      Simpson, J. T.     4.65   45.0    $209.25    $196.70
 10    17      56      Larson, Y. O.      3.90   22.5     $87.75     $82.49
 11    17     100      Adams, Z. W.       4.60   40.0    $184.00    $172.96
 12    17      83      Pitts, A. P.       5.55   10.0     $55.50     $52.17
 13    17     105      Homes, L. A.       6.01   35.0    $210.35    $197.73
 14    17      33      Thompson, N. C.    3.85    4.0     $15.40     $14.48
 15    17      01      Kelly, Q. D.       7.00   40.0    $280.00    $263.20
 16    18      72      Dobbs, E. S.       4.85   15.5     $75.18     $70.66
 17    18     105      Combs, E. E.       4.65   45.0    $209.25    $196.70
 18    18      60      Barnes, R. D.      3.85   25.5     $98.18     $92.28
 19    18      56      Tanner, H. S.      3.90   22.5     $87.75     $82.49
 20    18      83      Petis, B.          6.50   14.0     $91.00     $85.54
 21    18      41      Rich, I. W.        3.90   22.5     $87.75     $82.49
 22    18     115      Harris, K.         3.85    3.0     $11.55     $10.86
 23    18      23      Tonie, T. T.       5.50   11.5     $63.25     $59.46
 24    19      74      Farrington, W. A.  3.85   10.5     $40.43     $38.00
 25    19     101      Mitchel, T. H.     5.65   41.0    $231.65    $217.75
 26    19      56      Panelli, L. O.     3.95   27.5    $108.63    $102.11
 27    19     155      Dillard, J. V.     4.65   45.0    $209.25    $196.70
 28    19      83      Patterson, P.      6.50   12.0     $78.00     $73.32
 29    19     105      Harry, D.          3.85    5.0     $19.25     $18.09
```

Summary

This chapter has demonstrated reading multiple external files in a single DATA step, both concurrently and consecutively. The following major points were covered:

□ To read from different external files in the same DATA step, use multiple INFILE statements. As you read from each file, a pointer location is remembered so that you begin reading from that location the next time an INPUT statement reads from that file.

□ When reading multiple external files, use the END= option to prevent prematurely ending a DATA step by attempting to read past the end of a file.

□ To open and close different files consecutively in a DATA step, use the FILEVAR= option in the INFILE statement. Assign a value to the FILEVAR= variable that is the physical filename of the external file you want to read.

SAS Tools

This section summarizes syntax for the statements discussed in this chapter.

DO UNTIL(*condition*);
   SAS statements
END;
   executes the enclosed SAS statements until the specified condition is true. The condition can be any valid SAS expression, enclosed in parentheses. The condition is evaluated at the bottom of the loop, after the enclosed statements have been executed. If the condition is true, the DO loop is not executed again. Because the condition is evaluated at the bottom of the loop, the enclosed statements are always executed at least once.

DO WHILE(*condition*);
   SAS statements
END;
   executes the enclosed SAS statements as long as the specified condition is true. The condition can be any valid SAS expression, enclosed in parentheses. The condition is evaluated at the top of the loop, before the enclosed statements are executed. If the expression is true, the DO loop is executed. If the condition is false the first time it is evaluated, the DO loop is not executed at all.

INFILE '*input-file*' <*options*>;
   identifies an external file containing records of raw data and allows you to specify options that control how the records are read. The following options for the INFILE statement are discussed in this chapter:

   END=*variable*
      creates a variable, whose name you specify, that is automatically set to 1 when the last record from an input file is being processed. You can use the value of the END= variable to conditionally process SAS statements. This is useful, for example, for controlling a DO UNTIL loop. Using the value of the END= variable, you can prevent an INPUT statement from

(INFILE 'input-file' continued)

attempting to read past the end of a file and, thereby, bringing an abrupt halt to the DATA step.

FILEVAR=*variable*
creates a variable whose value controls the opening and closing of input files. When the FILEVAR= option is used in an INFILE statement, the value of the FILEVAR= variable is checked each time the INFILE statement executes. When that value changes, the current file is closed and a new file is opened.

Learning More

This section provides references for learning more about topics presented in this chapter.

□ Using the FILENAME or INFILE statement requires host-specific information. See the appropriate chapter in the SAS documentation for your host operating system.

□ For information on data-reading features provided by INFILE statement options that were not discussed in this chapter, see *SAS Language: Reference, Version 6, First Edition*, Chapter 9, "SAS Language Statements."

□ To read multiple raw data files consecutively, an alternate method is to use multiple INFILE statements and the END= option in DO loops. This method is especially useful if you need to use different statements to read each file.

Part 3

Using Advanced Programming Techniques

Chapter 6 Converting Variable Values

Introduction

In DATA step programming, you may sometimes need to convert the values of variables from one form to another, either character to numeric or numeric to character. Conversion occurs when new variables of the appropriate type are created. For efficiency, you should minimize automatic conversions whenever possible. Automatic conversion is resource-intensive and may produce undesirable results in output.

In this chapter
For cases in which you must convert, this chapter shows you how to convert

- numeric values to character values
- character values to numeric values
- packed decimal data to numeric values.

Prerequisites
To accomplish the tasks in this chapter, you should already be familiar with the following features of the SAS System:

- DATA step processing
- concatenation.

Converting Numeric Values to Character Values

Your reasons for producing a character value from a numeric value may vary. You may need to define numeric values as character values to accomplish specific programming objectives, such as concatenating variables. If you are transferring data between machines, you may also want to change numeric values to character values to circumvent the machine dependencies peculiar to numeric data. And because character variables in SAS data sets may require less storage space than the default length of numeric variables, you may want to convert numeric variables to character variables to save storage space when those variables are not being used in numeric calculations or comparisons.

The SAS System provides two ways to accomplish a numeric-to-character conversion:

□ automatically, by using a numeric value in one of the following situations:

   □ in an assignment to a character variable

   □ during a concatenation operation

   □ when used with a function that takes character arguments; for example, assigning a numeric variable to a macro variable by using the CALL SYMPUT routine.

   Note that automatic conversion can cause problems, such as trailing and leading blanks.

□ by using the PUT function in a SAS statement. Note that using the PUT function allows you greater computer efficiency and greater control over the results.

The following sections show you how to accomplish these conversions, both automatically and by using the PUT function. They also discuss advantages and disadvantages of each method.

To illustrate, a rainwear manufacturing company is changing its inventory procedures. Instead of recording an item by department and individual item number in two variables, it is adopting an identification code that combines the old department number and item number. Because the variable DEPT is numeric, it must be converted to a character value for the concatenation to work.

SAS Data Set Example

The following examples demonstrate numeric-to-character conversion. The data set used for the examples in this section contains the variables described in the following table:

Variable	Type	Length	Description
LINE	character	1	rainwear line: specialty (s) or regular (r)
DEPT	numeric	8	department in the rainwear manufacturing company
ITEM	character	5	specific rainwear model

The following PROC PRINT step displays the data set RAINWEAR.STOCK:*

```
libname rainwear 'SAS-data-library';

proc print data=rainwear.stock;
   title 'Printout of Inventory';
run;
```

Output 6.1 shows the results.

Output 6.1
Printout of
RAINWEAR.STOCK
Data Set

```
                     Printout of Inventory                      1

          OBS     LINE     DEPT     ITEM

           1       s       3070     20410
           2       s       3070     20411
           3       r       3070     20412
           4       s       3070     20413
           5       s       3070     20414
           6       r       3070     20415
           7       s       3070     20416
           8       s       3070     20417
           9       r       3070     20418
          10       s       3070     20419
          11       r       3070     20420
          12       r       3080     20430
          13       s       3080     20431
          14       r       3080     20432
          15       r       3080     20433
          16       s       3080     20434
          17       s       3080     20435
          18       s       3080     20436
          19       r       3080     20437
          20       r       3080     20438
          21       s       3080     20439
          22       r       3080     20440
```

The first example shows you how to convert the data automatically through concatenation.

---

* The DATA step that creates RAINWEAR.STOCK is shown in the Appendix.

Converting Numeric Values Automatically with Concatenation

As already noted, the SAS System converts numeric values to character values automatically under certain circumstances. Remember that the rainwear company is adopting an identification code that combines the old department number and item number. However, all department numbers have been stored as numeric values and item numbers as character values. The following example illustrates that numeric values are converted to character values automatically when those values are concatenated. In fact, if both DEPT and ITEM were numeric, the concatenation operation would convert both, since only character variables can be concatenated.

To concatenate a numeric variable such as DEPT and a character variable such as ITEM and to store the results in a new variable, you can simply use the concatenation operator in an assignment statement. The new variable is assigned the results of the concatenation. The assignment statement not only concatenates the two variables but makes the resulting variable (in this case, ID) character. Note that the original variable (in this case, DEPT) is not converted. Rather, as the result of the concatenation, the newly created variable is defined as a character variable. Here is the program that creates and prints the data set. In this example, the numeric variable DEPT is concatenated with a hyphen and the character variable ITEM. The result of the concatenation is stored in the new character variable ID.

```
libname rainwear 'SAS-data-library';

data rainwear.newstck1(drop=dept item);
   set rainwear.stock;
   id=dept||'-'||item;
run;

proc print data=rainwear.newstck1;
   title 'Inventory Printout, New Departmental System';
run;
```

The SAS log verifies that the SAS System converted the numeric values of the variable DEPT to character values as a result of the concatenation operation.*

```
NOTE: Numeric values have been converted to character
      values at the places given by: (Number of times) at (Line):(Column).
      22 at 36:7
```

Output 6.2 shows the results of the concatenation. By default, the SAS System uses the BEST12. format to convert the numeric values to character values, right-aligning the values so that this example contains no embedded spaces.

---

* A note in the log does not necessarily indicate a problem. You should understand what notes in the log imply and what action to take, if any.

Output 6.2
Converting
Numeric Values
Automatically with
Concatenation

```
                  Inventory Printout, New Departmental System            1

               OBS      LINE        ID

                1        s       3070-20410
                2        s       3070-20411
                3        r       3070-20412
                4        s       3070-20413
                5        s       3070-20414
                6        r       3070-20415
                7        s       3070-20416
                8        s       3070-20417
                9        r       3070-20418
               10        s       3070-20419
               11        r       3070-20420
               12        r       3080-20430
               13        s       3080-20431
               14        r       3080-20432
               15        r       3080-20433
               16        s       3080-20434
               17        s       3080-20435
               18        s       3080-20436
               19        r       3080-20437
               20        r       3080-20438
               21        s       3080-20439
               22        r       3080-20440
```

Although the conversion is successful and appears to produce no undesirable results, the CONTENTS procedure reveals that the new variable ID has a length of 18, 8 bytes more than is actually needed to store each value of ID. Of the 18 bytes, 12 come from the variable DEPT, 5 come from the variable ITEM, and 1 comes from the hyphen concatenated with the new values.

```
    -----Alphabetic List of Variables and Attributes-----


    #     Variable    Type    Len    Pos
    ------------------------------------
    2     ID          Char     18     1

    1     LINE        Char      1     0
```

To understand how to avoid this situation, see "Using the PUT Function to Convert Numeric Values to Character Values" later in this chapter.

Understanding How Unexpected Results Can Occur in an Automatic Conversion

The previous example produces acceptable output even though execution of the CONTENTS procedure reveals that it allocates more storage space than is actually needed. It is also possible, in some cases, for automatic conversion to produce unacceptable output.

To illustrate, in the previous example, only the variables DEPT and ITEM and a hyphen are concatenated. Suppose instead that the rainwear manufacturer decides to combine all of the variables from the data set RAINWEAR.STOCK to produce the new identification number so that the rainwear line—specialty or regular—is the first component of the variable ID.

To concatenate the variables LINE, DEPT, and ITEM and to store the results in a new variable, the concatenation operator is used in an assignment statement as in the previous example. Note that the character variable LINE is the first variable concatenated. The variable ID is again assigned the results of the concatenation. This concatenation automatically converts the numeric values of DEPT to character values with a default format of BEST12. Here is the program that creates and prints the data set.

```
libname rainwear 'SAS-data-library';

data rainwear.newstck2(drop=line dept item);
   set rainwear.stock;
   id=line||'-'||dept||'-'||item;
run;

proc print data=rainwear.newstck2;
   title 'Inventory Printout, New Departmental System';
run;
```

Again, the SAS log verifies that the SAS System converted the numeric values of the variable DEPT to character values as a result of the concatenation operation.

```
NOTE: Numeric values have been converted to character
      values at the places given by: (Number of times) at (Line):(Column).
      22 at 46:18
```

Output 6.3 shows the results of the concatenation. Note that the SAS System does not trim the embedded blanks that result from this operation.

Output 6.3
Producing Undesirable Results with Automatic Conversion

```
              Inventory Printout, New Departmental System          1

           OBS              ID

            1    s-         3070-20410
            2    s-         3070-20411
            3    r-         3070-20412
            4    s-         3070-20413
            5    s-         3070-20414
            6    r-         3070-20415
            7    s-         3070-20416
            8    s-         3070-20417
            9    r-         3070-20418
           10    s-         3070-20419
           11    r-         3070-20420
           12    r-         3080-20430
           13    s-         3080-20431
           14    r-         3080-20432
           15    r-         3080-20433
           16    s-         3080-20434
           17    s-         3080-20435
           18    s-         3080-20436
           19    r-         3080-20437
           20    r-         3080-20438
           21    s-         3080-20439
           22    r-         3080-20440
```

The printout of the CONTENTS procedure reveals that the new variable ID has a length of 20, 1 byte for the variable LINE, 1 byte for each hyphen, 12 bytes for the variable DEPT, and 5 bytes for the variable ITEM.

```
-----Alphabetic List of Variables and Attributes-----

     #   Variable   Type   Len   Pos
     -----------------------------------
     1   ID         Char    20    0
```

The next section shows you one way to control a numeric-to-character conversion so you get the results you want.

Using the PUT Function to Convert Numeric Values to Character Values

Sometimes automatic conversion produces undesirable results, as in the previous example. You can produce the output you want and minimize storage space by using the PUT function to convert numeric values to character values. The PUT function enables you to write the value of a SAS expression using a specified format.

To illustrate how the PUT function works, consider the previous example in which the variables LINE, DEPT, and ITEM are concatenated. To incorporate greater control into the operation, add the PUT function to the assignment statement. In the following assignment statement, the PUT function converts the numeric value of DEPT into a 4-byte character value. The SAS System then concatenates that value with the two other variables, LINE and ITEM, each separated from the value by a hyphen. The assignment statement evaluates the entire expression and stores the results in the newly created variable ID. Here is the program that creates and prints the data set.

```
libname rainwear 'SAS-data-library';

data rainwear.newstck3(drop=line dept item);
   set rainwear.stock;
   id=line||'-'||put(dept,4.)||'-'||item;
run;

proc print data=rainwear.newstck3;
   title 'Inventory Printout, New Departmental System';
run;
```

With the PUT function, the log produces no note indicating that conversion has occurred because conversion is specified rather than occurring automatically. Output 6.4 shows the results, which do not contain embedded blanks.

Output 6.4
Controlling a Numeric-to-Character Conversion with the PUT Function

```
          Inventory Printout, New Departmental System              1

                  OBS          ID

                   1        s-3070-20410
                   2        s-3070-20411
                   3        r-3070-20412
                   4        s-3070-20413
                   5        s-3070-20414
                   6        r-3070-20415
                   7        s-3070-20416
                   8        s-3070-20417
                   9        r-3070-20418
                  10        s-3070-20419
                  11        r-3070-20420
                  12        r-3080-20430
                  13        s-3080-20431
                  14        r-3080-20432
                  15        r-3080-20433

                                      (continued on next page)
```

```
(continued from previous page)
                      16    s-3080-20434
                      17    s-3080-20435
                      18    s-3080-20436
                      19    r-3080-20437
                      20    r-3080-20438
                      21    s-3080-20439
                      22    r-3080-20440
```

The CONTENTS procedure results reveal that the new variable ID has a length of 12, the exact number of nonblank characters and thus the exact number of bytes needed to store the string.

```
-----Alphabetic List of Variables and Attributes-----

         #    Variable   Type    Len   Pos
         ------------------------------------
         1    ID         Char     12    0
```

Converting Character Values to Numeric Values

You may have many reasons for converting character values to numeric values. For example, character values must be converted to numeric values to be used in a numeric operation. In addition, when you are reading external files with variable data fields, you might want to read an entire record into a single character variable. You can then scan that single character variable and apply informats to it, using the INPUT function to read the data.

The SAS System provides two ways to accomplish most character-to-numeric conversions:

□ automatically, by using a character value in one of the following numeric operations:

  □ in an arithmetic operation

  □ in a logical comparison with a numeric value

  □ when used with a function that takes numeric arguments

  □ in an assignment to a numeric variable

□ by using the INPUT function in a SAS statement.

The following sections show you how to accomplish these conversions, both automatically and by using the INPUT function.

Converting Character Values Automatically in an Arithmetic Operation

As already noted, the SAS System converts character values to numeric values automatically under certain circumstances. For example, the rainwear manufacturer wants to award post-production bonuses to its employees based on percentage of annual income. Annual incomes have been stored as character values; before calculating the bonuses, the company must convert those values to numeric values.

The following example shows an automatic character-to-numeric conversion. The data set used for the example in this section contains the variables described in the following table:

Variable	Type	Format	Length	Description
ID	character	$16.	16	employee identification number
SALARY	character		8	employee's annual income

The following PROC PRINT step displays the data set RAINWEAR.SALARIES:*

```
libname rainwear 'SAS-data-library';

proc print data=rainwear.salaries;
   title 'Printout of Salaries';
run;
```

Output 6.5 shows a printout of salaries before bonuses are calculated.

Output 6.5
Printout of
RAINWEAR.SALARIES
Data Set

```
                     Printout of Salaries                          1

          OBS            ID              SALARY

           1       8155-201-92-2498       35800
           2       8156-298-89-5671       32075
           3       8157-339-67-6980       29880
           4       8158-203-45-1897       30665
           5       8159-204-12-1269       28775
           6       8160-113-11-1398       37550
           7       8161-219-77-2908       39000
           8       8162-101-65-3008       27219
           9       8163-109-75-4009       40125
```

The following example illustrates character values being converted to numeric values automatically when those values are used in an arithmetic operation. In this case, one group of employees will be awarded 10 percent bonuses. The variable SALARY is multiplied by 10 percent to use its character values in the numeric operation. Note that the results are rounded using the ROUND function. Because no roundoff unit is specified, a default value of 1 is used, and the values are rounded to the nearest integer. Numeric values are produced and stored in

---

* The DATA step that creates RAINWEAR.SALARIES is shown in the Appendix.

the new variable BONUS. Here is the program that creates and prints the data set.

```
libname rainwear 'SAS-data-library';

data rainwear.bonuses1;
   set rainwear.salaries;
   bonus=round(.10*salary);
run;

proc print data=rainwear.bonuses1;
   title 'Production Bonuses';
run;
```

The SAS log verifies that the SAS System converted the character values of the variable SALARY to numeric values as a result of the arithmetic operation.

```
NOTE: Character values have been converted to numeric
      values at the places given by: (Number of times) at (Line):(Column).
      9 at 84:20
```

Output 6.6 shows the results.

Output 6.6
Converting
Character Values
by Using Them in
an Arithmetic
Operation

```
                        Production Bonuses                           1

         OBS        ID            SALARY    BONUS

          1    8155-201-92-2498    35800     3580
          2    8156-298-89-5671    32075     3208
          3    8157-339-67-6980    29880     2988
          4    8158-203-45-1897    30665     3067
          5    8159-204-12-1269    28775     2878
          6    8160-113-11-1398    37550     3755
          7    8161-219-77-2908    39000     3900
          8    8162-101-65-3008    27219     2722
          9    8163-109-75-4009    40125     4013
```

This conversion is successful and produces no undesirable results but requires more CPU time than explicit conversion does.

Understanding How Unexpected Results Can Occur in an Automatic Conversion

As with a numeric-to-character conversion, converting character values to numeric values sometimes produces undesirable results. In the previous example the values of SALARY are converted to numeric values, and a 10-percent bonus is calculated. Suppose instead that SALARY is not only stored as a character variable but that its values contain embedded dollar signs and commas. The data set used for the example in this section contains the variables described in the following table:

Variable	Type	Format	Length	Description
ID	character	$16.	16	employee identification number
SALARY	character		8	employee's annual income

The following PROC PRINT step displays the data set RAINWEAR.SALARY2:*

```
libname rainwear 'SAS-data-library';

proc print data=rainwear.salary2;
   title 'Production Bonuses';
run;
```

Output 6.7 shows a printout of salaries before bonuses are calculated.

Output 6.7
Printout of
RAINWEAR.SALARY2
Data Set

```
                         Production Bonuses                        1

            OBS          ID               SALARY

             1     8155-201-92-2498       $35,800
             2     8156-298-89-5671       $32,075
             3     8157-339-67-6980       $29,880
             4     8158-203-45-1897       $30,665
             5     8159-204-12-1269       $28,775
             6     8160-113-11-1398       $37,550
             7     8161-219-77-2908       $39,000
             8     8162-101-65-3008       $27,219
             9     8163-109-75-4009       $40,125
```

The same assignment statement as in the previous example is used to convert the character values of SALARY and to assign those values to the variable BONUS.

```
libname rainwear 'SAS-data-library';

data rainwear.bonuses2;
   set rainwear.salary2;
   bonus=round(.10*salary);
run;

proc print data=rainwear.bonuses2;
   title 'Production Bonuses';
run;
```

---

* The DATA step that creates RAINWEAR.SALARY2 is shown in the Appendix.

Output 6.8 shows the results, with missing values assigned to BONUS.

Output 6.8
Producing
Undesirable
Results with
Automatic
Conversion

```
                        Production Bonuses                           1

          OBS          ID          SALARY      BONUS

           1     8155-201-92-2498   $35,800       .
           2     8156-298-89-5671   $32,075       .
           3     8157-339-67-6980   $29,880       .
           4     8158-203-45-1897   $30,665       .
           5     8159-204-12-1269   $28,775       .
           6     8160-113-11-1398   $37,550       .
           7     8161-219-77-2908   $39,000       .
           8     8162-101-65-3008   $27,219       .
           9     8163-109-75-4009   $40,125       .
```

The log in Output 6.9 verifies that the SAS System converted the character values of the variable SALARY to numeric values in order to perform the arithmetic operation. However, it also shows that the SAS System considers those resulting numeric data invalid. Note the presence of the automatic variable _ERROR_, which has been assigned a value of 1 for all nine iterations of the DATA step to indicate an error during data conversion. Note also that the values of BONUS are considered missing. When data do not conform to the standard for *w.d* informats, automatic conversion does not work. In this case, the automatic conversion failed because of the embedded dollar signs and commas in the data values for SALARY.

Output 6.9
Producing
Undesirable
Results—the Log

```
    5          libname rainwear 'SAS-data-library';
NOTE: Libref RAINWEAR was successfully assigned as follows:
      Engine:        V606
      Physical Name: SAS-DATA-LIBRARY
    6          options pagesize=70;
    7          data rainwear.bonuses2;
    8             set rainwear.salary2;
    9             bonus=.10*salary;
   10          run;

NOTE: Invalid numeric data, SALARY='$35,800' , at line 9 column 14.
ID=8155-201-92-2498 SALARY=$35,800 BONUS=. _ERROR_=1 _N_=1
NOTE: Invalid numeric data, SALARY='$32,075' , at line 9 column 14.
ID=8156-298-89-5671 SALARY=$32,075 BONUS=. _ERROR_=1 _N_=2
NOTE: Invalid numeric data, SALARY='$29,880' , at line 9 column 14.
ID=8157-339-67-6980 SALARY=$29,880 BONUS=. _ERROR_=1 _N_=3
NOTE: Invalid numeric data, SALARY='$30,665' , at line 9 column 14.
ID=8158-203-45-1897 SALARY=$30,665 BONUS=. _ERROR_=1 _N_=4
NOTE: Invalid numeric data, SALARY='$28,775' , at line 9 column 14.
ID=8159-204-12-1269 SALARY=$28,775 BONUS=. _ERROR_=1 _N_=5
NOTE: Invalid numeric data, SALARY='$37,550' , at line 9 column 14.
ID=8160-113-11-1398 SALARY=$37,550 BONUS=. _ERROR_=1 _N_=6
NOTE: Invalid numeric data, SALARY='$39,000' , at line 9 column 14.
ID=8161-219-77-2908 SALARY=$39,000 BONUS=. _ERROR_=1 _N_=7
NOTE: Invalid numeric data, SALARY='$27,219' , at line 9 column 14.
ID=8162-101-65-3008 SALARY=$27,219 BONUS=. _ERROR_=1 _N_=8
NOTE: Invalid numeric data, SALARY='$40,125' , at line 9 column 14.
ID=8163-109-75-4009 SALARY=$40,125 BONUS=. _ERROR_=1 _N_=9
NOTE: Character values have been converted to numeric
      values at the places given by: (Number of times) at (Line):(Column).
      9 at 9:14
NOTE: Missing values were generated as a result of performing an operation
      on missing values.
      Each place is given by: (Number of times) at (Line):(Column).
      9 at 9:13
NOTE: The data set RAINWEAR.BONUSES2 has 9 observations and 3 variables.

   11          proc print data=rainwear.bonuses2;
   12             title 'Production Bonuses';
   13          run;

NOTE: The PROCEDURE PRINT printed page 1.
```

The following section shows you how to control a character-to-numeric conversion so you get the results you want.

Using the INPUT Function to Convert Character Values to Numeric Values

As the previous example illustrates, when data contain characters such as dollar signs and commas, automatic conversion does not work. However, you can produce the output you want by using the INPUT function to convert character values to numeric values. The INPUT function enables you to read the value of a SAS expression using a specified informat.

The following example simply adds the INPUT function to the assignment statement used in the previous example. The SAS System uses the COMMA7. informat to read the character values of SALARY as numeric values, first stripping out the unwanted dollar signs and commas. The resulting values are multiplied by 10 percent and rounded. The assignment statement evaluates the entire expression and stores the results in the newly created variable BONUS.

```
libname rainwear 'SAS-data-library';

data rainwear.bonuses3;
   set rainwear.salary2;
   bonus=round(.10*input(salary,comma7.));
run;

proc print data=rainwear.bonuses3;
   title 'Production Bonuses, by Employee';
run;
```

Output 6.10 shows the results of this successful conversion.

Output 6.10
*Controlling a
Character-to-Numeric
Conversion with
the INPUT
Function*

```
                    Production Bonuses, by Employee                1

          OBS        ID            SALARY      BONUS

           1    8155-201-92-2498   $35,800     3580
           2    8156-298-89-5671   $32,075     3208
           3    8157-339-67-6980   $29,880     2988
           4    8158-203-45-1897   $30,665     3067
           5    8159-204-12-1269   $28,775     2878
           6    8160-113-11-1398   $37,550     3755
           7    8161-219-77-2908   $39,000     3900
           8    8162-101-65-3008   $27,219     2722
           9    8163-109-75-4009   $40,125     4013
```

When the INPUT function is used, the log does not indicate that the data have been converted.

Converting Packed Decimal Data to Numeric Values

Numeric data are sometimes stored as packed decimals because this format allows for fields of varying sizes. In addition, packed decimal format consumes less storage space: through a technique called packing, two digits are fit into each byte and a sign occupies only a half of the last byte. However, if you want to use packed decimal data in a numeric operation, those data must first be converted to numeric values. This section shows you how to accomplish this conversion by using the PUT and INPUT functions with the appropriate formats and informats.

To illustrate, the rainwear company is planning a spring advertising campaign. The company must first determine when the sale should begin by taking into account the duration of the winter sale for different sites. The dates for that sale have been stored as packed decimal data. In the following example, which converts packed decimal data to SAS date values, each record contains the following fields:

Field	Description
t1	starting date of recent advertising campaign
t2	ending date of recent advertising campaign
site	area shopping site targeted for campaign

The values of T1 and T2 are integers representing month, day, and year, each occupying two places. However, these packed decimal data cannot be printed in a meaningful way until the appropriate SAS informats are used to read them. Although packed decimal data are stored differently on each operating system, the appropriate informat can read the data correctly.

Several steps are involved in converting packed decimal data to SAS date values. To read packed decimal data, use the PD*w.d* informat for the variables whose values are packed decimal data. This example uses the PD5. informat to read the values for the variables T1 and T2.

```
libname rainwear 'SAS-data-library';

data rainwear.dates(drop=t1 t2);
   infile 'input-file';
   input site $4. t1 pd5. t2 pd5.;
```

To write packed decimal data values as character values, use the PUT function with the appropriate format. Here, the values of T1 are written as character values using the PUT function with the 6. format.

```
put(t1,6.)
```

The next step is to read the character values resulting from the PUT function as SAS date values. Use the INPUT function to convert those character values to numeric values, applying the appropriate informat. Here, the MMDDYY6. informat reads the values as integers representing a two-digit month, a two-digit day, and a two-digit year. The assignment statement evaluates the entire expression and stores the results in the newly created variable START.

```
libname rainwear 'SAS-data-library';

data rainwear.dates;
   infile 'input-file';
   input site $4. t1 pd5. t2 pd5.;
   start=input(put(t1,6.),mmddyy6.);
```

The process is repeated for the variable T2. The PUT function writes the packed decimal values for variable T2 as character values, again using the 6. format.

```
put(t2,6.)
```

The INPUT function returns SAS date values for the variable T2, and the MMDDYY6. informat reads the values as integers representing a two-digit month, a two-digit day, and a two-digit year. The assignment statement evaluates the expression and stores the results in the newly created variable END. The value in the variable END is a SAS date value.

```
libname rainwear 'SAS-data-library';

data rainwear.dates;
   infile 'input-file';
   input site $4. t1 pd5. t2 pd5.;
   start=input(put(t1,6.),mmddyy6.);
   end=input(put(t2,6.),mmddyy6.);
```

An additional assignment statement subtracts the value of the numeric variable START from that of the numeric variable END. It evaluates the expression and stores the results in the newly created variable DURATION:

```
libname rainwear 'SAS-data-library';

data rainwear.dates(drop=t1 t2);
   infile 'input-file';
   input site $4. t1 pd5. t2 pd5.;
   start=input(put(t1,6.),mmddyy6.);
   end=input(put(t2,6.),mmddyy6.);
   duration=end-start;
run;
```

The last step in this example is to print the results. A FORMAT statement using the MMDDYY8. format is added to write the SAS date values as integers representing month, date, and year, separated by slashes.

```
libname rainwear 'SAS-data-library';

data rainwear.dates(drop=t1 t2);
   infile 'input-file';
   input site $4. t1 pd5. t2 pd5.;
   start=input(put(t1,6.),mmddyy6.);
```

```
        end=input(put(t2,6.),mmddyy6.);
        duration=end-start;
run;

proc print data=rainwear.dates;
    format start end mmddyy8.;
    title 'Packed Decimal Data Converted to SAS Date Values';
run;
```

Output 6.11 shows the results.

Output 6.11
Converting Packed Decimal Data to SAS Date Values

```
       Packed Decimal Data Converted to SAS Date Values              1

       OBS    SITE     START       END      DURATION

         1    HTTR    12/10/90   02/13/91       65
         2    WVMA    12/11/90   02/16/91       67
         3    ELMA    12/07/90   03/15/91       98
         4    HLMA    12/08/90   02/16/91       70
         5    SOBM    12/06/90   03/18/91      102
         6    GVDM    12/08/90   02/13/91       67
         7    VATR    12/08/90   03/15/91       97
         8    MDMA    12/09/90   03/16/91       97
         9    NOBM    12/10/90   02/12/91       64
        10    OPMA    12/11/90   02/14/91       65
        11    OTMA    12/09/90   03/16/91       97
```

Note that the variables START and END are formatted as expected.

Summary

The following points summarize how to convert variable values:

□ You can convert numeric values to character values either automatically or by using the PUT function.

□ Numeric values are converted to character values automatically in one of the following situations:

    □ in assignment to a character variable

    □ during concatenation

    □ when used with a function that takes character arguments.

Automatic conversion may produce unacceptable output, especially if the output has unwanted blanks.

□ The PUT function gives you greater control in converting numeric values to character values. It enables you to avoid the undesirable results you may get using automatic methods, and it uses less CPU time.

□ You can convert character values to numeric values either automatically or by using the INPUT function.

□ Character values are converted to numeric values automatically in one of the following situations:

   □ during an arithmetic operation

   □ in a logical comparison with a numeric value

   □ when used with a function that takes numeric arguments

   □ in an assignment to a numeric variable.

□ When data do not conform to the standard of *w.d* informats, you must use the INPUT function to convert character values to numeric values.

□ You can use packed decimal format to store data with fields of greatly varying sizes. This format also consumes less storage space. However, if you want to use packed decimal data in a numeric operation, you must first convert those data.

□ To convert packed decimal values to SAS date values, use the PUT function with a format and the INPUT function with the appropriate informat.

SAS Tools

This section summarizes syntax for the statements, functions, informats, formats, and automatic variable discussed in this chapter.

Statements

variable=expression;
   is an assignment statement. It causes the SAS System to evaluate the *expression* on the right side of the equal sign and assign the result to the *variable* on the left. You must select the name of the variable and create the proper expression for calculating its value. The same variable name can appear on the left and right sides of the equal sign because the SAS System evaluates the right side before assigning the result to the variable on the left side.

FORMAT *variables* <*format*>;
   associates formats with variables in a DATA step (permanent association) or a PROC step (temporary association).

Functions

INPUT(*source,informat*)
   returns the value produced when a source is read using a specified informat. *Source* contains the SAS expression to which you want to apply the *informat*.

PUT(*source,format*)
   returns a value using a specified format. *Source* contains the SAS expression whose value you want to reformat.

ROUND(*argument*<,*round-off-unit*>)

returns a value rounded to the nearest round-off unit. If *round-off-unit* is not provided, a default value of 1 is used, and *argument* is rounded to the nearest integer.

Informats

COMMA*w*.*d*

reads numeric values and removes embedded commas, blanks, dollar signs, percent signs, dashes, and right parentheses from the input data. This informat converts a left parenthesis at the beginning of a field to a minus sign. The *d* value range is 0 through 31. The *w* value must be greater than or equal to *d*+1.

MMDDYY*w*.

reads date values as integers representing month, day, and year. The month, day, and year can be separated by blanks or special characters. If delimiters are used, they should be placed between all fields in the value. Blanks can also be placed before and after the date.

PD*w*.*d*

reads packed decimal data. The *w* value can range from 1 to 16. The *d* value range is 0 through 10.

Formats

MMDDYY*w*.

writes a SAS date value as integers representing month, day, and year.

w.*d*

writes standard numeric values one digit per byte. The *w* value specifies the width of the output field including the decimal point. The *d* value optionally specifies the number of digits to the right of the decimal point in the numeric value.

Automatic variable

ERROR

indicates the occurrence of an error during an execution of the DATA step. The value assigned to the variable _ERROR_ is 0 when no error is encountered and 1 when an error is encountered.

Learning More

This section provides references for learning more about topics presented in this chapter.

□ For general rules on variable value conversion, see *SAS Language: Reference, Version 6, First Edition*, Chapter 4, "Rules of the SAS Language." For details specific to your host operating system, see the appropriate SAS companion provided by SAS Institute.

□ For detailed syntax information about the assignment and FORMAT statements, see *SAS Language: Reference*, Chapter 9, "SAS Language Statements."

□ For full syntax information concerning the INPUT, PUT, and ROUND functions, see *SAS Language: Reference*, Chapter 11, "SAS Functions."

□ For full syntax information concerning the COMMA*w.d*, MMDDYY*w.*, and PD*w.d* informats, see *SAS Language: Reference*, Chapter 13, "SAS Informats."

□ For full syntax information concerning the *w.d* and MMDDYY*w.* formats, see *SAS Language: Reference*, Chapter 14, "SAS Formats."

Chapter 7 Grouping Variables to Perform Repetitive Tasks Easily

Introduction

In DATA step programming you may often want to perform the same action on more than one variable. Although you can process variables individually, it is easier to handle them as a group. This technique is called array processing, and it provides an easy way to process a group of variables identically.

In this chapter
Using data from a rainwear manufacturing company, this chapter shows you how to

☐ arrange variables in one-dimensional groupings

☐ arrange variables in two-dimensional groupings

□   use array processing with bounded array dimensions

□   use shortcuts in array processing.

Prerequisites
To accomplish the tasks in this chapter, you should already be familiar with the following features of the SAS System:

□   DATA step processing

□   iterative processing with DO loops

□   simple array processing.

Note that this chapter begins with a review of simple array processing.

Arranging Variables in One-Dimensional Groupings

Simple array processing enables you to perform the same tasks for a series of variables using one-dimensional groupings. When processed, these groupings of variables produce results that can be presented in simple column format. These groupings are called *one-dimensional arrays*. The tasks described in this section include

□   performing repetitive calculations and recoding missing values for a group of variables

□   reading multiple records to create a single observation

□   assigning initial values to array elements

□   assigning temporary array elements.

Performing Repetitive Calculations and Recoding Missing Values

Often you may want to perform repetitive calculations and recode missing values for a group of variables. To perform the same action on more than one variable, do the following:

□   arrange the variables in a temporary grouping called an array*

□   perform the desired actions for all elements of the array.

---

*   If you have worked with arrays in other programming languages, note that arrays in the SAS System are different from those in many other languages. In the SAS System, an array is simply a convenient way of temporarily identifying a group of variables. It is not a data structure, and it exists only for the duration of the DATA step. The array's name identifies the array and distinguishes it from any other arrays in the same DATA step; it is not a variable.

The case of a rainwear manufacturing company illustrates this task. The company has been notified of a 12-percent price increase in the fabric it uses for its specialty garments. It plans to pass this price increase directly on to consumers. The company wants to accomplish two tasks:

□ calculate the price increase for its specialty garments

□ update its inventory by assigning missing values when a line is not available in a particular size category.

In this example, each record of raw data contains the following fields:

Field	Description
category	categories of sizes, each containing numerous individual sizes
classic	price of least expensive specialty rainwear
trench	price of moderately priced specialty rainwear
modern	price of higher priced specialty rainwear
europa	price of highest priced specialty rainwear

Here are the raw data records. Note that instances where a particular line is not available in a certain size category appear as values of **999**.

```
----+----1----+----2----+----3----+----4----+----5----+
women-regular  190.80   230.80   242.80   263.76
women-petite   207.75   258.25   276.70   295.00
women-large    200.00   240.85   260.90   280.75
men-regular    175.80   200.25   235.00   258.85
men-short      190.65   215.50   253.75   275.00
men-large      185.25   207.75      999   268.00
men-tall       195.00   225.00   260.75   285.90
junior         110.00      999   122.00   130.00
children        91.65      999      999   118.75
```

The two steps that accomplish the tasks follow.

Group the Variables

To put the variables to be processed into an array, first use an ARRAY statement. Note that arrays exist only for the duration of the DATA step. Here, the array is called ITEM and has four elements: CLASSIC, TRENCH, MODERN, and EUROPA.

```
libname rainwear 'SAS-data-library';

data rainwear.retail;
   input category $14. classic trench modern europa;
   array item{4} classic trench modern europa;
```

Perform the Desired Actions

After you group the variables, you can use a DO loop to process them identically. This section shows you how to

□ indicate the number of times you want to repeat the same action

□ specify the actions you want to perform

□ determine what variable, or array element, to process with each iteration of the repeated action.

First, to repeat the desired action for each array element, use an iterative DO loop. An iterative DO loop contains an index variable and other SAS statements. The DO loop iterates according to the instructions in the DO statement. The name of the index variable is arbitrary. To cause the loop to iterate as many times as there are elements in the array, specify that the values of the index variable are 1 to the number of array elements. The value of the index variable increases by 1 with each new iteration of the DO loop. When the value of the index variable exceeds the number of array elements, the END statement terminates the loop. In this example, the index variable is I. Because the array has four elements, I has a value of 1 to 4.

```
libname rainwear 'SAS-data-library';

data rainwear.retail;
   input category $14. classic trench modern europa;
   array item{4} classic trench modern europa;
   do i=1 to 4;
      more SAS statements
   end;
```

Next, specify the actions you want to perform. Here, use an IF-THEN statement to convert all values of 999 to missing values in order to update the inventory. Use an assignment statement to multiply all the nonmissing array elements by 1.12 to calculate the price increase. To prevent an unnecessary calculation from being performed for observations that have missing values for ITEM{i}, place this statement in an IF-THEN statement. At the same time that these statements specify the actions to perform, they also use the array reference for each array element to determine which element to process with each iteration of the DO loop. The value of the array reference is based on the value of the index variable.

```
libname rainwear 'SAS-data-library';

data rainwear.retail;
   input category $14. classic trench modern europa;
   array item{4} classic trench modern europa;
   do i=1 to 4;
      if item{i}=999 then item{i}=.;
      if item{i} ne . then item{i}=item{i}*1.12;
   end;
```

An array reference is assigned to each array element based on its position, or subscript, within the array. For example, here, the array reference for the variable TRENCH is ITEM{2} because TRENCH is the second item listed in the ARRAY statement. Because the value of the index variable within the DO loop is the subscript of the array reference, as the value of the index variable changes, the subscript of the array reference—and therefore the particular array element processed—also changes. Here, when I has a value of 1, the SAS System treats the array reference as ITEM{1} and performs the action on CLASSIC. It continues to process the statements within the DO loop, replacing the subscript I with its current value, which changes with each iteration. Because the index variable I has a value of 1 to 4, each statement is processed four times.

Here is the complete program, including the instream data records, that creates and displays the data set.

```
libname rainwear 'SAS-data-library';

data rainwear.retail;
    input category $14. classic trench modern europa;
    array item{4} classic trench modern europa;
    do i=1 to 4;
        if item{i}=999 then item{i}=.;
        if item{i} ne . then item{i}=item{i}*1.12;
    end;
    format classic trench modern europa dollar7.2;
    cards;
women-regular    190.80   230.80   242.80   263.76
women-petite     207.75   258.25   276.70   295.00
women-large      200.00   240.85   260.90   280.75
men-regular      175.80   200.25   235.00   258.85
men-short        190.65   215.50   253.75   275.00
men-large        185.25   207.75   999      268.00
men-tall         195.00   225.00   260.75   285.90
junior           110.00   999      122.00   130.00
children          91.65   999      999      118.75
;

proc print data=rainwear.retail;
    title 'Updated Inventory Reflecting Current Prices';
run;
```

Output 7.1 shows the results.

Output 7.1
Using Array Processing to Perform a Repetitive Calculation and Recode Missing Values

```
                   Updated Inventory Reflecting Current Prices                1

     OBS   CATEGORY         CLASSIC      TRENCH      MODERN      EUROPA    I

      1    women-regular    $213.70     $258.50     $271.94     $295.41    5
      2    women-petite     $232.68     $289.24     $309.90     $330.40    5
      3    women-large      $224.00     $269.75     $292.21     $314.44    5
      4    men-regular      $196.90     $224.28     $263.20     $289.91    5
      5    men-short        $213.53     $241.36     $284.20     $308.00    5
      6    men-large        $207.48     $232.68        .        $300.16    5
      7    men-tall         $218.40     $252.00     $292.04     $320.21    5
      8    junior           $123.20        .        $136.64     $145.60    5
      9    children         $102.65        .           .        $133.00    5
```

The RAINWEAR.RETAIL data set shows that the previous costs of CLASSIC, TRENCH, MODERN, and EUROPA have increased 12 percent as specified in the assignment statement of the DO loop; the values of 999 have been changed to missing (.). In addition, the data set now contains the index variable I with the value 5, the value that caused processing of the loop to stop in each observation. To omit the index variable from the printout, use the DROP= data set option to prevent the values of I from being written to the output data set.

Reading Multiple Records to Create a Single Observation

Usually you have data stored in a series of records that you want to store in a series of observations. However, you can also choose to read data from multiple records and create, for example, a single observation to make analyzing the results easier. In such cases, the data from each record become a separate variable or variables in the single observation. To accomplish this task, do the following:

□ arrange the variables in an array group

□ perform the desired actions for all elements of the array.

Recall the rainwear company mentioned earlier. The company is now weighing the results of a survey to rate the success of its international marketing strategies. To obtain representative survey results, the company polled consumers monthly in six major cities over 12 months. A composite rating of 1 to 10 was prepared for each city monthly, with the value of 10 indicating the highest degree and 1 the lowest degree of success. Results were recorded in a file with one record per month in most but not all cases. The company now wants to read all the records for one city and create a single observation for that city with a variable for each month. In the following example, each record of raw data contains the following fields:

Field	Description
city	major cities for which a monthly rating was developed
month	month of the year represented numerically
profile	numeric rating assigned to each city by month

Here is a partial listing of the raw data records:*

```
----+----1----+----2----+----3
Chicago      1      6
Chicago      2      3
Chicago      3      7
Chicago      4      4
Chicago      5      2
Chicago      6      8
Chicago      7      6
Chicago      8      5
Chicago      9      7
Chicago     10      9
Chicago     11      3
Chicago     12      5
Hong Kong    1      7
Hong Kong    2      7
Hong Kong    3      9
Hong Kong    4      1
Hong Kong    5      9
Hong Kong    6      4
Hong Kong    7      1
Hong Kong    8      9
London       1      7
London       2      7
London       5      4
London       6      7
London       7      5
London      10      7
London      11      7
London      12      8
     more data records
----+----1----+----2----+----3
```

The two steps that accomplish the task follow.

---

*   Refer to the Appendix for a complete listing of the input data.

Group the Variables

To put the variables that are to be processed into the array group, use an ARRAY statement. Here, the array is called PROFILE and has twelve elements: PROF1 through PROF12.

```
libname rainwear 'SAS-data-library';


data rainwear.profile;
   infile 'input-file';
   array profile{12} prof1-prof12;
```

Perform the Desired Actions

Now, process the variables identically by specifying the following actions:

□ indicate the number of times you want to repeat the same action

□ specify the particular actions you want to perform

□ determine what variable, or array element, to process with each iteration of the repeated action.

First, to create a single observation from all the records about a single city, use a DO WHILE loop containing an INPUT statement. Here, because there are six cities, the desired output contains six observations, each containing all information about a single city. The INPUT statement continues to read records as long as the value for CITY is the same. When the value for CITY changes, the program writes an observation and exits the DO WHILE loop. To determine when the value for CITY has changed, the INPUT statement in the DO WHILE loop must read two records. It reads the second record for the sole purpose of determining whether the record contains information about the same city. It reads the first field, assigns the value to a new variable named SITE, and holds the record in the input buffer because of the double trailing @ sign. If CITY and SITE are equal, the DO WHILE loop continues executing and building the current observation. When CITY is no longer equal to SITE, the DO WHILE loop ends and an observation is output automatically by the DATA step. The first record for the next city is held in the input buffer and read in its entirety during the next iteration of the DATA step.

```
libname rainwear 'SAS-data-library';


data rainwear.profile;
   length city $ 13 site $ 13;
   infile 'input-file';
   array profile{12} prof1-prof12;
   do while (site=city);
      input @1 city & $13. month profile{month} / site & $13.@@;
   end;
```

Note that the array PROFILE uses the value of the variable MONTH to ensure that the composite rating is assigned to the appropriate month, even if a record is missing for a given month. Note also the use of the LENGTH statement. It ensures that the variables CITY and SITE are properly created as character values, each with a length of 13 bytes.

The last step is to cause the final observation to be written to the data set. This example does not write the final observation to the DATA step because the INPUT statement goes past the end of the file the last time it tries to read a value for SITE. (The DATA step stops iterating when end-of-file is reached.) To cause the final observation to be written to the data set, use the EOF= option. This option defines a label that can be used to specify an action to be taken when the DATA step reaches the end of the input file. In this example, the statement following the label writes the final observation. Precede the label with a RETURN statement. The OUTPUT statement following the label turns off the automatic output feature of the DATA step so another OUTPUT statement is required prior to the label.

```
libname rainwear 'SAS-data-library';

data rainwear.profile;
   length city $ 13 site $ 13;
   infile 'input-file' eof=last;
   array profile{12} prof1-prof12;
   do while (site=city);
      input a1 city & $13. month profile{month}/site & $13.aa;
   end;
   output;
   return;
   last:
   output;
   drop site;
run;

proc print data=rainwear.profile;
   title 'Monthly Composite Rating for Selected Major Cities';
run;
```

Output 7.2 shows the results.

Output 7.2
Using an Array to Write Multiple Records to an Observation

```
                 Monthly Composite Rating for Selected Major Cities          1

                                                          P   P   P
                    C      P  P  P  P  P  P  P  P  P       R   R   R    M
                    I      R  R  R  R  R  R  R  R  R       O   O   O    O
           O        T      O  O  O  O  O  O  O  O  O       F   F   F    N
           B        Y      F  F  F  F  F  F  F  F  F       1   1   1    T
           S               1  2  3  4  5  6  7  8  9       0   1   2    H

           1  Chicago       6  3  7  4  2  8  6  5  7       9   3   5   12
           2  Hong Kong     7  7  9  1  9  4  1  9   .      .   .   .    8
           3  London        7  7  .  .  4  7  5   .   .     7   7   8   12
           4  Los Angeles   4  4  3  8  7  5  6  4  5       5   5   4   12
           5  New York      8  5  9  6  3  6  3  7  6       6   8   7   12
           6  Paris         6  8  2  7  8  9  9  8  2       3   7   7   12
```

Assigning Initial Values to Array Elements

In some cases, you may want to compare one set of values to a second set of values. If you want to use the first set of values as a standard of measurement, you can assign the values to a group of variables in an array and then measure the values of a second array group against them. To accomplish this task, do the following:

□ arrange the two sets of variables in two groups and assign initial values to one set

□ perform the desired actions for all elements in the target array.

To illustrate, again recall the rainwear company. The company had previously test marketed its specialty raincoats for aesthetic appeal and had derived composite ratings for each. The same coats were then marketed regionally using a different sampling method. For its quarterly stockholders' meeting, the company wants to report the highest ratings, whether they are the earlier composite ratings or the more recently acquired regional ratings. The company wants to accomplish two tasks:

□ for each of the four coat models, compare the earlier composite ratings with the more recent regional ratings

□ for each model, write the higher rating to an output data set.

In the following example, each record of raw data contains the following fields:

Field	Description
region	population area polled concerning rainwear
classic	regional rating of least expensive rainwear
trench	regional rating of moderately priced rainwear
modern	regional rating of higher priced rainwear
europa	regional rating of highest priced rainwear

Here are the raw data records for the regional ratings. Note that the composite ratings have already been derived; these values are not included in the data records.

```
----+----1----+----2----+----3
regiona   76   92   98   99
regionb   85   91   99   96
regionc   90   89   99   99
regiond   95   84   91   93
regione   90   99   96   94
regionf   92   94   95   99
regiong   92   94   96   98
regionh   91   95   99   97
regioni   90   96   96   95
regionj   94   95   98   90
```

The two steps that accomplish the task follow.

Group the Variables and Assign Values

In this example, two array groups are needed instead of one. First, to arrange a group with initial values, create an array and define the initial values parenthetically. Here, the array is called AVERAGE and has four elements, COMP1, COMP2, COMP3, and COMP4. The initial values, the values for the composite survey, are 96, 95, 98, and 94, respectively. Next, arrange a second array group. Here, the array RAINTEST has four elements: CLASSIC, TRENCH, MODERN, and EUROPA. Finally, to read in values for all of the elements for that array, include the array reference (in this case RAINTEST{*}) in the INPUT statement. This special syntax causes the SAS System to treat the array definition as a variable list.

```
libname rainwear 'SAS-data-library';

data rainwear.rating;
   array average{4} comp1-comp4 (96 95 98 94);
   array raintest{4} classic trench modern europa;
   input region $ raintest{*};
```

▶ *Caution* . . . . *The reference array-name{*} can be used only in certain situations.*
The reference *array-name*{*} can be used only in some situations, such as in the INPUT and PUT statements and in the arguments of some functions. ▲

Perform the Desired Actions

After grouping the variables and determining their values, you need to process them. Several steps are involved. First, to repeat the desired action for each array element, use an iterative DO loop. To cause the loop to iterate once for each array element, specify that the index variable is to have a value of 1 to the number of array elements. When the value exceeds that number, the END statement ends the loop. In the following example, the index value I has a value of 1 to 4.

```
libname rainwear 'SAS-data-library';

data rainwear.rating;
   array average{4} comp1-comp4 (96 95 98 94);
   array raintest {4} classic trench modern europa;
   input region $ raintest{*};
   do i=1 to 4;
      more SAS statements
   end;
```

Next, to specify that the values of the first array are to be compared with the values of the second array for each array element and the higher values for each assigned to a new variable, use an IF-THEN statement and an ELSE statement inside the DO group. To write the observations to the output data set, use the OUTPUT statement. Here, the array elements from AVERAGE are compared with those of RAINTEST and the higher values output to the new variable OVERALL. Note that four observations are output for each input record.

```
libname rainwear 'SAS-data-library';

data rainwear.rating;
   array average{4} comp1-comp4 (96 95 98 94);
   array raintest{4} classic trench modern europa;
   input region $ raintest{*};
   do i=1 to 4;
      if raintest{i}>average{i} then overall=raintest{i};
      else overall=average{i};
      output;
   end;
```

When I has a value of 1, the SAS System treats the array references as AVERAGE{1} and RAINTEST{1} and compares the values of COMP1 and CLASSIC. It continues to process the statements within the DO loop, replacing the subscript I with its current value, which changes with each iteration.

Here is the complete program, including the instream data records, that creates and displays the data set.

```
libname rainwear 'SAS-data-library';

data rainwear.rating;
   array average{4} comp1-comp4 (96 95 98 94);
   array raintest{4} classic trench modern europa;
   input region $ raintest{*};
   do i=1 to 4;
      if raintest{i}>average{i} then overall=raintest{i};
      else overall=average{i};
      output;
   end;
   cards;
regiona   76   92   98   99
regionb   85   91   99   96
regionc   90   89   99   99
regiond   95   84   91   93
regione   90   99   96   94
regionf   92   94   95   99
regiong   92   94   96   98
regionh   91   95   99   97
regioni   90   96   96   95
regionj   94   95   98   90
;

proc print data=rainwear.rating;
   title 'Ratings for Specialty Coats--Quarterly Meeting';
run;
```

Output 7.3 shows the results. Note that the variable OVERALL has been assigned the higher values based on a comparison of each element of the array AVERAGE with each element of the same position of the array RAINTEST. As a result, the output shows four observations for each region.

Output 7.3
Using Array
Processing to
Assign Initial
Values

```
                  Ratings for Specialty Coats--Quarterly Meeting                 1

 OBS COMP1 COMP2 COMP3 COMP4 CLASSIC TRENCH MODERN EUROPA REGION  I OVERALL

   1   96    95    98    94     76     92     98     99   regiona 1   96
   2   96    95    98    94     76     92     98     99   regiona 2   95
   3   96    95    98    94     76     92     98     99   regiona 3   98
   4   96    95    98    94     76     92     98     99   regiona 4   99
   5   96    95    98    94     85     91     99     96   regionb 1   96
   6   96    95    98    94     85     91     99     96   regionb 2   95
   7   96    95    98    94     85     91     99     96   regionb 3   99
   8   96    95    98    94     85     91     99     96   regionb 4   96
   9   96    95    98    94     90     89     99     99   regionc 1   96
  10   96    95    98    94     90     89     99     99   regionc 2   95
  11   96    95    98    94     90     89     99     99   regionc 3   99
  12   96    95    98    94     90     89     99     99   regionc 4   99
  13   96    95    98    94     95     84     91     93   regiond 1   96
  14   96    95    98    94     95     84     91     93   regiond 2   95
  15   96    95    98    94     95     84     91     93   regiond 3   98
  16   96    95    98    94     95     84     91     93   regiond 4   94
  17   96    95    98    94     90     99     96     94   regione 1   96
  18   96    95    98    94     90     99     96     94   regione 2   99
  19   96    95    98    94     90     99     96     94   regione 3   98
  20   96    95    98    94     90     99     96     94   regione 4   94
  21   96    95    98    94     92     94     95     99   regionf 1   96
  22   96    95    98    94     92     94     95     99   regionf 2   95
  23   96    95    98    94     92     94     95     99   regionf 3   98
  24   96    95    98    94     92     94     95     99   regionf 4   99
  25   96    95    98    94     92     94     96     98   regiong 1   96
  26   96    95    98    94     92     94     96     98   regiong 2   95
  27   96    95    98    94     92     94     96     98   regiong 3   98
  28   96    95    98    94     92     94     96     98   regiong 4   98
  29   96    95    98    94     91     95     99     97   regionh 1   96
  30   96    95    98    94     91     95     99     97   regionh 2   95
  31   96    95    98    94     91     95     99     97   regionh 3   99
  32   96    95    98    94     91     95     99     97   regionh 4   97
  33   96    95    98    94     90     96     96     95   regioni 1   96
  34   96    95    98    94     90     96     96     95   regioni 2   96
  35   96    95    98    94     90     96     96     95   regioni 3   98
  36   96    95    98    94     90     96     96     95   regioni 4   95
  37   96    95    98    94     94     95     98     90   regionj 1   96
  38   96    95    98    94     94     95     98     90   regionj 2   95
  39   96    95    98    94     94     95     98     90   regionj 3   98
  40   96    95    98    94     94     95     98     90   regionj 4   94
```

Assigning Temporary Array Elements

When elements of an array are constants needed only for the duration of the DATA step, you can omit variables from an array group and instead use *temporary array elements*. Although they behave like variables, temporary array elements do not appear in the output data set; they do not have names and can be referenced only by their array names and dimensions. Temporary array elements are automatically retained, instead of being reset to missing at the beginning of the next iteration of the DATA step. You can shorten execution time by using temporary array elements.

Consider the previous example where initial values in one array group were compared with the values of a second array group. The ARRAY statement for that example is as follows, with the array elements listed:

```
array average{4} comp1-comp4 (96 95 98 94);
```

To assign temporary array elements, replace the list of array elements with the
TEMPORARY argument as follows:

```
array average(4) _temporary_ (96 95 98 94);
```

The following program combines all of the elements of the previous example,
with the substitution of temporary array elements for actual variables:

```
libname rainwear 'SAS-data-library';

data rainwear.rating;
    array average(4) _temporary_ (96 95 98 94);
    array raintest(4) classic trench modern europa;
    input region $ raintest(*);
    do i=1 to 4;
        if raintest(i)>average(i) then overall=raintest(i);
        else overall=average(i);
        output;
    end;
    cards;
regiona  76  92  98   99
regionb  85  91  99   96
regionc  90  89  99   99
regiond  95  84  91   93
regione  90  99  96   94
regionf  92  94  95   99
regiong  92  94  96   98
regionh  91  95  99   97
regioni  90  96  96   95
regionj  94  95  98   90
;

proc print data=rainwear.rating;
    title 'Ratings for Specialty Coats--Quarterly Meeting';
run;
```

Output 7.4 shows the results. Note that the temporary array elements do not
appear in the output data set.

Output 7.4
Using Array
Processing to
Create Temporary
Array Elements

```
                  Ratings for Specialty Coats--Quarterly Meeting                 1

    OBS    CLASSIC    TRENCH    MODERN    EUROPA    REGION    I    OVERALL

     1        76        92        98        99      regiona   1      96
     2        76        92        98        99      regiona   2      95
     3        76        92        98        99      regiona   3      98
     4        76        92        98        99      regiona   4      99
     5        85        91        99        96      regionb   1      96
     6        85        91        99        96      regionb   2      95
     7        85        91        99        96      regionb   3      99
     8        85        91        99        96      regionb   4      96
     9        90        89        99        99      regionc   1      96
    10        90        89        99        99      regionc   2      95
    11        90        89        99        99      regionc   3      99
    12        90        89        99        99      regionc   4      99
    13        95        84        91        93      regiond   1      96
    14        95        84        91        93      regiond   2      95
    15        95        84        91        93      regiond   3      98
```

```
        16      95      84      91      93      regiond   4      94
        17      90      99      96      94      regione   1      96
        18      90      99      96      94      regione   2      99
        19      90      99      96      94      regione   3      98
        20      90      99      96      94      regione   4      94
        21      92      94      95      99      regionf   1      96
        22      92      94      95      99      regionf   2      95
        23      92      94      95      99      regionf   3      98
        24      92      94      95      99      regionf   4      99
        25      92      94      96      98      regiong   1      96
        26      92      94      96      98      regiong   2      95
        27      92      94      96      98      regiong   3      98
        28      92      94      96      98      regiong   4      98
        29      91      95      99      97      regionh   1      96
        30      91      95      99      97      regionh   2      95
        31      91      95      99      97      regionh   3      99
        32      91      95      99      97      regionh   4      97
        33      90      96      96      95      regioni   1      96
        34      90      96      96      95      regioni   2      96
        35      90      96      96      95      regioni   3      98
        36      90      96      96      95      regioni   4      95
        37      94      95      98      90      regionj   1      96
        38      94      95      98      90      regionj   2      95
        39      94      95      98      90      regionj   3      98
        40      94      95      98      90      regionj   4      94
```

Arranging Variables in Two-Dimensional Groupings

So far, the tasks presented in this chapter have involved simple groupings of variables that when processed produce results that can be presented in simple column format. These groupings are called one-dimensional arrays. However, your programming task may require you to arrange your variables in more complex groupings. When processed, their results could have two or more dimensions, such as columns and rows. These groupings are called *multidimensional arrays*. This section focuses on *two-dimensional arrays*, the most common among multidimensional arrays.

The same basic steps necessary to process a one-dimensional grouping are necessary to process a two-dimensional grouping:

□   arrange the variables in an array group

□   perform the desired actions for all elements of the array.

The rainwear manufacturer can again illustrate this point. In addition to its specialty garments, the company manufactures two less expensive lines: a low-cost bargain line and a higher cost standard line, each with three coat models. Concerned about the impact of the 12-percent price increase on all of these lines, the company wants to accomplish two tasks:

□   calculate a 12-percent price increase for the coats in the standard line and in the bargain line

□   present the results so that it is easy to compare the resulting prices of the two lines of coats.

In the following example, each record of raw data contains the following fields:

Field	Description
category	categories of sizes
high1	cost of standard model 1
high2	cost of standard model 2
high3	cost of standard model 3
low1	cost of bargain model 1
low2	cost of bargain model 2
low3	cost of bargain model 3

Here are the raw data records:

```
----+----1----+----2----+
1 165.80 180.80 190.80
  110.80 123.25 132.80
2 172.50 189.00 201.00
  116.75 130.00 140.00
3 155.95 174.65 183.75
  102.45 114.90 140.00
4 163.75 180.85 191.65
  108.80 120.75 132.86
```

The two steps that accomplish the task follow.

Group the Variables

To put the variables to be processed into an array group, use an ARRAY statement. To create a two-dimensional array, place the number of elements in each dimension after the array name, separated by a comma. The leftmost dimension represents rows, and the rightmost dimension represents columns. Note that the SAS System places variables in a multidimensional array by filling all rows in order, beginning at the upper left corner of the array (known as row-major order). In this example, the array is called COMPARE, it has two rows and three columns, and it has six elements: HIGH1 through HIGH3 and LOW1 through LOW3.

```
libname rainwear 'SAS-data-library';

data rainwear.coats;
   input category high1-high3 / low1-low3;
   array compare{2,3} high1-high3 low1-low3;
```

You can see graphically how this process works in Figure 7.1 The first dimension, to the left of the comma, is divided into the categories HIGH and LOW, whose positions in the first dimension are 1 and 2, respectively. The second dimension, to the right of the comma, includes the costs of the coat models in both categories. These are the values of the HIGH*n* and LOW*n* variables, and their positions in the second dimension are 1, 2, and 3 for the variables HIGH*n* and LOW*n*, respectively.

Figure 7.1
The COMPARE
Array

		models 1	2	3
	HIGH	1,1	1,2	1,3
category				
	LOW	2,1	2,2	2,3

Perform the Desired Actions

Now, process the variables identically by specifying the following actions:

□ indicate the number of times you want to repeat the same action

□ specify the particular actions you want to perform

□ determine what variable, or array element, to process with each iteration of the repeated action.

First, to repeat the desired action for each array element in both dimensions, use a nested DO loop. Here, to indicate that the first dimension has two components (HIGH*n* and LOW*n* variables), assign the index variable in the first DO loop a value of 1 to 2. To indicate that the second dimension has three components (*variable* 1, *variable* 2, and *variable* 3), assign the index variable in the second DO loop a value of 1 to 3. Close each DO loop with an END statement.

```
libname rainwear 'SAS-data-library';

data rainwear.coats;
   input category high1-high3 / low1-low3;
   array compare{2,3} high1-high3 low1-low3;
   do i=1 to 2;
      do j=1 to 3;
         more SAS statements
      end;
   end;
```

In the first iteration of the DATA step, the SAS System opens the first DO loop, accessing the first array dimension, the HIGH*n* variables. It then opens the second DO loop, performing the action for HIGH1 through HIGH3 for the first observation. The SAS System returns to the first DO loop, accessing the second array dimension, the LOW*n* variables. It then opens the second DO loop, performing the action for LOW1 through LOW3 for the first observation. It increases the values of the index variable by 1 with each new iteration of the DO loop. When the value of I is 3 and the value of J is 4, thus exceeding the number of array elements in each successive array dimension, the END statement ends array processing. Note that the outer DO loop causes the inner DO loop and its assignment statement to be processed twice. With each subsequent iteration of the DATA step, the SAS System continues to perform the same action for remaining observations.

Next, specify the actions you want to perform. Here, to multiply all the array elements by 1.12 to calculate the price increase, use an assignment statement. To round to the nearest integer, add the ROUND function. In the first iteration of the outer loop, the values in the first row are multiplied by 1.12; in the second iteration of the outer loop, the values in the second row are multiplied by 1.12.

```
libname rainwear 'SAS-data-library';

data rainwear.coats;
   input category high1-high3 / low1-low3;
   array compare(2,3) high1-high3 low1-low3;
   do i=1 to 2;
      do j=1 to 3;
         compare(i,j)=round(compare(i,j)*1.12);
      end;
   end;
```

At the same time these statements tell the SAS System what actions to perform, they also use the array reference for each array element to determine which element to process with each iteration of the DO loop. This process occurs as explained earlier in the chapter, with one exception: because these array elements are part of a two-dimensional array, each has a two-dimensional array reference to correspond with its position within the array. For example, the array reference for the variable HIGH2 is ITEM{1,2}. As the SAS System continues to process the statements within the DO loops, the value of the subscript changes with each iteration.

The following program combines all of the elements already discussed, as well as the instream data records:

```
libname rainwear 'SAS-data-library';

data rainwear.coats;
   input category high1-high3 / low1-low3;
   array compare(2,3) high1-high3 low1-low3;
   do i=1 to 2;
      do j=1 to 3;
         compare(i,j)=round(compare(i,j)*1.12);
      end;
   end;
   cards;
1 165.80 180.80 190.80
  110.80 123.25 132.80
2 172.50 189.00 201.00
  116.75 130.00 140.00
3 155.95 174.65 183.75
  102.45 114.90 140.00
4 163.75 180.85 191.65
  108.80 120.75 132.86
;
```

```
proc print data=rainwear.coats;
    title 'Updated Inventory for Standard Lines';
run;
```

Output 7.5 shows the results. Note the index variables I and J.

Output 7.5
Using a
Two-Dimensional
Array to Compare
Processing Results
for Two Variables

				Updated Inventory for Standard Lines					1
OBS	CATEGORY	HIGH1	HIGH2	HIGH3	LOW1	LOW2	LOW3	I	J
1	1	186	202	214	124	138	149	3	4
2	2	193	212	225	131	146	157	3	4
3	3	175	196	206	115	129	157	3	4
4	4	183	203	215	122	135	149	3	4

Using Array Processing with Bounded Array Dimensions

All arrays have upper and lower bounds, with the lower bound signifying the first element of a given dimension and the upper bound signifying the last element within a given dimension. The examples already shown in this chapter have lower bounds of 1. For example, in the following ARRAY statement, the lower bound is 1 and the upper bound is 4:

```
array raintest{4} classic trench modern europa;
```

In the next ARRAY statement, the first dimension has lower and upper boundaries of 1 and 2, respectively, corresponding to the number of rows; the second dimension has lower and upper boundaries of 1 and 3, respectively, corresponding to the number of columns:

```
array compare{2,3} high1-high3 low1-low3;
```

For most arrays, 1 is a convenient lower bound and the number of elements is a convenient upper bound, so you usually don't need to specify lower and upper bounds. However, specifying both bounds is useful when the array dimensions have a starting point other than 1. Note also that processing time is reduced if a lower bound of 0 is used because it decreases the computational time for subscript evaluation.

The rainwear company once more demonstrates this process. This company is analyzing the results of a consumer survey from a local department store. The company wants to produce a report that highlights the unanswered questions, which have been coded with 11s. Because the company wants to process only questions 15 through 24, it is convenient to specify array boundaries.

In the following example, each record of raw data contains the following fields:

Field	Description
q1—q24	survey questions, for which numeric responses are provided

Here are the raw data records:

```
----+----1----+----2----+----3----+----4----+----5----+
9 7 6 5 11 10 7 8 6 5 11 8 7 5 4 2 1 3 8 9 11 5 6 8
2 4 5 5 5 5 5 5 5 11 11 9 8 6 6 5 4 3 2 11 2 3 4 11
3 6 4 6 7 11 7 6 5 5 6 8 9 10 2 4 6 8 7 8 6 7 11 11
7 9 10 9 8 7 6 6 6 8 3 4 2 8 11 11 8 5 8 9 10 3 9 8
2 4 5 5 6 8 11 10 9 9 8 4 3 4 6 7 10 9 9 8 9 11 7 7
3 5 6 7 7 7 8 7 6 5 5 11 11 11 11 2 2 3 9 8 8 9 2 3
4 5 5 2 2 10 10 9 8 7 8 8 8 9 6 4 4 5 2 5 7 8 8 8
5 3 2 2 2 3 4 8 8 9 10 10 9 9 7 9 11 11 8 7 8 7 3 9
6 7 8 6 5 2 2 11 11 11 9 9 6 7 5 5 5 4 4 3 3 2 2 8
8 8 4 4 3 3 2 2 11 11 10 9 8 8 4 5 2 3 3 5 7 11 3 2
```

In order to consider only survey questions 15 through 24, the company uses the following simple array to develop this example. The array is called QUESTION and has 10 array elements: Q15 through Q24.

```
libname rainwear 'SAS-data-library';

data rainwear.survey;
   input q1-q24;
   array question{10} q15-q24;    /* using default bounds */
```

In this array, variable Q15 is QUESTION{1}, for example. The same example can be revised to use lower and upper array boundaries. Instead of writing the subscript as the number of array elements, write it as the lower boundary and then the upper boundary of the array, separated by a colon. The following ARRAY statement tells the SAS System to start processing with the 15th element and to stop after the 24th element. In this case, variable Q15 is QUESTION{15}, for example. Note that the bounded dimensions in the ARRAY statement correspond to the values assigned to the index variable in the DO statement. In other respects this example executes as did the first simple array in this chapter.

```
libname rainwear 'SAS-data-library';

data rainwear.survey;
   input q1-q24;
   array question{15:24} q15-q24;    /* specifying bounds */
   do i=15 to 24;
      if question{i}=11 then question{i}=.;
   end;
```

Here is the entire program, including the instream data records, that creates and displays the data set.

```
libname rainwear 'SAS-data-library';

data rainwear.survey;
   input q1-q24;
   array question{15:24} q15-q24;
   do i=15 to 24;
      if question{i}=11 then question{i}=.;
   end;
   cards;
9 7 6 5 11 10 7 8 6 5 11 8 7 5 4 2 1 3 8 9 11 5 6 8
2 4 5 5 5 5 5 5 5 11 11 9 8 6 6 5 4 3 2 11 2 3 4 11
3 6 4 6 7 11 7 6 5 5 6 8 9 10 2 4 6 8 7 8 6 7 11 11
7 9 10 9 8 7 6 6 6 8 3 4 2 8 11 11 8 5 8 9 10 3 9 8
2 4 5 5 6 8 11 10 9 9 8 4 3 4 6 7 10 9 9 8 9 11 7 7
3 5 6 7 7 7 8 7 6 5 5 11 11 11 11 2 2 3 9 8 8 9 2 3
4 5 5 2 2 10 10 9 8 7 8 8 8 9 6 4 4 5 2 5 7 8 8 8
5 3 2 2 2 3 4 8 8 9 10 10 9 9 7 9 11 11 8 7 8 7 3 9
6 7 8 6 5 2 2 11 11 11 9 9 6 7 5 5 5 4 4 3 3 2 2 8
8 8 4 4 3 3 2 2 11 11 10 9 8 8 4 5 2 3 3 5 7 11 3 2
;

proc print data=rainwear.survey;
   title 'Survey Results';
run;
```

Output 7.6 shows the results. Starting with the values of the 15th element, all 11s have been changed to missing values.

Output 7.6
Specifying Upper and Lower Array Bounds

Note that choosing numbers to specify upper and lower bounds is somewhat arbitrary. You can set the upper and lower dimensions to whatever numbers are meaningful to you, as long as the difference between the two corresponds to the number of elements in the array. For example, you could also rewrite the previous ARRAY statement as follows:

```
array question{1:10} q15-q24;
```

To use bounded array dimensions for multidimensional arrays, repeat the process used for a one-dimensional array, separating the dimensions by commas as you move from one dimension to another. For example, to put the two-dimensional array from "Arranging Variables in Two-Dimensional Groupings" into bounded array dimensions, rewrite it as follows:

```
array compare{1:2,1:3} high1-high3 low1-low3;
```

Using Shortcuts in Array Processing

Although array processing is a kind of shortcut programming, you can incorporate further shortcuts into that processing. The following sections show you quick ways to

□ specify an entire category of variables—numeric, character, or all variables

□ automate array processing to accommodate changes in data.

Specifying an Entire Category of Variables

In some cases, you may find it easier to specify array elements as a category instead of as individual elements. You can use this method if the array elements have already been defined in the DATA step. You can specify one of the following categories:

□ all currently defined numeric variables

□ all currently defined character variables

□ all currently defined variables. If you specify all currently defined variables, they must be of the same type—either character or numeric.

For example, to illustrate the first category, consider an earlier example in which the array elements are listed individually. The ARRAY statement appears as follows:

```
array item{*} classic trench modern europa;
```

To assign the array elements as a category, replace the list of array elements with the _NUMERIC_ argument. To avoid counting the elements, use the asterisk (*) as the dimension. The following ARRAY statement specifies that all numeric variables in the program data vector at that point are to be grouped into the array ITEM:*

```
array item{*} _numeric_;
```

---

* In Version 6 of the SAS System, the program data vector is a logical concept and does not imply a contiguous physical storage area.

Here is the entire program that creates and displays the data set:

```
libname rainwear 'SAS-data-library';

data rainwear.retail;
   input category $14. classic trench modern europa;
   array item(*) _numeric_;
   do i=1 to 4;
      if item(i)=999 then item(i)=.;
      if item(i) ne . then item(i)=item(i)*1.12;
   end;
   format classic trench modern europa dollar7.2;
   cards;
women-regular   190.80   230.80   242.80   263.76
women-petite    207.75   258.25   276.70   295.00
women-large     200.00   240.85   260.90   280.75
men-regular     175.80   200.25   235.00   258.85
men-short       190.65   215.50   253.75   275.00
men-large       185.25   207.75   999      268.00
men-tall        195.00   225.00   260.75   285.90
junior          110.00   999      122.00   130.00
children         91.65   999      999      118.75
;

proc print data=rainwear.retail;
   title 'Updated Inventory Reflecting Current Prices';
run;
```

Output 7.7 shows the results.

Output 7.7
*Using the
NUMERIC
Variable in Array
Processing*

```
                   Updated Inventory Reflecting Current Prices              1

   OBS    CATEGORY          CLASSIC     TRENCH      MODERN     EUROPA    I

    1     women-regular     $213.70    $258.50    $271.94    $295.41    5
    2     women-petite      $232.68    $289.24    $309.90    $330.40    5
    3     women-large       $224.00    $269.75    $292.21    $314.44    5
    4     men-regular       $196.90    $224.28    $263.20    $289.91    5
    5     men-short         $213.53    $241.36    $284.20    $308.00    5
    6     men-large         $207.48    $232.68          .    $300.16    5
    7     men-tall          $218.40    $252.00    $292.04    $320.21    5
    8     junior            $123.20          .    $136.64    $145.60    5
    9     children          $102.65          .          .    $133.00    5
```

If all of the currently defined variables were of the same type, substituting the special variable _ALL_ as shown in the next ARRAY statement would produce identical output:

```
array item(4) _all_;
```

Similarly, to assign as a category all array elements that have character values, replace the list of array elements with the _CHARACTER_ argument:

```
array item(4) _character_;
```

Automating Array Processing to Accommodate Changes in Data

Because array processing enables you to perform repetitive calculations easily, you are likely, over time, to reuse a program with an array, modifying it as needed. These modifications may include changing the data and thus the number of array elements processed. Although you can change the number of iterations in a DO loop by changing either the upper bound or the upper and lower bounds of the index variable whenever the number of array elements changes, you can simplify further by using SAS functions to return the number of elements in an array automatically. The following sections show you how to

□   change the upper bound of the index variable automatically

□   change both the upper and lower bounds of the index variable automatically.

Changing the Upper Bound of the Index Variable Automatically

To automatically return a total count of the number of elements in an array dimension, use the DIM function. Using the number that signifies the upper bound, the DIM function always returns a total count of the number of elements in an array dimension. To specify the dimension whose number of elements you want to know, add a numeric operand to the DIM function that corresponds to that dimension. If the numeric operand is omitted, its value is assumed to be 1.

To illustrate, consider the nested DO loop of an earlier example that uses a two-dimensional array; the value of the first index variable is 1 to 2 and the value of the second index variable is 1 to 3:

```
array compare{2,3} high1-high3 low1-low3;
do i=1 to 2;
   do j=1 to 3;
      compare{i,j}=compare{i,j}*1.12;
   end;
end;
```

Now automate the process with the DIM function. To return a total count of array elements in the first dimension, replace the upper bound of the index variable in the first DO statement with the DIM function, followed by its array name in parentheses. To return a total count of array elements in the second dimension, follow the same procedure, but use DIM2 to specify the second dimension:

```
array compare{2,3} high1-high3 low1-low3;
do i=1 to dim(compare);
   do j=1 to dim2(compare);
      compare{i,j}=compare{i,j}*1.12;
   end;
end;
```

Here is the entire program, including the instream data records, that creates and displays the data set.

```
libname rainwear 'SAS-data-library';

data rainwear.coats;
    input category high1-high3 / low1-low3;
    array compare{2,3} high1-high3 low1-low3;
    do i=1 to dim(compare);
        do j=1 to dim2(compare);
            compare{i,j}=round(compare{i,j}*1.12);
        end;
    end;
    cards;
1 165.80 180.80 190.80
  110.80 123.25 132.80
2 172.50 189.00 201.00
  116.75 130.00 140.00
3 155.95 174.65 183.75
  102.45 114.90 140.00
4 163.75 180.85 191.65
  108.80 120.75 132.86
;

proc print data=rainwear.coats;
    title 'Updated Inventory for Standard Lines';
run;
```

Output 7.8 shows the results.

Output 7.8
Using the DIM Function in Array Processing

		Updated Inventory for Standard Lines							1
OBS	CATEGORY	HIGH1	HIGH2	HIGH3	LOW1	LOW2	LOW3	I	J
1	1	186	202	214	124	138	149	3	4
2	2	193	212	225	131	146	157	3	4
3	3	175	196	206	115	129	157	3	4
4	4	183	203	215	122	135	149	3	4

Note that the output is identical to Output 7.5.

Changing the Upper and Lower Bounds of the Index Variable Automatically

When you use bounded array dimensions, you can use the LBOUND and HBOUND functions to produce the starting and stopping values of the index variable in the iterative DO loop. You can thus avoid changing the numeric values every time you change the bounds, or number of elements, of an array. You can use the LBOUND and HBOUND functions in the DO statement as a way to use the values of upper and lower bounds after they have been specified in the ARRAY statement.

To illustrate, consider an earlier example, where the ARRAY statement has a lower bound of 15 and an upper bound of 24. To return the lower bound of the array dimension, replace the starting value of 15 with the LBOUND function, followed by the name of the array in parentheses; to return the upper bound of the array dimension, replace the ending value of 24 with the HBOUND function, followed by the name of the array in parentheses. The program is identical to that in an earlier example, except that it uses the LBOUND and HBOUND functions instead of conventional bounded array dimensions:

```
libname rainwear 'SAS-data-library';

data rainwear.survey;
   input q1-q24;
   array question(15:24) q15-q24;
   do i=lbound(question) to hbound(question);
      if question(i)=11 then question(i)=.;
   end;
   cards;
9 7 6 5 11 10 7 8 6 5 11 8 7 5 4 2 1 3 8 9 11 5 6 8
2 4 5 5 5 5 5 5 5 11 11 9 8 6 6 5 4 3 2 11 2 3 4 11
3 6 4 6 7 11 7 6 5 5 6 8 9 10 2 4 6 8 7 8 6 7 11 11
7 9 10 9 8 7 6 6 6 8 3 4 2 8 11 11 8 5 8 9 10 3 9 8
2 4 5 5 6 8 11 10 9 9 8 4 3 4 6 7 10 9 9 8 9 11 7 7
3 5 6 7 7 7 8 7 6 5 5 11 11 11 11 2 2 3 9 8 8 9 2 3
4 5 5 2 2 10 10 9 8 7 8 8 8 9 6 4 4 5 2 5 7 8 8 8
5 3 2 2 2 3 4 8 8 9 10 10 9 9 7 9 11 11 8 7 8 7 3 9
6 7 8 6 5 2 2 11 11 11 9 9 6 7 5 5 5 4 4 3 3 2 2 8
8 8 4 4 3 3 2 2 11 11 10 9 8 8 4 5 2 3 3 5 7 11 3 2
;

proc print data=rainwear.survey;
   title 'Survey Results';
run;
```

Output 7.9 shows the results.

Output 7.9
Specifying Array
Bounds with SAS
Functions

```
                                 Survey Results                                1

     O                           Q  Q  Q  Q  Q Q Q  Q Q Q Q  Q Q Q Q
     B  Q  Q Q Q  Q  Q  Q  Q  Q  1  1  1  1  1 1 1  1 1 1 2  2 2 2 2
     S  1  2 3 4  5  6  7  8  9  0  1  2  3  4 5 6  7 8 9 0  1 2 3 4   I

  1  9  7  6 5 11 10  7  8  6  5 11  8  7  5 4 2  1 3 8 9  . 5 6 8  25
  2  2  4  5 5  5  5  5  5  5 11 11  9  8  6 6 5  4 3 2  . 2 3 4  . 25
  3  3  6  4 6  7 11  7  6  5  5  6  8  9 10 2 4  6 8 7 8  6 7 . .  25
  4  7  9 10 9  8  7  6  6  6  8  3  4  2  8 . .  8 5 8 9 10 3 9 8  25
  5  2  4  5 5  6  8 11 10  9  9  8  4  3  4 6 7 10 9 9 8  9 . 7 7  25
  6  3  5  6 7  7  7  8  7  6  5  5 11 11 11 . 2  2 3 9 8  8 9 2 3  25
  7  4  5  5 2  2 10 10  9  8  7  8  8  8  9 6 4  4 5 2 5  7 8 8 8  25
  8  5  3  2 2  2  3  4  8  8  9 10 10  9  9 7 9  . . 8 7  8 7 3 9  25
  9  6  7  8 6  5  2  2 11 11 11  9  9  6  7 5 5  5 4 4 3  3 2 2 8  25
 10  8  8  4 4  3  3  2  2 11 11 10  9  8  8 4 5  2 3 3 5  7 . 3 2  25
```

Note that the output is identical to Output 7.6.

Summary

The following points summarize array processing:

□ You can use array processing to perform repetitive actions on a group of variables. For example, for a group of variables, you might want to recode all missing values identically, perform the same numeric operation on all data values, or read a series of records to create a single observation.

□ Unlike arrays in some other programming languages, in the SAS System arrays are not a data structure but a convenient way to temporarily identify a group of variables.

□ To group selected variables, use an ARRAY statement, including the array name, number of array elements, and list of array elements. Use a DO loop to indicate the number of times you want to repeat the action and to determine which array element to process with each iteration of the repeated action. Within the DO loop nest the SAS statements that specify the actions you want to perform.

□ Simple array groupings are often called one-dimensional arrays. More complex groupings, which have two or more dimensions, are called multidimensional arrays.

□ Each array element is assigned an array reference based on the element's position, or subscript, in the array.

□ You can assign initial values to the elements of an array by listing the values parenthetically in the ARRAY statement. This technique is useful when you want to compare the values of elements from one array to another.

□ To create temporary array elements, use the _TEMPORARY_ argument. These elements do not have names and do not appear in the output data set.

□ All arrays have lower and upper boundaries. When an array has a lower bound with a value other than 1, it is useful to specify its boundaries. To do so, instead of using a single number in the ARRAY statement to indicate the number of array elements, use starting and ending numbers, separated by a colon.

□ You can add shortcuts to array processing. For the full list of array elements, substitute the following arguments, depending on whether the array elements are character or numeric:

□ Use the _NUMERIC_ argument for all numeric variables defined to that point in the program data vector.

□ Use the _CHARACTER_ argument for all character variables defined to that point in the program data vector.

□ Use the _ALL_ argument for all variables defined to that point in the program data vector. In this case, the elements must all be either numeric or character.

□ Instead of changing the number of array elements by changing either the upper bound or the upper and lower bounds of the index variable, you can use SAS functions to return the number of array elements automatically. Use the DIM function to change the upper bound of the index variable automatically. Use the LBOUND and HBOUND functions together to automatically change both the lower and upper bounds, respectively, of the index variable.

SAS Tools

This section summarizes syntax for the statements and functions discussed in this chapter.

Statements

ARRAY *array-name* {*number-of-array-elements*} *array-element-1*
     < . . . *array-element-n*>;
creates a named, ordered list of array elements that exists for processing of the current DATA step. The *array-name* must be a valid SAS name. Each *array-element* is the name of a variable to be included in the array. *Number-of-array-elements* is the number of array elements listed.

variable=expression;
is an assignment statement. It causes the SAS System to evaluate the *expression* on the right side of the equal sign and assign the result to the *variable* on the left. You must select the name of the variable and create the proper expression for calculating its value. The same variable name can appear on the left and right sides of the equal sign because the SAS System evaluates the right side before assigning the result to the variable on the left side.

DO *index-variable=n* TO *number-of-array-elements*;
     SAS statements
END;
is known as an iterative DO loop. In each execution of the DATA step, an iterative DO loop iterates based on the value of the *index-variable*. To create an index variable, simply use a SAS variable in an iterative DO statement. When you use iterative DO loops for array processing, the value of *index-variable* starts at *n* and increases by 1 before each iteration of the loop. When the value exceeds the *number-of-array-elements*, the SAS System stops processing the loop and proceeds to the next statement in the DATA step.

DO WHILE (*condition*);
     SAS statements
END;
executes the enclosed SAS statements as long as the specified condition is true. The condition can be any valid SAS expression, enclosed in parentheses. The condition is evaluated at the top of the loop, before the enclosed statements are executed. If the expression is true, the DO loop is executed. If the condition is false the first time it is executed, the DO loop is not executed at all.

IF *expression* **THEN** *statement*;
<**ELSE** <*action*>>;
>   for the observations from a file that meet the conditions specified in the IF
>   clause, executes the statement following the THEN clause. *Expression* is any
>   valid SAS expression, and *statement* is any executable SAS statement or DO
>   group. When *expression* is false, the ELSE statement may provide an
>   alternative *action*.

INFILE '*input-file*' EOF=*label*;
>   specifies the external file in which the input data are located. The EOF=
>   option specifies a statement label used to label a statement in the step. The
>   SAS System jumps to the labeled statement when an INPUT statement
>   attempts to read from a file that has no more records. The EOF= option is
>   often used with INPUT statements that read more than one data line at a
>   time.

INPUT <*specifications* / @@>;
>   reads a record of raw data either from an external file or instream data lines.
>   Use the slash (/) to advance the pointer to column 1 of the next input line.
>   Use the double trailing at sign (@@) to hold an input line for further
>   iterations of the DATA step. The @@ symbol is useful when each input line
>   contains values for several observations.

label: statement;
>   specifies any valid SAS name. Follow the label with a colon (:). *Statement*
>   specifies any executable statement in the same DATA step as the statement or
>   option that references it. Note that no two statements in a DATA step may
>   have the same label. If a statement in a DATA step is labeled, it should be
>   referenced by a statement or option in the step.

LENGTH *variable* <$> *length*;
>   assigns the number of bytes of storage (*length*) for a *variable*. Include a dollar
>   sign ($) if the variable is character. The LENGTH statement must appear
>   before the first use of the variable.

OUTPUT <*SAS-data-set*>;
>   immediately writes the current observation to the *SAS-data-set*. The
>   observation remains in the program data vector, and you can continue
>   programming with it, including outputting it again if you want. When an
>   OUTPUT statement appears in a DATA step, the SAS System doesn't
>   automatically output observations to the SAS data set; you must specify the
>   destination for all output in the DATA step with OUTPUT statements.

RETURN;
>   stops executing statements at the current point in the DATA step and returns
>   to a predetermined point before continuing execution. In this chapter,
>   examples show a return to the beginning of the DATA step.

Functions

DIM<*n*>(*array-name*)
> returns the number of elements in a one-dimensional array or the number of elements in a specified dimension of a multidimensional array when the lower bound of the dimension is 1.

HBOUND<*n*>(*array-name*)
> returns the upper bound of a one-dimensional array or the upper bound of a specified dimension of a multidimensional array.

LBOUND<*n*>(*array-name*)
> returns the lower bound of a one-dimensional array or the lower bound of a specified dimension of a multidimensional array.

ROUND(*argument,round-off-unit*)
> returns a value rounded to the nearest round-off unit. If *round-off-unit* is not provided, a default value of 1 is used and *argument* is rounded to the nearest integer.

Learning More

This section provides references for learning more about the topics presented in this chapter.

Array processing

□ For an introduction to array processing, see *SAS Language and Procedures: Usage, Version 6, First Edition*, Chapter 12, "Finding Shortcuts in Programming." For complete reference information, see *SAS Language: Reference, Version 6, First Edition*, Chapter 4, "Rules of the SAS Language."

□ For detailed syntax information about the ARRAY statement, see *SAS Language: Reference*, Chapter 9, "SAS Language Statements."

□ For further coverage of DO loops, see Chapter 3, "Reading Variable-Length Fields and Repeated Fields." For complete reference information, see *SAS Language: Reference*, Chapter 9, "SAS Language Statements."

□ For detailed syntax information about the DIM, HBOUND, LBOUND, and ROUND functions, see *SAS Language: Reference*, Chapter 11, "SAS Functions."

Reading data

□ For further information about reading raw data, see Part 2 of this book, "Reading Raw Data."

□ This chapter shows you how to use array processing to read multiple records in order to create a single observation. See Chapter 9, "Reshaping Data," for a similar example.

□ For detailed syntax information about the DO WHILE, IF-THEN/ELSE, INFILE, INPUT, LENGTH, OUTPUT, and RETURN statements, as well as the statement label, see *SAS Language: Reference*, Chapter 9, "SAS Language Statements."

Chapter 8 Classifying Variables into Categories

Introduction

In SAS programming that emphasizes the DATA step, the key to accomplishing what you want may be the way you manipulate variables. One way to manipulate variables is to classify them into categories. Often when you are evaluating data, the values of the variables, even collectively, may not lead you to a conclusion about their significance. However, if you redefine those values by classifying them into broader categories, they may become more meaningful. For example, the numeric value -107.89 may not be particularly meaningful, especially at a glance. Yet, assigning it to the category OVERDRAWN immediately attaches significance to the value and calls for a conclusion.

In this chapter
This chapter shows you how to redefine variables by

□   assigning values conditionally to a new variable

□   categorizing variable values with customized formats

□   changing variable values through logical expressions.

Prerequisites
To understand this chapter, you should be familiar with the following features of the SAS System:

□   DATA step processing

□   SELECT groups

□   how the SAS System evaluates compound expressions.

Understanding Logical Expressions

To understand some of the examples in this chapter, you must first understand logical expressions. In SAS software, expressions that are true have values of 1, and expressions that are false have values of 0. These are considered logical expressions. For example, suppose the value of the variable AMOUNT is 75000 for a particular observation. Consider the following expression:

```
(50000<=AMOUNT<100000)
```

When you substitute the value of the current observation for AMOUNT, you are in essence rewriting the expression as follows:

```
(50000<=75000<100000)
```

This logical expression is obviously true, so it has a value of 1. If the value of AMOUNT is instead 30,000, the same logical expression is false and has a value of 0. Note that each time the SAS System encounters an expression, it re-evaluates that expression. Logical expressions can return values of only 0 or 1; how you then put those values to work within your program is up to you.

Assigning Values Conditionally to a New Variable

You can make certain types of applications more meaningful by using the values of a variable conditionally to determine the values of a new variable. To illustrate, a new clothing manufacturing company has formed as the result of a merger between a rainwear manufacturing company and a resortwear manufacturing company. The new company is conducting an inventory of its current stock. However, because departments are numerically coded, the inventory printout does not indicate which departments produce rainwear and which departments produce resortwear. The company wants to make this indication on the inventory printout.

In the following example, which assigns values conditionally, each record of raw data contains the following fields:

Field	Description
dept	type of clothing department
item	clothing item, by number

Here are the raw data records:

```
----+----1----+
3070 20410
3070 20411
415  6002
3071 20500
3071 20501
411  2001
411  2002
3072 35102
412  3008
3071 20502
3072 35101
3073 36207
3074 38750
3074 38751
412  3009
414  5076
415  6001
3073 36205
3073 36206
413  4010
413  4011
414  5075
----+----1----+
```

The two steps that accomplish this task follow.

Create and Define a New Variable

The first step in assigning values conditionally to a new variable is to create and
define that variable. In the following example, the LENGTH statement establishes
TYPE as a character variable and sets its length as 10 bytes:

```
libname rainwear 'SAS-data-library';

data rainwear.newstock;
   input dept 1-4 item 6-12;
   length type $ 10;
```

Assign Values to the New Variable through Conditional Processing

The next step is to use conditional processing to assign values to the new variable.
You can use a SELECT group to execute the conditional statements in a program.
(Note that you can also use IF-THEN/ELSE statements for conditional processing.)
Specify each SELECT expression parenthetically within a WHEN statement,
followed by a statement specifying the intended action. Then use an OTHERWISE

statement to flag as invalid any values that fall outside of the ranges stated in the WHEN statements. For each record processed, the SAS System evaluates the WHEN expression in each WHEN statement, produces a result of true or false, and proceeds accordingly.

In this example, all clothing manufactured in departments whose values range between 3000 and 3999 is rainwear. All clothing manufactured in departments whose values range between 400 and 499 is resortwear. Therefore, the value `rainwear` is assigned to the variable TYPE when DEPT has values between 3000 and 3999, and the value `resortwear` is assigned to the variable TYPE when DEPT has values between 400 and 499.

```
select;
   when(3000<=dept<4000) type='rainwear';
   when(400<=dept<500) type='resortwear';
   otherwise type='invalid';
end;
```

Additional WHEN statements can be added as the manufacturer adds lines of clothing. The OTHERWISE statement can then be used only to flag invalid data entry. Note that the input lines do not currently contain invalid data.

Here is the entire program, including the in-stream data lines, that creates and prints the data set.

```
libname rainwear 'SAS-data-library';

data rainwear.newstock;
   input dept 1-4 item 6-12;
   length type $ 10;
   select;
      when(3000<=dept<4000) type='rainwear';
      when(400<=dept<500) type='resortwear';
      otherwise type='invalid';
   end;
   cards;
3070 20410
3070 20411
415  6002
3071 20500
3071 20501
411  2001
411  2002
3072 35102
412  3008
3071 20502
;

proc print;
   title 'Inventory by Stock Number and Clothing Line';
run;
```

Output 8.1 shows the results.

Output 8.1
*Assigning Values
Conditionally to a
New Variable*

```
                Inventory by Stock Number and Clothing Line                1

         OBS     DEPT     ITEM        TYPE

          1      3070    20410     rainwear
          2      3070    20411     rainwear
          3       415     6002     resortwear
          4      3071    20500     rainwear
          5      3071    20501     rainwear
          6       411     2001     resortwear
          7       411     2002     resortwear
          8      3072    35102     rainwear
          9       412     3008     resortwear
         10      3071    20502     rainwear
```

While Output 8.1 continues to list each item numerically, it identifies a department by the clothing line it manufactures in addition to its numeric department code. The descriptive values assigned to TYPE are more informative than the original numeric values assigned to DEPT.

Categorizing Variable Values with Customized Formats

The previous example used conditional processing to assign values to a new character variable based on values of an existing numeric variable. When conditions are likely to change often, you may want to avoid using SELECT groups. Instead, you can categorize the values of an existing variable using a format that you have defined. With this method, you don't have to alter the DATA step, and you can store the format in a centralized location so other programs can use it.

To illustrate, recall the clothing manufacturing company, which has sales data from several sites across the state. The company maintains monthly overhead and sales figures for each store, and in all cases, profit is calculated as the difference between sales and overhead costs.

In the following example, which creates a customized format, each record of raw data contains the following fields:

Field	Description
site	location of each department store
store	individual department store, by name
overhead	total operational costs, by month
sales	total sales revenues, by month

Here are the raw data records:

```
----+----1----+----2----+----3----+----4
HTTR Galloway         10000  50000
WVMA Smithy           15000  73000
ELMA Millers          18000  72000
HLMA Mathers          12000  88000
SOBM Galloway         33000  150000
GVDM Galloway         28000  142000
VATR Mathers          23000  117000
MDMA Millers          39000  189000
NOBM Smithy           29000  147000
OPMA Galloway         26000  132000
OTMA Millers          16000  90000
----+----1----+----2----+----3----+----4
```

The following program shows the assignment statement the manufacturer normally uses to calculate profit:

```
libname rainwear 'SAS-data-library';

data rainwear.profit;
   input site $ 1-4 store $ 6-23 overhead sales;
   profit=sales-overhead;
   cards;
HTTR Galloway         10000  50000
WVMA Smithy           15000  73000
ELMA Millers          18000  72000
HLMA Mathers          12000  88000
SOBM Galloway         33000  150000
GVDM Galloway         28000  142000
VATR Mathers          23000  117000
MDMA Millers          39000  189000
NOBM Smithy           29000  147000
OPMA Galloway         26000  132000
OTMA Millers          16000  90000
;

proc print data=rainwear.profit;
   title 'Monthly Profit Figures by Site';
run;
```

Output 8.2 shows the results.

Output 8.2
Monthly Profit Figures, Unformatted

```
                     Monthly Profit Figures by Site                    1

         OBS   SITE    STORE      OVERHEAD    SALES    PROFIT

          1    HTTR    Galloway     10000     50000    40000
          2    WVMA    Smithy       15000     73000    58000
          3    ELMA    Millers      18000     72000    54000
          4    HLMA    Mathers      12000     88000    76000
          5    SOBM    Galloway     33000    150000   117000
          6    GVDM    Galloway     28000    142000   114000
```

```
          7   VATR   Mathers    23000   117000    94000
          8   MDMA   Millers    39000   189000   150000
          9   NOBM   Smithy     29000   147000   118000
         10   OPMA   Galloway   26000   132000   106000
         11   OTMA   Millers    16000    90000    74000
```

However, the stockholders are not sufficiently knowledgeable about profit margins to interpret the numeric results of these calculations. Therefore, the CEO wants to reformat the values of PROFIT to indicate that those values are high, low, or somewhere in between.

The following example illustrates how to change variable values with customized formats using the following steps:

□ provide a means of storing a customized format

□ create a customized format

□ apply the customized format.

Provide a Means of Storing Customized Formats

When you create customized formats, you probably want to store them permanently so you can use them in subsequent SAS sessions without having to re-create them. Simply use the LIBRARY= option in the PROC FORMAT statement as follows to specify the SAS data library where you plan to store them:

```
libname library 'SAS-data-library';
proc format library=library;
```

Your formats are then written to a catalog named FORMATS in that SAS data library.

▶ *Caution* . . . . *Use the reserved libref LIBRARY when using customized formats.*
When you create customized formats, it is unimportant which libref you assign to the SAS data library where you store them. However, when you want to use these formats in a DATA step or a PROC step, you must use the reserved libref LIBRARY. When a user-written format is called by a DATA step or a PROC step, the SAS System looks for the format in a catalog named WORK.FORMATS and then in one named LIBRARY.FORMATS. ▲

Create a Customized Format

To create a customized format, use the FORMAT procedure with a VALUE statement. The PROC FORMAT statement invokes the FORMAT procedure, which creates a customized format that remains in effect for the duration of a session. The VALUE statement defines the format so the values of the variable can be associated with the new formatted values. The newly created values can be up to 40 characters and must be enclosed in quotes. You must assign the format a name that is not the name of a format supplied by the SAS System. (Note that the format name does not end with a period in the VALUE statement.) Be sure to place the PROC FORMAT step before your DATA step.

The following example uses the FORMAT procedure with the VALUE statement to reformat the profit margin values so stockholders can more easily interpret those profit margin values:

```
libname library 'SAS-data-library-to-contain-format';

proc format library=library;
   value gain      low-<50000='low'
                50000-<100000='average'
               100000-<150000='above average'
                 150000-high='high';
run;
```

In this example, the VALUE statement defines the format GAIN., which associates the character labels shown on the right side of the equal sign with the numeric values shown on the left side of the equal sign.

Apply the Customized Format

After you have created a customized format, you can use a FORMAT statement to associate the values of the format with the appropriate variable. Here, the format GAIN. is applied to the variable PROFIT.

```
libname library 'SAS-data-library-containing-format';
libname rainwear 'SAS-data-library';

proc print data=rainwear.profit;
   format profit gain. overhead sales dollar8.;
   title 'Monthly Profit Figures, by Site';
run;
```

Here is the entire program that creates and applies the customized format and that creates and prints the data set.

```
libname library 'SAS-data-library-containing-format';
libname rainwear 'SAS-data-library';

proc format library=library;
   value gain      low-<50000='low'
                50000-<100000='average'
               100000-<150000='above average'
                 150000-high='high';
run;

proc print data=rainwear.profit;
   format profit gain. overhead sales dollar8.;
   title 'Monthly Profit Figures, by Site';
run;
```

Output 8.3 shows the results.

Output 8.3
Categorizing Variable Values with a Customized Format

```
                    Monthly Profit Figures, by Site                    1

   OBS   SITE   STORE      OVERHEAD      SALES    PROFIT

    1    HTTR   Galloway    $10,000    $50,000    low
    2    WVMA   Smithy      $15,000    $73,000    average
    3    ELMA   Millers     $18,000    $72,000    average
    4    HLMA   Mathers     $12,000    $88,000    average
    5    SOBM   Galloway    $33,000   $150,000    above average
    6    GVDM   Galloway    $28,000   $142,000    above average
    7    VATR   Mathers     $23,000   $117,000    average
    8    MDMA   Millers     $39,000   $189,000    high
    9    NOBM   Smithy      $29,000   $147,000    above average
   10    OPMA   Galloway    $26,000   $132,000    above average
   11    OTMA   Millers     $16,000    $90,000    average
```

Changing Variable Values through Logical Expressions

When you are working with numeric groupings, you can write a very compact statement to produce those groupings. To demonstrate, consider the previous example, which starts with unformatted numeric values and uses the FORMAT procedure to categorize those values. Instead of creating a customized format as shown in the previous example, you can use logical expressions to create sequential categories with numeric values. This technique requires fewer programming statements and fewer steps than the previous example, which uses a PROC FORMAT step.

Suppose the four numeric categories of the previous example are profit standards within the clothing manufacturing company. They are immediately recognized as corresponding to low, average, above average, or high profits without being described as such. In fact, as a shorthand, the manufacturer prefers to use the upper bound for each numeric range as the category into which a given monthly profit can fall. Therefore, the numeric categories are

□ $50,000

□ $100,000

□ $150,000

□ $250,000.

To modify the unformatted example, first use the SET statement to read in the observations from the data set RAINWEAR.PROFIT. Then create a new variable whose values correspond to the values of the numeric categories listed earlier. Conditional processing can assign a value to the variable PROFGRP, based on the value of PROFIT with a series of IF-THEN and ELSE-IF statements as shown here:

```
if (0<=profit<=50000) then profgrp=50000;
else if (50000<profit<=100000) then profgrp=100000;
else if (100000<profit<=150000) then profgrp=150000;
else if (150000<profit) then profgrp=250000;
```

However, a more concise method achieves the same results by placing all four expressions in a single assignment statement. Only one of these expressions can be true (equal to 1) for a given observation. Using this fact, place all of these expressions in an assignment statement, multiply the result of each expression (which equals 1 or 0) by the value that represents the correct profit group, and add the results. Three expressions result in 0. These three 0s are added to the true expression (1), which is multiplied by the correct profit group value. This value is assigned to the variable PROFGRP for each observation.

```
libname rainwear 'SAS-data-library';

data rainwear.gains;
   set rainwear.profit;
   profgrp=50000*(0<=profit<=50000)+100000*(50000<profit<=100000)+
           150000*(100000<profit<=150000)+250000*(150000<profit);
run;
```

When each observation is processed, the current numeric value of PROFIT is evaluated against each parenthetical expression. For example, in the first observation, the value of PROFIT is 40000. Therefore, the first logical expression is true and takes a value of 1; the value 1 is multiplied by the value 50000, resulting in a total value of 50000 for that expression. When the remaining logical expressions are evaluated against the first observation, they prove to be false and have values of 0. Thus, for the first observation, the assignment statement is evaluated as follows:

```
profgrp=50000*(1)+100000*(0)+150000*(0)+250000*(0);
profgrp=50000+0+0+0;
profgrp=50000;
```

The SAS System continues processing each observation in the same way, using the values of PROFIT to determine the appropriate numeric category for the variable PROFGRP.

Here is the entire program that creates the variable PROFGRP, assigns it values, and prints the resulting data by its values.

```
libname rainwear 'SAS-data-library';

data rainwear.gains;
   set rainwear.profit;
   profgrp=50000*(0<=profit<=50000)+100000*(50000<profit<=100000)+
           150000*(100000<profit<=150000)+250000*(150000<profit);
run;

proc sort data=rainwear.gains;
   by profgrp;
run;
```

```
proc print data=rainwear.gains;
   by profgrp;
   id profgrp;
   format overhead sales profit profgrp dollar8.;
   title 'Monthly Profit Figures, by Site and Numeric Category';
run;
```

Output 8.4 shows the results.

Output 8.4
Determining
Numeric
Categories through
Logical
Expressions

```
               Monthly Profit Figures, by Site and Numeric Category              1

     PROFGRP     SITE     STORE      OVERHEAD        SALES        PROFIT

     $50,000     HTTR     Galloway   $10,000       $50,000       $40,000

     $100,000    WVMA     Smithy     $15,000       $73,000       $58,000
                 ELMA     Millers    $18,000       $72,000       $54,000
                 HLMA     Mathers    $12,000       $88,000       $76,000
                 VATR     Mathers    $23,000      $117,000       $94,000
                 OTMA     Millers    $16,000       $90,000       $74,000

     $150,000    SOBM     Galloway   $33,000      $150,000      $117,000
                 GVDM     Galloway   $28,000      $142,000      $114,000
                 MDMA     Millers    $39,000      $189,000      $150,000
                 NOBM     Smithy     $29,000      $147,000      $118,000
                 OPMA     Galloway   $26,000      $132,000      $106,000
```

Summary

The following points summarize how to classify variables into categories:

□ When you redefine values by classifying them into broader categories, they may become more meaningful. To redefine such values, you can use one of the following techniques:

□ assign values conditionally to a new variable

□ categorize variable values with customized formats

□ create new variable values through logical expressions.

□ To assign values conditionally to a new variable, you can use the SELECT statement combined with WHEN statements and an OTHERWISE statement. These statements, followed by an END statement, make up a SELECT group.

□ To categorize variable values with customized formats, define a format using the FORMAT procedure with a VALUE statement. Then use a FORMAT statement in the PROC PRINT step to associate that format with a variable. To provide a means of storing customized formats, use the LIBRARY= option in the PROC FORMAT statement to specify the SAS data library where you plan to store the formats. Use the reserved libref LIBRARY when using the customized formats.

□ When you are working with numeric groupings, you can use logical expressions, which return values of 0 (false) or 1 (true). Create an expression that corresponds to each numeric category, and place each expression parenthetically on the right side of an equation. On the left side of the equation, place a variable to which the results of the expressions are assigned.

SAS Tools

This section summarizes syntax for the statements and procedures discussed in this chapter.

Statements

variable = expression;
> is an assignment statement. It causes the SAS System to evaluate the *expression* on the right side of the equal sign and assign the result to the *variable* on the left. You must select the name of the variable and create the proper expression for calculating its value. The same variable can appear on the left and right sides of the equal sign because the SAS System evaluates the right side before assigning the result to the variable on the left side.

FORMAT *variables* <*format*>;
> associates formats with variables in the DATA step. The FORMAT statement can appear in the DATA step or the PROC step. To disassociate a format from a variable, use the variable's name in a FORMAT statement with no format.

LENGTH *variable*<$> *length*;
> assigns the number of bytes of storage (*length* for a *variable*). Include a dollar sign ($) if the variable is character. The LENGTH statement must appear before the first use of a character variable.

SELECT;
> **WHEN**-*1* (*condition-1*) *action-to-take*;
> <**WHEN**-*n* (*condition-n*) *action-to-take*;>
> <**OTHERWISE** *action-to-take*;>
END;
> is known as a SELECT group. Like a series of IF-THEN and ELSE statements, a SELECT group tests for conditions and then takes appropriate action. Especially if you have many conditions to specify, your code may be easier to read if you use a SELECT group.
>
> The *action-to-take* may be expressed in a single statement or in a DO group. It must be expressed as an executable statement, that is, one that can be processed conditionally.
>
> The OTHERWISE statement provides an alternative action when none of the valid conditions are met and is especially useful for error handling.

Procedures

PROC FORMAT <LIBRARY=*libref*>;
    VALUE *name value-1* ='*formatted-value-1*' < . . . *value-n*='*formatted-value-n*'>;

    PROC FORMAT <LIBRARY=*libref*>;
        begins the FORMAT procedure, which allows you to create your own
        formats and informats for character and numeric variables. The
        LIBRARY= option specifies the libref for a SAS data library containing a
        permanent catalog that contains formats or informats. (If the library does
        not already contain such a catalog, the SAS System automatically creates
        one.) When you specify a libref with the LIBRARY= option, all formats
        and informats you create in the PROC FORMAT step are permanent.

    VALUE *name value-1*='*formatted-value-1*'< . . . *value-n*='*formatted-value-n*'>;
        defines a format that writes a variable's value as a different value.

Learning More

This section provides references for learning more about the topics presented in
this chapter.

□   For more information about manipulating variables, see the other chapters in
     Part 3, "Using Advanced Programming Techniques." In particular, see
     Chapter 10, "Performing a Table Lookup," for other examples of using
     formats to manipulate variable values.

□   For further information to improve the efficiency of your SAS applications, see
     SAS Programming Tips: A Guide to Efficient SAS Processing. This book suggests
     efficient coding techniques, as well as guidelines for their use.

□   For general information about SAS formats, see *SAS Language: Reference,*
     Version 6, First Edition, Chapter 3, "Components of the SAS Language." See
     Chapter 14, "SAS Formats," for complete syntax information about individual
     SAS formats.

□   For detailed syntax information about the FORMAT procedure and the
     VALUE statement, see *SAS Procedures Guide, Version 6, Third Edition,*
     Chapter 18, "The FORMAT Procedure."

□   For detailed syntax information about the assignment, FORMAT, and
     LENGTH statements and about SELECT groups, see *SAS Language: Reference,*
     Chapter 9, "SAS Language Statements."

160

Chapter 9 Reshaping Data

Introduction

For some applications, you may need to perform mathematical calculations or generate reports that present the data from a particular vantage point. Doing so may require you to rearrange the values in the data set. This process is referred to as reshaping data.

In this chapter
This chapter describes four ways of reshaping data:

- creating multiple observations from a single observation
- creating one observation from multiple observations
- transposing observations and variables
- collapsing multiple variables into a single variable.

Prerequisites

To understand this chapter, you should be familiar with the following concepts:

□ DATA step processing

□ array processing

□ the equation that transforms binary values into decimal values.

Creating Multiple Observations from a Single Observation

Often, a single observation in a SAS data set contains numerous variables. If you want to perform calculations on the data in that data set, you may need to reshape the data so that information contained in a series of separate variables in one large observation becomes a single variable in a series of observations.

SAS Data Set Example

To illustrate, consider a company's marketing research department, which is conducting clinical trials to rate the texture of ten different brands of pasta. A test is repeated five times for each brand. This arrangement of data, where a measure is repeated several times, is called *repeated measures data*. The data set used for the examples in this section contains the variables described in the following table:

Variable	Type	Description
BRAND	character	brand of pasta, by code number
TEST1	numeric	score for first test (scale 1-100)
TEST2	numeric	score for second test (scale 1-100)
TEST3	numeric	score for third test (scale 1-100)
TEST4	numeric	score for fourth test (scale 1-100)
TEST5	numeric	score for fifth test (scale 1-100)

The following PROC PRINT step displays the data set IN.PASTA:*

```
libname in 'SAS-data-library';

proc print data=in.pasta;
   title 'Results of Clinical Trials, Pasta, 3/15';
run;
```

---

* The DATA step that creates IN.PASTA is shown in the Appendix.

Output 9.1 shows the results.

Output 9.1
*Printout of
IN.PASTA Data
Set*

```
                Results of Clinical Trials, Pasta, 3/15                1

    OBS    BRAND    TEST1    TEST2    TEST3    TEST4    TEST5

     1     X0123      70       80       85       90       96
     2     X0145      85       79       86       87       88
     3     X0144      63       85       79       80       81
     4     X0135      77       80       82       84       90
     5     X0136      82       82       89       93       85
     6     X0130      39       45       55       40       59
     7     X0129      62       64       70       71       68
     8     X0140      80       85       83       84       88
     9     X0126      76       78       74       71       80
    10     X0148      51       58       62       55       69
```

As already noted, a single observation contains values for six variables, five of which are values for repeated measures. To demonstrate whether some factor is lowering all scores for a certain test, the marketing research department wants to chart the mean of the overall rating for each of the five tests. Output 9.2 shows how the chart, a vertical bar chart, would appear:

Output 9.2
*Output Requiring
Rearrangement of
Data Set*

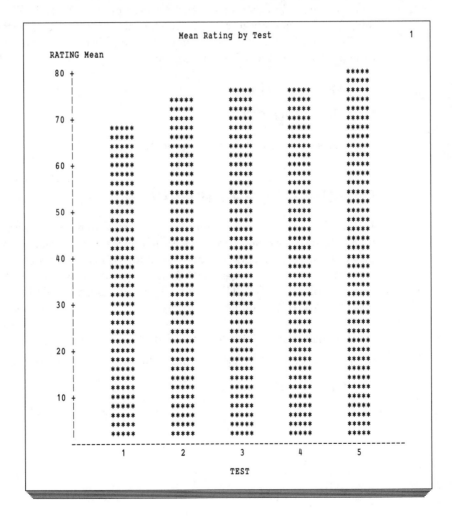

However, the current configuration of the data set does not allow such a chart to be produced. Generating this chart requires the creation of a new data set containing variables called RATING and TEST. The values of RATING can then be summarized and displayed in the bars, each bar representing one of the five tests. Here is the program used to generate the chart. Note that the SUMVAR= option names RATING as the variable to be summarized.

```
libname in 'SAS-data-library';

proc chart data=in.noodles;
   vbar test / sumvar=rating type=mean discrete;
   title 'Mean Rating by Test';
run;
```

Although the data set IN.PASTA already contains the variable BRAND, it doesn't contain a variable called RATING or a variable called TEST. As the next section demonstrates, RATING is a variable whose values reflect all of the test results—the values of TEST1, TEST2, TEST3, TEST4, and TEST5.

To produce such a chart, the company must calculate the overall rating of each brand and then calculate its mean. To calculate that overall rating, the company must first change the separate variables TEST1, TEST2, TEST3, TEST4, and TEST5 in one observation to one variable in a series of observations.

The next two sections show how to accomplish a task like the one in this example by using one of two methods:

□ a basic approach

□ a shortcut approach.

The first section demonstrates a basic approach.

Using a Basic Approach

When you want to change multiple variables in one observation to one variable in many observations, you can use a basic approach that requires a set of programming statements for each variable. You can follow a three-step process, repeating the process for each of the multiple variables. To change the variables TEST1, TEST2, TEST3, TEST4, and TEST5 to one variable in a series of observations, this example

□ assigns the test result to a new variable

□ creates a new variable containing the numeric order of the test

□ outputs the results.

An assignment statement assigns the value of the testing variable to a new variable. The SAS System reads the current value of TEST1 and stores the results in the newly created variable RATING.

```
libname in 'SAS-data-library';

data in.noodles;
   set in.pasta;
   rating=test1;
```

Another assignment statement creates a variable whose value corresponds to the numeric order of the test. The SAS System evaluates the numeric expression and stores the results in the newly created variable TEST.

```
libname in 'SAS-data-library';

data in.noodles;
   set in.pasta;
   rating=test1;
   test=1;
```

Finally, the OUTPUT statement writes the current observation to a SAS data set. Note that this happens immediately, not at the end of the DATA step.

```
libname in 'SAS-data-library';

data in.noodles;
   set in.pasta;
   rating=test1;
   test=1;
   output;
```

This process is repeated for each of the remaining testing variables, TEST2 through TEST5. With each iteration of the DATA step, the SAS System processes one observation from the original data set, assigns values to the variables RATING and TEST, and outputs five observations to the new data set. Here is the entire program that creates and prints the data set.

```
libname in 'SAS-data-library';

data in.noodles;
   set in.pasta;
   rating=test1;
   test=1;
   output;
   rating=test2;
   test=2;
   output;
   rating=test3;
   test=3;
   output;
   rating=test4;
   test=4;
```

```
            output;
            rating=test5;
            test=5;
            output;
            keep brand test rating;
        run;

        proc print data=in.noodles;
            title 'Results of Clinical Trials, Pasta, 3/15';
        run;
```

Output 9.3 shows the results.

Output 9.3
Using DATA Step
Processing to
Change a Series of
Variables in One
Observation to One
Variable in a
Series of
Observations

```
                Results of Clinical Trials, Pasta, 3/15              1

          OBS     BRAND     RATING     TEST

           1      X0123       70         1
           2      X0123       80         2
           3      X0123       85         3
           4      X0123       90         4
           5      X0123       96         5
           6      X0145       85         1
           7      X0145       79         2
           8      X0145       86         3
           9      X0145       87         4
          10      X0145       88         5
          11      X0144       63         1
          12      X0144       85         2
          13      X0144       79         3
          14      X0144       80         4
          15      X0144       81         5
          16      X0135       77         1
          17      X0135       80         2
          18      X0135       82         3
          19      X0135       84         4
          20      X0135       90         5
          21      X0136       82         1
          22      X0136       82         2
          23      X0136       89         3
          24      X0136       93         4
          25      X0136       85         5
          26      X0130       39         1
          27      X0130       45         2
          28      X0130       55         3
          29      X0130       40         4
          30      X0130       59         5
          31      X0129       62         1
          32      X0129       64         2
          33      X0129       70         3
          34      X0129       71         4
          35      X0129       68         5
          36      X0140       80         1
          37      X0140       85         2
          38      X0140       83         3
          39      X0140       84         4
          40      X0140       88         5
          41      X0126       76         1
          42      X0126       78         2
          43      X0126       74         3
          44      X0126       71         4
          45      X0126       80         5
          46      X0148       51         1
          47      X0148       58         2
          48      X0148       62         3
          49      X0148       55         4
          50      X0148       69         5
```

Now that the variables RATING and TEST have been created, it is possible to create the chart shown earlier in Output 9.2. The next section shows you how to shorten the process of reshaping variables to observations.

Taking a Programming Shortcut

If you have many variables to reshape, the program you create using the basic approach may become long and cumbersome. To illustrate, consider the previous example, which contains the following three programming statements for each variable to be reshaped (where the value of *n* corresponds to the number of the testing variable):

```
rating=testn;
test=n;
output;
```

This group of statements is executed five times to process the observations for all five sets of testing variables. While this basic approach works, given that only five variables require grouping, it could become burdensome with many more variables.

When you have many variables, you can shorten your program by using array processing to group the variables you want to change. Use the following two-step approach:

□ group the multiple variables

□ use iterative processing to simplify the task of changing a series of variables in one observation to a single variable in a series of observations.

To group the variables, use an ARRAY statement. Here, the array is called TESTING and has five elements: TEST1, TEST2, TEST3, TEST4, and TEST5.

```
libname in 'SAS-data-library';

data in.texture;
   array testing(5) test1-test5;
```

Now use iterative processing to simplify the task. To process the variables identically, indicate the number of times you want to repeat the action, specify the particular actions, and determine the array element to process with each iteration.

First, to cause the DO loop to iterate five times (the number of elements in the array), assign the index variable a value of 1 to 5. Use the END statement to end the loop.

```
libname in 'SAS-data-library';

data in.texture;
   array testing(5) test1-test5;
   set in.pasta;
   do test=1 to 5;
      more SAS statements
   end;
```

To continue to accomplish the task of reshaping all testing variables, embed within the DO loop programming statements similar to those used in the previous example.

```
libname in 'SAS-data-library';

data in.texture;
   array testing(5) test1-test5;
   set in.pasta;
   do test=1 to 5;
     rating=testing(test);
     output;
   end;
```

As the value of the index variable changes, the subscript of the array reference changes. For example, when TEST has a value of 3, the SAS System treats the array reference as TESTING{3} and performs the action on TEST3.

Here is the entire program that creates and prints the data set.

```
libname in 'SAS-data-library';

data in.texture;
   array testing(5) test1-test5;
   set in.pasta;
   do test=1 to 5;
     rating=testing(test);
     output;
   end;
   drop test1-test5;
run;

proc print data=in.texture;
   title 'Results of Clinical Trials, Pasta, 3/15';
run;
```

Output 9.4 shows the results, which are the same as those produced with a basic approach except that the order of variables presented differs.

Output 9.4
Using Array Processing to Change a Series of Variables in One Observation to One Variable in a Series of Observations

```
             Results of Clinical Trials, Pasta, 3/15              1

        OBS     BRAND     TEST     RATING

          1     X0123       1        70
          2     X0123       2        80
          3     X0123       3        85
          4     X0123       4        90
          5     X0123       5        96
          6     X0145       1        85
          7     X0145       2        79
          8     X0145       3        86
          9     X0145       4        87
         10     X0145       5        88
         11     X0144       1        63
         12     X0144       2        85
         13     X0144       3        79
         14     X0144       4        80
         15     X0144       5        81
         16     X0135       1        77
```

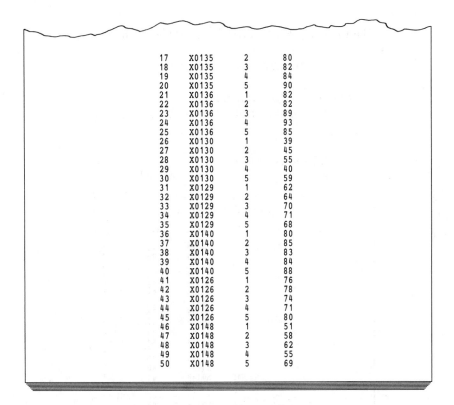

17	X0135	2	80
18	X0135	3	82
19	X0135	4	84
20	X0135	5	90
21	X0136	1	82
22	X0136	2	82
23	X0136	3	89
24	X0136	4	93
25	X0136	5	85
26	X0130	1	39
27	X0130	2	45
28	X0130	3	55
29	X0130	4	40
30	X0130	5	59
31	X0129	1	62
32	X0129	2	64
33	X0129	3	70
34	X0129	4	71
35	X0129	5	68
36	X0140	1	80
37	X0140	2	85
38	X0140	3	83
39	X0140	4	84
40	X0140	5	88
41	X0126	1	76
42	X0126	2	78
43	X0126	3	74
44	X0126	4	71
45	X0126	5	80
46	X0148	1	51
47	X0148	2	58
48	X0148	3	62
49	X0148	4	55
50	X0148	5	69

Creating One Observation from Multiple Observations

The previous example showed you how to rearrange a SAS data set by changing a series of variables in one observation to a single variable in a series of observations. Conversely, to facilitate reporting through DATA step or PROC step processing, you may want to rearrange a data set by changing a single variable in a series of observations to a series of variables in one observation.

SAS Data Set Example

To illustrate, suppose the marketing research department has its testing data arranged in a data set as shown in the following table. Note that instead of the five testing variables in the previous example, this data set has just one. Note also the variable RATING.

Variable	Type	Description
BRAND	character	brand of pasta, by code number
RATING	numeric	test score assigned to a brand of pasta (scale 1—100)
TEST	numeric	numeric order of the test

The following PROC PRINT step displays the data set IN.NOODLES:

```
libname in 'SAS-data-library';

proc print data=in.noodles;
   title 'Results of Clinical Trials, Pasta, 3/25';
run;
```

Output 9.5 shows the results.

Output 9.5
Printout of
IN.NOODLES
Data Set

```
              Results of Clinical Trials, Pasta, 3/25                    1

              OBS      BRAND      RATING      TEST

                1      X0123        70          1
                2      X0123        80          2
                3      X0123        85          3
                4      X0123        90          4
                5      X0123        96          5
                6      X0145        85          1
                7      X0145        79          2
                8      X0145        86          3
                9      X0145        87          4
               10      X0145        88          5
               11      X0144        63          1
               12      X0144        85          2
               13      X0144        79          3
               14      X0144        80          4
               15      X0144        81          5
               16      X0135        77          1
               17      X0135        80          2
               18      X0135        82          3
               19      X0135        84          4
               20      X0135        90          5
               21      X0136        82          1
               22      X0136        82          2
               23      X0136        89          3
               24      X0136        93          4
               25      X0136        85          5
               26      X0130        39          1
               27      X0130        45          2
               28      X0130        55          3
               29      X0130        40          4
               30      X0130        59          5
               31      X0129        62          1
               32      X0129        64          2
               33      X0129        70          3
               34      X0129        71          4
               35      X0129        68          5
               36      X0140        80          1
               37      X0140        85          2
               38      X0140        83          3
               39      X0140        84          4
               40      X0140        88          5
               41      X0126        76          1
               42      X0126        78          2
               43      X0126        74          3
               44      X0126        71          4
               45      X0126        80          5
               46      X0148        51          1
               47      X0148        58          2
               48      X0148        62          3
               49      X0148        55          4
               50      X0148        69          5
```

Instead of a single observation containing values for one brand and all of its test results, one observation contains values for a brand, its rating, and the corresponding test number. The marketing research department wants to use a chart to show how individual tests differ for each brand. The following chart, for instance, shows which brand achieves the highest rating for the first test, shown here as TEST1:

Output 9.6
*Output Requiring
Rearrangement of
Data Set*

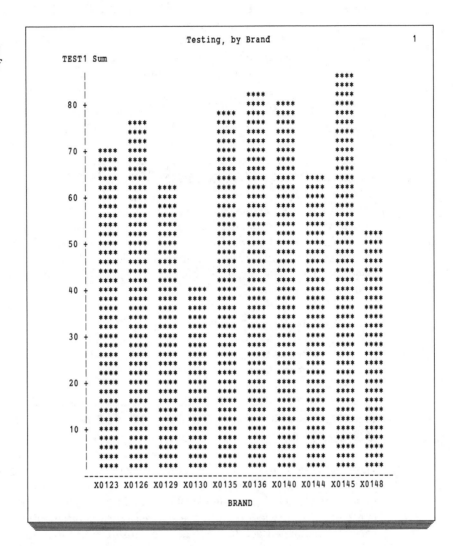

However, the current configuration of the data set IN.NOODLES does not allow such a chart to be produced using the PROC CHART step below. One way to generate this chart is to create a new data set containing a variable called TEST1. The values of TEST1 can then be summarized and displayed in the bars. Here is the program used to generate the chart. Note that the SUMVAR= option names TEST1 as the variable to be summarized.

```
libname in 'SAS-data-library';

proc chart data=in.reshape;
    vbar brand / sumvar=test1;
    title 'Testing, by Brand';
run;
```

Because only a collective testing variable, TEST, appears in the IN.NOODLES data set, this PROC CHART step can't produce these results for individual tests until new variables are created that correspond to each test. In this example, the goal is to reshape to one observation the five observations that reflect one set of data values for IN.NOODLES' variables RATING and TEST. Instead of the 50 observations that IN.NOODLES has, the new data set will have 10.

To accomplish this goal, do the following:

□ create and group the new variables

□ assign values to the new variables using iterative processing.

Create and Group New Variables

The first step is to create new variables that will reflect both a single variable and its data values from the original data set. To create and group the new variables, use an ARRAY statement. Here, the array is called COMBINE and has five elements: the newly created variables TEST1, TEST2, TEST3, TEST4, and TEST5. Note that these new variables reflect IN.NOODLES' variable TEST and the data values assigned to it.

```
libname in 'SAS-data-library';


data in.reshape;
   array combine{5} test1-test5;
```

Assign Data Values to the New Variables

The second step is to assign values to the new variables through iterative processing. In this example, the goal is to assign the values of IN.NOODLES' variable RATING to the new variables TEST1 through TEST5. Iterative processing is necessary to process each of the five array elements identically. The index variable is assigned a value of 1 to 5 to cause the DO loop to iterate five times.

```
libname in 'SAS-data-library';

data in.reshape;
   array combine{5} test1-test5;
   do i=1 to 5;
      more SAS statements
   end;
```

The next step is to place the necessary programming statements in the DO loop. Here, the SET statement reads observations for the data set IN.NOODLES. Note that the SET statement is embedded in the DO loop instead of preceding it so for each iteration of the DO loop five observations are read from IN.NOODLES

instead of one. In that way, the appropriate values are read for the array elements
TEST1 through TEST5 and five observations are condensed into one observation.

```
libname in 'SAS-data-library';

data in.reshape;
   array combine{5} test1-test5;
   do i=1 to 5;
      set in.noodles;
      combine{i}=rating;
   end;
```

The following assignment statement identifies a variable whose value
corresponds to the rating for each test. With each iteration of the DO loop, the
SAS System reads the current value of RATING based on the value of the index
variable I. For example, when I has a value of 5 and BRAND is X0123, the SAS
System assigns the value 96 to COMBINE{5}, that is TEST5.

```
libname in 'SAS-data-library';

data in.reshape;
   array combine{5} test1-test5;
   do i=1 to 5;
      set in.noodles;
      combine{i}=rating;
   end;
```

Here is the entire program that creates and prints the data set. Note that the
automatic output occurs after the END statement, so the five observations brought
in by the SET statement are output to one observation of the output data set.

```
libname in 'SAS-data-library';

data in.reshape(keep=brand test1-test5);
   array combine{5} test1-test5;
   do i=1 to 5;
      set in.noodles;
      combine{i}=rating;
   end;
run;

proc print data=in.reshape;
   title 'Results of Clinical Trials, Pasta, 4/18';
run;
```

Output 9.7 shows the results.

Output 9.7
Using DATA Step
Processing to
Change One
Variable in a
Series of
Observations to a
Series of Variables
in One Observation

```
                    Results of Clinical Trials, Pasta, 4/18                    1

      OBS    TEST1    TEST2    TEST3    TEST4    TEST5    BRAND

       1      70       80       85       90       96      X0123
       2      85       79       86       87       88      X0145
       3      63       85       79       80       81      X0144
       4      77       80       82       84       90      X0135
       5      82       82       89       93       85      X0136
       6      39       45       55       40       59      X0137
       7      62       64       70       71       68      X0129
       8      80       85       83       84       88      X0140
       9      76       78       74       71       80      X0126
      10      51       58       62       55       69      X0148
```

Transposing Observations and Variables in a SAS Data Set

Sometimes you may want to transpose the variables and observations in a SAS data set, perhaps to store the data in fewer observations or to make it easier to generate a tabular report.

SAS Data Set Example

To illustrate, again consider the marketing research company, whose testers are now testing five kitchen products for ease of use and effectiveness. They rate each product according to specific guidelines. The data set used in this example contains the variables described in the following table:

Variable	Type	Description
PERIOD	character	identification of test period
TESTER	numeric	identification number of tester
FOODPR1	numeric	rating for first food processor
FOODPR2	numeric	rating for second food processor
FOODPR3	numeric	rating for third food processor
COFFEEM1	numeric	rating for first coffee maker
COFFEEM2	numeric	rating for second coffee maker
MW_OVEN1	numeric	rating for first microwave oven
MW_OVEN2	numeric	rating for second microwave oven
DISHWHR1	numeric	rating for first dishwasher
DISHWHR2	numeric	rating for second dishwasher
DISHWHR3	numeric	rating for third dishwasher

The following PROC PRINT step displays the data set IN.PROD1:*

```
libname in 'SAS-data-library';

proc print data=in.prod1;
    title 'Results of Clinical Trials, Kitchen Products, 4/15';
run;
```

Output 9.8 shows the results.

Output 9.8
Printout of
IN.PROD1 Data
Set

```
                Results of Clinical Trials, Kitchen Products,  4/15                 1

                                    C     C    M    M    D    D    D
                     F     F    F   O     O    W    W    I    I    I
              T      O     O    O   F     F                   S    S    S     P
              E      O     O    O   F     F    O    O    H    H    H     E
              S      D     D    D   E     E    V    V    W    W    W     R
       O      T      P     P    P   E     E    E    E    H    H    H     I
       B      E      R     R    R   M     M    N    N    R    R    R     O
       S      R      1     2    3   1     2    1    2    1    2    3     D

       1     1001   115   45   65   83    78   55   113   82   45   77   initial
       2     1002    86   27   55   72    86   74    39   99   65   70   final
       3     1004    93   52   63   76    88   69   127  101   32   68   initial
       4     1015    73   35   43  112   108   47    98   78   51   73   initial
       5     1027   101  127   39   76    79   58   101  109   47   69   final
```

When the data were collected, it was convenient to enter each tester's identification number only once and to put the ratings for all of the kitchen products on one line. However, the data set needs to be reshaped to make it easier to use in later processing.

To accomplish the task in this example, do the following:

□ Use the TRANSPOSE procedure to convert rows in the data set to columns and columns to rows.

□ Name the transposed variables of the output data set.

□ List the variables to be transposed.

□ Optionally, make the necessary modifications to incorporate greater control over output results.

Convert Rows to Columns and Columns to Rows

To convert the rows (observations) of the data set IN.PROD1 to columns (variables) and the columns (variables) to rows (observations), use the TRANSPOSE procedure. This example reads in the data set IN.PROD1 and creates an output data set called IN.PROD2.

```
    proc transpose data=in.prod1 out=in.prod2;
```

---

*   The DATA step that creates IN.PROD1 is shown in the Appendix.

Name the Transposed Variables

To name the transposed variables of the output data set, add the ID statement after the PROC TRANSPOSE statement. In this case, the values of the variable TESTER from the input data set are used as the names of the transposed variables.

```
id tester;
```

Note that PROC TRANSPOSE changes the value of the ID variable if necessary to make the value into a valid SAS name. Because the values of TESTER are numeric, the SAS System precedes each transposed numeric variable with an underscore. If the resulting value has more than eight characters, it is truncated. Invalid characters are replaced by underscores; the characters +, -, and . are changed to P, N, and D, respectively.

▶ *Caution* . . . . *Duplicate occurrences of a formatted ID value require the LET option.*
If your data contain duplicate occurrences of a formatted ID value, the SAS System generates a warning message and stops processing. To prevent this occurrence, use the LET option in the PROC TRANSPOSE statement. The LET option allows duplicate values of an ID variable within the DATA= data set. Observations with missing values for the ID variable generate a warning message and cause the TRANSPOSE procedure to omit them from the output data set. ▲

List the Variables to Be Transposed

As a last step, to list the variables to transpose, add the VAR statement to the program.

```
var period foodpr1 foodpr2 foodpr3 coffeem1 coffeem2 mw_oven1
    mw_oven2 dishwhr1 dishwhr2 dishwhr3;
```

By default, PROC TRANSPOSE transposes all numeric variables in the input data set that are not listed in another statement. However, you must list character variables in a VAR statement if you want to transpose them. Any variables that are not transposed are omitted from the output data set unless they are listed in a COPY or a BY statement. Therefore, in this example, a VAR statement is necessary to transpose the character variable PERIOD and include it in the IN.PROD2 data set. Note that when a VAR statement is present, PROC TRANSPOSE transposes and includes in the output data set only the variables listed in the statement, whether numeric or character.

Here is the entire program that creates and prints the data set.

```
libname in 'SAS-data-library';

proc transpose data=in.prod1 out=in.prod2;
    id tester;
    var period foodpr1 foodpr2 foodpr3 coffeem1 coffeem2 mw_oven1
        mw_oven2 dishwhr1 dishwhr2 dishwhr3;
run;
```

```
proc print data=in.prod2;
   title 'Results of Clinical Trials, Kitchen Products, 4/15';
run;
```

Output 9.9 shows the results.

Output 9.9
*Transposing
Variables and
Observations with
the TRANSPOSE
Procedure*

```
               Results of Clinical Trials, Kitchen Products, 4/15            1

       _
       N
       A      _        _        _        _        _
 O     M      1        1        1        1        1
 B     E      0        0        0        0        0
 S     _      0        0        0        1        2
              1        2        4        5        7

  1 PERIOD  initial      final   initial  initial     final
  2 FOODPR1       115         86        93       73       101
  3 FOODPR2        45         27        52       35       127
  4 FOODPR3        65         55        63       43        39
  5 COFFEEM1       83         72        76      112        76
  6 COFFEEM2       78         86        88      108        79
  7 MW_OVEN1       55         74        69       47        58
  8 MW_OVEN2      113         39       127       98       101
  9 DISHWHR1       82         99       101       78       109
 10 DISHWHR2       45         65        32       51        47
 11 DISHWHR3       77         70        68       73        69
```

Notice that _1001, _1002, _1004, _1015, and _1027, which were
previously values of the variable TESTER, are now variables. Conversely,
PERIOD, FOODPR1 through FOODPR3, COFFEEM1 and COFFEEM2, MW_OVEN1
and MW_OVEN2, and DISHWHR1 through DISHWHR3, which were previously
variable names, are now values of the variable _NAME_.

Incorporate Greater Control Over Output Results

You can also achieve greater control over output results and make the information
you are reporting more informative by modifying the previous program slightly.
By default, the variable in the output data set that contains the name of the
transposed variables is called _NAME_. To assign a more descriptive name to
those values, use the NAME= option with the PROC TRANSPOSE statement.
Similarly, by default, the transposed variables in the output data set are called by
the assigned values in the input data. To assign a more descriptive name to these
variables, use the PREFIX= option with the PROC TRANSPOSE statement. In
this case, NAME=PRODUCT and PREFIX=TESTER, so the transposed variables
are named TESTER1, TESTER2, and so on.

The following program shows the previous program as well as the NAME=
and PREFIX= options. It omits the ID statement, which is no longer necessary
with the PREFIX= option.

```
libname in 'SAS-data-library';

proc transpose data=in.prod out=in.prod2 name=product prefix=tester;
   var period foodpr1 foodpr2 foodpr3 coffeem1 coffeem2 mw_oven1
       mw_oven2 dishwhr1 dishwhr2 dishwhr3;
run;
```

```
proc print data=in.prod2;
   title 'Results of Clinical Trials, Kitchen Products, 4/15';
run;
```

Output 9.10 shows the results.

Output 9.10
Making the PROC
TRANSPOSE Step
More Informative

```
                   Results of Clinical Trials, Kitchen Products, 4/15                    1

         P        T           T           T           T           T
         R        E           E           E           E           E
         O        S           S           S           S           S
         D        T           T           T           T           T
    O    U        E           E           E           E           E
    B    C        R           R           R           R           R
    S    T        1           2           3           4           5

    1 PERIOD    initial     final       initial     initial     final
    2 FOODPR1            115           86          93          73          101
    3 FOODPR2             45           27          52          35          127
    4 FOODPR3             65           55          63          43           39
    5 COFFEEM1            83           72          76         112           76
    6 COFFEEM2            78           86          88         108           79
    7 MW_OVEN1            55           74          69          47           58
    8 MW_OVEN2           113           39         127          98          101
    9 DISHWHR1            82           99         101          78          109
   10 DISHWHR2            45           65          32          51           47
   11 DISHWHR3            77           70          68          73           69
```

Collapsing Multiple Variables into a Single Variable

When you conduct a survey, it is to your advantage to allow the respondents flexibility in answering questions so they can respond as completely and as accurately as possible. Therefore, many market survey questions permit more than one answer. However, the more open-ended you make a survey, the more potentially complicated the process of analyzing the results.

Raw Data Example

To illustrate, consider a clothing manufacturer. Its market research department wants to poll customers concerning factors that influence their decisions for or against purchasing a raincoat. Customers are permitted to choose any combination of responses. The primary survey question reads as follows:

What factors influence your purchase of a raincoat? (circle all that apply)

A. I want the price to be as low as possible.
B. I want the raincoat to be washable.
C. I want the raincoat to have a zip-out lining.
D. I want the raincoat to have a hood.

This survey question has four responses, A, B, C, and D, which are used to create four variables. However, any subsequent data analysis can be greatly simplified if these variables are collapsed into one variable. This section shows you how to accomplish that task. In the following example, each record of raw data contains fields corresponding to the responses circled. Note that when a response is circled, it is assigned a value of 1; when not circled, it is assigned a value of 0. Several combinations of answers are possible.

Field	Description
A	response A of the survey
B	response B of the survey
C	response C of the survey
D	response D of the survey
sex	sex of the respondent

Here are the raw data records:

```
----+----1
0 0 0 1 m
1 1 0 0 f
0 0 0 1 f
0 1 1 0 f
1 1 0 0 m
1 0 1 1 m
0 0 0 0 m
0 1 1 0 f
1 1 1 1 f
1 0 0 1 f
0 0 1 1 m
1 0 1 1 m
1 0 1 1 f
1 0 1 0 f
0 0 1 0 m
----+----1
```

To analyze the responses to this question on the survey, the clothing manufacturer must do the following:

□   enter the values of the responses as four variables, one for each response

□   create a new variable, for which each value reflects a possible combination of answers

□   create a customized format that includes all of the new variable's possible values

□   associate the customized format with the newly created variable.

Enter the Values of the Responses as Four Variables

The first step is to enter the values of the responses as four variables, one for each response.

```
libname rainwear 'SAS-data-library';

data rainwear.survey;
   input A B C D sex $;
```

Again, when a response is selected, it is assigned a value of 1; otherwise, it is assigned a value of 0.

Create a Variable Whose Values Reflect All Possible Combinations of Answers

The next step is to create a variable whose values reflect all possible combinations of answers. As stated earlier, the primary survey question has four responses—A, B, C, and D. As before, when a response is circled, it is assigned a value of 1. When not circled, it is assigned a value of 0. Several different combinations of responses are possible. All of this information can be combined to create one variable whose various values represent each different combination of A, B, C, and D. To do this, the values of A, B, C, and D are treated as digits in a single binary number. Then the following mathematical equation that transforms binary values into decimal values is used to create a unique decimal value for each possible combination of the values of A, B, C, and D:

$$A(2^3) + B(2^2) + C(2^1) + D(2^0) = decimal\ value \quad .$$

The new decimal value is assigned to the variable NEWVAR.

```
libname rainwear 'SAS-data-library';

data rainwear.survey;
   input A B C D sex $;
   newvar=A*2**3+B*2**2+C*2+D;
```

The value of the new variable NEWVAR is set to a decimal value that represents the combination of answers for each observation.

The following table shows all possible values of A, B, C, and D that are represented by the variable NEWVAR's values:

NEWVAR	A	B	C	D	Meaning
0	0	0	0	0	circled no responses
1	0	0	0	1	circled D only
2	0	0	1	0	circled C only
3	0	0	1	1	circled C and D
4	0	1	0	0	circled B only
5	0	1	0	1	circled B and D
6	0	1	1	0	circled B and C
7	0	1	1	1	circled B, C, and D
8	1	0	0	0	circled A only
9	1	0	0	1	circled A and D
10	1	0	1	0	circled A and C
11	1	0	1	1	circled A, C, and D
12	1	1	0	0	circled A and B
13	1	1	0	1	circled A, B, and D
14	1	1	1	0	circled A, B, and C
15	1	1	1	1	circled all responses

The next step is to use the information in the table to create a user-defined format with the FORMAT procedure, as shown in the next section.

Create a Customized Format

The FORMAT procedure with a VALUE statement can be used to transfer the information from the earlier table to a form that the SAS System can use.

```
proc format;
   value choice  0='NONE'
                 1='D only'
                 2='C only'
                 3='C and D'
                 4='B only'
                 5='B and D'
                 6='B and C'
                 7='B, C, and D'
                 8='A only'
                 9='A and D'
                10='A and C'
                11='A, C, and D'
                12='A and B'
                13='A, B, and D'
```

```
                          14='A, B, and C'
                          15='A, B, C, and D';
            run;
```

In this example, the VALUE statement defines the format CHOICE., which associates the numeric values shown on the left-hand side of the equation with the character strings shown on the right. The format CHOICE. is associated with the variable NEWVAR in the PROC step shown later in this section.

Note that if you plan to store a format permanently so you can use it in subsequent sessions, you must use the LIBRARY= option with the reserved libref LIBRARY in the PROC FORMAT statement. For details, see Chapter 8, "Classifying Variables into Categories."

Now that a customized format has been created that includes all of NEWVAR's possible values, the next step is to associate the format with NEWVAR.

Apply the Customized Format

The last step is to apply the customized format. The FORMAT statement associates the format CHOICE. with the variable NEWVAR. Here is the entire program that creates and applies the customized format and creates and prints the data set.

```
libname rainwear 'SAS-data-library';

data rainwear.survey;
   input A B C D sex $;
   newvar=A*2**3+B*2**2+C*2+D;
   cards;
0 0 0 1 m
1 1 0 0 f
0 0 0 1 f
0 1 1 0 f
1 1 0 0 m
1 0 1 1 m
0 0 0 0 m
0 1 1 0 f
1 1 1 1 f
1 0 0 1 f
0 0 1 1 m
1 0 1 1 m
1 0 1 1 f
1 0 1 0 f
0 0 1 0 m
;

proc format;
   value choice  0='NONE'
                 1='D only'
                 2='C only'
                 3='C and D'
                 4='B only'
                 5='B and D'
```

```
                              6='B and C'
                              7='B, C, and D'
                              8='A only'
                              9='A and D'
                             10='A and C'
                             11='A, C, and D'
                             12='A and B'
                             13='A, B, and D'
                             14='A, B, and C'
                             15='A, B, C, and D';
            run;

            proc print data=rainwear.survey;
               format newvar choice.;
               title 'Rainwear Survey Results';
            run;
```

Output 9.11 shows the results.

Output 9.11
Collapsing
Multiple Variables
into a Single
Variable

```
                          Rainwear Survey Results                    1

          OBS   A   B   C   D   SEX   NEWVAR

           1    0   0   0   1    m    D only
           2    1   1   0   0    f    A and B
           3    0   0   0   1    f    D only
           4    0   1   1   0    f    B and C
           5    1   1   0   0    m    A and B
           6    1   0   1   1    m    A, C, and D
           7    0   0   0   0    m    NONE
           8    0   1   1   0    f    B and C
           9    1   1   1   1    f    A, B, C, and D
          10    1   0   0   1    f    A and D
          11    0   0   1   1    m    C and D
          12    1   0   1   1    m    A, C, and D
          13    1   0   1   1    f    A, C, and D
          14    1   0   1   0    f    A and C
          15    0   0   1   0    m    C only
```

The values of the new variable NEWVAR are now ready for further analysis, perhaps with the TABULATE procedure or the FREQ procedure.

Summary

The following points summarize how you can reshape data:

□ To create multiple observations from a single observation, you can use a three-step process, repeating the process for each variable you want to reshape.

  □ use an assignment statement to assign the value of the variable to a new variable

  □ create a new variable whose value corresponds to the numeric order of the test in a second assignment statement

  □ output the results.

□ As a shortcut approach to creating multiple observations from a single observation, use array processing.

□ To create a single observation from multiple observations, you can group the variables you want to reshape into an array. Then use iterative processing to complete the process.

□ To transpose observations and variables in a SAS data set, use the TRANSPOSE procedure. Use an ID statement to name the transposed variables. If you want to transpose any character variables, you must use a VAR statement. Once a VAR statement is used, it must include all of the variables to be transposed. To make your output more informative, add the NAME= and PREFIX= options to the PROC TRANSPOSE statement.

□ You can make it easier to analyze answers to multiple-response questions if you collapse the variables corresponding to the responses into one variable. Create a new variable whose values reflect all possible combinations of responses. Then create a customized format whose values reflect all of these possibilities. Associate the customized format with the new value you have created.

SAS Tools

This section summarizes syntax for the statements and procedures discussed in this chapter.

Statements

ARRAY *array-name* {*number-of-array-elements*} *array-element-1*
< . . . *array-element-n*>;
creates a named, ordered list of array elements that exists for processing the current DATA step. The *array-name* must be a valid SAS name. *Number-of-array-elements* is the number of array elements listed. Each *array-element* is the name of a variable to be included in the array.

variable=expression;
is an assignment statement. It causes the SAS System to evaluate the *expression* on the right side of the equal sign and assign the result to the *variable* on the left. You must select the name of the variable and create the proper expression for calculating its value. The same variable name can appear on the left and right sides of the equal sign because the SAS System evaluates the right side before assigning the result to the variable on the left side.

DO *index-variable=n* TO *number-of-array-elements*;
SAS statements
END;
is known as an iterative DO loop. In each execution of the DATA step, an iterative DO loop iterates based on the value of the *index-variable*. To create an index variable, simply use a SAS variable in an iterative DO statement. When you use iterative DO loops for array processing, the value of *index-variable* starts at *n* and increases by 1 before each iteration of the loop. When the value exceeds the *number-of-array-elements*, the SAS System stops processing the loop and proceeds to the next statement in the DATA step.

INPUT <*specifications*>;
    reads a record of raw data either from an external file or instream data lines.

OUTPUT <*SAS-data-set*>;
    immediately writes the current observation to the *SAS-data-set*. The observation remains in the program data vector, and you can continue programming with it, including outputting it again if you want. When an OUTPUT statement appears in a DATA step, the automatic output at the end of the DATA step no longer occurs.

Procedures

PROC FORMAT;
    VALUE *name value-1*='*formatted-value-1*'< . . . *value-n*='*formatted-value-n*'>;

    PROC FORMAT;
        begins the FORMAT procedure, which allows you to create your own formats and informats for character and numeric variables.

    VALUE *name value-1*='*formatted-value-1*'< . . . *value-n*='*formatted-value-n*'>;
        defines a format that writes a variable's value as a different value.

PROC TRANSPOSE <DATA=*SAS-data-set*> <OUT=*SAS-data-set*>
    <NAME=*variables-to-transpose*>
    <PREFIX=*name-of-variables-to-transpose*>;
    ID *name-of-variables-after-transpose*;
    VAR *variables-to-transpose*;

    PROC TRANSPOSE <DATA=*SAS-data-set*>
        <NAME=*variables-to-transpose*>
        <PREFIX=*name-of-variables-to-transpose*>;
    begins the TRANSPOSE procedure, which allows you to transpose the variables and observations in a SAS data set. The option NAME= specifies the name of the variable in the output data set that contains the name of the variable being transposed to create the current observation. The option PREFIX= specifies the prefix to use in constructing names of transposed variables in the output data set.

    ID *name-of-variables-after-transpose*;
        specifies a variable in the input data set. The formatted values of the ID variable are used as the names of the transposed variables in the output data set. Each formatted ID value should occur only once in the input data set or, if you use a BY statement, only once within a BY group.

    VAR *variables-to-transpose*;
        lists the variables to transpose. Without the VAR statement, all numeric variables in the input data set that are not listed in another statement are transposed.

Learning More

This section provides references for learning more about topics presented in this chapter.

□ For more information about manipulating variables, see the other chapters in Part 3, "Using Advanced Programming Techniques."

□ For further information about reading data, see Part 2, "Reading Raw Data."

□ See Chapter 7, "Grouping Variables to Perform Repetitive Tasks Easily," for greater coverage of array processing. For complete reference information, see *SAS Language: Reference, Version 6, First Edition*, Chapter 4, "Rules of the SAS Language."

□ See Chapter 3, "Reading Varying-Length Fields and Repeated Fields," and Chapter 7, "Grouping Variables to Perform Repetitive Tasks Easily," for greater coverage of iterative processing with DO loops. For complete reference information, see *SAS Language: Reference*, Chapter 9, "SAS Language Statements."

□ For information about ranking observations based on multiple variables, see Chapter 17, "Producing Summary Reports Using Descriptive Procedures."

□ For general information about SAS formats, see *SAS Language: Reference*, Chapter 3, "Components of the SAS Language." See Chapter 14, "SAS Formats," for complete syntax information about individual SAS formats.

□ For detailed syntax information about the ARRAY, assignment, DO, INPUT, OUTPUT, and SET statements, see *SAS Language: Reference*, Chapter 9, "SAS Language Statements."

□ For detailed syntax information about the FORMAT procedure and the VALUE statement, see *SAS Procedures Guide, Version 6, Third Edition*, Chapter 18, "The FORMAT Procedure."

□ For detailed syntax information about the TRANSPOSE procedure and the ID and VAR statements, as well as for the options used in this chapter with PROC TRANSPOSE, see *SAS Procedures Guide*, Chapter 41, "The TRANSPOSE Procedure."

Chapter 10 Performing a Table Lookup

Introduction

When you are programming, you may want to retrieve additional information from an auxiliary source based on the values of variables in that primary source. Known as *table lookup*, this processing technique is often used with the SAS System.

In this chapter
This chapter presents three ways to accomplish table lookup:

□ match-merging files based on values of a key variable. This kind of table lookup involves at least two files: a *primary file* that receives the additional information and a *lookup file* that provides the additional information.

□ using formatted data values as a lookup file to check data against a list, categorize data, or reshape variables to observations. This kind of table lookup can involve a single file that acts as the primary file and a set of SAS statements or multiple files that supply values and thus act as the lookup file.

□ retrieving selected information through direct access. This kind of table lookup involves two files, a primary file and a lookup file.

Prerequisites
To understand this chapter, you should be familiar with the following features of the SAS System:

□ DATA step processing

□ the SORT procedure

□ the FORMAT procedure

□ match-merging

□ array processing

□ the TODAY function

□ the PUT function.

Understanding Table Lookup

Table lookup is the technique you use to acquire additional information to supplement or replace information being processed. In its simplest form, table lookup involves only one file. You use a set of SAS programming statements to update the values in this file. In a more complex form, table lookup involves at least two files. The first, or primary file, is updated by associating one or more of its variables with key variables in a second file, known as a lookup file, and using that association to retrieve information. The information is then added to the primary file. In some cases, you may use more than one lookup file. The following section lists terms that are commonly used in discussions of table lookup.

Understanding Key Terms

Several terms are commonly used in discussions of table lookup. They are defined here for your reference:

primary file   is the file for which you want to obtain auxiliary information.

lookup file   is an auxiliary file that is maintained separately from the primary file and that is referenced for one or more of the observations of the primary file; sometimes a set of SAS statements provide values that act as the lookup file. The values of format tables also act as lookup files.

key variable   is the variable or variables whose values are the common elements between the primary file and the lookup file. Typically, key values are unique in the lookup file but not necessarily unique in the primary file.

lookup result   is the auxiliary information obtained using the key variable or variables as a reference into the lookup file.

seek operation   is the scanning or search operation involved in using the key variable or variables to access the lookup file.

Choosing Tools to Perform a Table Lookup

With the SAS System, several sets of tools are available to accomplish a table lookup:*

- □ array processing

- □ IF-THEN/ELSE statements or a SELECT group

- □ the MERGE statement and an associated BY statement referencing either a previously sorted variable or an indexed variable

- □ the SQL procedure

- □ the FORMAT procedure with the DATA step PUT function, with a FORMAT statement, or with array processing

- □ the SET statement with the POINT= option.

While you may be tempted to choose familiar tools, you should also consider the size of both your primary file and your lookup file. Some tools are recommended for smaller files and other tools are recommended for larger files.

The remaining sections in this chapter show you how to use some of the types of table lookup mentioned previously, beginning with a match-merge of two SAS data sets based on the common values of a key variable.

---

* Note that this chapter presents some but not all of the tools available for table lookup operations.

Match-Merging Two SAS Data Sets

Often you may have data in one file you want to combine with the data in a second file to create a third file that represents a superset or subset of the original data. If the two files contain a key variable, you can combine the two files by performing a match-merge operation. Note that match-merging requires both the primary file and the lookup file to be SAS data sets.

SAS Data Set Example

To illustrate, a hospital administration maintains many different data sets on patients. One data set—in this case, the primary file—contains information that enables the hospital to track the patients. Note that the data in this file are unique. The primary file, used for the examples in this section, contains the variables described in the following table:

Variable	Type	Description
LNAME	character	patient's last name
FNAME	character	patient's first name
STREET	character	patient's street address
IDCODE	character	identification code unique to each patient
PHONE	character	patient's phone number

The following PROC PRINT step displays the data set IN.PRIMARY:*

```
libname in 'SAS-data-library';

proc print data=in.primary;
   title 'Patients Tracking File';
run;
```

Output 10.1 shows the results.

Output 10.1
Printout of
IN.PRIMARY
Data Set

```
                              Patients Tracking File                           1

       OBS   LNAME       FNAME      STREET              IDCODE     PHONE

        1    Brown       Michael    1804 Downtown Dr.   BM684937   557-0074
        2    Bushnell    Wilbur     2904 Rosedale Ct.   BW129748   554-0552
        3    Coulston    Patrick    3038 Morone Rd.     CP061553   556-2581
        4    Dunlap      Lee        3015 Ignacius Street DL454167   553-8607
        5    Fuller      Deborah    1241 Ellis Place    FD518592   556-7076
        6    Geaghan     Jay        2269 Flyer Run      GJ133173   555-2605
```

---

*   The DATA step that creates IN.PRIMARY is shown in the Appendix.

```
     7   Graham      Patricia   130 Shasta Way        GP774960   555-7386
     8   Jones       Ian        924 Callinectes Ct.   JI927309   554-9994
     9   Kanehiro    Irene      3334 Islander Rd.     KI573115   554-5177
    10   Kcin        Regnad     1645 Stanton Drive    KR083870   553-3312
    11   Landing     William    1213 Moss Rd          LW631407   556-8780
    12   MacCormick  Bonnie     1049 Bianca St.       MB572315   555-7930
```

Another data set, the lookup file, contains information concerning the patients' current account balances. The lookup file contains the variables described in the following table:

Variable	Type	Format	Description
IDCODE	character		identification code unique to each patient
AMOUNT	numeric		amount of money the patient owes the hospital
DUEDATE	numeric	DATE7.	date payment is due

The following PROC PRINT step displays the data set IN.LOOKUP:*

```
libname in 'SAS-data-library';

proc print data=in.lookup;
   title 'Active Accounts';
run;
```

Output 10.2 shows the results.

Output 10.2
Printout of
IN.LOOKUP
Data Set

```
                     Active Accounts                         1

            OBS     IDCODE      AMOUNT    DUEDATE

             1      BM684937     948.25   06MAY91
             2      BW129748    1080.83   08APR91
             3      DL454167     150.99   01MAR91
             4      CP061553     632.98   26FEB91
             5      DS454167    2255.00   07MAY91
             6      FD518592    1600.80   11APR91
             7      GJ133173    2750.75   19FEB91
             8      GP774960    1365.90   11APR91
             9      JI927309     800.25   19FEB91
            10      KI573115     749.75   08MAY91
            11      KR083870     500.50   04MAR91
            12      LW631407     889.60   25FEB91
            13      MB572315     416.35   04APR91
```

---

* The DATA step that creates IN.LOOKUP is shown in the Appendix.

The variable common to both the IN.PRIMARY and IN.LOOKUP data sets is IDCODE. The SAS System can use the values of this variable as a key variable to accomplish the match-merge operation. Each of the next two sections shows you how to accomplish the match-merge operation. The first technique requires sorting prior to the merge, and the second doesn't.

Match-Merging Primary and Lookup Files, Preceded by Sorting

For more efficient record keeping, the hospital wants to match-merge IN.PRIMARY (the data set that tracks patients) with IN.LOOKUP (the data set for active accounts). This technique is recommended when both the primary file and the lookup file are large and, because its coding is simple, when programming time is a primary concern. Note that you can use the MERGE statement with a BY statement to access the information you want in the lookup file only if both the primary file and the lookup file are sorted by the key variable first.*

To merge the primary and lookup files, do the following:

□ make sure both data sets are sorted in ascending order of values of the key variable

□ merge the two data sets by the key variable to form a third data set

□ optionally, flag missing data from the match-merge operation for appropriate action.

Use the SORT procedure to sort the data sets. Optionally, you can use the OUT= option to specify the name of an output data set rather than replacing the original data set. Note that although this approach keeps the original data sets unchanged, it requires more storage space. The following example sorts the primary file IN.PRIMARY by IDCODE and outputs the results to the data set PRIMESRT. It sorts the lookup file IN.LOOKUP by IDCODE and outputs the results to the data set TRANSSRT. In each case, a temporary data set is created for the sorted data rather than replacing the original data set.

```
libname in 'SAS-data-library';

proc sort data=in.primary out=primesrt;
   by idcode;
run;

proc sort data=in.lookup out=transsrt;
   by idcode;
run;
```

---

* Note that if an index is present on the BY variable, the data do not have to be sorted.

After the data sets have been sorted, they can be match-merged. To match observations between two files according to the values of the BY variable, use the MERGE statement followed by a BY statement. Here, the data sets PRIMESRT and TRANSSRT are match-merged by the variable IDCODE.

```
data in.mrglook;
   merge primesrt transsrt;
   by idcode;
```

As a final step, you can flag missing data from the match-merge operation for appropriate action. Use the IN= data set option to create a variable that indicates whether the data set contributed data to the current observation. The value of the variable is 1 if it contributes to the observation and 0 if it doesn't. You can then use those values in further processing.

In this case, it is important to flag missing data from the primary file, PRIMESRT. The example creates a variable called TEST that indicates whether the data set PRIMESRT contributes data. When TEST is 0, the PUT statement writes the message, **data missing from PRIMESRT**, to the log:

```
data in.mrglook;
   merge primesrt(in=test) transsrt;
   by idcode;
   if test=0 then put 'data missing from PRIMESRT';
run;
```

Here is the entire program that sorts the primary and lookup files, performs the match-merge operation, prints the resulting data set, and writes the message to the SAS log:

```
libname in 'SAS-data-library';
options linesize=120;

proc sort data=in.primary out=primesrt;
   by idcode;
run;

proc sort data=in.lookup out=transsrt;
   by idcode;
run;

data in.mrglook;
   merge primesrt(in=test) transsrt;
   by idcode;
   if test=0 then put 'data missing from PRIMESRT';
run;

proc print data=in.mrglook;
   id idcode;
   title 'Tracking Information for Active Accounts';
run;
```

Output 10.3 shows the procedure output from the match-merge operation.

Output 10.3   *Accomplishing a Match-Merge Operation with the MERGE and BY Statements*

```
                        Tracking Information for Active Accounts                              1

        IDCODE     LNAME       FNAME       STREET                PHONE      AMOUNT    DUEDATE

        BM684937   Brown       Michael     1804 Downtown Dr.     557-0074   948.25    06MAY91
        BW129748   Bushnell    Wilbur      2904 Rosedale Ct.     554-0552   1080.83   08APR91
        CP061553   Coulston    Patrick     3038 Morone Rd.       556-2581   632.98    26FEB91
        DL454167   Dunlap      Lee         3015 Ignacius Street  553-8607   150.99    01MAR91
        DS454167                                                            2255.00   07MAY91
        FD518592   Fuller      Deborah     1241 Ellis Place      556-7076   1600.80   11APR91
        GJ133173   Geaghan     Jay         2269 Flyer Run        555-2605   2750.75   19FEB91
        GP774960   Graham      Patricia    130 Shasta Way        555-7386   1365.90   11APR91
        JI927309   Jones       Ian         924 Callinectes Ct.   554-9994   800.25    19FEB91
        KI573115   Kanehiro    Irene       3334 Islander Rd.     554-5177   749.75    08MAY91
        KR083870   Kcin        Regnad      1645 Stanton Drive    553-3312   500.50    04MAR91
        LW631407   Landing     William     1213 Moss Rd          556-8780   889.60    25FE●91
        MB572315   MacCormick  Bonnie      1049 Bianca St.       555-7930   416.35    04APR91
```

The following excerpt from the SAS log shows the message generated by the PUT statement.

```
data missing from PRIMESRT
NOTE: The data set IN.MRGLOOK has 13 observations and 7 variables.
```

The resulting data set IN.MRGLOOK contains seven variables: the key variable IDCODE from both data sets; LNAME, FNAME, STREET, and PHONE from the sorted data set PRIMESRT; and AMOUNT and DUEDATE from the sorted data set TRANSSRT. Note the absence of the variable TEST. Although the values of the IN= variables are available to program statements during the DATA step, the variables are not included in the SAS data set being created.

Joining Two Files without Prior Sorting

To perform the previous task without first having to make sure the two data sets are sorted or indexed, consider using the SQL procedure. Like the MERGE statement, the SQL procedure enables you to join corresponding observations from two or more SAS data sets into a single observation in a new SAS data set by the values of a key variable. However, unlike the MERGE statement, PROC SQL does not require sorted data or the creation of a new data set to store the results. Therefore, this technique saves disk space. This technique is also recommended when both the primary file and the lookup file are large.

Take the following steps to join two files using the SQL procedure:

□ create a PROC SQL view

□ retrieve the variables

□ reference the primary file and the lookup file as input sources

□ match values in the key variable to relate the two files

□ order the results by the key variable

□ print the results.

Explanations of the steps that accomplish this task follow.

Create a PROC SQL View

A *PROC SQL view* is a definition of a virtual data set that is named and stored for later use. This file contains no data, but it defines data that are stored in the PROC SQL view's underlying SAS data files or described by SAS/ACCESS views or other PROC SQL views. When data values are accessed through a PROC SQL view, the resulting data always reflect the most current values from the input sources (in this case, the primary file and the lookup file). Note that PROC SQL views are a type of SAS data view.

When you create a PROC SQL view, you must specify its name, the variables you want to select, and the source file or files of the data values. First, to create a PROC SQL view, use the CREATE statement with the keyword VIEW. In the following example, the CREATE statement tells the SAS System to create the view IN.COMBINE:

```
libname in 'SAS-data-library';

proc sql;
   create view in.combine as
```

Retrieve the Variables

To specify the variables to be retrieved, use the SELECT clause. List the variable names in the desired order of appearance, separated by commas.

```
libname in 'SAS-data-library';

proc sql;
   create view in.combine as
         select variable-1,variable-2,variable-3,variable-4,variable-5,
         variable-6,variable-7
```

Reference the Primary and Lookup Files as Input Sources

To designate an input source for the PROC SQL view, add the FROM clause to reference the primary file and the lookup file. In the following example, the FROM clause references the SAS data set IN.PRIMARY and assigns it an alias of P; it references the SAS data set IN.LOOKUP and assigns it an alias of L. Note that these aliases are used in the SELECT clause.

```
libname in 'SAS-data-library';

proc sql;
   create view in.combine as
         select p.idcode, lname, fname, street, phone, amount, duedate
         from in.primary as p, in.lookup as l
```

These aliases are temporary, alternate names assigned to qualify variable names so the correct variables are processed when the tables are joined. These aliases distinguish between variables that have identical names but that come from two different data sets.

Match Values in the Key Variable to Relate the Two Files

To relate the two files and ensure that the view selects only those observations for which the values of the key variable match, add a WHERE clause. Here, the WHERE clause specifies the condition that P.IDCODE, the key variable, must equal L.IDCODE.

```
libname in 'SAS-data-library';

proc sql;
   create view in.combine as
          select p.idcode, lname, fname, street, phone, amount, duedate
          from in.primary as p, in.lookup as l
          where p.idcode=l.idcode
```

Order the Results by the Key Variable

To specify the order in each observation, use the ORDER BY clause with the key variable. By default, the results are sorted in ascending order.

```
libname in 'SAS-data-library';

proc sql;
   create view in.combine as
          select p.idcode, lname, fname, street, phone, amount, duedate
          from in.primary as p, in.lookup as l
          where p.idcode=l.idcode
          order by p.idcode;
```

Print the Results

To print all the variables retrieved by the resulting view IN.COMBINE, use the asterisk (*) wildcard in a SELECT clause with a FROM clause (together, the two are known as a table expression). Note that the SQL procedure does not require a RUN statement or a PROC PRINT step; position the TITLE statement before the PROC SQL statement. However, to terminate the procedure, you must submit a QUIT statement or another PROC or DATA statement.

```
libname in 'SAS-data-library';
options linesize=120;
title 'Tracking Information for Active Accounts';
```

```
proc sql;
   create view in.combine as
         select p.idcode, lname, fname, street, phone, amount,duedate
         from in.primary as p, in.lookup as l
         where p.idcode=l.idcode
         order by p.idcode;
   select * from in.combine;
```

Output 10.4 shows the results.

Output 10.4   *Joining Two Files with the SQL Procedure*

```
                      Tracking Information for Active Accounts                         1

IDCODE     LNAME        FNAME       STREET                PHONE     AMOUNT  DUEDATE
----------------------------------------------------------------------------------------
BM684937   Brown        Michael     1804 Downtown Dr.     557-0074   948.25  06MAY91
BW129748   Bushnell     Wilbur      2904 Rosedale Ct.     554-0552  1080.83  08APR91
CP061553   Coulston     Patrick     3038 Morone Rd.       556-2581   632.98  26FEB91
DL454167   Dunlap       Lee         3015 Ignacius Street  553-8607   150.99  01MAR91
FD518592   Fuller       Deborah     1241 Ellis Place      556-7076   1600.8  11APR91
GJ133173   Geaghan      Jay         2269 Flyer Run        555-2605  2750.75  19FEB91
GP774960   Graham       Patricia    130 Shasta Way        555-7386   1365.9  11APR91
JI927309   Jones        Ian         924 Callinectes Ct.   554-9994   800.25  19FEB91
KI573115   Kanehiro     Irene       3334 Islander Rd.     554-5177   749.75  08MAY91
KR083870   Kcin         Regnad      1645 Stanton Drive    553-3312    500.5  04MAR91
LW631407   Landing      William     1213 Moss Rd          556-8780    889.6  25FEB91
MB572315   MacCormick   Bonnie      1049 Bianca St.       555-7930   416.35  04APR91
```

Using Formatted Data Values as a Lookup File

Table lookup can include data manipulation that falls into one of the following three categories:

□ checking data against a list

□ separating data into categories

□ reshaping variables to observations.

Although these forms of table lookup can include two separate files—one the primary file and the other the lookup file—they can also involve a primary file and a format table whose values act as a lookup file. Because formats can be created and stored separately from the program and data libraries, they are accessible to multiple users and can be altered without altering the DATA step. If you plan to store formats permanently so you can use them in subsequent sessions, you must use the LIBRARY= option with the reserved libref LIBRARY in the PROC FORMAT statement. For details, see Chapter 8, "Classifying Variables into Categories."

Checking Data Against a List

Often when you are processing a variable's data values, you may want to check those values against a list of entries. The point of this list-checking operation is to determine whether the value is present in the list and then take some action.*
This list checking is a form of table lookup that typically results in a subset of the original data values.

SAS Data Set Example

To illustrate, consider a hospital's surgery schedule. A master list of every surgeon and his or her surgical team is maintained; the list rarely changes. (This file is the primary file.) This master list is checked against two other lists of surgeons. One list contains the names of surgeons who operate on a Monday-Wednesday schedule, and the other list contains the names of surgeons who operate on a Tuesday-Thursday schedule. (These lists are lookup files.) These two lists change more often than the master list for reasons such as illness or vacation. This list-checking operation is performed weekly to create two surgical rosters: one for teams on a Monday-Wednesday schedule and one for teams on a Tuesday-Thursday schedule.

The following example shows the list-checking form of table lookup. The data set used for this example contains the variables described in the following table:

Variable	Type	Description
SURGEON	character	lead surgeon on surgical team
ASSIST	character	assisting surgeon on surgical team
SCRUB	character	scrub nurse on surgical team
ANESTH	character	anesthesiologist on surgical team

The following PROC PRINT step displays the data set IN.SURGTEAM, which is the master list (the primary file):**

```
libname in 'SAS-data-library';

proc print data=in.surgteam;
   title 'Surgical Team--Master List';
run;
```

---

* Data validation is one such action.

** The DATA step that creates IN.SURGTEAM is shown in the Appendix.

Output 10.5 shows the results.

Output 10.5
Printout of
IN.SURGTEAM
Data Set

```
                        Surgical Team--Master List                        1

      OBS     SURGEON      ASSIST        SCRUB        ANESTH

       1      Tran         Silva         Mohar        Rodwell
       2      Gerhard      Stewart       Ligon        West
       3      Johnson      Siu           MacKenzie    Short
       4      Estes        Petrie        Nuyen        Edelstein
       5      Frank        Robertson     Hoffman      McVeigh
       6      Cage         Landau        Lepone       Randall
       7      Ahmadi       Sherr         Just         Parker
       8      Sloan        Edwards       Kline        Tester
       9      Miller       Schwartz      Dingman      Perry
      10      Rhew         Cox-Lewis     Cesar        Biddle
      11      Junot        Meraz         Norton       d'Aubert
      12      O'Reilly     Donaldson     Willis       Marcantonio
      13      Grey         Wilson        Yancho       Edidin
      14      Matthews     Rice          Chang        Perez
      15      Smith        Caldwell      Sparkes      Winfield
      16      Wu           Jarvis        Stanton      Austin
      17      Taylor       Rippey        Campbell     Leff
      18      Potuzko      Martin        Truesdale    Zeng
```

Perform the following steps to do the list-checking operation:

□ create a format table or tables whose values act as the lookup file

□ check the primary file against the lookup file

□ use the checklist to create a subset of the data values from the primary file.

Create a Format Table Whose Values Act as the Lookup File

The first step in the list-checking operation is to create a format table that acts as a checklist against which to compare the master list. The values listed in this format table act as the lookup file. To create the format table, use a PROC FORMAT step. Use a VALUE statement to define the list of data values included in the format so the values of the variable can be associated with the new formatted values. Here, the goal is to develop a surgical roster for the Monday-Wednesday rotation. The following VALUE statement defines the format $SURGMW., which associates the character string `MW` with all the surgeons listed. While the names of surgeons can be added or removed, the lookup value remains the same.

```
proc format;
   value $surgmw 'Ahmadi','Frank','Junot',
                 "O'Reilly",'Potuzko','Rhew',
                 'Sloan','Tran','Wu'='MW';
run;
```

Note: The character value `O'Reilly` must be surrounded with double quotes because it includes a single quote.

Check the Primary File Against the Lookup File

To check the primary file against the lookup file, apply the customized format to the data values of the variable by using the PUT function. Here, the PUT function enables you to write the values of SURGEON with the $SURGMW. format. The result is a character string whose value matches the lookup result.

```
put(surgeon,$surgmw.)
```

Use the Checklist to Create a Subset of the Data Values

To create a subset of the primary file based on the formatted values, use the customized format within a subsetting IF statement:

```
libname in 'SAS-data-library';

data in.schedule;
   set in.surgteam;
   if put(surgeon,$surgmw.)='MW';
```

The SAS System evaluates the expression, which specifies that the format be applied to the values of the variable, as true or false. Here, the subsetting IF statement causes the DATA step to continue processing only the observations for which the value of SURGEON is **MW**. If the expression is false, the current observation is not written to the output data set.

Here is the entire program that creates and applies the customized format and creates and prints the data set.

```
libname in 'SAS-data-library';

proc format;
   value $surgmw 'Ahmadi','Frank','Junot',
                 "O'Reilly",'Potuzko','Rhew',
                 'Sloan','Tran','Wu'='MW';
run;

data in.schedule;
   set in.surgteam;
   if put(surgeon,$surgmw.)='MW';
run;

proc print data=in.schedule;
   title 'Monday-Wednesday Surgical Teams';
run;
```

Output 10.6 shows the current surgical roster for Mondays and Wednesdays.

```
                    Monday-Wednesday Surgical Teams                      1

     OBS     SURGEON      ASSIST        SCRUB        ANESTH

      1      Tran         Silva         Mohar        Rodwell
      2      Frank        Robertson     Hoffman      McVeigh
      3      Ahmadi       Sherr         Just         Parker
      4      Sloan        Edwards       Kline        Tester
      5      Rhew         Cox-Lewis     Cesar        Biddle
      6      Junot        Meraz         Norton       d'Aubert
      7      O'Reilly     Donaldson     Willis       Marcantonio
      8      Wu           Jarvis        Stanton      Austin
      9      Potuzko      Martin        Truesdale    Zeng
```

Separating Data into Categories

Often, for efficiency, you may want to use a lookup file to categorize data values. For example, a hospital's billing department sends out billing notices monthly. Because all accounts whose due dates fall within a certain range of time are treated identically, it is more efficient for the billing department to establish categories into which all accounts fall. An account is billed according to its assigned category.

SAS Data Set Example

The following example uses the SET statement to read the observations from the data set IN.MRGLOOK, created earlier in this chapter. The data set contains the variables described in the following table:

Variable	Type	Format	Description
LNAME	character		patient's last name
FNAME	character		patient's first name
STREET	character		patient's street address
IDCODE	character		identification code unique to each patient
PHONE	character		patient's phone number
AMOUNT	numeric		amount of money the patient owes the hospital
DUEDATE	numeric	DATE7.	date payment is due

The following PROC PRINT step displays the data set IN.MRGLOOK:

```
libname in 'SAS-data-library';
options linesize=120;

proc print data=in.mrglook;
   title 'Tracking Information for Active Accounts';
run;
```

Output 10.7 shows the results.

Output 10.7   *Printout of IN.MRGLOOK Data Set*

```
                        Tracking Information for Active Accounts                              1

    OBS    LNAME        FNAME      STREET              IDCODE     PHONE      AMOUNT   DUEDATE

     1     Brown        Michael    1804 Downtown Dr.   BM684937   557-0074    948.25  06MAY91
     2     Bushnell     Wilbur     2904 Rosedale Ct.   BW129748   554-0552   1080.83  08APR91
     3     Coulston     Patrick    3038 Morone Rd.     CP061553   556-2581    632.98  26FEB91
     4     Dunlap       Lee        3015 Ignacius Street DL454167  553-8607    150.99  01MAR91
     5                                                 DS454167              2255.00  07MAY91
     6     Fuller       Deborah    1241 Ellis Place    FD518592   556-7076   1600.80  11APR91
     7     Geaghan      Jay        2269 Flyer Run      GJ133173   555-2605   2750.75  19FEB91
     8     Graham       Patricia   130 Shasta Way      GP774960   555-7386   1365.90  11APR91
     9     Jones        Ian        924 Callinectes Ct. JI927309   554-9994    800.25  19FEB91
    10     Kanehiro     Irene      3334 Islander Rd.   KI573115   554-5177    749.75  08MAY91
    11     Kcin         Regnad     1645 Stanton Drive  KR083870   553-3312    500.50  04MAR91
    12     Landing      William    1213 Moss Rd        LW631407   556-8780    889.60  25FEB91
    13     MacCormick   Bonnie     1049 Bianca St.     MB572315   555-7930    416.35  04APR91
```

To place data in categories, do the following:

□ create a format table whose values act as the lookup file

□ create values in the primary file for comparison with the lookup values

□ categorize data from the primary file based on lookup values.

Create a Format Table Whose Values Act as the Lookup File

To create a customized format that categorizes data, use a PROC FORMAT step. Use a VALUE statement to define the values of each category it creates so the values of the variable can be associated with the new formatted values. As illustrated in the following list, the goal is to categorize accounts according to the number of days they remain unpaid.

□ Accounts unpaid for 0 to 30 days are considered due, and no reminders are sent.

□ Accounts unpaid for 31 to 60 days are considered overdue, and warnings are sent.

□ Accounts unpaid for at least 61 days are considered delinquent. Warnings are sent, and accounts are referred to a collection agency.

The following VALUE statement defines the format STATUS accordingly.

```
proc format;
    value status   0-30='due/no notice'
                  31-60='overdue/warning'
                 61-high='delinquent/referral';
run;
```

The values of this format table constitute the lookup file.

Create Values in the Primary File for Comparison with the Values in the Lookup File

The next step is to create a variable in the primary file whose values can be compared to the lookup values. Here, the goal is to create a variable whose values reflect the number of days an account remains unpaid. The example first creates a new data set and uses a SET statement to read observations from the data set IN.MRGLOOK. Then, it uses the TODAY function to return a SAS date value corresponding to the current date, which is assumed to be May 14, 1991. From that value, it subtracts the value of the variable DUEDATE for each observation. An assignment statement stores the results in the new variable DAYS:

```
libname in 'SAS-data-library';

data in.category;
   set in.mrglook;
   days=today()-duedate;
```

Categorize Data from the Primary File Based on Lookup Values

The final step is to use the categories established by the format table to categorize the data in the primary file. To apply the customized format to the data values of the variable, you can use a FORMAT statement in the PROC PRINT step if you want to report the values by category without creating a new variable. Here, the FORMAT statement associates the format STATUS. with the values of DAYS.

```
proc print data=in.category;
   format days status.;
   title 'Status of Active Accounts';
run;
```

Here is the entire program that creates and applies the customized format and creates and prints the data set.

```
libname in 'SAS-data-library';
options linesize=120;

proc format;
   value status  0-30='due/no notice'
                31-60='overdue/warning'
              61-high='delinquent/referral';
run;

data in.category(drop=duedate);
   set in.mrglook;
   days=today()-duedate;
run;
```

```
proc print data=in.category label;
   format days status.;
   title 'Status of Active Accounts';
   label days='account status';
run;
```

Output 10.8 shows the results.

Output 10.8   *Using a Lookup File to Categorize Data*

```
                              Status of Active Accounts                                    1

OBS   LNAME       FNAME      STREET              IDCODE      PHONE      AMOUNT    account status

  1   Brown       Michael    1804 Downtown Dr.   BM684937   557-0074    948.25   due/no notice
  2   Bushnell    Wilbur     2904 Rosedale Ct.   BW129748   554-0552   1080.83   overdue/warning
  3   Coulston    Patrick    3038 Morone Rd.     CP061553   556-2581    632.98   delinquent/referral
  4   Dunlap      Lee        3015 Ignacius Street DL454167  553-8607    150.99   delinquent/referral
  5                                               DS454167             2255.00   due/no notice
  6   Fuller      Deborah    1241 Ellis Place    FD518592   556-7076   1600.80   overdue/warning
  7   Geaghan     Jay        2269 Flyer Run      GJ133173   555-2605   2750.75   delinquent/referral
  8   Graham      Patricia   130 Shasta Way      GP774960   555-7386   1365.90   overdue/warning
  9   Jones       Ian        924 Callinectes Ct. JI927309   554-9994    800.25   delinquent/referral
 10   Kanehiro    Irene      3334 Islander Rd.   KI573115   554-5177    749.75   due/no notice
 11   Kcin        Regnad     1645 Stanton Drive  KR083870   553-3312    500.50   delinquent/referral
 12   Landing     William    1213 Moss Rd        LW631407   556-8780    889.60   delinquent/referral
 13   MacCormick  Bonnie     1049 Bianca St.     MB572315   555-7930    416.35   overdue/warning
```

Creating an Array Subscript to Reshape Variables to Observations

When you are updating a primary file with a lookup file, in some cases you may want to substitute variable values from the lookup file for variable values in the primary file (for example, to update data values or to replace character values with numeric values). And if you then want to process all of those values identically, as a further step, you may want to incorporate array processing into your table lookup operation. Note that this table lookup technique is favored not only for its efficiency in performing repetitive tasks but for two other reasons as well:

□ Array processing can be used to handle labels 1 to 200 characters long.

□ The lookup file can be stored and maintained separately.

This technique is recommended when both primary and lookup files are small.

SAS Data Set Example

To illustrate, a hospital accounting department bills for rooms by one of four daily rates based on the type of room a patient occupies:

□ intensive care unit

□ private room

□ semiprivate room

□ ward.

The daily rate for each room type fluctuates and is stored in a file called IN.TODAY, which contains the variables described in the following table:

Variable	Type	Description
RMTYPE1	numeric	daily rate for the intensive care unit
RMTYPE2	numeric	daily rate for a private room
RMTYPE3	numeric	daily rate for a semiprivate room
RMTYPE4	numeric	daily rate for a ward

The following PROC PRINT step displays the data set IN.TODAY (the lookup file):*

```
libname in 'SAS-data-library';

proc print data=in.today;
   title 'Daily Room Rates';
run;
```

Output 10.9 shows the results.

Output 10.9
Printout of
IN.TODAY
Data Set

```
                         Daily Room Rates                          1

           OBS    RMTYPE1    RMTYPE2    RMTYPE3    RMTYPE4

            1       800        500        350        100
```

Note that the variables RMTYPE1, RMTYPE2, RMTYPE3, and RMTYPE4 become the elements in the array RATES created later.

Another file called IN.RMINFO contains other occupancy information about patients whose files are active. This file contains the variables shown in the following table:

Variable	Type	Description
IDCODE	character	identification code unique to each patient
ROOM	character	type of room
NDAYS	numeric	number of days of occupancy

---

*   The DATA step that creates IN.TODAY is shown in the Appendix.

The following PROC PRINT step displays the data set IN.RMINFO (the primary file):*

```
libname in 'SAS-data-library';

proc print data=in.rminfo;
   title 'Patient Listing';
run;
```

Output 10.10 shows the results.

Output 10.10
Printout of
IN.RMINFO
Data Set

```
                             Patient Listing                                1

                   OBS     IDCODE     ROOM     NDAYS

                    1     BM684937     PVT       14
                    2     BW129748     WRD       11
                    3     CP061553     ICU       10
                    4     DL454167     SPT        4
                    5     FD518592     SPT        6
                    6     GJ133173     WRD        8
                    7     GP774960     ICU        7
                    8     JI927309     SPT        6
                    9     KI573115     PVT       12
                   10     KR083870     SPT       10
                   11     LW631407     WRD        3
                   12     MB572315     PVT        9
```

Every week, the accounting department performs two table lookup operations to update the file IN.RMINFO with the current room rates from the file IN.TODAY. The first operation determines the room type, and the second assigns room rates.

Take the following steps to perform two table lookup operations like those in the example:

□ create a format table whose values correspond to the array references in the array

□ read observations from both data sets and create the array group

□ perform both table lookup operations

□ perform the desired action to complete the task.

---

* The DATA step that creates IN.RMINFO is shown in the Appendix.

Create a Format Table Whose Values Act as a Lookup File

First, use a PROC FORMAT step to create a format table whose values act as a lookup file. The values of this customized format will correspond to the array references of the array group to be constructed later.* In the PROC FORMAT step, use a VALUE statement to define the format. Here, the VALUE statement defines the format $DAILY., which associates the character values ICU, PVT, SPT, and WRD with the values 1, 2, 3, and 4, respectively.

```
proc format;
    value $daily 'ICU'='1'
                 'PVT'='2'
                 'SPT'='3'
                 'WRD'='4';
run;
```

Note that the values ICU, PVT, SPT, and WRD are used as values for the variable ROOM in the data set IN.RMINFO. The values 1, 2, 3, and 4 will correspond to each array reference created by the array RATES.

Read Observations from Both Data Sets and Create the Array Group

When a lookup file contains only one observation, you need to read from that file just once. If you attempt to read past the end of the file, the DATA step stops. To prevent this, use the value of the automatic variable _N_ to control how many times the DATA step attempts to read from a file. In this example, the data set IN.TODAY is the lookup file that contains only a single observation, so the DATA step reads from it only on the first iteration.

```
libname in 'SAS-data-library';

data stay;
   if _n_=1 then
      set in.today;
```

Remember that the automatic variable _N_ counts the number of times the DATA step iterates or loops, incrementing by 1 with each iteration. Because _N_ is initially assigned a value of 1, observations for the data set IN.TODAY are read only once.

---

* Remember that an array reference is assigned automatically to an array element, with the form *array-name*{*subscript*}, where *subscript* is the position of the variable in the list. See Chapter 7, "Grouping Variables to Perform Repetitive Tasks Easily," for more information on array processing.

To arrange the variables from the lookup file into one group, use an ARRAY statement. Here, the variables RMTYPE1-RMTYPE4 are made to be elements of the array RATES.

```
libname in 'SAS-data-library';

data stay;
   if _n_=1 then
      set in.today;
   array rates{*} rmtype1-rmtype4;
```

To read observations from the primary file, add another SET statement. Here, the primary file is IN.RMINFO.

```
libname in 'SAS-data-library';

data stay;
   if _n_=1 then
      set in.today;
      array rates{*} rmtype1-rmtype4;
   set in.rminfo;
```

Perform Both Table Lookups to Assign Variable Values

The next step is to perform the table lookup operations necessary to reshape variable values. This example requires two table lookups, one to substitute the data values generated by the format $DAILY. for the variable ROOM, and the other to return a value for the variable RATE based on values of RMTYPE1 through RMTYPE4.

To write the values of ROOM as values corresponding to the array reference for each array element, the example uses the PUT function with the $DAILY. format created in the PROC FORMAT step.

```
put(room,$daily.);
```

Second, to read the results of the PUT function as numeric values, the example uses the INPUT function, applying the 1. informat.

```
input(put(room,$daily.),1.);
```

Finally, the resulting numeric value is used as the subscript of the array RATES to look up the value of RATE for each observation.

```
libname in 'SAS-data-library';

data in.stay;
   if _n_=1 then
      set in.today;
   array rates{4} rmtype1-rmtype4;
   set in.rminfo;
   rate=rates{input(put(room,$daily.),1.)};
```

For example, consider the value **PVT** for the variable ROOM. The value returned by the format $DAILY. is 2, which is written as a character value by the PUT function. When read by the INPUT function with the 1. informat, it becomes a numeric value, which is the array subscript. RATES{2} is the array reference for the variable RMTYPE2. A seek operation is performed on the array elements, and the value of 500 is returned.

Perform the Desired Action

The last step is to perform the desired action. The goal of this step is to calculate each patient's total bill by multiplying the values of the variable NDAYS by the values of the variable RATE. An assignment statement calculates the bill and assigns the value to the variable DOLLARS for each observation.

```
libname in 'SAS-data-library';

data in.stay;
   if _n_=1 then
      set in.today;
   array rates(4) rmtype1-rmtype4;
   set in.rminfo;
   rate=rates(input(put(room,$daily.),1.));
   dollars=ndays*rate;
```

The result is a total amount owed by each patient based on length of stay and room type. For example, the value of DOLLARS is 7000 for the patient whose identification number is BM684937, whose room type is private, and whose length of stay is 14 days.

Here is the entire program that performs both table lookup operations and prints the results.

```
libname in 'SAS-data-library';

proc format;
   value $daily 'ICU'='1'
                'PVT'='2'
                'SPT'='3'
                'WRD'='4';
run;

data in.stay;
   if _n_=1 then
      set in.today;
   array rates(4) rmtype1-rmtype4;
   set in.rminfo;
   rate=rates(input(put(room,$daily.),1.));
   dollars=ndays*rate;
   drop rmtype1-rmtype4;
run;
```

```
proc print data=in.stay;
   format dollars dollar6.;
   title 'Rooming Information, by Patient';
run;
```

Output 10.11 shows the results.

Output 10.11
Substituting
Lookup Values for
Primary Values
through Array
Processing

```
                     Rooming Information, by Patient                        1

        OBS      IDCODE      ROOM    NDAYS    RATE    DOLLARS

         1     BM684937      PVT      14      500     $7,000
         2     BW129748      WRD      11      100     $1,100
         3     CP061553      ICU      10      800     $8,000
         4     DL454167      SPT       4      350     $1,400
         5     FD518592      SPT       6      350     $2,100
         6     GJ133173      WRD       8      100       $800
         7     GP774960      ICU       7      800     $5,600
         8     JI927309      SPT       6      350     $2,100
         9     KI573115      PVT      12      500     $6,000
        10     KR083870      SPT      10      350     $3,500
        11     LW631407      WRD       3      100       $300
        12     MB572315      PVT       9      500     $4,500
```

Retrieving Lookup Records through Direct Access

As noted throughout this chapter, when you perform a table lookup, you must use the values of a key variable to look up information in an auxiliary file and add it to a primary file. This operation can be costly with large lookup files if you search the file sequentially until you match the values. It becomes crucial from an efficiency standpoint that you minimize the number of seek operations you perform to produce your lookup result. Instead of scanning a data set sequentially until you find the match you need, you can access the lookup result directly based on its location in the lookup file. This technique is known as *direct access*. If your files are entry-sequenced, you can obtain your lookup results directly, based on the physical location of a given value of the lookup variable. Note that direct access by observation number requires the lookup file to be a SAS data set.

To illustrate, a lending library has just been started for recovering patients of the thoracic unit (TH) and the cancer unit (CA); books have also been contributed by the Wellness Center (WC). The library contains a few books on medical and psychological topics of interest. If interest is sufficient, more books will be added and the library will continue to be supported. A primary file lists the books only by identification number and category (medical or psychology). A lookup file, which changes to reflect lending, lists the books by title. It also indicates the number of copies in and the number of copies out. After the first week of operation, staff in the thoracic unit perform a table lookup to update the primary file so they can determine the level of interest in books they have contributed.

To perform a table lookup like the one in this example and retrieve the lookup records through direct access, follow these steps:

□ assign the key variable's values in the primary file using an entry-sequenced method to indicate that record's location within the lookup file

□ store the lookup table as a SAS data set whose observations are sequenced to correspond to values of the key variable

□ use the key variable to access the lookup results.

Setting up the lookup file sequentially is essential to this kind of table lookup. Observations in the primary file may occur in any order as long as the key variable is assigned an appropriate value to associate it with the correct entry in the lookup file.

Assign the Key Variable's Values to Indicate Location

The first step is to assign the key variable's values to reflect a relative location in the respective lookup file when the primary file is created so the lookup records can be retrieved through direct access. Here, the book identification codes and categories are stored in the primary file IN.LIBRARY, which contains the variables described in the following table. The key variable is IDNO. Although the alphabetic portion of this variable varies, the numeric portion of the variable is sequential by unit or center, so the lookup records can be retrieved through direct access.

Variable	Type	Description
IDNO	character	identification code to each book
CATEGORY	character	type of book

The following PROC PRINT step displays the data set IN.LIBRARY:*

```
libname in 'SAS-data-library';

proc print data=in.library;
   title 'Library Inventory, Thoracic Unit';
run;
```

---

* The DATA step that creates IN.LIBRARY is shown in the Appendix.

Output 10.12 shows the results.

Output 10.12
Printout of
IN.LIBRARY
Data Set

```
                    Library Inventory, Thoracic Unit                    1

            OBS      IDNO       CATEGORY

             1      TH00001     medical
             2      WC00001     psychology
             3      TH00002     medical
             4      TH00003     psychology
             5      WC00002     psychology
             6      TH00004     psychology
             7      TH00005     medical
             8      TH00006     medical
             9      TH00007     medical
            10      TH00008     medical
            11      TH00009     medical
            12      CA00001     psychology
            13      TH00010     medical
            14      TH00011     medical
            15      TH00012     medical
            16      WC00003     medical
            17      TH00013     medical
            18      CA00002     medical
            19      TH00014     medical
```

Store Values in the Lookup Table Appropriately

The next step is to store the lookup table as a data set whose observations are sequenced to correspond to values of the key variable in the primary file. The lookup file IN.CHECKOUT contains the books' title information as well as their checkout status. This file contains the variables shown in the following table. The observation numbers and the values of SEQNO correspond sequentially to the numeric portion of the key variable in the primary file for a specific unit or center, in this case, thoracic. If the value of SEQNO does not reflect the correct location with respect to observation number and key variable value, the table lookup will not work.

Variable	Type	Description
SEQNO	numeric	sequence number assigned to a book
NUMIN	numeric	number of copies of a given book title currently available for lending
NUMOUT	numeric	number of copies of a given book title currently checked out
TITLE	character	title of book

The following PROC PRINT step displays the data set IN.CHECKOUT:*

```
libname in 'SAS-data-library';

proc print data=in.checkout;
    title 'Library Selections--Current Status, Thoracic Unit';
run;
```

Output 10.13 shows the results.

Output 10.13
Printout of
IN.CHECKOUT
Data Set

```
                 Library Selections--Current Status, Thoracic Unit              1

     OBS    SEQNO    NUMIN    NUMOUT    TITLE
      1       1        1        4       The Eight Week Cholesterol Cure
      2       2        2        2       Living With Heart Disease
      3       3        2        1       The Road Less Traveled
      4       4        1        0       Healthy Attitudes, Healthy Hearts
      5       5        2        4       Heart Disease:  Facts and Fiction
      6       6        3        4       Heart Attack:  Guide to Recovery
      7       7        2        3       Exercise Your Way to Better Health
      8       8        2        1       Changing Lifestyles
      9       9        1        0       Road to Recovery
     10      10        1        0       Treating Heart Disease
     11      11        2        3       The Oat Bran Story:  Myth or Miracle
     12      12        3        6       Stress:  Making an Enemy Your Ally
     13      13        1        4       Weight Loss the Sensible Way
     14      14        2        3       Heart Disease:  A Second Opinion
```

Use the Key Variable to Access the Lookup Results

The last step is to use the values of the key variable to access the lookup results. To perform the lookup operation, first read in observations from the primary file.

```
libname in 'SAS-data-library';

data lookup;
    set in.library;
```

You must use a portion of the key variable to gain access to the lookup file so you can read data values from it. Create a numeric variable (in this case, the variable FIND) whose values correspond to the location of each observation the SET statement reads from the lookup file. The first step you must take toward creating that variable is to remove the alphabetic portion of the key variable. To extract the numeric portion of the key variable, use the SUBSTR function. Here, the goal is to extract the string starting at position 3. The absence of a third argument specifies that the entire length of the remaining string is to be extracted.

```
substr(idno,3)
```

---

* The DATA set that creates IN.CHECKOUT is shown in the Appendix.

To convert the resulting character string to a numeric value, use the INPUT function with the desired informat. Here, the SAS System uses the 5. informat to read the character values as numeric values. It then uses the assignment statement to evaluate the expression and store the results in the variable FIND.

```
libname in 'SAS-data-library';

data lookup;
   set in.library;
   find=input(substr(idno,3),5.);
```

After a new numeric variable has been created, you can directly access observations from the lookup file. To access the correct observation in the lookup file, use the POINT= option in the SET statement. The POINT= option identifies the variable whose value represents the location (by observation number) of the observation you want the SET statement to read. In this example, the POINT= variable is FIND. Because the value of IDNO changes with each iteration, the value of FIND also changes. Here is the entire program that performs the table lookup operation and prints the resulting data set.

```
libname in 'SAS-data-library';

data lookup;
   set in.library;
   if substr(idno,1,2)='TH';
   find=input(substr(idno,3),5.);
   set in.checkout (drop=seqno) point=find;
run;

proc print data=lookup;
   title 'Current Status of Library, Thoracic Unit';
run;
```

Output 10.14 shows the results.

Output 10.14
Performing a Table Lookup Operation through Direct Access

```
                 Current Status of Library, Thoracic Unit                    1

    OBS   IDNO    CATEGORY   NUMIN NUMOUT  TITLE

     1  TH00001 medical       1      4    The Eight Week Cholesterol Cure
     2  TH00002 medical       2      2    Living With Heart Disease
     3  TH00003 psychology    2      1    The Road Less Traveled
     4  TH00004 psychology    1      0    Healthy Attitudes, Healthy Hearts
     5  TH00005 medical       2      4    Heart Disease:  Facts and Fiction
     6  TH00006 medical       3      4    Heart Attack:  Guide to Recovery
     7  TH00007 medical       2      3    Exercise Your Way to Better Health
     8  TH00008 medical       2      1    Changing Lifestyles
     9  TH00009 medical       1      0    Road to Recovery
    10  TH00010 medical       1      0    Treating Heart Disease
    11  TH00011 medical       2      3    The Oat Bran Story:  Myth or Miracle
    12  TH00012 medical       3      6    Stress:  Making an Enemy Your Ally
    13  TH00013 medical       1      4    Weight Loss the Sensible Way
    14  TH00014 medical       2      3    Heart Disease:  A Second Opinion
```

Note that the variable FIND, by default, is not added to the output data set because it is the POINT= variable. The POINT= variable is available anywhere in the DATA step, but it is not added to a new data set.

▶ *Caution* . . . . *The POINT= option does not work under certain circumstances.*
You cannot use the POINT= option with transport format data sets, compressed data sets, data sets in sequential format on tape or disk, and SAS/ACCESS views or the SQL procedure views that read from external files. ▲

Summary

The following points summarize how to perform table lookups:

□ Table lookup is a programming technique that enables you to retrieve a desired value or set of values from a SAS data set, an external file, or another source. One or more files can be involved. Several different sets of tools can be used to perform a table lookup. Consider the size of your files as you make your selection. Although many tasks are considered forms of table lookup, this chapter concentrates on match-merging files based on values of a key variable, using formatted data values as a lookup file, and retrieving lookup records through direct access.

□ The main file processed for which you want to obtain auxiliary information is known as a primary file. The auxiliary file that you access to obtain the additional information is known as the lookup file. These files must share a common variable, known as a key variable.

□ To match-merge files based on the values of a key variable, you can use the MERGE statement and the BY statement. You can use this technique only if both the primary file and the lookup file have been sorted by the key variable. Use the IN= data set option to create a variable that indicates whether the data sets contributed data to the current observation.

□ You can use the SQL procedure to join files without prior sorting. Use the CREATE statement to create a PROC SQL view, specifying its name, the variables you want to use, and the source files for the data. To specify the variables to be retrieved, use the SELECT clause, listing the variable names. Add the FROM clause to indicate the input source for the view, assigning temporary aliases to distinguish between variables from different sources with identical names. To make sure you keep only observations where the values of the key variable match, add the WHERE clause. Then add the ORDER BY clause to order the results.

□ You can use the FORMAT procedure to create a format table whose values act as a lookup file. This technique can be used in many different table lookup applications. In a list-checking operation, you can use a format table to determine whether a value from the primary file is specified in the list (lookup file) so you can take the appropriate action. For convenient processing, use the values of a format table to put the data values of a primary file into categories. A format table can be used to perform data substitution and to reshape variables to observations.

□ When your files are entry-sequenced, you can obtain lookup results based on the physical location of a given value of the lookup variable. This method is known as direct access. To use this method and thus obtain results in one seek operation, use the SET statement with the POINT= option.

SAS Tools

This section summarizes syntax for the statements, functions, data set option, procedures, and automatic variable discussed in this chapter.

Statements

ARRAY *array-name{number-of-array-elements} array-element-1*
    < . . . array-element-n>;
    creates a named, ordered list of array elements that exists for processing of the current DATA step. The *array-name* must be a valid SAS name. Each *array-element* is the name of an array element to be included in the array. *Number-of-array-elements* is the number of array elements listed.

variable=expression;
    is an assignment statement. It causes the SAS System to evaluate the *expression* on the right side of the equal sign and assign the result to the *variable* on the left. You must select the name of the variable and create the proper expression for calculating its value. The same variable name can appear on the left and right sides of the equal sign because the SAS System evaluates the right side before assigning the result to the variable on the left side.

BY *variable*;
    within a DATA step, controls the operation of the SET, MERGE, or UPDATE statement immediately preceding in the DATA step and sets up special grouping variables. The data sets listed in the SET, MERGE, or UPDATE statement must be sorted by the values listed in the BY statement or have an appropriate index.

FORMAT *variables <format>*;
    associates formats with variables in a DATA step.

IF *expression*;
    causes the DATA step to continue processing only those raw data records or observations from a SAS data set that meet the conditions of the expression specified in the subsetting IF statement. Therefore, the resulting SAS data set or SAS data sets contain a subset of the original external file or SAS data set.

IF *expression* **THEN** *statement*;
    for the observations from a file that meet the conditions specified in the IF clause, executes the statement following the THEN clause. *Expression* is any valid SAS expression, and *statement* is any executable SAS statement or DO group.

MERGE *data-set-name-1 <(data-set-options)>data-set-name-2*
    <(data-set-options)>;
    joins corresponding observations from two or more SAS data sets into single observations in a new SAS data set. The way the SAS System joins the observation depends on whether a BY statement accompanies the MERGE statement.

PUT *'character-string'*;
> writes the specified character string to the SAS log, by default.

SET *<data-set-name-1<(data-set-options-1)>>*
> *<... data-set-name-n<(data-set-options-n)>>*
> *<POINT=variable-name>;*
> reads observations from one or more SAS data sets. The SET statement reads
> all variables and all observations from the input data sets unless you tell it to
> do otherwise.
>> The following SET statement options are discussed in this chapter:

> *data-set-name*
>> specifies the name of the data set; in this chapter, two-level names are
>> used, but one-level names and special SAS data set names can also be
>> used.

> *(data-set-options)*
>> specifies actions the SAS System is to take when reading variables or
>> observations for processing.

> POINT=*variable-name*
>> reads SAS data sets using direct access by observation number.
>> *Variable-name* specifies the temporary variable whose value is the number
>> of the observation you want the SET statement to read. You must supply
>> the values of the POINT= variable.

Functions

INPUT(*source,informat*)
> returns the value produced when the source is read using a specified
> informat. *Source* contains the SAS expression to which you want to apply the
> *informat.*

PUT(*source,format*)
> returns a value using a specified format. *Source* contains the SAS expression
> whose value you want to reformat.

SUBSTR(*character-variable,position,n*)
> returns a portion of a value of a character variable when the SUBSTR
> function appears on the right side of the equal sign in an assignment
> statement.

TODAY ()
> returns the current date as a SAS date value.

Data set option

IN=*variable-list*
> in the SET, MERGE, or UPDATE statement, creates and names a variable that
> indicates whether the data set contributed data to the current observation.
> Within the DATA step, the value of the variable is 1 if the data set
> contributed data to the current observation and 0 otherwise.

Procedures

PROC FORMAT;
    VALUE *name value-1=’formatted-value-1’< . . . value-n=’formatted-value-n’>*;

    PROC FORMAT;
        begins the FORMAT procedure, which allows you to create your own
        formats and informats for character and numeric variables.

    VALUE *name value-1=’formatted-value-1’*
        < . . . value-n=’formatted-value-n’>;
        defines a format that writes a variable’s value as a different value.

PROC SQL;
    CREATE VIEW *view-name* AS *query-expression*;

    PROC SQL;
        begins the SQL procedure, which allows you to use Structured Query
        Language to create a report, a SAS data set, or both a SAS data set and a
        report from one or more data sets.

    CREATE VIEW *view-name* AS *query-expression*;
        creates a SAS data view as described in the *query-expression* that
        follows the keyword AS. A *query-expression* consists of clauses that
        describe the contents of the view. The following clauses are discussed
        in this chapter:

        SELECT *variable*< , . . . *variable-n*>
            specifies the variables to appear in the view. Place a comma
            between the variable names. You can list the variables by name
            only or as a variable name preceded by an alias and a period, as
            follows:

                alias.variable

        FROM *from-list*
            lists the SAS data set or data sets from which the new data
            view is to be constructed. The *from-list* can consist simply of
            data set names or of data set names and assigned aliases. If
            you list multiple data sets, separate them with commas.

        WHERE *where-expression*
            specifies one or more conditions for inclusion for each
            observation in the SAS data set or data sets in the FROM
            clause. A *where-expression* can consist of any valid SQL
            expression.

        ORDER BY *variable*
            specifies the variable by which the observations are to be
            sorted before the view is created.

Automatic variable

_N_

represents the number of times a DATA step has iterated. _N_ is initially set to 1. Each time the DATA step loops past the DATA statement, _N_ is incremented by 1.

Learning More

This section provides references for learning more about the topics presented in this chapter.

□ The SAS System has other tools available that you can use for table lookup operations. For a general overview of tools available, as well as examples, see "A Survey of Table Lookup Techniques for the SAS System" by Johnstone and Ray in *Proceedings of the Fourteenth Annual SAS Users Group International Conference*.

□ For complete reference information about array processing, see *SAS Language: Reference, Version 6, Third Edition*, Chapter 4, "Rules of the SAS Language." For more detailed usage information, see Chapter 7, "Grouping Variables to Perform Repetitive Tasks Easily", in this book.

□ For instruction on how to store formats permanently, see Chapter 8, "Classifying Variables into Categories", in this book. For general information about SAS formats, see *SAS Language Reference*, Chapter 3, "Components of the SAS Language." See Chapter 14, "SAS Formats," for complete syntax information about individual SAS formats.

□ For other examples of reshaping variables to observations, see Chapter 9, "Reshaping Data", in this book.

□ For detailed syntax information about the ARRAY, assignment, BY, FORMAT, subsetting IF, IF-THEN, MERGE, PUT, and SET statements, see *SAS Language: Reference*, Chapter 9, "SAS Language Statements."

□ For detailed syntax information about the INPUT, PUT, SUBSTR, and TODAY functions, see *SAS Language: Reference*, Chapter 11, "SAS Functions."

□ For detailed syntax information about the data set option IN=, see *SAS Language: Reference*, Chapter 15, "SAS Data Set Options."

□ For detailed syntax information about the FORMAT procedure and the VALUE statement, see *SAS Procedures Guide, Version 6, Third Edition*, Chapter 18, "The FORMAT Procedure." See Chapter 31, "The SORT Procedure," for detailed syntax information about the SORT procedure.

□ For complete reference and usage information about the SQL procedure and all of its statements and options, see *SAS Guide to the SQL Procedure, Usage and Reference, Version 6, First Edition*.

□ See *SAS Language: Reference*, Chapter 2, "The DATA Step," for further details on the automatic variable _N_.

Chapter 11 Smoothing Data

Introduction

When examining data collected over time, you may find considerable variation among observations. Decreasing the variation by smoothing the data can make it easier to determine trends when you graph the smoothed values. Replacing input with moving averages is a smoothing technique. When values are temporally ordered, you can substitute means over longer periods of time for individual observations to level off the peaks and valleys.

In this chapter
This chapter shows you how to calculate moving averages.

Prerequisites
To understand the example and discussion in this chapter, you should be familiar with the basics of DATA step programming.

SAS Data Set Example

In the example in this chapter, the manager of a bookstore is trying to determine trends for college textbook sales over the past year.* At this college, the spring semester lasts from early January until early May, and the fall semester lasts from the middle of August until the middle of December. Sales are high at the beginning of each semester, low in the middle of each semester, and moderate in exam months and summer months. Each observation in the data set contains values for the following variables:

Variable	Type	Description
MONTH	character	name of the month
SALES	numeric	number of books sold

---

* The DATA step that creates MYLIB.BOOKS is shown in the Appendix.

The following PROC PRINT step displays the data set MYLIB.BOOKS:

```
libname mylib 'SAS-data-library';

proc print data=mylib.books;
   title 'Textbook Sales';
run;
```

Output 11.1 shows the results.

Output 11.1
Printout of Data
Set MYLIB.BOOKS

```
                        Textbook Sales                              1

              OBS      MONTH      SALES

                1        jan        805
                2        feb        472
                3        mar         74
                4        apr        193
                5        may        340
                6        jun        518
                7        jul        215
                8        aug        947
                9        sep        636
               10        oct        102
               11        nov        181
               12        dec        505
```

Figure 11.1* shows the variation over time that makes this data set a candidate for smoothing. The plot demonstrates how sales of college textbooks vary from month to month over one year. In this case, demand changes over time because of how semesters are scheduled.

---

* Figure 11.1 and Figure 11.2 were produced with the GPLOT procedure, which is a feature of SAS/GRAPH software.

Figure 11.1   *Plot of Sales Values*

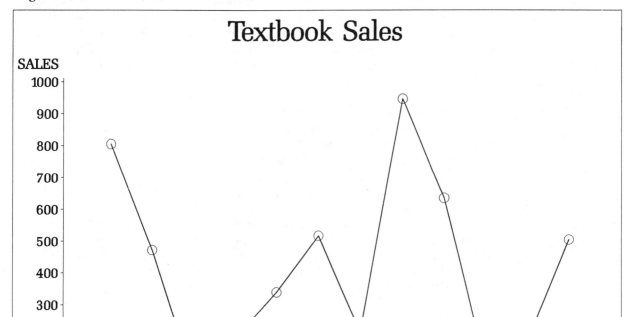

Understanding Moving Averages

When data seem erratic, a cyclic trend often explains the variation. Weather observations tend to vary considerably from month to month and season to season but remain relatively consistent from year to year. Consequently, sales of seasonal goods, such as short pants, umbrellas, earmuffs, sunglasses, rakes, and snow tires tend to fluctuate as well. Plotting smoothed data instead of actual values can help you determine trends more easily with a more compact, focused, and flowing curve. Visually, data smoothing transforms a series of lines with sharp connecting points into a curve with smooth turning points.

When analyzing such data, you may want to smooth your data by using a *moving average*. A moving average associates each observation with a mean of consecutive values. A two-point moving average takes the mean of two consecutive values. An example of a two-point moving average is replacing an observation for Sunday with the mean of the observations for Sunday and for Monday and replacing an observation for Monday with the mean of the observations for Monday and for Tuesday and so forth. In general, a *k*-point moving average takes the mean of *k* consecutive values.

Notice that this definition only requires consecutive values. For example, a four-point moving average for 1983 could be the mean of values for 1980, 1981, 1982, and 1983 or the mean of values for 1983, 1984, 1985, and 1986. Or the current observation could come in either of the middle positions. As long as you are consistent, you can let characteristics of the data suggest the number of points and the placement of the current observation.

Because of missing values before and after the range of time of a data set, a moving average with two or more points cannot be defined for each observation. For example, a five-point moving average for each day in January would be undefined for four observations. If the current observation were placed in the third position, the moving average would be undefined for the first, second, thirtieth, and thirty-first days. At each observation, this moving average would equal the mean of the current observation, the two previous observations, and the two following observations. For the first two days of the month, previous days would have missing values, and for the last two days of the month, following days would have missing values. The placement of the current observation determines where the moving average is undefined. If the current observation in this case were at the end of the string of five observations, the moving average would be undefined for the first four days of the month. In general, a k-point moving average is undefined at $k-1$ observations.

In the following example, a three-point moving average smooths data that change considerably from month to month. However, for data with elongated peaks and valleys over many months, a twelve-point moving average might be more appropriate. In this case, the current observation could be at the beginning, the end, or anywhere in the middle of the string of twelve observations, and the moving average would be undefined for eleven observations. For daily observations that show a cycle of one week, a seven-point moving average might be appropriate. This moving average would be undefined at six observations.

Calculating Moving Averages

To calculate a moving average, you need to compute means for strings of successive observations. These strings of observations are either a current observation with following observations, a current observation with previous observations, or a current observation with both following and previous observations. This example shows how to calculate a three-point moving average with the current observation in the middle position. At each observation, the moving average equals the mean of the following month, the current month, and the previous month.

To include values for following observations in your moving average, you can use SET statements with the FIRSTOBS= option. The FIRSTOBS= option causes data set processing to begin at the specified observation. For each following month included in your moving average, use a SET statement with the next-highest starting point specified in the FIRSTOBS= option and define a new variable to equal the value for that month. In this example, FIRSTOBS=2 means that the sales total for February is processed first. That value of SALES is set equal to the variable NEXTMON, and on the following iteration of the DATA step, the value of SALES for March is set equal to NEXTMON.

```
libname mylib 'SAS-data-library';

data smooth;
   set mylib.books(firstobs=2);
   nextmon=sales;
```

If this moving average included the values for two following months instead of one, the program would also need a SET statement with FIRSTOBS=3 and a new variable equal to the sales totals for the second month ahead.

To include values for previous observations in your moving average, you can use the LAG function. The LAG function returns a previous value of a variable. For each previous month included in your moving average, use a LAG function with the number of observations behind the current observation. In this example, on the first iteration of the DATA step, SALES equals the sales total for January, and LAG1(SALES) is missing. On the following iteration, SALES equals the sales total for February, and LAG1(SALES) equals the sales total for January.

To compute the moving average, define a variable equal to the sum of the included observations divided by the number of points. In this example, SMSALES equals one third of the sum of the previous month, the current month, and the following month.

```
   set mylib.books;
   smsales=(lag1(sales)+sales+nextmon)/3;
run;
```

If this moving average included the values for two previous months instead of one, the program would also need LAG2(SALES).

To print only those observations where the moving average is defined, you can use the FIRSTOBS= option with the PRINT procedure. To avoid printing observations whose previous values are not defined, specify the starting point as one more than the highest LAG function. This starting point is the first observation where all the components of the moving average are defined. In this example, FIRSTOBS=2 is specified with the PRINT procedure because LAG1 is the highest LAG function used. Since the DATA step stops executing when it encounters the end of the file given in the SET statement with the highest starting point specified in the FIRSTOBS= option, none of the observations with missing values for following observations are included in the new data set.

```
proc print data=smooth(firstobs=2);
```

Here is the complete program that produces and prints the three-point moving average for the textbook sales figures:

```
libname mylib 'SAS-data-library';

data smooth(drop=nextmon);
   set mylib.books(firstobs=2);
   nextmon=sales;
   set mylib.books;
   smsales=(lag1(sales)+sales+nextmon)/3;
run;

proc print data=smooth(firstobs=2);
   title 'Smoothed Textbook Sales';
run;
```

Output 11.2 shows the results.

Output 11.2
Calculating a
Moving Average

```
                      Smoothed Textbook Sales                        1

           OBS    MONTH    SALES    SMSALES

            2      feb      472     450.333
            3      mar       74     246.333
            4      apr      193     202.333
            5      may      340     350.333
            6      jun      518     357.667
            7      jul      215     560.000
            8      aug      947     599.333
            9      sep      636     561.667
           10      oct      102     306.333
           11      nov      181     262.667
```

Since the data set contains sales from only one calendar year, the three-point moving average is undefined for January and December due to a missing value for a neighboring month. Showing a value for SMSALES for these months would be misleading because the moving average would be based only on two months instead of three.

Figure 11.2 shows both SALES and SMSALES. Notice how much easier you can determine a trend by looking at the smoothed data. The new plot suggests a smooth curve and is much more compact.

Figure 11.2   *Plot of Smoothed Sales Values*

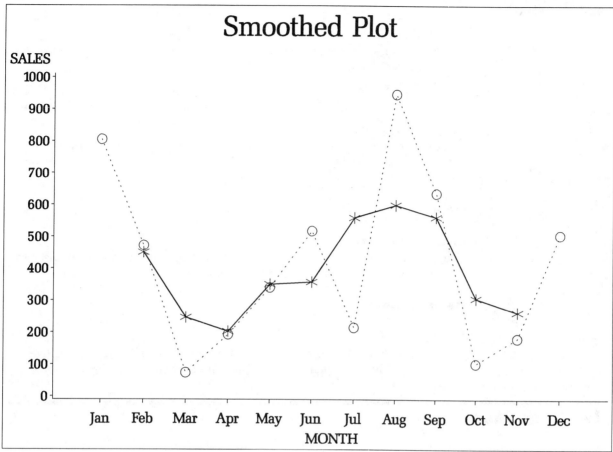

Summary

The following points summarize how to use the SAS System to smooth data:

□ To include values for following observations in your moving average, use additional SET statements with the FIRSTOBS= option and define variables to equal the values of following observations.

□ To include values for previous observations in your moving average, use the LAG function.

SAS Tools

This section summarizes syntax for the statements, functions, and data set options discussed in this chapter.

Statements

variable=expression;
> is an assignment statement that evaluates an expression and stores the result in a variable. *Variable* names a new or existing variable. *Expression* is any valid SAS expression.

Functions

LAG <*n*>(*argument*)
> returns a value from a queue where *n* is the length of the queue. *N* specifies the number of lagged values. *Argument* is numeric or character.

Data set options

FIRSTOBS=*n*
> causes processing to begin with the *n*th observation. *N* specifies a positive integer less than or equal to the number of observations in the data set.

Learning More

This section provides references for learning more about topics presented in this chapter.

□ Chapter 9, "SAS Language Statements," of *SAS Language: Reference, Version 6, First Edition* shows how to use multiple SET statements in a DATA step.

□ For detailed information about the LAG function, see Chapter 11, "SAS Functions," of *SAS Language: Reference*. Chapter 3, "Components of the SAS Language," discusses SAS functions in general.

□ To learn about the GPLOT procedure and other features of SAS/GRAPH software, see *SAS/GRAPH Software: Reference, Version 6, First Edition, Volume 1* and *Volume 2*.

Chapter **12** Taking Random Samples

Introduction

When working with a large data set, you may want to examine only a portion of observations to save time or money. This chapter shows you how to randomly select a smaller group of data from a large data set. Once you have taken a random sample properly, you can analyze it to answer questions about the original data set.

In this chapter
This chapter shows you how to take the following types of random samples:

☐ approximate-sized without replacement

☐ exact-sized without replacement

☐ exact-sized with replacement

☐ stratified of equal-sized groups

☐ stratified of unequal-sized groups.

Prerequisites

To understand the examples and discussions in this chapter, you should be familiar with the basics of DATA step programming.

SAS Data Set Example

In the examples in this chapter, the president of a small business is looking for alternate ways of sending products to regular customers. These buyers place their orders, and the company ships the goods by various mailing services. The data set contains the last names of the people who have been doing business with the company over the past year, the average monthly cost of sending packages and mail to them, and the location of the address (either inside or outside city limits). Each observation in the data set contains values for the following variables:

Variable	Type	Description
NAME	character	last name of the customer
COST	numeric	average monthly mailing cost
CITY	character	location of the address

The following PROC PRINT step displays the data set MYLIB.MAIL:*

```
libname mylib 'SAS-data-library';

proc print data=mylib.mail;
   title 'Mailing Costs';
run;
```

Output 12.1 shows the results.

Output 12.1
Printout of Data
Set MYLIB.MAIL

```
                      Mailing Costs                          1

           OBS    NAME        COST    CITY

            1     Agerton     17.28    in
            2     Allison     17.89    out
            3     Alverson    50.73    out
            4     Baldwin     67.66    out
            5     Beck        23.37    out
            6     Blevins     42.63    out
            7     Brown       48.67    out
            8     Chung       24.69    out
            9     Clark        3.23    in
           10     Cochran     38.62    out
           11     Dominger     8.83    out
           12     Dyer        62.88    in
           13     Fuller      58.99    out
           14     Goff        22.63    in
           15     Guillet     62.72    out
           16     Henzi        8.12    out
           17     Heuser      31.25    out
```

* The DATA step that creates MYLIB.MAIL is shown in the Appendix.

```
        18     Hibbert       77.83    out
        19     Holiday        9.46    out
        20     Krista        10.00    in
        21     Lanthier      52.63    out
        22     Lippert       23.84    out
        23     Magoulas      38.33    out
        24     McFann         8.33    out
        25     Moynihan       6.06    in
        26     Namboodri     24.38    out
        27     Newton         5.40    in
        28     Nist           8.35    in
        29     Parks         47.69    out
        30     Phelan        59.75    out
        31     Ritchie       76.01    out
        32     Rodriguez      5.78    in
        33     Rogers        33.45    out
        34     Salomon       25.36    out
        35     Sheldrick     58.26    out
        36     Slaton        38.78    out
        37     Terwilliger   88.22    out
        38     Veleff        54.72    out
        39     Vinson        49.53    in
        40     Whidby        52.25    out
```

Understanding Random Samples

When analyzing a large data set, you may want to take a random sample rather than conduct a census, or complete examination, because of limits on time, money, or computer resources. Further, you should randomly select observations so that your sample can be representative of the entire group. The examples in this chapter take samples of 10 from a list of 40 customers. You would probably choose to conduct a census if this were your actual data set. Taking random samples is a practical technique for analyzing data when you have much larger data sets containing hundreds or thousands of observations. Once you know the size of your sample and that you can generalize results from that sample to the larger group, then you are ready to decide which method of sampling is appropriate.

Two ways of taking a sample are with replacement and without replacement. The only difference is that when *sampling with replacement*, you can select each observation more than once, but when *sampling without replacement*, you can include each selected observation only once. If you want to make sure that no observation is repeated, take a random sample without replacement.

Another type of random sample discussed in this chapter is the *stratified random sample*. You can use a stratified random sample to select specific numbers of observations from different categories to include in your sample. For example, the president of the company might want to stratify the sample, or arrange the sample into classes, on the basis of whether or not the customer's address is in the city. The cost of mailing to local customers can be examined separately from the cost of mailing to the others since the solution for reducing expenses could be different for the two groups. The final decision might be to switch to a less expensive express mailing service for the out-of-town customers and to buy a van and hire a part-time employee to deliver mail locally.

Taking Random Samples without Replacement

Recall that sampling without replacement means that an observation does not go back into the pool of possible choices once it has been selected. In these two methods, each observation is included in the sample only once if it is selected. If you need a precise number of observations in your sample, you can take an exact-sized random sample, but if the sample size does not have to be exact, it is easier to take an approximate-sized random sample.

Taking Approximate-Sized Random Samples

Taking an approximate-sized random sample is the easier method when the size of your sample does not need to be exact. In this case, the target sample size is 10, but the actual sample contains 11 observations.

To specify a condition for randomly including observations in a sample, you can use a subsetting IF statement with the random number function RANUNI. The RANUNI function returns a (pseudo) random number from 0 to 1 for every observation in the large data set. The criterion for selection in your sample is that an observation's corresponding random number is less than or equal to the specified probability, or a chance from 0 to 1. Since MYLIB.MAIL has 40 observations, about one fourth of the customers should be selected to make a sample of approximately 10. Because the target sample size is one quarter the size of the original data set, the probability of each observation being included in the sample is .25.

```
libname mylib 'SAS-data-library';

data approx;
   set mylib.mail;
   if ranuni(7837599)<=.25;
```

In each iteration of the DATA step, the RANUNI function returns a random number from 0 to 1. In this example, only those observations with a corresponding number from 0 to .25 are included in the sample. With the RANUNI function, you must specify a nonnegative *seed*, or arbitrary starting point, less than 2,147,483,647. Here, a positive seed, 7,837,599, is specified with the function to begin generating random numbers. Every time this exact seed is given, the RANUNI function produces the same series of random numbers; therefore, the sample is the same size with the same observations. If you choose a positive seed, you can reproduce the sample by specifying the same seed. If you choose zero as the seed, the computer clock time at execution is used, but you may find it difficult to replicate your sample.

Here is the complete program that produces and prints the random sample of approximately ten customers with no repeated observations:

```
libname mylib 'SAS-data-library';

data approx;
   set mylib.mail;
   if ranuni(7837599)<=.25;
run;

proc print;
   title 'Approximate-Sized Random Sample';
run;
```

Output 12.2 shows the results.

Output 12.2
Taking an
Approximate-Sized
Random Sample

```
                 Approximate-Sized Random Sample                    1

       OBS    NAME        COST    CITY

         1    Blevins     42.63   out
         2    Brown       48.67   out
         3    Dyer        62.88   in
         4    Guillet     62.72   out
         5    Henzi        8.12   out
         6    Krista      10.00   in
         7    Lanthier    52.63   out
         8    Magoulas    38.33   out
         9    McFann       8.33   out
        10    Namboodri   24.38   out
        11    Whidby      52.25   out
```

Taking Exact-Sized Random Samples

With the previous technique for taking a random sample, the sample size is not always exact because the chance of selecting an observation remains constant. In fact, the proportion of random probabilities less than or equal to a specified probability usually changes from trial to trial. However, if you need to take a sample of a specific size with no duplicate observations, you can vary the probability of observations being selected according to the number of observations needed to complete your sample and the number of observations left to read in your data set.

To define two variables to represent the number of observations needed to complete your sample and the number of observations left to read in your data set, you can use the RETAIN statement. In the following example, K is the number of observations needed to complete the sample. K is initialized to 10 in the RETAIN statement because the sample size is ten. N is the number of observations left to read in the data set. Initially, 10 observations are needed to complete the sample, and 40 observations are left to read in the data set. These values change during the selection of the sample and are retained from one iteration to the next because of the RETAIN statement.

```
libname mylib 'SAS-data-library';

data exact;
   retain k 10 n;
```

When you don't know the total number of observations in your data set, you can initialize your variable representing the number of observations left to read by using the NOBS= option and an IF-THEN statement. (When you do know the total number of observations in your data set, it is easier to initialize the variable representing the number of observations left to read by listing that value after the variable in the RETAIN statement.) The NOBS= option creates and names a temporary variable whose value is the total number of observations in the data set. To set the variable representing the number of observations left to read in your data set equal to the total number of observations in your data set, use the automatic variable _N_ in an IF-THEN statement. Every DATA step creates an automatic variable denoted _N_. It is initially set at 1, and each time the DATA step iterates, _N_ increases by 1.

```
   if _n_=1 then n=total;
   set mylib.mail nobs=total;
```

In this example, the NOBS= option creates the variable TOTAL, which is equal to 40. On the first iteration of the DATA step, N is initialized to 40 because _N_ equals 1.

To randomly select observations for your sample based on a probability that varies with the number of observations needed to complete your sample and the number of observations left to read in your data set, you can use the RANUNI function in an IF-THEN statement followed by a DO group containing an OUTPUT statement. The criterion for selection in your sample is that an observation's corresponding random number is less than or equal to the number of observations needed to complete your sample divided by the number of observations left to read in your data set. If an observation is chosen for the sample, the OUTPUT statement immediately writes that observation to the specified SAS data set, and the number of observations needed to complete the sample decreases by 1. The number of observations left to read in the data set decreases by 1 whether or not the observation is included in the sample.

```
   if ranuni(747088789)<=k/n then
      do;
         output;
         k=k-1;
      end;
   n=n-1;
```

In this example, the arbitrary positive seed specified with the RANUNI function is 747,088,789. If the random number generated is less than or equal to K divided by N, which is initially one fourth, the observation is written to the data set EXACT, and K decreases by 1. N decreases by 1 at the end of each iteration.

To stop collecting observations when your sample reaches its specified size, you can use the STOP statement in an IF-THEN statement. When the number of observations needed to complete your sample is 0, the STOP statement stops the execution of the DATA step.

```
if k=0 then stop;
```

Here is the complete program that produces and prints the random sample of exactly ten customers with no repeated observations:

```
libname mylib 'SAS-data-library';

data exact(drop=k n);
   retain k 10 n;
   if _n_=1 then n=total;
   set mylib.mail nobs=total;
   if ranuni(747088789)<=k/n then
      do;
         output;
         k=k-1;
      end;
   n=n-1;
   if k=0 then stop;
run;

proc print;
   title 'Exact-Sized Random Sample';
run;
```

Output 12.3 shows the results.

Output 12.3
Taking an
Exact-Sized
Random Sample

```
                   Exact-Sized Random Sample                      1

          OBS     NAME          COST     CITY

            1     Fuller        58.99    out
            2     Goff          22.63    in
            3     Holiday        9.46    out
            4     Lippert       23.84    out
            5     Namboodri     24.38    out
            6     Newton         5.40    in
            7     Parks         47.69    out
            8     Rodriguez      5.78    in
            9     Rogers        33.45    out
           10     Terwilliger   88.22    out
```

Taking Random Samples with Replacement

Sampling with replacement means that an observation goes back into the pool of possible choices once it has been selected. The replication of an observation in the sample is likely when choosing 10 from a group of 40, but as the size of the data set increases relative to the size of the sample, the chance of any observation being included more than once decreases.

To randomly select observations by their observation number in your data set, you can use the POINT= option. The POINT= option names a variable whose value is the number of the observation that the SET statement reads. Instead of reading through the data set sequentially as in the previous examples, a SET statement with the POINT= option reads observations directly.

► *Caution* . . . . ***The POINT= option will not work under certain conditions.***
You cannot use it with transport format data sets, compressed data sets, data sets in sequential format on tape or disk, and SAS/ACCESS views or the SQL procedure views that read data from external files. ▲

In this example, the variable CHOICE, calculated using the INT function and the RANUNI function, contains the observation number in each iteration of the customer chosen for the sample.

```
libname mylib 'SAS-data-library';

data replace;
   choice=int(ranuni(36830)*n)+1;
   set mylib.mail point=choice nobs=n;
```

To define the variable that specifies the observation number, multiply the RANUNI function by the number of observations in your data set, truncate the decimal portion, and add 1. The variable that represents the total number of observations in your data set is defined in the NOBS= option. To truncate the decimal portion of a number, use the INT function. With each iteration of the DATA step, the RANUNI function generates a random number from 0 to 1. Here, this number is multiplied by N, the total number of observations in the data set, to produce a random number from 0 to 40. The INT function returns the integer portion, a random number from 0 to 39. Adding 1 specifies which of the observations, numbered 1 through 40, is chosen for the sample.

In general, if you need to generate a random number that is equally likely to fall in intervals of equal length anywhere between two points, multiply the RANUNI function by the difference between the endpoints and add the smaller endpoint. For example, to generate a random number between 30 and 50, multiply the RANUNI function by 20 and add 30. This evenly spread distribution where equal intervals are equally likely is called the uniform distribution. The SAS System can also generate random numbers from several other distributions.

To specify the number of observations in your sample, you can establish a counter and use the STOP statement in an IF-THEN statement. The STOP statement must be used with the POINT= option to stop the execution of the DATA step. In this example, the variable I counts the number of observations selected for the sample because it starts at 0 and increases by 1 with each iteration of the DATA step. When the sample reaches ten observations, the selection stops.

```
   i+1;
   if i>10 then stop;
```

Here is the complete program that produces and prints the random sample of ten customers with replacement:

```
libname mylib 'SAS-data-library';

data replace(drop=i);
   choice=int(ranuni(36830)*n)+1;
   set mylib.mail point=choice nobs=n;
   i+1;
   if i>10 then stop;
run;

proc print;
   title 'Random Sample with Replacement';
run;
```

Output 12.4 shows the results.

Output 12.4
Taking a Random Sample with Replacement

```
                    Random Sample with Replacement                    1

       OBS    NAME          COST    CITY

        1     Brown         48.67   out
        2     Guillet       62.72   out
        3     Lippert       23.84   out
        4     Newton         5.40   in
        5     Moynihan       6.06   in
        6     Krista        10.00   in
        7     Terwilliger   88.22   out
        8     Clark          3.23   in
        9     Terwilliger   88.22   out
       10     Namboodri     24.38   out
```

Taking Stratified Random Samples

When data contain observations from different categories, a random sample of the data will show membership in those categories in about the same proportion as in the original data set. Taking a stratified random sample lets you decide how many observations from each category are included in your sample. You can use several variables to define your categories, but in this chapter, the values of only one variable identify the categories of observations. The first method shows the specific case of equal category representation, and the second method shows the general case where you can specify the number of observations from each category to include in your sample. Both are examples of sampling without replacement.

Taking Stratified Random Samples of Equal-Sized Groups

If you want the same number of observations from each category included in your sample, it is easier to use this method to take a stratified random sample. This sample of ten observations consists of five customers inside the city and five customers outside the city. Since the process involves choosing a small sample from each of the subgroups of the data to make the entire random sample, you need to do the following:

- □ count the observations in each category

- □ sort the observations into categories

- □ combine the sorted data set with the category counts

- □ select the observations for the sample.

Count the Observations

To count the number of observations in each category, you can use the FREQ procedure. The following PROC FREQ step with a TABLES statement and the OUT= option counts the number of observations in each CITY category. To specify the input data set, use the DATA= option in the PROC FREQ statement. If this option is omitted, the FREQ procedure uses the most recently created SAS data set.

```
libname mylib 'SAS-data-library';

proc freq data=mylib.mail;
   tables city / out=bycount noprint;
run;
```

To specify the variable whose values identify the categories of observations, use the TABLES statement. In this example, the IN and OUT values of the CITY variable identify the categories of observations. To create an output SAS data set containing the variable values, frequency counts, and percentages, use the OUT= option. This data set contains a variable with the same name as the variable listed in the TABLES statement, a variable called COUNT, and a variable called PERCENT. In this example, the output SAS data set is named BYCOUNT.

Sort the Observations

To sort the observations into categories, you can use the SORT procedure with the BY statement. The BY statement specifies the variable whose values identify the categories of the data. The following PROC SORT step sorts the observations in the data set MYLIB.MAIL into categories based on the values of the CITY variable. To specify the input data set, use the DATA= option in the PROC SORT statement. If this option is omitted, the SORT procedure uses the most recently created SAS data set.

```
proc sort data=mylib.mail;
   by city;
run;
```

Combine the Data Sets

To combine your sorted data set with the observation counts by category, you can use the MERGE statement and the BY statement in a DATA step. The MERGE statement joins corresponding observations from SAS data sets into single observations in a new SAS data set. The BY statement names the variable by which the data sets are sorted. The following MERGE statement combines the newly created data set, BYCOUNT, with the sorted list of customers.

```
data strat1;
   merge mylib.mail bycount;
   by city;
```

Select the Observations

To randomly select the observations for your sample, you can start by using the RETAIN statement with the variable that specifies the number of observations from a category needed to complete the subsample from that category. In this example, the variable K is the number of observations from a value of CITY needed to complete the subsample from that value of CITY.

```
retain k;
```

To initialize this variable for each category, you can use the FIRST.*variable*. In the DATA step, the SAS System identifies the beginning and end of each BY group by creating the temporary variables FIRST.*variable* and LAST.*variable* for the BY variable. In this example, when the DATA step reads the first observation from a CITY category, K is set to 5.

```
if first.city then k=5;
```

To select the observations for your sample, you can use the RANUNI function to randomly choose the specified number of observations from each category. The variable COUNT, the total number of observations in a category, is created in the output data set of the PROC FREQ step. To set COUNT equal to the number of observations in a category left to read, decrease COUNT by 1 with each iteration of the DATA step. The following code is explained in detail earlier in this chapter in "Taking Exact-Sized Random Samples."

```
if ranuni(628825275)<=k/count then
   do;
      output;
      k=k-1;
   end;
count=count-1;
```

Here is the complete program that produces and prints the stratified random sample of five customers inside the city and five customers outside the city:

```
libname mylib 'SAS-data-library';

proc freq data=mylib.mail;
   tables city / out=bycount noprint;
run;
```

```
proc sort data=mylib.mail;
   by city;
run;

data strat1(drop=k count);
   merge mylib.mail bycount(drop=percent);
   by city;
   retain k;
   if first.city then k=5;
   if ranuni(628825275)<=k/count then
      do;
         output;
         k=k-1;
      end;
   count=count-1;
run;

proc print data=bycount;
   title 'Count of Customers by CITY';
run;

proc print data=strat1;
   title 'Stratified Random Sample of Equal-Sized Groups';
run;
```

Output 12.5 shows the results.

Output 12.5
Taking a Stratified
Random Sample of
Equal-Sized
Groups

```
                    Count of Customers by CITY                          1

              OBS    CITY     COUNT    PERCENT

               1     in        10        25
               2     out       30        75
```

```
              Stratified Random Sample of Equal-Sized Groups            2

                  OBS    NAME        COST    CITY

                   1     Clark        3.23    in
                   2     Dyer        62.88    in
                   3     Krista      10.00    in
                   4     Moynihan     6.06    in
                   5     Rodriguez    5.78    in
                   6     Dominger     8.83    out
                   7     Lanthier    52.63    out
                   8     Parks       47.69    out
                   9     Salomon     25.36    out
                  10     Sheldrick   58.26    out
```

Taking Stratified Random Samples of Unequal-Sized Groups

If you need to specify different numbers of observations from different categories to include in your sample, you can use this method of taking a stratified random sample. This example takes a stratified random sample of two customers inside the city and eight customers outside the city. To take a stratified random sample of unequal-sized groups, you need to do the following:

□ sort the observations into categories

□ specify the number of observations to select from each category

□ combine the sorted data set with the category counts

□ select the observations for the sample.

Sort the Observations

To sort the observations into categories, you can use the SORT procedure. The following PROC SORT step sorts the observations into categories based on the values of the variable CITY.

```
libname mylib 'SAS-data-library';

proc sort data=mylib.mail;
   by city;
run;
```

Specify the Number of Observations

To specify the number of observations to select from each category, you can create a SAS data set containing the values of the variable that identify the categories of observations, the number of observations in each category, and the number of observations to select from each category. To process only the variable whose values identify the categories of observations, use the KEEP= option with the SET statement. The BY statement names the variable by which the data set is sorted. The following DATA step creates a SAS data set, NSELECT, which contains the total number of observations in each CITY category and the number of observations to select from each CITY category.

```
data nselect;
   set mylib.mail(keep=city);
   by city;
```

To count the number of observations in each category, you can establish a counter and use the LAST.*variable*. In this example, N starts at 0 and increases by 1 with each iteration of the DATA step until it counts the number of observations in a CITY category. To specify the number of observations to select from each category, use a CARDS statement. To write the numbers of observations in your categories and the numbers of observations to select from your categories to the new data set, use the LAST.*variable* in a subsetting IF statement. In this example, if an observation is the last in a CITY category, K and N are written to the data set NSELECT, and N is reset to 0.

```
        n+1;
        if last.city;
        input k;
        output;
        n=0;
        cards;
2
8
;
```

When specifying the numbers of observations to select from your categories, list the numbers in order of the variable values that identify your categories. Since the SORT procedure orders the categories defined by a character variable alphabetically, the numbers must come in the same order. In this example, the value of K for the IN value of CITY, which is 2, must be listed before the value of K for the OUT value, which is 8.

In the special case of selecting an equal proportion of observations from each category, you can omit the INPUT and CARDS statements and data lines. To specify the same proportion for all categories, define the variable that represents the number of observations to select from a category in an assignment statement following the subsetting IF statement. That variable should be set equal to the CEIL function with the argument of the product of the proportion and the variable that represents the number of observations in that category. The CEIL function returns the smallest integer greater than or equal to the argument. In this example, K would be set equal to CEIL(N*.25) if the desired sample were to contain one fourth of the customers inside the city and one fourth of the customers outside the city. However, analyzing a sample instead of the population from which it is taken is valid only because the sample should be representative of that population. The only reason to stratify in this case is to obtain the precise numbers of observations.

Combine the Data Sets

To combine the sorted observations with the category counts, you can use the MERGE statement and the BY statement. The following MERGE statement combines the newly created data set, NSELECT, with the sorted list of customers.

```
data strat2;
   merge mylib.mail nselect;
   by city;
```

Select the Observations

To select the observations for the sample, you can use the RANUNI function to randomly choose the specified numbers of observations from the categories. In this example, K is the number of observations from a value of CITY needed to complete the subsample from that value of CITY, and N is the number of observations from a value of CITY left to read. The following code is explained in detail earlier in this chapter in "Taking Exact-Sized Random Samples."

```
if ranuni(332516)<=k/n then
   do;
      output;
      k=k-1;
   end;
n=n-1;
```

Here is the complete program that produces and prints the stratified random sample of two customers inside the city and eight customers outside the city:

```
libname mylib 'SAS-data-library';

proc sort data=mylib.mail;
   by city;
run;

data nselect;
   set mylib.mail(keep=city);
   by city;
   n+1;
   if last.city;
   input k;
   output;
   n=0;
   cards;
2
8
;

data strat2(drop=k n);
   merge mylib.mail nselect;
   by city;
   if ranuni(332516)<=k/n then
      do;
         output;
         k=k-1;
      end;
   n=n-1;
run;

proc print data=nselect;
   title 'Count of Customers by CITY';
run;
```

```
proc print data=strat2;
   title 'Stratified Random Sample of Unequal-Sized Groups';
run;
```

Output 12.6 shows the results.

Output 12.6
Taking a Stratified Random Sample of Unequal-Sized Groups

```
                    Count of Customers by CITY                     1

                    OBS    CITY    N    K

                     1     in     10    2
                     2     out    30    8
```

```
            Stratified Random Sample of Unequal-Sized Groups       2

            OBS     NAME           COST    CITY

             1      Agerton       17.28    in
             2      Clark          3.23    in
             3      Baldwin       67.66    out
             4      Heuser        31.25    out
             5      Hibbert       77.83    out
             6      Ritchie       76.01    out
             7      Rogers        33.45    out
             8      Salomon       25.36    out
             9      Sheldrick     58.26    out
            10      Terwilliger   88.22    out
```

Summary

The following points summarize how to use the SAS System to take random samples:

□ To select a percentage of observations for a sample, use the RANUNI function in a subsetting IF statement to assign each observation a random number from 0 to 1. Output only those observations with random numbers less than or equal to your specified proportion. This sequential acceptance or rejection of observations according to a constant probability results in an approximate-sized random sample without replacement.

□ To select a specific number of observations for a sample, vary the probability of acceptance according to the number of observations needed to complete the sample and the number of observations left to read in the data set. This results in an exact-sized random sample.

□ To generate a random number that is equally likely to fall in intervals of equal length anywhere between two points, multiply the RANUNI function by the difference between the endpoints and add the smaller endpoint. Truncate the decimal portion with the INT function to return an integer. You can randomly select observations by specifying their observation number in the data set with the POINT= option. This results in a random sample with replacement.

□ To create subsamples of observations from different categories, use the SORT procedure to sort the data set according to values of the category variables. Use the temporary variables, FIRST.*variable* and LAST.*variable*, to separate the selection process for the different categories. This results in a stratified random sample.

SAS Tools

This section summarizes syntax for the statements, functions, automatic variables, and procedures discussed in this chapter.

Statements

variable=expression;
>   is an assignment statement that evaluates an expression and stores the result in a variable. *Variable* names a new or existing variable. *Expression* is any valid SAS expression.

BY *variable*;
>   controls the operation of a SET or MERGE statement and sets up special grouping variables. *Variable* names each variable by which the data set is sorted or indexed. The data set can be sorted or indexed by more than one variable.

CARDS;
>   indicates that data lines follow.

DO;
>   *SAS statements*

END;
>   designates a group of statements to be executed as a unit.

IF *expression*;
>   is a subsetting IF statement that causes the DATA step to continue processing only those observations from a SAS data step that meet the condition of the expression. *Expression* is any valid SAS expression.

IF *expression* **THEN** *statement*;
>   executes a SAS statement for observations read from a SAS data set that meet the specified conditions. *Expression* is any valid SAS expression. *Statement* can be any executable SAS statement or DO group.

INPUT <*variable*>;
>   describes the arrangement of values in an input record and assigns input values to corresponding SAS variables. *Variable* names the variable whose value is read.

MERGE *data-set-name-1 data-set-name-2*;
>   joins corresponding observations from two SAS data sets into single observations in a new SAS data set. *Data-set-name* names two existing SAS data sets from which observations are read.

OUTPUT;
>   writes the current observation to the SAS data set immediately instead of at the end of the DATA step.

RETAIN <*element-list-1* <*initial-value-1*> < . . . *element-list-n* <*initial-value-n*>>>;
>   causes a variable whose value is assigned by an assignment statement to retain its value from the current iteration of the DATA step to the next. *Element-list* specifies variable names whose values are retained. *Initial-value* specifies an initial value for one or more of the preceding elements.

SET <*data-set-name*<(*data-set-options*)>> <*options*>;
>> reads observations from an existing SAS data set. *Data-set-name* specifies the name of the SAS data set. (*Data-set-options*) specifies actions the SAS System takes when reading variables or observations into the program data vector for processing.
>> The following options for the SET statement are discussed in this chapter.

> POINT=*variable-name*
>> reads SAS data sets using random (direct) access by observation number. *Variable-name* names a variable whose value is the number of the observation the SET statement reads.

> NOBS=*variable-name*
>> creates and names a temporary variable whose value is the total number of observations in the input data set.

STOP;
>> causes the SAS System to stop processing the current DATA step immediately and resume processing statements after the end of the current DATA step.

Functions

INT(*argument*)
>> returns the integer portion of the argument by truncating the decimal portion. *Argument* is numeric.

RANUNI(*seed*)
>> returns a random number from the uniform distribution on the interval (0,1). *Seed* is an arbitrary integer from 0 to 2,147,483,646.

Automatic variables

FIRST.*variable*
>> identifies the beginning of a BY group. *Variable* is the variable named in the BY statement.

LAST.*variable*
>> identifies the end of a BY group. *Variable* is the variable named in the BY statement.

_N_
>> represents the number of iterations of a DATA step. _N_ is initially set at 1, and each time the DATA step iterates, _N_ increases by 1.

Procedures

PROC FREQ <DATA=*SAS-data-set*>;
> **TABLES** *variables* </ *options*>;

> **PROC FREQ** <DATA=*SAS-data-set*>;
>> produces a frequency table showing the numbers of observations for categories of a variable. The DATA= option specifies the input SAS data set. If this option is omitted, the most recently created SAS data set is used. For each frequency table, put a table request in the TABLES statement.

TABLES *variables* </ *options*>;
specifies the variables that divide the data into categories.
The following options for the TABLES statement are used in this chapter:

NOPRINT
suppresses printing of the tables.

OUT=*SAS-data-set*
creates an output SAS data set containing variable values and frequency counts.

PROC SORT <DATA=*SAS-data-set*>;
BY *variable-1* <...*variable-n*>;

PROC SORT <DATA=*SAS-data-set*>;
sorts observations in a SAS data set by one or more variables. The DATA= option specifies the input SAS data set. If this option is omitted, the most recently created SAS data set is used. The BY statement must be included to specify the variables.

BY *variable-1* <...*variable-n*>;
lists the variables by which the data set is sorted.

Learning More

This section provides references for learning more about topics presented in this chapter.

□ To see other programs·for taking random samples, refer to *SAS Applications Guide, 1987 Edition*, Chapter 10, "Processing Large Data Sets with SAS Software."

□ For additional information about the RANUNI function and other random number functions, see *SAS Language: Reference, Version 6, First Edition*, Chapter 3, "Components of the SAS Language," and Chapter 11, "SAS Functions." Also, in the same book, Chapter 12, "SAS CALL Routines," discusses generating independent streams of random numbers with CALL routines.

□ For complete descriptions of the FREQ and SORT procedures, refer to *SAS Procedures Guide, Version 6, Third Edition*.

□ For another example of using the FIRST.*variable* and LAST.*variable*, see in Part 4, "Producing Reports," Chapter 15, "Producing Exceptions Reports," the section, "Determine Which Values Are Not Unique."

Part 4
Producing Reports

Chapter **13** Translating Data Values for Meaning and Readability

Introduction

The raw data you want to read to create a SAS data set may not always be recorded in ways that are appropriate to your application. If you have large amounts of data that must be entered into a file, you can design the process so that it promotes accuracy and efficiency for data entry but does not result in values exactly as you want to store them. Before writing these values to a variable and storing them, you can translate them into more useful ones. For example, a survey-taker may write the first three digits of a telephone number on each survey form. The person entering the data can simply enter the number as written, but a SAS program can translate that number into a marketing region code before writing it to a SAS data set.

Similarly, values stored in a SAS data set may be useful to one application but may need to be formatted differently to be meaningful in certain reports. Without changing the original data set or creating a new one, you can use a SAS program to group values for analysis as well as print variable values in ways that are more meaningful to a specific report.

In this chapter
This chapter shows you how to translate values so you can do the following:

□ read one value and store another in a SAS data set

□ group values for analysis and print them in a more meaningful form.

Prerequisites
To understand the examples in this chapter, you need to be familiar with the following concepts and tools:

□ modified list input

□ formatted input

□ the FORMAT procedure

□ the fundamentals of the TABULATE procedure, including the CLASS and TABLE statements. (The discussion of the TABULATE procedure in *SAS Language and Procedures: Usage* provides an adequate background for understanding the example in this chaper.)

Raw Data Example

This chapter uses data from a survey on radio-listening habits. In a telephone interview, the survey-takers asked each respondent questions and filled out the questionnaire shown in Figure 13.1.

Figure 13.1
Sample Radio
Listening Habits
Questionnaire

phone **967**

LISTENER SURVEY

1. **32** What is your age?

2. **F** What is your sex?

3. **5** On the average WEEKDAY, how many hours do you
listen to the radio?

4. **3** On the average WEEKEND-DAY, how many hours do you
listen to the radio?

Use codes 1-8 for question 5. Use codes 0-8 for 6-19.

0 Do not listen at that time
1 Rock   5 Classical
2 Top 40   6 Easy Listening
3 Country   7 News/Information/Talk
4 Jazz   8 Other

5. **5** What style of music or radio programming do you most
often listen to? (codes 1-8)

On a typical WEEKDAY, what kind of radio programming do you listen to	On a typical WEEKEND-DAY, what kind of radio programming do you listen to
6. **7** from 6-9 a.m.?	13. **0** from 6-9 a.m.?
7. **5** from 9 a.m. to noon?	14. **8** from 9 a.m. to noon?
8. **5** from noon to 1 p.m.?	15. **7** from noon to 1 p.m.?
9. **5** from 1-4 p.m.?	16. **0** from 1-4 p.m.?
10. **7** from 4-6 p.m.?	17. **0** from 4-6 p.m.?
11. **0** from 6-10 p.m.?	18. **8** from 6-10 p.m.?
12. **0** from 10 p.m. to 2 a.m.?	19. **0** from 10 p.m. to 2 a.m.?

Here are two sample records, showing how the data are entered from a single
survey:

```
----+----1----+----2----+----3
967 32 F 5 3 5
7 5 5 5 7 0 0 0 8 7 0 0 8 0
```

The data collected in this survey are read to create a SAS data set that contains the following variables:

Name	Type	Description
LOCATION	character	area of residency
AGE	numeric	age of respondent
SEX	character	sex of respondent
WEEKDAY	numeric	number of listening hours on a typical weekday
WEEKEND	numeric	number of listening hours on a typical weekend-day
STYLE	character	type of music or programming most listened to
TIME1-TIME7	character	type of music or programming listened to on a weekday during one of the following time periods, respectively: 6 a.m. to 9 a.m., 9 a.m. to noon, noon to 1 p.m., 1 p.m. to 4 p.m., 4 p.m. to 6 p.m., 6 p.m. to 10 p.m., 10 p.m. to 2 a.m.
TIME8-TIME14	character	type of music or programming listened to on a weekend-day during one of the time periods described for TIME1 through TIME7.

Reading and Storing Values Differently

As you can see from the form shown in Figure 13.1, the survey was designed to make the survey-taking process and the data-entry process as easy as possible. The answers can be entered into a file exactly as they are written down, requiring only 15 to 20 seconds per survey. The telephone exchange value, in particular, was designed to make it convenient for both the survey taker and the data-entry personnel. While the telephone rings, the survey-taker records the telephone exchange, thus saving time and making it unnecessary to ask a question about the respondent's location. This value is not particularly useful as is, but can easily be translated into a marketing region code that could be very useful to marketing personnel who want to use the survey results to help sell advertising. By using a customized (user-written) informat, you can easily translate values before they are written to a SAS data set without slowing down the data entry process. To do this, use the following steps:

□ provide a means of storing the user-written informats

□ create the informats

□ use the informats when you create the data set.

Provide a Means of Storing Customized Informats

When you create a customized informat, you can store it temporarily or permanently. If you plan to use a customized informat repeatedly, store it permanently by using the LIBRARY= option in the PROC FORMAT statement. Your informats are then written to a catalog named FORMATS in that SAS data library.

```
libname library 'SAS-data-library';
proc format library=library;
```

▶ *Caution* . . . . **Use the reserved libref LIBRARY when using permanently stored customized informats.** When you create customized informats, it is unimportant which libref you assign to the SAS data library in which you store them. When you want to use these informats in another DATA or PROC step, however, you must use the reserved libref LIBRARY. When a user-written informat is called by a DATA or PROC step, the system looks for the informat in a catalog named WORK.FORMATS and then in one named LIBRARY.FORMATS. ▲

Create Customized Informats

This example uses a customized informat to translate each respondent's three-digit telephone exchange number into a regional marketing code. To create a customized informat, use the INVALUE statement of the FORMAT procedure, as shown in the following template:

INVALUE *user-defined-character-informat 'old-value-1'=new-value-1* . . .
        'old-value-n'=new-value-n;

Note that you can create only character informats with the INVALUE statement.

This example creates a character informat named $LOC. and translates the three-digit telephone exchanges into regional marketing codes:

```
libname library 'SAS-data-library';

proc format library=library;
     invalue $loc               '732'='HILL'    /* Hillsborough     */
                                 '542'='PTBR'    /* Pittsboro        */
                                 '362'='APEX'    /* Apex             */
                                 '942'='CARR'    /* Carrboro         */
                         '467','677'='CARY'    /* Cary             */
                         '966','967'='CHPL'    /* Chapel Hill      */
                                 '833'='RAL1'    /* Raleigh - zone1  */
                         '848'-'851'='RAL2'    /* Raleigh - zone2  */
                         '856','859'='RAL3'    /* Raleigh - zone3  */
                 '779','781'-'783'='RAL4'    /* Raleigh - zone4  */
                                 '546'='RAL5'    /* Raleigh - zone5  */
                         '382'-'383'='DUR1'    /* Durham - zone1   */
                         '490'-'493'='DUR2'    /* Durham - zone2   */
```

```
                    '220'-'221'='DUR3'      /* Durham - zone3        */
                    '683'-'684'='DUR4'      /* Durham - zone4        */
                    '687'-'688'='DUR5'      /* Durham - zone5        */
                          '254'='RTP'       /* Research Triangle Park*/
                         OTHER='OUT'        /* all other areas       */
       ;
     run;
```

Note that in the INVALUE statement, you specify the name of the informat without the period. (The ending period is required when you use the informat to actually read data.) Then specify how you want each possible value translated. Place the current value on the left side of the equal sign and the new translated values on the right side. Remember, you must always specify character values in quotes.

Note that in each specification you can list a single value or multiple values. Multiple values can be specified as a range or individually, separated with commas. The following example uses both methods to translate the telephone exchanges 799 and 781 through 783 into the value RAL4:

```
    '779','781'-'783'='RAL4'     /* Raleigh - zone4                  */
```

Note also the special range OTHER. If any unexpected or erroneous values occur in your data, you can cause them all to be translated into a given value. This example uses the special range OTHER to translate all telephone exchanges not listed in the INVALUE statement into the value OUT.

Use the Informats When Creating a Data Set

Once you have created your own informats, you can use them as you read data to create a SAS data set. Note that the INPUT statement in the following DATA step uses the user-written informat $LOC. to translate values read in the raw data before assigning them to the variable LOCATION:

```
libname library 'SAS-data-library-containing-informats';
libname datalib 'SAS-data-library';

data datalib.radio;
   infile 'input-file' missover;
   length location $ 4;
   input location $loc3. age sex : $1. weekday weekend style $ /
         (time1-time14) ($1. +1);
run;
```

When you read a value with an informat, make certain you give the variable a length that is long enough to contain the new value assigned by the informat. In this example, the INPUT statement reads a three-digit telephone exchange in the raw data records, so it uses a length of 3 in the informat ($LOC3.) when reading a value to assign to LOCATION. The informat translates this three-digit value into a regional marketing code that can contain up to four digits, so the LENGTH statement must assign a length of 4 to the variable LOCATION.

Here is the entire program that creates and stores the user-written informat $LOC., creates a data set from the radio listener survey data, and prints the first 30 observations in the resulting SAS data set.

```
libname library 'SAS-data-library-containing-informats';

proc format library=library;
     invalue $loc              '732'='HILL'     /* Hillsborough          */
                               '542'='PTBR'     /* Pittsboro             */
                               '362'='APEX'     /* Apex                  */
                               '942'='CARR'     /* Carrboro              */
                         '467','677'='CARY'     /* Cary                  */
                         '966','967'='CHPL'     /* Chapel Hill           */
                               '833'='RAL1'     /* Raleigh - zone1       */
                         '848'-'851'='RAL2'     /* Raleigh - zone2       */
                         '856','859'='RAL3'     /* Raleigh - zone3       */
                   '779','781'-'783'='RAL4'     /* Raleigh - zone4       */
                               '546'='RAL5'     /* Raleigh - zone5       */
                         '382'-'383'='DUR1'     /* Durham - zone1        */
                         '490'-'493'='DUR2'     /* Durham - zone2        */
                         '220'-'221'='DUR3'     /* Durham - zone3        */
                         '683'-'684'='DUR4'     /* Durham - zone4        */
                         '687'-'688'='DUR5'     /* Durham - zone5        */
                               '254'='RTP'      /* Research Triangle Park*/
                             OTHER='OUT'        /* all other areas       */
      ;
run;

libname datalib 'SAS-data-library';

data datalib.radio;
   infile 'input-file' missover;
   length location $ 4;
   input location $loc3. age sex : $1. weekday weekend style $ /
         (time1-time14) ($1. +1);
run;

options ls=120 ps=50;

proc print data=datalib.radio(obs=30);
   title 'Sample of Survey Responses';
run;
```

Output 13.1 displays the results.

Output 13.1   *Displaying the First 30 Observations*

```
                                    Sample of Survey Responses                                        1
```

OBS	LOCATION	AGE	SEX	WEEKDAY	WEEKEND	STYLE	TIME1	TIME2	TIME3	TIME4	TIME5	TIME6	TIME7	TIME8	TIME9	TIME10	TIME11	TIME12	TIME13	TIME14
1	CHPL	32	f	5.0	3.0	5	7	5	5	5	7	0	0	0	8	7	0	0	8	0
2	RAL4	30	f	2.0	3.0	5	5	0	0	0	5	0	0	0	4	7	5	0	0	0
3	RAL3	39	f	1.0	0.0	5	1	0	0	0	1	0	0	0	0	0	0	0	0	0
4	RAL3	40	f	6.0	1.0	5	7	5	0	5	7	0	0	0	0	0	0	5	0	0
5	CARY	37	m	2.0	3.0	1	1	5	5	5	5	4	4	8	8	0	0	0	0	0
6	DUR3	35	f	3.0	1.0	7	7	0	0	0	7	0	0	0	7	0	0	0	0	0
7	RAL1	42	m	2.0	2.0	4	7	0	0	0	7	5	4	7	4	0	1	4	4	0
8	CHPL	39	f	0.5	1.0	7	7	0	0	0	7	7	0	0	0	0	0	0	8	0
9	CARY	28	m	0.5	0.5	7	7	0	0	0	0	0	0	0	0	0	0	0	0	0
10	RAL1	28	f	3.0	4.0	1	1	0	0	0	0	1	1	1	1	0	0	0	0	1
11	CARY	24	f	3.0	1.0	2	2	0	0	0	0	0	2	0	8	8	0	0	0	0
12	DUR5	32	m	5.0	2.0	4	4	5	5	0	4	8	0	0	5	0	8	0	0	0
13	PTBR	38	f	6.0	8.0	5	5	0	0	5	5	5	0	5	5	5	5	5	5	0
14	CARY	27	m	6.0	1.0	1	1	1	0	4	4	0	0	1	4	0	0	0	0	0
15	RAL4	37	f	2.5	4.0	7	7	0	0	0	7	7	0	7	7	4	4	7	8	0
16	APEX	31	f	1.0	2.0	2	8	0	0	0	8	0	0	0	0	0	8	8	0	0
17	RAL3	29	m	10.0	3.0	4	4	4	0	2	2	0	0	4	0	0	0	4	4	0
18	CARY	24	m	5.0	8.0	1	7	1	1	1	7	1	1	0	1	7	1	1	1	1
19	RAL2	34	m	1.0	2.0	8	0	0	0	0	8	0	0	0	4	0	0	0	8	0
20	RAL3	23	f	1.0	1.0	8	8	0	0	0	8	0	0	0	0	0	0	0	0	8
21	RAL4	34	f	9.0	3.0	1	2	1	0	1	4	4	4	0	1	1	1	1	4	4
22	RAL2	40	f	2.0	4.0	5	5	0	0	0	5	0	0	5	0	0	5	5	0	0
23	RAL4	34	m	3.0	2.0	4	7	0	0	0	7	4	4	0	0	4	4	0	0	0
24	RAL2	29	f	4.0	1.5	7	7	4	4	1	7	0	0	0	7	0	0	7	0	0
25	RAL2	28	f	1.0	2.0	2	2	0	2	0	2	0	0	0	0	2	2	2	0	0
26	RAL3	42	f	1.5	1.0	2	2	0	0	0	0	0	0	2	0	0	0	0	0	0
27	RAL3	29	m	0.5	0.5	5	5	0	0	0	1	0	0	0	0	8	8	5	0	0
28	RAL1	29	m	1.0	3.0	2	2	0	0	0	2	2	0	0	4	2	0	2	0	0
29	RAL3	23	f	10.0	3.0	1	1	5	0	8	8	1	4	0	1	1	1	1	1	4
30	RAL4	37	f	0.5	2.0	7	7	0	0	0	1	0	0	0	1	7	0	1	0	0

Grouping and Writing Values Differently to Create a Meaningful Report

Output 13.1 demonstrates that the data set DATALIB.RADIO was created, but it also shows that a detail report of individual survey responses is not particularly informative. To help you analyze such data, you can group values in meaningful units, for example, by age or sex. You can also write a better, more useful report by making values more readable. You can accomplish both of these goals by creating your own formats.

As an example, the marketing staff of a radio station that plays rock music and has a strong news department wants to use the radio survey data to determine the age and sex of people in the area who listen to rock or news during the morning or afternoon commute. By first grouping data with user-written formats, they can create a summary report that enables them to look at the data in this way. Figure 13.2 shows a template of the report to be created on the survey data.

Figure 13.2
Template of
Report on Radio
Survey Data

```
                                        Who's Listening to Rock or News

|                       |                       Morning Commute         |         Afternoon Commute                 |
|                       |-----------------------------------------------|-------------------------------------------|
|                       |          |          |News/Inform-|          |          |News/Inform-|
|                       |  Other   |Rock 'n Roll|ation/Talk|  Other   |Rock 'n Roll|ation/Talk|
|                       |----------+----------+----------+----------+----------+----------|
|                       | Number of| Number of| Number of| Numberof | Number of| Number of|
|                       | Listeners| Listeners| Listeners| Listeners| Listeners| Listeners|
|-----------------------+----------+----------+----------+----------+----------+----------|
|AGE         |SEX       |          |          |          |          |          |          |
|------------+----------|          |          |          |          |          |          |
|19 and under|f         |          |          |          |          |          |          |
|            |----------|----------+----------+----------+----------+----------+----------|
|            |m         |          |          |          |          |          |          |
|------------+----------+----------+----------+----------+----------+----------+----------|
|20s         |f         |          |          |          |          |          |          |
|            |----------|----------+----------+----------+----------+----------+----------|
|            |m         |          |          |          |          |          |          |
|------------+----------+----------+----------+----------+----------+----------+----------|
|30s         |f         |          |          |          |          |          |          |
|            |----------|----------+----------+----------+----------+----------+----------|
|            |m         |          |          |          |          |          |          |
|------------+----------+----------+----------+----------+----------+----------+----------|
|40s         |f         |          |          |          |          |          |          |
|            |----------|----------+----------+----------+----------+----------+----------|
|            |m         |          |          |          |          |          |          |
|------------+----------+----------+----------+----------+----------+----------+----------|
|50s         |f         |          |          |          |          |          |          |
|------------+----------+----------+----------+----------+----------+----------+----------|
|60 and over |m         |          |          |          |          |          |          |
|------------+----------+----------+----------+----------+----------+----------+----------|
|Total Number Within a  |          |          |          |          |          |          |
|Category               |          |          |          |          |          |          |
-------------------------------------------------------------------------------------------
```

To create such a report, perform the following tasks:

□ provide a means of storing the customized formats

□ create customized formats to group some values into useful units and to format other values so they can be printed more informatively

□ use the formats when you create a tabular report

□ enhance the report by showing more information and using titles and labels.

Provide a Means of Storing Customized Formats

To store customized formats, use the same method for storing customized informats shown earlier in this chapter. Use the LIBRARY= option in the PROC FORMAT statement to specify the SAS data library in which you plan to store the formats:

```
libname library 'SAS-data-library';

proc format library=library;
```

Remember that when you want to use permanently stored customized formats, you must assign the reserved libref LIBRARY to the SAS data library in which they are stored.

Create Customized Formats

To group observations by the value of a given variable, use the FORMAT procedure to create your own formats. Earlier in this chapter you saw how to use the INVALUE statement to create informats that can be used to translate data values as you read them. Now use the VALUE statement to create formats to reformat SAS variable values before writing them. Note that you can create numeric or character formats with the VALUE statement.

For example, the marketing staff probably isn't interested in how many 27-year olds are listening at any one time, but potential advertisers would be interested in knowing when a large number of people in their target audience, people in their twenties, thirties, and so forth, were listening. The following VALUE statement creates the numeric format AGEGRP. to group observations in the MYLIB.RADIO data set by age categories:

```
libname library 'SAS-data-library';

proc format library=library;
   value agegrp  LOW-19='19 and under'
                 20-29='20s'
                 30-39='30s'
                 40-49='40s'
                 50-59='50s'
               60-HIGH='60 and over';
```

Note how the special ranges LOW and HIGH are used:

```
  LOW-19='19 and under'
60-HIGH='60 and over'
```

If you do not know the highest or lowest values for a given variable in your data, you can use these special ranges instead of a numeric constant.

A second reason to customize formats is to make values more meaningful in a report. For example, look at the variables that report which style of music or radio programming is listened to during particular time periods (TIME1-TIME14). For simplicity in data entry and efficiency in storage, the values for style of music or programming most often listened to are represented simply as numbers. In a report, however, it is more useful to print them in a more descriptive way, as shown here:

```
value $music '1'="Rock 'n Roll"
             '7'='News/Information/Talk'
```

Note that the value `Rock 'n Roll` is enclosed in double quotes because it contains a single quote.

The object of this report is to see how many respondents listen only to rock or news during given time periods. The same format can use the special range OTHER to group all other values in a single group:

```
value $music   '1'="Rock 'n Roll"
               '7'='News/Information/Talk'
             OTHER='Other';
```

Note that the numerals 1 and 7 are enclosed in single quotes. Though these values are represented as numerals (1 through 8 in the data), they are stored as character values with a length of 1 to save space. (It is not necessary to store a numeral as a numeric value unless you plan to perform arithmetic with it.)

Create a Simple Tabular Report

After you create customized formats to group and print values, you can create a tabular report that summarizes your data with the TABULATE procedure.

```
libname library 'SAS-data-library-containing-formats';
libname datalib 'SAS-data-library';

proc tabulate data=datalib.radio;
```

Identify the formats the procedure should use in a FORMAT statement. This example uses the AGEGRP. format to group values for the numeric variable AGE and the $MUSIC. format to group and print the values for the character variables TIME1 and TIME5:

```
format age agegrp. time1 time5 $music.;
```

To create a report with PROC TABULATE, you must identify all the variables you want to appear in the report in either a VAR statement or a CLASS statement. Use a CLASS statement to specify the variables you want to organize into distinct categories. This example specifies the variables AGE, SEX, TIME1, and TIME5 in a CLASS statement:

```
class age sex time1 time5;
```

A VAR statement identifies variables for which you want the TABULATE procedure to compute statistics. Since the purpose of this report is simply to generate a frequency count on the number of listeners for two categories of programming during given time periods, no VAR statement is needed.

Specify exactly how you want a table to be built with a TABLE statement. First describe the rows and then describe the columns, as shown in the following template:

TABLE *row-description, column-description*;

In this report, each row represents a group of values of the variable AGE. (Remember that these groupings were created by applying the format AGEGRP. to AGE.) Each column represents one of the two time periods. Each of these columns is divided into the three possible values created by the $MUSIC. format. The following statements produce a simple tabular report from the radio survey data:

```
libname library 'SAS-data-library-containing-formats';
libname datalib 'SAS-data-library';

proc format library=library;
   value agegrp  LOW-19='19 and under'
                 20-29='20s'
                 30-39='30s'
                 40-49='40s'
                 50-59='50s'
               60-HIGH='60 and over';
   value $music  '1'="Rock 'n Roll"
                 '7'='News/Information/Talk'
               OTHER='Other';
run;

proc tabulate data=datalib.radio;
   format age agegrp. time1 time5 $music.;
   class age sex time1 time5;
   table age, time1 time5;
   title "Who's Listening to Rock or News";
run;
```

Output 13.2 shows the results.

Output 13.2   *Summarizing the Radio Survey Data in a Simple Table*

```
                        Who's Listening to Rock or News                              1
---------------------------------------------------------------------------------------
|               |           TIME1             |            TIME5                    |
|               |-----------------------------|-------------------------------------|
|               |        |         |News/Inform-|        |         |News/Inform-     |
|               | Other  |Rock 'n Roll| ation/Talk | Other  |Rock 'n Roll| ation/Talk |
|               |--------+---------+----------+--------+---------+------------|
|               |   N    |    N    |    N     |   N    |    N    |     N      |
|---------------+--------+---------+----------+--------+---------+------------|
|AGE            |        |         |          |        |         |            |
|---------------|        |         |          |        |         |            |
|19 and under   |  12.00 |   1.00  |    1.00  |  11.00 |   3.00  |      .     |
|---------------+--------+---------+----------+--------+---------+------------|
|20s            |  58.00 |  47.00  |   25.00  |  67.00 |  48.00  |    15.00   |
|---------------+--------+---------+----------+--------+---------+------------|
|30s            |  52.00 |  43.00  |   51.00  |  68.00 |  36.00  |    42.00   |
|---------------+--------+---------+----------+--------+---------+------------|
|40s            |  14.00 |   7.00  |   16.00  |  21.00 |   6.00  |    10.00   |
|---------------+--------+---------+----------+--------+---------+------------|
|50s            |   5.00 |    .    |    3.00  |   6.00 |    .    |     2.00   |
|---------------+--------+---------+----------+--------+---------+------------|
|60 and over    |   1.00 |    .    |     .    |   1.00 |    .    |      .     |
---------------------------------------------------------------------------------------
```

Create a More Informative Tabular Report

You can create a simple tabular report such as the one shown in Output 13.2, but by adding a few more features, you can create a report that is even more readable and informative. For example, you can

□ show more information by crossing variables

□ compute totals

□ add labels

□ format statistics.

You can look more closely at data for a given class variable by creating a subgroup within the class variable. For example, if data contain the age and sex for each observation, you can look at those data by grouping the observations into age groups and then grouping the observations within each age group by sex. Creating a group within another group is called *crossing variables*. In this report, crossing the variable AGE with the variable SEX demonstrates how many listeners of each sex appear in each age group.

```
table age*sex, time1 time5;
```

To calculate totals for a variable, use the keyword ALL.

```
table age*sex all, time1 time5;
```

To control how missing values are displayed, use the MISSTEXT= option. In this report, missing values can be represented with a zero.

```
table age*sex all, time1 time5 / misstext='0';
```

Label variables in a more meaningful way than the variable names with a LABEL statement.

```
label time1='Morning Commute';
label time5='Afternoon Commute';
```

TABULATE keywords, ALL (total) and N (frequency count) in this report, appear in the report unless you specify a more meaningful label with a KEYLABEL statement, as shown here:

```
keylabel all='Total Number Within Categories'
         n='Number of Listeners';
```

To control the way a statistic is printed in a report, use the FORMAT= option in the PROC TABULATE statement. This example specifies a numeric format without decimal places so that the frequency count of the number of listeners (the N statistic) prints in a more appropriate format.

```
proc tabulate data=datalib.radio format=10.;
```

Here are the PROC FORMAT and PROC TABULATE steps that organize the radio survey data into categories for analysis and create a more enhanced summary report than was shown in Output 13.2:

```
libname library 'SAS-data-library-containing-formats';
libname datalib 'SAS-data-library';

proc format library=library;
   value agegrp  LOW-19='19 and under'
                 20-29='20s'
                 30-39='30s'
                 40-49='40s'
                 50-59='50s'
               60-HIGH='60 and over';
   value $music   '1'="Rock 'n Roll"
                  '7'='News/Information/Talk'
               OTHER='Other';
run;

proc tabulate data=datalib.radio format=10.;
   class age sex time1 time5;
   format age agegrp. time1 time5 $music.;
   table age*sex all,time1 time5 / misstext='0';
   label time1='Morning Commute'
         time5='Afternoon Commute';
   keylabel all='Total Number Within Categories'
            n='Number of Listeners';
   title "Who's Listening to Rock or News";
run;
```

Output 13.3 shows the printed report.

Output 13.3   *Enhancing a Summary Report*

```
                               Who's Listening to Rock or News                             1
         -----------------------------------------------------------------------------------
         |                 |       Morning Commute        |      Afternoon Commute       |
         |                 |------------------------------|------------------------------|
         |                 |       |       |News/Info-|       |       |News/Info-|
         |                 |       | Rock 'n |rmation/T-|       | Rock 'n |rmation/T-|
         |                 | Other |  Roll   |   alk    | Other |  Roll   |   alk    |
         |                 |-------+-------+----------+-------+-------+----------|
         |                 |Number of|Number of|Number of |Number of|Number of|Number of |
         |                 |Listeners|Listeners|Listeners |Listeners|Listeners|Listeners |
         |-----------+------+---------+---------+----------+---------+---------+----------|
         |AGE        |SEX   |       |       |       |       |       |       |
         |-----------+------|       |       |       |       |       |       |
         |19 and under|f    |     8|     1|     1|     9|     1|     0|
         |           |------|------+-------+----------+-------+-------+----------|
         |           |m    |     4|     0|     0|     2|     2|     0|
         |-----------+------+---------+---------+----------+---------+---------+----------|
         |20s        |f    |    43|    33|    14|    47|    33|    10|
         |           |------|------+-------+----------+-------+-------+----------|
         |           |m    |    15|    14|    11|    20|    15|     5|
         |-----------+------+---------+---------+----------+---------+---------+----------|
         |30s        |f    |    39|    28|    25|    44|    24|    24|
         |           |------|------+-------+----------+-------+-------+----------|
         |           |m    |    13|    15|    26|    24|    12|    18|
         |-----------+------+---------+---------+----------+---------+---------+----------|
         |40s        |f    |    12|     5|     9|    17|     4|     5|
         |           |------|------+-------+----------+-------+-------+----------|
         |           |m    |     2|     2|     7|     4|     2|     5|
         |-----------+------+---------+---------+----------+---------+---------+----------|
         |50s        |f    |     5|     0|     3|     6|     0|     2|
         |-----------+------+---------+---------+----------+---------+---------+----------|
         |60 and over|m    |     1|     0|     0|     1|     0|     0|
         |-----------+------+---------+---------+----------+---------+---------+----------|
         |Total Number Within|       |       |       |       |       |       |
         |Categories   |    142|    98|    96|   174|    93|    69|
         -----------------------------------------------------------------------------------
```

Summary

The following points summarize how to translate data values before storing them in a SAS data set and how to translate data values so that you can create a useful summary report.

□ To store user-written informats or formats permanently, use the LIBRARY= option in the PROC FORMAT statement to specify a libref that has been assigned to the SAS data library where you want these items stored. To use these informats or formats in a subsequent DATA or PROC step, you must assign the libref LIBRARY to the SAS data library where they reside.

□ To translate a value being read into another value before storing it, you can read the value with an informat. To create your own customized (user-written) informats, use the INVALUE statement in the FORMAT procedure.

□ To group values into meaningful units in reports or to display values in a way that is more meaningful than the way they are stored, use formats. To create your own customized (user-written) formats, use the VALUE statement in the FORMAT procedure.

□ To summarize data so that you can make decisions based on comparisons, you can use a summary procedure such as PROC TABULATE. You can group variables in different ways to create many different reports. Using the

FORMAT procedure with the TABULATE procedure enables you to group the data in different ways for reports without altering the data or creating a different data set.

□ To create more readable and informative reports, you can cross variables, compute totals, add labels and titles, and format statistics.

SAS Tools

This section summarizes syntax for the statements and procedures discussed in this chapter.

Statements

LABEL *variable*='*label*' <. . . *variable-n*='*label-n*'>;
  specifies a label to be used in the table in the place of a variable name.

LIBNAME LIBRARY '*SAS-data-library*';
  assigns the reserved libref LIBRARY to a SAS data library. To use permanently stored user-defined formats or informats in a DATA or PROC step, you must assign the reserved libref LIBRARY to the SAS data library in which they are stored.

TITLE '*title*';
  specifies a title for the tabular report.

Procedures

PROC FORMAT <LIBRARY=*libref*>;
  INVALUE *user-defined-character-informat* '*value-1*'=*formatted-value-1*
    <. . . '*value-n*'=*formatted-value-n*>;
  VALUE *user-defined-format value-1*='*formatted-value-1*'
    <. . . *value-n*='*formatted-value-n*'>;

PROC FORMAT LIBRARY=*libref*;
  begins the FORMAT procedure, which allows you to create your own formats and informats for character and numeric variables. Use the LIBRARY= option to specify the libref of a SAS data library when you want to store customized informats or formats permanently.

INVALUE *user-defined-character-informat* '*value-1*'=*formatted-value-1*
    <. . . '*value-n*'=*formatted-value-n*>;
  defines a character informat that enables you to translate a value into a new value before writing it to a variable. Note that you can create a user-defined informat to read only character data. You can, however, choose to translate the value into a character or numeric value. Enclose the original character values in quotes. Enclose the new formatted values in quotes only if they are character values.

When specifying the values to be translated, you can specify a single value, multiple values separated by commas, or a range of values. Keywords are available for denoting special ranges, such as LOW, HIGH, and OTHER. The following special range is discussed in this chapter:

OTHER
  enables you to specify a new value into which all unspecified values will be translated. This special range is useful for grouping values as well as for error-handling.

VALUE *user-defined-format value-1='formatted-value-1'*
  <. . . value-n='formatted-value-n'>;
defines a numeric or character format that writes a variable's value as a different value. A user-defined format, whether character or numeric, always associates a variable value with a character value. Enclose the original value in quotes if it is a character value. Always enclose each new formatted value in quotes.

When specifying the values to be translated, you can specify a single value, multiple values separated by commas, or ranges of values. Keywords are available for denoting special ranges, such as LOW, HIGH, and OTHER. Each of these special ranges is discussed in this chapter:

LOW
  enables you to specify the lowest value without knowing the exact value, as in the following: LOW—19 = '19 and under'.

HIGH
  enables you to specify the highest value without knowing the exact value, as in the following: 60—HIGH = '60 and over'.

OTHER
  enables you to specify a new value into which all unspecified values will be translated. This special range is useful for grouping values.

PROC TABULATE *<DATA=SAS-data-set> <FORMAT=format>*;
  FORMAT *variable format <. . . variable-n format-n>*;
  CLASS *variables*;
  TABLE *row-description, column-description </ options>*;
  KEYLABEL *statistic='label' <. . . statistic-n='label-n'>*;

PROC TABULATE *<DATA=SAS-data-set> <FORMAT=format>*;
  begins the procedure for constructing a tabular report. Optionally, you can specify the input data set and a format to be used for formatting values in the table.

FORMAT *variable format <. . . variable-n format-n>*;
  associates a format with variable that is to appear in the report.

CLASS *variables*;
  specifies the variables that are to be organized into distinct categories. The variables that appear in the TABLE statement must also appear either in a CLASS or VAR statement.

(PROC TABULATE continued)

TABLE *row-description, column-description*;
 describes the appearance of the table, first by row and then by column. This chapter demonstrates the following elements of a *row-description* or *column-description*:

variables
 lists variables to be placed in the table, either in a row or column. Each of the variables listed must also appear in either a CLASS statement or a VAR statement.

variable-1*variable-2
 crosses two variables. By crossing two variables, you can break the data down into useful subcategories.

ALL
 specifies that totals be calculated for a variable.

The following TABLE statement option is used this chapter.

MISSTEXT='*text-string*'
 specifies a text string of up to 20 characters to print in table cells containing missing values.

KEYLABEL *statistic*='*label*' <. . . *statistic-n*='*label-n*'>;
 specifies a label to be used in the table in the place of the name of a statistic, such as N, or keyword, such as ALL.

Learning More

This section provides references for learning more about topics presented in this chapter.

□ To learn more about creating customized (user-defined) formats and informats, see the *SAS Procedures Guide, Version 6, First Edition*, Chapter 18, "The FORMAT Procedure."

□ To learn more about creating tabular reports, see the *SAS Procedures Guide*, Chapter 37, "The TABULATE Procedure." Also see the *SAS Guide to TABULATE Processing, 1987 Edition*.

Chapter 14 Reporting on Subsets of SAS Data Sets

Introduction

For many reasons, it is often useful to be able to report on only a subset of the observations in a SAS data set. For example, you can print a report that consists only of observations containing overdue accounts instead of a report of the entire data set you would have to search for these accounts.

In this chapter
This chapter shows you how to do the following:

□ report on a subset of observations in a single SAS data set by creating either just a report or a report and a new data set

□ report on a subset of observations in multiple SAS data sets by creating either just a report or a report and a new data set.

To process only a subset of observations from a SAS data set, you can use either the subsetting IF statement or WHERE processing.

The examples in this chapter focus on the special advantages of using WHERE processing and demonstrate its use with the DATA step, the PRINT procedure, and the SQL procedure. So you can select the best method for a particular DATA step application, this chapter discusses the differences between using WHERE processing and the subsetting IF statement.

Prerequisites

You should be familiar with the subsetting IF statement before reading the section "Understanding When to Choose WHERE Processing or the Subsetting IF Statement."

Understanding When to Choose WHERE Processing or the Subsetting IF Statement

To process only the observations from a SAS data set that meet your criteria, you can use either WHERE processing or the subsetting IF statement. The subsetting IF statement can be used only in a DATA step. *WHERE processing* enables you to conditionally select observations for processing in a DATA or PROC step by using a WHERE expression in a WHERE statement, a WHERE= data set option, a WHERE clause, or a WHERE command. A *WHERE expression* is a type of SAS expression that can be used to express a condition for selecting observations for processing. You can use WHERE expressions in

□ the WHERE statement of a DATA or PROC step

□ the WHERE= data set option

□ the WHERE clause of the SQL procedure's SELECT and CREATE statements

□ the WHERE command of the REPORT procedure.

Each method, WHERE processing and the subsetting IF statement, has special advantages and restrictions. Some of the differences between them depend on the timing of the observation selection process. When you express a condition in a WHERE expression in a DATA step, an observation is selected for processing before it is brought into the program data vector. However, when you use the subsetting IF statement, the selection is made after the observation has been brought into the program data vector. Knowing when the selection is made can help you choose between these methods in certain situations. In most cases, you can use either one. For a list of tasks that require you to use one instead of the other, refer to the following table:

Table 14.1
Choosing between WHERE Processing and the Subsetting IF Statement

If you want to . . .	Then use . . .
make the selection in a procedure without using a preceding DATA step	WHERE processing
take advantage of the efficiency available with indexed data sets	WHERE processing
use one of a group of special operators, including the following: BETWEEN-AND, CONTAINS, IS MISSING, IS NULL, LIKE, SAME-AND, or SOUNDS LIKE	WHERE processing

(*continued*)

	If you want to . . .	Then use . . .
Table 14.1 *(continued)*	base the selection on anything other than a variable value that already exists in a SAS data set—for example, on a value that is read from raw data or on a value that is calculated or assigned during the course of the DATA step	subsetting IF
	make the selection at some point during a DATA step rather than at the beginning	subsetting IF
	execute the selection conditionally	subsetting IF

If none of the restrictions in the previous table apply to your application, you can use either method. Keep in mind, however, that in most applications, WHERE processing is more efficient. If you are using a BY statement with the SET, MERGE, or UPDATE statements, you must realize that using WHERE processing can produce a different output data set than using a subsetting IF statement. This occurs because the SAS System assigns values to FIRST.*variable* and LAST.*variable* *before* the subsetting IF statement selects the observation, but *after* the WHERE statement selects.

Reporting on a Subset of Information in a Single SAS Data Set

If you are interested in only part of the data in a large SAS data set, you can create a report that includes only that subset of information. Based on the value of a specified variable, you can select observations for inclusion in the output data set.

For example, you can select an observation when the value of a numeric or character variable falls within a given range by using the BETWEEN-AND operator in a WHERE expression. You can also select an observation when the value of a character variable contains a specified character string. To do so, you can use the INDEX function in combination with a subsetting IF statement. However, a simple and more direct way to process only these observations is to use either the CONTAINS operator or the LIKE operator in a WHERE expression. The following examples demonstrate searching a file of real estate listings for houses that meet specified conditions.

SAS Data Set Example

The SAS data set MYLIB.HOUSES contains information on local real estate listings. Each observation contains the following variables:

Variable	Type	Description
ZONE	character	number representing a housing zone recognized by Realtors
TYPE	character	type of house
BEDR	numeric	number of bedrooms
BATH	numeric	number of bathrooms
SQFEET	numeric	square feet of heated living space
AGE	numeric	age of house
SCHOOLS	character	code representing the local district and schools
ADDRESS	character	street address
PRICE	numeric	asking price

The following PROC PRINT step displays the data set MYLIB.HOUSES:*

```
libname mylib 'SAS-data-library';

proc print data=mylib.houses;
    title 'Current Listings for Tri-County Area';
run;
```

Output 14.1 shows the results.

Output 14.1   *Printout of the Data Set MYLIB.HOUSES*

```
                              Current Listings for Tri-County Area                                      1
   OBS   ZONE   TYPE      BEDR   BATH   SQFEET   AGE     SCHOOLS         ADDRESS                  PRICE
    1     4    twostory    4     2.5    2538      6    920:340/400/368   211 Whitehall Way       154900
    2     1    twostory    4     2.5    2700      7    920:470/360/552   1800 Bridgeport         169900
    3     3    twnhouse    2     2.0    1595      6    320:332/366/312   154 Montrose            102000
    4     1    twostory    3     2.5    2750      0    920:628/388/348   4000 Skipjack Ct.       214900
    5     4    split       3     2.0    1306      0    920:576/512/436   5933 South Downs Dr.     95400
    6     2    twostory    3     3.5    2590      0    920:364/608/368   727 Crabtree Crossing   292400
    7     5    split       3     1.0    1959     31    680:308/316/332   627 Riverside Dr.        58900
    8     2    twnhouse    3     2.5    1374     15    920:304/604/368   907 Lexington Ct.        65500
    9     4    condo       2     2.0    1275      5    920:448/472/318   6010-102 Winterpoint     70000
   10     4    ranch       3     2.0    1526      6    920:476/424/428   6509 Orchard Knoll      107900
   11     1    split       3     1.5    1329     23    920:396/360/552   500 E. Millbrook Rd.     82900
```

---

* The DATA step that creates MYLIB.HOUSES is shown in the Appendix.

12	1	condo	2	3.5	1300	5	920:448/472/318	6010-101 Winterpoint	68900
13	8	twnhouse	2	2.0	1120	4	320:364/366/312	521 Woodwinds	84600
14	2	condo	2	2.0	1066	1	920:520/604/368	1324 Killiam Ct.	74900
15	4	split	4	2.5	2600	10	920:476/424/428	7141 Eastridge	198000
16	2	twnhouse	2	1.5	1150	15	920:304/400/368	1239 Donaldson Ct.	49900
17	4	ranch	3	2.5	2441	1	920:540/512/436	9356 Sauls Rd.	197000
18	1	split	3	1.0	1245	36	920:524/388/348	2414 Van Dyke	85000
19	7	twnhouse	2	1.5	1280	4	920:584/592/588	409 Galashiels	60000
20	4	ranch	3	3.0	2400	2	920:420/424/428	8122 Maude Steward Rd.	129900
21	2	duplex	2	2.5	1184	4	920:364/604/368	112 Lake Hollow	67900
22	6	duplex	3	1.0	1569	73	350:324/328/336	108 South Elm St.	100000
23	2	twnhouse	2	1.5	1040	9	920:414/604/316	216 Concannon Ct.	59900
24	4	condo	3	2.0	1448	5	920:448/472/318	6000-102 Winterpoint	79900
25	2	twnhouse	3	2.0	1471	1	920:364/604/368	765 Crabtree Crossing	184000
26	4	twostory	3	2.5	1940	4	920:328/312/316	1641 Pricewood Lane	195000
27	5	split	2	1.0	960	2	680:308/304/332	Rt.5 Yarbororugh Rd.	78900
28	8	twnhouse	2	2.0	1167	5	320:364/366/312	5001 Pine Cone	78500
29	2	condo	2	2.0	1246	4	920:364/604/316	721 Springfork	76900
30	1	twnhouse	2	1.0	980	4	920:304/360/552	1203 Berley Ct	72400
31	8	twostory	4	2.5	3446	0	320:313/316/356	Lot 10 Red Coach Rd.	225000
32	8	split	3	1.5	1441	28	320:315/316/356	5617 Laurel Crest Dr.	86900
33	5	twostory	3	2.5	1900	4	680:308/316/332	1532 St. Mary's Rd.	118500
34	8	split	3	2.0	1976	10	320:348/316/356	110 Skylark Way	123500
35	8	twnhouse	2	2.0	1276	6	321:360/304/356	8 Stonevillage	71000
36	5	split	3	2.0	1533	5	680:/308/316/32	603 Greentree Dr.	117800
37	2	twostory	4	2.5	2584	0	920:364/640/368	114 Grey Horse Dr.	189900
38	8	twostory	4	2.5	2608	0	320:362/366/312	2103 Carriage Way	189900
39	2	twnhouse	3	2.5	2080	4	920:530/400/318	108 Chattle Close	179900
40	5	twostory	3	2.5	2863	7	680:308/316/332	5521 Horseshoe Circle	199200
41	8	split	2	2.5	2900	38	320:315/316/356	2617 Snow Hill Rd	425000
42	3	twostory	4	2.5	3926	5	320:362/366/312	49 Birn Ham Lane	360000
43	4	split	3	1.0	1010	28	920:432/404/436	4341 Rock Quarry	60000
44	1	split	3	2.0	1662	12	920:488/360/552	6324 Lakeland, Lake Park	100000
45	2	split	3	2.0	2004	0	920:568/400/318	101 Meadowgladeo Ln.	179950
46	2	twostory	3	2.5	1650	0	920:364/608/368	100 Cumberland Green	143000
47	1	twostory	3	2.5	2416	6	920:568/356/318	6008 Brass Lantern Ct.	144500
48	4	ranch	3	2.5	2441	1	920:540/512/436	9356 Sauls Rd.	197000
49	1	twostory	5	3.5	4850	3	920:540/512/436	9317 Sauls Rd.	339950
50	4	split	3	1.5	1225	18	920:328/312/316	6424 Old Jenks Rd.	81900

Creating a Report

The listing in Output 14.1 is extensive and cumbersome to search visually. A Realtor may want to produce a listing that contains only the kind of house that has the specific characteristics a customer is interested in. For example, a family with frequent house guests and two athletic teenagers wants a house that has 2 to 3 1/2 bathrooms and that is convenient to an area school that has a cross-country team. WHERE processing is useful for creating such a report.

The following WHERE statement expresses the first condition. It uses the BETWEEN-AND operator to select observations in which the numeric variable BATH contains a value from 2 to 3.5.

```
libname mylib 'SAS-data-library ';

proc print data=mylib.houses;
   where bath between 2 and 3.5;
```

Note that the BETWEEN-AND operator is inclusive. This statement selects observations where the value for BATH is equal to 2, 3.5, or any value between them.

As a second condition, the clients want to be near one of the two schools in the area that have cross-country teams, either Waitley High School or Oak Ridge High School. Notice the values for the variable SCHOOL in the real estate data. Values for SCHOOL consist of a district code followed by three codes for individual schools. Figure 14.1 shows the structure of a sample value for the SCHOOL variable.

Figure 14.1
Sample Value for the Variable SCHOOL

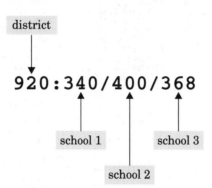

The real estate data contain codes for 167 schools in seven districts. To select the right school, the Realtor must search for both the correct district and school code. In an observation that specifies Waitley High School, the value of the SCHOOL variable begins with the district code **320**, ends with the school code **312**, and contains two other school codes between them. To specify a pattern against which the values of character variables can be checked, you can use the LIKE operator and percent sign (%) in a WHERE expression. The following WHERE expression selects all observations in which the value for SCHOOL begins with 320, ends with 312, and contains any values between them:

```
where (bath between 2 and 3.5) and (schools like '320%312');
```

To add conditions to a WHERE statement, specify additional operators and group expressions for processing by using parentheses. The following WHERE statement adds another condition. It selects an observation for a house that contains from 2 to 3.5 bathrooms and that is local to Waitley High School or to Oak Ridge High School. Note the use of parentheses to group expressions.

```
where (bath between 2 and 3.5) and
      ((schools like '320%312') or (schools like '920%348'));
```

The following program creates and prints a report that lists only houses in the MYLIB.HOUSES data set that meet these specified conditions.

```
libname mylib 'SAS-data-library ';

proc print data=mylib.houses;
   where (bath between 2 and 3.5) and
         ((schools like '320%312') or (schools like '920%348'));
   title1 'Houses With 2 to 3 1/2 Baths';
   title2 'Local to Waitley or Oak Ridge High School';
run;
```

Output 14.2 shows the requested real estate listings.

Output 14.2   *Using a WHERE Statement to Process Only a Subset of a SAS Data Set*

```
                                    Houses With 2 to 3 1/2 Baths                                        1
                                Local to Waitley or Oak Ridge High School

     OBS    ZONE    TYPE      BEDR    BATH    SQFEET    AGE     SCHOOLS          ADDRESS           PRICE

       3      3    twnhouse     2     2.0      1595      6    320:332/366/312    154 Montrose      102000
       4      1    twostory     3     2.5      2750      0    920:628/388/348    4000 Skipjack Ct. 214900
      13      8    twnhouse     2     2.0      1120      4    320:364/366/312    521 Woodwinds      84600
      28      8    twnhouse     2     2.0      1167      5    320:364/366/312    5001 Pine Cone     78500
      38      8    twostory     4     2.5      2608      0    320:362/366/312    2103 Carriage Way 189900
      42      3    twostory     4     2.5      3926      5    320:362/366/312    49 Birn Ham Lane  360000
```

Creating a Report and a Data Set

If you need a single report on a subset of information in a SAS data set, using the PRINT procedure is an efficient method. However, if you want to work further with only the subset of information, you can use the same WHERE statement in a DATA step to create an output data set. You can then print that data set with the PRINT procedure, or you can further manipulate it with DATA or PROC steps in subsequent SAS sessions.

The following program creates the same report shown in Output 14.2. It also creates an output data set named MYLIB.CHOSEN that can be used in subsequent SAS sessions. Note that the WHERE statement is the same, whether it is used in a DATA step or in a PROC step.

```
libname mylib 'SAS-data-library';

data mylib.chosen;
   set mylib.houses;
   where (bath between 2 and 3.5) and
         ((schools like '320%312') or (schools like '920%348'));
run;

proc print data=mylib.chosen;
   title1 'Houses With 2 to 3 1/2 Baths';
   title2 'Local to Waitley or Oak Ridge High School';
run;
```

Reporting on a Subset of Information in Multiple Data Sets

Sometimes data you want for a report reside in multiple data sets. For example, budget information can be in separate data sets, one for each department. In such cases, you must usually create the subset with a DATA step so you can read from multiple data sets. (Most base SAS procedures cannot process more than one data set at a time.) Using the SQL procedure, however, you can report on a subset of information from more than one SAS data set without having to first create a new data set. PROC SQL is the SAS System's implementation of Structured Query Language (SQL). If you are familiar with SQL, this procedure may be a natural choice for you even when you are manipulating only a single data set.

SAS Data Set Example

As an example, the following two data sets contain information on the travel plans and expenses for the marketing division of a software company. One data set contains the following variables and stores information about the travel plans for marketing representatives:

Variable	Type	Description
NAME	character	name of marketing representative
CONF	character	name of conference or trade show
BEGDATE	numeric	beginning date
ENDDATE	numeric	end date
CITY	character	destination
EXHIBIT	character	type of exhibit
SEMINAR	character	whether the representative made a seminar presentation

The other data set contains the following variables and stores information about the expenses incurred on each trip:

Variable	Type	Description
NAME	character	name of marketing representative
CITY	character	destination
BEGDATE	numeric	beginning date
ENDDATE	numeric	end date
AIRFARE	numeric	cost of airfare
GROUND	numeric	cost of ground transportation
HOTEL	numeric	cost of hotel expenses
FOOD	numeric	cost of food
ENTERTMT	numeric	cost of entertaining customers

The following PROC PRINT steps display these data sets:*

```
libname mylib 'SAS-data-library ';

proc print data=mylib.plan;
   title 'Conference Plans';
run;

proc print data=mylib.expense;
   title 'Conference Expenses';
run;
```

Output 14.3 and Output 14.4 show the results.

Output 14.3   *Printout of MYLIB.PLAN Data Set*

```
                                    Conference Plans                                              1
    OBS  NAME             CONF                            BEGDATE  ENDDATE  CITY          EXHIBIT              SEMINAR

     1   Judith Oslavsky  Chicago Electronics Trade Show  20MAY91  23MAY91  Chicago       music synthesizers     y
     2   Sandra Chen      Electronics Technologies Show   14APR91  17APR91  San Francisco electronics            y
     3   John Stephens    Entertainment Industries Show   24JUN91  28JUN91  Las Vegas     futures software       y
     4   Mark Goldstein   Entertainment Industries Show   24JUN91  28JUN91  Las Vegas     music software         n
     5   Rosa Rios        Entertainment Industries Show   24JUN91  28JUN91  Las Vegas     legal software         y
     6   Fred Washington  Western User's Group            11MAR91  13MAR91  Lake Tahoe    general software       y
     7   Gloria Faley     Western User's Group            11MAR91  13MAR91  Lake Tahoe    general software       n
     8   Harry Smith      Western User's Group            11MAR91  13MAR91  Lake Tahoe    general software       n
```

---

*   The DATA steps that create MYLIB.PLAN and MYLIB.EXPENSE are shown in the Appendix.

Output 14.4　　　　*Printout of MYLIB.EXPENSE Data Set*

```
                                    Conference Expenses                                              1
OBS   NAME              CITY          BEGDATE  ENDDATE    AIRFARE    GROUND      HOTEL      FOOD    ENTERTMT
  1   Judith Oslavsky   Chicago       20MAY91  23MAY91    $378.50    $23.00    $425.34   $325.88    $333.22
  2   Sandra Chen       San Francisco 14APR91  17APR91    $459.70    $25.00    $339.50   $170.15    $120.00
  3   John Stephens     Las Vegas     24JUN91  28JUN91    $220.35    $32.00    $698.22   $375.40    $420.98
  4   Mark Goldstein    Las Vegas     24JUN91  28JUN91    $220.35    $36.00    $702.56   $398.13    $235.18
  5   Rosa Rios         Las Vegas     24JUN91  28JUN91    $220.35    $30.00    $690.45   $380.78      $0.00
  6   Fred Washington   Lake Tahoe    11MAR91  13MAR91    $256.75    $22.00    $377.19   $280.10     $98.00
  7   Gloria Faley      Lake Tahoe    11MAR91  13MAR91    $256.75    $23.00    $372.90   $266.39      $0.00
  8   Harry Smith       Lake Tahoe    11MAR91  13MAR91    $256.75    $25.00    $398.00   $225.45    $195.00
```

Creating a Report

From the data sets MYLIB.PLAN and MYLIB.EXPENSE, managers can select information that reveals how much was spent on trips involving seminar presentations. To create a report that contains selected observations from one or more existing SAS data sets, use the SQL procedure. Begin with the PROC SQL statement and then title the report with a TITLE statement.

```
libname mylib 'SAS-data-library ';

proc sql;
    title 'Costs of Seminar Presentations';
```

Note that in a PROC SQL step you must place the TITLE statement before the statement that describes the report.

The next step is to describe the report with a SELECT statement. You can supply the following types of information in a SELECT statement:

□ the variables to display, including any new ones that must be calculated

□ any labels or formats

□ the data sets (tables in SQL terminology) from which to retrieve the variables

□ any conditions for including an observation in the report.

The following template demonstrates how to specify such information with a SELECT statement:

SELECT *variables and related-information*
FROM *SAS-data-sets (tables)*
WHERE *conditions-for-inclusion*;

To indicate the data set from which to select information, use a FROM clause. If some variables in the two data sets have the same name, you must indicate which variable you are specifying by identifying the data set in which it is located. Do this by giving each data set an alias when you specify it in the FROM clause. The following FROM clause assigns the aliases P and E to MYLIB.PLAN and MYLIB.EXPENSE, respectively:

```
from mylib.plan as p, mylib.expense as e
```

Once you assign aliases, you can specify the variables to be selected from each data set in the SELECT statement. Separate variable names with commas. The following partial SELECT statement specifies that the variables NAME and CITY are to be taken from the data set MYLIB.PLAN and that the variable CONF is also to be included.

```
select p.name, conf, p.city
    from mylib.plan as p, mylib.expense as e
```

The variables NAME and CITY reside in both data sets, so an alias is required. Because the variable CONF occurs in only one of the input data sets, no alias is required.

You can also calculate values and assign them to a new variable in a SELECT statement. This example adds the amounts reported for individual expenditures and assigns the sum to a new variable named TOTAL.

```
select p.name, conf, p.city,
        sum(airfare,ground,hotel,food,entertmt) as total
    from mylib.plan as p, mylib.expense as e
```

For readability in a report, you can assign labels and formats to variables in the SELECT statement. This example assigns the label **Total Expense** and the format DOLLAR10.2 to the variable TOTAL.

```
select p.name, conf, p.city,
        sum(airfare,ground,hotel,food,entertmt) as total
        label='Total Expense' format=dollar10.2
    from mylib.plan as p, mylib.expense as e
```

To finish describing a report on a subset of information, use a WHERE clause to state the condition for selecting an observation (row) from the data set (table).

▶ *Caution* .... *Restrict a join operation with a WHERE expression.*
When you join multiple tables with a SELECT statement, it is recommended that you always restrict the operation with a WHERE expression to avoid creating an unnecessarily large (and perhaps meaningless) table. ▲

In this example, the variables NAME and CITY are matched from each data set and only those observations for trips that included seminar presentations are chosen. Note that the alias identifying each data set precedes the variable names NAME and CITY.

```
select p.name, conf, p.city,
        sum(airfare,ground,hotel,food,entertmt) as total
        label='Total Expense' format=dollar10.2
    from mylib.plan as p, mylib.expense as e
    where p.name=e.name
        and p.city=e.city
        and seminar='y';
```

Here is the complete PROC SQL step that queries the data set and prints a report on expenditures for trips involving seminar presentations:

```
libname mylib 'SAS-data-library ';

proc sql;
    title 'Costs of Seminar Presentations';
    select p.name, conf, p.city,
            sum(airfare,ground,hotel,food,entertmt) as total
            label='Total Expense' format=dollar10.2
        from mylib.plan as p, mylib.expense as e
        where p.name=e.name
                and p.city=e.city
                and seminar='y';
```

Note that the SQL procedure does not require a RUN statement to produce the report. Output 14.5 shows the report generated.

Output 14.5   *Creating a Report from a Subset of Multiple SAS Data Sets*

```
                        Costs of Seminar Presentations                              1

                                                                    Total
   NAME              CONF                            CITY           Expense
   -----------------------------------------------------------------------------
   Judith Oslavsky   Chicago Electronics Trade Show  Chicago        $1,485.94
   Sandra Chen       Electronics Technologies Show   San Francisco  $1,114.35
   John Stephens     Entertainment Industries Show   Las Vegas      $1,746.95
   Rosa Rios         Entertainment Industries Show   Las Vegas      $1,321.58
   Fred Washington   Western User's Group            Lake Tahoe     $1,034.04
```

Creating a Report and a Data Set

As discussed earlier in this chapter, if you need only a single report, you probably do not want to create a data set from a subset of information that is already stored in a SAS data set. However, if you want to work further with only that subset, you can create a new SAS data set at the same time you generate a report with the SQL procedure. To create a new data set, use a CREATE statement. Then use a SELECT statement to create a report.

To illustrate, consider the PROC SQL step that generates the report in Output 14.5. The following program begins with that PROC SQL step and generates a SAS data set by using a CREATE statement. The SELECT statement in the previous program becomes a clause in the CREATE statement. A new SELECT statement creates the report by selecting all the variables in the data set created by the CREATE statement. The following PROC SQL step creates the same report as shown in Output 14.5 and creates a data set named MYLIB.SEMCOST:

```
libname mylib 'SAS-data-library';

proc sql;
   title 'Costs of Seminar Presentations';
   create table mylib.semcost as
      select p.name, conf, p.city,
             sum(airfare,ground,hotel,food,entertmt) as total
             label='Total Expense' format=dollar10.2
      from mylib.plan as p, mylib.expense as e
      where p.name=e.name
            and p.city=e.city
            and seminar='y';
   select * from mylib.semcost;
```

Summary

The following points summarize the differences between using a WHERE expression or a subsetting IF statement and also summarize how to create a report or a report and a new data set from a subset of information in one or more SAS data sets:

□ To create a subset of one or more SAS data sets, you can use either a WHERE expression or a subsetting IF statement. Each tool has special advantages and restrictions based on the time the observation selection process occurs.

□ When your application has the following requirements, use a subsetting IF statement:

   □ base the selection on anything other than a variable value that already exists in a SAS data set—for example, on a value that is read from raw data or on a value that is calculated or assigned during the course of the DATA step

   □ make the selection at some point during a DATA step rather than at the beginning

   □ execute the selection conditionally.

□   When your application has the one of following requirements, use a WHERE
expression:

□   make the selection in a procedure without using a preceding DATA step

□   take advantage of the efficiency available with indexed data sets

□   use one of the following operators: BETWEEN-AND, CONTAINS,
IS MISSING, IS NULL, LIKE, SAME-AND, or SOUNDS LIKE.

□   To create a report on a subset of a SAS data set, you can use a WHERE
expression in a PROC step. If you also want to create a new data set from the
subset, you can use the same WHERE expression in a DATA step and simply
print the report with a PROC step.

□   To create a report from a subset of information in multiple SAS data sets, you
must use either a DATA step or the SQL procedure. Using the SQL procedure
gives you the option of creating a new data set (called a table in SQL
terminology) and a report or just a report.

SAS Tools

This section summarizes syntax for the statements and procedure discussed in this
chapter.

Statements

WHERE *where-expression*;
specifies one or more conditions for the processing of an observation in the
current DATA or PROC step. You can specify any valid *where expression*. In
addition to a valid SAS expression, a where expression can include special
operators and characters that are available only in WHERE expressions. The
following special WHERE operators are discussed in this chapter:

LIKE
enables you to select observations by comparing the values of character
variables to patterns specified in the WHERE expression. The percent sign
(%) is a special character that you can use with the LIKE operator to
specify a pattern. The percent sign indicates that any number of
characters can occupy a certain position.

BETWEEN-AND
enables you to select observations in which the values of a character or
numeric variable fall within a range of values.

Procedure

PROC SQL;
    CREATE TABLE *SAS-data-set* AS *table-expression*;
    SELECT *table-expression*;

    PROC SQL;
        begins the SQL procedure, which allows you to use Structured Query
        Language to create a report, a SAS data set, or both a SAS data set and a
        report from one or more data sets (called a table in SQL terminology).

    CREATE TABLE *SAS-data-set* AS *table-expression*;
        creates a SAS data file (table) as described in the *table-expression* that
        follows the keyword AS. The table expression consists of the SELECT and
        FROM clauses, as well as other optional clauses. The following clauses are
        discussed in this chapter:

        SELECT *variable*<, . . . *variable-n*>
            specifies the variables to appear in the table. Place a comma between
            the variable names. You can list the variables by name only or as a
            variable name preceded by an alias and a period, as follows:
            alias.variable.

        FROM *from-list*
            lists the SAS data set(s) (SQL tables) from which the new data set is to
            be constructed. The *from-list* can consist simply of data set names or
            of data set names and assigned aliases. If you list multiple data sets,
            separate them with commas.

        WHERE *where-expression*
            specifies one or more conditions for inclusion for each observation
            (row) in the SAS data set(s) in a FROM clause. A *where-expression* can
            consist of any valid SQL expression.

    SELECT *table-expression*;
        creates a report as described in the *table-expression*. Use the SELECT
        statement instead of a CREATE statement when you want to create a
        report but no new data set. A *table-expression* consists of elements and
        clauses that describe the contents of the table. The following elements and
        clauses are discussed in this chapter:

        variable<, . . . *variable-n*>
            specifies the variables to include in the report. If a variable of the
            same name resides in more than one data set, you must precede the
            variable name with the appropriate alias (assigned in the FROM
            clause), in the following form:

            alias.variable.

(PROC SQL; continued)

FROM *from-list*
> lists the SAS data set(s) (SQL tables) from which the new data set is to be constructed. The *from-list* can consist simply of data set names or of data set names and assigned aliases. If you list multiple data sets, separate them with commas.

WHERE *where-expression*
> specifies one or more conditions for inclusion for each observation (row) in the SAS data set(s) in a FROM clause. A *where-expression* can consist of any valid SQL expression.

Learning More

This section provides references for learning more about topics presented in this chapter.

□ For a complete description of the WHERE statement, including the special operators available only in WHERE expressions, see *SAS Language: Reference, Version 6, First Edition*, Chapter 9, "SAS Language Statements."

□ To learn more details about using WHERE processing with base SAS software, including its use of indexes and its effect on BY processing, see *SAS Language: Reference*, Chapter 6, "SAS Files."

□ For a description of the WHERE= data set option, see *SAS Language: Reference*, Chapter 15, "SAS Data Set Options."

□ To learn more about producing reports and SAS data sets with the SQL procedure, see *SAS Guide to the SQL Procedure: Usage and Reference, Version 6, First Edition*.

Chapter 15 Producing Exceptions Reports

Introduction

Before you use data in a production process, you should ensure the data are free of errors, such as values that are miscoded, out-of-range, or logically inconsistent. You can use the SAS System to detect erroneous data and produce exceptions reports that list the data errors.

In this chapter
This chapter shows you how to produce reports that list the following categories of data errors:

- invalid values, such as character data in numeric fields and dates that are not valid for the informat specified

- missing, out-of-range, or miscoded values

- duplicate values

- values that are logically inconsistent relative to other values.

Using the information in the exceptions reports, you can refer to the original sources from which the data were entered to determine the correct values. Then you can make the necessary corrections in the raw data or SAS data set before using the data in a production program. (Although your data may be stored differently, this chapter uses instream data lines for easy reference.)

Prerequisites

Before reading this chapter, you should be familiar with the following:

□ the normal flow of the DATA step

□ the FORMAT procedure

□ the PUT function

□ the automatic variables FIRST.*variable* and LAST.*variable*.

Input Data Example

The four examples in this chapter use a DATA step to read raw data that were gathered by a financial institution from customers who opened certificates of deposit (CDs) in the amount of $10,000. The following table describes the fields in each record of raw data:

Field	Description
sequence number	unique identifier for each CD
issued	date of issue
months	term of CD in months, valid if 1 to 60 inclusive
interest code	paid as follows:
	C by check
	P to principal
	T to interest account
interest account	valid if the interest code equals T

Here are the raw data records:

```
----+----1----+----2----+----3----+----4
CD-05-234 12AUG91 )6 C 534-288-1476
CD-83-265 14AUG91
CD-22-067 16SEP91 60 T 534-203-4821
CD-83-266 9-18-91 06 P
CD-45-168 31NOV91 36 T 534-233-6751
CD-45-168 29NOV91 12 P 534-299-1832
CD-07-831 03DEC91 72 6
```

Listing Invalid Values

During data entry, invalid values can be introduced into raw data. Invalid values can include character data in numeric fields and values that do not match the informat listed on the INPUT statement. You can list these kinds of data entry errors easily if you execute a DATA step to do the following:

□ read all records in the raw data and check for errors

□ if errors exist, process the erroneous records appropriately.

To illustrate, look at the following set of errors in the CD raw data. Notice the highlighted values in the first, fourth, and fifth records. In the first record, the field containing months has a value of) 6, which is a character value in a numeric field. In the fourth record, the field containing the issue date has a value of 9-18-91, which is inconsistent with the format of the other dates. In the fifth record, the field containing the issue date has a value of 31NOV91 which is a nonexistent date; November has only 30 days.

```
----+----1----+----2----+----3----+----4
CD-05-234 12AUG91 )6 C 534-288-1476
CD-83-265 14AUG91
CD-22-067 16SEP91 60 T 534-203-4821
CD-83-266 9-18-91 06 P
CD-45-168 31NOV91 36 T 534-233-6751
CD-45-168 29NOV91 12 P 534-299-1832
CD-07-831 03DEC91 72 6
```

Read All Records and Check for Errors

To list the invalid values in the CD raw data, begin with a DATA step that reads all the records. After the INPUT statement, use an IF-THEN statement that includes the _ERROR_ automatic variable as the test condition.*

```
data _null_;
   input seqnum $9.
         a11 issued date7.
         a19 months 2.
         a22 incode $1.
         a24 inacct $12.;
   if (_error_) then
      do;
         statements that process an erroneous record
      end;
```

---

* If you only want to diagnose data errors, you can execute a DATA step that simply reads all the records and then you can review the SAS log for error messages. For details on using the SAS log to diagnose data errors, see *SAS Language and Procedures: Usage, Version 6, First Edition.*

For each DATA step, the SAS System creates the automatic variable _ERROR_. By default, the system sets _ERROR_ to 0 (false). However, when an error is encountered in the DATA step, _ERROR_ is set to 1 (true), and the SAS System writes the data line to the SAS log. (Note the expression _ERROR_ is the same as _ERROR_=1.)

You can use the value of the variable _ERROR_ as a test condition. If the value is 0, there is no error, and you can read the data line into the data set. If the value is 1, there is an error, and you'll need to process the erroneous record some other way.

Process the Erroneous Records

To process erroneous records, include certain statements in the DO group to do the following:

□ define an external print file

□ write an error message and record number to the print file

□ write the record contents to the print file

□ prevent the erroneous record from being written as an observation to the SAS data set.

Use the FILE statement to define a file to which the erroneous records are written. In this example, the PRINT file specification is used to send output to the procedure output file.

```
file print;
```

After the output file has been defined, use one or more PUT statements to write an error message to the output file. If you want to include the number of the erroneous record, add the _N_ automatic variable as a part of the error message.

For each DATA step, the SAS System creates the automatic variable _N_. Initially, _N_ is set to 1. Each time the DATA step loops past the DATA statement, _N_ is incremented by 1. Therefore, the value of _N_ represents the number of times the DATA step has iterated and it can be used to uniquely identify each input record.

```
put 'ERROR: In Record Number ' _n_;
put 'ERROR: Record Contents Follow:';
```

Next, write the contents of the current record to the output file that was defined in the FILE statement. You can do this with a PUT statement that uses an _INFILE_ specification.

```
put _infile_;
```

By adding a DELETE statement before closing the DO group, you can exclude erroneous records from the SAS data set. The DELETE statement tells the SAS System to stop processing the current observation. The observation is not written to any data set, and processing returns immediately to the beginning of the DATA step. The END statement closes the DO group.

```
    delete;
end;
```

The following DATA step combines all the elements discussed previously to list values that were entered incorrectly in the CD raw data. When the DATA step executes, the FILE statement and PUT statements in the DO group produce output, so no PROC PRINT step is needed.

```
title 'Invalid Values in CD Raw Data';

data _null_;
    input seqnum $9.
          @11 issued date7.
          @19 months 2.
          @22 incode $1.
          @24 inacct $12.;
    if (_error_) then
      do;
          file print;
          put 'ERROR: In Record Number ' _n_;
          put 'ERROR: Record Contents Follow:';
          put _infile_;
          delete;
      end;
    cards;
CD-05-234 12AUG91 )6 C 534-288-1476
CD-83-265 14AUG91
CD-22-067 16SEP91 60 T 534-203-4821
CD-83-266 9-18-91 06 P
CD-45-168 31NOV91 36 T 534-233-6751
CD-45-168 29NOV91 12 P 534-299-1832
CD-07-831 03DEC91 72 6
;
```

Output 15.1 shows the results.

Output 15.1

Listing Invalid Values

```
                         Invalid Values in CD Raw Data                    1
ERROR: In Record Number 1
ERROR: Record Contents Follow:
CD-05-234 12AUG91 )6 C 534-288-1476

ERROR: In Record Number 4
ERROR: Record Contents Follow:
CD-83-266 9-18-91 06 P

ERROR: In Record Number 5
ERROR: Record Contents Follow:
CD-45-168 31NOV91 36 T 534-233-6751
```

Using record numbers, such as the ones displayed in Output 15.1, you can find the missing, out-of-range, and miscoded values in the raw data. Then referring to the sources from which the data were originally entered, you can correct the values before proceeding to the next level of error detection.

Listing Missing, Out-of-Range, and Miscoded Data

Even when numeric fields contain only numeric values and dates are formatted correctly, the data can still contain errors. For example, the data can contain missing values, values that lie outside a valid range, or values that contain incorrect codes. Such errors will not be listed in a report like the one in the previous example because they do not affect the value of the _ERROR_ automatic variable. However, you can detect missing, out-of-range, and miscoded data by doing the following:

□ create formats to detect errors in the data

□ create and print a SAS data set that contains unformatted and formatted values of variables.

To illustrate, look at the following set of errors in the CD raw data. (The errors from the previous example have been corrected.) Notice the erroneous values in the second and the seventh records. In the second record, the fields for months and interest code both contain missing values. In the seventh record, the field containing months has a value of 72, which is out of the valid range of 1 to 60. Also in the seventh record, the field containing the interest code has a value of **6**, which is miscoded. The interest code should be either **C**, **P**, or **T**.

```
----+----1----+----2----+----3----+----4
CD-05-234 12AUG91 06 C 534-288-1476
CD-83-265 14AUG91 ▮▮ ▮
CD-22-067 16SEP91 60 T 534-203-4821
CD-83-266 18SEP91 06 P
CD-45-168 21NOV91 36 T 534-233-6751
CD-45-168 29NOV91 12 P 534-299-1832
CD-07-831 03DEC91 72 6
```

Create Formats to Detect Errors

None of the above data entry errors cause the SAS System to write notes or error messages to the log. Therefore, you need to detect the errors some other way. One way is to use a PROC FORMAT step to specify values that are valid, missing, out-of-range, and miscoded.

For example, the PROC FORMAT step below defines two formats, TERM. for numeric values and $PAYTO. for character values:

```
proc format;
   value term 1-60='Valid'
                  .='MISSING'
              other='OUT-OF-RANGE';
   value $payto 'C','P','T'='Valid'
                        ' '='MISSING'
                    other='MISCODED';
run;
```

Valid numeric and character values are defined as `Valid`. Missing numeric values (periods) and missing character values (blanks) are defined as `MISSING`. Any other values are detected using the keyword OTHER and are defined as `OUT-OF-RANGE` if they are numeric values or `MISCODED` if they are character values.

Note that the FORMAT procedure does not assign values to variables. It only defines formats that you can use later in a DATA or PROC step to display variable values.

Create and Print a SAS Data Set with Unformatted and Formatted Values

After you have defined formats to detect errors, create a DATA step to do the following:

□ read in the fields you want to check for errors

□ create new variables that contain formatted values.

The CD raw data contain a numeric field for months and a character field for the interest code. Create a DATA step that begins by reading these two fields.

```
data errors;
   input @19 months 2.
         @22 incode $1.;
```

In the exceptions report, the values of the variables should appear twice: first, unformatted the same as they are in the CD raw data, and second, formatted using the error-detection formats defined earlier in the PROC FORMAT step. Showing the values twice lets you see the actual data values, including errors, and the formatted values that describe the value as either `Valid`, `MISSING`, `OUT-OF-RANGE`, or `MISCODED`.

To list the unformatted values of the variables, you can use the variables MONTHS and INCODE because those values are the same as they are in the raw data. However, to list formatted values, create two new variables using assignment statements and the PUT function.

```
f_months=put(months,term.);
f_incode=put(incode,$payto.);
```

The assignment statements create two variables: F_MONTHS, which contains the formatted values of the variable MONTHS, and F_INCODE, which contains the formatted values of the variable INCODE. The values of the new variables are formatted with the user-defined formats TERM, and $PAYTO, respectively.

The following program combines all the elements discussed so far for listing missing, out-of-range, and miscoded values. In addition, the program includes a PROC PRINT step, which prints the observation numbers and unformatted and formatted values. The VAR statement lists the variables MONTHS, F_MONTHS, INCODE, and F_INCODE.

```
proc format;
    value term 1-60='Valid'
                   .='MISSING'
               other='OUT-OF-RANGE';
    value $payto 'C','P','T'='Valid'
                         ' '='MISSING'
                     other='MISCODED';
run;

data errors;
    input @19 months 2.
          @22 incode $1.;
    f_months=put(months,term.);
    f_incode=put(incode,$payto.);
    cards;
CD-05-234 12AUG91 06 C 534-288-1476
CD-83-265 14AUG91
CD-22-067 16SEP91 60 T 534-203-4821
CD-83-266 09SEP91 06 P
CD-45-168 21NOV91 36 T 534-233-6751
CD-45-168 29NOV91 12 P 534-299-1832
CD-07-831 03DEC91 72 6
;

proc print data=errors;
    var months f_months incode f_incode;
    title 'Missing, Out-of-Range, and Miscoded Values in CD Raw Data';
run;
```

Output 15.2 shows the results.

Output 15.2
Listing Missing,
Out-of-Range, and
Miscoded Data

```
         Missing, Out-of-Range, and Miscoded Values in CD Raw Data        1

   OBS     MONTHS    F_MONTHS         INCODE     F_INCODE

    1         6      Valid              C        Valid
    2         .      MISSING                     MISSING
    3        60      Valid              T        Valid
    4         6      Valid              P        Valid
    5        36      Valid              T        Valid
    6        12      Valid              P        Valid
    7        72      OUT-OF-RANGE       6        MISCODED
```

Listing Duplicate Values

Data errors can also include duplicate values that should actually be unique. For example, in the CD raw data the sequence number field should contain unique values that identify individual certificates of deposit. Otherwise, an error exists.

There are many ways you could use the SAS System to detect duplicate values—some more elaborate than others. However, a simple and effective way is to do the following:

□ read the data and assign each record a number

□ sort the data by the variable that should have unique values

□ determine which values are not unique.

To illustrate, look at the following set of errors in the CD raw data. (The errors from the previous example have been corrected.) Notice the values of the sequence numbers that are highlighted in the fifth and sixth data lines. Both values are `CD-45-168`. This is an error; the sequence numbers were not incremented correctly during data entry.

```
----+----1----+----2----+----3----+----4
CD-05-234 12AUG91 06 C 534-288-1476
CD-83-265 14AUG91
CD-22-067 16SEP91 60 T 534-203-4821
CD-83-266 18SEP91 06 P
CD-45-168 21NOV91 36 T 534-233-6751
CD-45-168 29NOV91 12 P 534-299-1832
CD-07-831 03DEC91 12 T
```

Read the Data and Assign Record Numbers

Use a DATA step to read the raw data. Also in the DATA step, you can assign a number to each record that corresponds to the record's position in the original data.

To assign each record a number that corresponds to its original position in the raw data file, you can use the automatic variable _N_. (For details, see "Listing Duplicate Values" earlier in this chapter.) In this example, the name of the new variable is RECORD.

```
data temp;
   input seqnum $9.;
   record=_N_;
   cards;
datalines
;
```

Sort the Data

Use a PROC SORT step to sort the observations by the variable that should have unique values, in this case, by the values of the variable SEQNUM.

```
proc sort data=temp;
   by seqnum;
run;
```

Determine Which Values Are Not Unique

In a second DATA step, use a SET statement to read the first data set. In this example, the second DATA step creates the data set DUPLICAT by reading in TEMP. Notice that the second DATA step also contains a BY statement for the variable SEQNUM.

```
data duplicat;
   set temp;
   by seqnum;
   more SAS statements
run;
```

When a BY statement is used with a SET statement, the SAS System automatically creates two special variables for each variable listed in the BY statement. These special variables are called FIRST.*variable* and LAST.*variable*.

Listed below are the possible values for FIRST.*variable* and LAST.*variable*:

FIRST.*variable*   equals 1 for the FIRST observation in a BY group, otherwise equals 0. (The expression FIRST.*variable* is the same as the expression FIRST.*variable*=1.)

LAST.*variable*   equals 1 for the LAST observation in a BY group, otherwise equals 0. (The expression LAST.*variable* is the same as the expression LAST.*variable*=1.)

You can use the values of FIRST.*variable* and LAST.*variable* to determine whether the value of another variable is duplicated in a SAS data set. For example, if the value of SEQNUM in the SAS data set TEMP is unique, then any given value is both the first *and* the last occurrence of that value in that BY group. Therefore, by adding the following subsetting IF statement to the second DATA step, you can output all values of the variable SEQNUM that are not both the first and the last occurrence.*

```
data duplicat;
   set temp;
   by seqnum;
   if not(first.seqnum and last.seqnum);
run;
```

The following program combines all the elements discussed so far for listing duplicate values. In addition, the program includes a PROC PRINT step, which prints the contents of the SAS data set DUPLICAT.

```
data temp;
   input seqnum $9.;
   record=_N_;
   cards;
CD-05-234 12AUG91 06 C 534-288-1476
CD-83-265 14AUG91 36 P
CD-22-067 16SEP91 60 T 534-203-4821
CD-83-266 18SEP91 06 P
CD-45-168 21NOV91 36 T 534-233-6751
CD-45-168 29NOV91 12 P 534-299-1832
CD-07-831 03DEC91 12 T
;

proc sort data=temp;
   by seqnum;
run;
```

---

*   You could also have written this condition as IF FIRST.SEQNUM AND LAST.SEQNUM THEN DELETE;

```
data duplicat;
   set temp;
   by seqnum;
   if not(first.seqnum and last.seqnum);
run;

proc print data=duplicat noobs;
   var record seqnum;
   title 'Duplicate Values in CD Raw Data';
run;
```

Output 15.3 shows the results.

Output 15.3
Listing Duplicate
Values

```
              Duplicate Values in CD Raw Data                    1

                   RCDNUM    SEQNUM

                      5     CD-45-168
                      6     CD-45-168
```

Listing Logically Inconsistent Data Using Related Fields

Another kind of error can exist in data when fields that relate logically to one another lack consistency. For example, in the CD raw data, the values of the interest code and the values of the variable transfer account number are logically related and should be cross validated to ensure consistency.

The following table shows the results of all the logical relationships that can exist between the values of the interest code and the interest account:

Interest Code	Interest Account	Results
C, P	missing	valid
C, P	acct. number	error
T	missing	error
T	acct. number	valid

Referring to the table, you can see that if the value of the interest code is C (meaning "pay the interest by check") or P (meaning "apply the interest to principal"), then no transfer account number is needed, and the value of the interest account should be missing. On the other hand, if the value of the interest code is T (meaning "transfer the interest to the interest account"), then the value of the interest account should contain a transfer account number. To detect such logical errors in data, do the following:

□ read the data and assign record numbers

□ test for conditions that are logically inconsistent.

To illustrate, look at the following set of errors in the CD raw data. (The errors from the previous example have been corrected.) Notice the erroneous values highlighted in the first, sixth, and seventh records.

In the first record, the interest code is **C**, which means "pay the interest by check." No interest account number is needed, but one exists. The same kind of logical error occurs in the sixth record. In that record, the interest code is **P**, which means "add the interest to principal"; however, the sixth record contains an interest account number where none is needed.

The seventh record has the opposite error. In that record, the interest code is **T**, which means "transfer to the interest account," but the interest account number is missing.

```
----+----1----+----2----+----3----+----4
CD-05-234 12AUG91 06 C 534-288-1476
CD-83-265 14AUG91 36 P
CD-22-067 16SEP91 60 T 534-203-4821
CD-83-266 18SEP91 06 P
CD-45-168 21NOV91 36 T 534-233-6751
CD-45-169 29NOV91 12 P 534-299-1832
CD-07-831 03DEC91 12 T
```

Read the Data and Assign Record Numbers

Use a DATA step to read the fields for which a logical relationship exists. The following DATA step also uses the value of the automatic variable _N_ to assign record numbers to each record in the CD raw data. (For details on using _N_ to assign record numbers, see the previous example, "Listing Duplicate Values.") As in the previous example, record numbers can help you locate individual records when you make corrections to the data.

```
data logical;
   input a22 incode $1.
         a24 inacct $12.;
   record=_N_;
   more SAS statements
   cards;
data lines
```

Test for Conditions that Are Logically Inconsistent

To select the records that are logically inconsistent, add a subsetting IF statement with the appropriate comparisons as its condition. In this example, the subsetting IF statement should select observations that meet the following conditions:

□ the value of INCODE is **C** and the value of INACCT is not missing

□ the value of INCODE is **P** and the value of INACCT is not missing

□ the value of INCODE is **T** and the value of INACCT is missing.

The following subsetting IF statement contains as its condition the three comparisons listed above:

```
if (incode='C' and inacct ne ' ') or
   (incode='P' and inacct ne ' ') or
   (incode='T' and inacct=' ');
```

The following program combines all the elements discussed so far for listing logically inconsistent data. In addition, the program includes a PROC PRINT step.

```
data logical;
   input @22 incode $1.
         @24 inacct $12.;
   record=_N_;
   if (incode='C' and inacct ne ' ') or
      (incode='P' and inacct ne ' ') or
      (incode='T' and inacct=' ');
   cards;
CD-05-234 12AUG91 06 C 534-288-1476
CD-83-265 14AUG91 36 P
CD-22-067 16SEP91 60 T 534-203-4821
CD-83-266 18SEP91 06 P
CD-45-168 21NOV91 36 T 534-233-6751
CD-45-169 29NOV91 12 P 534-299-1832
CD-07-831 03DEC91 12 T
;

proc print data=logical noobs;
   var record incode inacct;
   title 'Logically Inconsistent Fields in CD Raw Data';
run;
```

Output 15.4 shows the results.

Output 15.4
Listing Logically
Inconsistent Data
Using Related
Fields

```
          Logically Inconsistent Fields in CD Raw Data          1

          RCDNUM     INCODE     INACCT

             1          C        534-288-1476
             6          P        534-299-1832
             7          T
```

Summary

The following points summarize how to use the SAS System to list erroneous data:

□ To detect invalid values, use the DATA step and the _ERROR_ automatic variable and process them appropriately using the FILE statement and PUT statement.

□ To detect missing, out-of-range, or miscoded values, create formats that can be used with the PUT function and assignment statements.

□ To assign record numbers to raw data records, use the DATA step and the _N_ automatic variable.

□ To generate the special variables, FIRST.*variable* and LAST.*variable*, use the SET statement and the BY statement together.

□ To detect duplicate values, use the IF statement and the FIRST.*variable* and the LAST.*variable*.

□ To select values that are logically inconsistent relative to other values, use a compound subsetting IF statement.

SAS Tools

This section summarizes syntax for the statements, functions, procedures, and automatic variables discussed in this chapter.

Statements

BY *variable*;
controls the operation of a SET statement. Using a SET statement with a BY statement in a DATA step to read only one data set creates the FIRST.*variable* and the LAST.*variable*. The BY statement is also used in the SORT procedure to specify the sort variable.

DELETE;
stops processing of the current observation. The observation is not written to any data set, and the SAS System returns immediately to the beginning of the DATA step for another iteration.

DO;
designates a group of statements to be executed as a unit until a matching END statement is encountered.

END;
ends a DO group.

FILE PRINT;
specifies that output from PUT statements in the current DATA step be written to the procedure output file.

IF *expression* **THEN** *statement*;
causes the DATA step to continue processing only those raw data records or observations from a SAS data set that meet the condition of the expression specified in the IF statement. Therefore, the resulting SAS data set contains a subset of the original records or observations. *Expression* is any valid SAS expression. *Statement* is any executable SAS statement or DO group.

PUT _INFILE_;
> writes lines to the SAS log, to the SAS procedure file, or to the external file specified in the most recent FILE statement. _INFILE_writes the last record read from the file currently being used as input, either from the current input file or from data lines following a CARDS statement.

SET *data-set-name*;
> reads observations from a SAS data set. Using a SET statement with a BY statement in a DATA step to read only one data set creates the FIRST.*variable* and the LAST.*variable*.

Functions

PUT (*source, format*);
> returns a value using a specified format. *Source* identifies the SAS variable or constant whose value you want to reformat. *Source* can be character or numeric. *Format* identifies the SAS format you want applied to the variable or constant specified in the *source*. *Format* must be of the same type as *source*, either character or numeric.

Procedures

PROC FORMAT;
> **VALUE** *name value-1* ='*formatted-value-1*' < . . . *value-n*='*formatted-value-n*'>;

> **PROC FORMAT;**
>> begins the FORMAT procedure, which allows you to create your own formats and informats for character and numeric variables.

> **VALUE** *name value-1*='*formatted-value-1*'< . . . *value-n*='*formatted-value-n*'>;
>> defines a format that writes a variable's value as a different value. *Name* names the output format being created. *Value* specifies one or more values, a range of values, or a list of ranges that a variable written with the format can have. OTHER specifies a range of all other values. *Formatted-value* specifies the output to which the format converts the variable value.

Automatic variables

ERROR
> indicates whether an error is encountered, such as an input data error. By default, _ERROR_ is set to 0 but is set to 1 whenever an error is encountered.

FIRST.*variable*
> identifies the beginning of a BY group. *Variable* is the BY variable named in the BY statement.

LAST.*variable*
> identifies the ending of a BY group. *Variable* is the BY variable named in the BY statement.

_N_
> represents the number of times a DATA step has iterated. _N_ is initially set to 1. Each time the DATA step loops past the DATA statement, _N_ is incremented by 1.

Learning More

This section provides references for learning more about the topics presented in this chapter.

□ For complete documentation of the FORMAT procedure, see *SAS Procedures Guide: Version 6, Third Edition*, Chapter 18, "The FORMAT Procedure."

□ To learn how to use the PUT function for other purposes, see *SAS Language: Reference, Version 6, First Edition*, Chapter 11, "SAS Functions."

□ For complete documentation on the following topics, see the appropriate section in *SAS Language and Procedures: Usage, Version 6, First Edition*, and *SAS Language: Reference*:

  □ the PUT statement

  □ the FILE statement

  □ the automatic variable _ERROR_

  □ the automatic variables FIRST.*variable* and LAST.*variable*.

□ To learn how to prevent missing values and unmatched records from corrupting observations in a SAS data set, see Chapter 4, "Handling Missing and Invalid Values and Missing Records."

Chapter 16 Producing Multi-Panel Reports

Introduction

This chapter shows you how to produce *multi-panel reports*. Multi-panel reports are output that use sets of columns on a single page to display the values of variables. Each set of columns is called a *panel*. A familiar example of a multi-panel report is a telephone book, which displays multiple panels of names, addresses, and phone numbers on a single page.

In this chapter
This chapter shows you how to do the following:

☐ design the report

☐ set up the output file

☐ set up the panels

☐ fill in the panels with values.

Prerequisites
Before reading this chapter, you should understand DATA step processing. In addition, you should also know how to use DO loops to perform iterative processing. Additionally, you should be familiar with the PUT statement including line and column pointer controls and formats.

SAS Data Set Example

This chapter uses a SAS data set that contains information from a manufacturer of machine bolts. The data set contains 84 observations. The following table describes the variables in the data set:

Variable	Type	Description
PARTNMBR	character	part number of a particular size machine bolt
QUANTITY	numeric	quantity per box
PRICE	numeric	price per box

The PROC PRINT step below displays the first 15 observations of the machine bolts data set.*

```
libname macbolts 'SAS-data-library';

proc print data=macbolts.prices (obs=15);
   title 'Partial Printout of Machine Bolts Data Set';
run;
```

Output 16.1 shows the results.

Output 16.1
Partial Printout of Machine Bolts Data Set

```
                 Partial Printout of Machine Bolts Data Set            1

            OBS    PARTNMBR      QUANTITY    PRICE

             1     B01-03/06       100       5.75
             2     B02-03/08       100       6.60
             3     B03-03/10       100       7.25
             4     B04-03/12       100       7.80
             5     B05-03/14       100       8.40
             6     B06-03/16       100       7.95
             7     B07-03/20       100       8.80
             8     B08-03/25        50       4.25
             9     B09-03/30        50       7.40
            10     B10-03/06       100       7.10
            11     B11-03/08       100       7.20
            12     B12-03/10       100       7.70
            13     B13-03/12       100       8.00
            14     B14-03/14       100       8.80
            15     B15-03/16       100       9.05
```

* The DATA step that creates MACBOLTS.PRICES is shown in the Appendix.

Designing the Report

Before you begin coding, you should decide how you want the report to look. You should ask the following questions:

□   What is the page size?

□   How many panels do you need?

□   Where does each panel begin? (line number and column position)

□   Do you want descriptive headers printed at the top of each panel?

□   What values of variables do you want printed in columns within each panel?

□   Where does each column of values begin? (line numbers and column position).

A design, even a rough sketch, showing the column positions and line numbers of the panels and values will make it easier to write the DO loops and the PUT statements needed to generate the report.

To illustrate, consider Figure 16.1. It is a design of a multi-panel price list that uses the machine bolts data set, MACBOLTS.PRICES. The design of the price list has the following specifications:

□   40 lines per page

□   2 panels

□   The left panel begins on line 3 in column 4. The right panel begins on line 3 in column 45.

□   At the top of each panel is a descriptive header that reads, "`Part Number Quantity Price`."

□   The values of the variables PARTNMBR, QUANTITY, and PRICE are printed within each panel.

□   The values in the left panel begin on line 5 in column 5. The values in the right panel begin on line 5 in column 46. The values in both panels end on line 38, which leaves 2 blank lines at the bottom of the page.

Figure 16.1
Design of the
Machine Bolts
Price List

```
1   ----+----1----+----2----+----3----+----4----+----5----+----6----+----7----
0 (title line)            Machine Bolts Price List
1
2
3  Part Number  Quantity  Price        Part Number  Quantity  Price
4
5   B01-03/06     100     $5.75         B35-04/16      100     $9.05
6   B02-03/08     100     $6.60         B36-04/18      100     $9.60
7   B03-03/10     100     $7.25         B37-04/20      100     $8.80
8   B04-03/12     100     $7.80         B38-04/22      100    $11.20
9   B05-03/14     100     $8.40         B39-04/25       50     $5.25
10  B06-03/16     100     $7.95         B40-04/30       50     $5.50
11  B07-03/20     100     $8.80         B41-05/06      100    $11.80
12  B08-03/25      50     $4.25         B42-05/08      100     $6.40
13  B09-03/30      50     $7.40         B43-05/10      100     $6.60
14  B10-03/06     100     $7.10         B44-05/12      100     $6.80
15  B11-03/08     100     $7.20         B45-05/14      100     $7.70
16  B12-03/10     100     $7.70         B46-05/16      100     $6.60
17  B13-03/12     100     $8.00         B47-05/18      100     $7.95
18  B14-03/14     100     $8.80         B48-05/20      100     $7.20
19  B15-03/16     100     $9.05         B49-05/22      100     $8.80
20  B16-03/20     100     $9.20         B50-05/25       50     $4.15
21  B17-03/25      50     $5.75         B51-05/30       50     $4.60
22  B18-03/30      50     $8.00         B52-05/06      100    $13.75
23  B19-04/06     100    $10.10         B53-05/08      100     $7.05
24  B20-04/08     100     $5.90         B54-05/10      100     $7.10
25  B21-04/10     100     $6.40         B55-05/12      100     $7.70
26  B22-04/12     100     $6.80         B56-05/14      100     $7.95
27  B23-04/14     100     $7.50         B57-05/16      100     $8.15
28  B24-04/16     100     $6.95         B58-05/18      100     $8.45
29  B25-04/18     100     $7.95         B59-05/20      100     $8.90
30  B26-04/20     100     $7.20         B60-05/22      100    $10.40
31  B27-04/22     100     $9.60         B61-05/25       50     $4.85
32  B28-04/25      50     $3.95         B62-05/30       50     $5.25
33  B29-04/30      50     $4.60         B63-06/06      100    $12.20
34  B30-04/06     100    $11.60         B64-06/08      100     $7.00
35  B31-04/08     100     $6.70         B65-06/10      100     $7.20
36  B32-04/10     100     $7.10         B66-06/12      100     $7.45
37  B33-04/12     100     $7.70         B67-06/14      100     $7.95
38  B34-04/14     100     $8.80         B68-06/16      100     $8.05
39
40
```

Setting Up the Output File

After you have designed the report, you can begin coding. In the beginning of your code, you need to set up certain aspects of the output file. Specifically, you need to do the following:

□   specify the page size

□   specify the output file

□   make the entire output page available for writing.

To specify the number of lines per page of output, use the OPTIONS statement and the SAS system option PAGESIZE=.

```
options pagesize=40;
```

To specify the output file, use a FILE statement in a DATA step. In this example, output is directed to the procedure output file by the PRINT file specification in a FILE statement.

```
data _null_;
   file print;
```

To control the number of lines available for writing on each page of the output file, add the N= option to the FILE statement. To make the entire output page available, set N= to PAGESIZE. The value of PAGESIZE is the current specification of the SAS system option PAGESIZE=, which in this example is 40.

```
data _null_;
   file print n=pagesize;
```

Setting Up the Panels

The design of the machine bolts price list includes two panels. One panel begins in column 4 and the other in column 45. At the top of each panel is a header that reads, **Part Number Quantity Price**. The next two sections in this chapter show you how to set up the two panels by doing the following:

□ position the panels on the page

□ write the panel headers.

Position the Panels on the Page

Producing a multi-panel report can involve a great deal of repetitive processing, which makes it an excellent application for an iterative DO loop. As the following code illustrates, you can use an iterative DO loop to position the two panels in the correct columns on the output page.

The DO statement specifies an index variable named COLUMN, which has a value of 4 during the first iteration of the DO loop and a value of 45 during the second iteration. These values represent the left boundaries of each panel. Inside the DO loop is a statement that writes the panel headers.

```
do column=4,45;                    /* begin outer DO loop for panels */
    statement that writes the panel headers
end;                               /* end outer DO loop             */
```

Write the Panel Headers

Within the DO loop, use a PUT statement to write the panel headers. For example, the following PUT statement contains pointer control characters and character strings to specify where and what to write.

The first pointer control, which is #3, moves the pointer to line 3. The second pointer control, @COLUMN, moves the pointer to either column 4 or column 45, depending on the iteration of the DO loop.

Following the @COLUMN pointer control are three character strings enclosed in quotes, which specify the text of the panel headers, and a column pointer control, +2, which moves the character strings **QUANTITY** and **PRICE** two column positions to the right.

```
libname macbolts 'SAS-data-library';
options pagesize=40;
title 'Machine Bolts Price List';

data _null_;
   file print n=pagesize;
   do column=4,45;                    /* begin outer DO loop for panels */
      put #3 @column 'Part Number' +2 'Quantity' +2 'Price';
      inner DO loop fills in panels with values
   end;                               /* end outer DO loop             */
run;
```

When the DO loop executes, the header is written in the left panel first and then in the right panel. The report does not contain any values yet because no input file has been read. (An inner DO loop, represented above in italics, fills in the panels with values. The inner DO loop is discussed in detail in the next section.)

Output 16.2 shows the results of executing the code that exists so far.

Output 16.2
Writing the Panel
Headers

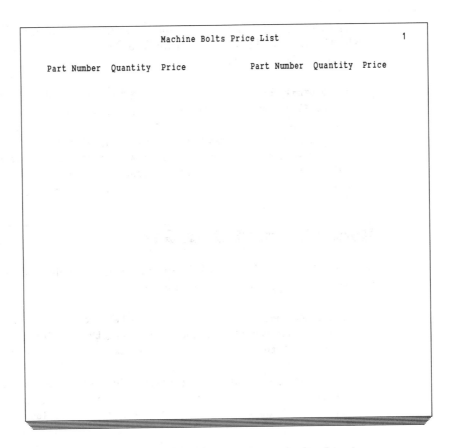

```
                              Machine Bolts Price List                        1

       Part Number  Quantity  Price              Part Number  Quantity  Price
```

Filling in the Panels with the Values of Variables

After you position the panels on the page and write the panel headers, you need
to fill in the panels with values. In this example, the values of variables from the
data set MACBOLTS.PRICES are written first in the left panel until that panel is
full. Then the values are written in the right panel.

To fill in the panels with the values of variables, you can add a second DO
loop inside the first DO loop. The inner DO loop should do the following:

□ position the lines within the panels

□ read the input data set

□ write the values

□ continue to another page.

Position the Lines within the Panels

The design of the machine bolts price list specifies lines 5 through 38 for writing
the values of variables. As the following code illustrates, you can accomplish this
task with a second DO loop that executes inside the first DO loop.

The DO statement specifies an index variable, which in this example is named LINE. The value of LINE ranges from 5 to 38 inclusive depending on the execution of the DO loop.

```
do column=4,45;                    /* begin outer DO loop for panels */
   put #3 @column 'Part Number' +2 'Quantity' +2 'Price';
   do line=5 to 38;          /* begin inner DO loop for lines  */
      statement that reads the input data set
      statements that process observations from the input data set
   end;                         /* end inner DO loop           */
end;                            /* end outer DO loop           */
```

Read the Input Data Set

After you have specified on which lines to write the values of the variables, use a SET statement to read the input data set.

```
do column=4,45;                    /* begin outer DO loop for panels */
   put #3 @column 'Part Number' +2 'Quantity' +2 'Price';
   do line=5 to 38;                /* begin inner DO loop for lines  */
      set macbolts.prices;
      statements that process observations from the input data set
   end;                         /* end inner DO loop           */
end;                            /* end outer DO loop           */
```

Write the Values

In the inner DO loop, use a PUT statement to write the values of the variables. Use pointer control characters, variable names, and formats to specify where, what, and how to write the values.

To illustrate, consider the PUT statement shown below. The first pointer control, #LINE, moves the pointer to the current value of the variable LINE, which is specified in the second DO statement. The current value of LINE is between 5 and 38 inclusive depending on the iteration of the inner DO loop.

The second pointer control character, @COLUMN, moves the pointer to the column position of the current value of the variable COLUMN, which is specified in the first DO statement. The current value of COLUMN is either 4 or 45, depending on the iteration of the outer DO loop.

Following the @COLUMN pointer control are three column pointer controls, the variable names PARTNMBR, QUANTITY, and PRICE, and formats that are appropriate for the variables.

```
do column=4,45;                    /* begin outer DO loop for panels */
   put #3 @column 'Part Number' +2 'Quantity' +2 'Price';
   do line=5 to 38;                /* begin inner DO loop for lines  */
      set macbolts.prices;
      put #line @column +1 partnmbr
                      +4 quantity 3.
                      +4 price dollar6.2;
   end;                         /* end inner DO loop           */
end;                            /* end outer DO loop           */
```

Continue to Another Page

If the input data set contains more observations than can be written on one page, you need to add a new output page before continuing to process observations. To write values to another page of output, do the following:

□ determine whether the current page is full

□ determine whether there are additional observations in the input data set

□ if needed, create a new output page.

Determine Whether the Current Page Is Full

You can use the fact that one DO loop is nested inside the other to determine whether the current page is full. As you have seen, the outer DO loop controls the panels. The inner DO loop controls the lines. During processing, if the final line (line 38 in this case) of the second panel (the one beginning in column 45) has been written, the current page is full and iteration of both DO loops is complete.

```
do column=4,45;        /* begin outer DO loop for panels */
   put #3 @column 'Part Number' +2 'Quantity' +2 'Price';
   do line=5 to 38;    /* begin inner DO loop for lines */
      set macbolts.prices;
      put #line @column +1 partnmbr
                        +4 quantity 3.
                        +4 price dollar6.2;
   end;                        /* end inner DO loop        */
end;                           /* end outer DO loop        */
```

Determine Whether There Are Additional Observations

To determine whether there are additional observations in the input data set, add the END= option to the SET statement. (The SET statement was shown in the earlier section, "Read the Input Data Set.") The END= option creates a temporary variable, the name of which you supply. In the revised SET statement that follows, the temporary variable is named ENDFILE.

```
set macbolts.prices end=endfile;
```

The value of the variable ENDFILE acts as an end-of-file marker or flag. That is, the value of ENDFILE is set initially to 0 and remains 0 until the final observation is read from the input data set. When the final observation is read, the value of ENDFILE is 1.

Create a New Output Page

To create a new output page, use an IF-THEN statement that appears outside both DO loops. The IF-THEN statement tests the value of the temporary variable ENDFILE and, if needed, creates a new output page. The new output page is created by a PUT statement and the _PAGE_ pointer control.

If there are more observations to be processed, the statement ENDFILE=0 is true; therefore, the PUT statement executes, the DATA step iterates again, and the remaining lines are written to the new output page.

On the other hand, if there are no more observations to be processed, the statement ENDFILE=0 is false, and the PUT statement does not execute.

The following program produces the machine bolts price list. The program includes all the statements and options discussed in this chapter including the END= option in the SET statement and an IF-THEN statement that appears outside the DO loops.

```
libname macbolts 'SAS-data-library';
options pagesize=40;
title 'Machine Bolts Price List';

data _null_;
   file print n=pagesize;
   do column=4,45;                      /* begin outer DO loop for panels */
      put #3 @column 'Part Number' +2 'Quantity' +2 'Price';
      do line=5 to 38;                  /* begin inner DO loop for lines  */
         set macbolts.prices end=endfile;
         put #line @column +1 partnmbr
                          +4 quantity 3.
                          +4 price dollar6.2;
      end;                              /* end inner DO loop          */
   end;                                 /* end outer DO loop          */
   if endfile=0 then put _page_;
run;
```

Output 16.3 shows the results.

Output 16.3
Filling in the
Panels with Values

```
                              Machine Bolts Price List                    1


     Part Number  Quantity  Price          Part Number  Quantity  Price

       B01-03/06    100     $5.75            B35-04/16    100      $9.05
       B02-03/08    100     $6.60            B36-04/18    100      $9.60
       B03-03/10    100     $7.25            B37-04/20    100      $8.80
       B04-03/12    100     $7.80            B38-04/22    100     $11.20
       B05-03/14    100     $8.40            B39-04/25     50      $5.25
       B06-03/16    100     $7.95            B40-04/30     50      $5.50
       B07-03/20    100     $8.80            B41-05/06    100     $11.80
       B08-03/25     50     $4.25            B42-05/08    100      $6.40
       B09-03/30     50     $7.40            B43-05/10    100      $6.60
       B10-03/06    100     $7.10            B44-05/12    100      $6.80
       B11-03/08    100     $7.20            B45-05/14    100      $7.70
       B12-03/10    100     $7.70            B46-05/16    100      $6.60
       B13-03/12    100     $8.00            B47-05/18    100      $7.95
       B14-03/14    100     $8.80            B48-05/20    100      $7.20
       B15-03/16    100     $9.05            B49-05/22    100      $8.80
       B16-03/20    100     $9.20            B50-05/25     50      $4.15
       B17-03/25     50     $5.75            B51-05/30     50      $4.60
       B18-03/30     50     $8.00            B52-05/06    100     $13.75
       B19-04/06    100    $10.10            B53-05/08    100      $7.05
       B20-04/08    100     $5.90            B54-05/10    100      $7.10
       B21-04/10    100     $6.40            B55-05/12    100      $7.70
       B22-04/12    100     $6.80            B56-05/14    100      $7.95
       B23-04/14    100     $7.50            B57-05/16    100      $8.15
       B24-04/16    100     $6.95            B58-05/18    100      $8.45
       B25-04/18    100     $7.95            B59-05/20    100      $8.90
       B26-04/20    100     $7.20            B60-05/22    100     $10.40
       B27-04/22    100     $9.60            B61-05/25     50      $4.85
       B28-04/25     50     $3.95            B62-05/30     50      $5.25
       B29-04/30     50     $4.60            B63-06/06    100     $12.20
```

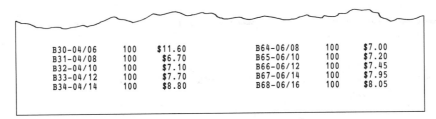

```
        B30-04/06    100    $11.60          B64-06/08    100    $7.00
        B31-04/08    100     $6.70          B65-06/10    100    $7.20
        B32-04/10    100     $7.10          B66-06/12    100    $7.45
        B33-04/12    100     $7.70          B67-06/14    100    $7.95
        B34-04/14    100     $8.80          B68-06/16    100    $8.05
```

```
                        Machine Bolts Price List                    2


        Part Number  Quantity  Price

           B69-06/18    100     $8.15
           B70-06/20    100     $9.40
           B71-06/22    100     $9.60
           B72-06/25     50     $4.65
           B73-06/30     50     $5.05
           B74-06/06    100    $15.25
           B75-06/08    100     $7.75
           B76-06/10    100     $7.90
           B77-06/12    100     $8.50
           B78-06/14    100     $8.75
           B79-06/16    100     $8.95
           B80-06/18    100     $9.20
           B81-06/20    100     $9.80
           B82-06/22    100    $11.80
           B83-06/25     50     $5.25
           B84-06/30     50     $5.75
```

Summary

The following points summarize how to use the DATA step to produce multi-panel reports:

□ To set up the output file, use the OPTIONS statement with the SAS system option PAGESIZE=, and the FILE statement with the PRINT option and the N=PAGESIZE option.

□ To control writing variable values in multiple panels, use nested DO loops and PUT statements.

□ To determine whether to write values on multiple output pages, use the END= option in a SET statement and an IF-THEN statement.

SAS Tools

This section summarizes syntax for the statements and system option discussed in this chapter.

Statements

FILE <PRINT <N=PAGESIZE>>;
> specifies the output file for PUT statements in the current DATA step. PRINT directs the lines produced by PUT statements to the same print file as the output produced by SAS procedures. N=PAGESIZE specifies the number of lines to make available to the output pointer in the current iteration of the DATA step which, in this chapter, is the number of lines specified in the PAGESIZE= SAS system option.

PUT <_PAGE_>;
> writes lines to the SAS log, to the SAS procedure output file, or to the external file specified in the most recent FILE statement. The _PAGE_ option advances the pointer to the first line on a new page. Pointer controls are provided in the PUT statement so that you can reset the pointer's column and line position. The following pointer controls are used in this chapter:

> *@numeric-variable*
>> moves the pointer to the column given by the value of *numeric-variable*.

> **+***n*
>> moves the pointer *n* columns.

> *#numeric-variable*
>> moves the pointer to the line given by the value of *numeric-variable*.

> *#n*
>> moves the pointer to line *n* .

SET *data-set-name* END=*variable-name*;
> reads observations from a SAS data set. *Data-set-name* specifies a one-level name, two-level name, or one of the special SAS data set names. END= creates a temporary variable that contains an end-of-file indicator. The variable, which is initialized to 0, is set to 1 when the SET statement reads the final observation in the last data set listed. *Variable-name* is a user-supplied name for the temporary variable.

System option

PAGESIZE=*number*;
> specifies the number of lines that can be printed per page of SAS output.

Learning More

This section provides references for learning more about the topics presented in this chapter.

SAS system options
Some SAS system options have host dependencies. For details, see the SAS documentation for your host operating system.

Using the DATA step
□ If you need introductory information about using DO loops, read *SAS Language and Procedures: Usage, Version 6, First Edition*, Chapter 12, "Finding Shortcuts in Programming."

□ To learn the basics of using line and column pointer controls, read *SAS Language and Procedures: Usage*, Chapter 29, "Writing Output."

□ You can also use negative integers as specifications in line and column pointer controls. For examples, see Chapter 2, "Reading Data in Different Record Formats and in Hierarchical Files," in this book.

□ For details about the PUT statement and pointer controls, refer to *SAS Language: Reference*, Chapter 9, "SAS Language Statements."

The REPORT procedure
You can also use PROC REPORT to produce various types of reports including multi-panel reports. For details, see *SAS Guide to the REPORT Procedure: Usage and Reference, Version 6, First Edition*.

Chapter 17 Producing Summary Reports Using Descriptive Procedures

Introduction

When analyzing a data set, you often want to compute characteristics to describe or compare observations or variables. This may require computing ranks of the observations or standardizing the variables to a new scale. This chapter shows you how to summarize a data set by using five of the descriptive procedures in base SAS software.

In this chapter
This chapter shows you how to do the following:

☐   compute ranks for variables across observations

☐   standardize variables to a given mean and standard deviation

☐   compute overall ranks based on multiple variables

☐   compute basic descriptive statistics for variables

☐   compute detailed descriptive statistics for distributions of variables

☐   measure strengths of relationships between variables.

Prerequisites

Knowledge of elementary statistics is needed to interpret some of the output, but mostly, these descriptive statistics are simple measurements of the data.

SAS Data Set Example

In the examples in this chapter, a small political organization is trying to determine which of the 36 newspapers in its area covers local, national, and international issues most completely and accurately. This organization consulted three published reports from different media critics who rated the papers' coverage of certain types of issues. The first critic critiques papers only on their coverage of local issues. The staff of the second critic reviews the papers on their coverage of national issues. The staff of the third critic evaluates the papers on their coverage of international issues. The political organization wants to analyze the ratings and combine them to compute overall rankings for the newspapers based equally on their local, national, and international coverage. The organization also gives papers categorical ratings based on their circulations. A paper with an average of 5,000 or more subscriptions is considered large, and a paper with an average of fewer than 5,000 subscriptions is considered small.

The first critic rated the papers on a scale of 1 to 4; the second critic rated the papers on a scale of 1 to 10; and the third critic rated the papers on a scale of 0 to 5. Higher scores indicate more complete and accurate coverage. Each observation in the data set contains values for the following variables:

Variable	Type	Description
NAME	character	name of the newspaper
LOCAL	numeric	rating from the first critic
NTL	numeric	rating from the second critic
INTNTL	numeric	rating from the third critic
CIRC	character	paper's circulation rating

The PROC PRINT step below displays the data set MYLIB.NEWS.*

```
libname mylib 'SAS-data-library';

proc print data=mylib.news;
   title 'Newspaper Ratings';
run;
```

---

* The DATA step that creates MYLIB.NEWS is shown in the Appendix.

Output 17.1 shows the results.

Output 17.1
Printout of Data
Set MYLIB.NEWS

```
                              Newspaper Ratings                           1

    OBS    NAME                              LOCAL    NTL    INTNTL    CIRC

      1    The Amsterdam Advocate             2.5      6       3.0      l
      2    The Auburntown Tribune             3.0      4       2.5      s
      3    The Bayside Observer               2.5      5       2.0      s
      4    The Bent Creek Gazette             2.5      3       1.5      s
      5    The Blue Ridge Neighborhood        3.5      7       3.0      l
      6    The Bramlett Courier               3.0      3       2.0      s
      7    The Cedar Park Edition             3.5      8       3.5      l
      8    The Clermont Weather and News      2.0      8       4.5      l
      9    The Community Spectator            1.5      5       2.0      s
     10    The Deakin Sentinel                2.5      6       2.0      s
     11    The Delta Voice                    2.0      3       2.0      s
     12    The Duckville Truth                3.5      4       2.0      s
     13    The Duplin Daily                   2.5      6       2.0      s
     14    The East Oak Corner Chronicle      3.0      7       3.0      s
     15    The Fort Washington Constitution   2.5      5       1.5      s
     16    The Glenhaven Herald               2.0      6       3.5      l
     17    The Greystone Planet and Sun       2.5      5       2.0      s
     18    The Harrison Review                3.0      6       2.5      l
     19    The Highbridge Record of Events    1.5      3       2.0      s
     20    The Historical Lakewalk            2.0      9       4.0      l
     21    The Hunts Point Bulletin           1.5      2       1.0      s
     22    The Lake Boone Heritage            2.5      5       2.0      l
     23    The Northwoods Examiner            4.0      5       1.5      s
     24    The Oxford Inquirer                2.5      4       2.0      s
     25    The Pine Hills Post                2.0      6       2.5      l
     26    The Rabbit Creek Star              2.0      3       1.0      l
     27    The Recent Past                    3.5      8       4.0      l
     28    The Riverside Globe                2.0      7       3.5      l
     29    The Samford Editorial              2.0      4       1.5      s
     30    The Seaside Journal                3.0      4       2.5      l
     31    The Sheep's Meadow Delivery        3.0      8       3.5      l
     32    Today's Headlines                  2.0      5       2.5      l
     33    The Tournament Times               1.5      7       4.0      l
     34    The Valley Free Press              1.5      6       3.0      l
     35    The Village Green Report           2.0      4       2.5      s
     36    The Warren Ponds Universal         1.5      7       4.0      l
```

Transforming Data

When analyzing a data set, you may want to use ranks of observations or standardized values rather than the actual values of the variables. *Ranking* transforms the data from the original measurements of the observations to the relative order of those measurements. When observations have multiple measurements on different scales, you may want to standardize the data. *Standardization* transforms the data from the original measurements of the observations to a new, consistent scale based on a given mean and standard deviation. This enables you to compute ranks weighted equally on many variables.

Computing Ranks for Variables across Observations

To compare values of a variable more easily, you may want to rank observations. Ranking orders observations, assigning them values from 1 to the number of total observations. By looking at values of a rank variable, you can compare observations based on the values of the original variable.

To compute ranks for variables, you can use the RANK procedure. In this example, the PROC RANK step computes ranks of the newspapers according to their ratings from the critics. To specify the input data set, use the DATA= option in the PROC RANK statement. If this option is omitted, the RANK procedure uses the most recently created SAS data set.

```
libname mylib 'SAS-data-library';

proc rank data=mylib.news;
```

To assign the largest value the rank of 1 and the next largest value the rank of 2 and so forth, use the DESCENDING option in the PROC RANK statement. Without this option, the RANK procedure ranks values from smallest to largest with the smallest value given the rank of 1. In this case, the rank of 1 is assigned to the paper with the highest rating.

```
proc rank data=mylib.news descending;
```

To specify what rank observations receive if they have the same value, use the TIES= option. TIES=MEAN, the default, gives tied observations the average of the ranks that the observations would have received if there had been no tie. For example, if four observations had the highest value, and you were assigning the rank of 1, the lowest possible rank, to the highest observation, each of the observations would receive a rank of 2.5, the mean of 1, 2, 3, and 4. TIES=HIGH gives the observations the highest possible rank, and TIES=LOW gives the observations the lowest possible rank. This example uses TIES=LOW because the highest rated papers receive the lowest ranks. If a critic gave two papers the highest rating, they would both receive a rank of 1, and the next highest rated paper(s) would receive a rank of 3.

```
proc rank data=mylib.news descending ties=low;
```

To specify the variables whose observations are ranked, use the VAR statement. These variables must be numeric. If you omit the VAR statement, the RANK procedure computes ranks for all numeric variables in the data set. The following VAR statement specifies LOCAL, NTL, and INTNTL as the variables whose observations are ranked:

```
var local ntl intntl;
```

To assign variable names to the ranks and include the original variables in your output data set, use the RANKS statement. If you omit the RANKS statement, the rank values replace the original variable values in the output data set. If you use a RANKS statement, you must include a VAR statement. The following RANKS statement assigns the ranks for LOCAL to the variable RANK1, the ranks for NTL to the variable RANK2, and the ranks for INTNTL to the variable RANK3:

```
ranks rank1 rank2 rank3;
```

Here is the complete program that produces and prints the rankings for the newspaper rating variables:

```
libname mylib 'SAS-data-library';

proc rank data=mylib.news(drop=circ) descending ties=low;
   var local ntl intntl;
   ranks rank1 rank2 rank3;
run;

proc print;
   title 'Newspaper Rankings';
run;
```

Output 17.2 shows the results.

Output 17.2
Computing Ranks
for Variables
across
Observations

```
                                  Newspaper Rankings                               1

OBS NAME                               LOCAL NTL INTNTL RANK1 RANK2 RANK3

  1 The Amsterdam Advocate              2.5   6   3.0     12    11    10
  2 The Auburntown Tribune              3.0   4   2.5      6    25    14
  3 The Bayside Observer                2.5   5   2.0     12    18    20
  4 The Bent Creek Gazette              2.5   3   1.5     12    31    31
  5 The Blue Ridge Neighborhood         3.5   7   3.0      2     6    10
  6 The Bramlett Courier                3.0   3   2.0      6    31    20
  7 The Cedar Park Edition              3.5   8   3.5      2     2     6
  8 The Clermont Weather and News       2.0   8   4.5     21     2     1
  9 The Community Spectator             1.5   5   2.0     31    18    20
 10 The Deakin Sentinel                 2.5   6   2.0     12    11    20
 11 The Delta Voice                     2.0   3   2.0     21    31    20
 12 The Duckville Truth                 3.5   4   2.0      2    25    20
 13 The Duplin Daily                    2.5   6   2.0     12    11    20
 14 The East Oak Corner Chronicle       3.0   7   3.0      6     6    10
 15 The Fort Washington Constitution    2.5   5   1.5     12    18    31
 16 The Glenhaven Herald                2.0   6   3.5     21    11     6
 17 The Greystone Planet and Sun        2.5   5   2.0     12    18    20
 18 The Harrison Review                 3.0   6   2.5      6    11    14
 19 The Highbridge Record of Events     1.5   3   2.0     31    31    20
 20 The Historical Lakewalk             2.0   9   4.0     21     1     2
 21 The Hunts Point Bulletin            1.5   2   1.0     31    36    35
 22 The Lake Boone Heritage             2.5   5   2.0     12    18    20
 23 The Northwoods Examiner             4.0   5   1.5      1    18    31
 24 The Oxford Inquirer                 2.5   4   2.0     12    25    20
 25 The Pine Hills Post                 2.0   6   2.5     21    11    14
 26 The Rabbit Creek Star               2.0   3   1.0     21    31    35
 27 The Recent Past                     3.5   8   4.0      2     2     2
 28 The Riverside Globe                 2.0   7   3.5     21     6     6
 29 The Samford Editorial               2.0   4   1.5     21    25    31
 30 The Seaside Journal                 3.0   4   2.5      6    25    14
 31 The Sheep's Meadow Delivery         3.0   8   3.5      6     2     6
 32 Today's Headlines                   2.0   5   2.5     21    18    14
 33 The Tournament Times                1.5   7   4.0     31     6     2
 34 The Valley Free Press               1.5   6   3.0     31    11    10
 35 The Village Green Report            2.0   4   2.5     21    25    14
 36 The Warren Ponds Universal          1.5   7   4.0     31     6     2
```

The new variable RANK1 compares the newspapers' ratings on local issues from the first critic. *The Northwoods Examiner,* the paper with the highest rating of 4 on local issues, receives the rank of 1 because of the DESCENDING option. The four papers with a rating of 3.5 receive a rank of 2 because TIES=LOW assigns tied values the lowest possible rank. The six papers with a rating of 3 receive a rank of 6; the nine papers with a rating of 2.5 receive a rank of 12; the ten papers with a rating of 2 receive a rank of 21; and the six papers with a rating of 1.5 receive a rank of 31. The variable RANK2 ranks the papers according to the second critic's ratings of their coverage of national issues, and the variable RANK3 ranks the papers according to the third critic's ratings of their coverage of international issues.

Standardizing Variables to a Given Mean and Standard Deviation

When observations are measured on scales with different characteristics, you may want to standardize variables to a consistent scale so that you can directly compare values originally measured on different scales. In this example, ratings from different critics cannot be compared because each critic evaluated the newspapers differently. A rating of 3 means something totally different to each critic. To simply average the three ratings to get an overall rating for each newspaper would give the variables different weights; that is, variables would have unequal influence on the outcome. Even if the critics had used the same scales, scores from one critic could not be compared directly with scores from another critic because the meaning of a score depends on how the critic rated that paper relative to the other papers. The meaning of that score depends on the mean of all the values for that variable and on the *standard deviation*, which is a measure of variation among values for that variable. Standardization converts variables to a consistent scale with new scores based on the mean and standard deviation of each variable. To standardize variables to a given mean and standard deviation, you need to do the following:

□   define the variables to be standardized

□   compute the values for the standardized variables.

Define the Variables

To preserve the original data, you need to define new variables to be standardized. The following DATA step sets three new variables — STAND1, STAND2, and STAND3 — equal to the original evaluation scores for the newspapers.

```
libname mylib 'SAS-data-library';

data rename;
   set mylib.news;
   stand1=local;
   stand2=ntl;
   stand3=intntl;
run;
```

Compute the Values

To compute the values for the standardized variables, you can use the STANDARD procedure. In this example, the PROC STANDARD step standardizes the new variables STAND1, STAND2, and STAND3 to means of 0 and standard deviations of 1. This creates new rating scales for the newspapers. To specify the input data set, use the DATA= option in the PROC STANDARD statement. If this option is omitted, the STANDARD procedure uses the most recently created SAS data set.

```
proc standard data=rename;
```

To change the mean and standard deviation of variables, you must specify a new mean and standard deviation in the PROC STANDARD statement. The most common standardization uses a mean of 0 and a standard deviation of 1 because a standardized value translates into how many standard deviations the original value is from the mean. The sign of a standardized value with these specifications indicates whether the original value is greater than or less than the mean.

```
proc standard data=rename mean=0 std=1;
```

To print the mean, standard deviation, and number of observations for each variable prior to standardization, use the PRINT option. The following PRINT option prints the statistics for the variables STAND1, STAND2, and STAND3:

```
proc standard data=rename mean=0 std=1 print;
```

To name the new SAS data set that contains the standardized variables, use the OUT= option. The OUT= data set contains all the variables from the input data set including those not standardized. The following OUT= option creates a permanent SAS data set named MYLIB.STAND:

```
proc standard data=rename mean=0 std=1 print out=mylib.stand;
```

To specify the variables that are standardized, use the VAR statement. If you do not use a VAR statement, all numeric variables are standardized. The following VAR statement specifies STAND1, STAND2, and STAND3 as the variables that are standardized:

```
var stand1 stand2 stand3;
```

Here is the complete program that produces and prints the standardized variables for the newspaper ratings:

```
libname mylib 'SAS-data-library';

data rename(drop=circ);
   set mylib.news;
   stand1=local;
   stand2=ntl;
   stand3=intntl;
run;

proc standard data=rename mean=0 std=1 print out=mylib.stand;
   var stand1 stand2 stand3;
   title 'Descriptive Statistics for the Original Ratings';
run;

proc print data=mylib.stand;
   title 'Standardized Ratings for Newspapers';
run;
```

Output 17.3 shows the results.

Output 17.3
Standardizing Variables to a Given Mean and Standard Deviation

```
            Descriptive Statistics for the Original Ratings          1

      NAME              MEAN              STD             N

      STAND1          2.430556         0.677735          36
      STAND2          5.388889         1.761132          36
      STAND3          2.541667         0.913197          36
```

		L O C A L	I N T N T L	S T A N D 1	S T A N D 2	S T A N D 3

O B S	N A M E				L O C A L	I N T L	S T A N D 1	S T A N D 2	S T A N D 3
1	The Amsterdam Advocate	2.5	6	3.0	0.10247	0.34700	0.50190
2	The Auburntown Tribune	3.0	4	2.5	0.84022	-0.78863	-0.04563
3	The Bayside Observer	2.5	5	2.0	0.10247	-0.22082	-0.59315
4	The Bent Creek Gazette	2.5	3	1.5	0.10247	-1.35645	-1.14068
5	The Blue Ridge Neighborhood	3.5	7	3.0	1.57797	0.91482	0.50190
6	The Bramlett Courier	3.0	3	2.0	0.84022	-1.35645	-0.59315
7	The Cedar Park Edition	3.5	8	3.5	1.57797	1.48263	1.04943
8	The Clermont Weather and News	2.0	8	4.5	-0.63529	1.48263	2.14448
9	The Community Spectator	1.5	5	2.0	-1.37304	-0.22082	-0.59315
10	The Deakin Sentinel	2.5	6	2.0	0.10247	0.34700	-0.59315
11	The Delta Voice	2.0	3	2.0	-0.63529	-1.35645	-0.59315
12	The Duckville Truth	3.5	4	2.0	1.57797	-0.78863	-0.59315
13	The Duplin Daily	2.5	6	2.0	0.10247	0.34700	-0.59315
14	The East Oak Corner Chronicle	3.0	7	3.0	0.84022	0.91482	0.50190
15	The Fort Washington Constitution	2.5	5	1.5	0.10247	-0.22082	-1.14068
16	The Glenhaven Herald	2.0	6	3.5	-0.63529	0.34700	1.04943
17	The Greystone Planet and Sun	2.5	5	2.0	0.10247	-0.22082	-0.59315
18	The Harrison Review	3.0	6	2.5	0.84022	0.34700	-0.04563
19	The Highbridge Record of Events	1.5	3	2.0	-1.37304	-1.35645	-0.59315
20	The Historical Lakewalk	2.0	9	4.0	-0.63529	2.05045	1.59695
21	The Hunts Point Bulletin	1.5	2	1.0	-1.37304	-1.92427	-1.68821
22	The Lake Boone Heritage	2.5	5	2.0	0.10247	-0.22082	-0.59315
23	The Northwoods Examiner	4.0	5	1.5	2.31572	-0.22082	-1.14068
24	The Oxford Inquirer	2.5	4	2.0	0.10247	-0.78863	-0.59315
25	The Pine Hills Post	2.0	6	2.5	-0.63529	0.34700	-0.04563
26	The Rabbit Creek Star	2.0	3	1.0	-0.63529	-1.35645	-1.68821
27	The Recent Past	3.5	8	4.0	1.57797	1.48263	1.59695
28	The Riverside Globe	2.0	7	3.5	-0.63529	0.91482	1.04943
29	The Samford Editorial	2.0	4	1.5	-0.63529	-0.78863	-1.14068
30	The Seaside Journal	3.0	4	2.5	0.84022	-0.78863	-0.04563
31	The Sheep's Meadow Delivery	3.0	8	3.5	0.84022	1.48263	1.04943
32	Today's Headlines	2.0	5	2.5	-0.63529	-0.22082	-0.04563
33	The Tournament Times	1.5	7	4.0	-1.37304	0.91482	1.59695
34	The Valley Free Press	1.5	6	3.0	-1.37304	0.34700	0.50190
35	The Village Green Report	2.0	4	2.5	-0.63529	-0.78863	-0.04563
36	The Warren Ponds Universal	1.5	7	4.0	-1.37304	0.91482	1.59695

(Standardized Ratings for Newspapers — page 2)

The first page of Output 17.3 shows the mean and standard deviation of all three variables prior to standardization. The standardized values in this example are computed by subtracting the mean of the variable from the rating and dividing by the standard deviation of the variable.

Because a mean of 0 and a standard deviation of 1 are specified for the standardization, the new variables indicate how many standard deviations of the original variable the original value is from the mean of the original variable. For example, *The Amsterdam Advocate*, *The Bayside Observer*, *The Bent Creek Gazette*, and all the other newspapers that received a rating of 2.5 for local coverage receive a standardized rating of .10247 for local coverage because 2.5 is .10247 units of the standard deviation above the mean. The variable LOCAL has a mean of 2.430556 and a standard deviation of .677735.

An example of a negative standardized rating is −.59315 for the papers that received a rating of 2 for their international coverage. This indicates that their rating is .59315 units of the standard deviation below the mean. The variable INTNTL has a mean of 2.541667 and a standard deviation of .913197.

Computing Overall Ranks Based on Multiple Variables

After you standardize the variables, you can compute overall rankings based equally on all the measurements. To compute overall rankings based on the standardized ratings, you need to do the following:

□ compute the overall ratings by averaging the standardized ratings

□ rank the observations according to their overall ratings.

Compute the Overall Ratings

To compute overall ratings for the observations, you can average the individual standardized ratings to give equal influence to each measurement scale. The following DATA step with the assignment statement and MEAN function creates an overall score for each newspaper by averaging the standardized ratings:

```
libname mylib 'SAS-data-library';

data overate;
   set mylib.stand;
   average=mean(stand1,stand2,stand3);
run;
```

The MEAN function computes the average of the nonmissing arguments in parentheses. The new variable, AVERAGE, is an overall rating of the newspapers based equally on the standardized opinions of all three critics.

Rank the Observations

To rank the observations according to their overall ratings, you can use the RANK procedure. The following PROC RANK step ranks the observations for the variable AVERAGE and assigns those ranks to the new variable OVERALL in the output data set OVERANK:

```
proc rank data=overate out=overank descending ties=low;
   var average;
   ranks overall;
```

Here is the complete program that produces and prints the overall rankings of the newspapers:

```
libname mylib 'SAS-data-library';

data overate(drop=local ntl intntl);
   set mylib.stand;
   average=mean(stand1,stand2,stand3);
run;

proc rank data=overate out=overank descending ties=low;
   var average;
   ranks overall;
run;

proc print data=overate;
   title 'Overall Ratings of Newspapers';
run;

proc print data=overank(drop=stand1 stand2 stand3);
   title 'Overall Rankings of Newspapers';
run;
```

Output 17.4 shows the results.

Output 17.4
Computing Overall
Ranks Based on
Multiple Variables

```
                          Overall Ratings of Newspapers                        1

OBS NAME                             STAND1    STAND2    STAND3   AVERAGE

  1 The Amsterdam Advocate           0.10247   0.34700   0.50190   0.31712
  2 The Auburntown Tribune           0.84022  -0.78863  -0.04563   0.00199
  3 The Bayside Observer             0.10247  -0.22082  -0.59315  -0.23717
  4 The Bent Creek Gazette           0.10247  -1.35645  -1.14068  -0.79822
  5 The Blue Ridge Neighborhood      1.57797   0.91482   0.50190   0.99823
  6 The Bramlett Courier             0.84022  -1.35645  -0.59315  -0.36980
  7 The Cedar Park Edition           1.57797   1.48263   1.04943   1.37001
  8 The Clermont Weather and News   -0.63529   1.48263   2.14448   0.99728
  9 The Community Spectator         -1.37304  -0.22082  -0.59315  -0.72900
 10 The Deakin Sentinel              0.10247   0.34700  -0.59315  -0.04790
 11 The Delta Voice                 -0.63529  -1.35645  -0.59315  -0.86163
 12 The Duckville Truth              1.57797  -0.78863  -0.59315   0.06539
 13 The Duplin Daily                 0.10247   0.34700  -0.59315  -0.04790
 14 The East Oak Corner Chronicle    0.84022   0.91482   0.50190   0.75231
 15 The Fort Washington Constitution 0.10247  -0.22082  -1.14068  -0.41968
 16 The Glenhaven Herald            -0.63529   0.34700   1.04943   0.25371
 17 The Greystone Planet and Sun     0.10247  -0.22082  -0.59315  -0.23717
 18 The Harrison Review              0.84022   0.34700  -0.04563   0.38053
 19 The Highbridge Record of Events -1.37304  -1.35645  -0.59315  -1.10755
 20 The Historical Lakewalk         -0.63529   2.05045   1.59695   1.00404
 21 The Hunts Point Bulletin        -1.37304  -1.92427  -1.68821  -1.66184
 22 The Lake Boone Heritage          0.10247  -0.22082  -0.59315  -0.23717
 23 The Northwoods Examiner          2.31572  -0.22082  -1.14068   0.31807
 24 The Oxford Inquirer              0.10247  -0.78863  -0.59315  -0.42644
 25 The Pine Hills Post             -0.63529   0.34700  -0.04563  -0.11130
 26 The Rabbit Creek Star           -0.63529  -1.35645  -1.68821  -1.22665
 27 The Recent Past                  1.57797   1.48263   1.59695   1.55252
 28 The Riverside Globe             -0.63529   0.91482   1.04943   0.44299
 29 The Samford Editorial           -0.63529  -0.78863  -1.14068  -0.85487
 30 The Seaside Journal              0.84022  -0.78863  -0.04563   0.00199
 31 The Sheep's Meadow Delivery      0.84022   1.48263   1.04943   1.12409
 32 Today's Headlines               -0.63529  -0.22082  -0.04563  -0.30058
 33 The Tournament Times            -1.37304   0.91482   1.59695   0.37958
 34 The Valley Free Press           -1.37304   0.34700   0.50190  -0.17471
 35 The Village Green Report        -0.63529  -0.78863  -0.04563  -0.48985
 36 The Warren Ponds Universal      -1.37304   0.91482   1.59695   0.37958
```

```
                        Overall Rankings of Newspapers                     2
       OBS   NAME                                    AVERAGE    OVERALL

        1    The Amsterdam Advocate                  0.31712      13
        2    The Auburntown Tribune                  0.00199      16
        3    The Bayside Observer                   -0.23717      22
        4    The Bent Creek Gazette                 -0.79822      31
        5    The Blue Ridge Neighborhood             0.99823       5
        6    The Bramlett Courier                   -0.36980      26
        7    The Cedar Park Edition                  1.37001       2
        8    The Clermont Weather and News           0.99728       6
        9    The Community Spectator                -0.72900      30
       10    The Deakin Sentinel                    -0.04790      18
       11    The Delta Voice                        -0.86163      33
       12    The Duckville Truth                     0.06539      15
       13    The Duplin Daily                       -0.04790      18
       14    The East Oak Corner Chronicle           0.75231       7
       15    The Fort Washington Constitution       -0.41968      27
       16    The Glenhaven Herald                    0.25371      14
       17    The Greystone Planet and Sun           -0.23717      22
       18    The Harrison Review                     0.38053       9
       19    The Highbridge Record of Events        -1.10755      34
       20    The Historical Lakewalk                 1.00404       4
       21    The Hunts Point Bulletin               -1.66184      36
       22    The Lake Boone Heritage                -0.23717      22
       23    The Northwoods Examiner                 0.31807      12
       24    The Oxford Inquirer                    -0.42644      28
       25    The Pine Hills Post                    -0.11130      20
       26    The Rabbit Creek Star                  -1.22665      35
       27    The Recent Past                         1.55252       1
       28    The Riverside Globe                     0.44299       8
       29    The Samford Editorial                  -0.85487      32
       30    The Seaside Journal                     0.00199      16
       31    The Sheep's Meadow Delivery             1.12409       3
       32    Today's Headlines                      -0.30058      25
       33    The Tournament Times                    0.37958      10
       34    The Valley Free Press                  -0.17471      21
       35    The Village Green Report               -0.48985      29
       36    The Warren Ponds Universal              0.37958      10
```

The variable AVERAGE is an overall rating based equally on the variables LOCAL, NTL, and INTNTL. The variable OVERALL ranks the newspapers according to their new rating. This ranking system combines the opinions of the three critics to give a complete comparison of news coverage. With this system, *The Recent Past* is the highest rated paper with an average standardized score of 1.55252, and *The Hunts Point Bulletin* is the lowest rated paper with a score of −1.66184.

Producing Descriptive Statistics

To compare or describe variables, you need to compute single numbers, called *descriptive statistics*, that represent the entire collection of observations. Descriptive statistics include measures of central tendency, such as the mean, median, and mode; measures of variation among observations, such as the standard deviation, variance, and interquartile range; and measures of the shape of the distribution, such as skewness and kurtosis. To compute descriptive statistics, you can use the MEANS and UNIVARIATE procedures.

Computing Basic Descriptive Statistics for Variables

To compute basic descriptive statistics for the variables in a data set, you can use the MEANS procedure. The MEANS procedure gives a concise summary of the data. For descriptive statistics that provide a more detailed analysis, you can use the UNIVARIATE procedure, which is described in the next section. In this example, the PROC MEANS step computes descriptive statistics for the variables LOCAL, NTL, and INTNTL for both levels of the variable CIRC. To specify the input data set, use the DATA= option in the PROC MEANS statement. If this option is omitted, the MEANS procedure uses the most recently created SAS data set.

```
libname mylib 'SAS-data-library';

proc means data=mylib.news;
```

The default statistics computed by the MEANS procedure are N, the number of observations having nonmissing values for the variable; MIN, the minimum value; MAX, the maximum value; MEAN, the mean; and STD, the standard deviation, which is a measure of variation among observations. You can request other statistics in the PROC MEANS statement.

To specify the variables for which statistics are computed, use the VAR statement. The MEANS procedure computes the statistics for each numeric variable listed in the VAR statement. If you do not use a VAR statement, the MEANS procedure analyzes all numeric variables in the input data set unless you use a BY, CLASS, FREQ, ID, or WEIGHT statement. The following VAR statement specifies LOCAL, NTL, and INTNTL as the variables for which statistics are computed:

```
var local ntl intntl;
```

To compute statistics separately for categories of observations, use a CLASS statement. *Class variables* may be either numeric or character, but normally each variable has a small number of discrete values, or unique levels, which define subgroups of the data. In this example, the variable CIRC divides the data into two levels based on circulation size so that the statistics are computed separately for every combination of rating variable and circulation size.

```
class circ;
```

Here is the complete program that produces and prints the basic descriptive statistics for the newspaper rating variables:

```
libname mylib 'SAS-data-library';

proc means data=mylib.news;
   var local ntl intntl;
   class circ;
   title 'Basic Descriptive Statistics for Newspaper Ratings';
run;
```

Output 17.5 shows the results.

Output 17.5
Computing Basic
Descriptive
Statistics for
Variables

```
            Basic Descriptive Statistics for Newspaper Ratings              1

CIRC  N Obs  Variable   N        Mean         Std Dev        Minimum
----------------------------------------------------------------------------
1       18   LOCAL      18     2.3888889      0.6978023      1.5000000
             NTL        18     6.4444444      1.5424283      3.0000000
             INTNTL     18     3.1388889      0.8711986      1.0000000

s       18   LOCAL      18     2.4722222      0.6745853      1.5000000
             NTL        18     4.3333333      1.2833779      2.0000000
             INTNTL     18     1.9444444      0.4501271      1.0000000
----------------------------------------------------------------------------

             CIRC  N Obs  Variable     Maximum
             -------------------------------------
             1       18   LOCAL       3.5000000
                          NTL         9.0000000
                          INTNTL      4.5000000

             s       18   LOCAL       4.0000000
                          NTL         7.0000000
                          INTNTL      3.0000000
             -------------------------------------
```

In Output 17.5, the MEANS procedure lists six values for every statistic. These values correspond to the three rating variables at each of the two levels of the circulation variable. The papers with large circulations have a mean of 2.3888889 for their ratings of local news coverage with a standard deviation of .6978023. The minimum value of these 18 ratings is 1.5 and the maximum is 3.5.

Computing Detailed Descriptive Statistics for Distributions of Variables

If you want a more detailed description of the variables in your data set, you can use the UNIVARIATE procedure. Using the UNIVARIATE procedure is usually the best way to begin analyzing data because the procedure provides such a complete description including percentiles, tables, and plots in addition to what the MEANS procedure provides. The output in this example also directly compares the ratings for the newspapers with high and low subscription rates with side-by-side plots of the distributions. To examine categories separately within a data set, you need to do the following:

□ sort the observations into categories

□ produce the statistics and plots for each category.

Sort the Observations

To sort the observations into categories, you can use the SORT procedure. The following PROC SORT step sorts the observations into categories based on the value of the CIRC variable.

```
libname mylib 'SAS-data-library';

proc sort data=mylib.news;
   by circ;
run;
```

Produce the Statistics and Plots

To produce descriptive statistics and plots for the distributions of the variables, you can use the UNIVARIATE procedure. In this example, the PROC UNIVARIATE step produces statistics and plots for the distributions of the newspaper rating variables at each circulation size. To specify the input data set, use the DATA= option in the PROC UNIVARIATE statement. If this option is omitted, the UNIVARIATE procedure uses the most recently created SAS data set.

```
proc univariate data=mylib.news;
```

To produce frequency tables, use the FREQ option in the PROC UNIVARIATE statement. A *frequency table* lists all the values of a variable, the number of observations with each value, the percentage of observations with each value, and the percentage of observations with values less than or equal to each value.

```
proc univariate data=mylib.news freq;
```

To produce stem-and-leaf plots, box plots, and normal probability plots, use the PLOT option in the PROC UNIVARIATE statement. If more than 48 observations fall into a single interval, the UNIVARIATE procedure produces a horizontal bar chart instead of a stem-and-leaf plot. If you use a BY statement, the UNIVARIATE procedure also produces side-by-side box plots comparing categories for each variable listed in the VAR statement. These diagrams help you visualize the distributions of the variables. A discussion of each type of plot follows the output in this section.

```
proc univariate data=mylib.news freq plot;
```

To specify the variables for which statistics are computed, use the VAR statement. The UNIVARIATE procedure computes the statistics for each numeric variable listed in the VAR statement. If you do not use a VAR statement, the UNIVARIATE procedure analyzes all numeric variables in the data set. The following VAR statement specifies LOCAL, NTL, and INTNTL as the variables for which statistics are computed:

```
var local ntl intntl;
```

To obtain separate analyses on categories of observations, you can use the BY statement to specify the variables used to define subgroups of the data. The input data set must be sorted in order of the BY variables. In this example, the variable CIRC is specified in the BY statement to produce separate analyses for the newspapers with large circulations and the newspapers with small circulations. So the UNIVARIATE procedure produces statistics and plots for both levels of circulation for the distributions of the three rating variables.

```
by circ;
```

To specify a variable whose values for the five largest and five smallest observations in each category appear in the printed output, use the ID statement. The values of the ID variable are truncated to eight characters in the output. The following ID statement prints the names of the five highest and five lowest rated newspapers in each category:

```
id name;
```

To request percentiles not automatically computed by the UNIVARIATE procedure, use the OUTPUT statement. The UNIVARIATE procedure automatically computes the 1st, 5th, 10th, 25th, 50th (often called the median), 75th, 90th, 95th, and 99th percentiles in addition to the minimum and maximum. To name the new SAS data set that contains the requested percentiles, use the OUT= option. The following OUT= option creates a new data set named DISTRIB:

```
output out=distrib;
```

To specify the requested percentiles, use the PCTLPTS= option. The PCTLPTS= option generates the additional percentiles and outputs them to the data set specified in the OUT= option. If you use the PCTLPTS= option, you must use the PCTLPRE= option to specify names for the percentiles. The following PCTLPTS= option requests the 20th, 40th, 60th, and 80th percentiles for the three rating variables at both levels of circulation size:

```
output out=distrib pctlpts=20 40 60 80;
```

To specify prefixes used to create variable names for the requested percentiles, use the PCTLPRE= option. These prefixes distinguish among the percentiles of different variables. If you request percentiles for more than one variable in the input data set, specify the prefixes to match the order of the variables in the VAR statement. The following PCTLPRE= option specifies the prefixes L, N, and I for the names of the percentiles for the variables LOCAL, NTL, and INTNTL. The variables containing the 20th percentiles are called L20, N20, and I20; the variables containing the 40th percentiles are called L40, N40, and I40; and so forth.

```
output out=distrib pctlpts=20 40 60 80 pctlpre=l n i;
```

Here is the complete program that produces and prints the detailed descriptive statistics for the distributions of the newspaper rating variables:

```
libname mylib 'SAS-data-library';

proc sort data=mylib.news;
   by circ;
run;
```

```
proc univariate data=mylib.news freq plot;
   var local ntl intntl;
   by circ;
   id name;
   title 'Detailed Descriptive Statistics for Newspaper Ratings';
   output out=distrib pctlpts=20 40 60 80 pctlpre=l n i;
run;

proc print data=distrib(drop=name);
   title 'Specified Percentiles for Newspaper Ratings';
run;
```

Output 17.6 shows the complete results for two of the six combinations of rating variable and circulation size. The pages of output are numbered in the top right corner. The first two pages of output are the analysis of the variable LOCAL for the large newspapers. Pages 3 through 6, the analyses of the variables NTL and INTNTL for the large papers, have been omitted along with pages 7 through 10, the analyses of the variables LOCAL and NTL for the small papers. Pages 11 and 12 of output, discussed in detail later, continue with the analysis of the variable INTNTL for the small newspapers. Pages 13, 14, and 15 of output show the side-by-side box plots comparing the levels of circulation for each variable. Page 16 gives the specified percentiles for all three variables.

Output 17.6
Computing
Detailed
Descriptive
Statistics for the
Distributions of
Variables

```
                Detailed Descriptive Statistics for Newspaper Ratings          1

--------------------------------- CIRC=1 ---------------------------------
                              Univariate Procedure

Variable=LOCAL

                                   Moments

                N              18   Sum Wgts           18
                Mean     2.388889   Sum                43
                Std Dev  0.697802   Variance     0.486928
                Skewness 0.444829   Kurtosis     -1.12919
                USS           111   CSS          8.277778
                CV       29.21033   Std Mean     0.164474
                T:Mean=0 14.52445   Prob>|T|       0.0001
                Num ¬= 0       18   Num > 0            18
                M(Sign)         9   Prob>|M|       0.0001
                Sgn Rank     85.5   Prob>|S|       0.0001


                              Quantiles(Def=5)

                100% Max      3.5        99%        3.5
                 75% Q3         3        95%        3.5
                 50% Med        2        90%        3.5
                 25% Q1         2        10%        1.5
                  0% Min      1.5         5%        1.5
                                          1%        1.5

                Range           2
                Q3-Q1           1
                Mode            2


                                  Extremes

                Lowest    ID       Highest    ID
                1.5(The Warr)         3(The Seas)
                1.5(The Vall)         3(The Shee)
                1.5(The Tour)       3.5(The Blue)
                  2(Today's )       3.5(The Ceda)
                  2(The Rive)       3.5(The Rece)
```

```
            Stem Leaf                      #          Boxplot
               3 555                       3             |
               3 000                       3          +-----+
               2 55                        2          |     |
               2 0000000                   7          *--+--*
               1 555                        3          |
                 ----+----+----+----+
```

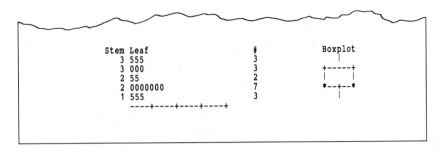

```
        Detailed Descriptive Statistics for Newspaper Ratings              2

        -------------------------------- CIRC=1 --------------------------------
                              Univariate Procedure

Variable=LOCAL

                            Normal Probability Plot
                                               *  *  ++*+++++
        3.75+                              *  **++++++++
            |                                 *+*+++
        2.75+                            ** **+**+*
            |                      *  *+*+++++
        1.75+           *
             +----+----+----+----+----+----+----+----+----+----+
                 -2        -1         0        +1        +2
```

```
                            Frequency Table

                          Percents                        Percents
        Value Count    Cell    Cum      Value Count    Cell    Cum
          1.5      3   16.7   16.7          3      3   16.7   83.3
            2      7   38.9   55.6        3.5      3   16.7  100.0
          2.5      2   11.1   66.7
```

```
        Detailed Descriptive Statistics for Newspaper Ratings             11

        -------------------------------- CIRC=s --------------------------------
                              Univariate Procedure

Variable=INTNTL

                                  Moments

            N                  18   Sum Wgts          18
            Mean         1.944444   Sum               35
            Std Dev      0.450127   Variance    0.202614
            Skewness     0.237388   Kurtosis    1.254767
            USS              71.5   CSS         3.444444
            CV           23.14939   Std Mean    0.106096
            T:Mean=0     18.32722   Prob>|T|      0.0001
            Num ¬= 0           18   Num > 0           18
            M(Sign)             9   Prob>|M|      0.0001
            Sgn Rank         85.5   Prob>|S|      0.0001


                            Quantiles(Def=5)

            100% Max            3   99%                3
             75% Q3             2   95%                3
             50% Med            2   90%              2.5
             25% Q1           1.5   10%              1.5
              0% Min            1   5%                 1
                                    1%                 1
            Range               2
            Q3-Q1             0.5
            Mode                2
```

(continued on next page)

(continued from previous page)

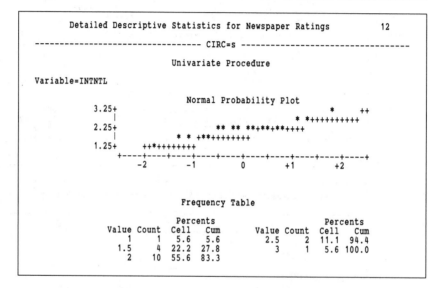

```
                            Extremes

                 Lowest     ID      Highest    ID
                      1(The Hunt)       2(The High)
                    1.5(The Samf)       2(The Oxfo)
                    1.5(The Nort)     2.5(The Aubu)
                    1.5(The Fort)     2.5(The Vill)
                    1.5(The Bent)       3(The East)


         Stem Leaf                      #         Boxplot
            3 0                         1            |
            2 55                        2            |
            2 0000000000               10         +-----+
            1 5555                       4         +--+--+
            1 0                          1            |
              ----+----+----+----+
```

```
        Detailed Descriptive Statistics for Newspaper Ratings        12

------------------------------- CIRC=s ------------------------------------

                         Univariate Procedure

Variable=INTNTL


                       Normal Probability Plot
        3.25+                                      *      ++
            |                              * *++++++++++
        2.25+                    ** ** **+**+**++++
            |           * * +**++++++++
        1.25+     ++*++++++++
            +----+----+----+----+----+----+----+----+----+----+
               -2        -1         0        +1        +2



                            Frequency Table

                       Percents                        Percents
        Value Count  Cell   Cum      Value Count  Cell    Cum
            1     1    5.6    5.6       2.5     2   11.1    94.4
          1.5     4   22.2   27.8         3     1    5.6   100.0
            2    10   55.6   83.3
```

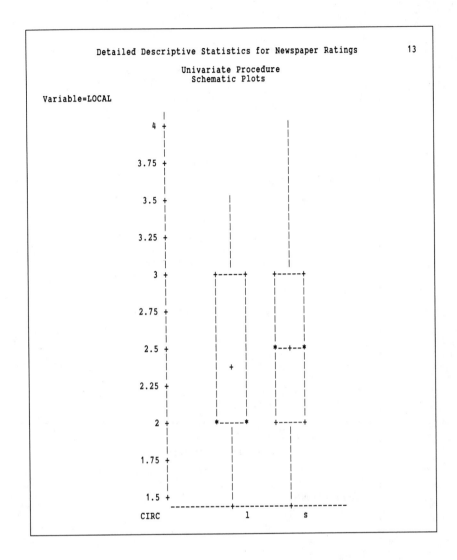

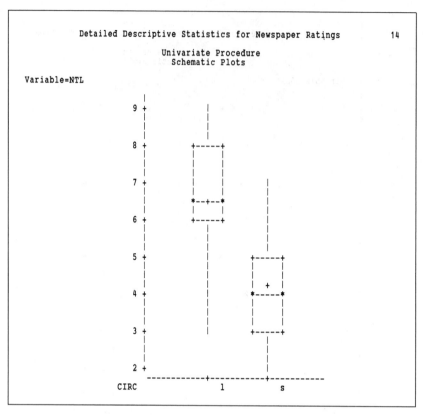

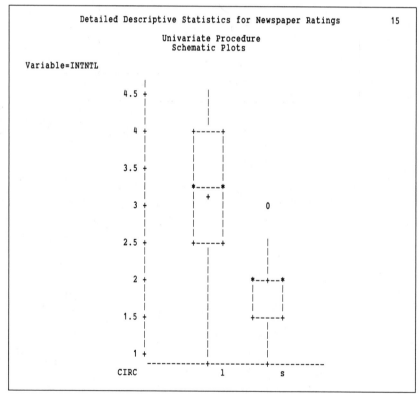

					Specified Percentiles for Newspaper Ratings							16
OBS	CIRC	L20	L40	L60	L80	N20	N40	N60	N80	I20	I40	I60	I80
1	l	2	2.0	2.5	3	5	6	7	8	2.5	3	3.5	4
2	s	2	2.5	2.5	3	3	4	5	5	1.5	2	2.0	2

For each category of each requested variable, the UNIVARIATE procedure output is divided into seven sections: moments, quantiles, extremes, the stem-and-leaf plot, the box plot, the normal probability plot, and the frequency table. The BY statement produces side-by-side box plots comparing the categories for each variable. The last page of output in this example is the table of the specified percentiles for all the variables.

Moments section

The moments section contains basic descriptive statistics along with several statistics not automatically provided by the MEANS procedure. *Skewness* is a measure of the tendency for the distribution of values to be more spread out on one side of the mean than on the other. A positive skewness indicates that values above the mean are more spread out than values below the mean, and a negative skewness indicates the opposite. The details for the final combination of size and variable begin in the moments section on page 11 of output. For the variable INTNTL for newspapers with a small circulation, the mean of the 18 ratings is 1.944444 with a standard deviation of .450127. The skewness is .237388, which indicates that the values above the mean are slightly more spread out than the values below the mean.

Kurtosis measures the "heaviness of the tails" of a distribution. Extremely nonnormal distributions may have kurtosis values far from zero, and nearly normal distributions have kurtosis values close to zero. A positive kurtosis indicates that the distribution has heavy tails. This means that the data contain some values far from the mean relative to most of the other values. A negative kurtosis indicates that the distribution has light tails. If a distribution has more extreme values than a normal distribution, it has a positive kurtosis, and if it has fewer extreme values than a normal distribution, it has a negative kurtosis. The kurtosis value for INTNTL for the papers with small circulations is 1.254767, which indicates a higher concentration of values away from the mean than in a normal distribution. You can visually identify skewness and kurtosis from the stem-and-leaf plot.

Quantiles section

The default percentiles — range, interquartile range, and mode — are listed in the quantiles section. A *percentile* is a value that is larger than a percentage of the values of the observations. For example, the 90th percentile for INTNTL for the small newspapers, shown on output page 11, is 2.5. This means that 2.5 is greater than 90 percent of the values of that variable and circulation size. The 75th percentile, or third quartile, is 2, which is also the median in this case. The 25th percentile, or first quartile, is 1.5. The *interquartile range*, denoted by Q3-Q1, is the difference between the third quartile and the first quartile. For this combination of variable and circulation size, the interquartile range is .5, the difference between the third quartile of 2 and the first quartile of 1.5. The *range* is the difference between the largest and smallest values. In this case, the range is 2, the difference between the maximum of 3 and the minimum of 1. The *mode* is the most frequent value. If there is a tie for the most frequent value, the smallest mode is given. Here, the mode is 2.

Extremes section

The five highest and five lowest values are listed in the extremes section. The extremes sections in this example show the highest and the lowest five values matched with the first eight characters of the names of the newspapers. Of the small papers, *The East Oak Corner Chronicle* has the highest rating for international coverage, shown on output page 11. *The Village Green Report* and *The Auburntown Tribune* each scored 2.5 to place second. Since there is a ten-way tie for the fourth-highest value, only two observations are listed to complete the set of five. *The Hunts Point Bulletin* scored the lowest with a 1, and *The Bent Creek Gazette*, *The Fort Washington Constitution*, *The Northwoods Examiner*, and *The Samford Editorial* scored next to the lowest with a 1.5.

Stem-and-leaf and box plots

The *stem-and-leaf plot* shows the distribution of the values for a variable. The stem values are to the left of the column of spaces, and the leaf values are to the right. Every leaf value represents one observation. The value of that observation, in this example, is one times the stem value plus one tenth times the leaf value. The column between the stem-and-leaf plot and the box plot shows the observation count for each line. The stem-and-leaf plot is valuable because it not only shows the shape of the distribution, but also gives the values of the observations.

The *box plot* is drawn on the same scale as the stem-and-leaf plot. The dashed lines on the box plot correspond to the 25th, 50th, and 75th percentiles. The 25th and 75th percentiles are the upper and lower bounds of the box. The plus sign indicates the mean. The vertical lines, or *whiskers*, stretch over the entire distribution, provided that all the values are within 1.5 interquartile ranges of the box. A value beyond the whisker range is represented by a zero if it is up to three interquartile ranges from the box or by an asterisk if it is beyond that. The box plot is valuable because it identifies quartiles and extreme values.

On page 11 of the output, the stem value is the number to the left of the decimal point, and the leaf value is the number to the right of the decimal point. The single leaf value of 0 with the stem of 3 indicates only one observation of 3.0. A zero is listed for this value in the box plot because it is more than 1.5 interquartile ranges above the third quartile. Since the third quartile is 2 and the interquartile range is .5, the value of 3 is two interquartile ranges above the third quartile.

The two leaf values of 5 with the stem value of 2 indicate two values of 2.5. These values are represented in the box plot by the whisker above the box. The box is defined by the first and third quartiles, which are 1.5 and 2.0. The stem-and-leaf plot shows ten values of 2.0 and four values of 1.5. The box plot does not show a separate dotted line for the median since it is the same as the third quartile. The single value of 1 is represented by the whisker below the box.

Normal probability plot

The *normal probability plot* compares the distribution of the data with a normal distribution. The plus signs, which represent a normal distribution, form a straight line. The normal distribution is a common, naturally occurring distribution that, when graphed, looks like a bell because of the high concentration of observations around the mean and the low concentration of observations in the tails of the distribution. The normal distribution is smooth, symmetric, and has only one value that represents the mean, the median, and the mode. The asterisks in the graph represent the input data. If the data are from a normal distribution, the asterisks form a straight line and cover most of the plus signs. A large number of visible plus signs indicates that the data are from a nonnormal distribution.

The normal probability plot on page 12 of the output shows the 18 values as asterisks with a straight line of plus signs representing a normal distribution. With only 18 values, this plot is not very helpful.

Frequency table

The frequency table on page 12 of the output shows that one observation has a value of 1, and 5.6 percent of the observations have a value of 1. This value is greater than or equal to 5.6 percent of the observations, which in this case is just itself. Four observations, which make up 22.2 percent of the observations, have a value of 1.5. This value is greater than or equal to 27.8 percent of the observations, those with values of 1.0 or 1.5. Ten observations have a value of 2, which represents 55.6 percent of the observations. The cumulative percentage is 83.3. The two values of 2.5 have a cell percentage of 11.1 and a cumulative percentage of 94.4. The maximum value of 3 represents 5.6 percent of the observations and is, by definition, greater than or equal to all the values.

Side-by-side box plots

Pages 13, 14, and 15 of the output show side-by-side box plots of the categories for all three variables. For the variable LOCAL, the higher plus sign in the box on the right indicates a higher mean for the small newspapers, and the higher whisker on the box on the right indicates a higher maximum value for the small papers. The minimum values and interquartile ranges are equal. For the variables NTL and INTNTL, the newspapers with large circulations scored so much better than the newspapers with small circulations that the boxes do not even overlap. Here, you can visually compare the means, quartiles, and extreme values of the large and small newspapers.

Specified percentiles

In this example, the final page of output lists the 20th, 40th, 60th, and 80th percentiles. The PCTLPTS= option lets you specify any percentile values from 0 to 100. These percentiles are given for all three variables and are split according to the value of the circulation variable. For the variable INTNTL, the rating of 2.5 is higher than 20 percent of the newspapers with a high subscription rate, and the rating of 1.5 is higher than 20 percent of the papers with a low subscription rate. The 40th percentile is 3 for the large papers and 2 for the small papers. The 60th percentile for INTNTL is 3.5 for the large papers and 2.0 for the small papers. A large paper with a score of 4 is rated higher than 80 percent of the large papers, and a small paper with a score of 2 is rated higher than 80 percent of the small papers.

Measuring Strengths of Relationships between Variables

When two different variables measure similar characteristics, the values of those variables may mirror each other. As the values of one variable increase, the values of an associated variable tend to increase or decrease. This association is called *correlation*. In this chapter, the newspapers that receive high marks for their coverage of international news also tend to receive high marks for their coverage of national news. The political organization could be confident in quoting a national story from a paper well respected for its international coverage. To

determine trends between variables, you can compute a single coefficient that indicates the direction and the strength of their relationship.

To measure the strengths of the relationships between variables, you can use the CORR procedure to compute correlation coefficients. A *correlation coefficient* ranges from -1 to 1 and indicates a trend between two variables. A large absolute value, or magnitude, indicates a strong relationship between variables. The sign of the correlation coefficient indicates whether the two variables are directly or inversely related. A negative value means that as one variable becomes larger, the other tends to become smaller. A positive correlation coefficient means that both variables tend to go in the same direction. Little relationship exists if the coefficient is close to 0. In this example, the PROC CORR step measures the strengths of the relationships between all possible combinations of the newspaper rating variables.

To specify the input data set, use the DATA= option in the PROC CORR statement. If this option is omitted, the CORR procedure uses the most recently created SAS data set.

```
libname mylib 'SAS-data-library';

proc corr data=mylib.news;
```

To request Pearson and Spearman correlation coefficients, use the PEARSON and SPEARMAN options. The Pearson correlation coefficient measures the strength of the relationship between two variables based on the actual values of those variables. The Spearman correlation coefficient is computed the same way as the Pearson except that it uses ranks of observations rather than actual values. You can request other correlation statistics in the PROC CORR statement.

```
proc corr data=mylib.news pearson spearman;
```

The CORR procedure computes correlation coefficients for all combinations of variables listed in the VAR statement. In this example, the three nontrivial pairings are LOCAL with NTL, LOCAL with INTNTL, and NTL with INTNTL.

```
var local ntl intntl;
```

Here is the complete program that produces and prints the Pearson and Spearman correlation coefficients for the newspaper rating variables:

```
libname mylib 'SAS-data-library';

proc corr data=mylib.news pearson spearman;
   var local ntl intntl;
   title 'Correlations of Newspaper Ratings';
run;
```

Output 17.7 shows the results.

Output 17.7
Measuring
Strengths of
Relationships
between Variables

```
                    Correlations of Newspaper Ratings                    1
                          Correlation Analysis

          3 'VAR' Variables:  LOCAL     NTL       INTNTL


                              Simple Statistics

       Variable     N      Mean    Std Dev    Median   Minimum   Maximum

       LOCAL       36     2.4306    0.6777    2.5000    1.5000    4.0000
       NTL         36     5.3889    1.7611    5.0000    2.0000    9.0000
       INTNTL      36     2.5417    0.9132    2.5000    1.0000    4.5000


     Pearson Correlation Coefficients / Prob > |R| under Ho: Rho=0 / N = 36

                         LOCAL              NTL              INTNTL

         LOCAL         1.00000           0.15493           -0.02981
                         0.0               0.3669            0.8630

         NTL           0.15493           1.00000            0.84238
                         0.3669            0.0               0.0001

         INTNTL       -0.02981           0.84238            1.00000
                         0.8630            0.0001            0.0


    Spearman Correlation Coefficients / Prob > |R| under Ho: Rho=0 / N = 36

                         LOCAL              NTL              INTNTL

         LOCAL         1.00000           0.12586           -0.02379
                         0.0               0.4645            0.8905

         NTL           0.12586           1.00000            0.81832
                         0.4645            0.0               0.0001

         INTNTL       -0.02379           0.81832            1.00000
                         0.8905            0.0001            0.0
```

Output 17.7 includes a correlation matrix for both the Pearson and Spearman coefficients. Any variable is perfectly correlated with itself, which is indicated by a coefficient of 1. There is no set value of the correlation coefficient that indicates a strong relationship; the coefficient must be examined in the context of the analysis.

The variables NTL and INTNTL are the most strongly related pair of the combinations with a Pearson correlation coefficient of .84238 and a Spearman correlation coefficient of .81832. You would expect a strong, positive correlation between these two variables just from reading the newspaper ratings because most of the papers that received a high rating from the second critic also received a high rating from the third critic and most that received a low rating from one received a low rating from the other.

The variables LOCAL and NTL are slightly directly related with a .15493 Pearson correlation coefficient and a .12586 Spearman correlation coefficient. The variables LOCAL and INTNTL are slightly inversely related with coefficients of −.02981 and −.02379. Because these correlation coefficients are close to 0, almost no relationship exists between these papers' ratings for local news and their ratings for international news and between their ratings for local news and national news.

The numbers below the coefficients are the probabilities of obtaining a coefficient of at least that magnitude given that the two variables are actually uncorrelated. The correlations in this example between LOCAL and NTL and between LOCAL and INTNTL could have easily occurred by chance alone. These probabilities can be used for hypothesis testing.

Summary

The following points summarize how to use five descriptive procedures of the SAS System to produce summary reports:

- □ To compute ranks for variables across observations, use the RANK procedure. You can use the VAR statement to specify the variables that are ranked and use the RANKS statement to name the new variables containing the ranks of the original variables.

- □ To standardize variables to a given mean and standard deviation, use the STANDARD procedure. You can specify a mean and standard deviation for the new distributions of the variables listed in the VAR statement.

- □ To compute just the basic descriptive statistics, such as the means and standard deviations, use the MEANS procedure. To obtain separate analyses on categories of observations, use the CLASS statement to specify variables that divide the data set into subgroups.

- □ To compute detailed descriptive statistics for the distributions of variables, use the UNIVARIATE procedure. You can request a stem-and-leaf plot, a box plot, a normal probability plot, a frequency table, and any percentiles for the variables listed in the VAR statement. To obtain separate analyses on categories of observations, use the SORT procedure and a BY statement in the UNIVARIATE procedure.

- □ To measure the strengths of the relationships between variables, use the CORR procedure. You can request Pearson and Spearman correlation coefficients for all possible combinations of variables listed in the VAR statement.

SAS Tools

This section summarizes syntax for the statements, functions, and procedures discussed in this chapter.

Statement

variable=expression;
    is an assignment statement that evaluates an expression and stores the result in a variable. *Variable* names a new or existing variable. *Expression* is any valid SAS expression.

Function

MEAN(*argument,argument, . . .*)
  returns the average of the nonmissing arguments. *Argument* is numeric.

Procedures

PROC CORR <DATA=*SAS-data-set*> <*types-options*>;
  VAR *variable-list*;

  PROC CORR <DATA=*SAS-data-set*> <*types-options*>;
    computes correlation coefficients between variables. The DATA= option specifies the input SAS data set. If this option is omitted, the most recently created SAS data set is used.
      The following *types-options* for the PROC CORR statement are discussed in this chapter:

      PEARSON   requests Pearson correlation coefficients.

      SPEARMAN   requests Spearman correlation coefficients.

  VAR *variable-list*;
    lists the variables for which correlation coefficients are computed.

PROC MEANS <DATA=*SAS-data-set*>;
  VAR *variable-list*;
  CLASS *variable-list*;

  PROC MEANS <DATA=*SAS-data-set*>;
    computes basic descriptive statistics for an entire SAS data set or for groups of observations. The DATA= option specifies the input SAS data set. If this option is omitted, the most recently created SAS data set is used.

  VAR *variable-list*;
    specifies the variables for which statistics are computed.

  CLASS *variable-list*;
    specifies variables whose values define categories of the data.

PROC RANK <DATA=*SAS-data-set*> <OUT=*SAS-data-set*><DESCENDING>
  <TIES=LOW>;
  VAR *variable-list*;
  RANKS *new-variable-list*;

  PROC RANK <DATA=*SAS-data-set*> <OUT=*SAS-data-set*>
    <DESCENDING> <TIES=LOW>;
    computes ranks of observations. The DATA= option specifies the input SAS data set. If this option is omitted, the most recently created SAS data set is used. The OUT= option names the output data set that contains the ranks. DESCENDING ranks the observations from largest to smallest with the largest observation receiving the rank of 1. TIES=LOW assigns the lowest possible rank to tied values.

(PROC RANK continued)

VAR *variable-list*;
specifies the variables whose observations are ranked.

RANKS *new-variable-list*;
names the new variables that contain the ranks.

PROC SORT <DATA=*SAS-data-set*>;
BY *variable-1* <. . .*variable-n*>;

PROC SORT <DATA=*SAS-data-set*>;
sorts observations in a SAS data set by one or more variables. The DATA= option specifies the input SAS data set. If this option is omitted, the most recently created SAS data set is used. The BY statement must be included to specify the variables.

BY *variable-1* <. . .*variable-n*>;
lists the variables by which the data set is sorted.

PROC STANDARD <DATA=*SAS-data-set*> *standardization-option-list*
<PRINT> <OUT=*SAS-data-set*>;
VAR *variable-list*;

PROC STANDARD <DATA=*SAS-data-set*> *standardization-option-list*
<PRINT> <OUT=*SAS-data-set*>;
standardizes some or all of the variables in a SAS data set to a given mean and standard deviation and produces a new SAS data set containing the standardized values. The DATA= option specifies the input SAS data set. If this option is omitted, the most recently created SAS data set is used. PRINT prints the mean, standard deviation, and number of observations for each variable prior to standardization. The OUT= option names the output data set that contains the standardized variables.
The following *standardization-options* for the PROC STANDARD statement are discussed in this chapter:

MEAN=*mean-value*
specifies the mean of the standardized variables.

STD=*std-value*
specifies the standard deviation of the standardized variables.

VAR *variable-list*;
specifies the variables that are standardized.

PROC UNIVARIATE <DATA=*SAS-data-set*> <*requests-options*>;
    VAR *variable-list*;
    BY *variable-list*;
    ID *variable*;
    OUTPUT <OUT=*SAS-data-set*>
       <PCTLPTS=*percentiles* PCTLPRE=*prefix-name-list*>;

PROC UNIVARIATE <DATA=*SAS-data-set*> <*requests-options*>;
    computes detailed descriptive statistics for distributions of variables. The
    DATA= option specifies the input SAS data set. If this option is omitted,
    the most recently created SAS data set is used.
       The following *requests-options* for the PROC UNIVARIATE statement
    are discussed in this chapter:

    FREQ   produces a frequency table.

    PLOT   produces a stem-and-leaf plot, a box plot, and a normal
              probability plot.

VAR *variable-list*;
    specifies the variables for which statistics are computed.

BY *variable-list*;
    specifies variables whose values define categories of the data.

ID *variable*;
    names a variable whose values for the five largest and five smallest
    observations in each category appear in the printed output.

OUTPUT <OUT=*SAS-data-set*>
    <PCTLPTS=*percentiles* PCTLPRE=*prefix-name-list*>;
    saves statistics in a new SAS data set. The OUT= option specifies the
    output data set. The PCTLPTS= option requests percentiles, and the
    PCTLPRE= option specifies prefixes to identify the percentiles for each
    variable listed in the VAR statement.

Learning More

This section provides references for learning more about topics presented in this
chapter.

□   *SAS System for Elementary Statistical Analysis* introduces statistics and
    statistical procedures in base SAS software. Chapter 5, "Understanding Some
    Basic Statistical Concepts," discusses the normal distribution.

□   For complete descriptions of the CORR, MEANS, RANK, SORT, STANDARD,
    and UNIVARIATE procedures, refer to *SAS Procedures Guide, Version 6,*
    Third Edition. Chapter 1, "SAS Elementary Statistics Procedures," compares
    procedures and provides statistical background.

□ See *SAS/STAT User's Guide, Version 6, Fourth Edition, Volumes 1* and *2* for documentation of other ranking procedures: NPAR1WAY, PRINQUAL, SCORE, and TRANSREG.

□ *JMP User's Guide* and *SAS/STAT User's Guide* discuss other methods of statistical analysis.

Chapter **18** Producing Calendars

Introduction

The CALENDAR procedure displays data from SAS data sets in a monthly calendar format. PROC CALENDAR can produce two basic types of calendars: *summary calendars* and *schedule calendars*. Summary calendars display activities that have durations of only one day. These calendars can include holidays as well as sum and mean calculations.

Schedule calendars display activities that have durations of one or more days. Schedule calendars can schedule activities around holidays, weekends, and other nonwork periods and can schedule activities in shifts.

In this chapter

This chapter shows you how to produce the following types of calendars:

□   summary calendars

□   schedule calendars.

Prerequisites

To understand the examples and discussions in this chapter, you should be familiar with the FORMAT procedure and SAS date values.

Producing Summary Calendars

When you want to summarize daily activities that occur repeatedly, you can use the CALENDAR procedure to produce summary calendars. For example, a bank could produce a summary calendar that displays the number of cash withdrawals successfully completed each day at an automatic teller machine. The summary calendar could include the total number of withdrawals performed each month as well as the average number of withdrawals.

This section uses a SAS data set as input and shows you how to do the following:

□   display a simple summary calendar

□   add holidays to the calendar

□   enhance the output

□   display totals and averages based on the number of activities

□   display averages based on the number of days in the month.

SAS Data Set Example for Summary Calendars

All the examples in this section use a SAS data set named ATM.ACTIVITY. It contains observations that a bank collected about daily use of an automatic teller machine (ATM). There is only one observation per day. Each observation contains a date and the number of ATM transactions successfully completed on that date. Each observation in the data set contains the following variables:

Variable	Type	Format	Description
ACTDATE	numeric	date7.	date of the activity, one for each day the ATM was in service
WITHDRAW	numeric		number of withdrawals of cash
INQUIRY	numeric		number of inquiries about account balances
TRANSFER	numeric		number of transfers of funds between accounts
DEPOSIT	numeric		number of deposits to accounts
PAYMENT	numeric		number of loan payments

The PROC PRINT step below produces a printout of the data set ATM.ACTIVITY.*

```
libname atm 'SAS-data-library';

proc print data=atm.activity noobs;
   format actdate date7.;
   title 'ATM Activity - January 1991';
run;
```

Output 18.1 shows the results of the PROC PRINT step.

Output 18.1
Printout of
Data Set
ATM.ACTIVITY

```
                    ATM Activity - January 1991                      1

    ACTDATE     WTHDRWL     INQUIRY     TRANSFR    DEPOSIT    PAYMENT
    01JAN91       129         14           5          11         16
    02JAN91       116         16           3           9          5
    03JAN91       174         40           6           8          4
    04JAN91       181         49           7           6          1
    05JAN91       166         44           2           6          0
    06JAN91       132         10           4           9          5
    07JAN91       134         19           3          10          6
    08JAN91       120         15           6           6          4

                                        (continued on next page)
```

---

* The DATA step that creates ATM.ACTIVITY is shown in the Appendix.

(continued from previous page)

09JAN91	121	12	2	7	18
10JAN91	195	49	5	10	17
11JAN91	227	59	12	6	0
12JAN91	188	41	1	0	1
13JAN91	117	15	10	7	4
14JAN91	135	17	9	8	8
15JAN91	119	13	5	15	7
16JAN91	122	20	4	19	5
17JAN91	160	39	6	9	6
18JAN91	192	44	3	10	4
19JAN91	175	32	4	8	6
20JAN91	138	14	6	9	12
21JAN91	130	15	10	7	6
22JAN91	129	12	4	7	5
23JAN91	133	22	5	9	14
24JAN91	222	58	8	11	3
25JAN91	223	62	10	10	2
27JAN91	225	60	12	4	2
28JAN91	188	.9	2	0	1
29JAN91	167	40	7	8	0
30JAN91	139	94	5	8	9
31JAN91	128	14	8	21	15

Notice that no observation exists for January 26, 1991. The ATM was out of service that day so no transactions were performed. The missing day becomes important when you use PROC CALENDAR to display averages. (See "Displaying Totals and Averages Based on Activities" later in this chapter.)

Displaying a Simple Summary Calendar

Often a simple summary calendar is all you need to display daily activities. If you decide to make the calendar more complex, you can build on the elements of the simple calendar.

To use PROC CALENDAR to display a simple summary calendar, do the following:

□ specify the line size and page size

□ specify the data set that contains the activities information

□ add the dates of the activities.

Specify the Page Size and Line Size

You need to specify the line size and page size to ensure the output page is large enough to accommodate your calendar. PROC CALENDAR always attempts to fit a calendar within a single page, as defined by the SAS system options PAGESIZE= and LINESIZE=.

All the examples in this chapter use the following OPTIONS statement to control the size of the output page:

```
options pagesize=66 linesize=132;
```

If your PAGESIZE= and LINESIZE= values do not allow enough room on the output page, PROC CALENDAR omits portions of the output, such as the values of variables. If portions of the output are omitted, the procedure writes messages to the SAS log.

Specify the Activities Data Set

To produce a summary calendar, you must have an *activities data set*. An activities data set for summary calendars is a SAS data set with the following characteristics:

□ no more than one observation can apply to one day

□ each observation must include an activity date expressed as either a SAS date or datetime value

□ the activities data set must be sorted (or indexed) by the activity dates.

To specify the activities data set, use a PROC CALENDAR statement with the DATA= option. The following PROC CALENDAR statement specifies ATM.ACTIVITY as the activities data set:

```
libname atm 'SAS-data-library';

proc calendar data=atm.activity;
```

Notice in Output 18.1 that the observations in the data set ATM.ACTIVITY are already arranged chronologically based on the values of the variable, ACTDATE. Therefore, the data set ATM.ACTIVITY does not need to be sorted or indexed.

PROC CALENDAR requires an activities data set. If you omit the DATA= option, PROC CALENDAR uses the most recently created SAS data set as the activities data set.

Add the Dates of the Activities

So that each activity appears on the correct day of the month, you must specify which variable in the activities data set contains the dates of the activities. For example, in the data set ATM.ACTIVITY, the variable ACTDATE contains the dates of the ATM transactions.

To specify the variable that contains the activity dates, use a START statement. The following START statement specifies the variable ACTDATE as the activity date variable:

```
libname atm 'SAS-data-library';

proc calendar data=atm.activity;
   start actdate;
   title 'Summary of ATM Activity - Completed Transactions';
run;
```

The START statement is required. Values of the activity date variable must be expressed as either a SAS date or datetime value.*

Output 18.2 shows the results of the PROC CALENDAR step.

Output 18.2   *A Simple Summary Calendar*

```
                        Summary of ATM Activity - Completed Transactions                      1
     ---------------------------------------------------------------------------------------
    |                                                                                       |
    |                                   January  1991                                       |
    |                                                                                       |
    |---------------------------------------------------------------------------------------|
    |   Sunday    |   Monday    |   Tuesday   |  Wednesday  |  Thursday   |   Friday    |  Saturday   |
    |-------------+-------------+-------------+-------------+-------------+-------------+-------------|
    |             |             |      1      |      2      |      3      |      4      |      5      |
    |             |             |             |             |             |             |             |
    |             |             |   129       |   116       |    174      |   181       |   166       |
    |             |             |    14       |    16       |     40      |    49       |    44       |
    |             |             |     5       |     3       |      6      |     7       |     2       |
    |             |             |    11       |     9       |      8      |     6       |     6       |
    |             |             |    16       |     5       |      4      |     1       |     0       |
    |-------------+-------------+-------------+-------------+-------------+-------------+-------------|
    |      6      |      7      |      8      |      9      |     10      |     11      |     12      |
    |             |             |             |             |             |             |             |
    |   132       |   134       |   120       |   121       |   195       |   227       |   188       |
    |    10       |    19       |    15       |    12       |    49       |    59       |    41       |
    |     4       |     3       |     6       |     2       |     5       |    12       |     1       |
    |     9       |    10       |     6       |     7       |    10       |     6       |     0       |
    |     5       |     6       |     4       |    18       |    17       |     0       |     1       |
    |-------------+-------------+-------------+-------------+-------------+-------------+-------------|
    |     13      |     14      |     15      |     16      |     17      |     18      |     19      |
    |             |             |             |             |             |             |             |
    |   117       |   135       |   119       |   122       |   160       |   192       |   175       |
    |    15       |    17       |    13       |    20       |    39       |    44       |    32       |
    |    10       |     9       |     5       |     4       |     6       |     3       |     4       |
    |     7       |     8       |    15       |    19       |     9       |    10       |     8       |
    |     4       |     8       |     7       |     5       |     6       |     4       |     6       |
    |-------------+-------------+-------------+-------------+-------------+-------------+-------------|
    |     20      |     21      |     22      |     23      |     24      |     25      |     26      |
    |             |             |             |             |             |             |             |
    |   138       |   130       |   129       |   133       |   222       |   223       |             |
    |    14       |    15       |    12       |    22       |    58       |    62       |             |
    |     6       |    10       |     4       |     5       |     8       |    10       |             |
    |     9       |     7       |     7       |     9       |    11       |    10       |             |
    |    12       |     6       |     5       |    14       |     3       |     2       |             |
    |-------------+-------------+-------------+-------------+-------------+-------------+-------------|
    |     27      |     28      |     29      |     30      |     31      |             |             |
    |             |             |             |             |             |             |             |
    |   225       |   188       |   167       |   139       |   128       |             |             |
    |    60       |    49       |    40       |    94       |    14       |             |             |
    |    12       |     2       |     7       |     5       |     8       |             |             |
    |     4       |     0       |     8       |     8       |    21       |             |             |
    |     2       |     1       |     0       |     9       |    15       |             |             |
     ---------------------------------------------------------------------------------------
```

---

*   If you use datetime values, you should specify the DATETIME option in the PROC CALENDAR statement. For details, see Chapter 7, "The CALENDAR Procedure," in *SAS Procedures Guide, Version 6, Third Edition.*

Adding Holidays to a Summary Calendar

You may also want to add to your calendars days of special significance, such as holidays. The following example uses a SAS data set that contains holiday information and shows you how to:

□ specify the data set that contains the holiday information

□ add the dates of the holidays

□ add the names of the holidays.

SAS Data Set Example

The SAS data set named ATM.HOLIDAYS contains one observation for the New Year's holiday, January 1, 1991. The observation contains the following variables:

Variable	Type	Format	Description
HOLSTRT	numeric	date7.	start date of the holiday
HOLNAME	character		name of the holiday

The PROC PRINT step below produces a printout of data set ATM.HOLIDAYS.*

```
libname atm 'SAS-data-library';

proc print data=atm.holidays noobs;
   format holstrt date7.;
   title 'Bank Holidays - January 1991';
run;
```

Output 18.3 shows the results of the PROC PRINT step.

Output 18.3
Printout of
Data Set
ATM.HOLIDAYS

```
                  Bank Holidays - January 1991                    1

                      HOLSTRT      HOLNAME

                      01JAN91   New Year's Day
```

---

* The DATA step that creates ATM.HOLIDAYS is shown in the Appendix.

Specify the Holidays Data Set

To include holidays in a calendar, you must have a *holidays data set* to use as input to PROC CALENDAR. A holidays data set for summary calendars is a SAS data set with the following characteristics:

□ no more than one observation can apply to one day

□ each observation must contain a holiday date expressed as either a SAS date or datetime value

□ the holidays data set does not need to be sorted (or indexed) in any particular order.

Optionally, you can include in the holidays data set a variable that contains the names of the holidays.

To specify a holidays data set, add the HOLIDATA= option to the PROC CALENDAR statement. The following PROC CALENDAR statement specifies ATM.HOLIDAYS as the holidays data set:

```
libname atm 'SAS-data-library';

proc calendar data=atm.activity
            holidata=atm.holidays;
   start actdate;
   title1 'Summary of ATM Activity - Completed Transactions';
   title2 'Holidays Included';
run;
```

Add the Dates of the Holidays

If you use a holidays data set, you must specify which variable in the holidays data set contains the dates of the holidays. To specify the holiday date variable, add a HOLISTART statement to the PROC CALENDAR step.

The following HOLISTART statement specifies the variable HOLSTRT from the data set ATM.HOLIDAYS as the variable that contains the holiday dates:

```
libname atm 'SAS-data-library';

proc calendar data=atm.activity
            holidata=atm.holidays;
   start actdate;
   holistart holstrt;
   title1 'Summary of ATM Activity - Completed Transactions';
   title2 'Holidays Included';
run;
```

Add the Names of the Holidays

If you want names of the holidays to appear on the calendar, specify the variable that contains the names of the holidays by including a HOLIVAR statement in the PROC CALENDAR step.

The following PROC CALENDAR step incorporates all the tasks discussed so far in this section including the HOLIVAR statement:

```
libname atm 'SAS-data-library';

proc calendar data=atm.activity
              holidata=atm.holidays;
   start actdate;
   holistart holstrt;
   holivar holname;
   title1 'Summary of ATM Activity - Completed Transactions';
   title2 'Holidays Included';
run;
```

Output 18.4 is partial output. It shows the first week of the calendar. Notice the value `New Year's Day` is displayed on January 1.

Output 18.4   *A Summary Calendar with Holidays*

```
                     Summary of ATM Activity - Completed Transactions                     1
                                    Holidays Included

 --------------------------------------------------------------------------------
|                                                                                |
|                                  January  1991                                 |
|                                                                                |
|--------------------------------------------------------------------------------|
|  Sunday  |  Monday  |  Tuesday  |  Wednesday  |  Thursday  |  Friday  |  Saturday |
|----------+----------+-----------+-------------+------------+----------+-----------|
|          |          |     1     |      2      |     3      |    4     |     5     |
|          |          |New Year's Day|          |            |          |           |
|          |          |   129     |    116      |   174      |   181    |   166     |
|          |          |    14     |     16      |    40      |    49    |    44     |
|          |          |     5     |      3      |     6      |     7    |     2     |
|          |          |    11     |      9      |     8      |     6    |     6     |
|          |          |    16     |      5      |     4      |     1    |     0     |
|----------+----------+-----------+-------------+------------+----------+-----------|
|          |          |           |             |            |          |           |
 --------------------------------------------------------------------------------
```

Enhancing the Output

By enhancing the output produced by PROC CALENDAR, you can make your calendars more informative and easier to read. For example, the calendar produced in Output 18.4 would be more informative if descriptions of the ATM transactions were printed along with the amounts. You can add such descriptions by using *picture formats*. Picture formats are templates or patterns that you define and can use in PROC CALENDAR and other SAS procedures to display the values of numeric variables.

To use picture formats, do the following:

□ define the picture formats

□ associate the picture formats with variables.

Define the Picture Formats

To define your own picture formats, use the FORMAT procedure and one or more PICTURE statements. The syntax of the PICTURE statement is as follows:

PICTURE *name range*='*picture*';

where **PICTURE** is a keyword, *name* is a format name you supply, *range* is a valid range of numeric values, and *picture* is a template for printing the numeric values.

For example, the following PROC FORMAT step contains five PICTURE statements:

```
proc format;
    picture wthfmt low-high = '000000 Withdrawals';
    picture inqfmt low-high = '000000    Inquiries';
    picture trnfmt low-high = '000000    Transfers';
    picture depfmt low-high = '000000     Deposits';
    picture payfmt low-high = '000000     Payments';
run;
```

The PICTURE statements define five picture formats named WTHFMT., INQFMT., TRNFMT., DEPFMT., and PAYFMT.. To define an all-inclusive range of numeric values, all five picture formats use the keywords LOW and HIGH.

Following the range specifications are the pictures in quotes. Each picture includes a string of zeros and a character string, such as the word **Withdrawals**. The zeros control the output of numeric values. The procedure inserts strings after the numeric digits are formatted.

When you associate the picture formats with numeric variables in a PROC step, the SAS System replaces the variable values in the output using the picture formats.*

---

* For more information on the PICTURE statement, see Chapter 18, "The FORMAT Procedure," in *SAS Procedures Guide*.

Associate the Picture Formats with Variables

To actually use picture formats in a procedure, you must associate the picture formats with numeric variables by adding a FORMAT statement to the PROC step. The following program includes the PROC FORMAT step discussed above and the same PROC CALENDAR step used in the previous example except that the PROC step now contains a FORMAT statement. The FORMAT statement associates the variables WITHDRAW, INQUIRY, TRANSFER, DEPOSIT, and PAYMENT with the appropriate picture formats:

```
proc format;
   picture wthfmt low-high = '000000 Withdrawals';
   picture inqfmt low-high = '000000   Inquiries';
   picture trnfmt low-high = '000000   Transfers';
   picture depfmt low-high = '000000    Deposits';
   picture payfmt low-high = '000000    Payments';
run;

libname atm 'SAS-data-library';

proc calendar data=atm.activity
              holidata=atm.holidays;
   start actdate;
   holistart holstrt;
   holivar holname;
   format withdraw wthfmt.
          inquiry inqfmt.
          transfer trnfmt.
          deposit depfmt.
          payment payfmt.;
   title 'Summary of ATM Activity - Completed Transactions';
run;
```

Output 18.5 is partial output. It shows the first week of the calendar produced by the procedure.

Output 18.5   *Summary Calendar Enhanced with Picture Formats*

```
                     Summary of ATM Activity - Completed Transactions                            1

-----------------------------------------------------------------------------------------------------
|                                                                                                   |
|                                         January  1991                                             |
|                                                                                                   |
-----------------------------------------------------------------------------------------------------
|    Sunday    |    Monday    |   Tuesday    |   Wednesday  |   Thursday   |    Friday    |  Saturday  |
-----------------------------------------------------------------------------------------------------
|              |              |      1       |       2      |       3      |      4       |     5      |
|              |              |*New Year's Day**|           |              |              |            |
|              |              | 129 Withdrawals| 116 Withdrawals| 174 Withdrawals| 181 Withdrawals| 166 Withdrawals|
|              |              |  14   Inquiries| 16   Inquiries| 40   Inquiries| 49   Inquiries| 44   Inquiries|
|              |              |   5   Transfers|  3   Transfers|  6   Transfers|  7   Transfers|  2   Transfers|
|              |              |  11   Deposits |  9   Deposits |  8   Deposits |  6   Deposits |  6   Deposits |
|              |              |  16   Payments |  5   Payments |  4   Payments |  1   Payments |  0   Payments |
-----------------------------------------------------------------------------------------------------
|              |              |              |              |              |              |            |
-----------------------------------------------------------------------------------------------------
```

Displaying Totals and Averages Based on Activities

In some of your summary calendars, you may want to display totals and averages of the numeric values from the activities data set. For example, the bank can display totals and averages of all the ATM transaction types. Legends for totals and averages are titled **Sum** and **Mean**, respectively, and appear at the bottom of the calendar page if there is room on the page or on the following page if there is no room.

To display the sums and means based on the number of observations in the activities data set, do the following:

□ specify the sum variables and formats

□ specify the mean variables and formats.

Specify the Sum Variables and Formats

To display totals, use a SUM statement to specify the names of the numeric variables in the activities data set for which you want totals. If you want to override the default format, include one or more FORMAT= options as a part of the SUM statement.

The following SUM statement specifies that totals for the five numeric variables WITHDRAW, INQUIRY, TRANSFER, DEPOSIT, and PAYMENT be displayed using the COMMA6.0 format:

```
sum  withdraw inquiry transfer deposit payment / format=comma6.0;
```

Note that the format specified is applied only to the results of the sum. The format does not affect the actual values of the variable.

Specify the Mean Variables and Formats

To display averages based on the number of nonmissing values of a variable, use a MEAN statement that specifies the names of the numeric variables in the activities data set for which you want averages.

The following PROC CALENDAR step contains all the statements discussed so far including a MEAN statement, which specifies that averages for the five numeric variables in the activities data set be displayed using the COMMA6.2 format.

```
libname atm 'SAS-data-library';

proc calendar data=atm.activity
              holidata=atm.holidays;
   start actdate;
   holistart holstrt;
   holivar holname;
   format withdraw wthfmt.
          inquiry inqfmt.
          transfer trnfmt.
          deposit depfmt.
          payment payfmt.;
   sum  withdraw inquiry transfer deposit payment / format=comma6.0;
   mean withdraw inquiry transfer deposit payment / format=comma6.2;
   title1 'Summary of ATM Activity - Completed Transactions';
   title2 'Sum and Mean by Number of Observations';
run;
```

Output 18.6 shows the results of the PROC CALENDAR step. Notice the legend at the bottom of the page, which contains the headers **Sum** and **Mean**, the names of the five numeric variables, and the totals and averages.

Output 18.6   *Displaying Totals and Averages Based on Activities*

```
                        Summary of ATM Activity - Completed Transactions                        1
                              Sum and Mean by Number of Observations
--------------------------------------------------------------------------------------------------
|                                                                                                |
|                                         January  1991                                          |
|------------------------------------------------------------------------------------------------|
|   Sunday    |   Monday    |   Tuesday   |  Wednesday  |  Thursday   |   Friday    |  Saturday   |
|-------------+-------------+-------------+-------------+-------------+-------------+-------------|
|             |             |      1      |      2      |      3      |      4      |      5      |
|             |             |*New Year's Day**|         |            |            |            |
|             |             | 129 Withdrawals | 116 Withdrawals | 174 Withdrawals | 181 Withdrawals | 166 Withdrawals |
|             |             |  14  Inquiries  |  16  Inquiries  |  40  Inquiries  |  49  Inquiries  |  44  Inquiries  |
|             |             |   5  Transfers  |   3  Transfers  |   6  Transfers  |   7  Transfers  |   2  Transfers  |
|             |             |  11  Deposits   |   9  Deposits   |   8  Deposits   |   6  Deposits   |   6  Deposits   |
|             |             |  16  Payments   |   5  Payments   |   4  Payments   |   1  Payments   |   0  Payments   |
|-------------+-------------+-------------+-------------+-------------+-------------+-------------|
|      6      |      7      |      8      |      9      |     10      |     11      |     12      |
| 132 Withdrawals | 134 Withdrawals | 120 Withdrawals | 121 Withdrawals | 195 Withdrawals | 227 Withdrawals | 188 Withdrawals |
|  10  Inquiries  |  19  Inquiries  |  15  Inquiries  |  12  Inquiries  |  49  Inquiries  |  59  Inquiries  |  41  Inquiries  |
|   4  Transfers  |   3  Transfers  |   6  Transfers  |   2  Transfers  |   5  Transfers  |  12  Transfers  |   1  Transfers  |
|   9  Deposits   |  10  Deposits   |   6  Deposits   |   7  Deposits   |  10  Deposits   |   6  Deposits   |   0  Deposits   |
|   5  Payments   |   6  Payments   |   4  Payments   |  18  Payments   |  17  Payments   |   0  Payments   |   1  Payments   |
|-------------+-------------+-------------+-------------+-------------+-------------+-------------|
|     13      |     14      |     15      |     16      |     17      |     18      |     19      |
| 117 Withdrawals | 135 Withdrawals | 119 Withdrawals | 122 Withdrawals | 160 Withdrawals | 192 Withdrawals | 175 Withdrawals |
|  15  Inquiries  |  17  Inquiries  |  13  Inquiries  |  20  Inquiries  |  39  Inquiries  |  44  Inquiries  |  32  Inquiries  |
|  10  Transfers  |   9  Transfers  |   5  Transfers  |   4  Transfers  |   6  Transfers  |   3  Transfers  |   4  Transfers  |
|   7  Deposits   |   8  Deposits   |  15  Deposits   |  19  Deposits   |   9  Deposits   |  10  Deposits   |   8  Deposits   |
|   4  Payments   |   8  Payments   |   7  Payments   |   5  Payments   |   6  Payments   |   4  Payments   |   6  Payments   |
|-------------+-------------+-------------+-------------+-------------+-------------+-------------|
|     20      |     21      |     22      |     23      |     24      |     25      |     26      |
| 138 Withdrawals | 130 Withdrawals | 129 Withdrawals | 133 Withdrawals | 222 Withdrawals | 223 Withdrawals |             |
|  14  Inquiries  |  15  Inquiries  |  12  Inquiries  |  22  Inquiries  |  58  Inquiries  |  62  Inquiries  |             |
|   6  Transfers  |  10  Transfers  |   4  Transfers  |   5  Transfers  |   8  Transfers  |  10  Transfers  |             |
|   9  Deposits   |   7  Deposits   |   7  Deposits   |   7  Deposits   |  11  Deposits   |  10  Deposits   |             |
|  12  Payments   |   6  Payments   |   5  Payments   |  14  Payments   |   3  Payments   |   2  Payments   |             |
|-------------+-------------+-------------+-------------+-------------+-------------+-------------|
|     27      |     28      |     29      |     30      |     31      |             |             |
| 225 Withdrawals | 188 Withdrawals | 167 Withdrawals | 139 Withdrawals | 128 Withdrawals |             |             |
|  60  Inquiries  |  49  Inquiries  |  40  Inquiries  |  94  Inquiries  |  14  Inquiries  |             |             |
|  12  Transfers  |   2  Transfers  |   7  Transfers  |   5  Transfers  |   8  Transfers  |             |             |
|   4  Deposits   |   0  Deposits   |   8  Deposits   |   8  Deposits   |  21  Deposits   |             |             |
|   2  Payments   |   1  Payments   |   0  Payments   |   9  Payments   |  15  Payments   |             |             |
--------------------------------------------------------------------------------------------------

                              -------------------------
                              |         | Sum  | Mean  |
                              | WTHDRWL | 4,725| 157.50|
                              | INQUIRY |  988 |  32.93|
                              | TRANSFR |  174 |   5.80|
                              | DEPOSIT |  258 |   8.60|
                              | PAYMENT |  186 |   6.20|
                              -------------------------
```

You can use as many SUM and MEAN statements as you like. By default, PROC CALENDAR calculates the average based on the number of nonmissing values of the variable being averaged. Notice in Output 18.6, the month has 31 days but there are only 30 observations. An observation for one of those days, the 26th, does not exist because the ATM was out of service that day.

Therefore, PROC CALENDAR calculates the average by dividing the totals by 30 instead of 31. For example, the average of withdrawals is calculated as follows:

4,725 withdrawals / 30 observations = 157.50

In the next example, you will see how to base the averages on the number of days displayed on the calendar.

Displaying Averages Based on Days in the Month

Displaying averages based on the number of days in the month gives you a true daily average. To display averages based on the number of days in the month rather than the number of nonmissing values, add the MEANTYPE=NDAYS option to the PROC CALENDAR statement.

To illustrate, the statement MEANTYPE=NDAYS has been added to the previous PROC CALENDAR step. The result is to calculate the average based on the number of days in January rather than the number of days the ATM was in service.

```
libname atm 'SAS-data-library';

proc calendar data=atm.activity
              holidata=atm.holidays
              meantype=ndays;
   start actdate;
   holistart holstrt;
   holivar holname;
   format withdraw wthfmt.
          inquiry inqfmt.
          transfer trnfmt.
          deposit depfmt.
          payment payfmt.;
   sum  withdraw inquiry transfer deposit payment / format=comma6.0;
   mean withdraw inquiry transfer deposit payment / format=comma6.2;
   title1 'Summary of ATM Activity - Completed Transactions';
   title2 'Sum and Mean by Number of Days';
run;
```

Output 18.7 is partial output: the first four weeks are not shown. Notice the legend, which follows the fifth week. It contains the averages that have changed from the previous output.

Output 18.7   *Displaying Averages Based on Days in the Month*

```
                       Summary of ATM Activity - Completed Transactions                    1
                                 Sum and Mean by Number of Days

 ------------------------------------------------------------------------------------------
|                                                                                          |
|                                      January  1991                                       |
|------------------------------------------------------------------------------------------|
|   Sunday    |   Monday    |   Tuesday   |  Wednesday  |  Thursday   |   Friday    | Saturday   |
|-------------+-------------+-------------+-------------+-------------+-------------+----------|
|             |             |             |             |             |             |          |
     .              .              .              .              .              .         .
     .              .              .              .              .              .         .
     .              .              .              .              .              .         .
|             |             |             |             |             |             |          |
|-------------+-------------+-------------+-------------+-------------+-------------+----------|
|    27       |    28       |    29       |    30       |    31       |             |          |
|             |             |             |             |             |             |          |
| 225 Withdrawals | 188 Withdrawals | 167 Withdrawals | 139 Withdrawals | 128 Withdrawals |     |          |
|  60  Inquiries  |  49  Inquiries  |  40  Inquiries  |  94  Inquiries  |  14  Inquiries  |     |          |
|  12  Transfers  |   2  Transfers  |   7  Transfers  |   5  Transfers  |   8  Transfers  |     |          |
|   4  Deposits   |   0  Deposits   |   8  Deposits   |   8  Deposits   |  21  Deposits   |     |          |
|   2  Payments   |   1  Payments   |   0  Payments   |   9  Payments   |  15  Payments   |     |          |
 ------------------------------------------------------------------------------------------

                              ---------------------------
                             |         |  Sum  |  Mean  |
                             |         |       |        |
                             | WTHDRWL |  4,725| 152.42 |
                             | INQUIRY |    988|  31.87 |
                             | TRANSFR |    174|   5.61 |
                             | DEPOSIT |    258|   8.32 |
                             | PAYMENT |    186|   6.00 |
                              ---------------------------
```

Producing Schedule Calendars

Schedule calendars can help you see how various activities relate to one another over time. For example, a bank that is converting to a new computer system can use PROC CALENDAR to produce schedule calendars that display various conversion tasks.

This section shows you how to do the following:

□   schedule activities for the entire week

□   schedule activities only during weekdays

□   add holidays to a schedule calendar

□   use workshifts to schedule activities.

SAS Data Set Example for Schedule Calendars

To produce a schedule calendar, you must start with an activities data set. An activities data set for a schedule calendar is a SAS data set with the following characteristics:

□ more than one observation can apply to one day

□ each observation can have a duration of more than one day

□ each observation must contain an activity start date expressed as either a SAS date or datetime value

□ each observation must contain a value for an activity duration variable*

□ the observations must be sorted (or indexed) by the activity start date variable.

To illustrate, all the examples in this section use the same SAS data set. It is named CONVERSN.ACTIVITY and it contains observations from a bank that is converting to a new computer system. The bank wants to produce a schedule calendar that displays all the activities of the conversion crew. Each observation in the data set CONVERSN.ACTIVITY contains the following variables:

Variable	Type	Format	Description
ACTSTRT	numeric	date7.	start date of the conversion activity
ACTTASK	character		description of the conversion activity
ACTPERS	character		person managing the activity
ACTDURA	numeric		duration of the activity in days

The PROC PRINT step below produces a printout of data set CONVERSN.ACTIVITY.**

```
libname conversn 'SAS-data-library';

proc print data=conversn.activity noobs;
   format actstrt date7.;
   title 'Computer Conversion Activities - July 1991';
run;
```

---

* Instead of an activity duration variable, you can use a finish date variable and name it in a FIN statement in the PROC CALENDAR step. For details, see Chapter 7, "The CALENDAR Procedure," in *SAS Procedures Guide*.

** The DATA step that creates CONVERSN.ACTIVITY is shown in the Appendix.

Output 18.8 shows the results of the PROC PRINT step.

Output 18.8
Printout of
Data Set
CONVERSN.ACTIVITY

```
              Computer Conversion Activities - July 1991                    1

     ACTSTRT    ACTTASK                    ACTPERS       ACTDURA

     01JUL91    Design Console Layout      R. Stiles       4.0
     05JUL91    Receive and Tag Cables     R. Stiles       1.5
     05JUL91    Receive CPU                C. Escobar      3.0
     10JUL91    Install CPU and Nodes      C. Escobar     10.0
     22JUL91    Redefine INIT Classes      S. Lee          3.0
     25JUL91    Test Utilities             R. Stiles       2.5
```

Notice that some of the conversion tasks overlap chronologically while others do not occur until a preceding task has completed. For example, the second and third tasks, `Receive and Tag Cables` and `Receive CPU`, both begin July 5, 1991. Based on the values of the variable ACTSTRT, the CALENDAR procedure displays these two as concurrent tasks.

On the other hand, the fourth task, `Install CPU and Nodes`, does not start until July 10 because it must be preceded by the `Receive CPU` task. Based on the values of the variable ACTSTRT, the CALENDAR procedure displays these two as sequential tasks.

Scheduling Activities for the Entire Week

When you have activities that can occur seven days a week, you can produce a simple schedule calendar that displays activities for the entire week. When you need to produce more complex schedules, you can start with a simple summary calendar that displays seven days a week and then add more complex statements and options.

To produce a simple schedule calendar, do the following:

□ specify the activities data set

□ add the start dates of the activities

□ add the durations of the activities.

Specify the Activities Data Set

To specify the activities data set, use a PROC CALENDAR statement with the DATA= option. The following statement specifies CONVERSN.ACTIVITY as the activities data set:

```
libname conversn 'SAS-data-library';

proc calendar data=conversn.activity;
```

Add the Start Dates of the Activities

After the PROC CALENDAR statement, you must specify the start dates of the
activities. To specify the start dates, use a START statement.

Recall that in the data set CONVERSN.ACTIVITY, the variable ACTSTRT
contains the start dates of the conversion activities. The following START
statement specifies the variable ACTSTRT as the one that contains the start dates:

```
libname conversn 'SAS-data-library';


proc calendar data=conversn.activity;
   start actstrt;
```

Add the Durations of the Activities

An important difference between summary calendars and schedule calendars is
the duration of the activities. Summary activities always have durations of only
one day; schedule activities can span one or more days. The DUR statement names
the activities duration variable from the activities data set.

PROC CALENDAR determines whether your output appears in summary or
schedule format based on the absence or presence of the DUR statement. If the
DUR statement (or FIN statement) is present, the procedure produces a schedule
calendar.

The following PROC CALENDAR step contains all the statements discussed so
far including a DUR statement that specifies the variable ACTDURA from the
activities data set as the variable that contains the activity durations:

```
libname conversn 'SAS-data-library';

proc calendar data=conversn.activity;
   start actstrt;
   dur actdura;
   title 'Schedule for Conversion Crew';
run;
```

Output 18.9 shows the results.

Output 18.9   *Scheduling Activities*

```
                                  Schedule for Conversion Crew                                    1
----------------------------------------------------------------------------------------------------
|                                                                                                  |
|                                          July  1991                                              |
|--------------------------------------------------------------------------------------------------|
|   Sunday   |   Monday   |   Tuesday  |  Wednesday |  Thursday  |   Friday   |   Saturday          |
|------------+------------+------------+------------+------------+------------+------------          |
|            |      1     |     2      |     3      |     4      |     5      |     6               |
|            |            |            |            |            |            |                     |
|            |            |            |            |            |            |                     |
|          ❶ |            |            |            |          ❷ +=====Receive CPU/C. Escobar======> ❸
|            +==================Design Console Layout/R. Stiles==================+ +Receive and Tag Cables/R. Stiles=+|
|------------+------------+------------+------------+------------+------------+------------          |
|     7      |      8     |     9      |    10      |    11      |    12      |    13               |
|            |            |            |            |            |            |                     |
|          ❽ |            |            |          ❹ |            |            |                   ❺ |
| <Receive CPU/C. +       |            | +==================Install CPU and Nodes/C. Escobar==================>|
|------------+------------+------------+------------+------------+------------+------------          |
|    14      |     15     |    16      |    17      |    18      |    19      |    20               |
|          ❻ |            |            |          ❼ |            |            |                     |
| <==================Install CPU and Nodes/C. Escobar==================+ |                          |
|------------+------------+------------+------------+------------+------------+------------          |
|    21      |     22     |    23      |    24      |    25      |    26      |    27               |
|            |            |            |            |            |            |                     |
|            +==========Redefine INIT Classes/S. Lee============+ +===========Test Utilities/R. Stiles==========+|
|------------+------------+------------+------------+------------+------------+------------          |
|    28      |     29     |    30      |    31      |            |            |                     |
|            |            |            |            |            |            |                     |
|            |            |            |            |            |            |                     |
|            |            |            |            |            |            |                     |
----------------------------------------------------------------------------------------------------
```

The following list corresponds to the reference numbers in Output 18.9:

❶ and ❷   Each activity begins and ends with a plus character (+).

❸   Activities that occur concurrently are displayed on parallel lines.

❹   For each day or part of a day, the duration of an activity is shown by a continuous line of equal signs (=).

❺ and ❻   If an activity continues from one week to another, PROC CALENDAR displays arrows (<>) at the points of continuation.

❼   Values of variables for each activity are printed on the same line separated by slashes (/). For example, for the week beginning July 14, the value `Install CPU and Nodes` of the variable ACTTASK is displayed followed by a slash. Then the value `C. Escobar` of the variable ACTPERS is displayed.

❽   If the length of all the values exceeds the available space, strings are truncated. For example, for July 7, the value `C. Escobar` is truncated to `C. .`

Scheduling Activities Only During Weekdays

In Output 18.9, the conversion activities were scheduled throughout the entire week—Sunday through Saturday. This is the default action. However, for some schedules you may want to exclude Saturdays and Sundays and thereby schedule activities only during weekdays.

Depending on the combinations of statements and options you use, there are several ways to control the number of days during which activities are scheduled. One simple way is to add the INTERVAL= option to the PROC CALENDAR statement.

The INTERVAL= option specifies how many days are in a weekly schedule and the length of each day. The INTERVAL= option has two valid settings: DAY and WORKDAY. If INTERVAL=DAY, which is the default, the schedule consists of seven days, Sunday through Saturday, all starting at 00:00 hours and lasting 24 hours. On the other hand, if INTERVAL=WORKDAY, the schedule consists of five workdays, Monday through Friday, all starting at 09:00 hours and lasting 8 hours. (You can change the schedule including the daily hours. For details, see "Using Workshifts to Schedule Activities" later in this chapter.)

In the PROC CALENDAR step below, INTERVAL=WORKDAY. Therefore, the conversion activities are scheduled Monday through Friday from 09:00 hours through 17:00 hours; no activities are scheduled on Saturday or Sunday.

```
libname conversn 'SAS-data-library';

proc calendar data=conversn.activity
             interval=workday;
   start actstrt;
   dur actdura;
   title 'Monday-Through-Friday Schedule for Conversion Crew';
run;
```

Output 18.10 shows the results.

Output 18.10   *Scheduling Activities*

```
                    Monday-Through-Friday Schedule for Conversion Crew                        1
--------------------------------------------------------------------------------------------
|                                                                                          |
|                                       July 1991                                          |
|                                                                                          |
|------------------------------------------------------------------------------------------|
|   Sunday   |   Monday   |  Tuesday   | Wednesday  |  Thursday  |   Friday   |  Saturday  |
|------------------------------------------------------------------------------------------|
|            |     1      |     2      |     3      |     4      |     5      |     6       |
|            |            |            |            |            |            |            |
|            |            |            |            |            |            |            |
|            |            |            |            |            |+Receive CPU/C. >|         |
|            |+=================Design Console Layout/R. Stiles=================+|+Receive and Tag>|
|------------------------------------------------------------------------------------------|
|     7      |     8      |     9      |     10     |     11     |     12     |     13      |
|            |            |            |            |            |            |            |
|            |            |            |            |            |            |            |
|            |<=====Receive CPU/C. Escobar======+|            |            |            |
|            |<Receive and Tag+|       |+=========Install CPU and Nodes/C. Escobar==========>|
|------------------------------------------------------------------------------------------|
|     14     |     15     |     16     |     17     |     18     |     19     |     20      |
|            |            |            |            |            |            |            |
|            |            |            |            |            |            |            |
|            |<============================Install CPU and Nodes/C. Escobar===============================>|
|------------------------------------------------------------------------------------------|
|     21     |     22     |     23     |     24     |     25     |     26     |     27      |
|            |            |            |            |            |            |            |
|            |            |            |            |            |            |            |
|            |+==========Redefine INIT Classes/S. Lee============+|            |            |
|            |<Install CPU and Nodes/C. Escobar=+|       |+====Test Utilities/R. Stiles=====>|
|------------------------------------------------------------------------------------------|
|     28     |     29     |     30     |     31     |            |            |            |
|            |            |            |            |            |            |            |
|            |            |            |            |            |            |            |
|            |<Test Utilities/+|        |            |            |            |            |
--------------------------------------------------------------------------------------------
```

Adding Holidays to a Schedule Calendar

In many of your schedule calendars, you may want to include special days, such as holidays, during which no activities are scheduled. For example, in Output 18.10, the first activity, `Design Console Layout`, runs through Thursday, July 4, which is Independence Day in the United States, a bank holiday. No conversion activities should be scheduled during that day.

This section uses a holidays data set and shows you how to do the following:

□ specify the data set that contains the holiday information

□ add the start dates of the holidays

□ add the names of the holidays

□ add the durations of the holidays.

Holidays Data Set Example

The remaining examples in this chapter use a holidays data set named CONVERSN.HOLIDAYS. It contains one observation for July 4, 1991. The data set contains the following variables:

Variable	Type	Format	Description
HOLSTRT	numeric	date7.	start date of the holiday
HOLNAME	character		description of the holiday
HOLDURA	numeric		duration of the holiday in days

The PROC PRINT step below produces a printout of data set CONVERSN.HOLIDAYS. *

```
libname conversn 'SAS-data-library';

proc print data=conversn.holidays noobs;
   format holstrt date7.;
   title 'Bank Holidays - July 1991';
run;
```

---

* The DATA step that creates CONVERSN.HOLIDAYS is shown in the Appendix.

Output 18.11 shows the results of the PROC PRINT step.

Output 18.11
Printout of
Data Set
CONVERSN.HOLIDAYS

```
                        Bank Holidays - July 1991                        1

              HOLSTRT        HOLNAME        HOLDURA

              04JUL91     Independ. Day        1
```

Specify the Holidays Data Set

To include holidays in a schedule calendar, you must have a holidays data set with the following characteristics:

□ no more than one observation can apply to one day

□ each observation must contain a holiday start date expressed as a SAS date or datetime value

□ each observation must contain a value for a holiday duration variable

□ the holidays data set does not need to be sorted (or indexed) in any particular order.

Optionally, you can include in the holidays data set a variable that contains the names of the holidays.

To specify a holidays data set, add the HOLIDATA= option to the PROC CALENDAR statement. The following PROC CALENDAR statement specifies CONVERSN.HOLIDAYS as the holidays data set:

```
libname conversn 'SAS-data-library';

proc calendar data=conversn.activity
              holidata=conversn.holidays
              interval=workday;
   start actstrt;
   dur actdura;
   title 'Monday-through-Friday Schedule for Conversion Crew';
run;
```

Add the Start Dates of the Holidays

If you use a holidays data set, you must specify which variable in the data set contains the start dates of the holidays. To specify the start dates of the holidays, add a HOLISTART statement to the PROC CALENDAR step.

The following HOLISTART statement specifies the variable HOLSTRT from the data set CONVERSN.HOLIDAYS as the variable that contains the holiday start dates:

```
libname conversn 'SAS-data-library';

proc calendar data=conversn.activity
              holidata=conversn.holidays
              interval=workday;
   start actstrt;
   dur actdura;
   holistart holstrt;
   title 'Monday-through-Friday Schedule for Conversion Crew';
run;
```

Add the Names of the Holidays

If you want names of the holidays to appear on the calendar, specify the variable that contains the names of the holidays by including a HOLIVAR statement in the PROC CALENDAR step.

The following HOLIVAR statement specifies the variable HOLINAME from the data set CONVERSN.HOLIDAYS as the variable that contains the holiday names:

```
libname conversn 'SAS-data-library';

proc calendar data=conversn.activity
              holidata=conversn.holidays
              interval=workday;
   start actstrt;
   dur actdura;
   holistart holstrt;
   holivar holname;
   title 'Monday-through-Friday Schedule for Conversion Crew';
run;
```

Add the Durations of the Holidays

The holidays duration variable is similar to the activities duration variable. (See "Add the Durations of the Activities" earlier in this chapter.) Both are used as a part of schedule calendars and define how long an event lasts. To specify the holiday duration variable, add a HOLIDUR statement to the PROC CALENDAR step.

The following PROC CALENDAR step incorporates all the tasks discussed so far in this section including the HOLIDUR statement. The PROC CALENDAR step produces a Monday-through-Friday schedule calendar for the bank's conversion to the new computer system. The HOLIDUR statement specifies the variable HOLDURA in the holidays data set as the variable that contains the holiday durations.

```
libname conversn 'SAS-data-library';

proc calendar data=conversn.activity
              holidata=conversn.holidays
              interval=workday;
   start actstrt;
   dur actdura;
   holistart holstrt;
   holivar holname;
   holidur holdura;
   title 'Monday-through-Friday Schedule for Conversion Crew';
run;
```

Output 18.12 shows the results.

Output 18.12   *Defining Events and Holidays*

```
                    Monday-through-Friday Schedule for Conversion Crew                      1
-------------------------------------------------------------------------------------------
|                                                                                         |
|                                        July  1991                                       |
|                                                                                         |
|-----------------------------------------------------------------------------------------|
|   Sunday   |   Monday   |   Tuesday  |  Wednesday |  Thursday  |   Friday   |  Saturday  |
|------------+------------+------------+------------+------------+------------+------------|
|            |     1      |     2      |     3      |     4      |     5      |     6      |
|            |            |            |            |**Independ. Day**|        |            |
|            |            |            |            |            |            |            |
|            |            |            |            |            |+Receive CPU/C. >|        |
|            |            |            |            |            |+Receive and Tag>|       |
|            |+==========Design Console Layout/R. Stiles==========>| <Design Console +|     |
|------------+------------+------------+------------+------------+------------+------------|
|     7      |     8      |     9      |     10     |     11     |     12     |     13     |
|            |            |            |            |            |            |            |
|            |            |            |            |            |            |            |
|            |<=====Receive CPU/C. Escobar======+   |            |            |            |
|            |<Receive and Tag+  |+=========Install CPU and Nodes/C. Escobar==========>|   |
|------------+------------+------------+------------+------------+------------+------------|
|     14     |     15     |     16     |     17     |     18     |     19     |     20     |
|            |            |            |            |            |            |            |
|            |            |            |            |            |            |            |
|            |<=============================Install CPU and Nodes/C. Escobar=============================>|
|------------+------------+------------+------------+------------+------------+------------|
|     21     |     22     |     23     |     24     |     25     |     26     |     27     |
|            |            |            |            |            |            |            |
|            |            |            |            |            |            |            |
|            |+==========Redefine INIT Classes/S. Lee=============+   |            |        |
|            |<Install CPU and Nodes/C. Escobar=+   | |+=====Test Utilities/R. Stiles=====>|         |
|------------+------------+------------+------------+------------+------------+------------|
|     28     |     29     |     30     |     31     |            |            |            |
|            |            |            |            |            |            |            |
|            |            |            |            |            |            |            |
|            |<Test Utilities/+|         |            |            |            |            |
-------------------------------------------------------------------------------------------
```

Using Workshifts to Schedule Activities

Some schedules require activities be completed in shifts. For example, you may have a 9-hour workshift during the weekdays and a 4-hour shift on Saturdays.

To schedule activities in shifts, do the following:

□   create a data set that defines the hours of each type of workshift you need

□   create another data set that associates the types of workshifts with days of the week.

Example Workdays Data Set

You can define daily workshifts in a schedule calendar by using a *workdays data set* as input to the PROC CALENDAR step. A workdays data set is a SAS data set in which each variable represents a type of workshift. The workshifts can vary according to any factors you choose. For example, workshifts could be based on the days of the week with one type of workshift for weekdays, another for Saturdays, and another for Sundays.

Each observation in a workdays data set represents either the beginning or ending time of a work period. The first value of a variable is the beginning of the first work period; the second value is the end of that work period. The third value is the beginning of the second work period; the fourth value is the end of that work period, and so on. (See Output 18.13.)

Workdays data sets must be sorted chronologically. That is, the first observation represents the earliest time, the second observation is later in time, and so on.

To illustrate, the example in this section uses a workdays data set named CONVERSN.WORKDAYS. It contains observations that define two workshifts—one for weekdays and another for Saturdays. Each observation in the workdays data set contains the following variables:

Variable	Type	Format	Description
WDAYHRS	numeric	time6.	hours of the weekday workshift
SATHRS	numeric	time6.	hours of the Saturday workshift

The PROC PRINT step below produces a printout of data set CONVERSN.WORKDAYS.*

```
libname conversn 'SAS-data-library';

proc print data=conversn.workdays noobs;
   format wdayhrs sathrs time6.;
   title 'Weekday and Saturday Hours for Conversion Crew';
run;
```

Output 18.13 shows the results of the PROC PRINT step.

Output 18.13
Printout of Data Set CONVERSN.WORKDAYS

```
            Weekday and Saturday Hours for Conversion Crew            1

                       WDAYHRS      SATHRS

                         8:00        8:00
                        12:00       12:00
                        13:00         .
                        17:00         .
```

---

* The DATA step that creates CONVERSN.WORKDAYS is shown in the Appendix.

Notice in Output 18.13 that the values of the variable WDAYHRS specify a 9-hour workshift: 4 hours of work beginning at 8:00 and ending at 12:00, an hour for lunch from 12:00 to 13:00, and 4 more hours of work beginning at 13:00 and ending at 17:00. The values of the variable SATHRS specify a 4-hour workshift beginning at 8:00 and ending at 12:00. Missing values, such as those of the variable SATHRS, default to 00:00 in the first observation in the data set and to 24:00 in all other observations. (Two consecutive values of 24:00 define a zero-period time, which is ignored.)

Example Calendar Data Set

To specify which daily workshifts apply to which days, you must include a *calendar data set* as input to the PROC CALENDAR step. A calendar data set is a SAS data set with variables that represent days of the week. Variables in a calendar data set must be named _SUN_, _MON_, _TUE_, _WED_, _THU_, _FRI_, and _SAT_.

Valid values for the variables in a calendar data set include HOLIDAY, which is a nonwork period predefined by PROC CALENDAR, and the names of variables in the workdays data set, in this example, WDAYHRS and SATHRS.

Each observation in a calendar data set represents the weekly work schedule for a single calendar of activities. (See Output 18.14.)

The following example uses a calendar data set. It is named CONVERSN.CALENDAR and contains one observation that represents the types of workshifts used by the conversion crew. Specifically, each observation in the data set contains the following variables:

Variable	Type	Description
SUN	character	type of workshift for Sundays
MON	character	type of workshift for Mondays
TUE	character	type of workshift for Tuesdays
WED	character	type of workshift for Wednesdays
THU	character	type of workshift for Thursdays
FRI	character	type of workshift for Fridays
SAT	character	type of workshift for Saturdays

The PROC PRINT step below produces a printout of data set CONVERSN.CALENDAR.*

```
libname conversn 'SAS-data-library';

proc print data=conversn.calendar noobs;
   title 'Weekly Schedule for Conversion Crew';
run;
```

---

* The DATA step that creates CONVERSN.CALENDAR is shown in the Appendix.

Output 18.14 shows the results of the PROC PRINT step.

Output 18.14
Printout of
Data Set
CONVERSN.CALENDAR

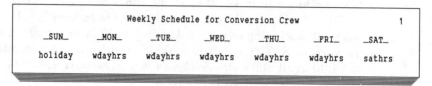

```
                      Weekly Schedule for Conversion Crew                    1

  _SUN_       _MON_       _TUE_       _WED_       _THU_       _FRI_      _SAT_

  holiday     wdayhrs     wdayhrs     wdayhrs     wdayhrs     wdayhrs    sathrs
```

Notice the values of the variables. The variable _SUN_ contains the value **HOLIDAY**, which is the nonwork period defined by the procedure. The variables _MON_ through _FRI_ contain the value **WDAYHRS**, which is defined in the workdays data set CONVERSN.WORKDAYS as a 9-hour workshift including an hour for lunch. The variable _SAT_ contains the value **SATHRS**, which is defined in the workdays data set CONVERSN.WORKDAYS as a 4-hour workshift.

Specify the Workdays Data Set

To specify the workdays data set, add the WORKDATA= option to the PROC CALENDAR statement. For example, the following PROC CALENDAR statement specifies CONVERSN.WORKDAYS as the workdays data set:

```
libname conversn 'SAS-data-library';

proc calendar data=conversn.activity
             holidata=conversn.holidays
             workdata=conversn.workdays
             interval=workday;
   start actstrt;
   dur actdura;
   holistart holstrt;
   holivar holname;
   holidur holdura;
   title 'Monday-through-Saturday Schedule for Conversion Crew';
run;
```

Specify the Calendar Data Set

To specify the calendar data set, add the CALEDATA= option to the PROC CALENDAR statement. The following PROC CALENDAR step contains all the tasks discussed so far including a CALEDATA= option that specifies CONVERSN.CALENDAR as the calendar data set:

```
libname conversn 'SAS-data-library';

proc calendar data=conversn.activity
              holidata=conversn.holidays
              workdata=conversn.workdays
              caledata=conversn.calendar
              interval=workday;
   start actstrt;
   dur actdura;
   holistart holstrt;
   holivar holname;
   holidur holdura;
   title 'Monday-through-Saturday Schedule for Conversion Crew';
run;
```

Output 18.15 shows the results.

Output 18.15   *Scheduling Different Workshifts*

```
                    Monday-through-Saturday Schedule for Conversion Crew                        1
 --------------------------------------------------------------------------------------------
|                                                                                             |
|                                        July  1991                                           |
 --------------------------------------------------------------------------------------------
|   Sunday     |    Monday    |   Tuesday    |  Wednesday   |   Thursday   |    Friday    |   Saturday   |
 -------------+-------------+-------------+-------------+-------------+-------------+-------------
|              |      1       |      2       |      3       |      4       |      5       |      6       |
|              |              |              |              |**Independ. Day**|           |              |
|              |              |              |              |              |              |              |
|              |              |              |              |              |+=====Receive CPU/C. Escobar=====>|
|              |              |              |              |              |+Receive and Tag Cables/R. Stiles=+|
|              |+==========Design Console Layout/R. Stiles==========>|    |<Design Console +|              |
 -------------+-------------+-------------+-------------+-------------+-------------+-------------
|      7       |      8       |      9       |     10       |     11       |     12       |     13       |
|              |              |              |              |              |              |              |
|              |              |              |              |              |              |              |
|              |              |              |              |              |              |              |
|              |<=====Receive CPU/C. Escobar======+|+==================Install CPU and Nodes/C. Escobar==================>|
 -------------+-------------+-------------+-------------+-------------+-------------+-------------
|     14       |     15       |     16       |     17       |     18       |     19       |     20       |
|              |              |              |              |              |              |              |
|              |              |              |              |              |              |              |
|              |              |              |              |              |              |              |
|              |<====================================Install CPU and Nodes/C. Escobar====================================>|
 -------------+-------------+-------------+-------------+-------------+-------------+-------------
|     21       |     22       |     23       |     24       |     25       |     26       |     27       |
|              |              |              |              |              |              |              |
|              |              |              |              |              |              |              |
|              |+==========Redefine INIT Classes/S. Lee============+|              |              |
|              |<Install CPU and+|            |              |+==============Test Utilities/R. Stiles==============+|
 -------------+-------------+-------------+-------------+-------------+-------------+-------------
|     28       |     29       |     30       |     31       |              |              |              |
|              |              |              |              |              |              |              |
|              |              |              |              |              |              |              |
|              |              |              |              |              |              |              |
|              |              |              |              |              |              |              |
 --------------------------------------------------------------------------------------------
```

Notice that the activities of the conversion crew now are scheduled on weekdays and Saturdays. Therefore, some of the activities end earlier than in the previous schedules. For example, notice the final task, `Test Utilities`, which begins July 25 and has a duration of 2.5 days. Previously, in Output 18.12, the final task ended Monday, July 29. With the 4-hour workshift on Saturdays, the final task now ends Saturday, July 27.

Summary

The following points summarize how to use the CALENDAR procedure to produce summary and schedule calendars:

- [ ] To specify an output page that is large enough to accommodate the output of PROC CALENDAR, use the SAS system options LINESIZE= and PAGESIZE=.

- [ ] To specify the activities data set, use the DATA= option of the PROC CALENDAR statement.

- [ ] To specify the dates of the activities in the activities data set for both summary and schedule calendars, use the START statement.

- [ ] To specify a holidays data set for both summary and schedule calendars, use the HOLIDATA= option of the PROC CALENDAR statement.

- [ ] To specify the dates of the holidays in the holidays data set for both summary and schedule calendars, use the HOLISTART statement.

- [ ] To specify the names of the holidays in the holidays data set for both summary and schedule calendars, use the HOLIVAR statement.

- [ ] To enhance summary calendar output, use PICTURE statements in a PROC FORMAT step to define picture formats, and use FORMAT statements in the PROC CALENDAR step to associate the picture formats with the values of variables.

- [ ] To display totals in a summary calendar, use a SUM statement and the appropriate specification of the FORMAT= option.

- [ ] To display averages in a summary calendar that are based on the number of nonmissing values, use a MEAN statement and the appropriate specification of the FORMAT= option.

- [ ] To display averages in a summary calendar that are based on the number of days in the calendar, use a MEAN statement and the appropriate specification of the FORMAT= option and add the MEANTYPE=NDAYS option to the PROC CALENDAR statement.

- [ ] To specify the durations of activities for a schedule calendar, use the DUR statement.

- [ ] To schedule activities only during weekdays, add the INTERVAL=WORKDAY option to the PROC CALENDAR statement.

- [ ] To specify the durations of holidays for a schedule calendar, use the HOLIDUR statement.

- [ ] To schedule activities in shifts, create a workdays data set that defines the workshifts and specify the data set using a WORKDATA= option in the PROC CALENDAR statement.

- [ ] To match the workshifts to days of the week, create a calendar data set and specify the data set using a CALEDATA= option in the PROC CALENDAR statement.

SAS Tools

This section summarizes syntax for the statement, system options, and procedures discussed in this chapter.

Statement

FORMAT *variable format*;
associates formats with variables.

    variable   names the variable or variables you want to associate with a format.

    format   specifies the format for writing the values of the variables.

SAS system options

LINESIZE = *nn*
specifies the width that can be printed per line of SAS output.

PAGESIZE = *nn*
specifies the number of lines that can be printed per page of SAS output.

Procedures

PROC CALENDAR *options*;
  statements;
displays data from SAS data sets in a monthly calendar format.
    The following options in the PROC CALENDAR statement are discussed in this chapter:

DATA=*SAS-data-set*
specifies the activities data set, which contains activities to be displayed in summary or schedule format.

HOLIDATA=*SAS-data-set*
specifies the holidays data set, which contains holidays.

WORKDATA=*SAS-data-set*
specifies the workdays data set, which contains definitions of workshifts.

CALEDATA=*SAS-data-set*
specifies the calendars data set, which contains weekly work schedules.

MEANTYPE=NDAYS
specifies the type of average to calculate for each month in a summary calendar.

INTERVAL=WORKDAY
specifies the number of days in a weekly schedule and the length of each day.

The following statements in the CALENDAR procedure are discussed in this chapter:

START *variable*;
> specifies the start dates of the events in the activities data set.

HOLISTART *variable*;
> specifies the start dates of events in the holidays data set.

HOLIVAR *variable*;
> specifies the variable in the holidays data set whose value is used to label the holidays.

HOLIDUR *variable*;
> specifies the duration of the events in the holidays data set.

DUR *variable*;
> specifies the duration of the events in the activities data set.

SUM *variables*;
> specifies numeric variables to total for each month of a summary calendar.

MEAN *variables*;
> specifies numeric variables to average for each month of a summary calendar.

PROC FORMAT;

> PICTURE *name range='picture'*;
> > defines informats and formats for character and numeric variables.

> | | |
> |---|---|
> | *name* | a user-supplied format name |
> | *range* | a valid range of numeric values |
> | *picture* | a template for printing the numeric values. |

Learning More

This section provides references for learning more about the topics presented in this chapter.

□ For complete documentation on the CALENDAR procedure, see the *SAS Procedures Guide: Version 6, Third Edition*, Chapter 7, "The CALENDAR Procedure."

□ If you want to use different characters to print outlines, dividers for the calendar cells, and identifying markers, such as asterisks and arrows, you can use the FORMCHAR= option as a part of the PROC CALENDAR statement or the FORMCHAR= SAS system option. For details, see *SAS Procedures Guide*, Chapter 7.

□ The CALENDAR procedure also includes the FIN statement, which enables you to specify finishing dates instead of using the DUR statement to specify durations. For details, see the *SAS Procedures Guide*, Chapter 7.

□ In addition to summary and schedule calendars, you can use PROC CALENDAR to produce multiple calendars. For details, see the *SAS Procedures Guide*, Chapter 7.

□ For information about using the CALENDAR procedure with PROC CPM in the SAS/OR product, see the *SAS/OR User's Guide: Version 6, First Edition*, Chapter 5, "The CPM Procedure."

Chapter 19 Plotting the Values of Variables Over Time

Introduction

By plotting the values of numeric variables over time, you can illustrate changes that occur in relationships among your data. For example, a water treatment company takes samples of ground water every three months. By plotting over time the levels of certain contaminants found in the samples, the company can demonstrate the effectiveness of the water cleanup system.

In this chapter

This chapter shows you how to plot the values of numeric variables over time by using the TIMEPLOT procedure. Specifically, you learn how to do the following:

□ plot variables on separate time plots

□ plot multiple variables on one time plot

□ enhance the appearance of time plots

□ plot variables in groups

□ organize data to reveal trends

□ add reference lines.

Prerequisites

Before reading this chapter, you should be familiar with plots in general such as the ones produced by the PLOT procedure. In addition, you should be familiar with BY-group processing of variables and know how to use the LABEL statement in the DATA step to assign labels to variables.*

Understanding Time Plots

The TIMEPLOT procedure produces a listing and a plot of observations in a SAS data set. The output produced by PROC TIMEPLOT is similar to the output produced by the PLOT and PRINT procedures. Figure 19.1 illustrates the basic elements of a time plot.

Figure 19.1
Elements of a
Time Plot

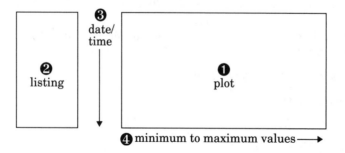

The following list corresponds to the reference numbers in Figure 19.1:

❶ the plot is printed on the right side of the output. Each observation appears on the plot sequentially on a separate line. Unlike the PLOT procedure, PROC TIMEPLOT does not hide observations.

❷ a listing of the variable values that are plotted is printed on the left side of the output.

---

* For details about the PLOT procedure, see *SAS Language and Procedures: Usage, Version 6, First Edition* and *SAS Procedures Guide, Version 6, Third Edition.* For details about BY-group processing and the LABEL statement, see *SAS Language and Procedures: Usage* and *SAS Language: Reference, Version 6, First Edition.*

❸ the vertical axis always represents the sequence of observations in the data set; therefore, if the observations are arranged in date and time order, the vertical axis represents time.

❹ the horizontal axis represents the values of the variables you are examining. Values appear in ascending order. Like the PLOT procedure, PROC TIMEPLOT can overlay multiple plots on one set of axes, so that each line of the time plot can contain values for more than one variable.

SAS Data Set Example

All the examples in this chapter use a SAS data set named CLEANUP.WELLS. The data come from a water treatment company that has installed a cleanup system at a site where the ground water was contaminated with cadmium and lead. To monitor the effectiveness of the cleanup system, the company tests water samples quarterly from two wells. The water treatment company uses the TIMEPLOT procedure to display the test results.

Each observation in the data set CLEANUP.WELLS contains the following variables:

Variable	Type	Format	Description
WELL	character		well from which water samples were taken, either 1 or 2
DATE	numeric	date7.	date on which water samples were taken
CD	numeric		parts per billion of cadmium in the water sample
PB	numeric		parts per billion of lead in the water sample

The following DATA step creates the data set CLEANUP.WELLS. Notice the LABEL statement in which the variable CD is assigned the label `Cadmium` and the variable PB is assigned the label `Lead`. These labels are used throughout the examples in this chapter.

```
libname cleanup 'SAS-data-library';

data cleanup.wells;
   input well $1.
         @3 date date7.
         @11 cd
         @15 pb;
   format date date7.;
   label cd='Cadmium' pb='Lead';
   cards;
1 02jul88  62  72
1 03oct88  60  60
more data lines
2 01oct90   6  45
2 04jan91   2  41
;
```

The following PROC PRINT step displays the data set CLEANUP.WELLS.*

```
libname cleanup 'SAS-data-library';

proc print data=cleanup.wells label noobs;
   title 'Contaminant Levels in Wells 1 and 2';
run;
```

Output 19.1 shows the results of the PROC PRINT step.

Output 19.1
Printout of
CLEANUP.WELLS
Data Set

```
                Contaminant Levels in Wells 1 and 2                    1

         WELL        DATE      Cadmium     Lead
           1       02JUL88        62        72
           1       03OCT88        60        60
           1       02JAN89        42        57
           1       03APR89        30        52
           1       05JUL89        25        49
           1       02OCT89        17        45
           1       03JAN90         9        40
           1       02APR90         7        35
           1       02JUL90         5        30
           1       01OCT90         3        28
           1       04JAN91         2        26
           2       02JUL88        72        78
           2       03OCT88        68        73
           2       02JAN89        55        64
           2       03APR89        43        59
           2       05JUL89        39        57
           2       02OCT89        28        52
           2       03JAN90        20        49
           2       02APR90        12        48
           2       02JUL90         8        47
           2       01OCT90         6        45
           2       04JAN91         2        41
```

Notice the observations are grouped first by the values of the variable WELL, either 1 or 2, and within each group are arranged in chronological order. For example, the first observation is for well 1, July 1988, the second observation is for well 1, October 1988, and so on.

If your data are not in chronological order, sort them by the date or datetime before using the data as input to PROC TIMEPLOT. If your data need to be grouped by the values of an identifying variable, sort them by the identifying variable and then by date or datetime.

Plotting Variables on Separate Time Plots

Plotting variables on separate time plots enables you to see how individual values change over time. For example, the water treatment company wants to plot the parts per billion of cadmium and lead in the water samples taken from wells 1 and 2. The company wants to produce one time plot for the values of the variable CD and a second time plot for the values of the variable PB. Each time plot should also list the values of certain variables, such as WELL and DATE, which are important to understanding the output.

---

* For a complete listing of the input data, refer to the Appendix.

To produce separate time plots, do the following:

□ specify the line size

□ specify which variable values to plot

□ include other important variables.

Specify the Line Size

You need to specify a line size wide enough to contain both the listing and the plot produced by PROC TIMEPLOT. The examples in this chapter use the following OPTIONS statement and the SAS system option LINESIZE=:

```
options linesize=132;
```

Specify Which Variable Values to Plot

Use the PROC TIMEPLOT statement and the DATA= option to begin the procedure. Then, to specify which values you want plotted, use a PLOT statement. The values that you specify in a PLOT statement are *plotting variables*. They must be numeric. The following PLOT statement specifies two plotting variables, CD and PB, and produces two separate time plots, one each for the two plotting variables:

```
proc timeplot data=cleanup.wells;
   plot cd pb;
```

You can specify any number of PLOT statements each time you invoke the procedure, and you can request any number of time plots on one PLOT statement. For example, the single PLOT statement above and the two PLOT statements below produce the same results:

```
plot cd;
plot pb;
```

Separate PLOT statements are useful when you want to apply different options to individual plots. (For example, see "Adding Reference Lines" later in this chapter.)

Include Other Important Variables

In addition to the plotting variables, you may want to print the values of other variables that help explain the output. For instance, the water treatment company wants to include in the listing to the left of the plot the values of the variables WELL and DATE because those values identify when and from where the water samples were taken.

To include the values of variables in addition to the plotting variables, use an ID statement. The following PROC TIMEPLOT step contains all the tasks discussed so far including an ID statement that specifies including the values of the variables WELL and DATE in the listing:

```
options linesize=132;

libname cleanup 'SAS-data-library';

proc timeplot data=cleanup.wells;
   plot cd pb;
   id well date;
   title1 'Contaminant Levels - Parts Per Billion';
   title2 'Identified by Well and Date';
run;
```

Output 19.2 shows the results of the PROC TIMEPLOT step.

Output 19.2   *Plotting Variables on Separate Time Plots*

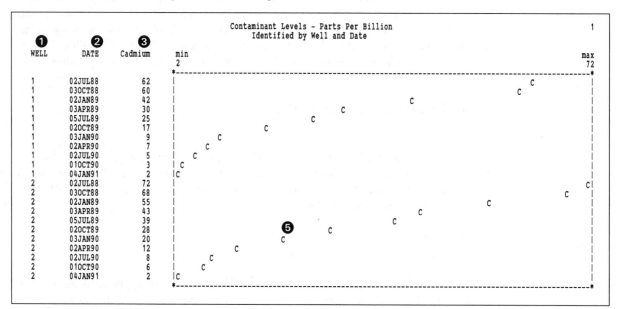

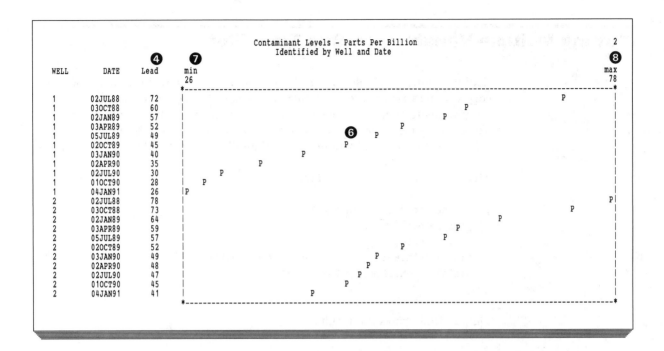

The following list corresponds to the reference numbers in Output 19.2:

❶ and **❷**   the values of the ID variables WELL and DATE are printed in the listing to the left of the plot, not on the plot itself.

❸ and **❹**   all the values of the variable CD appear on the first page of the time plot, and all the values of the variable PB appear on the second page.

       Also, the column headings use the labels `Cadmium` and `Lead`, which were created earlier in the section "SAS Data Set Example." PROC TIMEPLOT uses labels by default.

❺ and **❻**   also by default, PROC TIMEPLOT uses the first character of the variable name as the *plotting symbol*, which is the character used to plot the values of plotting variables.

       For example, the plotting symbol for the values of the variable PB is P (not L from the variable label `Lead`). Similarly, the plotting symbol for the values of the variable CD is the letter C.

       If you have two or more variables that begin with the same character, you can distinguish between them by specifying other characters to use as plotting symbols. For details, see "Specify a Character to Use as the Plotting Symbol" later in this chapter.

❼ and **❽**   the abbreviations MIN and MAX and, by default, the minimum and maximum values of the plotting variables are used as labels for the *plotting axis*. The plotting axis is the scale on which the values of the plotting variables are plotted. For details on overriding the default labels, see "Label the Plotting Axis" later in this chapter.

Plotting Multiple Variables on One Time Plot

By plotting multiple variables on one time plot, you can show how values of two or more variables relate to one another. For instance, the water treatment company wants to compare levels of cadmium and lead on one time plot.

To plot multiple variables on one time plot, add a slash (/) to the PLOT statement and the OVERLAY option as in the following PROC TIMEPLOT step:

```
libname cleanup 'SAS-data-library';

proc timeplot data=cleanup.wells;
   plot cd pb / overlay;
   id well date;
   title1 'Contaminant Levels - Parts Per Billion';
   title2 'Identified by Well and Date';
run;
```

Output 19.3 shows the results.

Output 19.3   *Plotting Multiple Variables on One Time Plot*

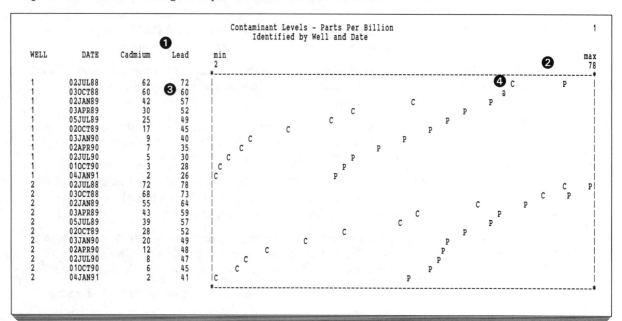

The following list corresponds to the reference numbers in Output 19.3:

❶ and **❷**   the values of the plotting variables CD and PB are overlaid in the listing and on the plot.

❸ and **❹**   for the second observation, the levels of cadmium and lead were both 60 parts per billion. As a result, an at sign (@) is printed as the plotting symbol for that observation. The @ is the default *overprint character* that PROC TIMEPLOT prints when two or more plotting symbols share the same print position.

Enhancing the Appearance of the Time Plot

By enhancing the appearance of the output produced by PROC TIMEPLOT, you can make your time plots easier to read and more consistent from one page of output to the next. The TIMEPLOT procedure contains several options that enable you to enhance the appearance of the output. The example in this section shows you how to enhance the output by specifying the following:

□ the overprint character

□ a character to use as a plotting symbol

□ labels for the plotting axis

□ the width of the plot.

Specify the Overprint Character

You can change the overprint character from an @ to any single character by adding the OVPCHAR= option to the PLOT statement. The OVPCHAR= option has been added to the following PLOT statement to specify an ampersand (&) as the overprint character:

```
plot cd pb / overlay ovpchar='&';
```

Specify a Character to Use as the Plotting Symbol

As illustrated in the previous example (Output 19.3), the TIMEPLOT procedure uses the first character of the variable name as the default plotting symbol. However, by adding an equal sign and a character enclosed in quotes to the PLOT statement, you can specify a different character to use as the plotting symbol. The following statement specifies the letter L as the plotting symbol for the values of the variable PB:

```
plot cd pb='L' / overlay ovpchar='&';
```

Label the Plotting Axis

Recall from the section "Include Other Important Variables" that, by default, PROC TIMEPLOT labels the plotting axis with the abbreviations MIN and MAX and the minimum and maximum values of the plotting variables.

For example, in Output 19.3 the minimum and maximum values of the plotting variables are 2 and 78, respectively, and the plotting axis is labeled from 2 to 78 as well. However, in some cases, you may want to use other values to label the plotting axis.

To illustrate, the water treatment company wants to change the time plots produced in the previous examples so that the plotting axis is always labeled 1 to 100 rather than varying with the values of the plotting variables.

To label the plotting axis, add the AXIS= option to the PLOT statement as the following statement illustrates:

```
plot cd pb='L' / overlay ovpchar='&' axis=1 to 100;
```

Any values of plotting variables that fall outside the plotting axis are indicated by a less than sign ($<$) or a greater than sign ($>$) on the left or right border of the plot, respectively.

Specify the Width of the Plot

Recall from the section "Specify the Line Size" that the line size was set to 132 to create an output page wide enough for the examples in this chapter. Within that space available on the output page, PROC TIMEPLOT prints the listing to the left of the plot, and by default uses the remaining columns for the plot itself. However, you can control the width of the plots by specifying the number of columns for the plot.

For example, the water treatment company wants each plot to contain 100 columns so there is a one-to-one correspondence between the range used to label the plotting axis (1 to 100) and the size of the plots (100 columns).

To specify the width of the plot, add the POS= option to the PLOT statement. The following PROC TIMEPLOT step incorporates all the tasks discussed so far including the POS= option to specify 100 columns for the plot:

```
libname cleanup 'SAS-data-library';

proc timeplot data=cleanup.wells;
   plot cd pb='L' / overlay ovpchar='&' axis=1 to 100 pos=100;
   id well date;
   title1 'Contaminant Levels - Parts Per Billion';
   title2 'Range from 1 to 100';
run;
```

Output 19.4 shows the results.

Output 19.4   *Enhancing the Appearance of the Time Plot*

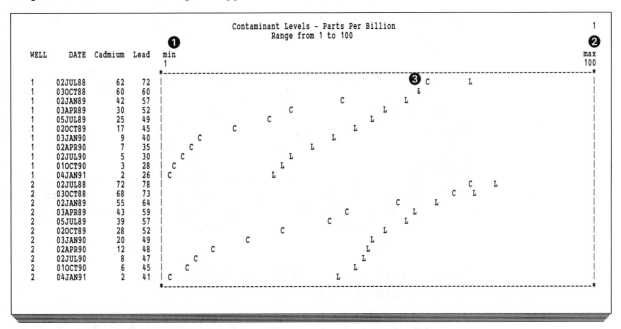

The following list corresponds to the reference numbers in Output 19.4:

❶ and ❷   the plot is 100 columns wide and the plotting axis uses the labels 1 and 100.

❸   the overprint character is an ampersand.

Plotting Variables in Groups

Sometimes you may want to display the values of variables based on groups of observations. For example, the water treatment company wants to see how the levels of the two contaminants relate when they are grouped according to the variable WELL.

To plot variables in groups, do the following:

□ specify the BY variable

□ prevent redundant printing of BY variable values.

Specify the BY Variable

To produce separate plots for observations in different groups, specify a BY variable in the BY statement. The following BY statement produces two time plots: one group each for well 1 and for well 2:

```
by well;
```

When you use a BY statement, the procedure prints the values of the BY variables in a BY line across the top of each time plot.

PROC TIMEPLOT expects the input data set to be sorted in order of the BY variables or indexed. In this example, there is no need to sort the input data set CLEANUP.WELLS because the values of the variable WELL are already in ascending order.

If your input data set is not sorted in ascending order, you can either use the SORT procedure with a similar BY statement to sort the data, or if appropriate, use the BY statement option NOTSORTED or DESCENDING. Also, within each BY group the data need to be sorted by date or datetime.

Prevent Redundant Printing of BY Variable Values

If the BY variable also appears in the ID statement, the values of the BY variable are printed twice: once in the BY line and again in the listing to the left of the plot. To prevent the redundant printing of values, remove the BY variable name from the ID statement.

The following PROC TIMEPLOT step includes the BY statement and an ID statement from which the variable WELL has been removed. Only the variable DATE remains in the ID statement.

```
libname cleanup 'SAS-data-library';

proc timeplot data=cleanup.wells;
   plot cd pb='L' / overlay ovpchar='&' axis=1 to 100 pos=100;
   by well;
   id date;
   title1 'Contaminant Levels - Parts Per Billion';
   title2 'Grouped by Well and Identified by Date';
run;
```

Output 19.5 shows the results.

Output 19.5 *Plotting Variables as BY Groups*

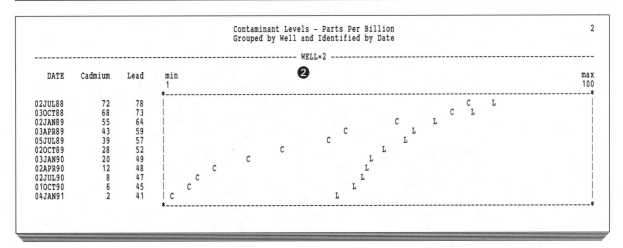

The following list corresponds to the reference numbers in Output 19.5:

❶ all the levels of cadmium and lead for well 1 appear on the first time plot.

❷ all the levels of cadmium and lead for well 2 appear on the second time plot.

Organizing Data to Reveal Trends

There are many ways you can organize your data to reveal trends. For example, using DATA step programming, the SORT procedure, and other SAS procedures, you can input data to PROC TIMEPLOT and reveal how trends in your data develop and change over time.

To illustrate, suppose the water treatment company wants to produce one time plot for cadmium and another for lead that do the following:

□   for every date that a water sample was taken, show how the level of a given contaminant in well 1 compares with the level of that same contaminant in well 2

□   show the decline over time of all contamination levels.

To reveal the above trends, the water treatment company needs to do the following:

□   designate a class variable

□   sort the data by a class variable

□   specify the class variable

□   specify a variable value to use as the plotting symbol

□   connect the high and low values.

Designate a Class Variable

Recall from the section "SAS Data Set Example" earlier in this chapter that the data set CLEANUP.WELLS is arranged first by well and then by date. In other words, all the observations for well 1 appear in chronological order followed by all the observations for well 2 in chronological order. However, in this example, the water treatment company wants to classify each observation according to the date the water samples were taken.

To classify each observation by the date of the sample, the water treatment company needs to designate the variable DATE as a *class variable*. Class variables organize your data into distinct categories. They can be either numeric or character, but usually each variable has a small number of discrete values, which form the classes.

Sort the Data by the Class Variable

Use the SORT procedure to sort the observations by the class variable. The following PROC SORT step sorts the observations in the data set CLEANUP.WELLS by the class variable DATE:

```
proc sort data=cleanup.wells;
   by date;
run;
```

When you sort the data by the class variable, the data are arranged in such a way that PROC TIMEPLOT can plot on each line of the time plot the date samples were taken, the level of a given contaminant in well 1 on that date, and the level of that same contaminant in well 2 on that same date.

Specify the Class Variable

To specify class variables in a PROC TIMEPLOT step, use a CLASS statement. The following CLASS statement specifies the variable DATE as a class variable:

```
proc timeplot data=cleanup.wells;
   plot cd pb='L' / ovpchar='&' axis=1 to 100 pos=100;
   class date;
run;
```

As with variables listed in an ID statement, PROC TIMEPLOT prints values of the class variables in the listing but does not plot them.

Specify a Variable Value to Use as the Plotting Symbol

In the examples so far in this chapter, the plotting symbol has been one of the following:

□   the first nonblank character of the plotting variable name, such as C for CD

□   a single character that you specify on the PLOT statement, such as L for PB.

However, in some time plots, you may want to show how the plotted values relate to the values of another variable. You can do this by specifying that variable's value as the plotting symbol, in which case PROC TIMEPLOT prints the first nonblank character of the variable's formatted value as the plotting symbol. If you want the symbol to apply to more than one plotting variable, enclose the list of plotting variables in parentheses.

For example, the water treatment company wants to show how the levels of contaminants relate over time to the wells from which the samples were taken.

In the following PROC TIMEPLOT step, the plotting variables CD and PB are enclosed in parentheses and the variable WELL is specified as the plotting symbol. When the step executes, the values of the variable WELL, either 1 or 2, are used as the plotting symbols rather than the first letters of the variables CD and PB. Also note that the OVERLAY option has been removed from the PLOT statement to produce separate plots for each contaminant:

```
proc timeplot data=cleanup.wells;
   plot (cd pb)=well / ovpchar='&' axis=1 to 100 pos=100;
   class date;
run;
```

Connect the High and Low Values

Often you may find it helpful to connect the leftmost plotting symbol to the rightmost plotting symbol. Connecting the plotting symbols with a line emphasizes the relationships between the values of plotting variables and can highlight trends in the data.

In this case, the water treatment company connects the values of the plotting variables to plot the levels and locations of contaminants over time.

To connect high and low values, add the HILOC option to the PLOT statement. The following program contains all the tasks discussed in this section including the HILOC option to connect the values of the plotting variables:

```
libname cleanup 'SAS-data-library';

proc sort data=cleanup.wells;
   by date;
run;

proc timeplot data=cleanup.wells;
   plot (cd pb)=well / ovpchar='&' axis=1 to 100 pos=100 hiloc;
   class date;
   title1 'Decline of Contaminant Levels - Parts Per Billion';
   title2 'Classified by Date';
run;
```

Output 19.6 shows the results of the PROC TIMEPLOT step.

Output 19.6   *Organizing Data to Reveal Trends*

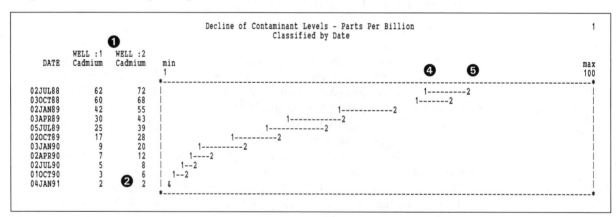

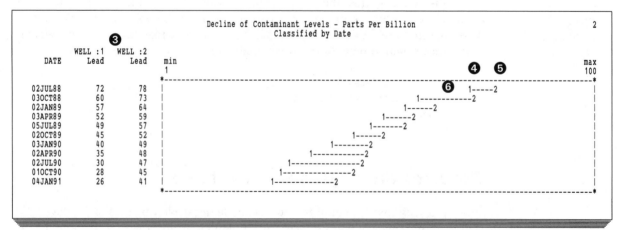

The following list corresponds to the reference numbers in Output 19.6:

❶ the levels of cadmium for both wells are displayed on page 1 of the output.

❷ PROC TIMEPLOT prints an ampersand as the plotting symbol because the levels of cadmium are the same for both wells on January 4, 1991.

❸ the values of the variable PB for both wells are displayed on page 2 of the output.

❹ and ❺ the values 1 and 2 of the variable WELL are specified as the plotting symbol and are printed on the plots.

❻ for each observation, lines connect the plotting symbols.

Adding Reference Lines

On some time plots, you may want to add reference lines. *Reference lines* are vertical lines printed on the plot that indicate whether the values of plotting variables are less than, greater than, or equal to a particular value.

For example, the water treatment company wants to produce two time plots that show how the levels of contamination relate to the levels that are safe for drinking water. The first time plot should plot the levels of cadmium and include a reference line at 10 to indicate that the safe level of cadmium is 10 parts per billion. The second time plot should plot the levels of lead and include a reference line at 50 to indicate that the safe level of lead is 50 parts per billion.

In the previous examples, one PLOT statement was used in each PROC step to produce two time plots: one for cadmium and one for lead. Using one PLOT statement for both time plots was possible because both time plots used the same options on the PLOT statement. Specifically, both time plots used the same specifications for the AXIS=, the POS=, the OVPCHAR=, and the HILOC options as the following PLOT statement illustrates:

```
plot (cd pb)=well / ovpchar='&' axis=1 to 100 pos=100 hiloc;
```

However, the safe levels of contamination are not the same for the two contaminants. Therefore, in this example, the water treatment company needs to specify two separate PLOT statements so that different options can be added to each time plot.

The following two PLOT statements contain the same options as the single PLOT statement in the previous example (Output 19.6), but are written separately so that options to specify different reference lines can be added:

```
plot cd=well / ovpchar='&' axis=1 to 100 pos=100 hiloc;
plot pb=well / ovpchar='&' axis=1 to 100 pos=100 hiloc;
```

To specify the reference line locations, add the REF= option to the PLOT statements. The following PROC TIMEPLOT step contains two PLOT statements with REF= options. The reference lines indicate the safe levels of the two contaminants.

```
libname cleanup 'SAS-data-library';

proc timeplot data=cleanup.wells;
   plot cd=well / ovpchar='&' axis=1 to 100 pos=100 hiloc ref=10;
   plot pb=well / ovpchar='&' axis=1 to 100 pos=100 hiloc ref=50;
   class date;
   title1 'Decline of Contaminant Levels - Parts Per Billion';
   title2 'Reference Lines Indicate Safe Levels';
run;
```

Output 19.7 shows the results of the PROC TIMEPLOT step.

Output 19.7   *Adding Reference Lines*

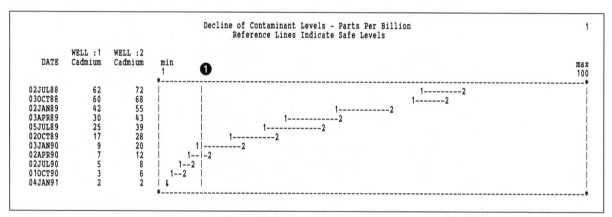

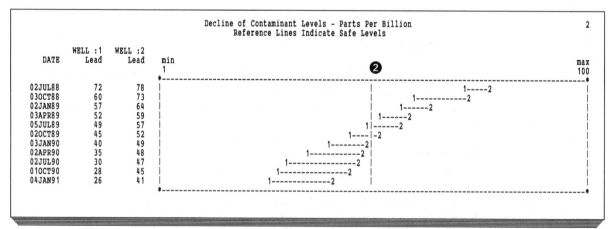

The following list corresponds to the reference numbers in Output 19.7:

❶ reference lines are printed at different locations. The location for the plotting variable CD is 10.

❷ It is 50 for the plotting variable PB.

Summary

The following points summarize how to use the TIMEPLOT procedure to produce time plots:

- □ To plot variables on separate time plots, use a PLOT statement to name the plotting variables.

- □ To include other important variable values in the listing, use an ID statement.

- □ To plot multiple variables on one time plot, use the OVERLAY option.

- □ To change the overprint character, use the OVPCHAR= option.

- □ To specify the plotting axis, use the AXIS= option.

- □ To specify the number of print positions, use the POS= option.

- □ To plot variables in groups, use a BY statement to specify the BY variable.

- □ To prevent redundant printing of values, remove the BY variable name from the ID statement.

- □ To plot variables as classes, use the CLASS statement to specify the class variable.

- □ To add reference lines, use the REF= option.

SAS Tools

This section summarizes syntax for the statements, system option, and procedures discussed in this chapter.

Statements

LABEL *variable label*;
    assigns labels to variables.

SAS system option

LINESIZE=*nn*
    specifies the width that can be printed per line of SAS output.

402 Learning More □ Chapter 19

Procedures

PROC SORT DATA=*SAS-data-set*;
    BY *by-variable*;
    sorts the *SAS-data-set* by the *by-variable*.

PROC TIMEPLOT DATA=*SAS-data-set*;
    produces a plot and a listing of observations in the *SAS-data-set*.
        The following TIMEPLOT statements are discussed in this chapter:

    BY *variable-list*;
        produces separate plots for observations in different BY groups.

    CLASS *variable-list*;
        groups data according to the values of the class variables.

    ID
        produces separate plots for observations in different BY groups.

    PLOT $</$ *plot-options*$>$;
        specifies the plots to produce.
            The following PLOT statement options are discussed in this chapter:

    OVERLAY
        plots multiple variables on one plot.

    OVPCHAR='*character*'
        specifies an overprint character.

    AXIS=*n* TO *nn*
        defines the plotting axis.

    POS=*nn*
        defines the size of the plots.

    HILOC
        connects high and low values.

    REF=*nn*
        adds reference lines.

Learning More

This section provides references for learning more about topics presented in this chapter.

□ For complete documentation of the TIMEPLOT procedure, see *SAS Procedures Guide, Version 6, Third Edition*, Chapter 40, "The TIMEPLOT Procedure."

□ The plots produced by the TIMEPLOT procedure are similar to the ones produced by the PLOT procedure. For details about the PLOT procedure, see *SAS Language and Procedures: Usage, Version 6, First Edition*, Chapter 27,

"Plotting the Relationship between Variables," and *SAS Procedures Guide*, Chapter 25, "The PLOT Procedure."

□ For details about BY-group processing and the LABEL statement, see *SAS Language and Procedures: Usage* and *SAS Language: Reference, Version 6, First Edition*.

Part 5

Working with Files

Chapter **20** Working with External Files

Introduction

In addition to SAS files, you often use external files when working with SAS software. For example, most DATA step programs read raw data from external files rather than from instream data. Writing a report usually means directing output to an external file. It is often convenient to manipulate these files and perform various file maintenance tasks from within your SAS session.

The DATA step provides you with tools for accomplishing many file maintenance tasks from within your SAS session that you would otherwise perform with various host operating system utilities. Knowing how to use base SAS software to perform these tasks enables you to manipulate external files on multiple operating systems without having to learn the system utilities on each one. Even on an operating system you know well, it can be convenient to copy or subset an external file without having to interrupt your SAS session.

In this chapter
This chapter shows you how to use many statements you are already familiar with to manipulate external files. It demonstrates the following tasks:

□ copying an entire file

□ copying parts of each record in a file

□ copying multiple files and adding new records

□ copying multiple files and adding new fields

□ subsetting a file based on a record number

□ subsetting a file based on contents

□ updating an external file in place

□ creating a file that contains carriage control characters

□ reading input data from a file that contains carriage control characters

□ writing and reading data files in different environments

□ reading and writing data at the bit level.

Prerequisites
To understand the examples in this chapter, you should be familiar with the following concepts and statements:

□ formatted input

□ the INFILE and FILE statements

□ the PUT statement

□ pointer controls in the INPUT and PUT statements.

Copying Files

Most operating systems provide utility programs for copying files. However, if you are working on an operating system you don't know well or if you want to copy all or part of a file during a SAS session or batch job, you can copy external files with SAS statements. Using SAS statements enables you to copy a file in the middle of a SAS job without exiting from the SAS System to use a host utility program. Further, knowing how to copy a file with SAS statements gives you the foundation for performing many other tasks with external files.

To copy an existing file, you can use a DATA step to read the input file and write each record to an external file or to the SAS log. The examples in this chapter illustrate the following tasks:

□ copying an external file

□ copying a contiguous section of each record in an external file

□ copying multiple external files and adding records

□ copying multiple external files and adding new fields.

Copying an Entire File

Copying a file is one of the simplest operations you can perform on an external file with a DATA step. The statements you use to copy a file form the basis for all tasks that use the DATA step for reading from and writing to external files and, therefore, for all examples in this chapter. To copy a file, follow these steps:

□ begin a DATA step that doesn't create a SAS data set

□ specify the external file to read

□ specify the external file to write

□ read each record from one external file

□ write each record to the other external file.

First, begin a DATA step whose sole purpose is to write to an external file, not create a SAS data set:

```
data _null_;
```

Specifying _NULL_ in the DATA statement saves computer resources because it indicates that the DATA step will not create a SAS data set.

Then specify an input file and an output file with the INFILE and FILE statements:

```
infile 'input-file';
file 'output-file';
```

▶ *Caution* . . . . *The new file may not necessarily have the same attributes.*
The new file may not have exactly the same attributes as the file being copied. To specify the attributes you want the new file to have, you can use options available in the FILE statement. See the SAS companion for your host operating system for relevant host-specific options in the FILE statement. ▲

Read a record from the input file by using a null INPUT statement:

```
input;
```

A null INPUT statement causes a new record to be read but does not assign any values to variables.

To write the contents of the current input record to the output file, use a PUT statement with the specification _INFILE_:

```
put _infile_;
```

With each iteration of the DATA step, the PUT _INFILE_ statement writes the current input record to the file specified in the FILE statement.

You now know all the statements needed to make a copy of a file. To increase efficiency, add an option. Use the SHAREBUFFERS option in the INFILE statement to make the copy operation require less CPU time for large files.

```
infile 'input-file' sharebuffers;
```

The SHAREBUFFERS option guarantees that the DATA step creates only one buffer, rather than the usual two, one for input and one for output. Consequently, it prevents the DATA step from performing an additional memory copy for each record it copies.

Here is the entire DATA step that copies the external file:

```
data _null_;
   infile 'input-file' sharebuffers;
   input;
   file 'output-file';
   put _infile_;
run;
```

The SAS log contains the following lines, reporting that the copy operation was successful:

```
NOTE: 1056 records were read from the infile 'input-file'.
NOTE: 1056 records were written to the file 'output-file'.
```

Copying Parts of Each Record in a File

If you need a contiguous portion of data contained in each record in a file, you can copy only the part that you need. For example, the following file from a human resources department file contains four records:

```
----+----1----+----2----+----3----+----4----+----5----+----6----+
L261  NC Aaronson, Star      6732 INTMAA@IDCVM    HUMANRES 1550
L139  NC Babcock, Paul       7237 INTJAB@IDCVM    HUMANRES 1221
L341  NC Callahan, Louanne   6211 INTEXC@IDCMVS   HUMANRES P596
L212  NC D'Aquanni, James    6748 INTJCD@IDCAPOLL HUMANRES 1599
```

The department wants to produce a file in which each record contains only an employee's name, extension number, and computer id in each record.

```
----+----1----+----2----+----3----+----4----+----5----+----6----+
Aaronson, Star      6732 INTMAAaIDCVM
Babcock, Paul       7237 INTJABaIDCVM
Callahan, Louanne   6211 INTEXCaIDCMVS
D'Aquanni, James    6748 INTJCDaIDCAPOLL
```

To create an output file in which each record contains only a contiguous portion of each record in the original file, you must control how much of each record is copied to the output file. To do this, begin with the statements shown earlier in this chapter. Then create and assign values to special variables that enable you to control how much of each record is copied.

The following statements copy each entire record to the output file:

```
data _null_;
   infile 'input-file'  sharebuffers;
   input;
   file 'output-file' ;
   put _infile_;
run;
```

Create the special variables you need to control how much of each record is copied by using the START= and LENGTH= options in the INFILE statement.

```
infile 'input-file'  start=firstcol length=lastcol sharebuffers;
```

Note that the variables FIRSTCOL and LASTCOL are created by the INFILE statement but are not assigned values. Next you must assign values to them.

The value of the START= option, FIRSTCOL in this example, controls the initial pointer position used by the PUT _INFILE_ statement. In this example, the PUT _INFILE_ statement should copy the contents of the input buffer beginning in column 10 instead of column 1. An assignment statement assigns the value 10 to FIRSTCOL.

```
firstcol=10;
```

The value of the LENGTH= variable, LASTCOL in this example, is automatically assigned a value by the INPUT statement. Each time the INPUT statement reads a record, LASTCOL is assigned a value equal to the length of the current record. When you do not want the entire record to be copied, you must override the value automatically assigned to the LENGTH= variable by the INPUT statement. In this case, LASTCOL should be set to 49, so that when the PUT _INFILE_ statement executes, it copies data from the input buffer only through column 49. The comments in the following statements demonstrate what happens when LASTCOL is given a value before the INPUT statement executes rather than after it executes:

```
/* incorrect order of statements /*
   firstcol=10;              /* FIRSTCOL equals 10.        */
   lastcol=49;              /* LASTCOL equals 49.        */
   input;                    /* LASTCOL equals the logical */
                            /* record length of the      */
                            /* current record.          */
```

Note that when the assignment statement comes before the INPUT statement, the value 49 is automatically written over when the INPUT statement executes. To prevent the INPUT statement from writing over the value of the LENGTH= variable, the INPUT statement should precede the assignment statement.

```
/* correct order of statements   /*
   firstcol=10;              /* FIRSTCOL equals 10.        */
   input;                    /* LASTCOL equals the logical */
                            /* record length of the      */
                            /* current record.          */
   lastcol=49;              /* LASTCOL equals 49.        */
```

The following DATA step creates a new file by copying only the information from columns 10 through 49 in the records of the original file:

```
data _null_;
   infile 'input-file'  start=firstcol length=lastcol sharebuffers;
   firstcol=10;
   input;
   lastcol=49;
   file 'output-file';
   put _infile_;
run;
```

The SAS log contains the following lines, indicating that the copy operation was successful:

```
NOTE: 4 records were read from the infile 'input-file'.
NOTE: 4 records were written to the file 'output-file'.
```

Copying Multiple Files and Adding New Records

When you copy a file with a DATA step, you can also write new records to the resulting file. For example, you may want to add a new record that notes when you made the copy or that identifies the original file.

You can also use a DATA step to copy several files into a single output file. You might want to copy four files to a single file on tape. Then you can copy a single file from the tape to another system. At the same time you need to add a record that indicates where one file ends and the other begins. For example, if there are four files to be copied, the contents of the output file might look like this:

```
records from first file
*** End of file: first-input-file ***
records from second file
*** End of file: second-input-file ***
records from third file
*** End of file: third-input-file ***
records from fourth file
*** End of file: fourth-input-file ***
```

To copy several files into a single output file and add a record at the end of each file that identifies it, do the following:

□ copy a single file

□ copy an entire file in a DO loop

□ provide the name of each input file at the appropriate time

□ write a new record that identifies the most recently copied file.

Copy a Single File

You already know how to copy the contents of a single file to another file. The following statements copy the file in this example:

```
data _null_;
   infile 'input-file' sharebuffers;
   file 'output-file';
   input;
   put _infile_;
run;
```

Now consider how to change the previous DATA step so that it can copy multiple files consecutively instead of copying only a single file. Currently, each iteration of the DATA step copies a single record, and the DATA step stops iterating when there are no more records to read. To copy records from multiple files, use the looping action of a DO loop to read an entire file. Stop the DO loop when there are no more records to read. Then use the looping action of the DATA step to change the input file. The DO loop then reads another entire file, and the process continues until there are no more records to read. Figure 20.1 contrasts copying one file and copying multiple files using a DATA step.

Figure 20.1 *Copying Files with a DATA Step*

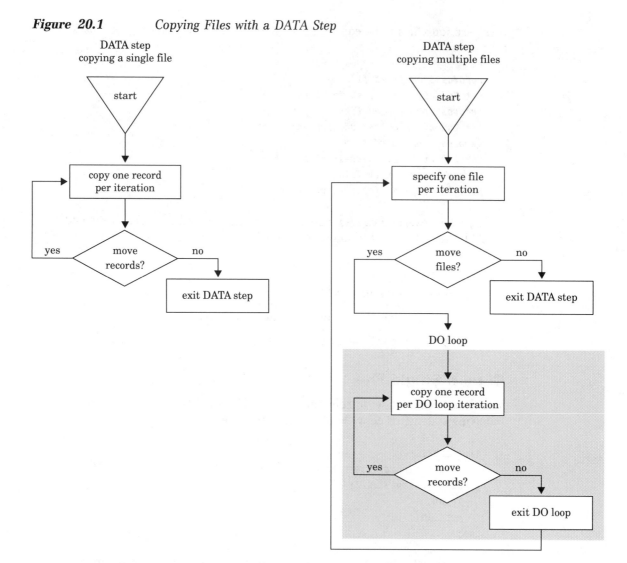

The next sections show you how to make the necessary changes to a DATA step to copy multiple files instead of only one.

Copy an Entire File with a DO Loop

To copy an entire file within a single iteration of the DATA step, put the statements that read from the input file and write to the output file in a DO loop. You must control the iterations of the DO loop, allowing it to execute the statements in the loop only until you read the end of the current input file. If you allow an INPUT statement to attempt to read past the end of a file, the DATA step stops. To prevent this from happening, use the END= option to create a variable whose value enables you to control the DO loop.

The END= variable, named DONE in this example, is equal to 1 when the end of a file is reached. To control the iterations of this DO loop, use a DO WHILE statement and specify that the DO loop should iterate only as long as DONE is not equal to 1.

```
infile 'input-file'  sharebuffers end=done;
file 'output-file';
do while(done ne 1);
   input;
   put _infile_;
end;
```

Note that you can use either a DO UNTIL statement or a DO WHILE statement in this example:

□ `do while(done ne 1);`

□ `do until(done=1);`

A DO WHILE statement is preferable in this kind of application because it prevents a fatal error. If you specify an empty file by mistake, the DATA step stops when the INPUT statement attempts to read from that file. Because the DO UNTIL statement does not check the value of the condition until the bottom of the loop, it always iterates once. If the file is empty, it causes a fatal error. The DO WHILE statement, on the other hand, checks the value of the END= variable at the top of the loop. If a file is empty, it does not allow the statements in the loop to execute, and the DATA step continues processing.

Supply the Names of the Input Files Consecutively

The next step is to add the statements that enable a single DATA step to copy several files consecutively. To read input files consecutively you must be able to do the following:

□ close the current file after you copy it

□ open a new file

□ supply the name of each input file you want to read.

You can open and close files consecutively with a DATA step by using the FILEVAR= option in the INFILE statement. Use this option to specify a variable that the INFILE statement uses to determine when to close one file and open another. Each time the INFILE statement executes, it checks the value of the FILEVAR= variable. If that value changes, it closes the current input file and opens a new one.

You can assign values to the FILEVAR= variable in the same ways you can assign values to any SAS variable. One way is to read the filenames from a file or instream data lines and assign a new name to the FILEVAR= variable on each iteration of the DATA step. This example creates a FILEVAR= variable named NOWREAD.

```
infile fileref sharebuffers end=done filevar=nowread;
```

Note that the INFILE statement no longer contains a *physical filename* (the name by which the operating system identifies the file) specified in quotes. When using the FILEVAR= variable, you must specify a valid SAS fileref in the INFILE statement. You may specify an unassigned fileref since the FILEVAR= variable is actually supplying the name of the input file. This example uses the fileref MYINPUT:

```
infile myinput sharebuffers end=done filevar=nowread;
```

On each iteration of this DATA step, the INPUT statement reads a physical filename from the data lines following the CARDS statement and assigns it to NOWREAD.

```
data _null_;
   input nowread $40.;
   infile myinput sharebuffers end=done filevar=nowread;
   file 'output-file' ;
   do while(done ne 1);
      input;
      put _infile_;
   end;
   cards;
input-file-1
input-file-2
input-file-3
input-file-4
;
```

▶ *Caution . . . . **You must assign valid filenames.***
The values assigned to the FILEVAR= variable must be valid physical filenames under your host operating system. Note that you do not enclose the filenames in quotes when assigning them as values to the FILEVAR= variable. ▲

Each iteration of this DATA step supplies a new value to NOWREAD. When NOWREAD changes, the INFILE statement closes the current file and opens a new one. Therefore, on each iteration of this DATA step, the INFILE statement closes one file and opens another.

Write a New Record

When copying files, you can add new records that identify the original file. For example, if you are combining files to transfer them as a single file to another operating system, you may want to be able to separate them later. You can do this easily if you write new records to the output file that mark the beginning and end of each file copied.

You can execute a PUT statement before and after each file is copied. To write the name of the file copied, use the FILEVAR= variable. Remember that the FILEVAR= variable contains the name of the current input file. This example uses the value of NOWREAD (the FILEVAR= variable) in the PUT statement to record the name of each file copied.

```
data _null_;
   input nowread $40.;
   infile myinput sharebuffers end=done filevar=nowread;
   file 'output-file';
   put '*** Beginning of file: ' nowread '***';
   do while(done ne 1);
      input;
      put _infile_;
   end;
   put '*** End of file: ' nowread '***';
   cards;
input-file-1
input-file-2
input-file-3
input-file-4
;
```

The resulting output file is shown below:

```
----+----1----+----2----+----3----+----4----+----5----+----6----+
*** Beginning of file: input-file-1 ***
L261  NC Aaronson, Star     6732 INTMAAaIDCVM    HUMANRES 1550
L139  NC Babcock, Paul      7237 INTJABaIDCVM    HUMANRES 1221
L341  NC Callahan, Louanne  6211 INTEXCaIDCMVS   HUMANRES 0596
L212  NC D'Aquanni, James   6748 INTJCDaIDCAPOLL HUMANRES 1599
*** End of file: input-file-1 ***
*** Beginning of file: input-file-2 ***
J261  NC Alonzo, J. D.      6732 INTCPAaIDCVM    QA       0995
J139  NC Badine, David      7237 INTMABaIDCVM    QA       1342
J341  NC Chen, Tae          6211 INTYZCaIDCMVS   QA       3552
J212  NC Droschak, Tricia   6748 INTCMDaIDCAPOLL QA       1467
*** End of file: input-file-2 ***
*** Beginning of file: input-file-3 ***
H261  NC Auxter, Jane       6732 INTJZAaIDCVM    MRKT     0046
H139  NC Bachteal, Marye    7237 INTPXBaIDCVM    MRKT     1978
H341  NC Cavanaugh, Sue     6211 INTSYCaIDCMVS   MRKT     7668
H212  NC Dhaliwal, D.       6748 INTKZDaIDCAPOLL MRKT     0889
*** End of file: input-file-3 ***
*** Beginning of file: input-file-4 ***
C153  NC Ayscue, Brendan    6732 INTBTAaIDCVM    TECHWRIT 0035
C197  NC Battaglia, Lisa    7237 INTLXBaIDCVM    TECHWRIT 1589
C222  NC Chu, Yao           6211 INTRWCaIDCMVS   TECHWRIT 7772
C201  NC Doshi, Radhika     6748 INTRZDaIDCAPOLL TECHWRIT 1356
*** End of file: input-file-4 ***
----+----1----+----2----+----3----+----4----+----5----+----6----+
```

Copying Multiple Files and Adding New Fields

When information comes from several sources, such as different departments or branches within a company, it may be useful to combine data from multiple files into a larger composite file. So that you can later identify the original source of a record, you can add a field identifying the source of each record as you write it to the composite file. Consider the following example of files containing real estate listings from multiple branches.

The central office of a real estate company receives a file from each branch that contains the new listings of residential property. Each record includes the following fields:

Field	Description
type	type of dwelling
space	square feet of living space
bed	number of bedrooms
bath	number of bathrooms
address	street address
price	asking price

Here are the records from the file showing new listings in branch eight:

```
----+----1----+----2----+----3----+----4----+----5----+----6
condo    1400   2  1.5 110 Market Street       80000
twostory 1810   4  3.0 47-B Garris Street      107000
condo    1390   3  2.5 3049 Hampshire Avenue   79350
condo    2105   4  2.5 509 Jeans Avenue        127150
```

Each branch has an identifying number, but those numbers are not in each file. The central office reads all files into a composite file. Adding the branch number to each record retains useful information. Here are the edited records, now showing the branch in which each listing originated:

```
----+----1----+----2----+----3----+----4----+----5----+----6
8 condo    1400   2  1.5 110 Market Street       80000
8 twostory 1810   4  3.0 47-B Garris Street      107000
8 condo    1390   3  2.5 3049 Hampshire Avenue   79350
8 condo    2105   4  2.5 509 Jeans Avenue        127150
```

Rather than edit each record in each file by hand, you can process all of them in a single DATA step, adding a field that identifies the source. Use the following steps:

□ copy each record, add a new field, and write the updated record to the output file

□ process each entire file in a DO loop

□ supply names of the input files consecutively

□ obtain a value that identifies the source of each record.

Copy and Add a New Field to Each Record

You have seen this basic copy operation throughout this chapter. To add a new field to each record, simply precede the _INFILE_ option in the PUT statement with a character string. The following DATA step copies all the records from the branch eight file and adds the number 8 and a blank space to the beginning of each record.

```
data _null_;
   infile 'input-file' ;
   file 'output-file';
   input;
   put '8 ' _infile_;
run;
```

Note that the INFILE statement does not use the SHAREBUFFERS option. The PUT statement writes a character and a space and then the contents of the original record. In this situation, using the SHAREBUFFERS option would cause a loss of information because the PUT statement would write over the first part of the original record in the input buffer.

▶ *Caution* . . . . *Longer records are created.*
This DATA step creates an output file that contains a longer record length than the file being copied. On some operating systems, you must consider record length when creating a file. ▲

As in the previous example, use this DATA step to create a DATA step that copies multiple files instead of one. The next two sections describe how to do this.

Process an Entire File in a DO Loop

You can place the statements that copy and update records in a DO WHILE loop and control the loop so that it does not attempt to read past the end of a file. Control the DO WHILE loop by using the value of the END= variable. The following DO WHILE loop iterates as long as DONE (the END= variable) does not equal 1—that is, as long as there are records to read.

```
infile 'input-file'  end=done;
file 'output-file';
do while(done ne 1);
   input;
   put '8 ' _infile_;
end;
```

When copying and updating more than one file with the same statements, you must use a variable instead of a character constant in the PUT statement to write the appropriate identifying value to each record. The first PUT statement shown in this example specifies the branch number as a character constant:

```
put '8 ' _infile_;
```

When the DATA step reads multiple files, the PUT statement must use a variable to produce the branch number.

```
put brnchnum _infile_;
```

Assigning a value to the variable that identifies the source of a record is discussed in a later section since it depends on other factors in an application, such as file naming conventions. For now, realize that the variable BRNCHNUM is assigned the appropriate branch number for the current input file.

The following statements read an entire input file in this example and build each observation:

```
infile 'input-file'  end=done;
file 'output-file';
do while(done ne 1);
   input;
   put brnchnum _infile_;
end;
```

Note that the INFILE and FILE statements precede the DO loop. You can place these statements in the DO loop, but placing them outside the loop is better programming practice because it prevents them from executing with each iteration of the DO loop.

Supply the Names of the Input Files Consecutively

Now that the statements that read and update each record have been placed in a DO loop, consider how to supply a new input filename. As shown earlier in this chapter, you can open and close input files consecutively by using an unassigned fileref and the FILEVAR= option in an INFILE statement.

In this example, the unassigned fileref used in the INFILE statement is CURRENT. The FILEVAR= variable is BRCHFILE. In each iteration of the DATA step, the INPUT statement reads a data line and assigns a new value to BRCHFILE. When the INFILE statement executes, as it will once for each iteration of the DATA step, the value of BRCHFILE is checked. With each iteration, BRCHFILE receives a new value. The current file is then closed and a new file is opened.

Here is the DATA step as constructed so far:

```
data _null_;
   input brchfile : $40.;
   statement that assigns a value to BRNCHNUM
   infile current filevar=brchfile  end=done;
   file 'output-file';
   do while(done ne 1);
      input;
      put brnchnum _infile_;
   end;
   cards;
branch3.dat
branch5.dat
```

```
branch6.dat
branch8.dat

;
```

▶ *Caution* . . . . ***You must assign valid filenames.***

The filenames shown here are for the purposes of illustration only. You must assign values to the FILEVAR= variable that are valid physical filenames on your operating system. Note that you do not enclose the filenames in quotes when assigning them as values to the FILEVAR= variable. ▲

Remember to specify a SAS fileref in an INFILE statement that uses the FILEVAR= option. You can use an unassigned fileref because the FILEVAR= variable, not the fileref, actually supplies the name of the input file.

The only task that remains is to obtain a value that identifies the original source of each record and assign it to the variable BRNCHNUM.

Obtain a Value That Identifies the Source of Each Record

How you obtain a value that identifies the original source of each record depends on your application. In this example, the naming conventions for the input files determine the method.

Each iteration of the DATA step assigns the name of a new input file to the FILEVAR= variable, BRCHFILE in this example. Note the structure of the filenames:

branch3.dat

branch5.dat

branch6.dat

branch8.dat

The seventh character in the value of BRCHFILE is the branch number. This example uses the SUBSTR function to extract the branch number from this value. Then an assignment statement assigns the resulting value to the variable BRNCHNUM. The SUBSTR function in the following assignment statement reads one character from the seventh position of the current value of the variable BRCHFILE:

```
brnchnum=substr(brchfile,7,1);
```

Now that BRNCHNUM contains the value of the branch for the current input file, the PUT statement can specify it along with the contents of the current input record (_INFILE_):

```
put brnchnum _infile_;
```

Here is the entire DATA step that reads four input files, copies each into a new composite file, and updates each record by adding a field that identifies the input file:

```
data _null_;
   input brchfile : $40.;
   brnchnum=substr(brchfile,7,1);
   infile current filevar=brchfile end=done;
   file 'output-file';
   do while(done ne 1);
      input;
      put brnchnum _infile_;
   end;
   cards;
branch3.dat
branch5.dat
branch6.dat
branch8.dat
;
```

The new composite file contains the contents of the four original files, along with an initial field in each record that identifies the source of the input record by branch:

```
----+----1----+----2----+----3----+----4----+----5----+----6
3 twostory 1040  2  1.0 89 Sanders Road      55850
5 ranch    1250  2  1.0 1610 Sheppard Avenue 64000
5 split    1190  1  1.0 2704 Rand Street     65000
5 ranch    1500  3  3.0 1605 Kemble Avenue   86865
5 ranch    1535  3  3.0 66-G State Highway   89100
5 twostory 1250  2  1.0 13-D Fairbanks Circle 69250
6 split    1615  4  3.0 23 West Drive        94450
6 split    1305  3  1.5 901 Graham Avenue    73660
8 condo    1400  2  1.5 110 Market Street    80000
8 twostory 1810  4  3.0 47-B Garris Street   107000
8 condo    1390  3  2.5 3049 Hampshire Avenue 79350
8 condo    2105  4  2.5 509 Jeans Avenue     127150
----+----1----+----2----+----3----+----4----+----5----+----6
```

Making a Subset of a File

When you want to create a subset of an external file, you can use a DATA step to select records in different ways. You can make a subset of a file by copying a group of consecutive records, or you can be more selective and include records according to content. For example, in a 2000-record file, you can copy a group of 300 records from the middle of the file to create a small file for testing purposes. In a file of daily orders received, you can create a subset that consists only of orders for a specific item or department. The following examples demonstrate creating a subset of an external file based on record number and on record content.*

Subsetting Based on Record Number

You can subset a file by reading only the records within a particular range of record numbers. For example, you can create a small file of data to use in testing by copying a group of records from a larger file. To create a subset, simply specify the first record to read with the FIRSTOBS= option and specify the number of the last record to read with the OBS= option. Otherwise, you use the same copy operation that you learned earlier in this chapter.

As an example, you may want to write a few records from a file to the SAS log. If you forget how the fields are laid out in the records, you can copy a few records from the input file to the SAS log so that you can write an INPUT statement correctly.

The following DATA step reads records 2, 3, and 4 from an external file and uses the LIST statement to write them to the SAS log along with a ruler that indicates the position of the fields.

```
data _null_;
   infile 'input-file'  firstobs=2 obs=4;
   input;
   list;
run;
```

You can use a PUT _INFILE_ statement to write records to the log, but it does not produce the ruler. This DATA step writes the following lines to the SAS log:

```
RULE:       ----+----1----+----2----+----3----+----4----+----5----+----6
2           5 ranch    1250    2  1.0 1610 Sheppard Avenue   64000
3           5 split    1190    1  1.0 2704 Rand Street       65000
4           5 ranch    1500    3  3.0 1605 Kemble Avenue     86865
NOTE: 3 records were read from the infile 'input-file'.
```

Subsetting Based on Contents

Sometimes you may want to retrieve selected records of data from a file. In these cases, you can create a smaller file that contains only those records. This example demonstrates reading a file of real estate listings and creating a subset that

---

* You can also randomly select records to create a subset. See Chapter 12, "Taking Random Samples."

contains only the listings in which a particular buyer is interested. The file contains the following fields:

Field	Description
type	type of dwelling
space	square feet of living space
bed	number of bedrooms
bath	number of bathrooms
address	street address
price	asking price

Here are the records in the file:

```
----+----1----+----2----+----3----+----4----+----5----+----6
twostory 1040  2  1.0 89 Sanders Road       55850
ranch    1250  2  1.0 1610 Sheppard Avenue   64000
split    1190  1  1.0 2704 Rand Street       65000
ranch    1500  3  3.0 1605 Kemble Avenue     86865
ranch    1535  3  3.0 66-G State Highway     89100
twostory 1250  2  1.0 13-D Fairbanks Circle  69250
split    1615  4  3.0 23 West Drive          94450
split    1305  3  1.5 901 Graham Avenue      73660
condo    1400  2  1.5 110 Market Street      80000
twostory 1810  4  3.0 47-B Garris Street    107000
condo    1390  3  2.5 3049 Hampshire Avenue  79350
condo    2105  4  2.5 509 Jeans Avenue      127150
----+----1----+----2----+----3----+----4----+----5----+----6
```

A DATA step can create a subset of this input file containing only the records that list condominium units. This task begins with the same basic copy operation shown previously in this chapter and adds the following two steps:

□ assign a value to a variable so you can test it

□ use conditional processing to determine when to write a record based on that variable's value.

If you want to write to an output file only records that contain a certain value, you must test that value in each record before executing a PUT statement. To test for a value, you must first assign it to a variable. The following DATA step assigns a value to the variable TYPE and writes a record to the output file only when the value of TYPE is equal to `condo`:

```
data _null_;
   infile 'input-file' sharebuffers;
   input type $;
   file 'output-file';
   if type='condo' then put _infile_;
run;
```

This DATA step writes the following records to the output file, creating a subset that contains only records listing information about condominium units.

```
----+----1----+----2----+----3----+----4----+----5----+----6
condo    1400    2  1.5 110 Market Street      80000
condo    1390    3  2.5 3049 Hampshire Avenue  79350
condo    2105    4  2.5 509 Jeans Avenue        127150
```

Updating an External File in Place

When you need to update information in an external file, you can use a DATA step to update the file in place without having to write the corrected version to another file. Updating records in a file may be as simple as changing each occurrence of one value to another. You can use a system editor to do this, or, if you are using a system with unfamiliar editing facilities, you can use a DATA step to update particular values in a file.

To understand how to change data values in records in an external file, consider the following example of updating a Human Resources Department file. The file contains, among other things, an employee's office number, name, phone number, and department. Here is a sample of the records in the file:

```
----+----1----+----2----+----3----+----4----+----5----+----6----+
J261  NC Aaronson, Star      6732 INTMAA@IDCVM    TECHWRIT 1550
H2139 NC Babcock, Paul       7237 INTJAB@IDCVM    QA       1221
E341  NC Callahan, Louanne   6211 INTEXC@IDCMVS   HUMANRES P596
H2212 NC D'Aquanni, James    6748 INTJCD@IDCAPOLL MRKT     1599
J263  NC Farrington, Mason   6732 INTMAA@IDCVM    TECHWRIT 1550
```

The Technical Writing Department is now called the Documentation Development Department, so each occurrence of TECHWRIT in this file must be changed to DOCDEV.

To update a field in a file, use the strategy shown in the previous example with one addition: specify the same file in the INFILE and FILE statements so that the DATA step updates the file in place instead of creating a new file. Note also that you must place the INFILE statement before the FILE statement in the DATA step in order to update a file in place.

▶ *Caution* .... *Create a back-up file.*
You should create a back-up file before updating an external file in place. ▲

The following DATA step updates an external file in place by changing each occurrence of `TECHWRIT` in the department field to `DOCDEV`.

```
data _null_;
   infile 'human-resources-file' sharebuffers;
   input @51 dept $;
   file 'human-resources-file';
   if dept='TECHWRIT' then put @51 'DOCDEV  ';
run;
```

Note that the new value DOCDEV is followed by two blank spaces. Because TECHWRIT is two characters longer than DOCDEV, the new value must contain two trailing blanks. Otherwise the resulting value in the department field would be DOCDEVIT instead of DOCDEV.

As a result of this DATA step, notes in the SAS log report how many records the DATA step read and how many records it corrected:

```
NOTE: 1359 records were read from the infile 'human-resources-file'.
NOTE: 276 records were written to the file 'human-resources-file'.
```

Here are the same sample records shown earlier, now showing the changes resulting from this DATA step. Note the different values in the first and fifth records.

```
----+----1----+----2----+----3----+----4----+----5----+----6----+----7
J261  NC Aaronson, Star      6732 INTMAAaIDCVM     DOCDEV   1550
H2139 NC Babcock, Paul       7237 INTJABaIDCVM     QA       1221
E341  NC Callahan, Louanne   6211 INTEXCaIDCMVS    HUMANRES P596
H2212 NC D'Aquanni, James    6748 INTJCDaIDCAPOLL  MRKT     1599
J263  NC Farrington, Mason   6732 INTMAAaIDCVM     DOCDEV   1550
```

Understanding the Impact of Separate Input and Output Buffers on Your Output

Looking at the results of the previous DATA step without the SHAREBUFFERS option demonstrates clearly what this option accomplishes. Here is the previous program without the SHAREBUFFERS option:

```
data _null_;
   infile 'human-resources-file';
   input a51 dept $;
   file 'human-resources-file';
   if dept='TECHWRIT' then put a51 'DOCDEV  ';
run;
```

Here are the contents of the updated file:

```
----+----1----+----2----+----3----+----4----+----5----+----6----+----7
                                                 DOCDEV
H2139 NC Babcock, Paul       7237 INTJABaIDCVM     QA       1221
E341  NC Callahan, Louanne   6211 INTEXCaIDCMVS    HUMANRES P596
H2212 NC D'Aquanni, James    6748 INTJCDaIDCAPOLL  MRKT     1599
                                                 DOCDEV
```

Because this DATA step writes to the same file, the contents of the second, third, and fourth records remain intact. Problems arise, however, with the updated records. Because the input and output buffers are separate when the SHAREBUFFERS option is not used, the output buffer contains only the information the PUT statement writes to it:

```
   if dept='TECHWRIT' then put a51 'DOCDEV  ';
```

Conversely, when you use the SHAREBUFFERS option, the output and input buffers are the same, so you do not have to specify the _INFILE_ option to copy the contents of the current record to the output buffer.

To produce the correct output without using the SHAREBUFFERS option— that is, when separate buffers exist—you must specify the _INFILE_ option. Then use a pointer control to write over the incorrect information. This example uses the _INFILE_ option to copy the current input record and then uses a pointer control (@51) to write over the incorrect value.

```
if dept='TECHWRIT' then put _infile_ @51 'DOCDEV ';
```

Creating and Reading Files That Contain Carriage Control Characters

So that you can easily print a file, you may want to add carriage control characters to its contents. You can use a DATA step to copy the contents of a file, add the appropriate carriage control characters, and create a new file that can be sent to certain printers.* You may want to read data from a file that contains carriage control characters. The DATA step enables you to do this without resorting to manually deleting the carriage control characters from the file.

The following example shows you how to copy the contents of a file and produce a file with carriage control characters. The second example shows you how to use a file containing carriage control characters as input to a DATA step.

Creating a File with Carriage Control Characters

So that you can conveniently print a file, you can copy its contents and add carriage control characters to create a new file. To do this, you perform the same basic read and write operation demonstrated throughout this chapter, with a few additions.

To specify that you want to create the new file with carriage control characters, use the PRINT option in a FILE statement. You can use the PAGESIZE= option in either the FILE statement or an OPTIONS statement to specify the page length. To ensure that you add only carriage control characters to the contents of the original file, you must also use other options. By default, using the PRINT option in a FILE statement also causes the following features to be added to the output file:

□ any current titles

□ the current date

□ page numbers.

---

* Carriage control characters are operating system specific. When you use SAS software to create an external file that contains carriage control characters, the resulting file contains characters appropriate to your host operating system.

To prevent these additional features from being added to the file you create, use the NOTITLES option in the FILE statement. (You can also specify the SAS system options NODATE and NONUMBER in an OPTIONS statement, but this is unnecessary since the NOTITLES options turns off all of these features.)

Here are the records of quality assurance data in the file used in this example. A machine fills 8-ounce cans with two-cycle engine oil additive. Each record contains sample weights of four cans.

```
----+----1----+----2----+
8.024 8.135 8.151 8.065
7.971 8.165 8.077 8.157
8.125 8.031 8.198 8.050
8.123 8.107 8.154 8.095
8.068 8.093 8.116 8.128
8.177 8.011 8.102 8.030
8.129 8.060 8.125 8.144
8.072 8.010 8.097 8.153
8.066 8.067 8.055 8.059
8.089 8.064 8.170 8.086
8.058 8.098 8.114 8.156
8.147 8.116 8.116 8.018
----+----1----+----2----+
```

The following DATA step reads this input file and creates another file that contains its contents plus carriage control characters:

```
data _null_;
    infile 'input-file' ;
    input;
    file 'output-file' print notitles pagesize=25;
    put _infile_;
run;
```

Reading Raw Data from a File That Contains Carriage Control Characters

As a rule, if a file containing raw data also contains carriage control characters, you can successfully read it with an INPUT statement without taking any special measures. Under most operating systems, SAS software can determine that a file has print attributes and compensate for it when reading the file with an INPUT statement.

For example, the following program reads the external file created in the previous example and ignores the carriage control characters to correctly construct and print a SAS data set.

```
data measures;
    infile 'input-file' ;
    input can1-can4;
run;
```

```
proc print data=measures;
    title 'Sample Weights for First 12-Hour Period';
run;
```

Output 20.1 shows that the data were read correctly.

Output 20.1
Using a File with
Carriage Control
Characters as
Input

```
                Sample Weights for First 12-Hour Period                  1

           OBS    CAN1     CAN2     CAN3     CAN4

            1    8.024    8.135    8.151    8.065
            2    7.971    8.165    8.077    8.157
            3    8.125    8.031    8.198    8.050
            4    8.123    8.107    8.154    8.095
            5    8.068    8.093    8.116    8.128
            6    8.177    8.011    8.102    8.030
            7    8.129    8.060    8.125    8.144
            8    8.072    8.010    8.097    8.153
            9    8.066    8.067    8.055    8.059
           10    8.089    8.064    8.170    8.086
           11    8.058    8.098    8.114    8.156
           12    8.147    8.116    8.116    8.018
```

Under some operating systems, the SAS System may not be able to detect that a file contains carriage control characters. In such a case, you can still read data from this file without having to delete the carriage control characters. To do so, simply use the PRINT option in an INFILE statement. In the INFILE statement, the PRINT option specifies that the input file contains carriage control characters, enabling the INPUT statement to read the data without mistakenly interpreting carriage control characters as data. If you have trouble reading such a file, rewrite the DATA step as follows, using the PRINT option. This DATA step produces the same data set shown in Output 20.1.

```
data measures;
    infile 'input-file' print;
    input can1-can4;
run;

proc print data=measures;
    title 'Sample Weights for First 12-Hour Period';
run;
```

Writing and Reading Data in Different Environments

Many users work in more than one computing environment or have to share files and data with others who must use them in different environments. Because numbers are stored differently on different operating systems, you must use some mechanism for ensuring that numbers written to a file under one operating system can be read correctly under a different operating system. The DATA step and a special group of informats and formats provide you with a means for creating an external file that any other user who also uses base SAS software can always read, regardless of the environment. You can also create an external file for an IBM 370 environment regardless of the operating system you are using to create the file.

▶ *Caution* . . . . *Floating-point representation may affect the numeric precision of your data.*
Under most situations, the fact that the SAS System stores numbers in
floating-point representation does not affect you as a user. However, knowing how
floating-point representation affects the precision and magnitude of your data can
help you understand some anomalies you may notice and can help you anticipate
and avoid certain problems. The problem of numeric precision is especially
relevant when you transfer data from one operating system to another. See the
discussion of numeric precision in Chapter 3, "Components of the SAS Language,"
in *SAS Language: Reference, Version 6, First Edition.* ▲

To create an external file for an IBM 370 environment, simply write the data
values using one of the S370 formats. To read the data after you move it to a
computing environment other than an IBM mainframe, simply use the
corresponding S370 informat.*

The examples of reading and writing data in different environments with an
S370 format use the following records:

```
----+----1----+----2----+----3
8.024 8.135 8.151 8.065
7.971 8.165 8.077 8.157
8.125 8.031 8.198 8.050
8.123 8.107 8.154 8.095
8.068 8.093 8.116 8.128
8.177 8.011 8.102 8.030
8.129 8.060 8.125 8.144
8.072 8.010 8.097 8.153
8.066 8.067 8.055 8.059
8.089 8.064 8.170 8.086
8.058 8.098 8.114 8.156
8.147 8.116 8.116 8.018
----+----1----+----2----+----3
```

Writing the Data

To create a file that contains data values in an IBM 370 format, first use an
INPUT statement to read the data values and assign them to variables. Then use a
PUT statement to write the variable values, in the correct format, to a file. In each
iteration of the following DATA step, the PUT statement writes a record that
contains the values of the four variables in the format S370FRB8.:

```
data _null_;
   infile 'file-1';
   input num1-num4;
   file 'file-2';
   put (num1-num4) (S370frb8.);
run;
```

---

* You can choose from several such formats and informats. See *SAS Language: Reference* for details.

Reading the Data

To read the file created in the previous example in an environment other than an IBM mainframe, use the S370FRB8. informat in an INPUT statement. This DATA step uses formatted input to read the data file created in the previous DATA step and to create a SAS data set that records sample weights of mechanically filled cans. The PRINT procedure displays the resulting SAS data set.

```
data measures;
   infile 'file-2';
   input (can1-can4) (s370frb8.);
run;

proc print data=measures;
   title 'Sample Weights for First 12-Hour Period';
run;
```

Output 20.2 shows the results.

Output 20.2
Creating a SAS
Data Set from
S370-Formatted
Raw Data

```
           Sample Weights for First 12-Hour Period                1

     OBS      CAN1      CAN2      CAN3      CAN4

      1      8.024     8.135     8.151     8.065
      2      7.971     8.165     8.077     8.157
      3      8.125     8.031     8.198     8.050
      4      8.123     8.107     8.154     8.095
      5      8.068     8.093     8.116     8.128
      6      8.177     8.011     8.102     8.030
      7      8.129     8.060     8.125     8.144
      8      8.072     8.010     8.097     8.153
      9      8.066     8.067     8.055     8.059
     10      8.089     8.064     8.170     8.086
     11      8.058     8.098     8.114     8.156
     12      8.147     8.116     8.116     8.018
```

Reading and Writing Data at the Bit Level

There are several reasons for needing to read and write data at the bit level. For example, when a file is damaged, you may be able to retrieve the data it contains if you can find the problem at the bit level and correct it. If you need to read a file with an INPUT statement, stray unprintable characters can prevent the INPUT statement from reading a value and can cause a variable value to be set to missing. In both of these cases, you may be able to salvage an otherwise unusable file or piece of data if you can correct a value at the bit level.

To correct a value at the bit level, you must be able to read what individual bytes contain, usually represented in hexadecimal representation, and write specific binary patterns of 0s and 1s to individual bytes. Since only a limited number of binary patterns in bytes correspond to printed characters, you probably need to use a hexadecimal literal to produce the binary pattern you need. Using a PUT statement, you can write a specified bit pattern to the correct location in an external file.

Raw Data Example

This example demonstrates salvaging a file that contains stray unprintable characters in data fields. The file was created on an ASCII-based system and then transferred to an EBCDIC-based system. The file contains the following records:

```
----+----1----+----2----+
8.024 8.135 8.151 8.065
7.971 8.165 8.077 8.157
8.125 8.031 8.198 8.050
8.123 8.107 8.154 8.095
8.068 8.093 8.116 8.128
8.177 8.011 8.102 8.030
8.129 8.060 8.125 8.144
8.072 8.010 8.097 8.153
8.066 8.067 8.055 8.059
8.089 8.064 8.170 8.086
8.058 8.098 8.114 8.156
8.147 8.116 8.116 8.018
----+----1----+----2----+
```

The following DATA step attempts to read these records with list input, assign values to the four variables NUM1, NUM2, NUM3, and NUM4 for each observation, and create a data set named MEASURES. Output 20.1 displays the MEASURES data set.

```
data measures;
   infile 'input-file';
   input num1-num4;
run;

proc print data=measures;
run;
```

Output 20.3
Creating a SAS
Data Set from Raw
Data Containing
Unprintable
Characters

```
                          The SAS System                               1

             OBS      NUM1      NUM2      NUM3      NUM4

              1      8.024     8.135     8.151     8.065
              2      7.971     8.165     8.077     8.157
              3      8.125     8.031     8.198     8.050
              4      8.123     8.107     8.154     8.095
              5      8.068     8.093     8.116       .
              6      8.177     8.011     8.102       .
              7      8.129     8.060     8.125     8.144
              8      8.072     8.010     8.097     8.153
              9      8.066     8.067     8.055     8.059
             10      8.089     8.064     8.170     8.086
             11      8.058     8.098     8.114     8.156
             12      8.147     8.116     8.116     8.018
```

Note that the values for NUM4 in the fifth and sixth observations are missing. The raw data contain no missing values, so the data are not the source of these missing values. Because values have been correctly assigned to the variable NUM4 in all the other observations, it's obvious that an incorrect INPUT statement is not the source of these missing values. To read these data correctly, use the following steps:

□ identify the problem by looking at the SAS log

□ correct the problematic records

□ verify that the correction was made.

Identify the Problem

When a problem occurs in reading raw data, first look at the SAS log. The following lines are written to the SAS log when the preceding program runs:

```
NOTE: Invalid data for NUM4 in line 5 19-24.
RULE:      ----+----1----+----2----+----3----+----4----+----5----+----6----+
CHAR       8.068 8.093 8.116 8.128.
ZONE       F4FFF4F4FFF4F4FFF4F4FFF0
NUMR       8B06808B09308B11608B1285
NUM1=8.068 NUM2=8.093 NUM3=8.116 NUM4=. _ERROR_=1 _N_=5
NOTE: Invalid data for NUM4 in line 6 19-24.
CHAR       8.177 8.011 8.102 8.030.
ZONE       F4FFF4F4FFF4F4FFF4F4FFF0
NUMR       8B17708B01108B10208B0305
NUM1=8.177 NUM2=8.011 NUM3=8.102 NUM4=. _ERROR_=1 _N_=6
NOTE: 12 records were read from the infile 'input-file'.
      The minimum record length was 23.
      The maximum record length was 24.
NOTE: The data set WORK.MEASURES has 12 observations and 4 variables.
```

As the note in the log shows, the problem is caused by the unprintable EBCDIC character '05'x that immediately follows the last piece of data in the fifth and sixth records. A tab character, entered in error from an ASCII keyboard ('09'x), was translated into an unprintable character ('05'x) on the EBCDIC-based system. This unprintable character occurs in the last field in the fifth and sixth records. Note that the unprintable character is represented with a period in the log.

Once you know where such a problem is in data records, you can correct the problem at the bit level.

Correct the Problem

▶ *Caution* .... *Create a back-up file.*
You should create a back-up file before updating an external file in place. ▲

Changing the last character in the fifth and sixth records to a blank corrects the problem. Because the sole purpose here is to correct a problem in two records, this DATA step reads only those records. To begin reading a file at any record other than the first, use the FIRSTOBS= option in an INFILE statement; likewise, to stop reading the file after reading a specified number of records, use the OBS= option. To correct a file in place, specify the same file in the INFILE and FILE statements and place the INFILE statement before the FILE statement.

```
filename trashed 'problematic-file';
data _null_;
   infile trashed sharebuffers firstobs=5 obs=6;
   file trashed;
```

To correct a problem at the bit level, you can use a PUT statement to write a new hex value over the incorrect one. In this example, the PUT statement writes the value '40'x (a blank on EBCDIC-based systems) over the incorrect value in column 24.

```
put @24 '40'x;
```

Note that the PUT statement specifies only the new value, not the rest of the record. This is possible because the SHAREBUFFERS option is specified in the INFILE statement. Because the input and output buffers are the same, you are required to specify only the values you are correcting rather than all the values in the record.

Here is the entire DATA step that changes the problematic value '05'x to '40'x in column 24 in the fifth and sixth records:

```
filename trashed 'problematic-file';
data _null_;
   infile trashed sharebuffers firstobs=5 obs=6;
   file trashed;
   input;
   put @24 '40'x;
run;
```

Verify the Correction

To verify that such a problem has been fixed in a raw data file, you can rerun the DATA step. Or you can first look at only the problematic records by writing them to the SAS log with the LIST statement:

```
filename trashed 'problematic-file' ;
data _null_;
   infile trashed firstobs=5 obs=6;
   input;
   list;
run;
```

Because the LIST statement lists hex values only for records that contain unprintable characters, the following lines written to the SAS log demonstrate that these two records no longer contain an unprintable character:

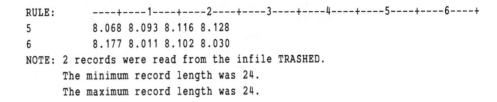

```
RULE:      ----+----1----+----2----+----3----+----4----+----5----+----6----+
5          8.068 8.093 8.116 8.128
6          8.177 8.011 8.102 8.030
NOTE: 2 records were read from the infile TRASHED.
      The minimum record length was 24.
      The maximum record length was 24.
```

Summary

The following points summarize how to read from and write to external files with a DATA step:

□ To use computer resources efficiently, you can choose not to build a SAS data set when you are using a DATA step to work with external files. Use the reserved data set name _NULL_ in the DATA statement.

□ To write the contents of the current input record to an external file or to the SAS log, use the _INFILE_ option in a PUT statement.

□ To copy a contiguous portion of a record to the SAS log or another file, use the START= and LENGTH= options in an INFILE statement. These options control how much of the input record is written by the PUT _INFILE_ statement.

□ When reading multiple input files, place the statements that read and write each record in a DO loop. To control the number of times these statements execute, use a DO WHILE statement and specify a condition so that the INPUT statement does not attempt to read past the end of a file.

□ To prevent prematurely ending a DATA step when reading from multiple input files, use the END= option in an INFILE statement. By checking the value of the END= variable, you can stop an INPUT statement from attempting to read past the end of a file.

□ To open and close different files consecutively in a DATA step, use the FILEVAR= option in an INFILE statement. Assign a value to the FILEVAR= variable that is the physical file name of the external file you want to read.

□ To read only selected records from an input file, use the FIRSTOBS= and OBS= options to specify the number of the first and last records you want to read.

□ To update an external file in place, specify the same file in both the INFILE and FILE statements. The INFILE statement must precede the FILE statement. As a precaution, consider creating a back-up file before updating a file in place.

□ When updating an external file in place, you can make more efficient use of computer resources and simplify the PUT statement by using the SHAREBUFFERS option in an INFILE statement. Using this option causes the INPUT and PUT statement to use the same buffer, thereby reducing the cost of copying or updating a large file.

□ To control such cosmetic features of an output file as the page size and the appearance of titles and page numbers, use the NOTITLES and PAGESIZE= options in a FILE statement.

□ To use a file that contains carriage control characters as input to a DATA step usually requires no special considerations. However, if you find that the INPUT statement reads the carriage control characters as if they were part of the file, use the PRINT option in the INFILE statement.

□ To copy a file and add carriage control characters so that you can print it, use a DATA step and specify the PRINT option in the FILE statement.

□ To write data values in an IBM mainframe format, no matter what operating system you are using, use the S370 formats. You can also use these formats to write data values that you can read on any other operating system by using a DATA step and the S370 informats in an INPUT statement.

□ To correct a problem at the bit level in a file, use the PUT statement to write a hex constant, for example, '40'x.

□ To display the hex values of unprintable characters in records, use the LIST statement to write the contents of the current input file to the SAS log. If a record contains unprintable characters, the LIST statement shows the hex values.

SAS Tools

This section summarizes syntax for the statements, function, informat, and format discussed in this chapter.

Statements

DATA _NULL_;
> begins a DATA step without creating a data set. Using the _NULL_ specification saves computer resources and is recommended when you are using a DATA step for report writing and processing external files.

DO WHILE(*condition*);
> *SAS statements*
END;
> executes the enclosed SAS statements as long as the specified condition is true. The condition can be any valid SAS expression enclosed in parentheses. The condition is evaluated at the top of the loop, before the enclosed statements execute. If the condition is false, the DO WHILE loop does not execute at all. Using a DO WHILE statement can prevent an INPUT statement from attempting to read from an empty file, and, therefore, prevent the DATA step from stopping unexpectedly.

FILE *fileref* | *'output-file'* <*options*>;
> identifies the output file for PUT statements in the current DATA step. In most cases, you can specify either a valid SAS fileref or the physical filename (the name by which the operating system identifies the file) enclosed in quotes.

The following FILE statement options are discussed in this chapter:

NOTITLES

> suppresses printing the current title lines, page numbers, and the current system date on pages of the output file. When you are writing to a file that contains carriage control characters, TITLES is in effect by default. To produce a file that contains carriage control characters but no titles, page numbers, or current date, you must specify NOTITLES.

PAGESIZE=*n*

> sets the number of lines per page. The value of *n* can range from 1 to 200. When you are creating a file that contains carriage control characters, use the PAGESIZE= option to determine where page breaks occur in the output file.

PRINT

> specifies that an output file written to by PUT statements in a DATA step contain carriage control characters appropriate for the operating system. By default, other features are also added to the output file. See the NOTITLES option.

INFILE *fileref* | *'input-file'* <*options*>;

> identifies the source of the input data and enables you to specify options that control how the data records are read. The external file used as input can be specified as a fileref or as the name of the physical file (enclosed in quotes). If you use the FILEVAR= option, you must specify a fileref in the INFILE statement.
>
> The following INFILE statement options are discussed in this chapter:

END=*variable*

> creates a variable, whose name you specify, that is automatically set to 1 when the last record in an input file is processed. You can use the value of an END= variable to process SAS statements conditionally in a DATA step—for example, to allow a statement to execute only during the last iteration of the DATA step. When the DATA step reads only one input file, the END= variable is set to 1 during the last iteration.

FILEVAR=*variable*

> creates a variable whose value controls the opening and closing of input files. When this option is used, the value of the FILEVAR= variable is checked each time the INFILE statement executes. When that value changes, the current file is closed and a new file is opened.

FIRSTOBS=*record-number*

> specifies that the DATA step begin reading the input file at the record number specified, rather than at the beginning of the file.

LENGTH=*variable*

> creates a variable whose value is automatically set to the length of the current input record. The LENGTH= variable is created by the INFILE statement but it is not assigned a value until an INPUT statement executes.

(INFILE fileref continued)

OBS=*record-number*
> specifies that the DATA step stop reading the input file at the record
> number specified, rather than at the end of the file.

START=*variable*
> creates a variable whose value controls the initial pointer position used by
> the PUT _INFILE_ statement. Use this option when you want to begin
> copying the contents of the current input record anywhere other than the
> beginning of the record.

SHAREBUFFERS
> specifies that no output buffer be created for the PUT statement. When
> you use this option in a DATA step to copy records from one file to
> another, you save computer resources since it prevents the DATA step
> from performing an additional memory copy for each record it copies.

LIST;
> at the end of the current iteration of a DATA step, writes to the SAS log the
> input data records for the current observation. The LIST statement also prints
> a column ruler above the first record. If a record contains an unprintable
> character, the LIST statement automatically prints the hexadecimal values.

PUT _INFILE_;
> writes the contents of the current record in the input buffer to the SAS log,
> an external file, or to the same destination as SAS procedure output. PUT
> _INFILE_ is especially useful for copying a record from one file to another.

Function

SUBSTR(*character-variable,position,n*)
> returns a portion of value of a character variable when the SUBSTR function
> appears on the right side of the equal sign in an assignment statement.

Informat

S370FRBw.d
> reads real binary (floating-point) data in IBM 370 format, regardless of which
> operating system you use.

Format

S370FRBw.d
> writes real binary (floating-point) data in IBM 370-format so that it can be
> read with SAS software, regardless of the operating system used.

Learning More

This section provides references for learning more about topics presented in this chapter.

□ To learn more about using external files in a SAS session, see the appropriate chapters in the SAS companion for your operating system.

□ To learn more options that enable you to control how an output file is written, see the FILE statement in *SAS Language: Reference*, Chapter 9, "SAS Language Statements." For options specific to the operating system under which you use SAS software, see the appropriate SAS companion.

□ To learn more options that enable you to control how an input file is read, see the INFILE statement in *SAS Language: Reference*, Chapter 9. For options specific to the operating system under which you use SAS software, see the appropriate SAS companion.

□ To learn more about the informats and formats that read and write data in an IBM 370 format, see *SAS Language: Reference*, Chapters 13 and 14, "SAS Informats" and "SAS Formats." See also the discussion of reading binary data in Chapter 2, "The DATA Step."

□ In addition to expressing a hex value as a constant, you can solve problems in a file at the bit level by using the INPUT function and the $HEX. informat to assign a hex value to a variable. To learn about using the INPUT function, see Chapter 6, "Converting Variable Values," in this book. To learn more about the $HEX. informat and format, see Chapters 13 and 14 in *SAS Language: Reference*.

□ To learn more about floating-point representation and numeric precision, see *SAS Language: Reference*, Chapter 3, "Components of the SAS Language."

Chapter 21 Using a Spell Checking Facility

Introduction

Whether you are working with SAS files or with external files, you can benefit from a facility that checks spelling and maintains dictionaries. The SAS System maintains a spell checking facility that includes a master dictionary and several auxiliary dictionaries. You can verify the spelling of a file against these dictionaries and, when necessary, generate suggested alternatives. Additionally, you can create other auxiliary dictionaries to use when appropriate.

In this chapter
The Spell Checking Facility is available both through the SPELL procedure and through the SAS Text Editor's SPELL and DICT commands. Note that this chapter documents the Spell Checking Facility only as it is accessed through PROC SPELL. Specifically, this chapter shows you how to

- [ ] use a master dictionary to verify correct spelling in an external file or in a SAS catalog entry of type HELP or CBT and, when necessary, generate suggested alternatives

- [ ] create an auxiliary dictionary, which contains a customized list of words

- [ ] use one or more auxiliary dictionaries with or without the master dictionary to verify correct spelling in an external file or in a SAS catalog entry of type HELP or CBT

- [ ] update an auxiliary dictionary.

Prerequisites

Before reading this chapter, you should be familiar with external files and SAS catalogs.

Understanding the Spell Checker

The Spell Checking Facility, also known as the spell checker, enables you to use a master dictionary to verify the correct spelling of words in an external file or in a SAS catalog entry of type HELP or CBT. This master dictionary contains approximately 50,000 words. Through this facility, you can also create and use one or more auxiliary dictionaries, either with or without the master dictionary, to verify the correct spelling of words in a file or in a catalog entry. You have four default auxiliary dictionaries available; you can also create your own customized dictionaries. If necessary, you can update the dictionaries you are using.

You can use the Spell Checking Facility either through the SPELL procedure or through the SAS Text Editor's SPELL and DICT commands. Regardless of the method you are using to run the SAS System, you can use PROC SPELL to accomplish the full range of spell-checking tasks available with this facility. Additionally, with the SAS Text Editor, you can use the SPELL and DICT commands in conjunction with the SPELL windows. You can use the SPELL command to verify the correct spelling of words and the DICT command to create, maintain, and invoke auxiliary dictionaries. Note that the SPELL and DICT commands are available for the convenience of your full-screen task. It is advisable to use the SPELL procedure rather than the DICT command to create any permanent auxiliary dictionaries since the word list used by the SPELL procedure acts as a record of the words contained in the auxiliary dictionary. Therefore, this chapter demonstrates only the SPELL procedure; references to the Spell Checking Facility here pertain only to its use through PROC SPELL.

To be able to use the SAS System's spell checker most efficiently, you should understand how it defines and verifies words and how it handles the case (either uppercase or lowercase) of words. The next two sections explain those processes.

Understanding How the Spell Checker Defines and Verifies Words

To verify spelling in a file, the spell checker first identifies strings of characters in potential words. It then checks to see if these words are in the dictionaries it is using. It follows several steps to identify and verify the spelling of potential words.

1. The spell checker scans the file, discarding characters until it finds an alphabetic character preceded by a blank, a special character, or a new-line character. The character it finds is the first character of a potential word. Special characters include the following:

    '   a single quote

    "   a double quote

    (a left parenthesis

[a left square bracket

{   a left brace

<   a left angle bracket or less-than sign.

2. The spell checker scans the characters until it reaches a character that is not valid in a word. A valid character is

    □   any alphabetic character

    □   a hyphen, if followed by an alphabetic character

    □   an apostrophe (or single quote), if followed by an alphabetic character.

    The characters starting with the first character of the potential word and ending with the last valid character form a potential word.
    Following these rules, the spell checker interprets the following character strings as potential words:

    ```
    doesn't
    copy-edit
    xxyy'zz
    ```

    The Spell Checker treats the following character string as three potential words: *embedded, nested,* and *quotation*:

    ```
    "'embedded (nested) quotation'"
    ```

3. The spell checker looks for the word in the currently defined dictionaries.

4. After determining whether the word is in the dictionaries, the spell checker begins to scan for another word. It repeats steps 1, 2, and 3 until it reaches the end of the file.

Understanding How the Spell Checker Handles the Case of Words

The spell checker is basically case sensitive. For example, the words PROC and proc are stored differently in a dictionary. However, in some situations it is case insensitive. Before using the spell checker, you should understand the rules it uses to choose which words to recognize.

□   If a lowercase word is in the dictionary, its uppercase counterpart is recognized (case insensitive).*

□   If an uppercase word is in the dictionary, its lowercase counterpart is not recognized (case sensitive).

---

*   Note that in this chapter the term "uppercase" is used to describe any word whose first letter is uppercase. Subsequent letters can be uppercase or lowercase.

□   If an uppercase word is not in the dictionary, the spell checker searches the dictionary for its lowercase counterpart. If it finds the lowercase counterpart, it recognizes the uppercase version in the file (case insensitive). This approach allows for a word position to vary within a sentence.

□   If a lowercase word is not in the dictionary, the spell checker does not search the dictionary for its uppercase counterpart. It simply does not recognize the word (case sensitive). In this situation, you are signaled when you inadvertently lowercase proper nouns.

External File Example

This chapter contains several examples that demonstrate how to use features of the spell checker. The examples demonstrate how the spelling is checked in a memo written to a printing company. This memo, which is contained in an external file, is shown in Figure 21.1. Note the misspelling of the word "restrictions."

Figure 21.1
Printing Memo,
Contained in an
External File

```
TO:    Bill Meyers
       T. K. Pierce and Company

FROM:  Jane K. Spencer
       Production Manager
       Publications Services

DATE: 05MAR91

REF:  Quote Request

GENERAL
The above mentioned project has a target shelf date of August 31, 1991.
The present plan allows 8 weeks for all materials, packaging, and
shipping; included in this is a 6-week window for book production.
Please be sure to include any scheduling restictions or problems in
your quotation.

Following is a list of specs for the entire project. I would like to
consider this a turn-key project and award all items to the same vendor.
However, I will be pricing the items out individually as well.  If your
company would rather bid only on certain items feel free to do so. When
bidding on single items, be sure to include scheduling windows, etc. so
that your information can be used in conjunction with another vendor's.

Camera ready copy will be sent for all printed materials.  Please send
specs as to how the diskette masters need be sent.

QUANTITY
10M and 15M
```

Figure 21.1
(continued)

OUTER CARTON
Sample enclosed. The same diecut configuration, amount of ink coverage
and stock weight will be used. Please quote this item with 2 options. 1)
4 color process plus 2 PMS/black--the software agreement will print on
the inside of the top box flap 2) 4 color process/black. The cost of
the die should be listed separately. We may be able to supply the die
from a previous job.

Cromalin proofs will be required.

USER'S GUIDES
This product will contain three separate books.

Size : 6 1/2 x 9

Page Counts: 1 volume at 512, 1 at 384 and 1 at 224.

Text: All three books will print in black ink on 40# Cougar or
comparable. as always the guidelines are that opacity not be less than
90 and brightness be as close to 86 as possible.

Covers : Each cover will print on 10 pt. C1S. Quote cover printing with
3 options; 1) 4 color process, 2 PMS and UV/black 2) 2 PMS, black plus
UV/black, and 3) 1 PMS plus black/black.

Proof: Blueline proofs will be required on each text and cover.

Binding: Otabind

DISKETTES
Samples enclosed. There will be a set of 7 diskettes to be replicated
labeled, collated and boxed.

Bronze master proofs will be required.

DISKETTE LABELS
The same stock, size, amount of coverage and finishing should be
quoted.

DISKETTE BOXES
Sample enclosed. The same diecut configuration, amount of coverage and
stock weight will be used. Please quote this item with 3 options. 1) 4
color process plus 2 PMS/0 2) 4 color process/0, and 3) 1 PMS and
black/0. The cost of the die should be listed separately. We may be
able to supply the die from a previous job.

Cromalin proofs will be required.

After the diskettes have been labeled, collated and inserted, the
diskette boxes will have to be shrinkwrapped. A WARNING label will then
have to be affixed to the shrinkwrap directing the user to read the
software agreement before breaking the wrap.

Figure 21.1
(continued)

```
REGISTRATION CARD
Sample enclosed.
A serialized registration card will also be included with this product.
Sample enclosed.

Size: 6 x 9

Stock and Ink:  Black and 1 PMS/Black on 110# Index or comparable.

Finishing:  1 Horizontal perforation and numbered in 2 places.

Proof:  Blueline proofs will be required.

SUPPLIED MATERIALS
An insert from BIX will be supplied and needs to be inserted into
the carton along with the above materials.
```

Checking Spelling Against a Master Dictionary

The SAS System maintains a master dictionary called
SASHELP.BASE.MASTER.DICTNARY. You can use it to check the spelling of
commonly used words in an external file or in a SAS catalog entry whose type is
HELP or CBT. To check the spelling of a file against the master dictionary, use the
SPELL procedure with the IN= and VERIFY options.

```
filename memo 'external-file-to-check';

proc spell in=memo verify;

   title 'List of Unrecognized Words';
run;
```

The IN= option identifies the file you want to check for spelling errors.* For an
external file, you can specify a fileref or the name of a physical file in quotes.**
For a catalog entry, use the form *libref.catalog.entry.type*. The VERIFY option tells
the SAS System that you want to verify the spelling in the file you specify.

   Note: If you use the VERIFY option, you cannot use the CREATE option or
the UPDATE option. If you do not specify at least one of these options, the
VERIFY option becomes the default. Therefore, specifying the VERIFY option is
not actually required in this example.

---

*   IN= is an alias for WORDLIST=. Both forms of the option identify the file to process. The file to
process can be either a list of words for creating or updating a dictionary or, as in this example, a file
to check for spelling errors. In this chapter, the form WORDLIST= is used only when it identifies a
word list.

**   On some host operating systems, you can use wildcards in the file specification instead of the literal
filename. See the SAS companion for your host operating system for details.

Output 21.1 shows the results of using the SPELL procedure to check the spelling in a file. Note that the fileref is displayed in the upper left portion of the output.

Output 21.1
Checking Spelling
Against a Master
Dictionary

```
                         List of Unrecognized Words                    1

       File: "MEMO"

       Unrecognized word          Freq      Line(s)

         Meyers                      1       1
         T                           1       2
         K                           2       2, 4
         Jane                        1       4
         Spencer                     1       4
         REF                         1       10
         restictions                 1       16
         specs                       2       19, 27
         diecut                      2       33, 72
         PMS                         7       35, 54 (2), 55, 74 (2), 92
         Cromalin                    2       40, 78
         x                           2       45, 90
         opacity                     1       50
         pt                          1       53
         C1S                         1       53
         UV                          2       54, 55
         Blueline                    2       57, 96
         Otabind                     1       59
         replicated                  1       62
         shrinkwrapped               1       81
         shrinkwrap                  1       82
         BIX                         1       99
```

Because the example memo contains unrecognized words—words that are misspelled or missing entirely from the master dictionary—the SPELL procedure generates output that includes the following information:

□ the unrecognized word

□ the number of times the word occurs in the file

□ the line number of the line or lines on which the unrecognized word appears.

To generate suggested alternatives for the unrecognized words, add the SUGGEST option to the PROC SPELL statement. Note that the VERIFY option must accompany the SUGGEST option so the SAS System can generate the list of suggestions.

```
filename memo 'external-file-to-check';

proc spell in=memo verify suggest;
   title 'List of Unrecognized Words and Suggestions';
run;
```

Output 21.2 shows the resulting list of suggestions.

Output 21.2
Checking Spelling
and Generating
Suggestions

```
                    List of Unrecognized Words and Suggestions              1

File: "MEMO"

 Unrecognized word              Freq     Line(s)

 Meyers                          1        1
      Suggestions: Meters, Meyerts

 T                               1        2
          Suggestions: A, I, AT, ET, IT, TO, TV

 K                               2        2, 4
          Suggestions: A, I, OK

 Jane                            1        4
          Suggestions: Cane, Dane, Lane, Mane, Pane, Sane, Vane, Wane, June,
                       Jade

 Spencer                         1        4
      Suggestions: Spender

 REF                             1        10
      Suggestions: RE, RED, REP, REV, REEF

 restictions                     1        16
      Suggestions: restrictions

 specs                           2        19, 27
      Suggestions: spews, speck, specks

 diecut                          2        33, 72
      Suggestions: die cut

 PMS                             7        35, 54 (2), 55, 74 (2), 92
      Suggestions: PAS

 Cromalin                        2        40, 78

 x                               2        45, 90
          Suggestions: a, i, ax, ox

 opacity                         1        50

 pt                              1        53
          Suggestions: at, et, it, pa, pi, apt, opt, pat, pet, pit, pot, put

 C1S                             1        53

 UV                              2        54, 55
      Suggestions: TV, UP, US

 Blueline                        2        57, 96
          Suggestions: Byueline, Blue line

 Otabind                         1        59

 replicated                      1        62
      Suggestions: replicate, replicamed
```

```
                    List of Unrecognized Words and Suggestions            2

    File: "MEMO"

      Unrecognized word              Freq     Line(s)

      shrinkwrapped                    1       81
            Suggestions: shrink wrapped

      shrinkwrap                       1       82
            Suggestions: shrink wrap

      BIX                              1       99
            Suggestions: FIX, MIX, NIX, SIX, BOX, BIB, BID, BIG, BIN, BIT
```

Using Auxiliary Dictionaries

In some cases, a file may contain specialized terms that are not in the master dictionary. Both to verify the correct spelling of these specialized terms and to prevent them from being listed as incorrect, you may want to create and use an auxiliary dictionary that contains these terms. Although the master dictionary is used by default, you can use one or more auxiliary dictionaries in addition to or instead of the master dictionary. This section shows you how to do the following:

□ create an auxiliary dictionary

□ check the spelling of a file against an auxiliary dictionary

□ update an auxiliary dictionary.

Note that the following four auxiliary dictionaries are stored in the catalog SASHELP.BASE and are available for your use, in addition to dictionaries you create yourself:

NAMES   contains common English first names.

CITIES   contains the names of cities in the United States.

CNTRIES   contains the names of countries.

STATES   contains the names of states and other entities identified by United States Post Office FIPS codes.

Creating an Auxiliary Dictionary

In addition to using the master dictionary, you may want to create a series of your own dictionaries, each tailored to the type of terminology you are likely to use in certain files.* For instance, one auxiliary dictionary may include only SAS keywords, while another may include terms common to a particular industry.

Consider the previous two examples, which check the spelling of an external file containing a letter to a printing company. Most of the unrecognized words from this file are printing terms. Therefore, the SPELL procedure can be used to

---

* Although it is possible to update a master dictionary, your site may place restrictions on your doing so.

check this file most efficiently if it is used with an auxiliary dictionary that contains printing terms. Do the following to create an auxiliary dictionary:

□ Create a word list of printing terms for the dictionary to use.

□ Build the auxiliary dictionary by following these steps:

□ specify the name of the dictionary

□ point to the appropriate word list

□ create the dictionary

□ specify the size of the dictionary.

Create a Word List

As a preliminary step to building an auxiliary dictionary, list the terms in an external file, with one term per line, as shown here.

```
----+----1----+
spec/s
diecut/s
PMS
Cromalin
opacity
UV
Blueline
Otabind
shrinkwrap/*
```

Following these conventions allows you to reduce the number of entries:

□ Encode words that can have a suffix of s by placing the character string /s at the end of the word.

□ Encode words that can have a suffix of s, ed, or ing by placing the character string /* at the end of the word.

Build the Auxiliary Dictionary

After you have formatted the word list you want, you can begin to build the auxiliary dictionary. To specify the name of the dictionary and point to the appropriate word list, use the PROC SPELL statement with the DICTIONARY= and the WORDLIST= options, as shown in this example.

```
libname in 'SAS-data-library';
filename wrdlst 'user-created-wordlist';

proc spell dictionary=in.spell.words wordlist=wrdlst;
```

The DICTIONARY= option names the dictionary, using the form *libref.catalog.entry*. The WORDLIST= option identifies the file that contains the formatted list of terms with the fileref WRDLST.

To actually create the dictionary and specify its size, add the CREATE and SIZE= options, specifying the number of bytes you want in the dictionary. By default, PROC SPELL creates a dictionary that is the same size as the master dictionary—about 86K—or large enough to contain 50,000 words. However, most auxiliary dictionaries require much less space, as little as 2K. In this case, the dictionary is 2048 bytes (based on a standard calculation of 1024 bytes for 1K).

```
libname in 'SAS-data-library';
filename wrdlst 'user-created-wordlist';

proc spell dictionary=in.spell.words wordlist=wrdlst create size=2048;
run;
```

In specifying the number of bytes, you must balance one goal of creating a dictionary small enough so you don't waste space with another goal of creating a dictionary large enough to minimize the chance that PROC SPELL accepts a word not in the dictionary. The probability of the SPELL procedure accepting a word not in the dictionary is a function of the number of words in the dictionary and the dictionary's size. Although the process of creating a dictionary does not generate procedure output, it does generate a message in the SAS log that indicates the chance of the SPELL procedure incorrectly identifying a word as correct.

Output 21.3 shows the log.

Output 21.3
Creating an
Auxiliary
Dictionary—the
Log

```
5          libname in 'SAS-data-library';
NOTE: Libref IN was successfully assigned as follows:
      Engine:        V606
      Physical Name: SAS-DATA-LIBRARY
6          filename wrdlst 'user-created-wordlist';
7
8          proc spell dictionary=in.spell.words wordlist=wrdlst
9          create size=2048;
10         run;

NOTE: Estimated chance of accepting a word not in WORDS using WORDS is
      9.801733E-30%.
```

The log shows that the auxiliary dictionary IN.SPELL.WORDS.DICTNARY has been created successfully. With this dictionary, the estimated chance of the SPELL procedure incorrectly identifying a word as correct is 9.801733E-30%. If you consider the chance specified in the log too high, you can re-create the dictionary, specifying more bytes. One recommendation is an estimated chance of .01 percent or less, although this amount may vary based on personal preference. You can estimate more specifically the bytes you need by reserving 10 bytes per word, decreasing the number of bytes per word as the number of words increases.

▶ *Caution* . . . . *Save your word lists; do not delete.*
After creating a dictionary, do not delete the dictionary's word list to save space. Only the SAS System can read the dictionary itself; to browse the entries, you must use the word list. Furthermore, to use a dictionary on a different host operating system, you must move the word list to that operating system and re-create the dictionary. ▲

Checking Spelling Against an Auxiliary Dictionary

The next step is to use the auxiliary dictionary to check the spelling of the file. As in the second example in this chapter, use the IN= option to identify the file you want to check, the VERIFY option to indicate that you want to verify the correct spelling, and the SUGGEST option to generate suggestions. In addition, to identify the dictionary to use to check the spelling, add the DICTIONARY= option, specifying the name of the dictionary created in the previous example.

```
libname in 'SAS-data-library';
filename memo 'external-file-to-check';

proc spell in=memo dictionary=in.spell.words verify suggest;
   title 'List of Unrecognized Words';
run;
```

Output 21.4 shows the results. Note that using an auxiliary dictionary tailored to your needs shortens the list of unrecognized words.

Output 21.4
Checking Spelling
Against Master
and Auxiliary
Dictionaries

```
                       List of Unrecognized Words                      1
     File: "MEMO"

     Unrecognized word                Freq      Line(s)

     Meyers                            1         1
           Suggestions: Meters, Meyerts

     T                                 1         2
            Suggestions: A, I, AT, ET, IT, TO, TV

     K                                 2         2, 4
            Suggestions: A, I, OK

     Jane                              1         4
            Suggestions: Cane, Dane, Lane, Mane, Pane, Sane, Vane, Wane, June,
                         Jade

     Spencer                           1         4
            Suggestions: Spender

     REF                               1         10
                Suggestions: RE, RED, REP, REV, REEF

     restictions                       1         16
                Suggestions: restrictions

     x                                 2         45, 90
                Suggestions: a, i, ax, ox

     pt                                1         53
                Suggestions: at, et, it, pa, pi, apt, opt, pat, pet, pit, pot, put

     C1S                               1         53

     replicated                        1         62
                Suggestions: replicate, replicamed

     shrinkwrapped                     1         81
                Suggestions: shrink wrapped

     BIX                               1         99
                Suggestions: FIX, MIX, NIX, SIX, BOX, BIB, BID, BIG, BIN, BIT
```

Note: By default, the master dictionary is used to check the spelling of a file in addition to any other dictionaries that are used. If you don't want to use the master dictionary, add the NOMASTER option to your PROC SPELL statement to suppress using this dictionary.

If you want to check your file against more than one auxiliary dictionary, simply list all dictionaries within parentheses after you specify the DICTIONARY= option, using a blank as the delimiter between dictionaries. The following example is identical to the previous one, except that it adds one of the default auxiliary dictionaries, SASHELP.BASE.NAMES, as well as a user-created auxiliary dictionary of SAS keywords, IN.SPELL.SASWORDS, and lists all dictionaries in parentheses.*

```
libname in 'SAS-data-library';
filename memo 'external-file-to-check';

proc spell in=memo dictionary=(in.spell.words sashelp.base.names
            in.spell.saswords)
          verify suggest;
   title 'List of Unrecognized Words';
run;
```

Output 21.5 shows the results of checking the file against three auxiliary dictionaries and the master dictionary.

Output 21.5
Checking Spelling Against Master and Auxiliary Dictionaries

```
                    List of Unrecognized Words                    1
    File: "MEMO"

      Unrecognized word            Freq      Line(s)

      Meyers                         1         1
            Suggestions: Meters, Meyerts

      T                              1         2
            Suggestions: A, I, R, AT, ET, IT, TO, TV

      K                              2         2, 4
            Suggestions: A, I, R, OK

      Spencer                        1         4
            Suggestions: Spender

      REF                            1         10
            Suggestions: RE, RED, REP, REV, REEF

      restictions                    1         16
            Suggestions: restrictions

      x                              2         45, 90
            Suggestions: a, i, ax, ox

      pt                             1         53
            Suggestions: at, et, it, pa, pi, apt, opt, pat, pet, pit, pot, put

      C1S                            1         53

      replicated                     1         62
            Suggestions: replicate, replicamed

                                        (continued on next page)
```

---
* Refer to the Appendix for the word list used to create the auxiliary dictionary IN.SPELL.SASWORDS.

```
(continued from previous page)

   shrinkwrapped              1        81
          Suggestions: shrink wrapped
   BIX                        1        99
            Suggestions: FIX, MIX, NIX, SIX, BOX, BIB, BID, BIG, BIN, BIT
```

In this case, the output is similar to the previous output because the external file being checked contains no SAS keywords and not all of the names in the memo are in the default auxiliary dictionary. However, using an auxiliary dictionary of SAS keywords to check a file containing numerous SAS keywords would make a big difference in the output.

Updating an Auxiliary Dictionary

If you continue to use an auxiliary dictionary over time, you may want to update it as terminology changes. To illustrate, consider the dictionary of SAS keywords, IN.SPELL.SASWORDS, that was one of three auxiliary dictionaries used previously in this chapter to verify the spelling in a file. The goal is to update that dictionary to add terms from an external file referenced by the fileref ADDITION. The word list is formatted as follows:

```
----+----1----+
FSFORM
DES
NEXTSCR
PREVSCR
=n
COPY
DELETE
FILE
FORMNAME
INCLUDE
PRINT
PRTFILE
SAVE
----+----1----+
```

To update the auxiliary dictionary as described, first use the WORDLIST= option to identify the list of words for updating the dictionary. Use the DICTIONARY= option to identify the dictionary you want to update; then add the UPDATE option, as shown here.

```
libname in 'SAS-data-library';
filename addition 'wordlist-update';

proc spell wordlist=addition dictionary=in.spell.saswords update;
run;
```

As with creating a dictionary, updating a dictionary does not generate procedure output. Output 21.6 shows the log that results from this process.

Output 21.6
Updating an
Auxiliary
Dictionary—the
Log

```
5          libname in 'SAS-data-library';
NOTE: Libref IN was successfully assigned as follows:
      Engine:        V606
      Physical Name: SAS-DATA-LIBRARY
6          filename addition 'wordlist-update';
7
8          proc spell wordlist=addition dictionary=in.spell.saswords update;
9          run;

NOTE: Estimated chance of accepting a word not in SASWORDS using SASWORDS
      is 1.220225E-26%.
```

Note: Although you can update a master dictionary the same way you update an auxiliary dictionary, no examples are shown in this book. You should consult your SAS Site Representative to determine when it is appropriate to update the master dictionary and when it is preferable to create an auxiliary dictionary.

Summary

The following points summarize how to use the Spell Checking Facility with the SPELL procedure:

□ The SAS System maintains a spell checking facility that includes a master dictionary and several auxiliary dictionaries. You can use this facility to verify the spelling of a file, generate suggested alternative spellings, and create other auxiliary dictionaries. Although the Spell Checking Facility is available both through the SPELL procedure and through the SAS Text Editor's SPELL and DICT commands, this chapter documents the facility only as it is accessed through PROC SPELL.

□ To verify the spelling of a file or catalog entry against the master dictionary and to generate suggested alternatives, use the PROC SPELL statement with the WORDLIST= (alias IN=) option to identify the file to process, followed by the VERIFY option and the SUGGEST option.

□ To create an auxiliary dictionary, you can use the following two-step approach:

  □ Before creating an auxiliary dictionary, create a word list by placing the terms in an external file, one term per line. To reduce the number of entries, encode words that can have a suffix of s by placing the character string /s at the end of the word. Encode words that can have a suffix of s, ed, or ing, by placing the character string /* at the end of the word.

  □ To build the auxiliary dictionary, first specify the dictionary name and point to the word list you want by using the PROC SPELL statement with the DICTIONARY= and the WORDLIST= (alias IN=) options. Then to actually create the dictionary and specify its size, use the CREATE and SIZE= options, specifying the number of bytes needed.

□ To check the spelling of a file against an auxiliary dictionary, use the same options that you use to check the spelling of a file against a master dictionary. Add the DICTIONARY= option, specifying the name of the auxiliary dictionary. To check your file against multiple auxiliary dictionaries, list all dictionaries by name in parentheses after you specify the DICTIONARY= option.

□ By default, a file continues to be checked against the master dictionary in addition to whatever auxiliary dictionary you specify. To suppress use of the master dictionary so that only the auxiliary dictionaries are used, add the NOMASTER option to the PROC SPELL statement.

□ To update an auxiliary dictionary, use the WORDLIST= option to identify the list of words for updating the dictionary, the DICTIONARY= option to identify the dictionary you want to update, and the UPDATE option.

SAS Tools

This section summarizes syntax for the SPELL procedure.

PROC SPELL WORDLIST=*file-to-process* <*option-list*>;
   begins the SPELL procedure, which allows you to check the spelling in an external file or in SAS catalog entries of type HELP or CBT. The SPELL procedure also allows you to maintain dictionaries. The alias for the WORDLIST= argument is IN=. *File-to-process* identifies a file that contains either a list of words for creating or updating a dictionary or some text to check for spelling errors. *File-to-process* can be either a fileref or the name of a physical file in quotes. The following options for the SPELL procedure are discussed in this chapter:

CREATE
   creates a dictionary.

DICTIONARY=
   names the dictionary to create or update or specifies one or more dictionaries to use to verify spelling.

NOMASTER
   suppresses use of the master dictionary.

SIZE=
   specifies the size of the dictionary in number of bytes.

SUGGEST
   writes suggestions for unrecognized words to SAS output.

UPDATE
   updates the specified dictionary.

VERIFY
   verifies the spelling in the specified file.

Learning More

This section provides references for learning more about topics presented in this chapter.

□ For further information about the Spell Checking Facility, see the *SAS Procedures Guide, Version 6, Third Edition*, Chapter 33, "The SPELL Procedure." Chapter 33 also provides complete syntax information for the SPELL procedure and all of its options.

□ As noted earlier, in addition to the SPELL procedure, you can use the Spell Checking Facility through the SAS Text Editor's SPELL and DICT commands in conjunction with the SPELL windows. For reference information about these commands, see *SAS Language: Reference, Version 6, First Edition*, Chapter 8, "SAS Text Editor."

□ For more information about SAS catalogs, see Chapter 22, "Managing SAS Catalogs." For complete reference information, see *SAS Language: Reference*, Chapter 6, "SAS Files."

□ For more information about external files, see Chapter 20, "Working with External Files." For reference information, see *SAS Language: Reference*, Chapter 2, "The DATA Step." For information specific to your host operating system, see the appropriate chapters in the SAS companion for your host system.

Chapter 22 Managing SAS® Catalogs

Introduction

This chapter shows you how to manage SAS *catalogs*. A catalog is a type of SAS file stored in a SAS data library. Catalogs can contain multiple entries. Each entry in a catalog has an entry name and entry type. Various entry types can be stored in an individual catalog.

Catalogs are used by base SAS software as well as other SAS software products. In base SAS software, catalogs contain information for use by various procedures, the SAS macro facility, and the SAS Display Manager System.

Managing SAS catalogs involves various tasks such as copying entries from one catalog to another, changing the names of catalog entries, and deleting entries from a catalog. You can use three methods in base SAS software to manage SAS catalogs: the DATASETS procedure, the CATALOG window in a windowing environment, or the CATALOG procedure.

With PROC DATASETS, you can manage entire catalogs, but you cannot manage entries within catalogs. With PROC CATALOG or the CATALOG window, you can manage entire catalogs as well as individual entries. Therefore, if you need to manage entries within catalogs, you should use PROC CATALOG or the CATALOG window rather than PROC DATASETS.

In this chapter

This chapter discusses the CATALOG procedure statements and options. In this chapter, you learn to do the following:

□ invoke the procedure

□ display the contents of a catalog

□ create new catalogs

□ specify a new catalog to process

□ maintain catalog entries

□ terminate execution of the procedure.

Prerequisites

Before you read this chapter, you should understand how the SAS System uses SAS data libraries to store SAS files such as data sets and catalogs. (See Chapter 6, "SAS Files," in *SAS Language: Reference, Version 6, First Edition*.) You should also be familiar with using PROC DATASETS to obtain information about SAS data libraries. (See *SAS Language and Procedures: Usage, Version 6, First Edition*, and the *SAS Procedures Guide: Version 6, Third Edition*.)

Understanding Procedure Execution

To understand the examples in this chapter, you need a basic understanding of the way PROC CATALOG executes. This section discusses how the CATALOG procedure executes, including how to invoke the procedure, how RUN groups work, how errors are processed, and ways to terminate execution of the procedure.

Using an Interactive Procedure

The CATALOG procedure is interactive; that is, it remains active after a RUN statement is executed. Once you submit a PROC CATALOG statement, you can continue to enter and execute statements without repeating the PROC CATALOG statement. In display manager, the message `PROC CATALOG running` is displayed until you terminate the procedure.

How RUN Groups Work

A *RUN group* is a set of subordinate procedure statements ending with a RUN statement. When you use the CATALOG procedure, you can specify subordinate procedure statements to make changes to catalog entries. PROC CATALOG implements the changes for a given group of statements when the procedure encounters a RUN statement. You can have more than one RUN statement among the sets of procedure statements. Error handling is based in part on the division of statements into RUN groups, as the next section describes.

How Errors Are Processed

If an error is encountered, statements in the current RUN group are not executed, and execution proceeds to the next RUN group. Even if the error occurs in the final statement of a RUN group, none of the statements in the RUN group takes effect.

▶ *Caution* . . . . *RUN groups affect deleting and renaming entries.*
Valid statements that lie outside the erroneous RUN group are executed. Therefore, be careful when setting up a processing sequence where the statements from one RUN group depend on the effects of a previous RUN group. Be especially careful when you are deleting or renaming entries. ▲

Ways to Terminate Procedure Execution

To terminate the CATALOG procedure, submit a QUIT statement, a DATA statement, another PROC statement, or end the SAS session with an ENDSAS statement or the BYE display manager command. When you enter a QUIT, DATA, or PROC statement, or end the SAS session, previous statements are executed before the CATALOG procedure terminates.

If you do not want to execute the statements in the current RUN group, submit a RUN CANCEL statement, which immediately terminates execution of the procedure.

SAS Data Library Examples

This chapter contains seven examples that illustrate how to use the CATALOG procedure. The examples use SAS files from the data processing department of an electronics supply company. The manager of the data processing department stores general ledger files in two SAS data libraries. One data library uses the libref PRODUCTN and contains production files, which are used routinely. The other data library uses the libref TESTLIB and periodically contains files that are used to test applications before they are put into production. Prototypes for the test files come from copies of the production files.

The following PROC DATASETS steps display the contents of the two SAS data libraries:

```
libname productn 'SAS-data-library';
libname testlib  'SAS-data-library';

proc datasets library=productn;
   contents data=_all_ nods;
run;

proc datasets library=testlib;
   contents data=_all_ nods;
run;

quit;
```

Output 22.1 shows the results.

Note: Output produced by the DATASETS procedure is specific to your host operating system. Procedure output produced on your operating system may not be exactly the same as Output 22.1.

Output 22.1
Contents
Descriptions of the
SAS Data Libraries
PRODUCTN and
TESTLIB

```
                          The SAS System                         1

                        DATASETS PROCEDURE

                       -----Directory-----

           Libref:            PRODUCTN
           Engine:            V606
           Physical Name:     'SAS-data-library'
           Unit:              DISK
           Volume:            ABC837
           Disposition:       OLD
           Device:            3380
           Blocksize:         6144
           Blocks per Track:  7
           Total Blocks Used: 28
           Highest Block Used: 28
        ❶ Members:            2

                        ❷        ❸
                  #  Name    Memtype  Indexes
                  ---------------------------
                  1  GLEDGER  CATALOG
                  2  GLEDGER  DATA
```

```
                          The SAS System                         2

                        DATASETS PROCEDURE

                       -----Directory-----

           Libref:            TESTLIB
           Engine:            V606
           Physical Name:     'SAS-data-library'
           Unit:              DISK
           Volume:            ABC837
           Disposition:       OLD
           Device:            3380
           Blocksize:         6144
           Blocks per Track:  7
           Total Blocks Used: 7
           Highest Block Used: 7
        ❹ Members:            0
```

The following list corresponds to the reference numbers in Output 22.1:

❶   the data library referenced by PRODUCTN contains two members.

❷ and ❸   both members are named GLEDGER, but the first one has a member type of CATALOG and the second one has a member type of DATA.

❹   the library referenced by TESTLIB contains no members at this point.

Invoking the Procedure

To invoke the CATALOG procedure, use the PROC CATALOG statement and the CATALOG= argument. In most cases, the CATALOG= argument is required. (For exceptions, see "Learning More" at the end of this chapter.)

The following statement invokes the procedure and specifies the catalog GLEDGER in the SAS data library referenced by PRODUCTN:

```
proc catalog catalog=productn.gledger;
```

Recall from "Understanding Procedure Execution" earlier in this chapter that once you submit a PROC CATALOG statement, you can continue to enter and execute statements without repeating the PROC CATALOG statement because the previous catalog specification remains active until you either specify a new catalog or terminate the procedure.

Note: The examples that follow assume the PROC CATALOG statement is active. Therefore, the PROC CATALOG statement is not repeated each time in the code that generates the examples.

Displaying the Contents of a Catalog

Before you copy, rename, or delete catalog entries, you probably want to see the contents of the catalog. The CATALOG procedure displays the number of entries in a catalog, along with the name, entry type, creation date, and a description of each entry.

To display the contents of a catalog, use the CONTENTS statement. The following CONTENTS statement displays the contents of the SAS catalog PRODUCTN.GLEDGER:

```
   contents;
run;
```

Output 22.2 shows the results.

Output 22.2
Contents of the
SAS Catalog
PRODUCTN.GLEDGER

```
                              The SAS System                              1

                       Contents of Catalog PRODUCTN.GLEDGER

     # Name       Type      Date       Description

     1 DMKEYS     KEYS      02/28/91   Display Manager Function Keys

     2 PGMEDIT    PMENU     02/28/91   Program Editor Description

     3 PROG010    SOURCE    03/01/91   Enter Transactions

     4 PROG020    SOURCE    03/01/91   Print Journals

     5 PROG030    SOURCE    03/01/91   Print Account Activity Detail Reports

     6 PROG040    SOURCE    03/01/91   Post Transactions

     7 PROG050    SOURCE    03/01/91   Print Trial Balance

     8 PROG060    SOURCE    03/01/91   Print Status of Reports
```

By default, the output of the CONTENTS statement is written to the procedure output file, such as the OUTPUT window of display manager.

A catalog can have entries of many different types. Each entry stores a different kind of information. The entries are sorted alphabetically first by entry type and then by entry name.

For example, notice that the catalog PRODUCTN.GLEDGER in Output 22.2 contains eight entries of various types. The first entry is a KEYS entry, which contains function key settings. The second entry is a PMENU entry, which contains pull-down menu definitions. The remaining six entries are SOURCE entries, which contain text from the NOTEPAD and PROGRAM EDITOR windows of display manager.

Creating New Catalogs

You can use existing catalogs or entries to create new ones. For example, if you have entries in a catalog in a SAS data library that is used for production applications, you may want to copy one or more of the entries to a catalog in a different SAS data library for running test applications.

In the next three sections, you learn how to

□ copy an entire catalog to a catalog in another SAS data library

□ limit processing to a specific type of entry

□ copy individual entries to a catalog in another SAS data library.

Copying an Entire Catalog

When you are managing SAS catalogs, you may want to copy all the entries from a catalog in one SAS data library to a catalog in another SAS data library. You can specify each catalog entry separately; however, it is simpler to copy the entire catalog at once.

To copy all the entries in one catalog to a catalog in another SAS data library, use the COPY statement and the OUT= argument. The OUT= argument is required. It names the catalog to which the entries are copied.

For example, the data processing manager of the electronics firm wants to copy all eight catalog entries from the catalog GLEDGER in the SAS data library PRODUCTN to a new catalog named RECEIVE in the SAS data library TESTLIB.

The following COPY statement contains an OUT= argument that specifies the two-level name TESTLIB.RECEIVE as the output data library and catalog. The previous PROC CATALOG statement, which is named PRODUCTN.GLEDGER, is still in effect.

```
    copy out=testlib.receive;
run;
```

Output 22.3 shows the results, which are written to the SAS log.

```
40            copy out=testlib.receive;
41        run;
NOTE: Copying object DMKEYS.KEYS from catalog PRODUCTN.GLEDGER to catalog
      TESTLIB.RECEIVE.
NOTE: Copying object PGMEDIT.PMENU from catalog PRODUCTN.GLEDGER to catalog
      TESTLIB.RECEIVE.
NOTE: Copying object PROG010.SOURCE from catalog PRODUCTN.GLEDGER to
      catalog TESTLIB.RECEIVE.
NOTE: Copying object PROG020.SOURCE from catalog PRODUCTN.GLEDGER to
      catalog TESTLIB.RECEIVE.
NOTE: Copying object PROG030.SOURCE from catalog PRODUCTN.GLEDGER to
      catalog TESTLIB.RECEIVE.
NOTE: Copying object PROG040.SOURCE from catalog PRODUCTN.GLEDGER to
      catalog TESTLIB.RECEIVE.
NOTE: Copying object PROG050.SOURCE from catalog PRODUCTN.GLEDGER to
      catalog TESTLIB.RECEIVE.
NOTE: Copying object PROG060.SOURCE from catalog PRODUCTN.GLEDGER to
      catalog TESTLIB.RECEIVE.
```

Limiting Processing to a Specific Type of Entry

Instead of copying all the entries in one catalog to another catalog, you may want to copy only catalog entries of a particular entry type. In this example, the data processing manager of the electronics firm wants to copy only the SOURCE entries from the catalog GLEDGER in the SAS data library PRODUCTN to a new catalog named PAYABLE, which is in the SAS data library TESTLIB.

To limit the processing of PROC CATALOG to a specific type of entry, use the ENTRYTYPE= option. To illustrate, the previous COPY statement has been revised in two ways: first, the OUT= argument specifies TESTLIB.PAYABLE as the catalog, and second, the ENTRYTYPE= option limits copying to entries with a type of SOURCE.

```
copy out=testlib.payable entrytype=source;
run;
```

Output 22.4 shows the contents of the SAS log after the revised COPY statement is submitted.

```
42            copy out=testlib.payable entrytype=source;
43        run;
NOTE: Copying object PROG010.SOURCE from catalog PRODUCTN.GLEDGER to
      catalog TESTLIB.PAYABLE.
NOTE: Copying object PROG020.SOURCE from catalog PRODUCTN.GLEDGER to
      catalog TESTLIB.PAYABLE.
NOTE: Copying object PROG030.SOURCE from catalog PRODUCTN.GLEDGER to
      catalog TESTLIB.PAYABLE.
NOTE: Copying object PROG040.SOURCE from catalog PRODUCTN.GLEDGER to
      catalog TESTLIB.PAYABLE.
NOTE: Copying object PROG050.SOURCE from catalog PRODUCTN.GLEDGER to
      catalog TESTLIB.PAYABLE.
NOTE: Copying object PROG060.SOURCE from catalog PRODUCTN.GLEDGER to
      catalog TESTLIB.PAYABLE.
```

You can use the ENTRYTYPE= option as a part of all statements in the CATALOG procedure except the CONTENTS statement. The ENTRYTYPE= option in the PROC CATALOG statement specifies the entry type for all statements that follow.

Copying Individual Entries

In the previous example, you learned how to limit processing of catalog entries to those of the same entry type. In some cases, you may want to copy individual catalog entries. For example, the data processing manager wants to copy only three SOURCE entries from the catalog PRODUCTN.GLEDGER to a third catalog in TESTLIB. The name of the third catalog is INSTOCK, and the SOURCE entries to be selected for copying are the first, second, and fifth ones in PRODUCTN.GLEDGER, which are named PROG010, PROG020, and PROG050, respectively. (See "Displaying the Contents of a Catalog" earlier in this chapter.)

To copy selected entries to a catalog in another SAS data library, use the COPY statement, the OUT= argument, and either the SELECT or EXCLUDE statement. The following COPY statement contains an OUT= argument that specifies the two-level name TESTLIB.INSTOCK as the output catalog. The SELECT statement specifies which three SOURCE entries to select from PRODUCTN.GLEDGER.

```
copy out=testlib.instock entrytype=source;
    select prog010 prog020 prog050;
run;
```

Output 22.5 shows the contents of the SAS log after the COPY and SELECT statements are submitted.

Output 22.5
SAS Log Notes
about the COPY
Statement Using
the SELECT
Option

```
44          copy out=testlib.instock entrytype=source;
45              select prog010 prog020 prog050;
46          run;

NOTE: Copying object PROG010.SOURCE from catalog PRODUCTN.GLEDGER to
      catalog TESTLIB.INSTOCK.
NOTE: Copying object PROG020.SOURCE from catalog PRODUCTN.GLEDGER to
      catalog TESTLIB.INSTOCK.
NOTE: Copying object PROG050.SOURCE from catalog PRODUCTN.GLEDGER to
      catalog TESTLIB.INSTOCK.
```

You can use the EXCLUDE statement instead of the SELECT statement to copy the same entries. For example, the following COPY and EXCLUDE statements copy the same entries that were copied in the previous example, Output 22.5:

```
copy out=testlib.instock;
    exclude prog030 prog040 prog060;
run;
```

You cannot use the SELECT and EXCLUDE statements at the same time within a single COPY statement in a RUN group, but you can use one or the other multiple times.

Specifying a New Catalog to Process

As discussed earlier in "Understanding Procedure Execution," the CATALOG procedure is interactive. Therefore, once you submit a PROC CATALOG statement, you can continue to enter and execute statements without repeating the PROC CATALOG statement. A previous catalog specification remains active until you either specify a new catalog or terminate the procedure. When you want to process entries in a catalog that is different from the currently active catalog specification, submit a new PROC CATALOG statement and CATALOG= argument.

For example, the data processing manager wants to work with individual SOURCE entries in one of the new catalogs, INSTOCK. However, the following PROC CATALOG statement and CATALOG= argument were specified earlier in the chapter in the section "Invoking the Procedure":

```
proc catalog catalog=productn.gledger;
```

That specification is still active. To change the catalog specification to TESTLIB.INSTOCK, the data processing manager submits the following PROC CATALOG statement and CATALOG= argument. The ENTRYTYPE= option limits subsequent processing to SOURCE entries.

```
proc catalog catalog=testlib.instock entrytype=source;
```

The remaining PROC CATALOG statements in this chapter apply to the catalog INSTOCK in the SAS data library referenced by TESTLIB.

Maintaining Catalog Entries

After you have created new catalogs, you may need to maintain them by performing duties such as changing the names of entries or deleting entries.

In the next two sections, you learn how to do the following:

□ change the names of entries

□ delete entries.

Changing the Names of Entries

When you copy entries from one catalog to another, you may want to rename the entries in the new catalog to conform to a naming convention. To change the names of entries in a catalog, use the CHANGE statement.

The following statement applies to TESTLIB.INSTOCK and changes the name of the SOURCE entry PROG050 to TEMP050:

```
change prog050=temp050;
run;
```

Output 22.6 shows the contents of the SAS log after the CHANGE statement is submitted.

Output 22.6
SAS Log Notes
about the
CHANGE
Statement

```
47            change prog050=temp050;
48        run;
NOTE: Changing object PROG050.SOURCE to TEMP050.SOURCE in catalog
      TESTLIB.INSTOCK.
```

Deleting Entries

When you no longer need a catalog entry, you can delete it using the DELETE
statement. For example, after testing the three SOURCE entries in
TESTLIB.INSTOCK, the data processing manager determines the SOURCE entry
TEMP050 is not needed and deletes it from the catalog.

```
    delete temp050;
run;
```

Output 22.7 shows the contents of the SAS log after the DELETE statement is
submitted.

Output 22.7
SAS Log Note
about the DELETE
Statement

```
49            delete temp050;
50        run;
NOTE: Deleting object TEMP050.SOURCE in catalog TESTLIB.INSTOCK.
```

Terminating Procedure Execution

Several ways of terminating execution of the CATALOG procedure are discussed
in "Understanding Procedure Execution" earlier in this chapter. However, the
simplest way to terminate execution is by submitting a QUIT statement, in which
case statements in the current RUN group are executed before the CATALOG
procedure terminates.

For example, the following QUIT statement terminates the PROC CATALOG
step:

```
quit;
```

Output 22.8 shows the contents of the SAS log after the QUIT statement is
submitted.

Output 22.8
SAS Log Note
about Procedure
Termination

```
51        quit;
NOTE: The PROCEDURE CATALOG used 0.04 CPU seconds and 3311K.
```

Summary

The following points summarize how to use the CATALOG procedure to manage SAS catalogs:

□ To display the contents of a catalog, use the PROC CATALOG statement and the CATALOG= argument to invoke the procedure and the CONTENTS statement to specify the contents.

□ To copy all entries in one catalog to a catalog in another SAS data library, use the COPY statement and the OUT= argument.

□ To limit processing to a specific type of entry, use the ENTRYTYPE= option.

□ To copy individual entries to a catalog in another SAS data library, use the COPY statement, the OUT= argument, and either the SELECT or the EXCLUDE statement.

□ To specify a new catalog to process, use another PROC CATALOG statement and CATALOG= argument.

□ To change the names of entries, use the CHANGE statement.

□ To delete entries from a catalog, use the DELETE statement.

□ To execute statements in the current RUN group and then terminate the CATALOG procedure, submit a QUIT statement, a DATA statement, another PROC statement, or end the SAS session with an ENDSAS statement or the BYE display manager command.

□ To terminate execution of the CATALOG procedure immediately without executing any previous statements, submit a RUN statement with the CANCEL option.

SAS Tools

This section summarizes syntax for the procedure discussed in this chapter.

PROC CATALOG CATALOG=*<libref.>catalog-name*;
  manages entries in catalogs in SAS data libraries. CATALOG= specifies the catalog to be processed.

CONTENTS;
  displays the contents of the catalog specified in the most recent CATALOG= argument.

COPY OUT=*<libref.>catalog-name* <ENTRYTYPE=*entrytype*> ;
  copies entries to the catalog specified in the OUT= argument. ENTRYTYPE= limits processing to the type of entries specified.

(COPY OUT= continued)

The COPY statements discussed in this chapter are

SELECT *entry-list*;
    selects for copying only those entries named in *entry-list*.

EXCLUDE *entry-list*;
    excludes from copying those entries named in *entry-list*.

CHANGE *oldname=newname*;
    renames one or more catalog entries.

DELETE *entry-list*;
    deletes from the catalog those entries in *entry-list*.

QUIT;
    terminates execution of the procedure.

Learning More

This section provides references for learning more about topics presented in this chapter.

□ In a full-screen windowing environment, you can use the CATALOG window instead of the CATALOG procedure. The CATALOG window supports most of the features of the CATALOG procedure. For more information on using the CATALOG window, see *SAS Language and Procedures: Usage, Version 6, First Edition*, Chapter 39, "Mastering Your Environment with Selected Windows," and *SAS Language: Reference, Version 6, First Edition*, Chapter 17, "SAS Display Manager Windows."

□ By default, the output of the CONTENTS statement is written to the procedure output file, such as the OUTPUT window of display manager. You can also send the output to an external file by using the FILE= option in the CONTENTS statement, or to a SAS data set by using the OUT= option. For details on these options, see the *SAS Procedures Guide, Version 6, Third Edition*, Chapter 8, "The CATALOG Procedure."

□ To invoke the CATALOG procedure, you use the PROC CATALOG statement and the CATALOG= argument. In most cases, the CATALOG= argument is required. Without the CATALOG= argument the procedure fails because there is no default catalog name. However, if you use the CATALOG= option in the CONTENTS statement or the IN= option in the COPY statement, the CATALOG= argument is not required.

□ For details about how PROC CATALOG treats multiple occurrences of the ENTRYTYPE= option, see the section "Using the ENTRYTYPE= Option in Subordinate Statements" in Chapter 8 of the *SAS Procedures Guide*.

□ In addition to base SAS software, catalogs are used by other SAS products, such as SAS/FSP, SAS/AF, SAS/IML, and SAS/GRAPH software, to store several types of information. For a complete list of entry types, their contents, and how they are created and used, see the section "Release 6.06: SAS Catalogs" in *SAS Language Reference*, Chapter 6, "SAS Files."

□ To specify a new catalog to process, you can also use the IN= option in the COPY statement to override the current CATALOG= specification. For details, see "COPY Statement" in the *SAS Procedures Guide*, Chapter 8.

Chapter 23 Comparing SAS® Data Sets

Introduction

At times, you may need to compare two SAS data sets to determine differences that exist between the data sets. For example, you may need to compare two data sets to determine which variables and observations do not match.

This chapter shows you how to use the COMPARE procedure to determine whether matches exist between attributes and contents of two SAS data sets. You can also use PROC COMPARE to make comparisons within a single data set. To illustrate, an agricultural research firm can determine whether lack of rain negatively affects nutrient levels in certain crops by comparing a data set that contains levels of nutrients obtained during a drought with one containing levels obtained during a period of normal rainfall.

PROC COMPARE produces a variety of reports based on the comparisons it performs. A wide selection of options enables you to control the kinds of output to produce, the kinds of comparisons to make, and the degree of detail to report.

In this chapter
This chapter shows you how to use the COMPARE procedure to

☐ display a brief report of the differences between variables and observations

☐ restrict the comparison to values of specific variables

☐ compare similar variables that have different names

☐ compare variables within a single data set.

Prerequisites

To understand the examples and discussions in this chapter, you should be familiar with the basics of DATA step processing.

SAS Data Set Examples

The examples in this chapter use two SAS data sets as input for the COMPARE procedure. Both data sets come from an agricultural research firm that conducted tests to determine the nutritional value of different kinds of vegetables.

The first data set is named NUTRIENT.NORMAL, and it contains data collected from tests conducted during a year in which there was normal rainfall. The data set NUTRIENT.NORMAL contains the following variables:

Variable	Type	Description
CROP	character	a vegetable tested for nutrients
CALCIUM	numeric	milligrams of calcium per cup
IRON	numeric	milligrams of iron per cup
VITA_B1	numeric	milligrams of vitamin B_1 per cup
VITA_B2	numeric	milligrams of vitamin B_2 per cup
VITA_C	numeric	milligrams of vitamin C per cup

The following PROC PRINT step displays the data set NUTRIENT.NORMAL:*

```
libname nutrient 'SAS-data-library';

proc print data=nutrient.normal;
   id crop;
   title 'Milligrams of Nutrients Per Cup';
run;
```

Output 23.1 shows the results.

Output 23.1
Printout of SAS
Data Set
NUTRIENT.NORMAL

```
                      Milligrams of Nutrients Per Cup                    1

            CROP          CALCIUM      IRON     VITA_B1    VITA_B2    VITA_C

            beets            32         1.2       0.07       0.06       0.9
            corn              8         1.4       0.13       0.12       0.5
            cauliflower      28         1.3       0.09       0.08       1.0
            green beans      54         1.5       0.12       0.11       1.9
            lettuce          11         0.3       0.03       0.03       1.3
            peas             30         3.0       0.14       0.13       1.5
```

---

* The DATA step that creates NUTRIENT.NORMAL is shown in the Appendix.

The second data set is named NUTRIENT.DROUGHT, and it contains data collected from tests conducted during a year in which a severe shortage of rainfall occurred. The data set NUTRIENT.DROUGHT contains the following variables:

Variable	Type	Description
CROP	character	a vegetable tested for nutrients
CALCIUM	numeric	milligrams of calcium per cup
IRON	numeric	milligrams of iron per cup
VITA_B1	numeric	milligrams of vitamin B_1 per cup
RIBOFLVN	numeric	milligrams of riboflavin (vitamin B_2) per cup

The following PROC PRINT step displays the data set NUTRIENT.DROUGHT:*

```
libname nutrient 'SAS-data-library';

proc print data=nutrient.drought;
   id crop;
   title 'Milligrams of Nutrients Per Cup';
run;
```

Output 23.2 shows the results.

Output 23.2
Printout of SAS
Data Set
NUTRIENT.DROUGHT

```
                  Milligrams of Nutrients Per Cup                    1

       CROP          CALCIUM   IRON   VITA_B1   RIBOFLVN

       beets            28      1.2    0.06      0.05
       corn              8      1.2    0.13      0.11
       cauliflower      28      1.3    0.08      0.08
       green beans      54      1.3    0.12      0.10
```

Understanding a Simple Comparison

To understand how the COMPARE procedure makes comparisons, consider a simple comparison of the data sets NUTRIENT.NORMAL and NUTRIENT.DROUGHT. Assume that neither data set has attributes set by the TYPE= or LABEL= options in the DATA statement.

As Output 23.1 and Output 23.2 illustrate, the data sets NUTRIENT.NORMAL and NUTRIENT.DROUGHT vary slightly. Specifically, the two data sets are similar in that they both contain an ID variable named CROP. The data sets also contain three *matching variables*: CALCIUM, IRON, and VITA_B1. Matching variables are variables that have the same name. Also, both data sets contain four *matching observations*: the ones with the values **BEETS**, **CORN**, **CAULIFLOWER**, and **GREEN BEANS** for the ID variable CROP. Matching observations are observations in

---

* The DATA step that creates NUTRIENT.DROUGHT is shown in the Appendix.

which the ID variables contain the same value. (If you do not use the ID statement, matching observations are observations that occur in the same position in the data sets.)

On the other hand, the two data sets are different in that NUTRIENT.NORMAL contains six observations, but NUTRIENT.DROUGHT contains only four observations. In other words, NUTRIENT.NORMAL contains two observations for CROP (LETTUCE and PEAS) for which NUTRIENT.DROUGHT has no matching observations. Also, NUTRIENT.NORMAL contains two variables, VITA_B2 and VITA_C, for which there are no matching variables in NUTRIENT.DROUGHT.

When you use PROC COMPARE to compare two data sets such as NUTRIENT.NORMAL and NUTRIENT.DROUGHT, the procedure first compares the following:

□ data set attributes (set by the TYPE= and LABEL= options in the DATA statement)

□ variables; that is, the COMPARE procedure checks each variable in one data set to determine whether it matches a variable in the other data set

□ attributes of matching variables (type, length, labels, formats, and informats)

□ observations; that is, the COMPARE procedure checks each observation in one data set to determine whether it matches an observation in the other data set.

After making these comparisons, the COMPARE procedure only compares values in the parts of the data set that match. Observations in which values are equal are not displayed. For example, when the COMPARE procedure compares the data set NUTRIENT.NORMAL and the data set NUTRIENT.DROUGHT, it compares values only for the three matching variables (CALCIUM, IRON, and VITA_B1) and the four matching observations (those in which the value of the ID variable is either BEETS, CORN, CAULIFLOWER, or GREEN BEANS).

In Figure 23.1 the shaded areas illustrate the matching variables and matching observations in the data sets NUTRIENT.NORMAL and NUTRIENT.DROUGHT.

Figure 23.1
Matching Parts of
Data Sets
NUTRIENT.NORMAL
and
NUTRIENT.DROUGHT

Data Set NUTRIENT.NORMAL

Milligrams of Nutrients Per Cup

CROP	CALCIUM	IRON	VITA_B1	VITA_B2	VITA_C
beets	32	1.2	.05	.02	.9
corn	8	1.4	.13	.08	.5
cauliflower	28	1.3	.09	.13	1.0
green beans	54	1.5	.12	.09	1.9
lettuce	11	.3	.03	.03	1.3
peas	30	3.0	.14	.43	1.5

Data Set NUTRIENT.DROUGHT

Milligrams of Nutrients Per Cup

CROP	CALCIUM	IRON	VITA_B1	RIBOFLVN
beets	28	1.2	.05	.02
corn	8	1.2	.13	.07
cauliflower	28	1.3	.08	.11
green beans	54	1.3	.12	.09

By default, PROC COMPARE produces five reports. If you have a large number of matching variables and matching observations in your data sets, all five default reports may be too much detailed output. However, you can use one or more procedure options to limit the number of reports.

The next section shows how to reduce the number of reports produced by PROC COMPARE by displaying one brief report of the differences between two data sets. All subsequent examples in this chapter use the same brief report to illustrate other ways to use PROC COMPARE.

Displaying a Brief Report of Differences between Data Sets

Although the COMPARE procedure produces a wide variety of reports, you may want to limit the amount of output by displaying a brief report of the differences between data sets.

For example, the agricultural research firm does not need all the details produced by the COMPARE procedure's five default reports. Instead, the research firm wants to produce a report that only shows any decline in nutrient values as a result of drought conditions. For each matching nutrient that compares unequally, the report should show the differences expressed as negative numbers and percentages.

To base the comparisons on normal rainfall, the research firm uses the data set NUTRIENT.NORMAL as the *base data set* and the data set NUTRIENT.DROUGHT as the *comparison data set*. A base data set is a SAS data set used as the basis of a comparison. A comparison data set is a SAS data set that is compared to the base.

To display a brief report, do the following in a PROC COMPARE statement:

□ specify the base data set

□ specify the comparison data set

□ request a brief report.

To specify the base data set in a PROC COMPARE statement, use the BASE= option. The following PROC COMPARE statement specifies the data set NUTRIENT.NORMAL as the base data set:

```
proc compare base=nutrient.normal;
```

To specify the comparison data set, use the COMPARE= option. The following PROC COMPARE statement contains the COMPARE= option that specifies the data set NUTRIENT.DROUGHT as the comparison data set:

```
proc compare base=nutrient.normal compare=nutrient.drought;
```

To display a brief report of the differences between data sets, use the BRIEF option. The following PROC COMPARE step contains all of the options discussed so far, including the BRIEF option to limit the output:

```
libname nutrient 'SAS-data-library';

proc compare base=nutrient.normal compare=nutrient.drought brief;
   title 'Decline in the Amount of Nutrients';
run;
```

The BRIEF option suppresses the first four default summaries and produces only the fifth report, the value comparison results. (See "Learning More" at the end of this chapter for more information on default reports.)

Output 23.3 shows the results.

Output 23.3
Displaying a Brief
Report

```
                          Decline in the Amount of Nutrients                    1

                                    COMPARE Procedure
                    Comparison of NUTRIENT.NORMAL with NUTRIENT.DROUGHT
                                      (Method=EXACT)

         NOTE: Data set NUTRIENT.NORMAL contains 2 observations not in
               NUTRIENT.DROUGHT.
         NOTE: Values of the following 3 variables compare unequal: CALCIUM IRON
               VITA_B1


                          Value Comparison Results for Variables

                    ❶          ❷          ❸          ❹          ❺
               _____

                      ||      Base     Compare
                 Obs  ||    CALCIUM     CALCIUM     Diff.      % Diff
               _____ ||  _____
                      ||
                  1   ||    32.0000     28.0000    -4.0000    -12.5000
               _____


                      ||      Base     Compare
                 Obs  ||      IRON       IRON       Diff.      % Diff
               _____ ||  _____
                      ||
                  2   ||     1.4000      1.2000    -0.2000    -14.2857
                  4   ||     1.5000      1.3000    -0.2000    -13.3333
               _____


                      ||      Base     Compare
                 Obs  ||    VITA_B1     VITA_B1     Diff.      % Diff
               _____ ||  _____
                      ||
                  1   ||     0.0700      0.0600    -0.0100    -14.2857
                  3   ||     0.0900      0.0800    -0.0100    -11.1111
               _____
```

The value comparison results report produced with the BRIEF option contains five parts. The following list corresponds to the reference numbers in Output 23.3:

❶ This column lists the observation numbers.

❷ This column lists the values of the variables in the base data set.

❸ This column lists the values of the variables in the comparison data set.

❹ For numeric variables, this column lists the difference between the two values.

❺ For numeric variables, this column lists the percent difference between the two values.

Restricting the Comparison to Values of Specific Variables

In some cases you may want to restrict the comparison to the values of specific variables. For example, the research firm wants to compare only the values of the variable CALCIUM. By default, the COMPARE procedure compares the values of all matching variables. However, you can restrict the comparison to values of specific variables by naming the variables in a VAR statement, as in the following step:

```
libname nutrient 'SAS-data-library';

proc compare base=nutrient.normal compare=nutrient.drought brief;
   var calcium;
      title 'Decline in the Amount of Calcium';
run;
```

Output 23.4 shows the results.

Output 23.4
Restricting the Comparison to Values of Specific Variables

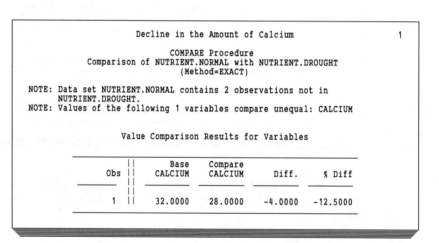

```
                     Decline in the Amount of Calcium                      1

                             COMPARE Procedure
              Comparison of NUTRIENT.NORMAL with NUTRIENT.DROUGHT
                              (Method=EXACT)
    NOTE: Data set NUTRIENT.NORMAL contains 2 observations not in
          NUTRIENT.DROUGHT.
    NOTE: Values of the following 1 variables compare unequal: CALCIUM


                    Value Comparison Results for Variables


                   ||
                   ||     Base     Compare
              Obs  ||   CALCIUM    CALCIUM      Diff.      % Diff
                   ||
                   ||
                1  ||   32.0000    28.0000    -4.0000    -12.5000
```

Comparing Similar Variables That Have Different Names

Sometimes you may want to compare variables in one data set with similar variables that have different names in another data set. For example, both data sets contain a variable for vitamin B_2. In the data set NUTRIENT.NORMAL, the variable is named VITA_B2, but in the data set NUTRIENT.DROUGHT, the variable is named RIBOFLVN. The agricultural research firm wants to compare the amounts of vitamin B_2 in the two data sets.

To compare variables in the base data set with similar variables having different names in the comparison data set, you need to

□ specify the variables in the base data set

□ specify the variables in the comparison data set.

Specify the Variables in the Base Data Set

To specify variables in the base data set, use a VAR statement. The following VAR statement specifies the variable VITA_B2 from the data set NUTRIENT.NORMAL:

```
proc compare base=nutrient.normal compare=nutrient.drought brief;
   var vita_b2;
```

Specify the Variables in the Comparison Data Set

To specify variables in the comparison data set, list them in a WITH statement. The first variable you list in the WITH statement corresponds to the first variable you list in the VAR statement, the second corresponds to the second, and so on. When you use a WITH statement, you must use a VAR statement.

To illustrate, the following PROC COMPARE step contains all the statements discussed so far, including a WITH statement that compares the values of the variable VITA_B2 in the base data set NUTRIENT.NORMAL with the values of the variable RIBOFLVN in the comparison data set NUTRIENT.DROUGHT:

```
libname nutrient 'SAS-data-library';

proc compare base=nutrient.normal compare=nutrient.drought brief;
   var vita_b2;
   with riboflvn;
   title 'Decline in the Amount of Vitamin B2 (Riboflavin)';
run;
```

Output 23.5 shows the results.

Output 23.5
Comparing Similar Variables with Different Names

```
           Decline in the Amount of Vitamin B2 (Riboflavin)              1

                            COMPARE Procedure
            Comparison of NUTRIENT.NORMAL with NUTRIENT.DROUGHT
                            (Method=EXACT)

NOTE: Data set NUTRIENT.NORMAL contains 2 observations not in
      NUTRIENT.DROUGHT.
NOTE: Values of the following 1 variables compare unequal:
      VITA_B2¬=RIBOFLVN


                Value Comparison Results for Variables

          ||       Base     Compare
      Obs ||     VITA_B2    RIBOFLVN      Diff.      % Diff
   _____||_____
          ||
        1 ||      0.0600      0.0500     -0.0100    -16.6667
        2 ||      0.1200      0.1100     -0.0100     -8.3333
        4 ||      0.1100      0.1000     -0.0100     -9.0909
```

Comparing Variables within a Single Data Set

For some comparisons, you may want to see how variable values within a single data set compare with one another. Variables that are used as the basis of the comparison are referred to as the *base variables*. The variables to which the base variables are compared are called the *comparison variables*.

For example, the research firm wants to make two comparisons using variables in the data set NUTRIENT.NORMAL. The first comparison shows the differences between the levels of minerals. The basis of the comparison is iron, to which calcium is compared. The second comparison shows the differences between the levels of B vitamins. The basis of the comparison is vitamin B_2, to which vitamin B_1 is compared.

To compare variables within a single data set, specify the following:

□   a single data set

□   the base variables for that data set

□   the comparison variables for that data set.

Specify a Single Data Set

To specify a single data set, use a PROC COMPARE statement that uses only the BASE= option; do not include the COMPARE= option.

The following PROC COMPARE statement uses the BASE= option to name one data set, NUTRIENT.NORMAL. The PROC COMPARE statement does not contain the COMPARE= option. As in the previous examples, the BRIEF option limits the amount of output:

```
proc compare base=nutrient.normal brief;
```

Specify the Base Variables

To specify the base variable or variables, use the VAR statement. The following VAR statement specifies the variables IRON and VITA_B2 as the base variables:

```
proc compare base=nutrient.normal brief;
   var iron vita_b2;
```

Specify the Comparison Variables

To specify the comparison variable or variables, use the WITH statement. The first variable you list in the WITH statement corresponds to the first variable you list in the VAR statement, the second corresponds to the second, and so on. When you use a WITH statement, you must use a VAR statement.

The following PROC COMPARE step includes all the statements discussed so far, including a WITH statement that specifies the variables CALCIUM and VITA_B1 as the comparison variables:

```
libname nutrient 'SAS-data-library';

proc compare base=nutrient.normal brief;
   var iron vita_b2;
   with calcium vita_b1;
   title 'Normal Levels of Iron/Calcium and Vitamins B2/B1';
run;
```

Output 23.6 shows the results.

Output 23.6
Comparing
Variables within a
Single Data Set

```
             Normal Levels of Iron/Calcium and Vitamins B2/B1           1

                          COMPARE Procedure
                 Comparisons of variables in NUTRIENT.NORMAL
                            (Method=EXACT)

NOTE: Values of the following 2 variables compare unequal: IRON¬=CALCIUM
      VITA_B2¬=VITA_B1


                  Value Comparison Results for Variables


                 ||    Base      Compare
           Obs   ||    IRON      CALCIUM      Diff.      % Diff
           _____||
                 ||
             1   ||   1.2000     32.0000     30.8000        2567
             2   ||   1.4000      8.0000      6.6000    471.4286
             3   ||   1.3000     28.0000     26.7000        2054
             4   ||   1.5000     54.0000     52.5000        3500
             5   ||   0.3000     11.0000     10.7000        3567
             6   ||   3.0000     30.0000     27.0000    900.0000



                 ||    Base      Compare
           Obs   ||   VITA_B2    VITA_B1      Diff.      % Diff
           _____||
                 ||
             1   ||   0.0600     0.0700      0.0100     16.6667
             2   ||   0.1200     0.1300      0.0100      8.3333
             3   ||   0.0800     0.0900      0.0100     12.5000
             4   ||   0.1100     0.1200      0.0100      9.0909
             6   ||   0.1300     0.1400      0.0100      7.6923
```

A variable name can appear any number of times in a VAR statement or a WITH statement. By selecting VAR and WITH statement lists, you can compare the variables in any permutation.

Summary

The following points summarize how to use the COMPARE procedure to compare SAS data sets:

□ To display a brief report of the differences between data sets, in the PROC COMPARE statement, use the BASE= option to specify the base data set, use the COMPARE= option to specify the comparison data set, and use the BRIEF option to limit the output produced.

□ To restrict the comparison to values of specific variables, use the VAR statement.

□ To compare similar variables that have different names, use the VAR statement and the WITH statement.

□ To compare variables within a single data set, use only the BASE= option in the PROC COMPARE statement; do not include the COMPARE= option. Also, use the VAR statement to specify the base variable or variables and the WITH statement to specify the comparison variable or variables.

SAS Tools

This section summarizes syntax for the statements discussed in this chapter.

PROC COMPARE <*options*>;
compares SAS data sets. The following options in the PROC COMPARE statement are discussed in this chapter:

BASE=	specifies the base data set.
COMPARE=	specifies the comparison data set.
BRIEF	limits procedure output to a value comparison results report.

VAR *variable-list*;
restricts comparisons of the values of one or more variables.

WITH *variable-list*;
specifies one or more comparison variables in the comparison data set if two data sets are used or in the base data set if the comparison is among values in a single data set.

Learning More

To learn more about the following topics, see the *SAS Procedures Guide: Version 6, Third Edition*, Chapter 11, "The COMPARE Procedure":

Default reports
By default, PROC COMPARE produces five reports:

data set summary
> lists the attributes of the data sets being compared.

variables summary
> compares the variables in the two data sets but not the values of the variables.

observation summary
> provides information about observations in the base and comparison data sets.

values comparison summary
> in two parts; part one summarizes the kinds of differences that occur, part two summarizes values of variables that are unequal.

value comparison results
> consists of a table for each pair of matching variables that are unequal at one or more observations.

Additional procedure options
The COMPARE procedure supports a wide variety of options that enable you to do the following:

□ specify data set names including output data sets

□ specify the contents of the output data set

□ control comparisons of data values

□ control the detail of procedure output

□ control the listing of variables and observations.

BY statement
You can use a BY statement with PROC COMPARE to do the following:

□ compare corresponding BY groups

□ compare each BY group in the base data set with the entire comparison data set.

ID statement
You can use an ID statement with PROC COMPARE to match variables in the base data set with corresponding observations in the comparison data set.

Part 6

Creating a Customized SAS® Environment

Chapter 24 Creating Customized Windows

Introduction

When you develop applications for other people to use, you can include customized windows to make your applications interactive. Using customized windows makes it easy to display text and variable values and accept input from the keyboard. You can group related text in one window and display the windows independently of each other. You can also create multiple windows and, by including simple programming statements and error messages, use customized windows to verify data interactively.

Customized windows in base SAS software use the normal flow of the DATA step. Therefore, you do not need any additional software or expertise beyond DATA step programming to create user-friendly interfaces. The customized windows you create in the DATA step can be easily integrated into existing DATA step programming.

Customized windows can be included in applications that run under the SAS
Display Manager System, interactive line mode, or noninteractive mode.
(Customized windows do not work in batch mode because no terminal is
connected to a batch executing process.)

In this chapter
This chapter teaches you how to use the WINDOW statement and the DISPLAY
statement to create customized windows. Specifically, this chapter shows you how
to do the following:

□ create a window that accepts input from the keyboard

□ create groups to display calculated values

□ create multiple windows

□ verify data interactively.

Prerequisites
Before reading this chapter, you should be familiar with the following:

□ the flow of action of the DATA step

□ row (or line) pointer control (#) and column pointer control (@)

□ IF-THEN/ELSE statements

□ sum statements

□ the UPCASE function.

SAS Data Set Example

All the examples in this chapter use the same SAS data set as input. The data set
is named CLOSING.INFO and contains information about real estate closings
performed by a law firm. The data set CLOSING.INFO contains the following
variables:

Variable	Type	Description
FILENMBR	character	number of the file containing the closing information
BUYER	character	buyer of the real estate
SELLER	character	seller of the real estate

The following PROC PRINT step displays the data set CLOSING.INFO:*

```
libname closing 'SAS-data-library';

proc print data=closing.info;
   title 'Real Estate Closing Information';
run;
```

Output 24.1 shows the results.

Output 24.1
Printout of SAS
Data Set
CLOSING.INFO

```
                   Real Estate Closing Information                    1

          OBS     FILENMBR     BUYER        SELLER

           1      9212-01      Sharpe       Keller
           2      9212-02      Dunlap       Nash
           3      9212-03      Wilson       Hendrick
           4      9212-04      Marsalla     Currin
           5      9212-05      Richards     Lee
           6      9212-06      Downey       Turner
           7      9212-07      Upton        Chang
           8      9212-08      Salinski     Winslow
           9      9212-09      Patel        Kramer
```

Creating a Window That Accepts Input

When your applications require users to input data values from the keyboard, you can create customized windows as a part of normal DATA step processing. These customized windows can display text, display variable values, and prompt the user for data.

For example, the law firm wants a real estate application that uses a DATA step to read the closing information file, CLOSING.INFO. In the DATA step, a customized window should display text and variable values from the input data set. The window also should accept as input from the keyboard the names of paralegals who will be assigned to research the legal documents used during real estate closings.

To create a customized window that accepts input from the keyboard, do the following:

□ name the window

□ specify the position and contents of fields

□ protect fields from data entry

□ display the window.

Name the Window

To name a window, use a WINDOW statement within a DATA step. The following statements create a SAS data set named CLOSING.ASIGNMTS. The SET statement

---
* The DATA step that creates CLOSING.INFO is shown in the Appendix.

reads the data set CLOSING.INFO, which was created earlier in the section "SAS Data Set Example." The WINDOW statement defines a window named ASSIGN. The contents of the window are discussed in the next section. The semicolon following the contents specification ends the WINDOW statement.

```
libname closing 'SAS-data-library';

data closing.asignmts;
   set closing.info;
   window assign
         contents of window;
run;
```

When the DATA step finishes executing, the observations in the new data set, CLOSING.ASIGNMTS, will contain variable values from the input data set CLOSING.INFO and variable values that were input from the keyboard by the user.

Specify the Position and Contents of Fields

As a part of customized windows, you can specify fields that contain text or variables. To display fields, you must specify their position and contents. You specify the position of a field using a row (or line) pointer control (#) and a column pointer control (@). For the contents of a field, you can use character strings enclosed in quotes and variables.

For example, the law firm wants five rows displayed in the ASSIGN window. The first row is displayed on row 10 beginning in column 27 and contains a text string that describes the purpose of the window.

```
window assign
      #10 @27 "REAL ESTATE CLOSING ASSIGNMENTS"
```

If you omit the row pointer control in the first field definition of a window, the SAS System uses row 1 of the window. If you omit the row pointer control in a later field definition, the SAS System continues on the row that contains the previous field.

If you omit the column pointer control, the SAS System uses column 1 (the left border of the window). Although you can specify either row or column first, the examples in this chapter show the row pointer control first.

The second, third, and fourth rows of the ASSIGN window are displayed on rows 12, 13, and 14 of the terminal, respectively. Beginning in column 10, each row contains a text field. Beginning in column 25 of each row is a field that contains the name of one of the variables from the data set CLOSING.INFO (either FILENMBR, BUYER, or SELLER).

```
window assign
      #10 @27 "REAL ESTATE CLOSING ASSIGNMENTS"
      #12 @10 "File Number:" @25 filenmbr
      #13 @10 "Buyer's Name:" @25 buyer
      #14 @10 "Seller's Name:" @25 seller
```

The fifth and final row in the ASSIGN window is used for entering data from the keyboard. The field prompts the user to enter the name of a paralegal and contains the name of a character variable, PARALEGL. Notice that the variable PARALEGL is not from the SAS data set CLOSING.INFO. (See "SAS Data Set Example" earlier in this chapter.) Instead, PARALEGL is a new variable created by the current DATA step. PARALEGL receives values when, as a part of executing the DATA step, the ASSIGN window is displayed and the user enters the names of paralegals.

```
window assign
       #10 @27 "REAL ESTATE CLOSING ASSIGNMENTS"
       #12 @10 "File Number:" @25 filenmbr
       #13 @10 "Buyer's Name:" @25 buyer
       #14 @10 "Seller's Name:" @25 seller
       #15 @10 "Enter Paralegal's Name:" @34 paralegl $;
```

Protect Fields from Data Entry

In some windows, you may want to protect certain fields from being overwritten by input from the keyboard. For example, in the ASSIGN window the law firm wants to protect the fields that contain the values of the variables FILENMBR, BUYER, and SELLER. That is, the data entry person should not be able to change the values of these variables by typing over what is displayed in the ASSIGN window.

To protect a field from being overwritten, add the PROTECT= option to the WINDOW statement, as the highlighted portions of the following code illustrate:

```
window assign
       #10 @27 "REAL ESTATE CLOSING ASSIGNMENTS"
       #12 @10 "File Number:" @25 filenmbr protect=yes
       #13 @10 "Buyer's Name:" @25 buyer protect=yes
       #14 @10 "Seller's Name:" @25 seller protect=yes
       #15 @10 "Enter Paralegal's Name:" @34 paralegl $;
```

Use the PROTECT= option only for fields containing variable names; fields containing text are automatically protected. The default specification is PROTECT=NO.

Display the Window

The WINDOW statement in a DATA step only defines windows; it does not display windows. To display a window previously defined, add a DISPLAY statement to the DATA step.

The following DATA step includes all the statements and options discussed so far, including a DISPLAY statement that specifies the ASSIGN window:

```
libname closing 'SAS-data-library';

data closing.asignmts;
   set closing.info;
   window assign
         #10 @27 "REAL ESTATE CLOSING ASSIGNMENTS"
         #12 @10 "File Number:" @25 filenmbr protect=yes
         #13 @10 "Buyer's Name:" @25 buyer protect=yes
         #14 @10 "Seller's Name:" @25 seller protect=yes
         #15 @10 "Enter Paralegal's Name:" @34 paralegl $;
   display assign;
run;
```

Display 24.1 shows the results during the first iteration of the DATA step.

Display 24.1
*First Iteration of
the DATA Step*

```
┌ASSIGN─────────────────────────────────────────────────────────
│ Command ===>




                        REAL ESTATE CLOSING ASSIGNMENTS

          File Number:   9212-01
          Buyer's Name:  Sharpe
          Seller's Name: Keller
          Enter Paralegal's Name: David




                                                                 R
```

A DATA step containing WINDOW and DISPLAY statements follows the normal flow of DATA step processing. For example, a DATA step that displays windows also creates a SAS data set (unless DATA _NULL_ is specified).

In Display 24.1, values of the variables FILENMBR, BUYER, and SELLER from the first observation of the input data set CLOSING.INFO are displayed. (Notice the first file number, 9212-01, is displayed.) Also, the value **David** has been entered from the keyboard and appears in the field containing the variable PARALEGL. When the data entry person presses ENTER or RETURN, the first observation is written to the output data set CLOSING.ASIGNMTS. Then the DATA step begins a new iteration, and the SET statement reads the next observation from the data set CLOSING.INFO.

Each time a window is displayed that contains fields where you can enter values, such as the field containing PARALEGL in this example, you must either enter a value or press ENTER or RETURN at each unprotected field. You cannot skip any fields. While a window is being displayed, you can use commands to view other windows, change the size of the current window, and so on.

Once you display a window, it remains visible until you overlay it with another window or until the end of the DATA step.

Display 24.2 shows the results during the ninth iteration of the DATA step in this example.

Display 24.2
Final Iteration of the DATA Step

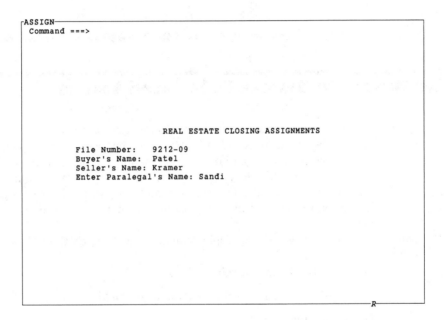

```
┌ASSIGN─────────────────────────────────────────────────────────────┐
│ Command ===>                                                       │
│                                                                    │
│                                                                    │
│                                                                    │
│                                                                    │
│                                                                    │
│                                                                    │
│                         REAL ESTATE CLOSING ASSIGNMENTS            │
│                                                                    │
│             File Number:   9212-09                                 │
│             Buyer's Name:  Patel                                   │
│             Seller's Name: Kramer                                  │
│             Enter Paralegal's Name: Sandi                          │
│                                                                    │
│                                                                  ─R│
└────────────────────────────────────────────────────────────────────┘
```

You can end the execution of a DATA step that displays a window in one of two ways. One, as in any DATA step, you can allow a step that displays a window to continue to execute until the final observation read by a SET, MERGE, UPDATE, or INPUT statement has been processed or until a STOP or ABORT statement is executed. Two, you can end execution of a DATA step that displays a window by issuing the END command on the command line of the window.

In Display 24.2, eight of the nine closings have been assigned and the DATA step is in the ninth iteration. (Notice the ninth file number, 9212-09, is displayed.) So far, the paralegal David has three assignments, Nancy has three, and Sandi has two. Also, Sandi's name has been typed in, but not yet entered, for the final observation. When the data entry person presses ENTER or RETURN, the final observation is output to the data set, CLOSING.ASIGNMTS, and the DATA step ends. At that point, the data set CLOSING.ASIGNMTS contains nine observations.

The following PROC PRINT step displays the data set CLOSING.ASIGNMTS:

```
libname closing 'SAS-data-library';

proc print data=closing.asignmts;
   title 'Real Estate Closing Assignments';
run;
```

Output 24.2 shows the results.

Output 24.2
Printout of SAS
Data Set
CLOSING.ASIGNMTS

```
                        Real Estate Closing Assignments                    1

        OBS    FILENMBR    BUYER       SELLER      PARALEGL

         1     9212-01     Sharpe      Keller      David
         2     9212-02     Dunlap      Nash        David
         3     9212-03     Wilson      Hendrick    David
         4     9212-04     Marsalla    Currin      Nancy
         5     9212-05     Richards    Lee         Nancy
         6     9212-06     Downey      Turner      Nancy
         7     9212-07     Upton       Chang       Sandi
         8     9212-08     Salinski    Winslow     Sandi
         9     9212-09     Patel       Kramer      Sandi
```

Creating Groups to Display Calculated Values

Within a single window definition, you can specify various groups of related fields and display them independently. Grouping enables you to separate fields within a window according to the kind of information the fields provide. For example, the law firm can modify the ASSIGN window to include two groups of related fields. The first group can display running totals as paralegals are assigned to closings. The second group can display closing information and prompt the user to enter data.

To create groups to display calculated values, do the following:

□ name the groups of related fields

□ specify the position and contents of the fields

□ display the groups

□ increment the counter variables

□ protect the groups from data entry.

Name the Groups of Related Fields

To name groups of related fields, use the GROUP= option in the WINDOW statement. The GROUP= name must be a valid SAS name. The complete name of a group is its *window.group* specification.

The following WINDOW statement contains two GROUP= option specifications. The first group is named ASSIGN.COUNTER and contains fields that display running totals of the closing assignments. The second group is named ASSIGN.ENTRY and contains the fields that display the closing information and enable data entry. Also notice the semicolon that ends the single WINDOW statement. Both group definitions are contained within the one WINDOW statement:

```
libname closing 'SAS-data-library';

data closing.asignmts;
   set closing.info;
   window assign
         group=counter
               contents of assign.counter
         group=entry
               contents of assign.entry;
```

Specify the Position and Contents of Fields

To define the position of fields, use row pointer controls and column pointer controls. For the contents of a field, you can use character strings enclosed in quotes or variables.

The following group specification uses pointer controls, text strings in quotes, and variable names to specify the position and contents of the ASSIGN.COUNTER group. ASSIGN.COUNTER contains four rows of fields that appear on rows 1, 3, 4, and 5 of the ASSIGN window. The first row contains text that describes the purpose of the group. It is displayed on row 1 beginning in column 27. The next three rows contain text fields that display the name of a paralegal, either David, Nancy, or Sandi, and variable values, which show running totals of the assignments for each paralegal.

Notice the variables D, N, and S. They are created in the current DATA step and serve as counter variables; that is, their values will be the number of real estate closings assigned to a given paralegal at any given iteration of the DATA step (see "Increment the Counter Variables" later in this example).

```
group=counter
      #1 @27 "CLOSINGS PER PARALEGAL"
      #3 @10 "David has" @21 d
      #4 @10 "Nancy has" @21 n
      #5 @10 "Sandi has" @21 s
```

The second group of related fields is the ASSIGN.ENTRY group. ASSIGN.ENTRY contains the same information as the ASSIGN window, which was defined earlier (see "Creating a Window That Accepts Input"), with one exception: the header in row 10 has been abbreviated and moved to column position 32. All the other fields remain the same as in the ASSIGN window.

```
group=entry                            /* similar to ASSIGN window */
    #10 ə32 "ASSIGNMENTS"
    #12 ə10 "File Number:" ə25 filenmbr protect=yes
    #13 ə10 "Buyer's Name:" ə25 buyer protect=yes
    #14 ə10 "Seller's Name:" ə25 seller protect=yes
    #15 ə10 "Enter Paralegal's Name:" ə34 paralegl $;
```

Display the Groups

To display a group, use the *window.group* name in a DISPLAY statement. The following DISPLAY statements display COUNTER and ENTRY groups of the ASSIGN window:

```
display assign.counter;
display assign.entry;
```

Increment the Counter Variables

As discussed earlier, fields in the ASSIGN.COUNTER group include three variables created in the current DATA step: D, N, and S. These three variables serve as counter variables; that is, their values will be the number of real estate closings assigned to a given paralegal.

The value of D, N, or S is based on the value of the variable PARALEGL at any given iteration of the DATA step. The value of the variable PARALEGL is input from the keyboard in response to the prompt in the ASSIGN.ENTRY group.

To increment the counter variables, use IF-THEN/ELSE statements that test the value of PARALEGL and sum statements that increment the counter variables, as the following lines of code illustrate:

```
display assign.counter;
display assign.entry;
if paralegl="David" then d+1;
else if paralegl="Nancy" then n+1;
else if paralegl="Sandi" then s+1;
```

Protect Groups from Data Entry

When a window contains groups of related fields that are designed only to display information, you may want to protect those groups from being overwritten by input from the keyboard. For example, the ASSIGN.COUNTER group only displays totals; it is not designed for input by the user.

To protect an entire group from data entry, you can either add the PROTECT=YES option following each field, or you can simply add the NOINPUT option to the DISPLAY statement for the group.

For example, the following DATA step contains all the statements and options discussed so far, including the NOINPUT option in the DISPLAY statement to protect the entire ASSIGN.COUNTER group:

```
libname closing 'SAS-data-library';

data closing.asignmts;
   set closing.info;
   drop d n s;
   window assign
         group=counter
               #1 a27 "CLOSINGS PER PARALEGAL"
               #3 a10 "David has" a21 d
               #4 a10 "Nancy has" a21 n
               #5 a10 "Sandi has" a21 s
         group=entry                    /* similar to ASSIGN window */
               #10 a32 "ASSIGNMENTS"
               #12 a10 "File Number:" a25 filenmbr protect=yes
               #13 a10 "Buyer's Name:" a25 buyer protect=yes
               #14 a10 "Seller's Name:" a25 seller protect=yes
               #15 a10 "Enter Paralegal's Name:" a34 paralegl $;
   display assign.counter noinput;
   display assign.entry;
   if paralegl="David" then d+1;
   else if paralegl="Nancy" then n+1;
   else if paralegl="Sandi" then s+1;
run;
```

Display 24.3 shows the results during the fourth iteration of the DATA step.

Display 24.3
Creating Groups to Display Calculated Values

```
┌ASSIGN───────────────────────────────────────────────────────────┐
│ Command ===>                                                      │
│                            CLOSINGS PER PARALEGAL                 │
│                                                                   │
│         David has  3                                              │
│         Nancy has  0                                              │
│         Sandi has  0                                              │
│                                                                   │
│                                                                   │
│                                ASSIGNMENTS                        │
│                                                                   │
│         File Number:   9212-04                                    │
│         Buyer's Name:  Marsalla                                   │
│         Seller's Name: Currin                                     │
│         Enter Paralegal's Name: Nancy                             │
│                                                                   │
│                                                                   │
│                                                                   │
│                                                                   │
│                                                                 R │
└───────────────────────────────────────────────────────────────── ┘
```

If you use the NOINPUT option in all DISPLAY statements in the DATA step, you must include a STOP statement to stop processing the DATA step.

Creating Multiple Windows

For some applications, you may want to create two or more separate windows that contain related information. When you have two or more windows, you can make your applications more interactive by displaying the windows conditionally based on data input by the user.

To display multiple windows, do the following:

□ name the windows

□ specify the sizes of the windows

□ specify the position and contents of fields

□ display the windows.

In the following example, the real estate application is modified to display two separate windows instead of one window with two groups.

Name the Windows

To name multiple windows, use separate WINDOW statements for each one. For example, the following WINDOW statements define two windows, TOTALS and PROMPT. Notice that semicolons appear at the end of each WINDOW statement.

```
libname closing 'SAS-data-library';

data closing.asignmts;
   set closing.info;
   drop d n s;
   window totals
         contents of totals window;
   window prompt
         contents of prompt window;
```

Specify the Sizes of the Windows

The size of a window is defined by the number of rows and columns it contains. You define rows with two options in the WINDOW statement: the ROWS= option, which specifies the number of rows in the window (excluding borders), and the IROW= option, which specifies the initial row within the display at which the window is displayed. (You define columns with the COLUMNS= option and the ICOLUMN= option. For details, see the WINDOW statement in *SAS Language: Reference, Version 6, First Edition,* Chapter 9, "SAS Language Statements."

You can use one or more of the row and column options to control the size of windows. For example, the following options in the WINDOW statements define the size of the two windows, TOTALS and PROMPT. The first two options, IROW=1 and ROWS=11, apply to the window TOTALS. By default, TOTALS uses all available columns. The third option, IROW=12, begins the PROMPT window on row 12. By default, the PROMPT window uses all remaining rows and all available columns:

```
data closing.asignmts;
   set closing.info;
   drop d n s;
   window totals irow=1 rows=11
         contents of totals window;
   window prompt irow=12
         contents of prompt window;
```

Specify the Position and Contents of Fields

As shown in the previous examples, a field is identified by its position and contents. The position of a field in a window is its beginning row and column. The contents of a field can be character strings or variables.

The following lines of code specify the positions and contents of fields in the TOTALS window and the PROMPT window. The TOTALS window contains four fields, which are similar to the four fields in the ASSIGN.COUNTER group defined in the previous example. The PROMPT window contains five fields, which are similar to the five fields in the ASSIGN.ENTRY group also defined in the previous example.

Also, as in the previous example, row and column pointer controls are used to specify the placement of the fields within the window. However, notice that the row pointer controls now refer to fields within separate windows: rows 1, 3, 4, and 5 in the TOTALS window and rows 1, 3, 4, 5, and 6 in the PROMPT window.

```
libname closing 'SAS-data-library';

data closing.asignmts;
   set closing.info;
   drop d n s;

      /* similar to ASSIGN.COUNTER group   */
   window totals irow=1 rows=11
            #1 @27 "CLOSINGS PER PARALEGAL"
            #3 @10 "David has" @21 d
            #4 @10 "Nancy has" @21 n
            #5 @10 "Sandi has" @21 s;
```

```
                       /* similar to ASSIGN.ENTRY group */
              window prompt irow=12
                   #1 @32 "ASSIGNMENTS"
                   #3 @10 "File Number:" @25 filenmbr protect=yes
                   #4 @10 "Buyer's Name:" @25 buyer protect=yes
                   #5 @10 "Seller's Name:" @25 seller protect=yes
                   #6 @10 "Enter Paralegal's Name:" @34 paralegl $;
```

Display the Windows

Use a separate DISPLAY statement to specify each window you want to display. Note that the position of the DISPLAY statements within the DATA step determines when the windows appear.

The following DATA step contains all the statements and options discussed so far including two DISPLAY statements. Notice the first DISPLAY statement; it displays the TOTALS window and includes the NOINPUT option to protect all fields in the window from input by the user:

```
   libname closing 'SAS-data-library';

data closing.asignmts;
   set closing.info;
   drop d n s;

       /* similar to ASSIGN.COUNTER group   */
   window totals irow=1 rows=11
          #1 @27 "CLOSINGS PER PARALEGAL"
          #3 @10 "David has" @21 d
          #4 @10 "Nancy has" @21 n
          #5 @10 "Sandi has" @21 s;

       /* similar to ASSIGN.ENTRY group */
   window prompt irow=12
          #1 @32 "ASSIGNMENTS"
          #3 @10 "File Number:" @25 filenmbr protect=yes
          #4 @10 "Buyer's Name:" @25 buyer protect=yes
          #5 @10 "Seller's Name:" @25 seller protect=yes
          #6 @10 "Enter Paralegal's Name:" @34 paralegl $;
   display totals noinput;
   display prompt;
   if paralegl="David" then d+1;
   else if paralegl="Nancy" then n+1;
   else if paralegl="Sandi" then s+1;
run;
```

Display 24.4 shows the results during the sixth iteration of the DATA step.

Display 24.4
Creating Two
Windows

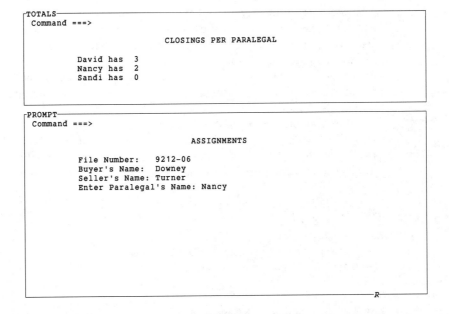

```
┌TOTALS────────────────────────────────────────────────────────────┐
│  Command ===>                                                      │
│                          CLOSINGS PER PARALEGAL                    │
│                                                                    │
│          David has  3                                              │
│          Nancy has  2                                              │
│          Sandi has  0                                              │
│                                                                    │
│                                                                    │
└────────────────────────────────────────────────────────────────────┘
┌PROMPT─────────────────────────────────────────────────────────────┐
│  Command ===>                                                      │
│                              ASSIGNMENTS                           │
│                                                                    │
│          File Number:   9212-06                                    │
│          Buyer's Name:  Downey                                     │
│          Seller's Name: Turner                                     │
│          Enter Paralegal's Name: Nancy                             │
│                                                                    │
│                                                                    │
│                                                                    │
│                                                                  R─┘
```

Verifying Data Interactively

When you combine aspects of DATA step programming with the creation of customized windows, you can add a great deal of interactivity to your applications including the ability to verify data interactively. Verifying data interactively enables you to detect data entry errors immediately after the errors are entered and notify the user before the errors become part of a data set.

For example, the law firm wants the real estate application to check the names of the paralegals as they are entered from the keyboard. Only three names are allowed: David, Nancy, or Sandi. Although mixed case letters should be accepted, the names must be spelled correctly. If the user enters erroneous data, such as `Sandy` instead of `Sandi`, the application should send an error message and enable the user to try again.

To modify the previous DATA step to include features that verify data interactively, do the following:

□ allow for mixed case input

□ add an error message and a conditional statement to display the message

□ enable re-entering of data.

Allow for Mixed Case Input

The SAS System distinguishes between uppercase and lowercase letters in comparisons. For example, the values `David` and `DAVID` are not equivalent. However, when prompted to enter a character string, a user can enter the string in numerous ways; all uppercase letters, all lowercase, or some combination of uppercase and lowercase. To allow for all combinations of input, use the UPCASE function to produce an uppercase value; then make the comparison between two uppercase values.

For example, the UPCASE function has been added here to the IF-THEN/ELSE statements that increment the counter variables D, N, and S. As a result, when the user enters the name of a paralegal, the value is converted to uppercase and compared with the values `DAVID`, `NANCY`, and `SANDI`.

```
display totals noinput;
display prompt;
if upcase(paralegl)="DAVID" then d+1;
else if upcase(paralegl)="NANCY" then n+1;
else if upcase(paralegl)="SANDI" then s+1;
```

Add an Error Message

When a WINDOW statement executes, the SAS System creates an automatic variable named _MSG_. The variable _MSG_ is a character variable with a length of 80; its value is set to blank after each execution of a DISPLAY statement. You can use the variable _MSG_ to display error messages by equating _MSG_ with a character string enclosed in quotes and by adding conditional statements to display the message.

The following ELSE statement and DO group have been added to the existing IF-THEN/ELSE statements. If the value of the variable PARALEGL is entered incorrectly from the keyboard, the final ELSE statement enables the DO statement to execute and display the error message. The END statement ends the DO group:

```
if upcase(paralegl)="DAVID" then d+1;
else if upcase(paralegl)="NANCY" then n+1;
else if upcase(paralegl)="SANDI" then s+1;
else do;
    _msg_="INVALID NAME. ENTER David, Nancy, OR Sandi";
end;
```

Enable Re-entering of Data

When you develop applications that verify data interactively, you can add program statements that enable the user to re-enter data if a mistake is made. For example, if the user of the real estate application misspells the name of a paralegal during data entry, the DATA step should enable the user to try again as many times as necessary.

There are many ways to program iterative processing; however, one simple but effective way is to add a GOTO statement and a statement label. The GOTO statement should appear after the data entry error is detected. The GOTO statement names the statement label and tells the SAS System to jump immediately to the label and begin executing statements from that point.

The statement label should appear at the beginning of the data entry structure. A colon following the statement label identifies it as the target of the GOTO statement. Both the GOTO statement and the statement label must appear within the same DATA step.

The following example shows the entire DATA step needed to produce two windows, PROMPT and TOTALS, and to verify the data entry interactively. The label GETINFO appears before the PROMPT window, and the statement GOTO GETINFO appears inside the ELSE-DO structure.

```
libname closing 'SAS-data-library';

data closing.asignmts;
   set closing.info;
   drop d n s;
   window totals irow=1 rows=11
         #1 a27 "CLOSINGS PER PARALEGAL"
         #3 a10 "David has" a21 d
         #4 a10 "Nancy has" a21 n
         #5 a10 "Sandi has" a21 s;
   window prompt irow=12
         #1 a32 "ASSIGNMENTS"
         #3 a10 "File Number:" a25 filenmbr protect=yes
         #4 a10 "Buyer's Name:" a25 buyer protect=yes
         #5 a10 "Seller's Name:" a25 seller protect=yes
         #6 a10 "Enter Paralegal's Name:" a34 paralegl $;
   display totals noinput;
   getinfo:
   display prompt;
   if upcase(paralegl)="DAVID" then d+1;
   else if upcase(paralegl)="NANCY" then n+1;
   else if upcase(paralegl)="SANDI" then s+1;
   else do;
         _msg_="ERROR: INVALID NAME. ENTER David, Nancy, OR Sandi";
         goto getinfo;
   end;
run;
```

Display 24.5 shows the results during the seventh iteration of the DATA step.

Display 24.5
Verifying Data
Interactively

```
┌TOTALS────────────────────────────────────────────────────────────┐
│ Command ===>                                                       │
│                                                                    │
│                        CLOSINGS PER PARALEGAL                      │
│                                                                    │
│          David has  3                                              │
│          Nancy has  3                                              │
│          Sandi has  0                                              │
│                                                                    │
│                                                                    │
└────────────────────────────────────────────────────────────────────
┌PROMPT────────────────────────────────────────────────────────────┐
│ Command ===>                                                       │
│ ERROR: INVALID NAME. ENTER David, Nancy, OR Sandi                  │
│                        ASSIGNMENTS                                 │
│                                                                    │
│          File Number:   9212-07                                    │
│          Buyer's Name:  Upton                                      │
│          Seller's Name: Chang                                      │
│          Enter Paralegal's Name: Sandy                             │
│                                                                    │
│                                                                    │
│                                                                    │
│                                                                    │
│                                                                    │
│                                                                    │
│                                                                  ─R│
└────────────────────────────────────────────────────────────────────
```

Notice the PROMPT window in Display 24.5 contains the error message that appears under the command line and reads, "ERROR: INVALID NAME. ENTER David, Nancy, OR Sandi." The error message resulted when the data entry person incorrectly entered the name `Sandy` instead of `Sandi` during the seventh iteration of the DATA step. In the TOTALS window you can see that six closing assignments have been made, three to `David` and three to `Nancy`. The seventh assignment for file number 9212-07 is displayed pending re-entry of the paralegal's name.

Summary

The following points summarize how to use the WINDOW and DISPLAY statements to create customized windows:

□ To create a window that accepts input, name the window using the WINDOW statement, specify the postion and contents of fields using row and column pointer controls with text and variable values, protect non-input fields from data entry using the PROTECT= option, and display the window using the DISPLAY statement.

□ To specify groups of related fields and display them independently, name the groups using the GROUP= option in the WINDOW statement; define the position of the fields using row and column pointer controls; display the groups using DISPLAY statements; and, protect groups from data entry by adding the PROTECT=YES option after each field or add the NOINPUT option to the DISPLAY statement for the group.

□ To create multiple windows, name the windows using the WINDOW statement; specify the sizes of the windows using the ROWS= option, the IROW= option, the COLUMNS= option, and the ICOLUMN= option; specify the postion and contents of fields using row and column pointer controls with text and variable values; and display the windows using the DISPLAY statement.

□ To verify data interactively, allow for mixed case input using the UPCASE function, add an error message using the DO statement and the automatic variable _MSG_, and enable data re-entry using the GOTO statement and statement label.

SAS Tools

This section summarizes syntax for the statements, function, and automatic variable discussed in this chapter.

Statements

DISPLAY *window<.group>* <NOINPUT>;
   displays a window defined with the WINDOW statement. *Window* names a window. *Window.group* names a group of fields within a window. NOINPUT protects all unprotected fields in a window or group from keyboard input.

DO-END
   specifies a group of statements to be executed as a unit.

GOTO *statement-label*
   moves program execution immediately to *statement-label*.

IF-THEN/ELSE
   executes a SAS statement for observations meeting specific conditions.

Variable+expression;
   adds the result of an expression to a counter variable.

WINDOW *window* <*window-options*> *field-definitions*;
   defines customized windows. *Window* names a window. The following *window-options* are discussed:

PROTECT=	protects fields from input
GROUP=	defines groups of related fields
ROWS=	specifies the number of rows in a window
IROW=	specifies the initial row of a window
COLUMNS=	specifies the number of columns in a window
ICOLUMN=	specifies the initial column of a window.

Field-definitions use row pointer control (#) and column pointer control (@) to specify the position of text and variable values.

Function

UPCASE
>   converts all letters in an argument to uppercase.

Automatic variable

MSG
>   contains a message you specify to be displayed in the message area of a window.

Learning More

This section provides references for learning more about topics presented in this chapter.

The %WINDOW and %DISPLAY statements
The %WINDOW and %DISPLAY statements in the SAS macro language create and display windows controlled by the macro facility. For more information, see *SAS Guide to Macro Processing: Version 6, Second Edition*, Chapter 3, "Macro Program Statements."

The automatic variable _CMD_
The WINDOW statement also creates an automatic variable named _CMD_, which contains the last command from the current window's command line that was not processed by display manager. For details, see the WINDOW statement in *SAS Language: Reference*, Chapter 9, "SAS Language Statements."

The WINDOW statement
In addition to PROTECT=, you can specify other characteristics of fields. Characteristics include the color of a field, whether a field can be left blank, and whether the contents of a field persists from one iteration of the DATA step to the next. For details on these and other characteristics of fields, see the WINDOW statement in *SAS Language: Reference*, Chapter 9, "SAS Language Statements."

The DISPLAY statement
The DISPLAY statement also includes a BLANK option that clears a window and a BELL option that produces a sound when a window is displayed (if your terminal has a speaker). For more information, see the DISPLAY statement in *SAS Language: Reference*, Chapter 9, "SAS Language Statements."

Chapter **25** Customizing a SAS® Environment for Individual Users

Introduction

As an individual user of SAS software, you are probably part of a community of other SAS users. Starting with shipment of SAS software from SAS Institute Inc., many of the decisions concerning your computing environment are made for you based on what users and developers have found to be most useful and efficient. Once SAS software arrives at your site, however, you have the tools to take a powerful software package and customize it to best serve your particular needs. If you are a SAS Software Representative, you can customize it during installation for all the users at your site. However, whether you are a SAS Software Representative or an individual user, you can customize it as necessary to meet your individual needs.

In this chapter

This chapter shows you how to customize a SAS environment for individual users, either for yourself or for another SAS software user. Specifically, this chapter shows you how to

□ customize a SAS programming environment

□ tailor the SAS WORK library to individual needs

□ tailor the SASUSER library to individual needs

□ customize output

□ use the SAS sample library.

How you customize your SAS environment is host-specific. Note that this chapter stops short of providing host-specific instructions. Where the same functionality is available across host operating systems but the specific details vary by system, only the functionality is described. Note that the syntax shown in this chapter may be host-specific in some cases. It is generally consistent with the syntax of your host operating system but may include additional or alternate punctuation. To use the documentation in this chapter to meet your objectives, you should use it in conjunction with the SAS companion provided by SAS Institute for your host operating system.

Prerequisites

In addition to having access to a companion for your host operating system, you should be familiar with the following features of the SAS System:

□ DATA step processing

□ the SAS Display Manager System

□ SAS system options

□ generating output.

Understanding Initialization and Invocation

Much of this chapter focuses on invocation and initialization. Therefore, it is important that you understand the distinction between the two. *SAS invocation* is the process of calling or starting up the SAS System by an individual user who executes the SAS command. Invoking the SAS System begins initialization. *SAS initialization* is setting global characteristics that must be in place at startup for a SAS programming environment. The SAS System performs initialization by setting certain SAS system options called initialization options. These initialization options control setting up the SAS System as well as hardware and software interfacing. Although other kinds of options that also have global impact are available, the difference between other global options and initialization options is that other global options do not have to be specified at startup. Here are some of the default settings specified during initialization.*

□ the location for output outside of display manager mode

□ the location of the SASHELP library

□ the listing or nonlisting of SAS system option settings in the configuration file.

Note that invocation always precedes initialization. For example, consider the following SAS command under VMS:

```
sas/batch/verbose
```

First, the SAS command is used to invoke or call the SAS System. Then the SAS System initializes itself, first setting the options as specified in a default configuration file and, on some operating systems, additionally in any other configuration files that are defined. Second, it uses the specifications in the SAS command, which in this case are BATCH and VERBOSE.**

Customizing a SAS Programming Environment

As an individual user, you can customize your SAS programming environment by:

□ using your user configuration file to set SAS system options at initialization

□ setting SAS system options by entering them directly in the SAS command at invocation

□ using your autoexec file to execute SAS statements immediately after initialization.

---

* This chapter discusses many of the tasks accomplished during initialization. In addition, Table 25.1 provides a list of initialization options.

** After using the settings in the SAS command, the SAS System uses the specifications from any autoexec files that are defined, although this is not considered part of the initialization phase. Initialization options cannot be specified in an autoexec file.

Note that initialization options cannot be set in an autoexec file; they can be set only directly in the SAS command or in a configuration file. (See Table 25.1 for a list of portable initialization options.) If you specify the same SAS system option in the SAS command that you have specified in the configuration file but the settings differ from one place to another, the options are concatenated, with the setting in the SAS command overriding the setting in the configuration file. If you specify the same system option in the SAS command that you have specified in the autoexec file but the settings differ from one place to another, the setting in the SAS command is overridden by the setting in the autoexec file. Figure 25.1 shows the order in which the SAS System searches for option settings. Figure 25.2 shows the subsequent order of precedence.

Figure 25.1
SAS System Options—Order of Search

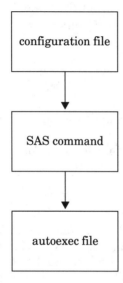

Figure 25.2
SAS System Options—Order of Precedence

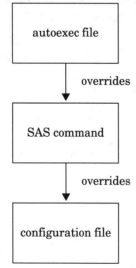

The following sections show you how to use these methods to customize your programming environment.

Setting SAS System Options in a Configuration File

If you want to set SAS system options when you invoke the SAS System, you can keep them in a special file called a configuration file. A configuration file contains SAS system options that are set automatically at initialization. Among other things, this file may identify files that are used by your session and determine default parameters. Although you can also set SAS system options during initialization by entering them directly in the SAS command, using a configuration file is more convenient if you have a number of options to set, especially if you are unlikely to change their settings often.

Note that it is possible for the SAS System to use three kinds of configuration files:

□ a system configuration file, which can be used to customize the SAS environment for a group of users, usually for an entire site

□ a user configuration file, which you can use as an individual user to customize your own working environment.

□ a group configuration file, which can be used to customize the SAS environment for a group of users, usually for a subgroup at a site.

The presence and contents of these configuration files depends not only on the host operating system but on the site. Most sites, but not all, have both system configuration files and user configuration files. Fewer sites have group configuration files. Note that the settings in a user configuration file override the settings in a system configuration file.

In addition to these variations among operating systems and sites, you can create multiple configuration files and use each for a specific type of task.

Create a Customized Configuration File

To customize your SAS session automatically at initialization, create a customized configuration file by writing SAS system options to an operating system file (for example, with a text editor or by using a PUT statement in DATA step processing) in the same form as you would use in the OPTIONS operand in the SAS command on your operating system. Specify one or more options per line. For example, under MVS, a configuration file could appear as follows:

```
nostimer linesize=76 pagesize=50 nomemrpt
nodate dms work=work sasuser=sasuser
nooplist
nonews
```

Note: No embedded blanks are allowed in the options specifications. You can use any SAS system option in this file except the CONFIG= option, which specifies the configuration file. If you include it in your configuration file, the SAS System ignores it, providing no warning or error message.

Activate a Configuration File

To specify the operating system file that contains the configuration options, use the SAS system option CONFIG= at invocation in the SAS command. Note that it is only at invocation that you can specify this option. The settings you put into effect remain in effect for the duration of your session unless overridden by options set in an autoexec file, in an OPTIONS statement, or in the OPTIONS window.

Setting SAS System Options in the SAS Command

When you invoke the SAS System, you can specify SAS system options directly in the SAS command. These option settings take effect immediately and are in effect for the duration of your SAS session unless they are overridden by option settings in an autoexec file, in an OPTIONS statement of a SAS program, or in the OPTIONS window of display manager.

The following examples show how options are specified under different host operating systems. Here, the DMS option is used, which specifies that the SAS Display Manager System is to be used for a session. How you specify options varies by operating system and method of operation. For an interactive invocation under CMS, specify

```
sas (dms
```

Under VMS and AOS/VS, specify

```
sas/dms
```

Under MVS, specify

```
sas options('dms')
```

Under OS/2, PRIMOS, and UNIX, specify

```
sas -dms
```

Issuing SAS Statements in an Autoexec File

If you have SAS statements that you want to execute immediately after the SAS System has fully initialized and before other SAS input source statements have been processed, you may want to store them in an autoexec file. Using an autoexec file makes customizing your SAS session more convenient in much the same way that using a configuration file does. The autoexec file is one of only two ways to execute SAS program statements before statements from the SYSIN file. (Note that an autoexec file can contain only SAS statements.) Setting the SAS system option INITSTMT= allows you to specify a SAS statement to be executed after SAS statements in the autoexec file and before SAS statements from the SYSIN file.

Create an Autoexec File

To create an autoexec file, write SAS statements to an operating system file (for example, with a text editor or by using a PUT statement in DATA step processing) in the same form as you would use in the PROGRAM EDITOR window of display manager or in a batch file on your operating system. Note that the SAS statements in an autoexec file can include SAS system options. Unlike the SAS statements in a configuration file, they must be part of a valid SAS statement. In the following MVS example, the autoexec file includes an OPTIONS statement, a LIBNAME statement, a FILENAME statement, and a DM statement.

```
options pagesize=50 linesize=72;
libname mydata 'SAS-data-library';
filename myfile 'input-file';
dm notepad 'zoom; nums on';
```

Putting a DM statement in your autoexec file is especially useful because it allows you to submit SAS display manager or text editor commands as one of a series of SAS statements.

Note: Initialization options cannot be specified in an OPTIONS statement and thus cannot be used in an autoexec file.

Activate the Autoexec File

To specify the name of your operating system file, use the SAS system option AUTOEXEC=. Note that you can specify this option at invocation listed directly in the SAS command, in a configuration file, or by using the system default.

By default, SAS statements submitted from an autoexec file are not displayed in the SAS log. To tell the SAS System to write the source lines from your autoexec file to the SAS log, use the ECHOAUTO option, either in the SAS command or in the configuration file. To disable the option, use the NOECHOAUTO option, either in the SAS command or in the configuration file.

Choosing SAS System Options to Customize Initialization

In addition to the options described earlier in this chapter, the SAS System has other options that control SAS System initialization and that allow you to make choices about your hardware and software interfacing. Table 25.1 shows the initialization options that work on all host operating systems. In addition, your host operating system may have host-specific initialization options. Consult your SAS companion for details.

Table 25.1
Initialization
Options

Option	Description
ALTLOG=	specifies a destination to which a copy of the SAS log is written.
ALTPRINT=	specifies a destination to which a copy of procedure output is written.
AUTOEXEC=	specifies the autoexec file. The autoexec file is a file containing SAS statements that are executed automatically whenever the SAS System is invoked.
BATCH	specifies whether the batch set of SAS system option default values is in effect when the SAS System executes.
CONFIG=	specifies the configuration file. The configuration file contains SAS system options that are executed automatically after the SAS System is invoked. The SAS System usually supplies a default configuration file, but you can create your own configuration file and store it in a location of your choice. The name of the configuration file is host-specific.
DMR	invokes a remote SAS session on a host computer in order to run SAS/CONNECT software.
DMS	specifies whether the SAS Display Manager System is to be active in a SAS session.
ECHOAUTO	echoes autoexec input to the SAS log.
INITSTMT=	specifies a SAS statement or statements to be executed before any SAS statements from the SYSIN file and after any statements in the autoexec file.
LOG=	specifies a destination to which the SAS log is written when executing SAS programs in modes other than display manager.
NEWS=	specifies a file that contains messages to be written to the SAS log. Typically, the file contains information for users such as news items about the system.
PRINT=	specifies the destination to which SAS output is written when executing SAS programs in modes other than display manager.
REMOTE=	specifies the kind of communications device used for SAS/CONNECT software.
SASHELP=	specifies the SASHELP library, which is where help files are stored.
SASMSG=	specifies the library that contains SAS messages.
SASUSER=	specifies the SASUSER library, which contains a user's profile catalog. The library and catalog are created automatically by the SAS System; you do not have to create them explicitly.

(continued)

	Option	Description
Table 25.1 *(continued)*	SETINIT	allows alteration of site license information.
	SITEINFO=	specifies a file that contains site-specific information. If the SITEINFO command is issued within display manager and the SITEINFO system option is specified, site-specific information is displayed in the SITEINFO window.
	SYSIN=	specifies a file containing a SAS program. This option is applicable only when you are processing noninteractively.
	TERMINAL	specifies whether a terminal is attached at SAS invocation. The SAS System defaults to the appropriate setting for the TERMINAL system option based on whether the session is invoked in the foreground or background.
	VERBOSE	writes the settings of all SAS system options in the configuration file. Some hosts may list additional information such as the name of the configuration file.
	WORK=	specifies the SAS WORK data library.
	WORKINIT	controls whether the SAS WORK data library is initialized at SAS System invocation.

Tailoring the SAS WORK Data Library to Individual Needs

The SAS WORK data library is an operating system location the SAS System creates by default at the beginning of a SAS session or SAS job; without it, the SAS System will not run. The WORK library is temporary by default. Some host operating systems optionally allow the WORK library to be routed to memory rather than to a temporary disk. On most operating systems, both the SAS system options WORKTERM and WORKINIT are in effect. The WORKTERM option specifies that files from the current WORK data library are to be cleared at the end of the current SAS session. The WORKINIT option specifies that files from the current WORK library are to be cleared at invocation.* Use the NOWORKTERM option to specify that files are not to be erased from the current SAS WORK data library. Use the NOWORKINIT option to prevent the SAS WORK library from being cleared at invocation. To access a data set in the WORK library, you can choose between two sets of statements, one using a one-level name and one using a two-level name. The following example illustrates that the data set TOPICS can be referred to as TOPICS or WORK.TOPICS:

```
proc print data=topics;
run;

proc print data=work.topics;
run;
```

---

* On some operating systems, alias names with less than 8 bytes are required.

The SAS WORK data library can be made permanent by routing it to an alternate permanent location with the USER= option. Once the USER library is assigned, it becomes the default location of files specified with a one-level name.

The WORK data library contains data sets as well as some utility files created by SAS procedures such as PROC TABULATE and PROC SORT. It also contains catalogs for macros and macro variables.

Handling Storage Space in the WORK Library

Depending on the operating system you are using, storage in a SAS data library is either a logical concept or both a logical and physical concept. On directory-based systems where the library is strictly a logical concept, you can't tell the SAS System how much space to assign the WORK library. If you need more space on these systems, you can move the WORK library to another disk that has more disk space available. On operating systems that implement a SAS data library both physically and logically, you can choose one of three ways to compensate for lack of storage:

□ increase the size of the WORK library by designating a larger, alternate file or disk

□ delete the files you don't need in the WORK library to make room for others

□ move the files that are part of the WORK library to a different library.

First, you can increase the size of your WORK library by designating a larger, alternate file or disk at invocation either in the SAS command or as part of the configuration file. Use one of two methods:

□ Use the SAS system option WORK= to assign a valid alternate library specification.

□ Use the SAS system option USER= to specify the name of the default SAS data library. Note that by default no value is assigned to USER. Once you have specified this option, you can use a one-level name to reference SAS files in another SAS data library in SAS statements.

Second, to conserve space by deleting SAS files that you no longer need, use the DATASETS procedure with the DELETE statement. For example, in the following program, the file TOPICS is deleted:

```
proc datasets library=work;
   delete topics;
run;
```

Third, you can move SAS files from the WORK library to another data library, making the new library the size you need it to be. Use a permanent or temporary location for the library and store it on disk or on tape. Use a two-level name for the SAS data set and a LIBNAME statement to associate a libref with the SAS data library.

Storing SAS Statements in the WORK Library for Later Use

If you want to reuse SAS statements that you are processing in your current session, or just allow for the possibility of doing so, use the SAS system option SPOOL to tell the SAS System to write any SAS statements automatically from your current session to a utility file in the WORK library. After you have enabled the SPOOL option, you can use the %INCLUDE statement to resubmit some or all of the SAS statements or the %LIST statement to redisplay some or all of the SAS statements. For example, to resubmit lines 1 through 20, use the %INCLUDE statement with one of the following two conventions:

```
%inc 1:20;
%inc 1-20;
```

To redisplay the same lines, use the %LIST statement with one of the following two conventions:

```
%list 1:20;
%list 1-20;
```

Unless you disable it, the SPOOL option remains in effect for the duration of your SAS session. Specify the following to disable it:

```
options nospool;
```

Note: When you are processing in interactive line mode, the SPOOL option must be in effect if you want to use the %LIST statement to see the lines entered previously.

Tailoring the SASUSER Data Library to Individual Needs

The SASUSER library is a SAS data library that contains SAS catalogs that enable you to tailor features of the SAS System to your needs. For example, you can store the following customized features in the user profile catalog of your SASUSER data library:

□ function key settings

□ window command settings

□ notepads from display manager's NOTEPAD window

□ customized forms.

Understanding the Default SASUSER Library

The SASUSER library is assigned automatically only when you invoke the SAS Display Manager System or when you invoke a full-screen or graphics procedure outside of display manager. By default, files placed in the SASUSER library are permanent and are retained for future sessions. Note that default settings originally provided with the SAS System are stored in the SASHELP library. If you do not make any changes to settings, the SAS System uses the default settings. If you do make changes, the new information is stored in your SASUSER data library. To return to the original default settings stored in the SASHELP library, use the CATALOG procedure or the CATALOG window to delete the appropriate entries from your user profile catalog. By default, the SAS System then uses the corresponding entry from the SASHELP library.

   Note: Even if a SASUSER library is not created at your site, the SAS System will continue to create a profile catalog that it uses to store profile information for your SAS session. It will simply locate it in the WORK library.

Designating Your Own SASUSER Library

At invocation either entered directly in the SAS command or as part of the configuration file, you can designate an alternate location for your default SASUSER library in much the same way that you can for the WORK data library. To specify the name of the default SASUSER library, use the SAS system option SASUSER=, specifying a physical filename or a logical name, depending on your host operating system.

Storing and Using Customized Function Key Settings

Unless you change the default SASUSER library, by default, your function key settings are stored in the SASUSER.PROFILE catalog in the entry DMKEYS with a type of KEYS. You can customize those function key settings in one of the following ways:

□　by typing over the definition within the KEYS window

□　by using the KEYDEF command or the %KEYDEF macro statement outside of the KEYS window.

The new definition takes effect immediately.

Customizing Function Keys within the KEYS Window

When you change a function key setting by typing over the definition in the KEYS window, the status of that setting is handled differently based on which command you subsequently execute.

□ The END command closes the window and permanently saves the key settings, both in the current session of the KEYS window and to the appropriate entry in your SASUSER.PROFILE catalog.

□ The CANCEL command closes the window and reinstates the key settings in the current session of the KEYS window, reversing any changes made since the most recent execution of the END command. The CANCEL command leaves the entry in the default catalog unaltered.

□ The SAVE command leaves the window open and permanently saves the current key settings to the entry in the default catalog. However, the key settings in the current session of the KEYS window are subject to cancellation by the CANCEL command.

With the SAVE command, you can either replace the default definitions in your SASUSER.PROFILE catalog with the new definitions or store the new definitions as a separate catalog entry. Without an argument, the SAVE command writes the settings to the default catalog, as noted earlier. To write the customized settings to another catalog entry, specify a one-, two-, three-, or four-level name to designate the libref, catalog, entry, and type, respectively. Any level not specified causes the SAS System to use the default. Note that a type of KEYS is required.

In the following example, the SAVE command writes the contents of the window to the catalog entry NEWKEYS in the SASUSER.PROFILE catalog:

```
save sasuser.profile.newkeys.keys
```

Customizing Function Keys outside of the KEYS Window

For convenience, you can change key settings outside of the KEYS window by using the KEYDEF command. When you execute the KEYDEF command outside of the KEYS window, one of two things happens. Issued without an argument, the KEYDEF command acts as a query that causes the SAS System to echo the current setting. For example, suppose you execute the KEYDEF command as follows:

```
keydef f10
```

Depending on your operating system, the SAS System may echo the current setting as follows:

```
NOTE: F10 set to "command".
```

You can also change settings with the KEYDEF command, as shown in the following example, which changes the F1 function key from the currently defined command to the NEXTWIND command:

```
keydef f1 nextwind
```

Once you execute the KEYDEF command, the new setting appears in the KEYS window. However, the setting that you have created with the KEYDEF command is not stored in your default catalog unless you do one of the following:

□   invoke the KEYS window, make any change in it, and execute the END command

□   invoke the KEYS window and execute the SAVE command.

The SAS System uses the key settings that are currently in the KEYS window. To use a customized group of key settings that you have stored in a catalog entry rather than those stored in your default catalog, use the COPY command to copy the catalog entry into the KEYS window. Executing the COPY command without an argument cancels any of the changes you have made in the KEYS window during your current session and copies into the window the definitions previously stored in your default catalog.

Storing and Using Customized Window Command Settings

Within display manager, you can customize your windows in many different ways. For example, you can redefine the active window by using the WDEF command to specify new starting rows and columns. Executing the WDEF command with the following numeric arguments in the NOTEPAD window keeps the window almost the same size as the default but moves it down and centers it horizontally on the display:

```
wdef 10 15 30 45
```

Note that 10 signifies the starting row, 15 the starting column, 30 the number of rows including the border, and 45 the number of columns including the border.

The active window is thus resized and moved to a different location. However, by default, this new window configuration is in effect only while the window remains open. To save the command settings put into effect, use the WSAVE command. The WSAVE command saves the command settings even after you close the window or end the current SAS session. When executed with no argument, the WSAVE command saves the current settings in the active window only; when executed with the ALL argument, the WSAVE command saves all command settings that can be saved with the WSAVE command in all currently open windows.* By default, the command settings are saved to your SASUSER.PROFILE catalog to an entry whose name matches the name of the active window; the type is WSAVE. For example, executing the WSAVE command with no argument from the NOTEPAD window generates the following message:

```
Window saved to object NOTEPAD.wsave.
```

---

*   Note the difference between an active window and an open window: a window is typically opened with a window-call command and remains open until specifically closed even if it is obscured by other windows. An active window is open, displayed, and contains the cursor.

The settings are retained until you change them again within the window or until you delete the WSAVE entries in your default catalog. To do the latter, invoke the CATALOG window, and type **SASUSER** and **PROFILE** in the **Libref** and **Catalog** fields, respectively. Then press ENTER or RETURN. A listing of current entries for your SASUSER.PROFILE catalog appears on the display. To delete the NOTEPAD entry, move the cursor to the selection field adjacent to it, type the selection-field command **D**, and press ENTER or RETURN. The selection field is then highlighted, and you are prompted with a message to verify or cancel the operation. Move your cursor again to the selection field adjacent to the listing, type **V**, and press ENTER or RETURN. You can now issue the END command to exit the CATALOG window and return to the previously active window for processing.

You can use the WSAVE command to save other customized settings, including the following:

□ window color and attributes

□ window size and position

□ the presence of scroll bars

□ the presence of the PMENU facility's action bar.

Simply configure your window as you want it to remain, and execute the WSAVE command. Your customized setting remains in effect until you make further changes.

For example, to change the border of the PROGRAM EDITOR window to cyan, specify

```
color border cyan
```

To retain this customized color, execute the WSAVE command. The customized setting is stored in your SASUSER.PROFILE in the entry PROGRAM with the type WSAVE. It becomes the default unless you re-execute the COLOR command in the PROGRAM EDITOR window or delete this entry in the CATALOG window. Note that if you do the latter, you must end your current session before the change appears to have taken effect, since the PROGRAM EDITOR window cannot be closed. You can also change the color and issue the WSAVE command again.

To change your window size and position, you can choose from a number of commands. For example, the CASCADE command creates a layered display of all open windows, and the TILE command creates a mosaic of all open windows. The RESIZE command returns the window to the configuration prior to the tiled or cascaded pattern. In addition, your host operating system has commands that enable you to move, shrink, and enlarge windows. You can store these command settings in your SASUSER.PROFILE catalog and make their resulting configurations the default. Remember that when you use the WSAVE command to store in your default catalog commands that customize more than the active window (for example, TILE and CASCADE), you must use the ALL argument.

Storing and Using Customized Notepads

In display manager, the NOTEPAD window is a full-screen editor, similar to the PROGRAM EDITOR window, for entering and altering text and for saving information from session to session. Once you have entered the text you want in your notepad, you can use the SASUSER.PROFILE catalog to store your notepads and reuse them in later sessions.

To store your customized notepad in the SASUSER library, execute the SAVE command with a one-, two-, three-, or four-level name to designate the libref, catalog, entry, and type, respectively. Any level not specified causes the SAS System to use the default. By default, notepads are stored in the SASUSER.PROFILE catalog. The default catalog entry is the origin of the notepad. Issuing a SAVE command with no argument stores a notepad in the catalog entry most recently specified in a SAVE or COPY command.

To copy a customized notepad into the NOTEPAD window for reuse, execute the COPY command with a one-, two-, three-, or four-level name to designate the libref, catalog, entry, and type, respectively. Any level not specified causes the SAS System to use the default as documented for the SAVE command. Issuing a COPY command with no argument copies into the NOTEPAD window the notepad in the catalog entry most recently specified in a SAVE or COPY command.

Thus, you can keep several notepads stored in your SASUSER.PROFILE catalog at a time, using and modifying them as needed. You can also have several instances of the NOTEPAD window open at one time.

Customizing Output

Previous sections have explained how to customize your environment. The objective has been to modify your environment as a means to achieving other goals. For example, storing and using customized key settings allows you to use function keys to execute the commands you are most likely to use.

This section shows you how to customize the result of your programming efforts; that is, your output. It discusses how to do the following:

□ customize the appearance of procedure output

□ customize the appearance of the SAS log

□ customize the destination of output

□ customize the printing of output.

SAS Data Set Example

The examples in this section process real estate data from the data set IN.HOUSES. Each observation in the SAS data set IN.HOUSES contains the following variables:

Variable	Type	Description
ZONE	character	number representing a housing zone recognized by Realtors
TYPE	character	type of house
BEDR	numeric	number of bedrooms
BATH	numeric	number of bathrooms
DR	character	whether the house has a dining room
GARAGE	numeric	number of cars the garage can hold
SF	numeric	square feet of heated living space
AGE	numeric	age of house
FP	numeric	number of fireplaces
SCHOOLS	character	code representing the elementary, middle, and high schools for which the property is zoned
ADDRESS	character	street address
PRICE	numeric	asking price

The following PROC PRINT step displays the data set IN.HOUSES:*

```
libname in 'SAS-data-library';

proc print data=in.houses;
   title 'Felspar County Real Estate Listing';
run;
```

---

* The DATA step that creates IN.HOUSES is shown in the Appendix.

Output 25.1 shows the results.

Output 25.1
*Printout of Data
Set IN.HOUSES*

```
                    Felspar County Real Estate Listing                    1

OBS  ZONE  TYPE      BEDR  BATH  DR  GARAGE    SF   AGE  FP     SCHOOLS
      1    4    twostory    4    2.5   y     2     2538    6    2   920:340/400/368
      2    1    twostory    4    2.5   y     2     2700    7    1   920:470/360/552
      3    3    twnhouse    2    2.0   y     0     1595    6    1   320:332/366/312
      4    1    twostory    3    2.5   y     1     2750    0    1   920:628/388/348
      5    4    split       3    2.0   y     1     1306    0    1   920:576/512/436
      6    2    twostory    3    3.5   y     2     2590    0    2   920:364/608/368
      7    5    split       3    1.0   n     0     1959   31    0   680:308/316/332
      8    2    twnhouse    3    2.5   y     0     1374   15    0   920:304/604/368
      9    4    condo       2    2.0   y     0     1275    5    1   920:448/472/318
     10    4    ranch       3    2.0   y     1     1526    6    1   920:476/424/428
     11    1    split       3    1.5   y     1     1329   23    0   920:396/360/552
     12    1    condo       2    3.5   n     0     1300    5    1   920:448/472/318
     13    8    twnhouse    2    2.0   y     0     1120    4    1   320:364/366/312
     14    2    condo       2    2.0   y     0     1066    1    1   920:520/604/368
     15    4    split       4    2.5   y     3     2600   10    2   920:476/424/428
     16    2    twnhouse    2    1.5   y     0     1150   15    0   920:304/400/368
     17    4    ranch       3    2.5   y     0     2441    1    0   920:540/512/436
     18    1    split       3    1.0   n     0     1245   36    0   920:524/388/348
     19    7    twnhouse    2    1.5   y     0     1280    4    1   920:584/592/588
     20    4    ranch       3    3.0   n     0     2400    2    1   920:420/424/428
     21    2    duplex      2    2.5   y     0     1184    4    1   920:364/604/368
     22    6    duplex      3    1.0   y     1     1569   73    2   350:324/328/336
     23    2    twnhouse    2    1.5   y     0     1040    9    1   920:414/604/316
     24    4    condo       3    2.0   y     0     1448    5    1   920:448/472/318
     25    2    twnhouse    3    2.0   y     2     1471    1    1   920:364/604/368
     26    4    twostory    3    2.5   y     0     1940    4    1   920:328/312/316

OBS  ADDRESS                 PRICE
      1   211 Whitehall Way        154900
      2   1800 Bridgeport          169900
      3   154 Montrose             102000
      4   4000 Skipjack Ct.        214900
      5   5933 South Downs Dr.      95400
      6   727 Crabtree Crossing    292400
      7   627 Riverside Dr.         58900
      8   907 Lexington Ct.         65500
      9   6010-102 Winterpoint      70000
     10   6509 Orchard Knoll       107900
     11   500 E. Millbrook Rd.      82900
     12   6010-101 Winterpoint      68900
     13   521 Woodwinds             84600
     14   1324 Killiam Ct.          74900
     15   7141 Eastridge           198000
     16   1239 Donaldson Ct.        49900
     17   9356 Sauls Rd.           197000
     18   2414 Van Dyke             85000
     19   409 Galashiels            60000
     20   8122 Maude Steward Rd.   129900
     21   112 Lake Hollow           67900
     22   108 South Elm St.        100000
     23   216 Concannon Ct.         59900
     24   6000-102 Winterpoint      79900
     25   765 Crabtree Crossing    184000
     26   1641 Pricewood Lane      195000
```

```
                    Felspar County Real Estate Listing                    2

OBS  ZONE  TYPE      BEDR  BATH  DR  GARAGE    SF   AGE  FP     SCHOOLS
     27    5    split       2    1.0   n     0      960    2    0   680:308/304/332
     28    8    twnhouse    2    2.0   y     0     1167    5    1   320:364/366/312
     29    2    condo       2    2.0   n     0     1246    4    1   920:364/604/316
     30    1    twnhouse    2    1.0   n     0      980    4    0   920:304/360/552
     31    8    twostory    4    2.5   y     2     3446    0    2   320:313/316/356
     32    8    split       3    1.5   y     0     1441   28    1   320:315/316/356
     33    5    twostory    3    2.5   y     0     1900    4    0   680:308/316/332
     34    8    split       3    2.0   y     2     1976   10    1   320:348/316/356
     35    8    twnhouse    2    2.0   n     0     1276    6    1   321:360/304/356
     36    5    split       3    2.0   n     0     1533    5    1   680:/308/316/32
     37    2    twostory    4    2.5   y     2     2584    0    0   920:364/640/368
```

```
   38    8    twostory    4    2.5  y    2    2608     0    0    320:362/366/312
   39    2    twnhouse    3    2.5  y    0    2080     4    1    920:530/400/318
   40    5    twostory    3    2.5  y    2    2863     7    1    680:308/316/332
   41    8    split       2    2.5  n    0    2900    38    1    320:315/316/356
   42    3    twostory    4    2.5  y    2    3926     5    1    320:362/366/312
   43    4    split       3    1.0  n    0    1010    28    0    920:432/404/436
   44    1    split       3    2.0  y    0    1662    12    1    920:488/360/552
   45    2    split       3    2.0  y    2    2004     0    2    920:568/400/318
   46    2    twostory    3    2.5  y    2    1650     0    1    920:364/608/368
   47    1    twostory    3    2.5  y    2    2416     6    1    920:568/356/318
   48    4    ranch       3    2.5  y    0    2441     1    0    920:540/512/436
   49    1    twostory    5    3.5  y    2    4850     3    0    920:540/512/436
   50    4    split       3    1.5  n    2    1225    18    1    920:328/312/316

   OBS   ADDRESS                      PRICE

   27    Rt.5 Yarbororugh Rd.         78900
   28    5001 Pine Cone               78500
   29    721 Springfork               76900
   30    1203 Berley Ct               72400
   31    Lot 10 Red Coach Rd.        225000
   32    5617 Laurel Crest Dr.        86900
   33    1532 St. Mary's Rd.         118500
   34    110 Skylark Way             123500
   35    8 Stonevillage               71000
   36    603 Greentree Dr.           117800
   37    114 Grey Horse Dr.          189900
   38    2103 Carriage Way           189900
   39    108 Chattle Close           179900
   40    5521 Horseshoe Circle       199200
   41    2617 Snow Hill Rd           425000
   42    49 Birn Ham Lane            360000
   43    4341 Rock Quarry             60000
   44    6324 Lakeland, Lake Park    100000
   45    101 Meadowglade Ln.         179950
   46    100 Cumberland Green        143000
   47    6008 Brass Lantern Ct.      144500
   48    9356 Sauls Rd.              197000
   49    9317 Sauls Rd.              339950
   50    6424 Old Jenks Rd.           81900
```

Output 25.2 shows the SAS log generated by this PROC PRINT step. Note the system messages that the SAS System generates and writes to the log automatically.

Output 25.2
Printout of Data Set IN.HOUSES— SAS Log

```
5          libname in 'SAS-data-library';
NOTE: Libref IN was successfully assigned as follows:
      Engine:        V606
      Physical Name: SAS-DATA-LIBRARY
6          proc print data=in.houses;
7             title 'Felspar County Real Estate Listing';
8          run;

NOTE: The PROCEDURE PRINT printed pages 1-2.
```

The next two sections show you how to customize the appearance of your procedure output and the SAS log, starting with procedure output.

Customizing the Appearance of Procedure Output

The default characteristics of your output depend not only on your programming environment but on many other factors including the procedure you are using, your host operating system, and your site. This section concentrates on how you as an individual user can customize the appearance of your output by tailoring a few SAS statements and system options to your needs.

Consider Output 25.1 and the enhancements that would improve its appearance. The output would be more readable if you could fit an entire observation on one line and if the columns were better spaced. Additionally, since the output is lengthy, the observations printed should include only those needed for analysis.

To increase the line size, use the SAS system option LINESIZE=. To print only selected observations at the beginning of a data set, use the SAS system option OBS=. The following example has a linesize of 120; only the first ten observations are printed:

```
libname in 'SAS-data-library';
options linesize=120 obs=10;


proc print data=in.houses;
    title 'Felspar County Real Estate Listing';
run;
```

The LINESIZE= option specifies the printer line width for both the SAS log and the procedure output. The OBS= option specifies the last observation that the SAS System processes. The SAS System counts a line of input data as one observation even if the raw data for several SAS data set observations are on a single line. Note that you can assign a value of MAX as well as a numeric argument to the OBS= option. Output 25.3 shows the much improved results.

Output 25.3   *Customizing Procedure Output with the SAS System Options LINESIZE= and OBS=*

```
                                      Felspar County Real Estate Listing                                                 1

  OBS  ZONE  TYPE      BEDR  BATH  DR  GARAGE   SF   AGE  FP     SCHOOLS        ADDRESS                   PRICE

    1    4   twostory    4   2.5   y     2     2538   6   2   920:340/400/368  211 Whitehall Way        154900
    2    1   twostory    4   2.5   y     2     2700   7   1   920:470/360/552  1800 Bridgeport          169900
    3    3   twnhouse    2   2.0   y     0     1595   6   1   320:332/366/312  154 Montrose             102000
    4    1   twostory    3   2.5   y     1     2750   0   1   920:628/388/348  4000 Skipjack Ct.        214900
    5    4   split       3   2.0   y     1     1306   0   1   920:576/512/436  5933 South Downs Dr.      95400
    6    2   twostory    3   3.5   y     2     2590   0   2   920:364/608/368  727 Crabtree Crossing    292400
    7    5   split       3   1.0   n     0     1959  31   0   680:308/316/332  627 Riverside Dr.         58900
    8    2   twnhouse    3   2.5   y     0     1374  15   0   920:304/604/368  907 Lexington Ct.         65500
    9    4   condo       2   2.0   y     0     1275   5   1   920:448/472/318  6010-102 Winterpoint      70000
   10    4   ranch       3   2.0   y     1     1526   6   1   920:476/424/428  6509 Orchard Knoll       107900
```

As another step, you can suppress the title of the output. You can remove the TITLE statement, which causes the SAS System to supply the default title "The SAS System." If you prefer that your output remain untitled, use a null TITLE statement as shown here.

```
libname in 'SAS-data-library';
options linesize=120 obs=10;


proc print data=in.houses;
    title;
run;
```

Output 25.4 shows the untitled output.

Output 25.4   *Customizing Procedure Output with a Null TITLE Statement*

```
                                                                                        1

 OBS  ZONE  TYPE       BEDR  BATH  DR  GARAGE    SF  AGE  FP    SCHOOLS        ADDRESS              PRICE

  1    4    twostory    4    2.5   y     2     2538   6   2   920:340/400/368  211 Whitehall Way    154900
  2    1    twostory    4    2.5   y     2     2700   7   1   920:470/360/552  1800 Bridgeport      169900
  3    3    twnhouse    2    2.0   y     0     1595   6   1   320:332/366/312  154 Montrose         102000
  4    1    twostory    3    2.5   y     1     2750   0   1   920:628/388/348  4000 Skipjack Ct.    214900
  5    4    split       3    2.0   y     1     1306   0   1   920:576/512/436  5933 South Downs Dr.  95400
  6    2    twostory    3    3.5   y     2     2590   0   2   920:364/608/368  727 Crabtree Crossing 292400
  7    5    split       3    1.0   n     0     1959  31   0   680:308/316/332  627 Riverside Dr.     58900
  8    2    twnhouse    3    2.5   y     0     1374  15   0   920:304/604/368  907 Lexington Ct.     65500
  9    4    condo       2    2.0   y     0     1275   5   1   920:448/472/318  6010-102 Winterpoint  70000
 10    4    ranch       3    2.0   y     1     1526   6   1   920:476/424/428  6509 Orchard Knoll   107900
```

Note that if you routinely prefer to keep your output untitled, you can put a null TITLE statement in an autoexec file, which would then be executed after initialization.

Customizing the Appearance of the SAS Log

In addition to customizing procedure output, you can customize the log that accompanies it. As Output 25.2 demonstrates, the SAS log typically contains the SAS statements from the program that generated it and notes about the program. In addition, if the program contains errors, the log displays error messages and indicates when the SAS System detects the error.

If the program is error-free, you may want to suppress the notes in the log. To do so, add the SAS system option NONOTES to the OPTIONS statement, as shown here.

```
libname in 'SAS-data-library';
options linesize=120 obs=10 nonotes;

proc print data=in.houses;
   title;
run;
```

Output 25.5 shows the SAS log; notes have been suppressed.

Output 25.5   *Suppressing Notes to the SAS Log*

```
5          libname in 'SAS-data-library';
6          options linesize=120 obs=10 nonotes;
7          proc print data=in.houses;
8             title;
9          run;
```

On most operating systems, by default, SAS source statements are written to the SAS log. You can prevent these statements from being written to the log by specifying NOSOURCE as in the following example:

```
libname in 'SAS-data-library';
options linesize=120 obs=10 nosource;

proc print data=in.houses;
   title;
run;
```

Output 25.6 shows the SAS log; SAS source statements have been suppressed.

Output 25.6   *Suppressing SAS Source Statements to the SAS Log*

```
5          libname in 'SAS-data-library';
NOTE: Libref IN was successfully assigned as follows:
      Engine:        V606
      Physical Name: SAS-DATA-LIBRARY
6          options linesize=120 obs=10 nosource;

NOTE: The PROCEDURE PRINT printed page 1.
```

Specify the SOURCE option to return to the default log listing.

You can also customize the log by adding the appropriate statements and options to an autoexec file or the appropriate options to a configuration file.

Note: Notes and SAS source statements must be specified for SAS programs that are sent to SAS Institute for problem determination and resolution.

Customizing the Destination of Output

You can customize the destination of your output, choosing from the methods listed here.

□ To route the SAS log and procedure output from their destinations to an alternate destination, use the PRINTTO procedure. You can also use PROC PRINTTO to return to the default destination.

□ To redefine the default destination for an entire session or program, at invocation use the SAS system option PRINT= for procedure output and the SAS system option LOG= for the SAS log. Remember that you can specify these options either in the SAS command or in a configuration file.

Instructions for using both of these techniques are included in *SAS Language and Procedures: Usage, Version 6, First Edition*, Chapter 22, "Directing the SAS Log and Output."

You can also specify default locations to which copies of the SAS log and the SAS print file are written. To specify a destination for a copy of the log, use the SAS system option ALTLOG=. Use the SAS system option ALTPRINT= to specify a destination for a copy of the procedure output.

Customizing the Printing of Your Output

Default printing parameters are usually established for an entire site and vary by both site and host operating system. However, if the default parameters at your site do not meet your individual needs, you can use the FORM window subsystem to customize these parameters as you want. For more complete information about the FORM window subsystem, see *SAS Language: Reference, Version 6, First Edition*, Chapter 17, "SAS Display Manager Windows." For host-specific information, see the SAS companion for your host operating system.

In addition, extensive help is available online for the FORM window. From any display manager window, you can obtain help information by issuing the HELP command on the command line or with a function key. If you are using the PMENU facility, select the help item from the action bar and proceed accordingly. Within the FORM window you can obtain help information for a highlighted feature by executing the HELP command, moving the cursor to the highlighted feature, and pressing ENTER or RETURN.*

The FORM window subsystem includes the following six frames, which enable you to create a FORM catalog entry tailored to your operating system environment and default printer. Note that the frames are listed in the sequence in which they fall, as shown here:

1. Printer Selection

2. Text Body and Margin Information

---

* The method of highlighting may vary across systems; on some systems, a contrasting color is used.

3. Carriage Control Information

4. Print File Parameters

5. Font Control Information

6. Printer Control Language.

You can move among the frames by executing the PREVSCR or NEXTSCR command or by executing the =*n* command, where *n* has a value of 1 to 5 and invokes the frames in sequence, starting with the Text Body and Margin Information frame and ending with the Printer Control Language frame.*

You can use a FORM catalog entry to send output from various procedures or commands to your printer. Specifications include printer margins, printer control language, and font control information. Although a default form is available, you can use the FORM window subsystem to change that default, as explained in the next section.

Changing the Default Destination of the FORM Window Subsystem

To change the destination and customize other features that affect output generated by the PRINT command, do the following:

1. To display your default form, specify the following:**

   ```
   fsform default
   ```

   If your SASUSER.PROFILE catalog contains a form named DEFAULT, it is displayed. Otherwise, the Printer Selection frame is displayed. When you select a printer from the Printer Selection frame, the default form for that printer is copied into your SASUSER.PROFILE catalog.

2. Modify your default form to change the default destination and number of copies to suit your needs. As necessary, you can move backward with the PREVSCR command and forward with the NEXTSCR command among all of the frames except the Printer Selection frame.

3. To save your changes, issue the END command. Issue the CANCEL command if you don't want to save your changes.

---

*   Note that the Print File Parameters frame is optional and may not be available at your site. If it is not available, issuing =3 displays the Font Control Information frame and issuing =4 displays the Printer Control Language frame.

**   Note that although FORM is the name of the window, FSFORM is its window-call command.

Creating a New Form

To add a form to the FORM window subsystem, simply specify the window-call name followed by a valid SAS name for the form. You can then modify the form as described in the previous section. For example, to add a new form called PRTFORM, specify the following:

```
fsform prtform
```

By default, this entry is stored in your SASUSER.PROFILE catalog.

Selecting a Printer

When you are creating a new form, the Printer Selection Frame is displayed. You can customize the form by typing in a description of up to 40 characters; this description is displayed in the CATALOG window. You can also select the printer you want to use by browsing the list of printers, moving your cursor to the printer you want, and pressing ENTER or RETURN. Your selection takes effect, and the next frame is displayed. Note that to move to a new window, you must select a printer. The printer you select influences the information that appears in the frames that follow.

Specifying Page Formats

After you select a printer, the Text Body and Margin Information frame is displayed automatically.* This frame enables you to specify page formats by filling in values for features such as the number of characters per line; the number of lines per page; and the left, top, and bottom margins on a given page.

Specifying Carriage Control Information

The next frame displayed, the Carriage Control Information frame, enables you to specify whether you want carriage control information displayed with the output and where you want to signal page breaks. By default, carriage control information is displayed with output. To maintain the default, keep your cursor on the **YES** field and press ENTER or RETURN; otherwise, move your cursor to the **NO** field and press ENTER or RETURN. To specify where you want page breaks signaled, browse the list of choices, move your cursor to the one you want, and press ENTER or RETURN.

Modifying Print File Parameters

Use the Print File Parameter frame to change the printing parameters. Note that parameters differ among operating systems, both in availability and naming; values may vary by site. In addition, for some operating systems, a secondary Print File Parameter frame is available in which you can specify further information. Simply tab to the **SELECT** field and press ENTER or RETURN to display the second frame. You can use the Print File Parameter frame to modify

---

* Note that if you are *editing* and not creating a form, this window is the first one displayed. Starting with this window, you then follow the same sequence as when you create a form.

parameters such as the number of copies to print, the destination for the output, and the job characteristics.

Note that the names of these parameters vary by operating system, and their values vary by site. For further information, see your SAS Site Representative or contact the data center at your site.

Specifying Printer Control Characters and Text Attributes

To specify printer control characters and text attributes, use the Font Control Information frame. The attributes defined in this frame are based on the printer you selected in the Printer Selection frame. The top part of the frame has spaces for you to define up to eight special characters that represent printer control characters. For each control character you define, you specify the special character, its decimal representation, and a description.

These characters are then used in the bottom portion of the frame to define text attributes, which are special colors and highlighting that you can use in text to define printing modes. These color and highlighting attributes are associated with the control codes used by your printer for printing in the special mode. The SAS System supplies some default text attribute definitions with the correct start and stop sequences for each special printing mode supported by available printers. You can scroll these definitions to verify the defaults available for your printer. You can also change these color and highlighting attributes. To obtain information on the acceptable values of a field, type a question mark (?) in a given field and press ENTER or RETURN.

Note that this frame is particularly printer- and site-specific. For further details, refer to your printer manual or see your SAS Software Consultant.

Composing Printing Control Sequences

Finally, use the Printer Control Language frame to compose the control sequences that are sent to the printer in the following situations:

□ before text is sent

□ between pages of text

□ after all text is sent.

Use this frame to change the paper trays and the default font for a page or to perform tasks that you cannot specify within the Font Control Information frame. The following labels, each placed on a line by itself preceding the control sequence it sends, signify the appropriate control sequence, as indicated here:

PRINT INIT section   sends the listed control sequences before sending text to the print file; these control sequences are sent once per print file.

PAGE *n* section   sends the listed control sequences before sending the specified page, where *n* signifies the page number. Specify a PAGE label with no control sequences to stop the control sequences from repeating.

PAGE LAST section   sends the listed control sequences after all text is sent for a single item.

PRINT TERM section   sends the listed control sequences after all text is sent for all items.

Refer to your printer manual to determine the control language sequences you need.

Using the SAS Sample Library

In addition to customizing output from SAS programs that you build yourself, you can customize output from programs that SAS Institute builds for you and maintains in the SAS Sample Library. The SAS Sample Library is a diverse collection of SAS programs that illustrate specific applications of SAS software and that demonstrate different approaches to programming problems. Every release of SAS software includes sample programs that demonstrate the features of that release. Each SAS software product has its own sample library that is shipped with each new release of the product. Installation instructions for the sample programs are included with the installation instructions for the SAS System on your operating system. Although the SAS Sample Library is shipped to every site, it is not loaded and available at every site. To determine the availability of or to request access to the library at your site, consult your SAS Site Representative. If the SAS Sample Library is available, the SAS Site Representative can tell you how to access it.

By using the SAS Sample Library, you can choose an example program, study it, run it, examine the output, modify the program to suit your needs and run it again to get the output you want. The sample programs can help you select the right procedure for a specific purpose or the best approach to a particular programming problem.

Most of the programs in the SAS Sample Library are stand-alone and can be executed as they are. External files supplied in the sample library are listed with the programs, and any permanent SAS data sets needed to run the sample programs are provided in a single SAS data library. This data library is referenced by a libref that can be assigned automatically when the SAS System is initialized. In some cases, you must supply your own data, either cards data or data in an external file.

Each program in the SAS Sample Library contains two parts: the header and the program statements. The header includes information about the program's function, the operating system required, and the tools (for example, SAS procedures and functions) the program uses. It also includes notes about the program.

You can generate an index to the programs in the SAS Sample Library either interactively or through batch processing.

Summary

The following points summarize how to customize your SAS environment for an individual user. Note that the specifics of this process vary by site and host operating system; for detailed information, refer to the SAS companion for your host operating system.

□ To customize your SAS programming environment, use one of the following methods:

□ use your user configuration file to set SAS system options at initialization

□ set SAS system options at invocation by including them in the SAS command

□ use your autoexec file to execute certain SAS statements immediately after initialization.

□ To use an autoexec file, use an operating system file to store the SAS statements you want to use. Then when you invoke the SAS System, use the SAS system option AUTOEXEC= to specify that file.

□ The SAS WORK data library is a library the SAS System creates by default at the beginning of a session; it is temporary by default.

□ How you handle insufficient storage space in the WORK library depends on your host operating system. You can increase the size of the WORK library by designating a larger, alternate file or disk. You can conserve space by using PROC DATASETS with the DELETE statement to delete the SAS files you do not need. Finally, you can move files that are part of the WORK library to a different library.

□ The SASUSER data library enables you to store and use customized features including the following:

□ function key settings

□ window command settings

□ notepads from the NOTEPAD window

□ customized forms.

□ To customize function key settings, type over a definition in the KEYS window or use the KEYDEF command outside the window. Use the SAVE or END command within the KEYS window to store the changes in your SASUSER.PROFILE catalog.

□ You can store customized window command settings in your SASUSER.PROFILE catalog, such as window size and position and window color, and make the customized settings the default. To do this, use the WSAVE command.

□ To store a customized notepad, execute the SAVE command.

□ You can choose from many SAS statements and SAS system options to customize the appearance of your output. For example, you can use the LINESIZE= option to alter the line size of your output, the OBS= option to print a subset of observations, and a null TITLE statement to suppress all titles. You can add these customized features to your program or activate them through autoexec and configuration files.

□ You can customize the destination of your output. To route the SAS log and procedure output to an alternate destination, use the PRINTTO procedure. To redefine the default destination for an entire session or program, at invocation use the SAS system option PRINT= for procedure output and the SAS system option LOG= for the SAS log. To write copies of the SAS log and the SAS print file to alternate destinations, use the SAS system options ALTLOG= and ALTPRINT=.

□ To customize the printing of your output, use the FORM window subsystem. This subsystem includes six different frames that enable you to create a FORM catalog entry tailored to your operating system environment and default printer.

□ The SAS Sample Library is a diverse collection of SAS programs that illustrate specific applications of SAS software and that demonstrate different approaches to programming problems. You can choose any program from this library and execute it, first modifying the program to serve your needs. In this way, you can select the right procedure for a specific purpose or the best approach to a particular programming problem.

SAS Tools

This section summarizes syntax for the statements, SAS system options, display manager commands, and procedures in this chapter.

Statements

%INCLUDE *source-1* < . . . *source-n*>;
 includes SAS statements and data lines from lines entered earlier in the same session, lines entered from the keyboard, or external files.

%LIST <*n*<:*m* | −*m*>>;
 lists lines *n* through *m* entered in the current session using either of the conventions shown.

OPTIONS *option-1* < . . . *option-n*>;
 changes the value of one or more SAS system options.

TITLE;
 cancels all existing titles.

SAS system options

LINESIZE=*n*
 specifies the printer line width for the SAS log and the standard print file used by the DATA step and procedures.

NOTES | NONOTES
 controls whether notes are written to the SAS log.

OBS=*n*
> specifies which observation from a data set the SAS System reads last.

SPOOL | NOSPOOL
> controls whether SAS statements are written to a utility data set in the WORK data library for later use by a %INCLUDE or %LIST statement.

SOURCE | NOSOURCE
> controls whether SAS source statements are written to the SAS log.

Display manager commands

CANCEL
> in the KEYS window, closes the window and reinstates the key settings in the current session of the KEYS window, reversing changes made since the most recent execution of the END command.

COPY <*catalog-entry*>;
> copies a catalog entry into a window. *Catalog-entry* specifies the SAS data library, catalog name, entry name, and entry type. You can specify one-, two-, three-, and four-level names. The complete specification is *libref.catalog.entry.type*.

END
> in the KEYS window, closes the window and permanently saves the key settings, both in the current session of the KEYS window and to the appropriate entry in the SASUSER.PROFILE catalog.

FSFORM <*catalog-name.*>*form-name*
> invokes the FORM window, which enables you to specify the type of printer, text format, and destination for output. *Catalog-name* specifies the name of the SAS catalog that contains the form; *form-name* specifies the name of the form.

KEYDEF *key-name* <*display-manager-command* | ~*text-string*>
> redefines or identifies a function key setting outside the KEYS window. *Key-name* represents any function key in the KEYS window. *Display-manager-command* | ~*text-string* represents any display manager command or text string to which you assign the function key specified with the KEYDEF command.

SAVE
> in the KEYS window, leaves the window open and permanently saves the current key settings to the entry in the default catalog.

WDEF *starting-row starting-col nrows ncols*
> redefines the active window by specifying a new starting row and column and by specifying a size by the number of rows and columns in the window. *Starting-row* specifies the starting row, by number, for the window border; *starting-col* specifies the starting column, by number, for the window border. *Nrows* specifies the number of rows inside the window, including the border; *ncols* specifies the number of columns inside the window, including the border.

Procedures

PROC DATASETS LIBRARY=*libref*;
    DELETE *member-list*;

    PROC DATASETS LIBRARY=*libref*;
        begins the DATASETS procedure, which lists, copies, renames and
        manages SAS files, as well as managing indexes for and appending SAS
        data sets in a SAS data library. The option LIBRARY= refers to the SAS
        data library to be processed.

    DELETE *member-list*;
        specifies members to be deleted from the SAS data library.

Learning More

This section provides references for learning more about the topics presented in
this chapter.

□   For host-specific details for the SAS WORK data library, the SASUSER data
library, configuration files, autoexec files, and the FORM window subsystem,
see the SAS companion provided by SAS Institute for your host operating
system. Many of the tools in this chapter have host-specific features; refer to
your SAS companion for information about these features also.

□   For more information about SAS output and how you can customize it, see
SAS Language: Reference, Version 6, First Edition, Chapter 5, "SAS Output."
For details on customizing the destination of output with the PRINTTO
procedure and with the SAS system options PRINT= and LOG=, see
SAS Language and Procedures: Usage, Version 6, First Edition, Chapter 22,
"Directing the SAS Log and Output." For complete reference information
about the PRINTTO procedure, see the *SAS Procedures Guide, Version 6,
Third Edition*, Chapter 28, "The PRINTTO Procedure."

□   See SAS Technical Report U-114, *A Guide to the SAS Notes, Sample Library,
and Online Customer Support Facility, Release 6.06*, for details on the SAS
Sample Library. See also *SAS Language: Reference*, Appendix 2, "SAS Sample
Library."

□   For detailed syntax information about the statements discussed in this chapter,
see *SAS Language: Reference*, Chapter 9, "SAS Language Statements."

□   For complete reference information about the SAS system options discussed in
this chapter, see *SAS Language: Reference*, Chapter 3, "Components of the SAS
Language," and Chapter 16, "SAS System Options."

□   For more information about function keys and the KEYS window, see
SAS Language: Reference, Chapter 17, "SAS Display Manager Windows." See
Chapter 17 also for reference information about the FORM window
subsystem.

□ For complete syntax for the display manager commands discussed in this chapter, see *SAS Language: Reference*, Chapter 18, "SAS Display Manager Commands."

□ See the *SAS Procedures Guide*, Chapter 17, "The DATASETS Procedure," for complete reference information about the DATASETS procedure.

Part 7
Appendix

Appendix   **Raw Data and DATA Steps**

Raw Data and DATA Steps

Appendix

Introduction

Chapters in this book generally show you how to create the data sets used in the chapter. However, some chapters show only partial data when the input data are lengthy or the actual contents of the data sets are not crucial for understanding the examples. When partial data are shown in the chapter, the complete raw data or DATA steps appear in this appendix.

Chapter 5

Raw Data for RPTDATA

Records from *daily-order-file*

```
----+----1----+----2
BA01  2000    190
BA02 17000   1700
CA01 33000   3500
CN01  7000    600
ZA01  7500    635
```

Records from *customer-reference-file*

```
----+----1----+----2----+----3----+----4----+----5----+----6----+----7----+
AP01 Appleton Construction   P.O. Box 1923    Apex, NC 27516
BA01 Barnet and Sons         P.O. Box 1172    Raleigh, NC 27742
BA02 Baxter Brothers Asphalt P.O. Box 95      Fuquay-Varina, NC 27732
CN01 Concord Concrete        P.O. Box 13      Concord, NC  27832
CU01 Custom Construction     P.O. Box 68      Fuquay-Varina, NC 27732
DE01 Drummens Hauling        P.O. Box 42118   Durham, NC   27704
DE01 Dixon Plumbing, Co      P.O. Box 560     Apex,NC   27516
FR01 Frazier Concrete        P.O. Box 1539    Raleigh, NC 27742
GA01 Glazier Remodeling      P.O. Box 190     Durham, NC 27704
HA01 Hamilton Roofing, Co    P.O. Box 22      Fuquay-Varina, NC 27732
HI01 Hicks Utilities         P.O. Box 5466    Apex, NC 27516
JJ01 JJ's Insulating         P.O. Box 145     Fuquay-Varina, NC 27732
MI01 Miller Building, Inc    P.O. Box 4511    Concord, NC  27832
MI02 Mitchel's Asbestos      P.O. Box 16      Durham, NC  27704
PE02 Precision Exteriors     P.O. Box 49      Raleigh, NC 27704
QU01 Quality Homes           P.O. Box 110     Chapel Hill, NC 27514
RA01 Raleigh Reality         P.O. Box 87618   Raleigh, NC  27704
RJ01 RJ Construction         P.O. Box 7655    Durham, NC   27704
SA01 Sanford and Son         P.O. Box 41      Chapel Hill, NC 27514
TJ01 TJ's Woodworks, Co      P.O. Box 42355   Apex,NC   27516
TR01 Tri-City Homes          P.O. Box 21      Chapel Hill, NC 27514
WE01 Wellington Builders, Inc P.O. Box 9221   Raleigh, NC 27742
WI01 Wilson & Associates     P.O. Box 654     Raleigh, NC 27742
YA01 Yang Brothers Grading   P.O. Box 229     Chapel Hill, NC 27514
YO01 York Contractors        P.O. Box 804     Apex, NC 27516
----+----1----+----2----+----3----+----4----+----5----+----6----+----7----+
```

Raw Data for PARTTIME

Records from *store-1-input-file*

```
----+----1----+----2----+----3----+----4
16 79 Carson, E. A.  3.85 13.5
16 101 Alvarez, J. T.  4.65 45.0
16 56 Ianelli, L. O.  3.90 26.5
16 50 Daniels, J. T.  4.10 20.5
16 83 Patel, H.  7.50 11.0
16 105 Huang, L.  4.00 3.0
16 22 Woods, H.  5.50 15.0
```

Records from *store-2-input-file*

```
----+----1----+----2----+----3----+----4
17 79 Covington, T. A.  3.85 13.5
17 101 Simpson, J. T.  4.65 45.0
17 56 Larson, Y. O.  3.90 22.5
17 100 Adams, Z. W.  4.60 40.0
17 83 Pitts, A. P.  5.55 10.0
17 105 Homes, L. A.  6.01 35.0
17 33 Thompson, N. C.  3.85 4.0
17 01 Kelly, Q. D.  7.00 40.0
```

Records from *store-3-input-file*

```
----+----1----+----2----+----3----+----4
18 72 Dobbs, E. S.  4.85 15.5
18 105 Combs, E. E.  4.65 45.0
18 60 Barnes, R. D.  3.85 25.5
18 56 Tanner, H. S.  3.90 22.5
18 83 Petis, B.  6.50 14.0
18 41 Rich, I. W.  3.90 22.5
18 115 Harris, K.  3.85 3.0
18 23 Tonie, T. T.  5.50 11.5
```

Records from *store-4-input-file*

```
----+----1----+----2----+----3----+----4
19 74 Farrington, W. A.  3.85 10.5
19 101 Mitchel, T. H.  5.65 41.0
19 56 Panelli, L. O.  3.95 27.5
19 155 Dillard, J. V.  4.65 45.0
19 83 Patterson, P.  6.50 12.0
19 105 Harry, D.  3.85 5.0
```

Chapter 6

DATA Step to Create RAINWEAR.STOCK

```
libname rainwear 'SAS-data-library';

data rainwear.stock;
   input line $ 1 dept 3-6 item $ 8-12;
   cards;
s 3070 20410
s 3070 20411
r 3070 20412
s 3070 20413
s 3070 20414
```

```
r 3070 20415
s 3070 20416
s 3070 20417
r 3070 20418
s 3070 20419
r 3070 20420
r 3080 20430
s 3080 20431
r 3080 20432
r 3080 20433
s 3080 20434
s 3080 20435
s 3080 20436
r 3080 20437
r 3080 20438
s 3080 20439
r 3080 20440
;
```

DATA Step to Create RAINWEAR.SALARIES

```
libname rainwear 'SAS-data-library';

data rainwear.salaries;
   input id $ 16. salary $ 19-26;
   cards;
8155-201-92-2498   35800
8156-298-89-5671   32075
8157-339-67-6980   29880
8158-203-45-1897   30665
8159-204-12-1269   28775
8160-113-11-1398   37550
8161-219-77-2908   39000
8162-101-65-3008   27219
8163-109-75-4009   40125
;
```

DATA Step to Create RAINWEAR.SALARY2

```
libname rainwear 'SAS-data-library';

data rainwear.salary2;
input id $ 16. salary $ 19-26;
  cards;
8155-201-92-2498   $35,800
8156-298-89-5671   $32,075
8157-339-67-6980   $29,880
```

```
8158-203-45-1897  $30,665
8159-204-12-1269  $28,775
8160-113-11-1398  $37,550
8161-219-77-2908  $39,000
8162-101-65-3008  $27,219
8163-109-75-4009  $40,125
;
```

Raw Data for RAINWEAR.DATES (Unpacked)

```
----+----1----+----2
HTTR 121090  021391
WVMA 121190  021691
ELMA 120790  031591
HLMA 120890  021691
SOBM 120690  031891
GVDM 120890  021391
VATR 120890  031591
MDMA 120990  031691
NOBM 121090  021291
OPMA 121190  021491
OTMA 120990  031691
----+----1----+----2
```

Chapter 7

Raw Data for RAINWEAR.PROFILE

```
----+----1----+----2----+
Chicago      1      6
Chicago      2      3
Chicago      3      7
Chicago      4      4
Chicago      5      2
Chicago      6      8
Chicago      7      6
Chicago      8      5
Chicago      9      7
Chicago     10      9
Chicago     11      3
Chicago     12      5
Hong Kong    1      7
Hong Kong    2      7
Hong Kong    3      9
Hong Kong    4      1
Hong Kong    5      9
Hong Kong    6      4
----+----1----+----2----+
```

```
----+----1----+----2----+
Hong Kong      7      1
Hong Kong      8      9
London         1      7
London         2      7
London         5      4
London         6      7
London         7      5
London        10      7
London        11      7
London        12      8
Los Angeles    1      4
Los Angeles    2      4
Los Angeles    3      3
Los Angeles    4      8
Los Angeles    5      7
Los Angeles    6      5
Los Angeles    7      6
Los Angeles    8      4
Los Angeles    9      5
Los Angeles   10      5
Los Angeles   11      5
Los Angeles   12      4
New York       1      8
New York       2      5
New York       3      9
New York       4      6
New York       5      3
New York       6      6
New York       7      3
New York       8      7
New York       9      6
New York      10      6
New York      11      8
New York      12      7
Paris          1      6
Paris          2      8
Paris          3      2
Paris          4      7
Paris          5      8
Paris          6      9
Paris          7      9
Paris          8      8
Paris          9      2
Paris         10      3
Paris         11      7
Paris         12      7
----+----1----+----2----+
```

Chapter 9

DATA Step to Create IN.PASTA

```
libname in 'SAS-data-library';

data in.pasta;
   input brand $ test1-test5;
   cards;
X0123 70 80 85 90 96
X0145 85 79 86 87 88
X0144 63 85 79 80 81
X0135 77 80 82 84 90
X0136 82 82 89 93 85
X0130 39 45 55 40 59
X0129 62 64 70 71 68
X0140 80 85 83 84 88
X0126 76 78 74 71 80
X0148 51 58 62 55 69
;
```

DATA Step to Create IN.PROD1

```
libname in 'SAS-data-library';

data in.prod1;
   input tester foodpr1-foodpr3 coffeem1 coffeem2 mw_oven1
         mw_oven2 dishwhr1-dishwhr3 period $;
   cards;
1001 115 45 65 83 78 55 113 82 45 77 initial
1002 86 27 55 72 86 74 39 99 65 70 final
1004 93 52 63 76 88 69 127 101 32 68 initial
1015 73 35 43 112 108 47 98 78 51 73 initial
1027 101 127 39 76 79 58 101 109 47 69 final
;
```

Chapter 10

DATA Step to Create IN.PRIMARY

```
libname in 'SAS-data-library';

data in.primary;
    input lname $14. fname $12. street $21. idcode $9. phone $;
    cards;
Brown        Michael      1804 Downtown Dr.     BM684937 557-0074
Bushnell     Wilbur       2904 Rosedale Ct.     BW129748 554-0552
Coulston     Patrick      3038 Morone Rd.       CP061553 556-2581
Dunlap       Lee          3015 Ignacius Street  DL454167 553-8607
Fuller       Deborah      1241 Ellis Place      FD518592 556-7076
Geaghan      Jay          2269 Flyer Run        GJ133173 555-2605
Graham       Patricia     130 Shasta Way        GP774960 555-7386
Jones        Ian          924 Callinectes Ct.   JI927309 554-9994
Kanehiro     Irene        3334 Islander Rd.     KI573115 554-5177
Kcin         Regnad       1645 Stanton Drive    KR083870 553-3312
Landing      William      1213 Moss Rd          LW631407 556-8780
MacCormick   Bonnie       1049 Bianca St.       MB572315 555-7930
;
```

DATA Step to Create IN.LOOKUP

```
libname in 'SAS-data-library';

data in.lookup;
    input idcode $ amount @20 duedate mmddyy8.;
    format duedate date7.;
    cards;
BM684937 948.25    05/06/91
BW129748 1080.83   04/08/91
DL454167 150.99    03/01/91
CP061553 632.98    02/26/91
DS454167 2255      05/07/91
FD518592 1600.8    04/11/91
GJ133173 2750.75   02/19/91
GP774960 1365.9    04/11/91
JI927309 800.25    02/19/91
KI573115 749.75    05/08/91
KR083870 500.5     03/04/91
LW631407 889.6     02/25/91
MB572315 416.35    04/04/91
;
```

DATA Step to Create IN.SURGTEAM

```
libname in 'SAS-data-library';

data in.surgteam;
   input surgeon $15. +1 assist $15. +1 scrub $15. +1 anesth $15.;
   cards;
Tran            Silva           Mohar           Rodwell
Gerhard         Stewart         Ligon           West
Johnson         Siu             MacKenzie       Short
Estes           Petrie          Nuyen           Edelstein
Frank           Robertson       Hoffman         McVeigh
Cage            Landau          Lepone          Randall
Ahmadi          Sherr           Just            Parker
Sloan           Edwards         Kline           Tester
Miller          Schwartz        Dingman         Perry
Rhew            Cox-Lewis       Cesar           Biddle
Junot           Meraz           Norton          d'Aubert
O'Reilly        Donaldson       Willis          Marcantonio
Grey            Wilson          Yancho          Edidin
Matthews        Rice            Chang           Perez
Smith           Caldwell        Sparkes         Winfield
Wu              Jarvis          Stanton         Austin
Taylor          Rippey          Campbell        Leff
Potuzko         Martin          Truesdale       Zeng
;
```

DATA Step to Create IN.TODAY

```
libname in 'SAS-data-library';

data in.today;
   input rmtype1-rmtype4;
   cards;
800 500 350 100
;
```

DATA Step to Create IN.RMINFO

```
libname in 'SAS-data-library';

data in.rminfo;
   input idcode $ room $ ndays;
   cards;
BM684937 PVT 14
BW129748 WRD 11
CP061553 ICU 10
DL454167 SPT 4
```

```
FD518592 SPT 6
GJ133173 WRD 8
GP774960 ICU 7
JI927309 SPT 6
KI573115 PVT 12
KR083870 SPT 10
LW631407 WRD 3
MB572315 PVT 9
;
```

DATA Step to Create IN.LIBRARY

```
libname in 'SAS-data-library';

data in.library;
   input idno $ category $16.;
   cards;
TH00001 medical
WC00001 psychology
TH00002 medical
TH00003 psychology
WC00002 psychology
TH00004 psychology
TH00005 medical
TH00006 medical
TH00007 medical
TH00008 medical
TH00009 medical
CA00001 psychology
TH00010 medical
TH00011 medical
TH00012 medical
WC00003 medical
TH00013 medical
CA00002 medical
TH00014 medical
;
```

DATA Step to Create IN.CHECKOUT

```
libname in 'SAS-data-library';

data in.checkout;
   input seqno numin numout title $46.;
   cards;
1 1 4 The Eight Week Cholesterol Cure
2 2 2 Living With Heart Disease
3 2 1 The Road Less Traveled
4 1 0 Healthy Attitudes, Healthy Hearts
```

```
5 2 4 Heart Disease:  Facts and Fiction
6 3 4 Heart Attack:  Guide to Recovery
7 2 3 Exercise Your Way to Better Health
8 2 1 Changing Lifestyles
9 1 0 Road to Recovery
10 1 0 Treating Heart Disease
11 2 3 The Oat Bran Story:  Myth or Miracle
12 3 6 Stress:  Making an Enemy Your Ally
13 1 4 Weight Loss the Sensible Way
14 2 3 Heart Disease:  A Second Opinion
;
```

Chapter 11

DATA Step to Create MYLIB.BOOKS

```
libname mylib 'SAS-data-library';

data mylib.books;
   input month $3.
         sales 5.;
   cards;
jan 805
feb 472
mar  74
apr 193
may 340
jun 518
jul 215
aug 947
sep 636
oct 102
nov 181
dec 505
;
```

Chapter 12

DATA Step to Create MYLIB.MAIL

```
libname mylib 'SAS-data-library';

data mylib.mail;
   input name $ 1-12 cost 15-21 city $ 22-27;
   cards;
Agerton       17.28  in
Allison       17.89  out
Alverson      50.73  out
Baldwin       67.66  out
Beck          23.37  out
Blevins       42.63  out
Brown         48.67  out
Chung         24.69  out
Clark          3.23  in
Cochran       38.62  out
Dominger       8.83  out
Dyer          62.88  in
Fuller        58.99  out
Goff          22.63  in
Guillet       62.72  out
Henzi          8.12  out
Heuser        31.25  out
Hibbert       77.83  out
Holiday        9.46  out
Krista        10.00  in
Lanthier      52.63  out
Lippert       23.84  out
Magoulas      38.33  out
McFann         8.33  out
Moynihan       6.06  in
Namboodri     24.38  out
Newton         5.40  in
Nist           8.35  in
Parks         47.69  out
Phelan        59.75  out
Ritchie       76.01  out
Rodriguez      5.78  in
Rogers        33.45  out
Salomon       25.36  out
Sheldrick     58.26  out
Slaton        38.78  out
Terwilliger   88.22  out
Veleff        54.72  out
Vinson        49.53  in
Whidby        52.25  out
;
```

Chapter 13

Raw Data for DATALIB.RADIO

```
967 32 f 5 3 5
7 5 5 5 7 0 0 0 8 7 0 0 8 0
781 30 f 2 3 5
5 0 0 0 5 0 0 0 4 7 5 0 0 0
859 39 f 1 0 5
1 0 0 0 1 0 0 0 0 0 0 0 0 0
859 40 f 6 1 5
7 5 0 5 7 0 0 0 0 0 0 5 0 0
467 37 m 2 3 1
1 5 5 5 5 4 4 8 8 0 0 0 0 0
220 35 f 3 1 7
7 0 0 0 7 0 0 0 7 0 0 0 0 0
833 42 m 2 2 4
7 0 0 0 7 5 4 7 4 0 1 4 4 0
967 39 f .5 1 7
7 0 0 0 7 7 0 0 0 0 0 0 8 0
677 28 m .5 .5 7
7 0 0 0 0 0 0 0 0 0 0 0 0 0
833 28 f 3 4 1
1 0 0 0 0 1 1 1 1 0 0 0 1 1
677 24 f 3 1 2
2 0 0 0 0 0 0 2 0 8 8 0 0 0
688 32 m 5 2 4
5 5 0 4 8 0 0 5 0 8 0 0 0 0
542 38 f 6 8 5
5 0 0 5 5 5 0 5 5 5 5 5 5 0
677 27 m 6 1 1
1 1 0 4 4 0 0 1 4 0 0 0 0 0
779 37 f 2.5 4 7
7 0 0 0 7 7 0 7 7 4 4 7 8 0
362 31 f 1 2 2
8 0 0 0 8 0 0 0 0 0 8 8 0 0
859 29 m 10 3 4
4 4 0 2 2 0 0 4 0 0 0 4 4 0
467 24 m 5 8 1
7 1 1 1 7 1 1 0 1 7 1 1 1 1
851 34 m 1 2 8
0 0 0 0 8 0 0 0 4 0 0 0 8 0
859 23 f 1 1 8
8 0 0 0 8 0 0 0 0 0 0 0 0 8
781 34 f 9 3 1
2 1 0 1 4 4 4 0 1 1 1 1 4 4
851 40 f 2 4 5
5 0 0 0 5 0 0 5 0 0 5 5 0 0
783 34 m 3 2 4
7 0 0 0 7 4 4 0 0 4 4 0 0 0
848 29 f 4 1.5 7
```

```
7 4 4 1 7 0 0 0 7 0 0 7 0 0
851 28 f 1 2 2
2 0 2 0 2 0 0 0 0 2 2 2 0 0
856 42 f 1.5 1 2
2 0 0 0 0 0 0 2 0 0 0 0 0 0
859 29 m .5 .5 5
5 0 0 0 1 0 0 0 0 0 0 8 8 5 0
833 29 m 1 3 2
2 0 0 0 2 2 0 0 4 2 0 2 0 0
859 23 f 10 3 1
1 5 0 8 8 1 4 0 1 1 1 1 1 4
781 37 f .5 2 7
7 0 0 0 1 0 0 0 1 7 0 1 0 0
833 31 f 5 4 1
1 0 0 0 1 0 0 0 4 0 4 0 0 0
942 23 f 4 2
1 0 0 0 1 0 1 0 1 1 0 0 0 0
848 33 f 5 4 1
1 1 0 1 1 0 0 0 1 1 1 0 0 0
222 33 f 2 0 1
1 0 0 0 1 0 0 0 0 0 0 0 0 0
851 45 f .5 1 8
8 0 0 0 8 0 0 0 0 0 8 0 0 0
848 27 f 2 4 1
1 0 0 0 1 1 0 0 4 1 1 1 1 1
781 38 m 2 2 1
5 0 0 0 1 0 0 0 0 0 1 1 0 0
222 27 f 3 1 2
2 0 2 0 2 2 0 0 2 0 0 0 0 0
467 34 f 2 2 1
1 0 0 0 0 1 0 1 0 0 0 0 1 0
833 27 f 8 8 1
7 0 1 0 7 4 0 0 1 1 1 4 1 0
677 49 f 1.5 0 8
8 0 8 0 8 0 0 0 0 0 0 0 0 0
849 43 m 1 4 1
1 0 0 0 4 0 0 0 4 0 1 0 0 0
467 28 m 2 1 7
7 0 0 0 7 0 0 7 0 0 1 0 0 0
732 29 f 1 0 2
2 0 0 0 2 0 0 0 0 0 0 0 0 0
851 31 m 2 2 2
2 5 0 6 0 0 8 0 2 2 8 2 0 0
779 42 f 8 2 2
7 2 0 2 7 0 0 0 0 0 0 0 2 0
493 40 m 1 3 3
3 0 0 0 5 3 0 5 5 0 0 0 1 1
859 30 m 1 0 7
7 0 0 0 7 0 0 0 0 0 0 0 0 0
833 36 m 4 2 5
7 5 0 5 0 5 0 0 7 0 0 0 5 0
467 30 f 1 4 1
0 0 0 0 1 0 6 0 0 1 1 1 0 6
```

```
859 32 f 3 5 2
2 2 2 2 2 2 6 6 2 2 2 2 2 6
851 43 f 8 1 5
7 5 5 5 0 0 0 4 0 0 0 0 0 0
848 29 f 3 5 1
7 0 0 0 7 1 0 0 1 1 1 1 1 0
833 25 f 2 4 5
7 0 0 0 5 7 0 0 7 5 0 0 5 0
783 33 f 8 3 8
8 0 8 0 7 0 0 0 8 0 5 4 0 5
222 26 f 10 2 1
1 1 0 1 1 0 0 0 3 1 1 0 0 0
222 23 f 3 2 2
2 2 2 2 7 0 0 2 2 0 0 0 0 0
859 50 f 1 5 4
7 0 0 0 7 0 0 5 4 4 4 7 0 0
833 26 f 3 2 1
1 0 0 1 1 0 0 5 5 0 1 0 0 0
467 29 m 7 2 1
1 1 1 1 1 0 0 1 1 1 0 0 0 0
859 35 m .5 2 2
7 0 0 0 2 0 0 7 5 0 0 4 0 0
833 33 f 3 3 6
7 0 0 0 6 8 0 8 0 0 0 8 6 0
221 36 f .5 1 5
0 7 0 0 0 7 0 0 7 0 0 7 7 0
220 32 f 2 4 5
5 0 5 0 5 5 5 0 5 5 5 5 5 5
684 19 f 2 4 2
0 2 0 2 0 0 0 0 0 2 2 0 0 0
493 55 f 1 0 5
5 0 0 5 0 0 0 0 7 0 0 0 0 0
221 27 m 1 1 7
7 0 0 0 0 0 0 0 5 0 0 0 5 0
684 19 f 0 .5 1
7 0 0 0 0 1 1 0 0 0 0 0 1 1
493 38 f .5 .5 5
0 8 0 0 5 0 0 0 5 0 0 0 0 0
221 26 f .5 2 1
0 1 0 0 0 1 0 0 5 5 5 1 0 0
684 18 m 1 .5 1
0 2 0 0 0 0 1 0 0 0 0 1 1 0
684 19 m 1 1 1
0 0 0 1 1 0 0 0 0 0 1 0 0 0
221 29 m .5 .5 5
0 0 0 0 0 5 5 0 0 0 0 0 5 5
683 18 f 2 4 8
0 0 0 0 8 0 0 0 8 8 8 0 0 0
966 23 f 1 2 1
1 5 5 5 1 0 0 0 0 1 0 0 1 0
493 25 f 3 5 7
7 0 0 0 7 2 0 0 7 0 2 7 7 0
683 18 f .5 .5 2
```

```
1 0 0 0 0 0 5 0 0 1 0 0 0 1
382 21 f 3 1 8
0 8 0 0 5 8 8 0 0 8 8 0 0 0
683 18 f 4 6 2
2 0 0 0 2 2 2 0 2 0 2 2 2 0
684 19 m .5 2 1
0 0 0 0 1 1 0 0 0 1 1 1 1 5
684 19 m 1.5 3.5 2
2 0 0 0 2 0 0 0 0 0 2 5 0 0
221 23 f 1 5 1
7 5 1 5 1 3 1 7 5 1 5 1 3 1
684 18 f 2 3 1
2 0 0 1 1 1 1 7 2 0 1 1 1 1
683 19 f 3 5 2
2 0 0 2 0 6 1 0 1 1 2 2 6 1
683 19 f 3 5 1
2 0 0 2 0 6 1 0 1 1 2 0 2 1
221 35 m 3 5 5
7 5 0 1 7 0 0 5 5 5 0 0 0 0
221 43 f 1 4 5
1 0 0 0 5 0 0 5 5 0 0 0 0 0
493 32 f 2 1 6
0 0 0 6 0 0 0 0 0 0 0 0 4 0
221 24 f 4 5 2
2 0 5 0 0 2 4 4 4 5 0 0 2 2
684 19 f 2 3 2
0 5 5 2 5 0 1 0 5 5 2 2 2 2
221 19 f 3 3 8
0 1 1 8 8 8 4 0 5 4 1 8 8 4
221 29 m 1 1 5
5 5 5 5 5 5 5 5 5 5 5 5 5 5
221 21 m 1 1 1
1 0 0 0 0 0 5 1 0 0 0 0 0 5
683 20 f 1 2 2
0 0 0 0 2 0 0 0 2 0 0 0 0 0
493 54 f 1 1 5
7 0 0 5 0 0 0 0 0 0 5 0 0 0
493 45 m 4 6 5
7 0 0 0 7 5 0 0 5 5 5 5 5 5
850 44 m 2.5 1.5 7
7 0 7 0 4 7 5 0 5 4 3 0 0 4
220 33 m 5 3 5
1 5 0 5 1 0 0 0 0 0 0 0 5 5
684 20 f 1.5 3 1
1 0 0 0 1 0 1 0 1 0 0 1 1 0
966 63 m 3 5 3
5 4 7 5 4 5 0 5 0 0 5 5 4 0
683 21 f 4 6 1
0 1 0 1 1 1 1 0 1 1 1 1 1 1
493 23 f 5 2 5
7 5 0 4 0 0 0 0 1 1 1 1 1 0
493 32 f 8 8 5
7 5 0 0 7 0 5 5 5 0 0 7 5 5
```

```
942 33 f 7 2 5
0 5 5 4 7 0 0 0 0 0 0 7 8 0
493 34 f .5 1 5
5 0 0 0 5 0 0 0 0 6 0 0 0
382 40 f 2 2 5
5 0 0 0 5 0 0 5 0 0 5 0 0 0
362 27 f 0 3 8
0 0 0 0 0 0 0 0 0 0 0 8 0
542 36 f 3 3 7
7 0 0 0 7 1 0 0 0 7 1 1 0 0
966 39 f 3 6 5
7 0 0 0 7 5 0 0 7 0 5 0 5 0
849 32 m 1 .5 7
7 0 0 0 5 0 0 0 7 4 4 5 7 0
677 52 f 3 2 3
7 0 0 0 0 7 0 0 0 7 0 0 3 0
222 25 m 2 4 1
1 0 0 0 1 0 0 0 1 0 1 0 0 0
732 42 f 3 2 7
7 0 0 0 1 7 5 5 7 0 0 3 4 0
467 26 f 4 4 1
7 0 1 0 7 1 0 0 7 7 4 7 0 0
467 38 m 2.5 0 1
1 0 0 0 1 0 0 0 0 0 0 0 0 0
382 37 f 1.5 .5 7
7 0 0 0 7 0 0 0 3 0 0 0 3 0
856 45 f 3 3 7
7 0 0 0 7 5 0 0 7 7 4 0 0 0
677 33 m 3 2 7
7 0 0 4 7 0 0 0 7 0 0 0 0 0
490 27 f .5 1 2
2 0 0 0 2 0 0 0 2 0 2 0 0 0
362 27 f 1.5 2 2
2 0 0 0 1 0 4 0 1 0 0 0 4 4
783 25 f 2 1 1
1 0 0 0 1 7 0 0 0 0 1 1 1 0
546 30 f 8 3 1
1 1 1 1 1 0 0 1 0 5 5 0 0 0
677 30 f 2 0 1
1 0 0 0 0 1 0 0 0 0 0 0 0 1
221 35 f 2 2 1
1 0 0 0 1 0 1 0 1 1 1 0 0 0
966 32 f 6 1 7
7 1 1 1 7 4 0 1 7 1 8 8 4 0
222 28 f 1 5 4
7 0 0 0 4 0 0 4 4 4 4 0 0 0
467 29 f 5 3 4
4 5 5 5 1 4 4 5 1 1 1 1 4 4
467 32 m 3 4 1
1 0 1 0 4 0 0 0 4 0 0 0 1 0
966 30 m 1.5 1 7
7 0 0 0 7 5 0 7 0 0 0 0 5 0
967 38 m 14 4 7
```

```
7 7 7 7 7 0 4 8 0 0 0 0 4 0
490 28 m 8  1  1
7 1 1 1 1 0 0 7 0 0 8 0 0 0
833 30 f .5 1 6
6 0 0 0 6 0 0 0 0 6 0 0 6 0
851 40 m 1 0 7
7 5 5 5 7 0 0 0 0 0 0 0 0 0
859 27 f 2 5 2
6 0 0 0 2 0 0 0 0 0 0 2 2 2
851 22 f 3 5 2
7 0 2 0 2 2 0 0 2 0 8 0 2 0
967 38 f 1 1.5 7
7 0 0 0 7 5 0 7 4 0 0 7 5 0
856 34 f 1.5 1 1
0 1 0 0 0 1 0 0 4 0 0 0 0 0
222 33 m .1 .1 7
7 0 0 0 7 0 0 0 0 0 7 0 0 0
856 22 m .50 .25 1
0 1 0 0 1 0 0 0 0 0 0 0 0 0
677 30 f 2 2 4
1 0 4 0 4 0 0 0 4 0 0 0 0 0
859 25 m 2 3 7
0 0 0 0 0 7 0 0 7 0 2 0 0 1
833 35 m 2 6 7
7 0 0 0 7 1 1 0 4 7 4 7 1 1
677 35 m 10 4 1
1 1 1 1 1 8 6 8 1 0 0 8 8 8
848 29 f 5 3 8
8 0 0 0 8 8 0 0 0 8 8 8 0 0
688 26 m 3 1 1
1 1 7 1 1 7 0 0 0 8 8 0 0 0
490 41 m 2 2 5
5 0 0 0 0 0 5 5 0 0 0 0 0 5
493 35 m 4 4 7
7 5 0 5 7 0 0 7 7 7 7 0 0 0
677 27 m 15 11 1
1 1 1 1 1 1 1 1 1 1 1 1 1 1
848 27 f 3 5 1
1 1 0 0 1 1 0 0 1 1 1 1 0 0
362 30 f 1 0 1
1 0 0 0 7 5 0 0 0 0 0 0 0 0
783 29 f 1 1 4
4 0 0 0 4 0 0 0 4 0 0 0 4 0
467 39 f .5 2 4
7 0 4 0 4 4 0 0 4 4 4 4 4 4
677 27 m 2 2 7
7 0 0 0 7 0 0 7 7 0 0 7 0 0
221 23 f 2.5 1 1
1 0 0 0 1 0 0 0 0 0 0 0 0 0
677 29 f 1 1 7
0 0 0 0 7 0 0 0 7 0 0 0 0 0
783 32 m 1 2 5
4 5 5 5 4 2 0 0 0 0 3 2 2 0
```

```
833 25 f 1 0 1
1 1 0 0 0 0 0 0 0 0 0 0 0 0
859 24 f 7 3 7
1 0 0 0 1 0 0 0 0 1 0 0 1 0
677 29 m 2 2 8
0 8 8 0 8 0 0 0 8 8 8 0 0 0
688 31 m 8 2 5
7 5 5 5 5 7 0 0 7 7 0 0 0 0
856 31 m 9 4 1
1 1 1 1 1 0 0 0 0 0 0 0 1 0
856 44 f 1 0 6
6 0 0 0 6 0 0 0 0 0 0 0 0 0
677 37 f 3 3 1
0 0 1 0 0 0 0 0 4 4 0 0 0 0
859 27 m 2 .5 2
2 2 2 2 2 2 2 2 0 0 0 0 0 2
781 30 f 10 4 2
2 0 0 0 2 0 2 0 0 0 0 0 0 2
362 27 m 12 4 3
3 1 1 1 1 3 3 3 0 0 0 0 3 0
362 33 f 2 4 1
1 0 0 0 7 0 0 7 1 1 1 1 1 0
222 26 f 8 1 1
1 1 1 1 0 0 0 1 0 0 0 0 0 0
779 37 f 6 3 1
1 1 1 1 1 0 0 1 1 0 0 0 1 0
467 32 f 1 1 2
2 0 0 0 0 0 0 0 2 0 0 2 0 0
859 23 m 1 1 1
1 0 0 0 1 1 0 1 0 0 0 0 1 1
781 33 f 1 .5 6
6 0 0 0 6 0 0 0 0 0 0 0 0 0
779 28 m 5 2 1
1 1 1 1 1 0 0 0 0 7 7 1 1 0
677 28 m 3 1 5
7 5 5 5 5 6 0 0 6 6 6 6 6 0
677 25 f 9 2 5
1 5 5 5 5 1 1 0 1 1 1 1 1 1
848 30 f 6 2 8
8 0 0 0 2 7 0 0 0 2 0 2 0
546 36 f 4 6 4
7 0 0 0 4 4 0 5 5 5 5 2 4 4
222 30 f 2 3 2
2 2 0 0 2 0 0 0 2 0 2 2 0 0
383 32 m 4 1 2
2 0 0 0 2 0 0 2 0 0 0 0 0 0
851 43 f 8 1 6
4 6 0 6 4 0 0 0 0 0 0 0 0 0
222 27 f 1 3 1
1 1 0 1 1 1 0 0 1 0 0 0 4 0
833 22 f 1.5 2 1
1 0 0 0 1 1 0 0 1 1 1 0 0 0
467 29 f 2 1 8
```

```
8 0 8 0 8 0 0 0 0 0 8 0 0 0
856 28 f 2 3 1
1 0 0 0 1 0 0 0 1 0 0 1 0 0
580 31 f 2.5 2.5 6
6 6 6 6 6 6 6 6 1 1 1 1 6 6
688 39 f 8 8 3
3 3 3 3 3 3 3 3 3 3 3 3 3 3
677 37 f 1.5 .5 1
6 1 1 1 6 6 0 0 1 1 6 6 6 0
859 38 m 3 6 3
7 0 0 0 7 3 0 0 3 0 3 0 0 0
677 25 f 7 1 1
0 1 1 1 2 0 0 0 1 2 1 1 1 0
848 36 f 7 1 1
0 1 0 1 1 0 0 0 0 0 0 1 1 0
781 31 f 2 4 1
1 0 0 0 1 1 0 1 1 1 1 1 0 0
781 40 f 2 2 8
8 0 0 8 8 0 0 0 0 0 8 8 0 0
677 25 f 3 5 1
1 6 1 6 6 3 0 0 2 2 1 1 1 1
779 33 f 3 2 1
1 0 1 0 0 0 1 0 1 0 0 0 1 0
677 25 m 7 1.5 1
1 1 0 1 1 0 0 0 0 0 1 0 0 0
362 35 f .5 0 1
1 0 0 0 1 0 0 0 0 0 0 0 0 0
677 41 f 6 2 7
7 7 0 7 7 0 0 0 0 0 8 0 0 0
677 24 m 5 1 5
1 5 0 5 0 0 0 0 1 0 0 0 0 0
833 29 f .5 0 6
6 0 0 0 6 0 0 0 0 0 0 0 0 0
362 30 f 1 1 1
1 0 0 0 1 0 0 0 1 0 0 0 0 0
850 26 f 6 12 6
6 0 0 0 2 2 6 6 6 0 0 6 6
467 25 f 2 3 1
1 0 0 6 1 1 0 0 0 0 1 1 1 1
967 29 f 1 2 7
7 0 0 0 7 0 0 7 7 0 0 0 0 0
833 31 f 1 1 7
7 0 7 0 7 3 0 0 3 3 0 0 0 0
859 40 f 7 1 5
1 5 0 5 5 1 0 0 1 0 0 0 0 0
848 31 m 1 2 1
1 0 0 0 1 1 0 0 4 4 1 4 0 0
222 32 f 2 3 3
3 0 0 0 0 7 0 0 3 0 8 0 0 0
783 33 f 2 0 4
7 0 0 0 7 0 0 0 4 0 4 0 0 0
856 28 f 8 4 2
0 2 0 2 2 0 0 0 2 0 2 0 4 0
```

```
781 30 f 3 5 1
1 1 1 1 1 1 0 0 1 1 1 1 1 0
850 25 f 6 3 1
7 5 0 5 7 1 0 0 7 0 1 0 1 0
580 33 f 2.5 4 2
2 0 0 0 2 0 0 0 0 0 8 8 0 0
677 38 f 3 3 1
1 0 0 0 1 0 1 1 1 0 1 0 0 4
677 26 f 2 2 1
1 0 1 0 1 0 0 0 1 1 1 0 0 0
467 52 f 3 2 2
2 6 6 6 6 2 0 0 2 2 2 2 0 0
542 31 f 1 3 1
1 0 1 0 1 0 0 0 1 1 1 1 1 0
859 50 f 9 3 6
6 6 6 6 6 6 6 6 6 3 3 3 6 6
779 26 f 1 2 1
7 0 1 0 1 1 4 1 4 1 1 1 1 4 4
779 36 m 1.5 2 4
1 4 0 4 4 0 0 4 4 4 4 0 0 0
222 31 f 0 7
1 0 0 0 7 0 0 0 0 0 0 0 0 0
362 27 f 1 1 1
1 0 1 0 1 4 0 4 4 1 0 4 4 0
967 32 f 3 2 7
7 0 0 0 7 0 0 0 1 0 0 1 0 0
362 29 f 10 2 2
2 2 2 2 2 2 2 2 2 2 7 0 0
677 27 f 3 4 1
0 5 1 1 0 5 0 0 0 1 1 1 0 0
546 32 m 5 .5 8
8 0 0 0 8 0 0 0 8 0 0 0 0 0
688 38 m 2 3 2
2 0 0 0 2 0 0 0 2 0 0 0 1 0
362 28 f 1 1 1
1 0 0 0 1 1 0 4 0 0 0 0 4 0
851 32 f .5 2 4
5 0 0 0 4 0 0 0 0 0 0 0 2 0
967 43 f 2 2 1
1 0 0 0 1 0 0 1 7 0 0 0 1 0
467 44 f 10 4 6
7 6 0 6 6 0 6 0 0 0 0 0 0 6
467 23 f 5 3 1
0 2 1 2 1 0 0 0 1 1 1 1 1 1
783 30 f 1 .5 1
1 0 0 0 1 0 0 0 0 0 0 7 0 0
677 29 f 3 1 2
2 2 2 2 0 0 0 0 0 0 0 0 0
859 26 f 9.5 1.5 2
2 2 2 2 0 0 2 2 0 0 0 0 0
222 28 f 3 0 2
2 0 0 0 2 0 0 0 0 0 2 0 0 0
966 37 m 2 1 1
```

```
7 1 1 1 7 0 0 0 7 0 0 0 0 0
859 31 f 10 10 1
0 1 1 1 1 0 0 0 1 1 0 0 1 0
781 27 f 2 1 2
2 0 0 0 1 0 0 0 4 0 0 0 0 0
677 31 f .5 .5 6
7 0 0 0 0 0 0 0 6 0 0 0 0 0
848 28 f 5 1 2
2 2 0 2 0 0 0 0 2 0 0 0 0 0
781 24 f 3 3 6
1 6 6 6 1 6 0 0 0 0 1 0 1 1
856 27 f 1.5 1 6
2 6 6 6 2 5 0 2 0 0 5 2 0 0
382 30 m 1 2 7
7 0 0 0 7 0 4 7 0 0 0 7 4 4
848 25 f 9 3 1
7 1 1 5 1 0 0 0 1 1 1 1 1 0
382 30 m 1 2 4
7 0 0 0 7 0 4 7 0 0 0 7 4 4
688 40 m 2 3 1
1 0 0 0 1 3 1 0 5 0 4 4 7 1
856 40 f .5 5 5
3 0 0 0 3 0 0 0 0 0 5 5 0 0
966 25 f 2 .5 2
1 0 0 0 2 6 0 0 4 0 0 0 0 0
859 30 f 2 4 2
2 0 0 0 0 2 0 0 0 0 2 0 0 0
849 29 m 10 1 5
7 5 5 5 7 5 5 0 0 0 0 0 7 0
781 28 m 1.5 3 4
1 0 0 0 1 4 4 0 4 4 1 1 4 0
467 35 f 4 2 6
7 6 7 6 6 7 6 7 7 7 7 7 7 6
222 32 f 10 5 1
1 1 0 1 1 0 0 1 1 1 0 0 1 0
677 32 f 1 0 1
1 0 1 0 0 0 0 0 0 0 0 0 0 0
222 54 f 21 4 3
5 0 0 0 7 0 0 7 0 0 0 0 0 0
677 30 m 4 6 1
7 0 0 0 0 1 1 1 7 1 1 0 8 1
683 29 f 1 2 8
8 0 0 0 8 0 0 0 0 8 8 0 0 0
467 38 m 3 5 1
1 0 0 0 1 0 0 1 1 0 0 0 0 0
781 29 f 2 3 8
8 0 0 0 8 8 0 0 8 8 0 8 8 0
781 30 f 1 0 5
5 0 0 0 0 5 0 0 0 0 0 0 0 0
783 40 f 1.5 3 1
1 0 0 0 1 4 0 0 1 1 1 0 0 0
851 30 f 1 1 6
6 0 0 0 6 0 0 0 6 0 0 6 0 0
```

```
851 40 f 1 1 5
5 0 0 0 5 0 0 0 0 1 0 0 0 0
779 40 f 1 0 2
2 0 0 0 2 0 0 0 0 0 0 0 0 0
467 37 f 4 8 1
1 0 0 0 1 0 3 0 3 1 1 1 0 0
859 37 f 4 3 3
0 3 7 0 0 7 0 0 0 7 8 3 7 0
781 26 f 4 1 2
2 2 0 2 1 0 0 0 2 0 0 0 0 0
859 23 f 8 3 3
3 2 0 2 3 0 0 0 1 0 0 3 0 0
967 31 f .5 0 1
1 0 0 0 0 0 0 0 0 0 0 0 0 0
851 38 m 4 2 5
7 5 0 5 4 0 4 7 7 0 4 0 8 0
467 30 m 2 1 2
2 2 0 2 0 0 0 0 2 0 2 0 0 0
848 33 f 2 2 7
7 0 0 0 0 7 0 7 7 0 0 0 7 0
688 35 f 5 8 3
2 2 2 2 2 0 0 3 3 3 3 3 0 0
467 27 f 2 3 1
1 0 1 0 0 1 0 0 1 1 1 0 0 0
783 42 f 3 1 1
1 0 0 0 1 0 0 0 1 0 1 1 0 0
687 40 m 1.5 2 1
7 0 0 0 1 1 0 0 1 0 7 0 1 0
779 30 f 4 8 7
7 0 0 0 7 0 6 7 4 2 2 0 0 6
222 34 f 9 0 8
8 2 0 2 8 0 0 0 0 0 0 0 0 0
467 28 m 3 1 2
2 0 0 0 2 2 0 0 0 2 2 0 0 0
222 28 f 8 4 2
1 2 1 2 2 0 0 1 2 2 0 0 2 0
542 35 m 2 3 2
6 0 7 0 7 0 7 0 0 0 2 2 0 0
677 31 m 12 4 3
7 3 0 3 3 4 0 0 4 4 4 0 0 0
783 45 f 1.5 2 6
6 0 0 0 6 0 0 6 6 0 0 0 0 0
942 34 f 1 .5 4
4 0 0 0 1 0 0 0 0 0 2 0 0 0
222 30 f 8 4 1
1 1 1 1 1 0 0 0 1 1 0 0 0 0
967 38 f 1.5 2 7
7 0 0 0 7 0 0 7 1 1 1 1 0 0
783 37 f 2 1 1
6 6 1 1 6 6 0 0 6 1 1 1 6 0
467 31 f 1.5 2 2
2 0 7 0 7 0 0 7 7 0 0 0 7 0
859 48 f 3 0 7
```

```
7 0 0 0 0 0 0 0 0 7 0 0 0 0
490 35 f 1 1 7
7 0 0 0 7 0 0 0 0 0 0 0 8 0
222 27 f 3 2 3
8 0 0 0 3 8 0 3 3 0 0 0 0 0
382 36 m 3 2 4
7 0 5 4 7 4 4 0 7 7 4 7 0 4
859 37 f 1 1 2
7 0 0 0 0 2 0 2 2 0 0 0 0 2
856 29 f 3 1 1
1 0 0 0 1 1 1 1 0 0 1 1 0 1
542 32 m 3 3 7
7 0 0 0 0 7 7 7 0 0 0 0 7 7
783 31 m 1 1 1
1 0 0 0 1 0 0 0 1 1 1 0 0 0
833 35 m 1 1 1
5 4 1 5 1 0 0 1 1 0 0 0 0 0
782 38 m 30 8 5
7 5 5 5 5 0 0 4 4 4 4 4 0 0
222 33 m 3 3 1
1 1 1 1 1 1 1 1 4 1 1 1 1 1
467 24 f 2 4 1
0 0 1 0 1 0 0 0 1 1 1 0 0 0
467 34 f 1 1 1
1 0 0 0 1 0 0 1 1 0 0 0 0 0
781 53 f 2 1 5
5 0 0 0 5 5 0 0 0 0 5 5 5 0
222 30 m 2 5 3
6 3 3 3 6 0 0 0 3 3 3 3 0 0
688 26 f 2 2 1
1 0 0 0 1 0 0 0 1 0 1 1 0 0
222 29 m 8 5 1
1 6 0 6 1 0 0 1 1 1 1 0 0 0
783 33 m 1 2 7
7 0 0 0 7 0 0 0 7 0 0 0 7 0
781 39 m 1.5 2.5 2
2 0 2 0 2 0 0 0 2 2 2 0 0 0
850 22 f 2 1 1
1 0 0 0 1 1 1 0 5 0 0 1 0 0
493 36 f 1 0 5
0 0 0 0 7 0 0 0 0 0 0 0 0 0
967 46 f 2 4 7
7 5 0 5 7 0 0 0 4 7 4 0 0 0
856 41 m 2 2 4
7 4 0 0 7 4 0 4 0 0 0 7 0 0
546 25 m 5 5 8
8 8 0 0 0 0 0 0 0 0 0 0 0 0
222 27 f 4 4 3
2 2 2 3 7 7 0 2 2 2 3 3 3 0
688 23 m 9 3 3
3 3 3 3 3 7 0 0 3 0 0 0 0 0
849 26 m .5 .5 8
8 0 0 0 8 0 0 0 0 8 0 0 0 0
```

```
783 29 f 3 3 1
1 0 0 0 4 0 0 4 1 0 1 0 0 0
856 34 f 1.5 2 1
7 0 0 0 7 0 0 7 4 0 0 7 0 0
966 33 m 3 5 4
7 0 0 0 7 4 5 0 7 0 0 7 4 4
493 34 f 2 5 1
1 0 0 0 1 0 0 0 7 0 1 1 8 0
467 29 m 2 4 2
2 0 0 0 2 0 0 2 2 2 2 2 2 2
677 28 f 1 4 1
1 1 1 1 1 0 0 0 1 0 1 0 0 0
781 27 m 2 2 1
1 0 1 0 4 2 4 0 2 2 1 0 1 4
467 24 m 4 4 1
7 1 0 1 1 1 0 7 1 0 0 0 0 0
859 26 m 5 5 1
1 1 1 1 1 1 1 1 1 1 1 1 1 1
848 27 m 7 2 5
7 5 0 5 4 5 0 0 0 7 4 4 0 4
677 25 f 1 2 8
8 0 0 0 0 5 0 0 8 0 0 0 2 0
222 26 f 3.5 0 2
2 0 0 0 2 0 0 0 0 0 0 0 0 0
833 32 m 1 2 1
1 0 0 0 1 0 0 0 5 0 1 0 0 0
781 28 m 2 .5 7
7 0 0 0 7 0 0 0 4 0 0 0 0 0
783 28 f 1 1 1
1 0 0 0 1 0 0 0 0 0 1 1 0 0
222 28 f 5 5 2
2 6 6 2 2 0 0 0 2 2 0 0 2 2
851 33 m 4 5 3
1 0 0 0 7 3 0 3 3 3 3 3 7 5
859 39 m 2 1 1
1 0 0 0 1 0 0 0 0 0 0 1 0 0
848 45 m 2 2 7
7 0 0 0 7 0 0 0 7 0 0 0 0 0
467 37 m 2 2 7
7 0 0 0 0 7 0 0 0 7 0 0 7 0
859 32 m .25 .25 1
1 0 0 0 0 0 0 0 1 0 0 0 0 0
```

Chapter 14

DATA Step to Create MYLIB.HOUSES

```
libname mylib 'SAS-data-library';

data mylib.houses;
   input zone $1. +1 type : $8. bedr bath sqfeet age
         schools : $15. / address & $25. price;
cards;
4 twostory 4 2.5 2538 6 920:340/400/368
211 Whitehall Way  154900
1 twostory 4 2.5 2700 7 920:470/360/552
1800 Bridgeport  169900
3 twnhouse 2 2 1595 6 320:332/366/312
154 Montrose  102000
1 twostory 3 2.5 2750 0 920:628/388/348
4000 Skipjack Ct.  214900
4 split 3 2 1306 0 920:576/512/436
5933 South Downs Dr.  95400
2 twostory 3 3.5 2590 0 920:364/608/368
727 Crabtree Crossing  292400
5 split 3 1 1959 31 680:308/316/332
627 Riverside Dr.  58900
2 twnhouse 3 2.5 1374 15 920:304/604/368
907 Lexington Ct.  65500
4 condo 2 2 1275 5 920:448/472/318
6010-102 Winterpoint  70000
4 ranch 3 2 1526 6 920:476/424/428
6509 Orchard Knoll  107900
1 split 3 1.5 1329 23 920:396/360/552
500 E. Millbrook Rd.  82900
1 condo 2 3.5 1300 5 920:448/472/318
6010-101 Winterpoint  68900
8 twnhouse 2 2 1120 4 320:364/366/312
521 Woodwinds  84600
2 condo 2 2 1066 1 920:520/604/368
1324 Killiam Ct.  74900
4 split 4 2.5 2600 10 920:476/424/428
7141 Eastridge  198000
2 twnhouse 2 1.5 1150 15 920:304/400/368
1239 Donaldson Ct.  49900
4 ranch 3 2.5 2441 1 920:540/512/436
9356 Sauls Rd.  197000
1 split 3 1 1245 36 920:524/388/348
2414 Van Dyke  85000
7 twnhouse 2 1.5 1280 4 920:584/592/588
409 Galashiels  60000
```

```
4 ranch 3 3 2400 2 920:420/424/428
8122 Maude Steward Rd.  129900
2 duplex 2 2.5 1184 4 920:364/604/368
112 Lake Hollow  67900
6 duplex 3 1 1569 73 350:324/328/336
108 South Elm St.  100000
2 twnhouse 2 1.5 1040 9 920:414/604/316
216 Concannon Ct.  59900
4 condo 3 2 1448 5 920:448/472/318
6000-102 Winterpoint  79900
2 twnhouse 3 2 1471 1 920:364/604/368
765 Crabtree Crossing  184000
4 twostory 3 2.5 1940 4 920:328/312/316
1641 Pricewood Lane  195000
5 split 2 1 960 2 680:308/304/332
Rt.5 Yarbororugh Rd.  78900
8 twnhouse 2 2 1167 5 320:364/366/312
5001 Pine Cone  78500
2 condo 2 2 1246 4 920:364/604/316
721 Springfork  76900
1 twnhouse 2 1 980 4 920:304/360/552
1203 Berley Ct  72400
8 twostory 4 2.5 3446 0 320:313/316/356
Lot 10 Red Coach Rd.  225000
8 split 3 1.5 1441 28 320:315/316/356
5617 Laurel Crest Dr.  86900
5 twostory 3 2.5 1900 4 680:308/316/332
1532 St. Mary's Rd.  118500
8 split 3 2 1976 10 320:348/316/356
110 Skylark Way  123500
8 twnhouse 2 2 1276 6 321:360/304/356
8 Stonevillage  71000
5 split 3 2 1533 5 680:/308/316/322
603 Greentree Dr.  117800
2 twostory 4 2.5 2584 0 920:364/640/368
114 Grey Horse Dr.  189900
8 twostory 4 2.5 2608 0 320:362/366/312
2103 Carriage Way  189900
2 twnhouse 3 2.5 2080 4 920:530/400/318
108 Chattle Close  179900
5 twostory 3 2.5 2863 7 680:308/316/332
5521 Horseshoe Circle  199200
8 split 2 2.5 2900 38 320:315/316/356
2617 Snow Hill Rd  425000
3 twostory 4 2.5 3926 5 320:362/366/312
49 Birn Ham Lane  360000
4 split 3 1 1010 28 920:432/404/436
4341 Rock Quarry  60000
1 split 3 2 1662 12 920:488/360/552
6324 Lakeland, Lake Park  100000
2 split 3 2 2004 0 920:568/400/318
101 Meadowglade Ln.  179950
```

```
2 twostory 3 2.5 1650 0 920:364/608/368
100 Cumberland Green  143000
1 twostory 3 2.5 2416 6 920:568/356/318
6008 Brass Lantern Ct.  144500
4 ranch 3 2.5 2441 1 920:540/512/436
9356 Sauls Rd.  197000
1 twostory 5 3.5 4850 3 920:540/512/436
9317 Sauls Rd.  339950
4 split 3 1.5 1225 18 920:328/312/316
6424 Old Jenks Rd.  81900
;
```

DATA Step to Create MYLIB.PLAN

```
libname mylib 'SAS-data-library';

data mylib.plan;
   input name & $18. conf & $40. begdate : date7. enddate date7. /
         city & $14. exibit & $18. seminar : $1.;
   cards;
Judith Oslavsky  Chicago Electronics Trade Show  20MAY91 23MAY91
Chicago  music synthesizers  y
Sandra Chen  Electronics Technologies Show  14APR91 17APR91
San Francisco  electronics  y
John Stephens  Entertainment Industries Show  24JUN91 28JUN91
Las Vegas  futures software  y
Mark Goldstein  Entertainment Industries Show  24JUN91 28JUN91
Las Vegas  music software  n
Rosa Rios  Entertainment Industries Show  24JUN91 28JUN91
Las Vegas  legal software  y
Fred Washington  Western User's Group  11MAR91 13MAR91
Lake Tahoe  general software  y
Gloria Faley  Western User's Group  11MAR91 13MAR91
Lake Tahoe  general software  n
Harry Smith  Western User's Group  11MAR91 13MAR91
Lake Tahoe  general software  n
;
```

DATA Step to Create MYLIB.EXPENSE

```
libname mylib 'SAS-data-library';

data mylib.expense;
   input name $ 1-18 city $ 21-34 +2 begdate date7. +1 enddate date7. /
         airfare ground hotel food entertmt;
   cards;
Judith Oslavsky    Chicago         20MAY91 23MAY91
   378.50   23.00   425.34  325.88  333.22
```

```
Sandra Chen          San Francisco   14APR91 17APR91
   459.70    25.00  339.50  170.15  120.00
John Stephens         Las Vegas      24JUN91 28JUN91
   220.35    32.00  698.22  375.40  420.98
Mark Goldstein        Las Vegas      24JUN91 28JUN91
   220.35    36.00  702.56  398.13  235.18
Rosa Rios             Las Vegas      24JUN91 28JUN91
   220.35    30.00  690.45  380.78    0.00
Fred Washington       Lake Tahoe     11MAR91 13MAR91
   256.75    22.00  377.19  280.10   98.00
Gloria Faley          Lake Tahoe     11MAR91 13MAR91
   256.75    23.00  372.90  266.39    0.00
Harry Smith           Lake Tahoe     11MAR91 13MAR91
   256.75    25.00  398.00  225.45  195.00
;
```

Chapter 16

DATA Step to Create MACBOLTS.PRICES

```
libname macbolts 'SAS-data-library';

data macbolts.prices;
   input       partnmbr $10.
          @11 quantity 3.
          @15 price 6.2;
   cards;
B01-03/06 100  5.75
B02-03/08 100  6.60
B03-03/10 100  7.25
B04-03/12 100  7.80
B05-03/14 100  8.40
B06-03/16 100  7.95
B07-03/20 100  8.80
B08-03/25  50  4.25
B09-03/30  50  7.40
B10-03/06 100  7.10
B11-03/08 100  7.20
B12-03/10 100  7.70
B13-03/12 100  8.00
B14-03/14 100  8.80
B15-03/16 100  9.05
B16-03/20 100  9.20
B17-03/25  50  5.75
B18-03/30  50  8.00
B19-04/06 100 10.10
B20-04/08 100  5.90
B21-04/10 100  6.40
B22-04/12 100  6.80
```

```
B23-04/14 100   7.50
B24-04/16 100   6.95
B25-04/18 100   7.95
B26-04/20 100   7.20
B27-04/22 100   9.60
B28-04/25  50   3.95
B29-04/30  50   4.60
B30-04/06 100  11.60
B31-04/08 100   6.70
B32-04/10 100   7.10
B33-04/12 100   7.70
B34-04/14 100   8.80
B35-04/16 100   9.05
B36-04/18 100   9.60
B37-04/20 100   8.80
B38-04/22 100  11.20
B39-04/25  50   5.25
B40-04/30  50   5.50
B41-05/06 100  11.80
B42-05/08 100   6.40
B43-05/10 100   6.60
B44-05/12 100   6.80
B45-05/14 100   7.70
B46-05/16 100   6.60
B47-05/18 100   7.95
B48-05/20 100   7.20
B49-05/22 100   8.80
B50-05/25  50   4.15
B51-05/30  50   4.60
B52-05/06 100  13.75
B53-05/08 100   7.05
B54-05/10 100   7.10
B55-05/12 100   7.70
B56-05/14 100   7.95
B57-05/16 100   8.15
B58-05/18 100   8.45
B59-05/20 100   8.90
B60-05/22 100  10.40
B61-05/25  50   4.85
B62-05/30  50   5.25
B63-06/06 100  12.20
B64-06/08 100   7.00
B65-06/10 100   7.20
B66-06/12 100   7.45
B67-06/14 100   7.95
B68-06/16 100   8.05
B69-06/18 100   8.15
B70-06/20 100   9.40
B71-06/22 100   9.60
B72-06/25  50   4.65
B73-06/30  50   5.05
B74-06/06 100  15.25
B75-06/08 100   7.75
```

```
B76-06/10 100   7.90
B77-06/12 100   8.50
B78-06/14 100   8.75
B79-06/16 100   8.95
B80-06/18 100   9.20
B81-06/20 100   9.80
B82-06/22 100  11.80
B83-06/25  50   5.25
B84-06/30  50   5.75
;
```

Chapter 17

DATA Step to Create MYLIB.NEWS

```
libname mylib 'SAS-data-library';

data mylib.news;
   input name $ 1-37 local 38-44 ntl 45-48 intntl 49-54 circ $ 55-58;
   cards;
The Amsterdam Advocate                2.5   6   3.0   1
The Auburntown Tribune                3.0   4   2.5   s
The Bayside Observer                  2.5   5   2.0   s
The Bent Creek Gazette                2.5   3   1.5   s
The Blue Ridge Neighborhood           3.5   7   3.0   1
The Bramlett Courier                  3.0   3   2.0   s
The Cedar Park Edition                3.5   8   3.5   1
The Clermont Weather and News         2.0   8   4.5   1
The Community Spectator               1.5   5   2.0   s
The Deakin Sentinel                   2.5   6   2.0   s
The Delta Voice                       2.0   3   2.0   s
The Duckville Truth                   3.5   4   2.0   s
The Duplin Daily                      2.5   6   2.0   s
The East Oak Corner Chronicle         3.0   7   3.0   s
The Fort Washington Constitution      2.5   5   1.5   s
The Glenhaven Herald                  2.0   6   3.5   1
The Greystone Planet and Sun          2.5   5   2.0   s
The Harrison Review                   3.0   6   2.5   1
The Highbridge Record of Events       1.5   3   2.0   s
The Historical Lakewalk               2.0   9   4.0   1
The Hunts Point Bulletin              1.5   2   1.0   s
The Lake Boone Heritage               2.5   5   2.0   1
The Northwoods Examiner               4.0   5   1.5   s
The Oxford Inquirer                   2.5   4   2.0   s
The Pine Hills Post                   2.0   6   2.5   1
The Rabbit Creek Star                 2.0   3   1.0   1
The Recent Past                       3.5   8   4.0   1
The Riverside Globe                   2.0   7   3.5   1
The Samford Editorial                 2.0   4   1.5   s
The Seaside Journal                   3.0   4   2.5   1
```

```
The Sheep's Meadow Delivery          3.0   8   3.5   l
Today's Headlines                    2.0   5   2.5   l
The Tournament Times                 1.5   7   4.0   l
The Valley Free Press                1.5   6   3.0   l
The Village Green Report             2.0   4   2.5   s
The Warren Ponds Universal           1.5   7   4.0   l
;
```

Chapter 18

DATA Step to Create ATM.ACTIVITY

```
libname atm 'SAS-data-library';

data atm.activity;
   input    actdate date7.
         @9 withdraw
         @14 inquiry
         @19 transfer
         @24 deposit
         @29 payment;
   cards;
01jan91   129   14    5    11   16
02jan91   116   16    3     9    5
03jan91   174   40    6     8    4
04jan91   181   49    7     6    1
05jan91   166   44    2     6    0
06jan91   132   10    4     9    5
07jan91   134   19    3    10    6
08jan91   120   15    6     6    4
09jan91   121   12    2     7   18
10jan91   195   49    5    10   17
11jan91   227   59   12     6    0
12jan91   188   41    1     0    1
13jan91   117   15   10     7    4
14jan91   135   17    9     8    8
15jan91   119   13    5    15    7
16jan91   122   20    4    19    5
17jan91   160   39    6     9    6
18jan91   192   44    3    10    4
19jan91   175   32    4     8    6
20jan91   138   14    6     9   12
21jan91   130   15   10     7    6
22jan91   129   12    4     7    5
```

```
23jan91  133   22    5    9   14
24jan91  222   58    8   11    3
25jan91  223   62   10   10    2
27jan91  225   60   12    4    2
28jan91  188   49    2    0    1
29jan91  167   40    7    8    0
30jan91  139   94    5    8    9
31jan91  128   14    8   21   15
;
```

DATA Step to Create ATM.HOLIDAYS

```
libname atm 'SAS-data-library';

data atm.holidays;
   input holstrt date7.
         holname $ 9-24;
   cards;
01jan91 New Year's Day
;
```

DATA Step to Create CONVERSN.ACTIVITY

```
libname conversn 'SAS-data-library';

data conversn.activity;
   input actstrt date7.
         acttask $   9-32
         actpers $ 34-47
         actdura 49-52;
   cards;
01jul91 Design Console Layout    R. Stiles    4
05jul91 Receive and Tag Cables   R. Stiles    1.5
05jul91 Receive CPU              C. Escobar   3
10jul91 Install CPU and Nodes    C. Escobar   10
22jul91 Redefine INIT Classes    S. Lee       3
25jul91 Test Utilities           R. Stiles    2.5
;
```

DATA Step to Create
CONVERSN.HOLIDAYS

```
libname conversn 'SAS-data-library';

data conversn.holidays;
   input holstrt date7.
         holname $ 9-24
         holdura;
   cards;
04jul91 Independ. Day    1
;
```

DATA Step to Create
CONVERSN.WORKDAYS

```
libname conversn 'SAS-data-library';

data conversn.workdays;
   input wdayhrs time6.
         sathrs    time6.;
   cards;
 8:00  8:00
12:00 12:00
13:00
17:00
;
```

DATA Step to Create
CONVERSN.CALENDAR

```
libname conversn 'SAS-data-library';

data conversn.calendar;
   input _Sun_ $   1- 7
         _Mon_ $   9-15
         _Tue_ $  17-23
         _Wed_ $  25-31
         _Thu_ $  33-39
         _Fri_ $  41-47
         _Sat_ $  49-54;
   cards;
holiday wdayhrs wdayhrs wdayhrs wdayhrs wdayhrs sathrs
;
```

Chapter 19

DATA Step to Create CLEANUP.WELLS

```
libname cleanup 'SAS-data-library';

data cleanup.wells;
   input well $1.
         @3 date date7.
         @11 cd
         @15 pb;
   format date date7.;
   label cd='Cadmium' pb='Lead';
   cards;
1 02jul88  62  72
1 03oct88  60  60
1 02jan89  42  57
1 03apr89  30  52
1 05jul89  25  49
1 02oct89  17  45
1 03jan90   9  40
1 02apr90   7  35
1 02jul90   5  30
1 01oct90   3  28
1 04jan91   2  26
2 02jul88  72  78
2 03oct88  68  73
2 02jan89  55  64
2 03apr89  43  59
2 05jul89  39  57
2 02oct89  28  52
2 03jan90  20  49
2 02apr90  12  48
2 02jul90   8  47
2 01oct90   6  45
2 04jan91   2  41
;
```

Chapter 21

Raw Data for IN.SPELL.SASWORDS

```
----+----1
SAS
SYMPUT
libname
proc
CPU
BEST12
Len
Pos
informat/s
COMMA7
pd5
MMDDYY6
MMDDYY8
COMMAwd
MMDDYYw
----+----1
```

Chapter 23

DATA Step to Create NUTRIENT.NORMAL

```
libname nutrient 'SAS-data-library';

data nutrient.normal;
   input crop $11.
         @13 calcium
         @16 iron
         @20 vita_b1
         @24 vita_b2
         @28 vita_c;
   cards;
beets      32 1.2 .07 .06  .9
corn        8 1.4 .13 .12  .5
cauliflower 28 1.3 .09 .08 1.0
green beans 54 1.5 .12 .11 1.9
lettuce    11  .3 .03 .03 1.3
peas       30 3.0 .14 .13 1.5
;
```

DATA Step to Create
NUTRIENT.DROUGHT

```
libname nutrient 'SAS-data-library';

data nutrient.drought;
   input crop $11.
         @13 calcium
         @16 iron
         @20 vita_b1
         @24 riboflvn;
   cards;
beets        28 1.2 .06 .05
corn          8 1.2 .13 .11
cauliflower  28 1.3 .08 .08
green beans  54 1.3 .12 .10
;
```

Chapter 24

DATA Step to Create CLOSING.INFO

```
libname closing 'SAS-data-library';

data closing.info;
 input filenmbr $ buyer $ seller $;
 cards;
9212-01 Sharpe Keller
9212-02 Dunlap Nash
9212-03 Wilson Hendrick
9212-04 Marsalla Currin
9212-05 Richards Lee
9212-06 Downey Turner
9212-07 Upton Chang
9212-08 Salinski Winslow
9212-09 Patel Kramer
;
run;
```

Chapter 25

DATA Step to Create IN.HOUSES

```
libname in 'SAS-data-library';

data in.houses;
   input zone $1. +1 type $ @12 bedr bath dr $1. +1 garage sf
         age fp schools $15. @48 address $25. @72 price;
   cards;
4 twostory 4 2.5 y 2 2538 6 2 920:340/400/368   211 Whitehall Way      154900
1 twostory 4 2.5 y 2 2700 7 1 920:470/360/552   1800 Bridgeport        169900
3 twnhouse 2 2 y 0 1595 6 1 320:332/366/312     154 Montrose           102000
1 twostory 3 2.5 y 1 2750 0 1 920:628/388/348   4000 Skipjack Ct.      214900
4 split    3 2 y 1 1306 0 1 920:576/512/436     5933 South Downs Dr.    95400
2 twostory 3 3.5 y 2 2590 0 2 920:364/608/368   727 Crabtree Crossing  292400
5 split    3 1 n 0 1959 31 0 680:308/316/332    627 Riverside Dr.       58900
2 twnhouse 3 2.5 y 0 1374 15 0 920:304/604/368  907 Lexington Ct.       65500
4 condo    2 2 y 0 1275 5 1 920:448/472/318     6010-102 Winterpoint    70000
4 ranch    3 2 y 1 1526 6 1 920:476/424/428     6509 Orchard Knoll     107900
1 split    3 1.5 y 1 1329 23 0 920:396/360/552  500 E. Millbrook Rd.    82900
1 condo    2 3.5 n 0 1300 5 1 920:448/472/318   6010-101 Winterpoint    68900
8 twnhouse 2 2 y 0 1120 4 1 320:364/366/312     521 Woodwinds           84600
2 condo    2 2 y 0 1066 1 1 920:520/604/368     1324 Killiam Ct.        74900
4 split    4 2.5 y 3 2600 10 2 920:476/424/428  7141 Eastridge         198000
2 twnhouse 2 1.5 y 0 1150 15 0 920:304/400/368  1239 Donaldson Ct.      49900
4 ranch    3 2.5 y 0 2441 1 0 920:540/512/436   9356 Sauls Rd.         197000
1 split    3 1 n 0 1245 36 0 920:524/388/348    2414 Van Dyke           85000
7 twnhouse 2 1.5 y 0 1280 4 1 920:584/592/588   409 Galashiels          60000
4 ranch    3 3 n 0 2400 2 1 920:420/424/428     8122 Maude Steward Rd. 129900
2 duplex   2 2.5 y 0 1184 4 1 920:364/604/368   112 Lake Hollow         67900
6 duplex   3 1 y 1 1569 73 2 350:324/328/336    108 South Elm St.      100000
2 twnhouse 2 1.5 y 0 1040 9 1 920:414/604/316   216 Concannon Ct.       59900
4 condo    3 2 y 0 1448 5 1 920:448/472/318     6000-102 Winterpoint    79900
2 twnhouse 3 2 y 2 1471 1 1 920:364/604/368     765 Crabtree Crossing  184000
4 twostory 3 2.5 y 0 1940 4 1 920:328/312/316   1641 Pricewood Lane    195000
5 split    2 1 n 0 960 2 0 680:308/304/332      Rt.5 Yarbororugh Rd.    78900
8 twnhouse 2 2 y 0 1167 5 1 320:364/366/312     5001 Pine Cone          78500
2 condo    2 2 n 0 1246 4 1 920:364/604/316     721 Springfork          76900
1 twnhouse 2 1 n 0 980 4 0 920:304/360/552      1203 Berley Ct          72400
8 twostory 4 2.5 y 2 3446 0 2 320:313/316/356   Lot 10 Red Coach Rd.   225000
8 split    3 1.5 y 0 1441 28 1 320:315/316/356  5617 Laurel Crest Dr.   86900
5 twostory 3 2.5 y 0 1900 4 0 680:308/316/332   1532 St. Mary's Rd.    118500
8 split    3 2 y 2 1976 10 1 320:348/316/356    110 Skylark Way        123500
8 twnhouse 2 2 n 0 1276 6 1 321:360/304/356     8 Stonevillage          71000
5 split    3 2 n 0 1533 5 1 680:/308/316/32     603 Greentree Dr.      117800
2 twostory 4 2.5 y 2 2584 0 0 920:364/640/368   114 Grey Horse Dr.     189900
8 twostory 4 2.5 y 2 2608 0 0 320:362/366/312   2103 Carriage Way      189900
2 twnhouse 3 2.5 y 0 2080 4 1 920:530/400/318   108 Chattle Close      179900
5 twostory 3 2.5 y 2 2863 7 1 680:308/316/332   5521 Horseshoe Circle  199200
8 split    2 2.5 n 0 2900 38 1 320:315/316/356  2617 Snow Hill Rd      425000
```

```
3 twostory 4 2.5 y 2 3926 5 1 320:362/366/312   49 Birn Ham Lane          360000
4 split    3 1 n 0 1010 28 0 920:432/404/436     4341 Rock Quarry           60000
1 split    3 2 y 0 1662 12 1 920:488/360/552     6324 Lakeland, Lake Park 100000
2 split    3 2 y 2 2004 0 2 920:568/400/318      101 Meadowglade Ln.       179950
2 twostory 3 2.5 y 2 1650 0 1 920:364/608/368    100 Cumberland Green      143000
1 twostory 3 2.5 y 2 2416 6 1 920:568/356/318    6008 Brass Lantern Ct.    144500
4 ranch    3 2.5 y 0 2441 1 0 920:540/512/436    9356 Sauls Rd.            197000
1 twostory 5 3.5 y 2 4850 3 0 920:540/512/436    9317 Sauls Rd.            339950
4 split    3 1.5 n 2 1225 18 1 920:328/312/316   6424 Old Jenks Rd.         81900
;
```

Glossary

access method
a set of instructions used to read from or write to a file. See also engine.

action bar
a list of selections that enable you to perform an action. To use an action bar, place your cursor on the selection that you want and press ENTER. If you are using a mouse, point and click on your selection. Making a selection executes a command, displays a pull-down menu, or displays a dialog box.

activities data set
in the CALENDAR procedure, a SAS data set that contains observations that define activities to be displayed in a summary or schedule calendar. See also schedule calendar and summary calendar.

aggregate storage location
a group of distinct files on an operating system. Different host operating systems call an aggregate grouping of files different names, such as a directory, a maclib, or a partitioned data set. The standard form for referencing an aggregate storage location from within the SAS System is *fileref(name)*, where *fileref* is the entire aggregate and *(name)* is a specific file or member of that aggregate. See also fileref.

alias
an alternative name, usually in a shortened form, for a keyword, format, option, or other SAS language element.

analysis variable
a numeric variable used to calculate statistics. In the CORR, MEANS, SUMMARY, and TABULATE procedures, you identify analysis variables in a VAR statement. In the REPORT procedure, all numeric variables are, by default, analysis variables. Usually analysis variables contain quantitative or continuous values, but this is not required. You can request a variety of descriptive statistics for analysis variables.

argument
(1) in the DATA step, the values or expressions a user supplies within parentheses on which a SAS function or CALL routine performs the indicated operation.
(2) in syntax descriptions, any word that follows the keyword in a SAS statement or command.

arithmetic operators
the symbols ($+, -, /, *$, and $**$) used to perform addition, subtraction, division, multiplication, and exponentiation in SAS expressions.

array
(1) a group of variables of the same type available for processing under a single name. See also multidimensional array, one-dimensional array, and two-dimensional array.
(2) a logical construct.

array name
a name selected to identify a group of variables or temporary data elements. It must be a valid SAS name that is not the name of a variable in the same DATA step or SCL program. See also array.

array reference
a reference to the element to be processed in an array. See also array.

ASCII
an acronym for the American Standard Code for Information Interchange. ASCII is a 7-bit character coding scheme (8 bits when a parity check bit is included) including graphic (printable) and control (nonprintable) codes.

ASCII collating sequence
an ordering of characters that follows the order of the characters in the American Standard Code for Information Interchange (ASCII) character coding scheme. The SAS System uses the same collating sequence as its host operating system. See also EBCDIC collating sequence.

autoexec file
a file containing SAS statements that are executed automatically when the SAS System is invoked. The autoexec file can be used to specify some SAS system options, as well as librefs and filerefs that are commonly used.

automatic variable
a variable that is created automatically by the DATA step, some DATA step statements, some SAS procedures, and the SAS macro facility.

base data set
in the COMPARE procedure, a SAS data set used as the basis of a comparison.

base SAS software
software that includes a programming language that manages your data, procedures for data analysis and reporting, procedures for managing SAS files, a macro facility, help menus, and a windowing environment for text editing and file management.

base variable
in the COMPARE procedure, a variable within a base data set whose values are compared to the values of another variable in the comparison data set.

batch mode
a method of executing SAS programs in which you prepare a file containing SAS statements and any necessary operating system commands and submit the program to the computer's batch queue. While the program executes, control of the SAS System returns to the user. Batch mode is sometimes referred to as running in background. The job output can be written to files or printed on an output device.

bit mask
a string of bits with a specific pattern of binary 0s and 1s that you use to compare with other values.

Boolean operator

See logical operator.

box plot

a plot that displays summary statistics for the distribution of a variable.

    In the UNIVARIATE procedure, dashed lines (- -) represent quartiles; a plus sign (+) represents the mean; and vertical lines (|), zeroes, and asterisks (*) represent values outside the box.

BY group

all observations with the same values for all BY variables.

BY-group processing

the process of using the BY statement to process observations that are ordered, grouped, or indexed according to the values of one or more variables. Many SAS procedures and the DATA step support BY-group processing. For example, you can use BY-group processing with the PRINT procedure to print separate reports for different groups of observations in a single SAS data set.

BY value

the value of a BY variable.

calendar data set

in the CALENDAR procedure, a SAS data set that contains observations that define one weekly work schedule. Observations in a calendar data set must use character variables named _SUN_, _MON_, _TUE_, _WED_, _THU_, _FRI_, and _SAT_ to specify which workshift applies to which day of the week.

CALL routine

(1) a program that can be called in a DATA step or in SCL programs by issuing a CALL statement. A CALL routine may change the value of some of the arguments passed to it, but it does not return a value as a function does.
(2) an alternate form of one of the SAS random number functions that allows more control over the seed stream and random number stream.

carriage-control character

a specific symbol that tells the printer how many lines to advance the paper, when to begin a new page, when to skip a line, and when to hold the current line for overprint.

catalog

See SAS catalog.

catalog entry

a separate storage unit within a SAS catalog. Each entry has an entry type that identifies its structure to the SAS System. See also entry type.

cell

a single unit of a table produced by a SAS procedure, such as the TABULATE or FREQ procedure. The value contained in the cell is a summary statistic for the input data set. The contents of the cell are described by the page, row, and column that contain the cell.

character comparison

a process in which character operands are compared character by character from left to right, yielding a numeric result. If the character operands are equal, the result is the value 1; if they are not equal, the result is the value 0.

character constant

one or more characters enclosed in quotes in a SAS statement (sometimes called a character literal). The maximum number of characters allowed is 200. See also character string.

character format

an instruction to the SAS System to write character data values using a specific pattern.

character function

a function that enables you to perform character string manipulations, comparisons, evaluations, or analyses.

character informat

an instruction to the SAS System to read character data values into character variables using a specific pattern.

character literal

See character constant.

character string

one or more alphanumeric or other keyboard characters or both. See also character constant.

character value

a value that can contain alphabetic characters, numeric characters 0 through 9, and other special characters. See also character variable.

character variable

a variable whose values can consist of alphabetic and special characters as well as numeric characters.

class variable

in some SAS procedures, a variable used to group data. Class variables can be character or numeric. Class variables can have continuous values, but they typically have a few discrete values that define the classifications of the variable. In base SAS software, you identify a class variable in the CLASS statement.

collating sequence

See ASCII collating sequence and EBCDIC collating sequence.

column input

in the DATA step, a style of input that gives column specifications in the INPUT statement for reading data in fixed columns.

column output

in the DATA step, a style of output that gives column specifications in the PUT statement for writing data in fixed columns.

comment

the descriptive text within a program that explains or documents the program. In the SAS language, a comment begins with the symbols /* and ends with the symbols */; a comment can also begin with an asterisk (*) and end with a semicolon (;).

comparison data set

in the COMPARE procedure, a SAS data set that the procedure compares to a base data set.

comparison operator

a symbolic or mnemonic instruction that tests for a particular relationship between two values. In SAS software, if the comparison is true, the result of executing the instruction is the value 1; if the comparison is false, the result is the value 0.

comparison variable

in the COMPARE procedure, a variable within a comparison data set whose values are compared to the values of another variable in the base data set.

compilation

the process of checking syntax and translating a portion of a program into a form that the computer can execute.

composite index

an index that locates observations in a SAS data set by the values of two or more key variables. See also index and simple index.

compound expression

an expression containing more than one operator.

concatenating

(1) for SAS data sets, a process in which the SAS System combines two or more SAS data sets, one after the other, into a single data set.
(2) for character values, a process in which the SAS System combines two or more character values, one after the other, into a single character value.
(3) for external files, the process that enables the SAS System to access two or more files as if they were one by specifying the filenames one after another in the same SAS statement.

condition

in a SAS program, one or more numeric or character expressions that result in a value upon which some decision depends.

configuration file

an external file containing SAS system options. The options in the file are put into effect when the SAS System is invoked.

configuration option

a SAS option that can be specified in the SAS command or in a configuration file. Configuration options affect how the SAS System interfaces with the computer hardware and operating system.

constant
a number or a character string that indicates a fixed value. Character constants must be enclosed in quotation marks.

converting SAS files
the process of changing the format of a SAS file from the format appropriate to one version of the SAS System to the format appropriate to another version running under the same operating system. The V5TOV6 procedure converts files from Version 5 to Version 6 format.

correlation
the tendency for the values of a variable to become larger or smaller as the values of a variable increase or decrease.

correlation coefficient
a statistic, ranging from -1 to 1, measuring the strength of the linear relationship between two series of values.

crossing
in the TABULATE procedure, the process that combines the effects of two or more elements.

data error
a type of execution error that occurs when a SAS program analyzes data containing invalid values. For example, a data error occurs if you specify numeric variables in the INPUT statement for character data. Data errors do not cause a program to stop but, instead, to generate notes in the SAS log. See also programming error and syntax error.

data file
See SAS data file.

data model
See SAS data model.

data set label
in a SAS data set, a user-defined attribute of up to 40 characters used for documenting the SAS data set.

data set option
an option that appears in parentheses after a SAS data set name. Data set options specify actions that apply only to the processing of the preceding SAS data set. See also SAS system option.

DATA step
a group of statements in a SAS program that begins with a DATA statement and ends with either a RUN statement, another DATA statement, a PROC statement, the end of the job, or the semicolon that immediately follows instream data lines. The DATA step enables you to read raw data or other SAS data sets and use programming logic to create a SAS data set, write a report, or write to an external file.

data value

(1) a unit of character or numeric information in a SAS data set. A data value represents one variable in one observation.

(2) in the SAS data model, an element in a collection of data values that are organized and presented to the SAS System in a rectangular structure of columns and rows. A data value represents the intersection of a row and a column.

date and time format

an instruction that tells the SAS System how to write numeric values as dates, times, and datetimes.

date and time informat

an instruction that tells the SAS System how to read numeric values represented as dates, times, and datetimes.

date value

See SAS date value.

declarative statement

a statement that supplies information to the SAS System and that takes effect when the system compiles program statements.

delimiter

a character that serves as a boundary separating the elements of a character string, programming statement, data line, or list of arguments.

descriptive statistic

a quantity that characterizes, rather than draws inference from, a collection of values. Types of descriptive statistics are measures of central tendency, measures of variation among values, and measures of the shape of the distribution of values.

descriptor information

(1) the information the SAS System creates and maintains identifying the attributes of a SAS data set and its contents.

(2) in the SAS data model, the logical component of a SAS data set that supplies the SAS System with information about the data set and its contents.

detail record

one of the two types of records found in a hierarchical file. In a hierarchical file, related data occur in groups. Each record group begins with a header record and usually contains one or more detail records. For example, in a customer order file, a header record may contain name and address information about the customer, and each detail record may contain information about an item ordered. See also header record and hierarchical file.

detail report

output that lists all the data that are processed.

dialog box

a data entry window opened when certain items are selected from a pull-down menu. Menu items that open dialog boxes have an ellipsis (...) following the item name. Dialog boxes are used when additional information is required to perform the action indicated in the menu item.

dimension expression

in the TABULATE procedure, the portion of the TABLE statement that defines what variables and statistics make up a single dimension of the table. The format of a dimension expression is the same for any of the three dimensions page, row, and column.

direct access

in table lookup applications, a technique for retrieving records by observation number instead of searching a data set sequentially to find a match. This technique cannot be used with a BY statement, a WHERE statement, or a WHERE= data set option. It also cannot be used with transport format data sets, compressed data sets, data sets in sequential format on tape or disk, or SAS/ACCESS views or the SQL procedure views that read data from external files.

directory

(1) in a SAS data library, a list of the members and associated information.
(2) in a SAS catalog, a list of entries and associated information.

display manager

See SAS Display Manager System.

display manager mode

an interactive method of running SAS programs in which you edit a group of statements, submit the statements, and then review the results of the statements in various windows.

DO group

a sequence of statements headed by a simple DO statement and ended by a corresponding END statement. See also DO loop.

DO loop

a sequence of statements headed by an iterative DO, DO WHILE, or DO UNTIL statement; ended by a corresponding END statement; and executed (usually repeatedly) according to directions in the DO statement. See also DO group.

double trailing at sign (@@)

a special symbol used to hold a line in the input buffer across iterations of the DATA step.

duration

a value representing the difference, in elapsed time or days, between any two time or date values.

EBCDIC

an acronym for Extended Binary Coded Decimal Interchange Code. EBCDIC is an 8-bit character coding scheme including graphic (printable) and control (nonprintable) codes.

EBCDIC collating sequence

an ordering of characters that follows the order in the Extended Binary Coded Decimal Interchange Code (EBCDIC) character coding scheme. The SAS System uses the same collating sequence as its host operating system. See also ASCII collating sequence.

engine
a part of the SAS System that reads from or writes to a file. Each engine allows the SAS System to access files with a particular format. There are several types of engines.

entry
a unit of information stored in a SAS catalog. Catalog entries differ widely in content and purpose. See also entry type.

entry type
a characteristic of a SAS catalog entry that identifies its structure and attributes to the SAS System. When you create an entry, the SAS System automatically assigns the entry type as part of the name.

executable statement
a SAS statement that causes some action to occur during DATA step execution. See also declarative statement.

execution
(1) the process of performing the actions defined in a portion of a program (such as a DATA or PROC step or a macro).
(2) the process in the DATA step in which the SAS System carries out statements for each observation or record in the file.
(3) in contexts other than the DATA step, such as SAS macros, procedures, and global statements, the process in which the SAS System performs the actions indicated.

explicit array
an array that consists of a valid SAS name, reference to the number of variables or temporary data elements, and an optional list of the array elements. In an explicit array, you must explicitly specify the subscript in the reference when referring to an element. See also explicit array reference and implicit array.

explicit array reference
a description of the element to be processed in an explicit array. See also explicit array and implicit array reference.

expression
See SAS expression.

external file
(1) a file maintained by the host operating system rather than by the SAS System. External files can contain raw data, SAS programming statements, procedure output, or output created by the PUT statement. See also fileref.
(2) in a DATA step, a file the SAS System can read using INFILE and INPUT statements, or a file the SAS System can write to using FILE and PUT statements.

field
(1) in an external file, the smallest logical unit of data. See also file and record.
(2) in windowing environments, a window area that is defined to contain a value that users usually can view, enter, or modify.

file

a collection of related records treated as a unit. SAS files are processed and controlled through the SAS System and are stored in a SAS data library.

file reference

See fileref.

fileref

a name temporarily assigned to an external file or an aggregate storage location and used to identify it to the SAS System. You assign a fileref with a FILENAME statement or with an operating-system command.

Do not confuse filerefs with librefs. Filerefs are used for external files; librefs are used for SAS data libraries. See also libref.

first-level name

See libref.

FIRST.*variable*

a temporary variable that the SAS System creates to identify the first observation of each BY group. The variable is not added to the SAS data set. See also LAST.*variable*

floating-point representation

a compact form of storing real numbers on a computer, similar to scientific notation. Floating-point representation techniques vary by operating system.

format

an instruction the SAS System uses to display or write each value of a variable. Some formats are supplied by SAS software. Other formats can be written by the user with the FORMAT procedure in base SAS software or with SAS/TOOLKIT software. See also user-written format.

format modifier

a special symbol used in the INPUT and PUT statements that enables you to control the way the SAS System reads input data and writes output data.

formatted input

a style of input that uses special instructions called informats in the INPUT statement to determine how values entered in data fields should be interpreted. See also informat.

formatted output

a style of output that uses special instructions called formats in the PUT statement to determine how to write variable values. See also format.

frequency table

a table that lists the values of a variable and the number of observations with each value.

In the UNIVARIATE procedure, the frequency table also lists the percentage of observations with each value and the percentage of observations with values less than or equal to each value.

function

a routine that can accept arguments, perform an operation, and return a value. For example, the ABS function returns the absolute value of a numeric argument. Functions can return either numeric or character results.

global option

See SAS system option.

header record

a record that begins a record group in a hierarchical file. Header records are usually followed by one or more detail records. For example, in a customer order file, a header record may contain name and address information about the customer, and each detail record may contain information about an item ordered. See also detail record and hierarchical file.

header routine

a group of DATA step statements that you identify with the HEADER= option in the FILE statement. A header routine begins with a statement label, ends with a RETURN statement, and produces page headers in print files.

heading

(1) in reporting procedures, a label that describes the contents of some portion of the table. This includes page, row, and column headings in the TABULATE procedure and column headings in many other procedures.
(2) in SAS output, the text located near the beginning of each page of output. This includes text produced by a HEADER= option in a FILE statement, titles written with a TITLE statement, and default information such as date and page numbers.

hierarchical file

a file in which records containing related data occur in groups. Each record group begins with a header record and usually contains one or more detail records. See also detail record and header record.

holidays data set

in the CALENDAR procedure, a SAS data set that contains observations that define holidays to be displayed in a summary or schedule calendar. See also schedule calendar and summary calendar.

implicit array

in the DATA step, an array that consists of an array name, an optional index variable, and a list of array elements. Using implicit arrays is not recommended for new programmers. See also explicit array and implicit array reference.

implicit array reference

a description of the element to be processed in an implicit array. See also explicit array reference and implicit array.

index

a component of a SAS data set that contains the data values of a key variable or variables paired with a location identifier for the observation containing the value. The value/identifier pairs are ordered in a structure that enables the SAS System to search by a value of a variable. See also composite index and simple index.

infix operator
a symbol specifying an operation applied to two operands, one on each side (for example, the greater-than symbol in 8>6). There are four general kinds of infix operators: arithmetic, comparison, logical or Boolean, and other (minimum, maximum, and concatenation).

informat
an instruction the SAS System uses to read raw data values to create variable values. Some informats are supplied by SAS software. Other informats can be written by the user with the FORMAT procedure in base SAS software or with SAS/TOOLKIT software. See also user-written informat.

initialization option
a configuration option specified at start-up for a SAS programming environment that controls setting up the SAS System as well as hardware and software interfacing. See also SAS initialization.

input buffer
the temporary area of memory into which each record of data is read when the INPUT statement executes. Note that the input buffer is a logical concept independent of physical implementation.

input/output operation
any operation of physically reading data from a storage medium, such as a disk or tape, or writing data to a storage medium.

interactive facility
a system that alternately accepts and responds to input. An interactive facility is conversational; that is, a continuous dialog exists between user and system. The SAS Display Manager System is interactive.

interactive line mode
a method of running SAS programs in which you enter one line of a SAS program at a time at the SAS session prompt. The SAS System processes each line immediately after you press the ENTER or RETURN key. Procedure output and informative messages are returned directly to the display monitor.

interleaving
a process in which the SAS System combines two or more sorted SAS data sets into one sorted SAS data set based on the values of the BY variables.

interquartile range
the difference between the third quartile, or 75th percentile, and the first quartile, or 25th percentile.

join
in the SQL procedure, the combination of data from two or more tables (or SAS data views) to produce a single result table. A conventional, or *inner*, join returns a result table for all the rows in a table that have one or more matching rows in the other tables(s), as specified by the sql-expression.

key variable
(1) a variable that is used to index SAS data sets.
(2) in table lookup applications, the variable that resides in both the primary file and the lookup file. The values of the key variable are the common elements between the files. Typically, key values are unique in the lookup file but not necessarily in the primary file.

KEYS entry
a type of catalog entry that contains function key settings for interactive windowing procedures.

keyword
See SAS keyword.

kurtosis
a measure of the "heaviness of the tails" of a distribution relative to the normal distribution, which has a kurtosis of zero.

label
See data set label, statement label, and label, variable.

label, variable
a descriptive label of up to 40 characters that can be printed by certain procedures instead of, or in addition to, the variable name.

LAST.*variable*
a temporary variable that the SAS System creates to identify the last observation of each BY group. This variable is not added to the SAS data set. See also FIRST.*variable*

length, variable
the number of bytes used to store each of a variable's values in a SAS data set.

library reference
See libref.

libref
(1) the name temporarily associated with a SAS data library. You assign a libref with a LIBNAME statement or with operating system control language.
(2) the first part of a multilevel SAS filename indicating the SAS data library in which the file is stored. For example, in the name SASUSER.ACCOUNTS, the name SASUSER is the libref.

line-hold specifier
a special symbol used in INPUT and PUT statements that enables you to hold a record in the input or output buffer for further processing. Line-hold specifiers include the trailing at sign (@) and the double trailing at sign (@@).

line mode
See interactive line mode.

list input, modified

a style that uses special instructions called informats and format modifiers in the INPUT statement to scan input records for data values that are separated by at least one blank or other delimiter, and in some cases, by two blanks.

list input, simple

a style that gives only variable names and dollar signs ($) in the INPUT statement to scan input records for data values that are separated by at least one blank or other delimiter.

list output

a style in which a character string or variable is specified in a PUT statement without explicit directions that specify where the SAS System should place the string or value.

literal

any character or numeric value in a SAS program that is not the value of a variable, but the literal value of numbers or characters representing it. Character literals are usually enclosed in quotes. See also numeric constant.

logical data model

a framework into which engines fit information for processing by the SAS System. It is a logical representation of data or files, not a physical structure.

logical operator

an operator used in expressions to link sequences of comparisons. The logical operators are AND, OR, and NOT.

lookup file

an auxiliary file that is maintained separately from the primary file and that is referenced for one or more of the observations of the primary file. A set of SAS statements can provide values that serve as the lookup file. The values of format tables also serve as lookup files. See also primary file.

lookup result

in table lookup applications, the auxiliary information obtained using the key or keys as a reference into the lookup file.

macro

an entry in a catalog containing compiled macro program statements and stored text.

macro facility

a portion of the SAS System used for extending and customizing the SAS System and for reducing the amount of text that must be entered to do common tasks. It consists of the macro processor and the macro language.

macro language

the programming language used to communicate with the macro processor.

macro variable

a variable belonging to the macro language whose value is a string that remains constant until you change it. A macro variable is also called a symbolic variable.

master data set

in an update operation, the data set containing the information you want to update. See also transaction data set.

match-merging

a process in which the SAS System joins observations from two or more SAS data sets according to the values of the BY variables. See also one-to-one merging.

matching observations

in the COMPARE procedure, observations that have the same values for all ID variables you specify or, if you do not use the ID statement, observations that occur in the same position in the data sets.

matching variables

in the COMPARE procedure, variables that have the same name or variables that you explicitly pair by using the VAR and WITH statements.

MEA

See Multiple Engine Architecture (MEA).

member

a file in a SAS data library.

member type

a name assigned by the SAS System that identifies the type of information stored in a SAS file. Member types include ACCESS, DATA, CATALOG, PROGRAM, and VIEW.

menu

a display presenting choices a user can make. Menus include action bars, pull-down menus, block menus, and selection lists.

merging

the process of combining observations from two or more SAS data sets into a single observation in a new SAS data set. See also match-merging and one-to-one merging.

methods of running the SAS System

standard methods of operation used to run SAS System programs. These methods are display manager mode, interactive line mode, noninteractive mode, and batch mode.

missing value

a value in the SAS System indicating that no data are stored for the variable in the current observation. By default, the SAS System prints a missing numeric value as a single period and a missing character value as a blank space.

In the SQL procedure, a missing value is equivalent to an SQL NULL value.

mnemonic operator

an arithmetic or logical (Boolean) operator composed of letters rather than symbols (for example, EQ rather than =).

mode

the most frequent value of a variable.

modified list input

a style that combines the scanning feature of list input with informats. Combining scanning with informats enables you to read unaligned data values that are nonstandard, longer than 8 bytes long, or contain single embedded blanks.

moving average

an average of a specified number of consecutive values that move according to the current observation.

Multiple Engine Architecture (MEA)

a feature of the SAS System that enables it to access a variety of file formats through sets of instructions called engines. See also engine.

multi-panel report

output that use sets of columns on a page to display the values of variables. For example, telephone books are usually arranged in multi-panels of names, addresses, and phone numbers on a single page.

multidimensional array

a grouping of variables of the same type under a single name with at least two dimensions. When processed, this grouping of variables produces results in columns, rows, and, depending on the array, higher dimensions. See also one-dimensional array and two-dimensional array.

name, variable

the identifying attribute of a variable. A variable name must conform to SAS naming rules.

named input

a style in which equal signs appear in the INPUT statement to read data values in the form *variable=data-value*.

named output

a style in which equal signs appear in the PUT statement to write variable values in the form *variable=data-value*.

noninteractive mode

a method of running SAS programs in which you prepare a file of SAS statements and submit the program to the operating system. The program runs immediately and occupies your current session.

nonstandard data

data that the SAS System can read or write only with the aid of informats or formats. Examples of nonstandard data are hexadecimal or binary values.

normal probability plot

a plot that compares the distribution of input data with the normal distribution.

In the UNIVARIATE procedure, asterisks represent the input data and plus signs form the reference line.

normalization

in the analysis of test scores, the process of converting each set of original scores to some standard scale. One method in common use is to determine percentiles of the scores and then express them as corresponding deviations from the mean of a normal distribution.

numeric constant

a number that appears in a SAS expression. See also literal.

numeric format

an instruction to the SAS System to write numeric variable values using a specific pattern.

numeric informat

an instruction to the SAS System to read numeric data values using a specific pattern.

numeric value

a value that usually contains only numbers, including numbers in E-notation and hexadecimal notation. A numeric value can sometimes contain a decimal point (.), plus sign ($+$), or minus sign ($-$). Numeric values are stored in numeric variables.

numeric variable

a variable that can contain only numeric values. The SAS System stores all numeric variables in floating-point representation by default.

observation

a row in a SAS data set that contains the specific data values for a single object.

one-dimensional array

a grouping of variables of the same type under a single name. When processed, this grouping of variables produces results that can be presented in simple column format. See also multidimensional array and two-dimensional array.

one-to-one matching

the process of combining observations from two or more data sets into one observation using two or more SET statements to read observations independently from each data set. See also match-merging.

one-to-one merging

the process of using the MERGE statement (without a BY statement) to combine observations from two or more data sets based on the observations' positions in the data sets. See also match-merging.

operands

the variables and constants in a SAS expression that contains operators, variables, and constants.

operators

symbols that request a comparison, logical operation, or arithmetic calculation. In the SAS System, there are two major kinds of operators: prefix operators and infix operators.

output buffer

in the DATA step, the area of memory to which a PUT statement writes before writing to a designated file or output device.

overprint character

the character printed when two or more plotting symbols share the same print position. In most procedures, the default overprint character is the at sign (@).

page

(1) the number of bytes of data that the SAS System moves between external storage and memory in one input/output operation.
(2) the portion of a SAS data set that can occupy the number of bytes specified by the page size attribute. See also page size.

page size

the number of bytes of data that the SAS System moves between external storage and memory in one input/output operation. Page size is analogous to buffer size for SAS data sets.

panel

each set of columns in a multi-panel report. See also multi-panel report.

password

a valid SAS name a user must correctly specify to gain access to SAS files. Passwords can grant read, write, or alter access.

percentile

a variable value that is larger than a particular percentage of the values of the variable. For example, the 95th percentile is larger than 95 percent of the values of that variable.

permanent SAS data library

a library that is not deleted when the SAS session terminates; it is available for subsequent SAS sessions. Unless the USER libref is defined, you use a two-level name to access a file in a permanent library. The first-level name is the libref, and the second-level name is the member name.

permanent SAS file

a file in a SAS data library that is not deleted when the SAS session or job terminates.

physical filename

the name the operating system uses to identify a file.

physical order

the order in which observations appear in their storage structure.

picture

in the FORMAT procedure, a template for printing the values of numeric variables.

picture format

in the FORMAT procedure, a user-defined format for displaying numeric values. Picture formats are defined with the PICTURE statement.

plotting axis

the scale on which the procedure plots the values of the plotting variables. The abbreviations MIN and MAX print above the horizontal axis along with the values that make up the plotting axis.

plotting symbol

the character the procedure uses to plot the values of plotting variables. By default, the TIMEPLOT procedure uses the first character of the variable name as the plotting symbol.

plotting variables

the variables that you specify in a PLOT statement. Plotting variables must be numeric.

PMENU entry

a type of catalog entry that contains definitions for pull-down menus, action bars, and dialog boxes created by the PMENU procedure.

PMENU facility

a menuing facility in the SAS System that is used instead of the command line as a way to execute commands. The PMENU facility consists of an action bar, pull-down menus, and dialog boxes.

pointer

in the DATA step, a programming tool the SAS System uses to keep track of its position in the input or output buffer.

pointer control

the process of instructing the SAS System to move the pointer before reading or writing data.

prefix operator

a symbol specifying an operation applied to the variable, constant, function, or parenthetical expression immediately following it (for example, the minus sign in $-6*a$).

primary file

in table lookup applications, the file for which you want to obtain auxiliary information. See also lookup file.

primary windows

the core windows that compose the SAS Display Manager System. The four primary windows are the PROGRAM EDITOR, LOG, OUTPUT (LISTING), and OUTPUT MANAGER windows.

print file

an external file containing carriage-control (printer-control) information. See also carriage-control character.

PROC SQL view

a definition of a virtual data set that is named and stored for later use. This file contains no data, but it defines data that are stored in the PROC SQL view's underlying SAS data files, or described by SAS/ACCESS views or other PROC SQL views. Its output table can be a subset or a superset of one or multiple underlying structures. However, in Release 6.06, you cannot reference a PROC SQL view to update its underlying data. See also view.

PROC step

a group of SAS statements that call and execute a procedure, usually with a SAS data set as input.

procedure

See SAS procedure.

procedure output file

an external file that contains the result of the analysis or the report produced. Most procedures write output to the procedure output file by default. Reports that DATA steps produce using PUT statements and a FILE statement with the PRINT destination also go to this file.

PROFILE catalog

a SAS catalog in a special SAS data library that contains information used by the SAS System to control various aspects of your display manager session. See also SASUSER library.

program data vector

the temporary area of memory, or storage area, where the SAS System builds a SAS data set, one observation at a time. Note that the program data vector is a logical concept that is independent of physical implementation.

programming error

a flaw in the logic of a SAS program that can cause it to fail or to perform differently than the programmer intended. See also data error and syntax error.

pull-down menu

the list of choices displayed vertically in a rectangular box when you choose an item from an action bar or from another pull-down menu. The choices in the list are called items.

query-expression (query)

a table-expression or multiple table-expressions that can be linked with set operators. The primary purpose of a query-expression is to retrieve data from tables, PROC SQL views, or SAS/ACCESS views. In the SQL procedure, the SELECT statement is contained in a query-expression.

random access

(1) the ability to retrieve records in a file without reading all records sequentially. (2) in the SAS data model, a pattern of access by which the SAS System processes observations according to the value of some indicator variable without processing all observations sequentially.

range

the difference between the largest and smallest values of a variable.

ranking

the process of ordering observations according to values of particular variables.

raw data

(1) data that have not been read into a SAS data set.
(2) in statistical analysis, data (including SAS data sets) that have not had a particular operation, such as standardization, performed on them.

raw data file

an external file whose records contain data values in fields. A DATA step can read a raw data file by using the INFILE and INPUT statements.

record

a logical unit of information consisting of fields of related data. A collection of records makes up a file.

reference lines

in the TIMEPLOT procedure, the vertical lines printed on the plot that indicate whether the values of plotting variables are less than, greater than, or equal to a particular value.

repeated measures data

an arrangement of data where multiple measurements that are responses to the same experimental factor are contained in a single observation for each experimental unit. For example, a patient's blood pressure at different times or in response to different levels of medication is a repeated measure.

RUN group

in SAS procedures, a set of statements ending with a RUN statement.

sampling with replacement

a method of taking a sample that allows you to select an item more than once.

sampling without replacement

a method of taking a sample that does not allow you to select an item more than once.

SAS catalog

a SAS file that stores many different kinds of information in smaller units called catalog entries. A single SAS catalog can contain several different types of catalog entries.

SAS compilation

the process of converting statements in the SAS language from the form in which you enter them into a form ready for the SAS System to use.

SAS data file

(1) a SAS data set that contains both the data values and the descriptor information.

(2) in the SAS data model, a SAS data set that is implemented in a form that contains both the data values and the descriptor information. SAS data files have the type DATA.

SAS data library

(1) a collection of one or more SAS files that are recognized by the SAS System. Each file is a member of the library.

(2) in the SAS data model, a collection of SAS files accessed by the same library engine and recognized as a logical unit by the SAS System.

SAS data model

the framework into which engines put information for SAS processing. The SAS data model is a logical representation of data or files, not a physical structure.

SAS data set

(1) descriptor information and its related data values organized as a table of observations and variables that can be processed by the SAS System. A SAS data set can be either a SAS data file or a SAS data view.

(2) in the SAS data model, a logical structure into which engines fit data for processing by the SAS System. The logical model has three components: descriptor information, data values, and indexes.

SAS data set option

See data set option.

SAS data view

(1) a SAS data set in which the descriptor information and the observations are obtained from other files. SAS data views store only the information required to retrieve data values or descriptor information.

(2) in the SAS data model, a SAS data set that is implemented in a form that obtains the descriptor information or data values, or both, from other files. Only the information necessary to derive the descriptor information or retrieve the data values is stored in the file of member type VIEW.

SAS date constant

a string in the form '*ddMMMyy*'d or '*ddMMMyyyy*'d representing a date in a SAS statement. The string should be enclosed in quotes and followed by the character d (for example '06JUL91'd).

SAS date value

an integer representing a date in the SAS System. The integer represents the number of days between January 1, 1960, and another specified date. (For example, the SAS date value 366 represents the calendar date January 1, 1961.)

SAS datetime constant

a string in the form '*ddMMMyy:hh:mm:ss*'dt or '*ddMMMyyyy:hh:mm:ss*'dt representing a date and time in the SAS System. The string should be enclosed in quotes and followed by the characters dt (for example, '06JUL91:09:53:22'dt).

SAS datetime value

an integer representing a date and time in the SAS System. The integer represents the number of seconds between midnight, January 1, 1960, and another specified date and time. (For example, the SAS datetime value for 9:30 a.m., June 5, 1989, is 928661400.)

SAS Display Manager System

an interactive windowing environment in which actions are performed by issuing commands. Display manager commands can be issued by typing them on the command line, pressing function keys, or selecting items from pull-down menus. Within one session, multiple tasks can be accomplished. Display manager can be used to prepare and submit programs, view and print the results, and debug and resubmit the programs.

SAS execution

the process of following the instructions given by SAS statements to perform an action.

SAS expression

a sequence of operands and operators forming a set of instructions that the SAS System performs to produce a result value. A single variable name, constant, or function is also a SAS expression.

SAS file

a specially structured file that is created, organized, and, optionally, maintained by the SAS System. A SAS file can be a SAS data set, a catalog, a stored program, or an access descriptor.

SAS initialization

the setting of global characteristics that must be in place at start-up for a SAS programming environment. The SAS System performs initialization by setting certain SAS system options called initialization options. Invoking the SAS System initiates SAS initialization. See also SAS invocation.

SAS invocation

the process of calling or starting up the SAS System by an individual user through execution of the SAS command. Invoking the SAS System initiates SAS initialization. See also SAS initialization.

SAS keyword

a literal that is a primary part of the SAS language. Keywords are the words DATA and PROC, statement names, function names, macro names, and macro function names.

SAS log

a file that contains the SAS statements you have submitted, messages about the execution of your program, and, in some cases, output from the DATA step and from certain procedures.

SAS name

a name whose construction follows certain rules and that can appear in a SAS statement (for example, names of variables and SAS data sets). SAS names can be up to eight characters long. The first character must be a letter or an underscore. Subsequent characters can be letters, numbers, or underscores. Blanks and special characters (except the underscore) are not allowed.

SAS operator

See operators.

SAS procedure

a program accessed with a PROC statement that produces reports, manages files, or analyzes data. Many procedures are included with the SAS System. In addition, users can write their own procedures using SAS/TOOLKIT software; these are called user-written procedures.

SAS program

a series of SAS statements that, taken together, guide the SAS System through a process or series of processes.

SAS session

an environment created by invoking the SAS System in which you can give commands, submit SAS statements, receive responses to the commands, and receive results of the SAS statements until you exit the environment or until the environment is terminated.

SAS statement

a string of SAS keywords, SAS names, and special characters and operators ending in a semicolon that instructs the SAS System to perform an operation or gives information to the SAS System.

SAS system option

an option that affects the processing of the entire SAS program or interactive SAS session from the time the option is specified until it is changed. Examples of items controlled by SAS system options include the appearance of SAS output, the handling of some of the files used by the SAS System, the use of system variables, the processing of observations in SAS data sets, the features of SAS System initialization, the SAS System's interface with your computer hardware, and the SAS System's interface with the host operating system.

SAS Text Editor

a full-screen editing facility available in some windows of the SAS Display Manager System, as well as in windows of SAS/AF and SAS/FSP software.

SAS time constant

a string in the form '*hh:mm:ss*'t representing a time in a SAS statement. The string should be enclosed in quotes and followed by the character t (for example, '09:53:22't).

SAS time value

an integer representing a time in the SAS System. The integer represents the number of seconds between midnight of the current day and another specified time value. (For example, the SAS time value for 9:30 a.m. is 34200.)

SAS windowing environment

See SAS Display Manager System.

SAS WORK data library

a SAS data library the SAS System creates by default at the beginning of a SAS session or SAS job that contains data sets, utility files created by certain SAS procedures, and catalogs for macros and macro variables. Without the SAS WORK library, the SAS System will not run. It is temporary by default.

SASHELP library

a SAS data library supplied by SAS software that stores the text for HELP windows, default function key and window definitions, and menus.

SASUSER library

a default permanent SAS data library that is created at the beginning of your first SAS session. It contains a PROFILE catalog that stores the tailoring features you specify for the SAS System. You can also store other SAS files in this library. See also PROFILE catalog and SAS data library.

schedule calendar

in the CALENDAR procedure, procedure output that displays observations from one or more SAS data sets in month-by-month calendars. A schedule calendar can display activities that can have durations of more than one day.

seed

an initial value from which a random number function or CALL routine calculates a random variate.

seek operation

in table lookup applications, the scanning or search operation involved in using the key variable to access the lookup file.

sequential access

a method of file access in which the records are read or written one after the other from the beginning of the file to the end.

simple expression

a SAS expression that uses only one operator.

simple index

an index that locates observations by the values of one variable. See also composite index and index.

skewness

a measure of the deviation from symmetry of a distribution, or the tendency of values to be more spread out on one side of the mean than the other.

SOURCE entry

a type of catalog entry that contains text from SAS Text Editor windows.

SQL

See Structured Query Language (SQL).

standard data
data that are stored with one digit or character per byte.

standard deviation
a statistical measure of the variability of a group of data values. This measure, which is the most widely used measure of the dispersion of a frequency distribution, is equal to the positive square root of the variance.

standardization
a method of transforming values of a variable to a different scale based on a particular mean and standard deviation.

statement label
a SAS name followed by a colon that prefixes a statement in a DATA step so that other statements can direct execution to that statement as necessary, bypassing other statements in the step.

statement option
a word that you specify in a given SAS statement that affects only the processing that that statement performs.

stem-and-leaf plot
a plot that shows the shape of a distribution with each value separated into a base number, plotted in the stem, and the remaining portion, plotted in the leaf.

step boundary
a point in a SAS program at which the SAS System recognizes that a DATA step or PROC step is complete.

stratified random sample
a sample obtained by dividing a population into nonoverlapping parts, called strata, and randomly selecting items from each stratum.

string
See character string.

Structured Query Language (SQL)
the standardized, high-level query language used in relational database management systems to create and manipulate database management system objects. The SAS System implements SQL through the SQL procedure.

summary calendar
in the CALENDAR procedure, procedure output that displays observations from SAS data sets in month-by-month calendars. A summary calendar can display activities that have durations of only one day.

summary table
output that provides a concise overview of the information in a data set.

syntax checking
a process in which the SAS System checks each SAS statement for proper usage, correct spelling, proper SAS naming conventions, and so on.

syntax error

an error in the spelling or grammar of SAS statements. The SAS System finds syntax errors as it compiles each SAS step before execution. See also data error and programming error.

table

in the SQL procedure, a SAS data file. See also SAS data file.

table alias

a temporary, alternate name for a table that is specified in the FROM clause. Table aliases are optionally used to qualify column names when tables are joined. See also table.

table lookup

a processing technique used to retrieve additional information from an auxiliary source based on the values of variables in the primary source.

target variable

the variable to which the result of a function or expression is assigned.

temporary array elements

array elements that behave like variables but that do not appear in the output data set. They have no names and can be referenced only by their array names and dimensions. They are automatically retained, instead of being reset to missing at the beginning of the next iteration of the DATA step.

temporary SAS data library

a library that exists only for the current SAS session or job. The most common temporary library is the WORK library.

temporary SAS file

a SAS file in a SAS data library (usually the WORK data library) that is deleted at the end of the SAS session or job.

title

a heading printed at the top of each page of SAS output or of the SAS log.

toggle

an option, parameter, or other mechanism that enables you to turn on or turn off a processing feature.

trailing at sign (@)

a special symbol used to hold a line so that you can read from it or write to it with another INPUT or PUT statement.

transaction data set

in an update operation, the data set containing the information needed to update the master data set. See also master data set.

two-dimensional array
a grouping of variables of the same type under a single name with two dimensions. When processed, this grouping of variables produces results that can be displayed in columns and rows. See also multidimensional array and one-dimensional array.

type, variable
See variable type.

updating
a process in which the SAS System replaces the values of variables in the master data set with values from observations in the transaction data set.

USER data library
a SAS data library defined with the libref USER. When the libref USER is defined, the SAS System uses it as the default libref for one-level names.

user-written format
a format you define with the FORMAT procedure or with C, PL/I, FORTRAN, or IBM 370 assembler using SAS/TOOLKIT software. See also format.

user-written informat
an informat you define with the FORMAT procedure or with C, PL/I, FORTRAN, or IBM 370 assembler using SAS/TOOLKIT software. See also informat.

value
See data value.

variable
(1) a column in a SAS data set. A variable is a set of data values that describe a given characteristic across all observations. See also macro variable.
(2) in the SAS data model, a vertical component of a SAS data set.

variable attributes
the name, label, format, informat, type, and length associated with a particular variable.

variable list
a list of variables. You can use abbreviated variable lists in many SAS statements instead of listing all the variable names.

variable type
the classification of a variable as either numeric or character. Type is an attribute of SAS variables.

view
a definition of a virtual data set that is named and stored for later use. This file contains no data but describes or defines data stored elsewhere. See also PROC SQL view and SAS data view.

WHERE expression

a type of SAS expression used to specify a condition for selecting observations for processing by a DATA or PROC step. WHERE expressions can contain special operators not available in other SAS expressions. WHERE expressions can appear in a WHERE statement, a WHERE= data set option, a WHERE clause, or a WHERE command. See also SAS expression and WHERE processing.

WHERE processing

a method of conditionally selecting observations for processing in a DATA or PROC step. WHERE processing involves using a WHERE expression in a WHERE statement, a WHERE= data set option, a WHERE clause, or a WHERE command. See also WHERE expression.

whisker

a vertical line on a box plot that represents values larger than the third quartile or smaller than the first quartile but within 1.5 interquartile ranges of the box.

window

a resizable, movable division of the display.

windowing environment

See SAS Display Manager System.

WORK data library

the temporary library automatically defined by the SAS System at the beginning of each SAS session or job to store temporary files. When the libref USER is not defined, the SAS System uses WORK as the default library for one-level names.

workdays data set

in the CALENDAR procedure, a SAS data set that contains observations that define workshifts named in a calendar data set. Each variable in the workdays data set contains one daily schedule of alternating work and nonwork periods. See also calendar data set.

Index

Special Characters

Your Turn

If you have comments or suggestions about *SAS Language and Procedures: Usage 2, Version 6, First Edition*, please send them to us on a photocopy of this page.

Please return the photocopy to the Publications Division (for comments about this book) or the Technical Support Division (for suggestions about the software) at SAS Institute Inc., SAS Campus Drive, Cary, NC 27513.